FRANK WOOD'S

Book-keeping and Accounts

SIXTH EDITION

Frank Wood BSc(Econ), FCA

and

Sheila Robinson BA(Hons), Cert Ed, FMAAT

FT Prentice Hall
FINANCIAL TIMES

An imprint of **Pearson Education**

Harlow, England • London • New York • Boston • San Francisco • Toronto • Sydney • Singapore • Hong Kong
Tokyo • Seoul • Taipei • New Delhi • Cape Town • Madrid • Mexico City • Amsterdam • Munich • Paris • Milan

Pearson Education Limited

Edinburgh Gate
Harlow
Essex CM20 2JE
England

and Associated Companies throughout the world

Visit us on the World Wide Web at:
www.pearsoned.co.uk

First published 1981
Sixth edition published 2004

© Longman Group Limited 1981
© Longman Group UK Limited 1986, 1992
© Financial Times Professional Limited 1997
© Pearson Education Limited 2001, 2004

The rights of Frank Wood and Sheila Robinson to be identified as authors
of this work have been asserted by them in accordance with the Copyright,
Designs and Patents Act 1988.

ISBN: 0 273 68548-1

British Library Cataloguing-in-Publication Data
A catalogue record for this book is available from the British Library

10 9 8 7 6 5 4 3 2 1
08 07 06 05 04

Typeset in 10.5/12.5pt Garmond Book by 35
Printed and bound by Ashford Colour Press Ltd., Gosport

The publisher's policy is to use paper manufactured from sustainable forests.

Contents

Part 4 Adjustments for financial statements

Part 5 Financial statements of other organisations

Preface to the sixth edition

This sixth edition of *Book-keeping and Accounts* continues its development as a well established book for foundation intermediate level accountancy students. The scope of the book has been broadened so that it is suitable as a study text for the various examining bodies offering accountancy at this level.

I have introduced the chapter dealing with value added tax at an earlier stage and include VAT on all subsequent topics. A new chapter has been included, Extended trial balance, in view of the increasing use of this in accounting practices. It is also appearing as an examination topic. The chapter has many worked examples and exercises to familiarise students with possible examination questions. A step-by-step guide is provided in the chapter that is applied to a fully worked example.

Step-by-step guides, using fully worked examples, are provided in some other chapters on various topics including the preparation of the financial statements of different organisations.

The learning objectives for each chapter have been reviewed and updated as appropriate. Each chapter now has a summary as a quick reference and subject reminder for students and Appendix A contains a glossary of accounting terms.

Many new questions have been introduced and include actual examination questions from the bodies noted in the acknowledgements. Model layouts for the preparation of financial statements can be found in Appendix B together with blank worksheets for other topics such as the extended trial balance. A Solutions Manual is available with answers to those questions with suffix 'X'. This is available free to teaching staff who recommend this book.

This comprehensive text embraces the requirements of the various examining bodies at accountancy foundation intermediate level. It is, however, necessary for students and tutors to be fully conversant with the syllabus of the bodies whose examinations they intend to take.

Sheila Robinson

Acknowledgements

The authors and publishers are grateful to the following examining bodies for their permission to use past assessment papers, and sample questions from examination papers:

Association of Accounting Technicians (AAT)

Assessment and Qualifications Alliance (AQA) – and the various GCSE examining bodies. Please note that the AQA (SEG) questions used on pages 123, 191, 290, 301, 324, 395, 396, 421, 423 and 462 are *NOT* from the live examinations for the current specification. For GCSE subjects new specifications were introduced in 2003.

City & Guilds Pitman qualifications

Oxford, Cambridge and RSA Examinations (OCR)

I wish to thank Joanne Tyler for her keen interest and diligent work reading and checking the manuscript and to Malcolm Robinson for his support, encouragement and help throughout the production of this text.

Sheila Robinson
Frank Wood

Part 1

Introduction to double entry accounting

This part of the book is concerned with the basic principles of the double entry system of book-keeping.

Introduction to accounting

1.1 Aims of a business

Almost every business is started with the aim of making money for its owners. To achieve this aim, they will have to trade with other people and businesses, which means selling goods and/or services.

Money is the medium of exchange used almost universally in trading, and it allows a monetary value to be given to goods or services that are offered to potential customers. It follows that the control of money in a business is vital if it is to be successful and a profit is to be made (*see* Exhibit 1.1).

The owners of a business need to know how much money is coming into the business from the sale of goods and/or services. They also need to know how much it is costing to run the business. In other words, they need to 'account' for every pound coming into and going out of the business. This process is known as **accounting**, and keeping books provides the basic method used by accountants in the financial control of a business.

1.2 Basic concept of financial control

All businesses whether small, i.e. sole trader, through to very large ones such as multinational corporations use the same concept of financial control. This can best be illustrated using a straightforward example such as a market trader who buys and sells goods. Such a person would operate his or her business as shown in Exhibit 1.2.

Exhibit 1.1 The basis of a business

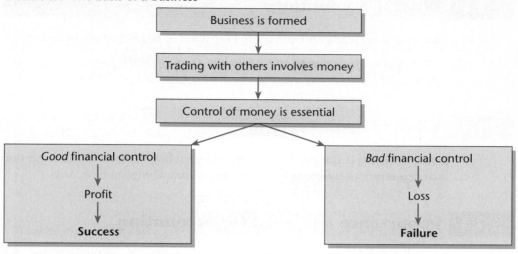

Exhibit 1.2

Financial control	
Trader invests in goods using his own money	Buys goods for £10,000
Being a good salesperson he is able to sell goods at more than he paid for them	Sells all the goods for £15,000
The difference between the cost of goods and selling price is profit	£ Selling price 15,000 *Less* Cost price 10,000 **Profit** 5,000
However, he has incurred expenses in actually selling the goods, i.e. market rents, transport, which must be deducted from this profit	*Less* Expenses 3,000 **Profit now** £2,000

Financial control is a major function of a business but there are other aspects which are needed to provide success:

● a competitive product and/or service
● a good strategy
● a competent workforce.

None of these would be of any use unless there was a market (people or businesses willing to buy).

It is, however, a fact that businesses, which practice good recording of financial data, will have the information to make sound management decisions with a far better chance of success.

1.3 What is accounting?

Accounting is clearly and concisely described in the following definition:

The skill or practice of maintaining accounts and preparing reports to aid the financial control and management of a business.

1.4 What is book-keeping?

Book-keeping is the process of recording, in books of accounts or on computer, the financial effect of business transactions and managing such records.

1.5 Importance and need for accounting

As stated earlier, businesses must operate profitably otherwise they will cease to exist. The **financial statements** produced by a business's accounting department aim to show clearly the profit or loss which has been made and the financial position of the business.

The two most important statements are:

1 the trading and profit and loss account
2 the balance sheet.

Both these statements have to be checked and verified by a firm of auditors as part of the legal requirements for correct financial reporting. It is essential that accurate financial information is available to the auditors to enable them to fulfil their functions properly.

There are, however, other groups who are keenly interested in the activities of the business. These include:

● Inland Revenue – they collect employees' tax, National Insurance contributions, and tax on the profits of the business.
● Customs and Excise – they are responsible for the collection or refund of monies for a business which is registered for value added tax (VAT) purposes.
● Investors – these may be private individuals, companies or banks, any or all of which will want to monitor the performance of the business to ensure that they will get a return for their investment.
● Suppliers – this group will need to be sure of the financial stability of the business before accepting orders.
● Customers – they will need to be sure of the financial stability of the business before placing orders.
● Employees – a sound business with a good working environment will help to keep employees' moral high and will be able to attract high-calibre new staff.

In order that the business can satisfy all these interested parties, it must follow certain accounting procedures and practices in a formal sequence. Essentially this sequence can be stated as shown in Exhibit 1.3. Each part of the sequence can be explained briefly, as set out next.

Exhibit 1.3 **The accounting sequence**

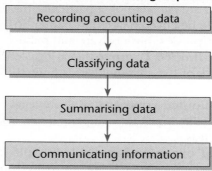

Recording accounting data

Each business must install a system to collect and record all the financial transactions that are carried out. This includes cash received and paid out, goods bought and sold, items bought for use in the business, and so on.

Classifying data

Once the data has been recorded, it has to be classified so that it can be of use to the business. For instance, if a leisure business sells both sports equipment and camping gear, it would be of value to the proprietor to know the sales figures for the separate parts of the business.

Summarising data

Summarising the data of the various financial transactions provides the managers of the business with information in a concise form.

Communicating information

When the information from the three preceding procedures has been prepared, it then needs to be presented in a formal way as the business's accounts and business reports.

1.6 Types of organisations

Organisations are classified according to their structure and financial make-up and are mainly classified as shown below. The classification will determine an organisation's legal status and what financial reporting is required of the organisation. Thus, we have the following:

- A **sole trader** is an individual trading alone in his or her own name, or under a recognised trading name. He or she is solely liable for all business debts, but when the business is successful the trader takes all the profits.

- A **partnership** is a group of more than two people and a maximum of twenty, who together are carrying on a particular business with a view to making a profit. This topic will be covered later in Chapter 36.
- **Limited companies**, both private and public:
  - A **private limited company** is a legal entity with at least two shareholders. The liability of the shareholders is limited to the amount that they have agreed to invest.
  - A **public limited company** is also a legal entity with limited shareholder liability, but unlike a private company it can ask the public to subscribe for shares in its business.
- **Non-trading organisations** include clubs, associations and other non-profit making organisations which are normally run for the benefit of their members to engage in a particular activity and not to make a profit. Their financial statements will take the form of income and expenditure accounts, to be covered in Chapter 34.

Chapter summary

- The basis of business is trading with others and good financial control is essential if the organisation is to succeed.
- Financial control means ensuring that the sales of a business are greater than the cost incurred by the business thus providing a profit.
- The two most important financial statements are:
  - the trading and profit and loss account
  - the balance sheet.
- A number of groups or agencies have a keen interest in the financial performance of a business:
  - Inland Revenue
  - Customs and Excise
  - investors
  - suppliers
  - customers
  - employees.
- The accounting sequence is as follows:
  - recording accounting data
  - classifying data
  - summarising data
  - communicating information.
- Organisations can include:
  - sole traders
  - partnerships
  - private limited companies
  - public limited companies
  - non-trading organisations.

Note: A glossary of New Terms can be found in Appendix A at the end of the book.

CHAPTER 2

The accounting equation and the balance sheet

Learning objectives

After you have studied this chapter you should be able to:

- understand what is meant by assets, liabilities and capital
- understand the accounting equation
- draw up balance sheets after different transactions have occurred
- explain the meaning of the terms assets, capital, liabilities, debtors and creditors.

2.1 The accounting equation

The whole of financial accounting is based upon a simple idea called the **accounting equation**. This sounds complicated but is, in fact, easy to understand. It can be explained by saying that if a business decides to set up and start trading, it will require resources. Assuming that the owner of the new business supplies all the resources then this can be shown as:

> Resources supplied by the owner = Resources in the business

In accounting, special terms are used to describe many things. The amount of the resources supplied by the owner is called **capital**. The actual resources that are then in the business are called **assets**. This means that when the owner has supplied all of the resources, the accounting equation can be shown as:

> Capital = Assets

Usually, however, other people besides the owner have supplied some of the assets. **Liabilities** is the name given to the amounts owing to these people for these assets. The accounting equation has now changed to:

> Capital = Assets − Liabilities

This is the most common way in which the accounting equation is presented. It can be seen that the two sides of the equation will have the same totals. This is because we are dealing with the same thing from two different points of view – the value of the owners' investment in the business and the value of what is owned by the owners.

Unfortunately, with this form of the accounting equation, we can no longer see at a glance what value is represented by the resources in the business. You can see this more clearly if you switch assets and capital around to give an alternative form of the accounting equation:

$$\text{Assets} = \text{Capital} + \text{Liabilities}$$

This can then be replaced with words describing the resources of the business:

Resources: what they are = Resources: who supplied them
(Assets)   (Liabilities)

It is a fact that no matter how you present the accounting equation, the totals of both sides will always equal each other, and this will always be true no matter how many transactions there may be. The actual assets, capital and liabilities may change, but the total of the assets will always equal the total of capital + liabilities. Or, reverting to the more common form of the accounting equation, the capital will always equal the assets of the business minus the liabilities.

Assets consist of property of all kinds, such as buildings, machinery, stocks of goods and motor vehicles. Other assets include debts owed by customers and the amount of money in the bank account.

Liabilities include amounts owed by the business for goods and services supplied to the business and for expenses incurred by the business that have not yet been paid for. They also include funds borrowed by the business.

Capital is often called the owner's **equity** or **net worth**. It comprises the funds invested in the business by the owner plus any profits retained for use in the business less any share of the profits paid out of the business to the owner.

2.2 The balance sheet and the effects of business transactions

The accounting equation is expressed in a financial statement called the **balance sheet**. The balance sheet shows the financial position of an organisation at a point in time. In other words, it presents a snapshot of the organisation at the date when the balance sheet was prepared. The balance sheet is not the first accounting record to be made, nor the first that you will learn how to record, but it is a convenient place to start to consider accounting.

Let's now see how a series of transactions affects the balance sheet.

The introduction of capital (1)

On 1 January 2008, K Astley started in business and put £20,000 into a bank account for the business. The balance would appear:

K Astley
Balance Sheet as at 1 January 2008

	£
Assets: Cash at bank	20,000
Capital	20,000

Note how the top part of the balance sheet contains the assets and the bottom part contains the capital. This is always the way information is presented in the balance sheet.

The purchase of an asset by cheque (2)

On 3 January 2008, Astley buys a building for £10,000. The effect of this transaction on the balance sheet is that the money in the bank is decreased and the new asset, building, is added:

K Astley
Balance Sheet as at 3 January 2008

	£
Assets: Building	10,000
Cash at bank	10,000
	20,000
Capital	20,000

Note how the two parts of the balance sheet 'balance', that is, both totals are the same. This is always the case with balance sheets.

The purchase of an asset and the incurring of a liability (3)

On 5 January 2008, Astley buys some goods for £3,000 from D Moore and agrees to pay for them some time within the next two weeks. The effect of this is that a new asset, **stock** of goods, is acquired, and a liability for the goods is created. A person to whom money is owed for goods is known in accounting language as a **creditor**. The balance sheet becomes:

K Astley
Balance Sheet as at 5 January 2008

		£
Assets: Building		10,000
Stock of goods		3,000
Cash at bank		10,000
		23,000
Less: Creditor		3,000
		20,000
Capital		20,000

Note how the liability (the creditor) is shown as a deduction from the assets. This is exactly the same calculation as is presented in the most common form of the accounting equation.

Sale of an asset on credit (4)

On 10 January 2008, goods which cost £1,000 were sold to P Hall for the same amount, the money to be paid at a later date. The effect is a reduction in the stock of goods and the creation of a new asset. A person who owes the firm money is known in accounting terms as a **debtor**. The balance sheet now appears as:

K Astley
Balance Sheet as at 10 January 2008

		£
Assets:	Building	10,000
	Stock of goods	2,000
	Debtor	1,000
	Cash at bank	10,000
		23,000
Less:	Creditor	3,000
		20,000
Capital		20,000

Sale of an asset for immediate payment (5)

On 15 January 2008, goods which cost £500 were sold to M Clark for the same amount. Clark paid for them immediately by cheque. Here one asset, stock of goods, is reduced, while another asset, bank, is increased. The balance sheet after these transactions is now shown:

K Astley
Balance Sheet as at 15 January 2008

		£
Assets:	Building	10,000
	Stock of goods	1,500
	Debtor	1,000
	Cash at bank	10,500
		23,000
Less:	Creditor	3,000
		20,000
Capital		20,000

The payment of a liability (6)

On 17 January 2008, Astley pays a cheque for £1,500 to D Moore in part payment of the amount owing. The asset of bank is therefore reduced, and the liability to the creditor is also reduced. The balance sheet now appears as shown below:

K Astley
Balance Sheet as at 17 January 2008

		£
Assets:	Building	10,000
	Stock of goods	1,500
	Debtor	1,000
	Cash at bank	9,000
		21,500
Less:	Creditor	1,500
		20,000
Capital		20,000

Note how the total of each part of the balance sheet has not changed. The business is still worth £20,000 to the owner K Astley.

Collection of an asset (7)

P Hall, who owed Astley £500, makes a part payment of £250 by cheque on 31 January 2008. The effect is to reduce one asset, debtor, and to increase another asset, bank. The balance sheet after these transactions is now shown:

K Astley
Balance Sheet as at 31 January 2008

		£
Assets:	Building	10,000
	Stock of goods	1,500
	Debtor	750
	Cash at bank	9,250
		21,500
Less:	Creditor	1,500
		20,000
Capital		20,000

2.3 Equality of the accounting equation

It can be seen that every transaction has affected two items. Sometimes it has changed two assets by reducing one and increasing the other. In other cases, the effect has been different. You will notice, however, that in all cases apart from the very first (when the owner started the business by putting in cash of £20,000) no change has been made to the total of either section of the balance sheet and the equality between their two totals has remained the same. The accounting equation has held true throughout the example and, in fact, always will.

The effect of each of the seven accounting transactions, shown above, upon the two sections of the balance sheet is now illustrated in Exhibit 2.1.

Exhibit 2.1

Type of transaction	Effect	
1 Owner pays capital into the bank	⬆ Increase asset (Bank)	⬆ Increase capital
2 Purchase of a building by cheque	⬇ Decrease asset (Bank)	⬆ Increase asset (Building)
3 Buy goods on credit	⬆ Increase asset (Stock of goods)	⬆ Increase liability (Creditors)
4 Sale of goods on credit	⬇ Decrease asset (Stock of goods)	⬆ Increase asset (Debtors)
5 Sale of goods for cash or cheque	⬆ Increase asset (Cash or bank)	⬇ Decrease asset (Stock of goods)
6 Pay creditor	⬇ Decrease asset (Bank)	⬇ Decrease liability (Creditor)
7 Debtor pays money owing by cheque	⬆ Increase asset (Bank)	⬇ Decrease asset (Debtors)

Each transaction has, therefore, maintained the same total for assets as for capital + liabilities. This can be shown:

Number of transactions as above	Assets	Capital and Liabilities	Effect on balance sheet totals
1	+	+	Each side added to equally
2	– +		A minus and a plus both on the assets side thus cancelling out each other
3	+	+	Each side added to equally
4	– +		A minus and a plus on the assets side
5	+ –		A plus and a minus both on the assets side cancelling out each other
6	–	–	Each side reduced equally
7	+ –		A plus and a minus on the assets side

2.4 More detailed presentation of the balance sheet

The balance sheets shown in this chapter are presented in what is referred to as the 'vertical presentation'. This method will be used throughout the book since it is the most common method of presentation used today.

A more detailed balance sheet of K Astley is now shown in line with how you will learn to present the information in later stages of your studies:

K Astley
Balance Sheet as at 31 January 2008

		£
Fixed assets		
Buildings		10,000
Current assets		
Stock of goods	1,500	
Debtor	750	
Cash at bank	9,250	
	11,500	
Less: Current Liabilities		
Creditor	1,500	10,000
		20,000
Capital		20,000

You will have noticed the use of the terms 'fixed assets', 'current assets' and 'current liabilities'. Chapter 9 contains a full and proper examination of these terms. At this point we will simply say that:

- **fixed assets** are assets to be kept as such for a few years at least, e.g. buildings, machinery, fixtures, motor vehicles;
- **current assets** are assets which change from day to day, e.g. the value of stock in hand goes up and down as it is bought and sold. Similarly, the amount of money owing to us by debtors will change quickly, as we sell more to them on credit and they pay their debts. The amount of money in the bank will also change as we receive and pay out money;
- **current liabilities** are those liabilities which have to be paid within the near future, e.g. creditors for goods bought.

Note: Generally, the figures used for exhibits and for exercises have been kept down to relatively small amounts. This has been done deliberately to make the work of the user of this book that much easier. Constantly handling large figures does not add anything to the study of the principles of accounting; instead, it simply wastes a lot of students' time, and they will probably make many more errors if larger figures are used. This approach could lead to the accusation of not being 'realistic' with the figures given, but we believe that it is far more important to make learning easier for the student.

Chapter summary

- The whole of accounting is based on the accounting equation namely that resources supplied by the owner (the capital) will always equal the resources in the business (the assets).
- Other people may also supply some of the assets to the business. The name given to any amounts that are owed by the business to other people are called liabilities.

- When assets are supplied by other people as well as the owner of the business the accounting equation becomes Capital = Assets − Liabilities.
- The two sides of the accounting equation are represented by the two sections of the balance sheet.
- The balance sheet is a financial statement prepared at a particular point in time. It contains assets, capital and liabilities.
- The totals of each part of the balance sheet should always agree, i.e. balance.
- Every transaction affects two items in the accounting equation. Sometimes that may involve the same item being affected twice, once positively (going up) and once negatively (going down).
- Every transaction affects two items in the balance sheet.

Reminder: There is a Glossary of accounting terms in Appendix A at the end of the book.

Exercises

*Note: Questions with the suffix 'X' shown after the question number do **not** have answers shown at the back of the book. Answers to the other questions are shown in Appendix E.*

2.1 Examine the following table and complete the gaps:

	Assets £	Liabilities £	Capital £
(a)	34,282	7,909	?
(b)	276,303	?	213,817
(c)	?	6,181	70,919
(d)	?	109,625	877,138
(e)	88,489	?	78,224
(f)	456,066	51,163	?

2.2X Examine the following table and complete the gaps:

	Assets £	Liabilities £	Capital £
(a)	?	59,997	604,337
(b)	346,512	?	293,555
(c)	47,707	?	42,438
(d)	108,129	11,151	?
(e)	515,164	77,352	?
(f)	?	19,928	179,352

2.3 Determine which are assets and which are liabilities from the following list:

(a) Computer equipment
(b) Stock of goods
(c) Loan from H Barlow
(d) Motor vehicles
(e) What we owe for advertising materials
(f) Bank balance.

2.4X   Which of the following are assets and which are liabilities?

(*a*) Premises
(*b*) Debtors
(*c*) Cash in hand
(*d*) Creditors
(*e*) Loan from finance company
(*f*) Owing to bank
(*g*) Machinery
(*h*) Motor vehicles.

2.5   State which of the following are shown under the wrong headings for S Murphy's business:

Assets	Liabilities
Cash in hand	Money owing to bank
Creditors	Debtors
Premises	Stock of goods
Motor vehicles	
Loan from C Shaw	
Machinery	

2.6X   Which of the following are shown under the wrong headings?:

Assets	Liabilities
Cash at bank	Machinery
Computer equipment	Motor vehicles
Creditors	Loan from W Barlow
Capital	
Debtors	
Stock of goods	

2.7   Ann Wood decides to open a retail shop selling greetings cards and gifts. Her uncle lends her £30,000 to help her with financing the venture. Ann buys shop premises costing £50,000, a motor vehicle for £10,000 and stock of goods for £5,000. Ann did not pay for her stock of goods in full and still owes £2,100 to her suppliers in respect of them. After the events described above and before she starts trading, Ann has £100 cash in hand and £7,000 cash at the bank.

You are required to calculate the amount of capital that Ann invested in her business.

2.8X   Suman Patel decides to start his own retail business and his father agrees to lend him £3,000. Before starting trading he decides to buy some shop fittings costing £4,000 and a secondhand motor van costing £6,100.

Suman also buys a stock of goods for £5,720 paying £3,000 when he placed the order, the balance being due in two months. After paying for the above items Suman has £4,200 in the bank and £120 in cash.

You are required to calculate Suman's capital.

2.9   Draw up T Lymer's balance sheet, using the vertical presentation method, from the following information as at 31 December 2007.

	£
Capital	34,823
Delivery van	12,000
Debtors	10,892
Office furniture	8,640
Stock of goods	4,220
Cash at bank	11,722
Creditors	12,651

2.10X Draw up A Pennington's balance sheet as at 31 March 2008 from the following information:

	£
Premises	50,000
Plant and machinery	26,500
Debtors	28,790
Creditors	32,320
Bank overdraft	3,625
Stock	21,000
Cash in hand	35
Capital	90,380

2.11 Complete the columns to show the effects of the following transactions:

Effects upon

Assets   *Capital*   *Liabilities*

(*a*) Bought goods on credit £400.
(*b*) F Drew lends the firm £500 by cheque.
(*c*) We return goods £50 to a supplier whose account
    was still outstanding.
(*d*) We pay a creditor £330 by cheque.
(*e*) The owner of the business introduces £5,000 into
    the firm by cheque.
(*f*) Bought computer £880 for office use paying by cheque.
(*g*) Sold goods for cash £45.
(*h*) A debtor pays us in cash £77.

For each item shown above, you are required to state how it changes assets, capital or liabilities.

    For example the answer to (*a*) will be:

(*a*) *Assets*   *Capital*   *Liabilities*
    + £400   –   + £400

CHAPTER 3

The double entry system for assets, liabilities and capital

Learning objectives

After you have studied this chapter, you should be able to:

● understand what is meant by the double entry system
● explain how the double entry system follows the rules of the accounting equation
● understand the rules for double entry book-keeping
● be able to draw up 'T-accounts' and understand the terms 'debit' and 'credit'
● be able to record transactions affecting assets, liabilities and capital in the T-accounts.

3.1 Nature of a transaction

In Chapter 2 we saw how various events changed two items in the balance sheet. Events which result in such changes are known as **transactions**. This means that if the proprietor of a business asks the price of some goods but does not buy them, then there is no transaction. If he later asks the price of some goods and then buys them, in this second case there is a transaction, since it would mean that two balance sheet items, i.e. stock of goods and cash at bank, will have changed.

3.2 The double entry system

The system of double entry book-keeping is a method of recording transactions in the books of account of a business. In the previous chapter we saw how every transaction affected two items. We now need to show these effects when the transaction is first recorded in the books of account. The information for every item that is entered into the books of account is obtained from a source document, i.e. invoice, credit note, cheque book stub, paying in book etc. The next important stage is to understand the double entry system of book-keeping.

Business transactions deal with money or money's worth and each transaction always affects two things. For example, if a firm buys goods valued at £500 and pays for them by cheque, two things have occurred:

1 the money in the firm's bank account will have decreased by £500

2 the stock of goods is increased.

Here is another example: if a firm buys a motor van costing £10,000 and pays for it by cheque then again two things have been affected:

1 the money in the firm's bank account will have decreased by £10,000

2 the motor van will have been acquired for the business and that asset account will have increased.

This is the book-keeping stage of accounting and the process used is called **double entry**; sometimes this may also be referred to as **double entry book-keeping**, either term is correct.

In the previous chapter a new balance sheet was drawn up after each transaction. This can be done quite easily if there are only a few transactions per day. However, if there are hundreds of transactions per day then it will become impossible to draw up numerous balance sheets. There simply would not be enough time to carry out such a task.

Therefore, instead of constantly drawing up amended balance sheets after each transaction what we have instead is the double entry system. The basis of this system is that the transactions that have occurred are entered in the books of account, as mentioned above. An **account** shows us the 'history of' a particular business transaction. It is the place in the records where all the information referring to a particular asset, liability or capital is entered, for example, the bank account or motor van account. If manual records are kept, then each account is usually shown on a separate page; if a computerised system is used, then each account is given a separate code number and the information is stored on the accounting package and back-up discs.

3.3 The accounts for double entry

Each account should be shown on a separate page. The double entry system divides each page into two halves. The left-hand side of each page is called the **debit** side, while the the right-hand side is called the **credit** side. The title of each account is written across the top of the account at the centre – see Exhibit 3.1. Note that the word 'Debit' is often shown in a short form as *Dr*, whilst 'Credit' is often shown as *Cr*.

Exhibit 3.1

Title of account written here					
Date	Details	£	Date	Details	£

Left-hand side of the page.
This is the 'debit' side.

Right-hand side of the page.
This is the 'credit' side.

The words 'debit' and 'credit' in book-keeping terms do not mean the same as in normal language and should be viewed differently from the start to avoid confusion. Students new to studying double entry may find it useful to think of 'IN' when looking at the entry of a debit item, and to think of 'OUT' when looking at the entry of a credit item. We will consider this later in Section 3.5.

3.4 Rules for double entry

Double entry is relatively easy to learn and understand if the following four rules are learnt and understood:

1 Double entry means that every transaction affects two things and should, therefore, be entered twice: once on the *Debit* side and once on the *Credit* side.
2 The order in which the items are entered does not matter – although students may find it easier to deal with any cash or bank transaction first using the 'IN' and 'OUT' principle.
3 A **Debit entry** is always an asset or an expense. A **Credit entry** is a liability, capital or income.
4 To increase or decrease assets, liabilities or capital, as seen in Chapter 2, the double entry rules are as shown in Exhibit 3.2.

Exhibit 3.2

Accounts	To record	Entry in the account
Assets	↑ an increase ↓ a decrease	Debit Credit
Liabilities	↑ an increase ↓ a decrease	Credit Debit
Capital	↑ an increase ↓ a decrease	Credit Debit

Let's look once again at the accounting equation:

	Capital =	Assets –	Liabilities
To increase each item	Credit	Debit	Credit
To decrease each item	Debit	Credit	Debit

The double entry rules for liabilities and capital are the same, but they are the opposite of those for assets. Looking at the accounts the rules will appear as:

Capital account		Any asset account		Any liability account	
Decreases	Increases	Increases	Decreases	Decreases	Increases
−	+	+	−	−	+

In a real business, at least one full page would be taken for each account in the accounting books. However, as we have not enough space in this textbook to put each account on a separate page, we will list the accounts under each other.

3.5 The 'IN' and 'OUT' approach

To help students having difficulty in deciding on which side of each account the items should be entered, a useful hint is for them to think of the debit side being 'IN' to the account, and the credit side being 'OUT' of the account.

To give two examples of this approach, we will use the following:

Example 1: Paid cash £200 to buy machinery

The double entry for this transaction would be as follows:

Effect	Action
(a) Machinery comes 'IN'	A *debit* entry in the Machinery account
(b) Cash goes 'OUT'	A *credit* entry in the Cash account

Example 2: Took £500 out of the cash in hand of the business and paid it into the bank account of the business.

The double entry for this transaction would be as follows:

Effect	Action
(a) Money comes 'IN' to the bank	A *debit* entry in the Bank account
(b) Cash goes 'OUT' of the cash till	A *credit* entry in the Cash account

3.6 T accounts

The type of accounts that are going to be demonstrated are known as **T accounts**. This is because the accounts are in the shape of a T, as illustrated in Exhibit 3.3.

Exhibit 3.3

Account title here: the top stroke of the T

Debit side | Credit side

The line divides the two sides and is the downstroke of the T.

3.7 Worked examples

The entry of a few transactions can now be attempted:

Example 3: The proprietor starts the firm with £10,000 in cash on 1 August 2006.

Effect	Action
(a) Increases the *asset* of cash (b) Increases the *capital*	Debit the cash account – cash goes 'IN' Credit the capital account – cash comes 'OUT' of the owner's money

These are entered as follows:

Cash Account

Dr   Cr

2006	£	
Aug 1	10,000	

Capital Account

Dr   Cr

		2006	£
		Aug 1	10,000

The date of the transaction has already been entered. Now there remains the description which is to be entered alongside the amount. The double entry to the item in the cash account is completed by an entry in the capital account, and therefore the word 'Capital' will appear in the cash account. Similarly, the double entry to the item in the capital account is completed by an entry in the cash account, and therefore the word 'Cash' will appear in the capital account.

The finally completed accounts are therefore:

Cash Account

Dr   Cr

2006		£	
Aug 1	Capital	10,000	

Capital Account

Dr   Cr

		2006		£
		Aug 1	Cash	10,000

This method of entering transactions therefore fulfils the requirements of the double entry rules as shown in Section 3.4. Now let us look at the entry of some more transactions.

Example 4: A motor van is bought for £7,500 cash on 2 August 2006.

Effect	Action
(a) Decreases the *asset* of cash	Credit the cash account – Cash goes 'OUT'
(b) Increases the *asset* of motor van	Debit the motor van account – Motor van comes 'IN'

Cash Account

Dr				Cr
		2006		£
		Aug 2 Motor van		7,500

Motor Van Account

Dr				Cr
2006		£		
Aug 2 Cash		7,500		

Example 5: Fixtures bought on credit from Shop Fitters for £1,500 on 3 August 2006.

Effect	Action
(a) Increases the *asset* of Fixtures	Debit the Fixtures account – Fixtures go 'IN'
(b) Increases the *liability* to Shop Fitters	Credit the Shop Fitters' account – Fixtures come 'OUT' of the supplier's account

Fixtures Account

Dr				Cr
2006		£		
Aug 3 Shop Fitters		1,500		

Shop Fitters' Account

Dr				Cr
		2006		£
		Aug 3 Fixtures		1,500

Example 6: Paid the amount owing in cash to Shop Fitters on 17 August 2006.

Effect	Action
(a) Decreases the *asset* of cash	Credit the cash account – Cash goes 'OUT'
(b) Decreases the *liability* to Shop Fitters	Debit the Shop Fitters' account – Cash goes 'IN' to the supplier's account

Cash Account

Dr				Cr
		2006		£
		Aug 17 Shop Fitters		1,500

Shop Fitters' Account

Dr		Cr
2006	£	
Aug 17 Cash	1,500	

***Example* 7**: Transactions to date.

Taking the transactions numbered 3 to 6 above, the records will now appear thus:

Cash Account

Dr			Cr
2006	£	2006	£
Aug 1 Capital	10,000	Aug 2 Motor Van	7,500
		Aug 17 Shop Fitters	1,500

Capital Account

Dr		Cr
	2006	£
	Aug 1 Cash	10,000

Motor Van Account

Dr		Cr
2006	£	
Aug 2 Cash	7,500	

Shop Fitter's Account

Dr			Cr
2006	£	2006	£
Aug 17 Cash	1,500	Aug 3 Fixtures	1,500

Fixtures Account

Dr		Cr
2006	£	
Aug 3 Shop Fitters	1,500	

Before you read further, you are required to work through Exercises 3.1 and 3.2 at the end of the chapter.

***Example* 8**: Now you have actually made some entries in accounts, you are to go carefully through the example shown in Exhibit 3.4. Make certain you can understand every entry.

Exhibit 3.4

Transactions	Effect	Action	IN/OUT
2006 May 1 Started an engineering business putting £10,000 into a business bank account.	⬆ Increases *asset* of bank. ⬆ Increases *capital* of owner.	Debit bank account. Credit capital account.	IN OUT
May 3 Bought works machinery on credit from Unique Machines £2,750.	⬆ Increases *asset* of machinery. ⬆ Increases *liability* to Unique Machines.	Debit machinery account. Credit Unique Machines account.	IN OUT
May 4 Withdrew £2,000 cash from the bank and placed it in the cash box.	⬇ Decreases *asset* of bank. ⬆ Increases *asset* of cash.	Credit bank account. Debit cash account.	OUT IN
May 7 Bought a motor van paying in cash £1,800.	⬇ Decreases *asset* of cash. ⬆ Increases *asset* of motor van.	Credit cash account. Debit motor van account.	OUT IN
May 10 Sold some of the machinery for £150 on credit to B Barnes.	⬇ Decreases *asset* of machinery. ⬆ Increases *asset* of money owing from B Barnes.	Credit machinery account. Debit B Barnes account.	OUT IN
May 21 Returned some of the machinery, value £270 to Unique Machines.	⬇ Decreases *asset* of machinery. ⬇ Decreases *liability* to Unique Machines.	Credit machinery account. Debit Unique Machines account.	OUT IN
May 28 B Barnes pays the firm the amount owing, £150, by cheque.	⬆ Increases *asset* of bank. ⬇ Decreases *asset* of money owing by B Barnes.	Debit bank account. Credit B Barnes account.	IN OUT
May 30 Bought another motor van for £4,200, paying by cheque.	⬇ Decreases *asset* of bank. ⬆ Increases *asset* of motor vans.	Credit bank account. Debit motor van account.	OUT IN
May 31 Paid the amount of £2,480 to Unique Machines by cheque.	⬇ Decreases *asset* of bank. ⬇ Decreases *liability* to Unique Machines.	Credit bank account. Debit Unique Machines account.	OUT IN

In account form this is shown thus:

Bank Account

Dr   Cr

2006		£	2006		£
May 1	Capital	10,000	May 4	Cash	2,000
May 28	B Barnes	150	May 30	Motor van	4,200
			May 30	Unique Machines	2,480

Cash Account

Dr   Cr

2006		£	2006		£
May 4	Bank	2,000	May 7	Motor van	1,800

Capital Account

Dr   Cr

			2006		£
			May 1	Bank	10,000

Machinery Account

Dr   Cr

2006		£	2006		£
May 3	Unique Machines	2,750	May 10	B Barnes	150
			May 21	Unique Machines	270

Motor Van Account

Dr   Cr

2006		£			
May 7	Cash	1,800			
May 30	Bank	4,200			

Unique Machines Account

Dr   Cr

2006		£	2006		£
May 21	Machinery	270	May 3	Machinery	2,750
May 31	Bank	2,480			

B Barnes Account

Dr   Cr

2006		£	2006		£
May 10	Machinery	150	May 28	Bank	150

3.8 Abbreviation of 'Limited'

In this book, when we come across transactions with limited companies the letters
'Ltd' are used as the abbreviation for 'Limited Company'. Thus you will know that, if

you see the name of a firm as 'T Lee Ltd', that business will be a limited company. In our books, the transactions with T Lee Ltd will be entered in the same way as for any other customer or supplier.

Chapter summary

- The chapter covers the concept of double entry book-keeping whereby every transaction affects two things. Each item has to be entered twice in the book-keeping records, once on the debit side of an account and once on the credit side of an account.
- Double entry follows the rules of the accounting equation.
- Transactions are entered into the accounts rather than directly into numerous balance sheets.
- The use of 'T accounts' to record information is discussed.
- The chapter contains a fully worked example illustrating how transactions cause increases and decreases in asset, liability and capital accounts.

Exercises

3.1 Complete the following table showing which accounts are to be credited and which to be debited:

	Account to be debited	Account to be credited
(a) Bought motor van for cash		
(b) Bought office machinery on credit from J Grant & Son		
(c) Introduced capital in cash		
(d) A debtor, J Beach, pays us by cheque		
(e) Paid a creditor, A Barrett, in cash.		

3.2X Complete the following table showing which accounts are to be debited and which accounts are to be credited:

	Account to be debited	Account to be credited
(a) Bought computer equipment for office paying by cheque		
(b) A debtor, Bush Ltd, pays us by cheque		
(c) Owner of the business puts further money into the business by cheque		
(d) Paid a creditor, Ash & Co, by cheque		
(e) Bought office chair paying by cash		
(f) Bought a motor car paying by cheque		
(g) Mike Meredith lent the business £5,000 paying by cheque		
(h) Sold old motor van, received cash, £600		
(i) Paid a creditor, Skinners Ltd, by cash		
(j) Bought desk for computer paying by cheque.		

3.3 Write up the asset and liability and capital accounts to record the following transactions in the records of G Powell.

2008
July 1 Started business with £2,500 in the bank
July 2 Bought office furniture by cheque, £150
July 3 Bought machinery £750 on credit from Planers Ltd
July 5 Bought a second-hand van paying by cheque, £600
July 8 Sold some of the office furniture – not suitable for the firm – for £60 on credit to J Walker & Sons
July 15 Paid the amount owing to Planers Ltd, £750, by cheque
July 23 Received the amount due from J Walker, £60, in cash
July 31 Bought more machinery by cheque, £280.

3.4X You are required to open the asset, liability and capital accounts and record the following transactions for May 2008 in the records of John Morgan & Co.

2008
May 1 Started in business with £12,000 in cash
May 2 Paid £11,750 of the opening cash into a bank account for the business
May 4 Bought office furniture on credit from Office Supplies Ltd for £770
May 11 Bought computer equipment £2,000 paying by cheque
May 17 Bought benches for workroom on credit from Baxter's Ltd, £1,500
May 22 Returned one of the work benches, costing £500, which was broken to Baxter's Ltd. They agreed to credit our account.
May 24 Paid amount owing to Office Supplies Ltd by cheque
May 28 Bought secondhand motor van paying by cheque, £3,000
May 30 Bought secondhand work bench paying by cash, £100
May 31 Paid the amount outstanding to Baxter's Ltd by cheque.

3.5 Write up the asset, capital and liability accounts in the books of A Burton to record the following transactions:

2008
July 1 Started in business with £15,000 in the bank
July 3 Bought motor car and paid by cheque, £6,500
July 9 Bought office furniture from Cheetham & Co £1,150 paid by cheque
July 12 Bought computer on credit from Computext Ltd, £2,400
July 17 Took £200 out of the bank and put it in the cash till
July 19 Bought office chair and paid by cash, £42
July 25 Paid Computext Ltd £1,000 on account
July 27 Bought secondhand motor van, £2,450 paid by cheque
July 29 Bought desk for reception area and paid cash, £100
July 31 Paid the outstanding account to Computext Ltd by cheque.

3.6X Write up the various accounts needed in the books of S Russell to record the following transactions:

2008
April 1 Opened business with £10,000 in the bank
April 3 Bought office equipment for £700 on credit from J Saunders Ltd
April 6 Bought motor van, paying by cheque, £3,000
April 8 Borrowed £1,000 from H Thompson – he gave us the money by cheque
April 11 Russell put further capital into the firm in the form of cash, £500

April 12 Paid £350 of the cash in hand into the bank account

April 15 Returned some of the office equipment costing £200 – it was faulty – to J Saunders Ltd

April 17 Bought more office equipment, paying by cash, £50

April 19 Sold the motor van, as it had proved unsuitable, to R Jones for £3,000. R Jones will settle for this by three payments later this month

April 21 Received a loan in cash from J Hawkins, £400

April 22 R Jones paid us a cheque for £1,000

April 23 Bought a suitable motor van £3,600 on credit from Phillips Garages Ltd

April 26 R Jones paid us a cheque for £1,800

April 28 Paid £2,000 by cheque to Phillips Garages Ltd

April 30 R Jones paid us cash, £200.

CHAPTER 4

The double entry system for the asset of stock

Learning objectives

After you have studied this chapter you should be able to:

- understand the terms cost price and selling price, the monetary difference between the two being the profit which is one of the main aims of a business
- understand the need to use various accounts in recording the movement of stock, i.e. sales, purchases, returns inwards and returns outwards accounts
- record the purchase and sale of goods both by credit and cash using the double entry system
- record the return of goods in the returns inwards account using the double entry system when customers return goods to the firm
- record the return of goods in the returns outwards account using the double entry system when the firm returns goods to their supplier
- explain the meanings of the terms 'purchases' and 'sales' as used in accounting
- understand the differences in recording sales for cash compared with sales made on credit.

4.1 Introduction

One of the main aims of organisations is to make a **profit** and continue to remain in business. To achieve this aim many firms buy goods at cost price and sell them to their customers at the higher selling price, the difference being **profit**. The same applies to a firm offering services to their customers. If, however, goods and services are sold for less than their cost, the difference is a **loss**. Firms cannot sustain a loss indefinitely as eventually they would cease to be able to trade. In Chapter 2 it was assumed that all the goods were sold at the same price that they were bought, which of course is extremely unusual. We will now consider the accounts needed to record the purchase at cost price and the sale of goods at selling price.

4.2 Stock movements

A business, on any particular date, will normally have goods which have been bought previously and have not yet been sold. These unsold goods are known as the business's 'stock' of goods. The stock of goods in a business is therefore constantly changing because some of it is bought, some of it is sold, some is returned to the suppliers and some is returned by the firm's customers.

To keep a check on the movement of stock, various accounts are opened as shown in the table below:

Account	Reason
Purchases Account	For the purchase of goods
Sales Account	For the sale of goods
Returns Inwards Account	For goods returned to the firm by its customers
Returns Outwards Account	For goods returned by the firm to its suppliers

As stock is an asset, and these four accounts are all connected with this asset, the double entry rules are those used for assets.

We shall now look at some specific entries in the following sections.

4.3   Purchase of stock on credit

On 1 August 2006, goods costing £165 are bought on credit from D Henry. First, the twofold effect of the transaction must be considered so that the book-keeping entries can be worked out. We have the following:

(a) *The asset of stock is increased.* An increase in an asset needs a debit entry in an account. Here, the account is a stock account showing the particular movement of stock; in this case it is the purchases movement, so the account must be the purchases account.

(b) *There is an increase in a liability.* This is the liability of the firm to D Henry because the goods supplied have not yet been paid for. An increase in a liability needs a credit entry, and so in order to enter this part of the transaction a credit entry is made in D Henry's account.

Here again, we can use the idea of the debit side being 'IN' to the account, and the credit side being 'OUT' of the account. In this example, purchases have come 'IN', thus creating a debit in the Purchase Account; and the goods have come 'OUT' of D Henry, needing a credit in the account of D Henry. Thus:

Purchases Account

Dr				Cr
2006		£		
Aug 1 D Henry		165		

D Henry Account

Dr				Cr
			2006	£
			Aug 1 Purchases	165

4.4 Purchases of stock for cash

On 2 August 2006, goods costing £220 were bought, cash being paid for them immediately. As a result:

(*a*) *The asset of stock is increased.* Thus, a debit entry will be needed. The movement of stock is that of a purchase, so it is the Purchases Account which needs debiting. (Purchases have come 'IN' – debit the Purchases Account.)

(*b*) *The asset of cash is decreased.* To reduce an asset a credit entry is called for, and the asset is that of cash so the Cash Account needs crediting. (Cash has gone 'OUT' – credit the Cash Account.)

Purchases Account

Dr			Cr
2006	£		
Aug 2 Cash	220		

Cash Account

Dr			Cr
		2006	£
		Aug 2 Purchases	220

4.5 Sales of stock on credit

On 3 August 2006, a business sold goods on credit for £250 to K Leach. Then:

(*a*) *An asset account is increased.* This is the account showing that K Leach is a debtor for the goods. The increase in the asset of debtors requires a debit and the debtor is K Leach, so the account concerned is that of K Leach. (Goods have gone 'IN' to K Leach – debit K Leach's account.)

(*b*) *The asset of stock is decreased.* For this, a credit entry to reduce an asset is needed. The movement of stock is that of 'Sales' and so the account credited is the Sales Account. (Sales have gone 'OUT' – credit the Sales Account.)

Thus:

K Leach Account

Dr			Cr
2006	£		
Aug 3 Sales	250		

Sales Account

Dr			Cr
		2006	£
		Aug 3 K Leach	250

4.6 Sales of stock for cash

On 4 August 2006, goods are sold for £55, the cash for them being paid immediately. Then:

(a) *The asset of cash is increased.* A debit in the cash account is needed to show this. (Cash has come 'IN' – debit the Cash Account.)

(b) *The asset of stock is reduced.* The reduction of an asset requires a credit and the movement of stock is represented by 'Sales'. So the entry needed is a credit in the Sales Account. (Sales have gone 'OUT' – credit the Sales Account.)

Cash Account

Dr				Cr
2006	£			
Aug 4 Sales	55			

Sales Account

Dr				Cr
		2006		£
		Aug 4 Cash		55

4.7 Returns inwards

Returns inwards represent goods sold which have subsequently been returned by a customer. This could be for various reasons, such as:

● the goods sent to the customer are of the incorrect size, colour or model
● the goods have been damaged in transit
● the goods are of poor quality.

An alternative name for a returns inwards account is a sales returns account.

Just as the original sale was entered in the double entry system, so the return of those goods must also be entered.

On 5 August 2006, goods which had previously been sold to F Lowe for £29 have been returned by him. As a result:

(a) *The asset of stock was increased by the goods returned.* A debit representing an increase of an asset is needed, and this time the movement of stock is that of 'Returns Inwards'. The entry required therefore is a debit in the Returns Inwards Account. (The goods have come 'IN' – debit the Returns Inwards Account.)

(b) *An asset is decreased.* The debt of F Lowe to the firm is now reduced, and to record this a credit is required in F Lowe's account. (The goods have come 'OUT' of F Lowe – credit the F Lowe Account.)

The movements are shown thus:

Returns Inwards Account

Dr			Cr
2006	£		
Aug 5 F Lowe	29		

F Lowe Account

Dr			Cr
		2006	£
		Aug 5 Returns inwards	29

4.8 Returns outwards

These represent goods which were purchased, and are now being returned to the supplier. As the original purchase was entered in the double entry system, so also is the return to the supplier of those goods.

On 6 August 2006, goods previously bought for £96 are returned by the firm to K Howe. Thus:

(a) *The liability of the firm to K Howe is decreased by the value of the goods returned to him.* The decrease in a liability needs a debit, this time in the K Howe Account. (The goods have gone 'IN' to K Howe – debit the K Howe Account.)

(b) *The asset of stock is decreased by the goods sent out.* A credit representing a reduction in an asset is needed, and the movement of stock is that of 'Returns Outwards', so the entry will be a credit in the returns outwards account. (The returns have gone 'OUT' – credit the Returns Outward Account.)

K Howe Account

Dr			Cr
2006	£		
Aug 6 Returns outwards	96		

Returns Outwards Account

Dr			Cr
		2006	£
		Aug 6 K Howe	96

An alternative name for a returns outwards account is a purchases returns account.

4.9 A worked example

Enter the following transactions in suitable double entry accounts:

2006
May 1 Bought goods on credit £68 from D Small
May 2 Bought goods on credit £77 from A Lyon & Son
May 5 Sold goods on credit to D Hughes for £60
May 6 Sold goods on credit to M Spencer for £45
May 10 Returned goods £15 to D Small
May 12 Goods bought for cash, £100
May 19 M Spencer returned £16 goods to us
May 21 Goods sold for cash, £150
May 22 Paid cash to D Small, £53
May 30 D Hughes paid the amount owing by him £60 in cash
May 31 Bought goods on credit £64 from A Lyon & Son.

The double entry accounts can now be shown as:

Purchases Account

Dr		£		Cr
2006				
May 1	D Small	68		
May 2	A Lyon & Son	77		
May 12	Cash	100		
May 31	A Lyon & Son	64		

Sales Account

Dr				Cr
		2006		£
		May 5	D Hughes	60
		May 6	M Spencer	45
		May 21	Cash	150

Returns Outwards Account

Dr				Cr
		2006		£
		May 10	D Small	15

Returns Inwards Account

Dr		£		Cr
2006				
May 19	M Spencer	16		

D Small Account

Dr   Cr

2006		£	2006		£
May 10	Returns outwards	15	May 1	Purchases	68
May 22	Cash	53			

A Lyon & Son Account

Dr   Cr

			2006		£
			May 2	Purchases	77
			May 31	Purchases	64

D Hughes Account

Dr   Cr

2006		£	2006		£
May 5	Sales	60	May 30	Cash	60

M Spencer Account

Dr   Cr

2006		£	2006		£
May 6	Sales	45	May 19	Returns inwards	16

Cash Account

Dr   Cr

2006		£	2006		£
May 21	Sales	150	May 12	Purchases	100
May 30	D Hughes	60	May 22	D Small	53

4.10 Special meaning of 'sales' and 'purchases'

It must be emphasised that 'sales' and 'purchases' have a special meaning in accounting language.

Purchases in accounting means 'the purchase of those goods which the firm buys with the prime intention of selling'. Sometimes the goods may be altered, added to or used in the manufacture of something else, but it is the element of *resale* that is important. To a firm that trades in computers, for instance, computers are purchases. If something else is bought, such as a motor van, such an item cannot be called purchases, even though in ordinary language it may be said that a motor van has been purchased. The prime intention of buying the motor van is for use by the company and not for resale.

Similarly, **sales** means the 'sale of those goods in which the firm normally deals and that were bought with the prime intention of resale'. The description 'sales' must never be given to the disposal of other items.

If we did not keep to these meanings, it would result in the different kinds of stock accounts containing something other than goods sold or for resale.

4.11 Comparison of cash and credit transactions for purchases and sales

The difference between the records needed for cash and credit transactions can now be seen.

The complete set of entries for purchases of goods where they are paid for immediately by cash would be:

(*a*) **debit the purchases account**
(*b*) **credit the cash account**.

On the other hand, the complete set of entries for the purchase of goods on credit can be broken down into two stages. First, the purchase of the goods and second, the payment for them. The first part is:

(*a*) **debit the purchases account**
(*b*) **credit the supplier's account**.

The second part is:

(*c*) **debit the supplier's account**
(*d*) **credit the cash account**.

The difference can now be seen. With the cash purchase, no record is kept of the supplier's account. This is because cash passes immediately and therefore there is no need to keep a check of indebtedness (money owing) to a supplier. On the other hand, in the credit purchase the records should show to whom money is owed until payment is made. A study of cash sales and credit sales will reveal a similar difference.

Cash Sales	Credit Sales
Complete entry: ● debit cash account ● credit sales account	First part: ● debit customer's account ● credit sales account Second part: ● debit cash account ● credit customer's account

Chapter summary

- To make a profit goods are bought at one price, the cost price, and sold at a higher price, the selling price; the difference is profit.
- If goods and/or services are sold for less than their cost, the difference, is a loss.
- One of the main objectives of all businesses is to make a profit and remain in business.
- Various accounts are used to record the movement of stock because stock is normally sold at a higher price than its cost.

- The accounts used to record the movement of stock are:
  - **purchases account** to record the purchases of stock as debit entries in the account since the goods come 'IN' to the firm
  - **sales account** for the sale of the goods as credit entries in the account because the goods go 'OUT' of the firm
  - **returns inwards account** to record goods that a customer returns to the firm as debit entries since the goods are returned 'IN' to the firm
  - **returns outwards account** to record goods that the firm returns to its suppliers as the goods go 'OUT' of the firm.
- The special meaning in accounting terms of 'purchases' and 'sales', namely that purchases refer to goods bought for resale. Purchases of assets such as a motor van to be used in the business, are recorded separately in the asset account, motor van. Sales refers to goods sold in the normal course of business. The disposal of an asset such as equipment should never be recorded in the sales account but recorded separately in a disposal account to be discussed later.
- Purchases for cash are *never* entered in the supplier's account whilst purchases on credit are *always* entered in the supplier's (creditor's) account.
- Sales for cash are *never* entered in the customer's account whilst sales on credit are *always* entered in the customer's (debtor's) account.

Exercises

4.1 Complete the following table showing which accounts are to be credited and which are to be debited:

	Account to be debited	Account to be credited
(a) Goods bought on credit from P Hart		
(b) Goods sold for cash		
(c) Bought motor car from Morgan Motors on credit		
(d) Bought goods on credit from Cohens Ltd		
(e) Returned some of the goods, which were faulty, to P Hart		
(f) Sold goods on credit to H Perkins		
(g) Goods sold, a cheque being received on the sale		
(h) Sold some of the office furniture for cash		
(i) H Perkins returned some of the goods to us		
(j) Goods brought on credit from P Griffith.		

4.2X   Complete the following table:

	Account to be debited	Account to be credited
(a) Bought goods on credit from J Needham		
(b) Bought goods paying by cheque		
(c) Sold goods for cash		
(d) We returned goods to J Needham		
(e) Bought computer for the office on credit from Smith Computers Ltd		
(f) Sold goods on credit to H Broad		
(g) Goods returned to us by H Broad		
(h) Bought goods for cash		
(i) We paid a creditor, W Simms, by cheque		
(j) Bought motor car on credit from Smithy Garage.		

4.3   Paul Garner decided to start his own business and asks you to assist him by entering the following transactions in the books of account for March 2006:

2006
March 1 Started business with £4,000 in cash
March 2 Bought goods £1,230 on credit from Flynn Bros
March 4 Bought goods for cash, £345
March 7 Sold goods for cash, £120
March 10 Opened a bank account and took £3,500 out of the cash and put it in the bank
March 14 Bought a computer to use in the office paid by cheque, £1,000
March 16 Sold goods on credit to D Knott, £600
March 20 Bought goods £450 on credit from Flynn Bros
March 23 Sold goods on credit to Bateson's Ltd, £570
March 25 We returned goods to Flynn Bros, £75
March 27 Paid the amount due to Flynn Bros by cheque
March 30 Bateson's Ltd returned some faulty goods to us value, £109.

4.4   The following are the business transactions of Grace Andrews, a retailer of ladies wear, for the month of September 2005:

2005
Sept 1 Started in business with £10,000 in the bank and £100 of cash
Sept 3 Bought shop fittings £1,900 on credit from Duffy & Son
Sept 5 Bought goods on credit from Barrett's Fashions, £2,378
Sept 9 Bought computer for use within the business, £1,020 paid by cheque
Sept 10 Bought desk for office, £65 and paid cash
Sept 12 Sales of goods £800 paid into bank
Sept 15 Returned faulty goods to Barrett's Fashions, £180
Sept 22 Paid Duffy & Son by cheque, £1,900
Sept 25 Sales of goods £600 paid into bank
Sept 28 Bought goods on credit from Barrett's Fashions, £1,434
Sept 30 Sold goods for cash, £280
Sept 30 Bought secondhand motor car, £4,750.

As accounts assistant you have been asked to record the above transactions in the books of account for September 2005.

4.5X Ahmed's Ltd has just started his own business selling computer equipment and software. The following transactions took place during his first month of trading, June 2006. You are required to enter them into the books of account:

2006
June 1 Started in business with £20,000 in the bank
June 3 Bought stock of computers for resale £8,000 on credit from Computers Wholesale Ltd
June 4 Bought shop fittings paying by cheque, £1,690
June 8 Bought stock of software for resale, £1,000 paid by cheque
June 9 Bought motor car paying by cheque, £7,000
June 12 Sold goods, £1,700 by cheque
June 16 Returned faulty goods to Computers Wholesale Ltd, £900
June 20 Sold goods for cash, £340
June 26 Bought desk and chair for office, £300 paying by cheque
June 28 Sold goods on credit to Law & Co, £1,600
June 29 Paid Computers Wholesale Ltd £5,000 on account by cheque
June 30 Bought goods from Computers Wholesale Ltd on credit, £850
June 30 Law & Co return goods to us, £220
June 30 Sold goods, £2,300 by cheque.

4.6X You are to enter the following in the accounts needed:

2005
June 1 Started business with £1,000 cash
June 2 Paid £800 of the opening cash into a bank account for the firm
June 3 Bought goods on credit from H Grant, £330
June 4 Bought goods on credit from D Clark, £140
June 6 Sold goods on credit to B Miller, £90
June 8 Bought office furniture on credit from Barrett's Ltd, £400
June 10 Sold goods for cash, £120
June 13 Bought goods on credit from H Grant, £200
June 14 Bought goods for cash, £60
June 15 Sold goods on credit to H Sharples, £180
June 16 We returned goods worth £50 to H Grant
June 17 We returned some of the office furniture, cost £30, to Barrett's Ltd
June 18 Sold goods on credit to B Miller, £400
June 21 Paid H Grant's account by cheque, £480
June 23 B Miller paid us the amount owing in cash, £490
June 24 Sharples returned to us £50 of goods
June 25 Goods sold for cash, £150
June 28 Bought goods for cash, £370
June 30 Bought motor van on credit from J Kelly, £600.

CHAPTER 5

The double entry system for expenses and revenues

Learning objectives

After you have studied this chapter you should be able to:

- understand the concept of profit and loss by comparing revenue with expenses
- see the effects of profits and losses on capital and the relationship to the accounting equation
- understand why separate accounts are used for each type of expense and revenue
- be able to record expenses and revenues using the double entry system
- understand the term 'drawings', be able to record them and recognise the effects of drawings on capital.

5.1 The nature of profit or loss

To an accountant, **profit** means the amount by which **revenues** are greater than **expenses** for a set of transactions. The term 'revenues' means the sales value of goods and services that have been supplied to customers. The term **expenses** means the value of all the assets that have been used up to obtain those revenues.

If, therefore, we had supplied goods and services valued for sale at £100,000 to customers, and the expenses incurred by us to be able to supply those goods and services amounted to £70,000, then the result would be a profit calculated as follows:

		£
Revenues	Goods and services supplied to customers for the sum of	100,000
Less Expenses	Value of all the assets used up to enable us to supply the above goods and services	70,000
Profit		30,000

On the other hand, it is possible for our expenses to exceed our revenues for a set of transactions. In this case the result is a loss. For example a **loss** would be incurred given the following.

		£
Revenues	What we have charged to our customers in respect of all the goods and services supplied to them	60,000
Less Expenses	Value of all the assets used up to supply these goods and services to our customers	(80,000)
Loss is therefore		(20,000)

5.2 The effect of profit and loss on capital

Businesses exist to make profits and so increase their capital. Let's look at the relationship between profits and capital in an example.

On 1 January the assets and liabilities of a firm are:

● Assets: Fixtures £10,000, Stock £7,000,
            Cash at the bank £3,000.
● Liabilities: Creditors £2,000.

The capital is found from the accounting equation:

> **Capital = Assets − Liabilities**

In this case capital works out at Assets £10,000 + £7,000 + £3,000 − Liabilites £2,000 = £18,000.

During January the whole of the £7,000 stock is sold for £11,000 cash. On 31 January the assets and liabilities have become:

● Assets: Fixtures £10,000, Stock nil, Cash at the bank £14,000.
● Liabilities: Creditors £2,000.

The capital can be calculated:

Assets £10,000 + £14,000 − Liabilities £2,000 = £22,000

It can be seen that capital has increased from £18,000 to £22,000 = £4,000 increase because the £7,000 stock was sold for £11,000, a profit of £4,000. Profit, therefore, increases capital.

> **Old Capital + Profit = New Capital**
> **£18,000 + £4,000 = £22,000**

On the other hand, a loss would *reduce* the capital so:

> **Old Capital − Loss = New Capital**

5.3 Profit or loss and sales

Profit will be made when goods are sold at more than cost price, while the opposite will mean a **loss**.

5.4   Profit or loss and expenses

In Section 5.1 it was shown that profit was made when the goods were sold for more than the cost price. As well as the cost of the goods, a firm incurs other **expenses** such as rent, salaries, wages, telephone costs, motor expenses, and so on. Every £1 of expenses will mean £1 less profit.

All expenses could be charged to one Expense Account, but it would then be difficult to identify specific areas of the firms expenditure, such as the amount spent on motor running costs or rent. To facilitate the need to know different types of expenses, a separate account is opened for each type of expense, for instance:

- Rent Account
- Telephone Account
- Stationery Account
- Salaries Account
- Advertising Account
- Motor Expenses Account
- Wages Account
- Insurance Account
- Postages Account

In the same way that separate accounts are opened for each type of expense, separate accounts are also opened for any additional *revenue* that the business may receive, such as rent received or bank interest received. Again, separate revenue accounts can be opened as follows:

- Rent Receivable Account
- Commission Received Account
- Bank Interest Received Account

It is purely a matter of choice in a business as to the name of each expense or revenue account. For example, an account for postage stamps could be called 'Postage Stamp Account', 'Postage Account' or even 'Communication Expenses Account'. Also some businesses amalgamate expenses – for example, 'Printing, Stationery and Advertising Account'. Infrequent or small items of expense are usually put into a 'Sundry Expenses Account' or 'General Expenses Account'.

5.5   Debit or credit?

We have to decide whether expense accounts are to be debited or credited with the costs involved. Assets involve expenditure by the firm and are shown as debit entries. Expenses also involve expenditure by the firm and therefore should also be debit entries. Why? Because assets and expenses must ultimately be paid for. This payment involves a credit to the bank account (or to the cash account) so the original entry in the asset account or in the expense account must be a debit.

An alternative explanation may also be used for expenses. Every expense results in a decrease in an asset or an increase in a liability, and because of the accounting equation this means that the capital is reduced by each expense. The decreases in capital needs a debit entry and therefore expense accounts contain debit entries for expenses.

Revenue is the opposite of expenses and, therefore, appears on the opposite side to expenses – that is, revenue accounts appear on the credit side of the books. Pending the periodical calculation of profit, therefore, revenue is collected together in appropriately named accounts, and until it is transferred to the profit calculations it will need to be shown as a credit.

Consider, too, that expenditure of money pays for expenses, which are used up in the short term, or assets, which are used up in the long term – both for the purpose of winning revenue. Both of these are shown on the debit side of the accounts, while the revenue which has been won is shown on the credit side of the accounts.

5.6 Effect of transactions

A few illustrations will demonstrate the double entry required.

Example 1: Rent of £200 is paid in cash. Here the twofold effect is:
(*a*) *The total of the expenses of rent is increased* – a benefit goes 'IN'. As expense entries are shown as debits, and the expense is rent, so the action required is the debiting of the Rent Account.
(*b*) *The asset of cash is decreased* – money goes 'OUT'. This means crediting the Cash Account to show the decrease of the asset.

Summary: ● debit the rent account with £200 – 'IN'
● credit the cash account with £200 – 'OUT'.

Example 2: Motor expenses are paid with a cheque for £230. The twofold effect is:
(*a*) *The total of the motor expenses paid is increased* – a benefit is received 'IN'. To increase an expenses account needs a debit, and so the action required is to debit the Motor Expenses Account.
(*b*) *The asset of money in the bank is decreased* – money goes 'OUT'. This means crediting the Bank Account to show the decrease of the asset.

Summary: ● debit the motor expenses account with £230 – 'IN'
● credit the bank account with £230 – 'OUT'.

Example 3: £60 cash is paid for telephone expenses.
(*a*) *The total of telephone expenses is increased* – a benefit received goes 'IN'. Expenses are shown by a debit entry, and therefore to increase the expense account in question the action required is to debit the Telephone Expenses Account.
(*b*) *The asset of cash is decreased* – money goes 'OUT'. This needs a credit in the Cash Account to decrease the asset.

Summary: ● debit telephone expenses account with £60 – 'IN'
● credit the cash account with £60 – 'OUT'.

It is now possible to study the effects of some more transactions showing the results in the form of a table. See Exhibit 5.1.

Exhibit 5.1

	Increase	Action	Decrease	Action
2006 June 1 Paid for postage stamps by cash £20	Expense of postages	Debit postages account	Asset of cash	Credit cash account
2 Paid for advertising by cheque £290	Expense of advertising	Debit advertising account	Asset of bank	Credit bank account
3 Paid wages by cash £900	Expense of wages	Debit wages account	Asset of cash	Credit cash account
4 Paid insurance by cheque £420	Expense of insurance	Debit insurance account	Asset of bank	Credit bank account

The above four examples can now be shown in account form:

Cash Account

Dr			Cr
		2006	£
		June 1 Postages	20
		June 3 Wages	900

Bank Account

Dr			Cr
		2006	£
		June 2 Advertising	290
		June 4 Insurance	420

Advertising Account

Dr			Cr
2006	£		
June 2 Bank	290		

Insurance Account

Dr			Cr
2006	£		
June 4 Bank	420		

Postage Account

Dr			Cr
2006	£		
June 1 Cash	20		

Wages Account

Dr			Cr
2006	£		
June 3 Cash	900		

Sometimes the owner of a business will want to take cash out of the business for his or her private use. These are known as **drawings**. Any money taken out as drawings will reduce capital.

The capital account is a very important account. To help to stop it getting full of small details, each item of drawings is not entered in the capital account. Instead, a drawings account is opened and the debits are entered there. The following worked example illustrates the entries for drawings.

Example 4: On 25 August 2006 a proprietor takes £50 cash out of her business for her own use.

Effect	Action
1 Capital is decreased by £50 2 Cash is decreased by £50	Debit the drawings account £50 Credit the cash account £50

Cash Account

Dr		Cr
	2006	£
	Aug 25 Drawings	50

Drawings Account

Dr		Cr
2006	£	
Aug 25 Cash	50	

Sometimes *goods* (rather than money) are taken for private use. These are also known as drawings. Entries for such transactions will be described later in the book.

5.7 Revenues and double entry

We have just looked at instances of expenses being recorded. There will also be the need to record revenues. We will now look at an example.

Example 5: On 5 June 2006 it is decided that part of a firm's premises are not needed at the moment. The firm lets someone else use the surplus space and receives rent of £140 by cheque. Here, the twofold effect is:

(*a*) *The asset of the bank is increased* – money comes 'IN'. This means debiting the bank account to show the increase of the asset.

(*b*) *The total of the revenue of rent received is increased* – the benefit comes 'OUT' of rent received, so the action required is the crediting of the rent received account.

Summary: ● debit the bank account with £140 – 'IN'

  ● credit the rent received account with £140 – 'OUT'.

This will therefore appear as:

Bank

2006	£
June 5 Rent received	140

Rent Received

	2006	£
	June 5 Bank	140

Chapter summary

● The calculation of profit is achieved by comparing revenues with expenses incurred in running the business.

● A loss occurs when the expenses incurred are more than the revenue earned.

● If a business makes a profit, that profit belongs to the owner of the business and consequently their capital is increased by that amount.

● When a loss is incurred then the owner must bear the losses and such a loss will reduce their capital account.

● The importance of recording expenses in separate expense accounts to enable the business to identify various areas of expense such as motor expenses, stationery etc.

● Different types of revenue should also be recorded in separate accounts to provide information of the income received.

● The procedure for recording expenses and revenue in the various accounts using the double entry system.

● The meaning of the term 'drawings' and how they are recorded in a separate account. They are then deducted from the owner's capital account and are never an expense of the business.

Exercises

5.1 Complete the following table:

	Account to be debited	Account to be credited
(a) Paid rent by cash		
(b) Paid for goods by cash		
(c) Received by cheque a refund of rates already paid		
(d) Paid general expenses by cheque		
(e) Received commissions in cash		
(f) Goods returned by us to T Jones		
(g) Goods sold for cash		
(h) Bought office fixtures by cheque		
(i) Paid wages in cash		
(j) Took cash out of business for private use.		

5.2X   Complete the following table

	Account to be debited	Account to be credited
(a) Sold surplus stationery, receiving proceeds in cash		
(b) Paid salaries by cheque		
(c) Rent received for premises sublet, by cheque		
(d) Goods returned to us by Royal Products		
(e) Commission received by us previously in error, now refunded by cheque		
(f) Bought machinery by cheque		
(g) Paid lighting expenses in cash		
(h) Insurance rebate received by cheque		
(i) Buildings bought by cheque		
(j) Building repairs paid in cash.		

5.3   You are required to enter the following transactions in the double entry accounts of B Cartwright:

2005
Jan 1 Started business with £20,000 capital, which was deposited in the bank
Jan 3 Paid rent for premises by cheque, £1,000
Jan 4 Bought goods on credit from M Parkin for £580 and J Kane for £2,400
Jan 4 Purchased motor van for £5,000, paying by cheque
Jan 5 Cash sales of £1,005
Jan 10 Paid motor expenses in cash, £75
Jan 12 Paid wages in cash, £120
Jan 17 Bought goods on credit from M Parkin, £670
Jan 19 Paid insurance by cheque, £220
Jan 25 Sold goods for £800, payment being received as a cheque, which was banked immediately
Jan 31 Paid wages in cash, £135, and electricity by cheque, £78.

5.4X   The following are the transactions of G Dunn for the month of May 2007. You are required to enter the transactions in the appropriate accounts using the double entry system.

2007
May   1 Started in business with £12,000 in the bank
May   2 Purchased goods £1,750 on credit from M Mills
May   3 Bought fixtures and fittings for £1,500, paying by cheque
May   5 Sold goods for cash, £1,300
May   6 Bought goods on credit for £1,140 from S Waite
May 10 Paid rent by cash, £250
May 12 Bought stationery, £87, paying by cash
May 18 Goods returned by us to M Mills, £230
May 21 Let off part of the premises receiving rent by cheque, £100
May 23 Sold goods on credit to M Street for £770
May 24 Bought a motor van, paying by cheque £3,000
May 30 Paid wages for the month, £648, by cash
May 31 The proprietor, G Dunn, took cash for himself amounting to £200.

5.5   You are required to enter the following transactions, completing the double entry in the records of K Walsh for the month of July 2006.

2006

July 1 Started in business with £8,000 in the bank

July 2 Paid for rent of premises by cheque, £375

July 3 Bought shop fittings for £800 paid by cheque

July 5 Bought goods on credit from A Jackson, £450; D Hill, £675; and E Frudd, £1,490

July 6 Paid insurance by cheque, £130

July 7 Bought motor van for £5,000 on credit from High Lane Motors

July 11 Cash Sales of £1,500

July 13 Paid for printing and stationery by cheque, £120

July 15 Paid wages in cash, £200

July 18 Bought goods from A Jackson, £890, on credit

July 21 Cash sales, £780

July 25 Paid motor expenses, £89, by cash

July 30 Paid High Lane Motors, £5,000

July 31 Paid wages in cash, £300, and stationery, £45, in cash.

5.6X   Write up the following transactions in the books of J Blake for March 2006:

2006

March 1 Started business with £15,000 capital in cash

March 2 Paid £14,000 of the cash into a bank account for the business

March 2 Bought goods on credit from J Paul for £592

March 4 Paid for rent of premises by cash, £250, and bought a motor van for £3,000, paying by cheque

March 5 Bought goods, paying by cheque for £2,100

March 9 Sold goods to E Ford for £323 and received a cheque

March 11 Paid for printing of stationery, £45, by cash

March 14 Cash sales of £490

March 18 Goods returned by us to J Paul, £67

March 19 Bought goods from J Paul on credit, £720

March 21 Paid for advertising, £60, by cheque

March 24 Sold goods for cash, £500

March 25 Paid the following expenses by cheque: wages, £540; motor expenses, £110; stationery, £82

March 28 Paid J Paul £1,245 by cheque

March 31 Sold goods for cash, £526.

5.7X   Enter the following transactions using double entry for S Littleton for the month of April 2005

2005

April 1 Started in business with capital of £7,500 in the bank account and £1,000 in cash

April 3 Bought a motor car, £4,000, paying by cheque

April 5 Paid for rent of office, £275 in cash

April 7 Paid for motor expenses, £50 in cash

April 9 Paid for telephone charges, £95 by cheque

April 14 Bought stock of goods on credit from K Woodburn, £2,300, and A Veale, £2,600

April 16 Sold goods, £1,900, receiving the money by cheque

April 19 Paid for motor expenses, £60 in cash

April 20 Returned faulty goods to A Veale, £240

April 25 Cash sales of £875, paid for insurance, £180 in cash

April 28 Paid salaries, £1,210 by cheque

April 29 Paid K Woodburn £1,500 on account by cheque

April 30 Bought further goods from K Woodburn on credit, £770.

CHAPTER 6

Balancing off accounts

Learning objectives

After you have studied this chapter you should be able to:

- understand what is meant by 'balancing off' accounts
- balance off accounts at the end of a period and bring down the opening balance to the next period
- distinguish between a debit balance and a credit balance
- prepare accounts in a three-column format, as used in computerised accounts.

6.1 Introduction

In the preceding chapter the entries into the various accounts have been shown. However, at the end of a period, usually monthly, each account will require 'balancing off'. Balancing off simply means finding the difference between the total of the debit entries and the total of the credit entries in a particular account. The 'difference' between the two sides is known as the 'balance' and this figure is inserted on the side of the account that shows the least amount of money. If both sides of the account are then totalled up, they should agree, having inserted the 'balance'; if they do not add up correctly, then an error may have been made in the calculation of the balance or perhaps in adding up the account. The calculation will then need to be rechecked.

Sometimes an account simply requires closing off; this is when both the debit and credit sides total up to exactly the same amount and thus there is no balance.

In the following examples we will consider balancing off accounts at the end of a period and bringing down the balances to the next accounting period.

6.2 Accounts for debtors

Where debtors have paid their accounts

So far we have considered how to record transactions in the accounting books by means of debit and credit entries. At the end of each accounting period the figures in each account are examined to see what they reveal. One of the most obvious reasons for this is to find out how much money our customers owe us for goods we have sold to them. As mentioned above this procedure is usually carried out monthly.

We will now look at the account of one of our customers, K Tandy, for transactions in August 2005.

K Tandy Account

Dr		£			Cr
2005		£	2005		£
Aug 1	Sales	144	Aug 22	Bank	144
Aug 19	Sales	300	Aug 28	Bank	300

This shows that during the month of August we sold a total of £444 in goods to Tandy, and have been paid a total of £444 by him. At the close of business at the end of August he therefore owes us nothing; his account can be closed off on 31 August 2005 by inserting the totals on each side, as follows:

K Tandy Account

Dr		£			Cr
2005		£	2005		£
Aug 1	Sales	144	Aug 22	Bank	144
Aug 19	Sales	300	Aug 28	Bank	300
		444			444

Notice that totals in accounting are shown with a single line above them, and a double line underneath. Totals on accounts at the end of a period are always shown on a level with one another, as shown in the following completed account for C Lee:

C Lee Account

Dr		£			Cr
2005		£	2005		£
Aug 11	Sales	177	Aug 30	Bank	480
Aug 19	Sales	203			
Aug 22	Sales	100			
		480			480

In this account, C Lee also owed us nothing at the end of August 2005, as she had paid us for all sales to her.

If an account contains only one entry on each side and they are equal, you don't need to include totals. For example:

K Wood Account

Dr		£			Cr
2005		£	2005		£
Aug 6	Sales	214	Aug 12	Bank	214

Where debtors still owe for goods

Not all customers will have paid their accounts by the end of the month and indeed some customers may still have amounts outstanding on their account. In these cases, the totals of each side would not equal each other. Let us look at the account of D Knight for August 2005:

D Knight Account

Dr   Cr

2005		£	2005		£
Aug 1	Sales	158	Aug 28	Bank	158
Aug 15	Sales	206			
Aug 30	Sales	118			

If you add the figures, you will see that the debit side adds up to £482 and the credit side adds up to £158. You should be able to see what the difference of £324 (i.e. £482 – £158) represents. It consists of sales of £206 and £118 not paid for and therefore still owing to us on 31 August 2005.

In double entry, we only enter figures as totals if the totals on both sides of the account agree. We do, however, want to close off the account for August, but showing that Knight owes us £324. If he owes £324 at close of business on 31 August 2005, then he will still owe us that same figure when the business opens on 1 September 2005. We show this by **balancing the account**, which is done in five stages:

1 Add up both sides to find out their totals. Do not write anything in the account at this stage.
2 Deduct the smaller total from the larger total to find the balance.
3 Now enter the balance on the side with the smallest total. This now means the totals will be equal.
4 Enter totals on a level with each other.
5 Now enter the balance on the line below the totals. The balance below the totals should be on the opposite side to the balance shown above the totals.

Against the balance above the totals, complete the date column by showing the last day of that period. Below the totals, show the first day of the next period against the balance. The balance above the totals is described as **balance *carried down***. The balance below the total is described as **balance *brought down***.

Knight's account when 'balanced off' will appear as shown in Exhibit 6.1.

Exhibit 6.1

D Knight Account

Dr   Cr

2005		£	2005		£
Aug 1	Sales	158	Aug 28	Bank	158
Aug 15	Sales	206	Aug 31	Balance	
Aug 30	Sales	118		carried down	324
		482			482
Sept 1	Balance brought down	324			

Stage 5: enter balance to start off entries for following month.

Stage 4: enter totals level with each other.

Stage 3: enter balance here so that totals will be equal.

We can now look at another account prior to balancing:

H Henry Account

Dr				Cr
2005	£	2005		£
Aug 5 Sales	300	Aug 24 Returns inwards		50
Aug 28 Sales	540	Aug 29 Bank		250

We will abbreviate 'carried down' to 'c/d' and 'brought down' to 'b/d' from now on.

H Henry Account

Dr				Cr
2005	£	2005		£
Aug 5 Sales	300	Aug 24 Returns inwards		50
Aug 28 Sales	540	Aug 29 Bank		250
		Aug 31 Balance c/d		540
	840			840
Sept 1 Balance b/d	540			

Notes:

● The date given for the balance c/d is the last day of the period which is finishing and that for the balance b/d is given as the opening date of the next period.
● As the total of the debit side originally exceeded the total of the credit side, the balance is said to be a debit balance. This being a personal account (i.e. for a person), the person concerned is said to be a debtor – the accounting term for anyone who owes money to the firm. The use of the term 'debtor' for a person whose account has a debit balance can again thus be seen.

If accounts contain only one entry, it is unnecessary to enter the total. A double line ruled under the entry will mean that the entry is its own total. For example:

B Walters Account

Dr				Cr
2005	£	2005		£
Aug 18 Sales	51	Aug 31 Balance c/d		51
Sept 1 Balance b/d	51			

6.3 Accounts for creditors

Exactly the same principles apply when the balances are carried down to the credit side. We can look at two accounts of suppliers which are to be balanced off.

E Williams Account

Dr				Cr
2005	£	2005		£
Aug 21 Bank	100	Aug 2 Purchases		248
		Aug 18 Purchases		116

K Patterson Account

Dr				Cr
2005	£	2005		£
Aug 14 Returns outwards	20	Aug 8 Purchases		620
Aug 28 Bank	600	Aug 15 Purchases		200

We now add up the totals and find the balance, i.e. stages 1 and 2 of the five-stage process. When balanced, these will appear as shown in Exhibit 6.2.

Exhibit 6.2

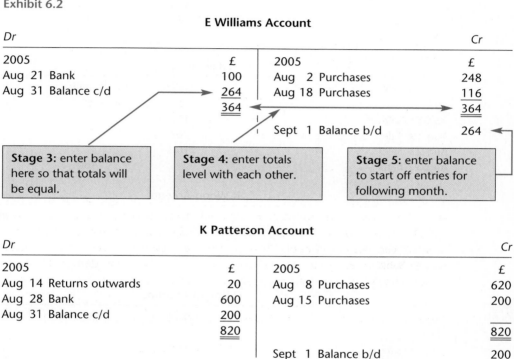

E Williams Account

Dr				Cr
2005	£	2005		£
Aug 21 Bank	100	Aug 2 Purchases		248
Aug 31 Balance c/d	264	Aug 18 Purchases		116
	364			364
		Sept 1 Balance b/d		264

Stage 3: enter balance here so that totals will be equal.

Stage 4: enter totals level with each other.

Stage 5: enter balance to start off entries for following month.

K Patterson Account

Dr				Cr
2005	£	2005		£
Aug 14 Returns outwards	20	Aug 8 Purchases		620
Aug 28 Bank	600	Aug 15 Purchases		200
Aug 31 Balance c/d	200			
	820			820
		Sept 1 Balance b/d		200

Before you read further, attempt Exercises 6.1 and 6.2 at the end of this chapter.

The type of accounts which have been demonstrated so far are often known as 'T accounts' (see Section 3.6) since the accounts are in the shape of a letter T. The following accounts show the three-column method, which is used in computerised accounting systems.

6.4 Three-column accounts

Through the main part of this book, the type of account used shows the left-hand side of the account as the debit side and the right-hand side as the credit side. However, when most computers are used, the style of the ledger account is different. It appears as three columns of figures, there being one column for debit entries, another column for credit entries, and the last column for the balance. If you have a current account at a bank, your bank statements will normally be shown using this method.

The accounts used in this chapter will now be redrafted to show the ledger accounts drawn up in this way.

K Tandy Account

	Debit	Credit	Balance (and whether debit or credit)
2005	£	£	£
Aug 1 Sales	144		144 Dr
Aug 19 Sales	300		444 Dr
Aug 22 Bank		144	300 Dr
Aug 28 Bank		300	0

C Lee Account

	Debit	Credit	Balance
2005	£	£	£
Aug 11 Sales	177		177 Dr
Aug 19 Sales	203		380 Dr
Aug 22 Sales	100		480 Dr
Aug 30 Bank		480	0

K Wood Account

	Debit	Credit	Balance
2005	£	£	£
Aug 6 Sales	214		214 Dr
Aug 12 Bank		214	0

D Knight Account

	Debit	Credit	Balance
2005	£	£	£
Aug 1 Sales	158		158 Dr
Aug 15 Sales	206		364 Dr
Aug 28 Cash		158	206 Dr
Aug 31 Sales	118		324 Dr

H Henry Account

	Debit	Credit	Balance
2005	£	£	£
Aug 5 Sales	300		300 Dr
Aug 24 Returns		50	250 Dr
Aug 28 Sales	540		790 Dr
Aug 29 Bank		250	540 Dr

B Walters Account

	Debit	Credit	Balance
2005	£	£	£
Aug 18 Sales	51		51 Dr

E Williams Account

	Debit	Credit	Balance	
2005	£	£	£	
Aug 2 Purchases		248	248	Cr
Aug 18 Purchases		116	364	Cr
Aug 21 Bank	100		264	Cr

K Patterson Account

	Debit	Credit	Balance	
2005	£	£	£	
Aug 8 Purchases		620	620	Cr
Aug 14 Returns	20		600	Cr
Aug 15 Purchases		200	800	Cr
Aug 28 Bank	600		200	Cr

You will notice in the above accounts that the balance is calculated after every entry. This can be done quite simply when using a computer accounting package since the software can automatically calculate the new balance after each entry is made.

However, when manual methods are being used, it is often too much work to have to calculate a new balance after each entry. Also, the greater the number of calculations, the greater the possibility of errors. For these reasons, it is usual for students to use two-sided accounts. However, it is important to note that there is no difference in principle; the final balances are the same using either method.

Chapter summary

- This chapter describes what is meant by 'balancing off' accounts at the end of a period.
- Balance off appropriate accounts at the end of a period and bring down the opening balance to the beginning of the next period.
- Opening balances brought down on the debit side are referred to as debit balances whereas those brought down on the credit side are known as credit balances.
- 'Debtors' are people or organisations who owe money to the business. Their accounts in your accounting records show a greater value on the debit side, hence they are your debtors.
- 'Creditors' are people or organisations that the business owes money to. Their accounts in your accounting records show a greater value on the credit side, hence they are your creditors.
- 'T accounts' are used generally for recording transactions where there is a manual system of accounting.
- Computerised accounting packages use three-column accounts. Illustrations of preparing three-column accounts are shown.
- Both the 'T accounts' and the three-column accounts show the same information and the balances will be identical whichever method is used.

Exercises

6.1 Enter the following items in the appropriate debtors' accounts (i.e. your customers' accounts) only; do *not* write up other accounts. Then balance off each of these personal accounts at the end of the month. (Keep your answer – it will be used as a basis for question 6.3.)

2008
May   1 Sales on credit to D Binns £1,035, C Cade £450, H Teate £630
May   3 Sales on credit to J Watts £627, M Lowe £99
May   9 Returns inwards from D Binns £60, H Teate £30
May 12 C Cade paid us by cheque, £450
May 16 H Teate paid us by cheque, £600
May 25 D Binns paid us £450 on account in cash
May 31 Sales on credit to J Watts, £135.

6.2 Enter the following in the appropriate creditors' accounts (i.e. your suppliers' accounts) only. Do *not* write up the other accounts. Then balance off each of these personal accounts at the end of the month. (Keep your answer – it will be used as the basis for question 6.4X.)

2005
July   2 Purchases on credit from G Birks £687, A Weale £180, T Potts £1,012
July   5 Purchases on credit from K Lee £150, B Dixon £1,320
July 11 We returned goods to T Potts £33, G Birks £87
July 17 Purchases on credit from G Birks, £120
July 21 We paid B Dixon by cheque, £1,320
July 27 We paid G Birks £300 on account by cash
July 31 We returned goods to A Weale, £42.

6.3 Redraft each of the accounts given in your answer to 6.1 as three-column ledger-style accounts.

6.4X Redraft each of the accounts given in your answer to 6.2 as three-column ledger-style accounts.

6.5 Enter the following in the personal accounts (i.e. the creditor and debtor accounts) only; do *not* write up the other accounts. Balance off each personal account at the end of the month. After completing this, state which of the balances represent debtors and which represent creditors.

2006
Oct   1 Sales on credit to T Tickle £690, S Ames £330,
Oct   3 Purchases on credit D Stott £116, D Owen £347, J Rhodes £98
Oct   9 Sales on credit to S Ames £645, T Johnson £376
Oct 11 Purchases on credit from D Owen £135, J Ahmed £367
Oct 14 Returns inwards from S Ames £45, T Tickle £46
Oct 19 We returned goods to D Owen £36, D Stott £19
Oct 23 We paid D Stott by cheque, £97
Oct 25 T Tickle paid us by cheque, £674
Oct 29 We paid J Ahmed by cash, £367
Oct 30 S Ames paid us £500 on account by cheque
Oct 31 T Johnson paid us by cheque, £376.

6.6X Enter the following in the necessary personal accounts; do *not* write up the other accounts. Balance each personal account at the end of the month. (Keep your answer – it will be used as the basis of question 6.8X.)

2006

Aug 1 Sales on credit to L Sterling £445, L Lindo £480, R Spencer £221
Aug 4 Goods returned to us by L Sterling £15, R Spencer £33
Aug 8 Sales on credit to L Lindo £66, R Spencer £129, L Banks £465
Aug 9 We received a cheque for £430 from L Sterling
Aug 12 Sales on credit to R Spencer £235, L Banks £777
Aug 19 Goods returned to us by L Banks £21, R Spencer £25
Aug 22 We received cheques as follows: R Spencer £300, L Lindo £414
Aug 31 Sales on credit to L Lindo £887, L Banks £442.

6.7X Enter the following, which are personal accounts only. Bring down balances at end of the month. After completing this, state which of the outstanding balances represent debtors and which represent creditors.

2006

May 1 Credit sale B Flynn £241, R Kelly £29, J Long £887, T Fryer £124
May 2 Credit purchases from S Wood £148, T DuQuesnay £27, R Johnson £77, G Henriques £108
May 8 Credit sales to R Kelly £74, J Long £132
May 9 Credit purchases from T DuQuesnay £142, G Henriques £44
May 10 Goods returned to us by J Long £17, T Fryer £44
May 12 Cash paid to us by T Fryer, £80
May 15 We returned goods to S Wood £8, G Henriques £18
May 19 We received cheques from J Long £500, B Flynn £241
May 21 We sold goods on credit to B Flynn £44, R Kelly £280
May 28 We paid by cheque the following: S Wood £140; G Henriques £50; R Johnson £60
May 31 We returned goods to G Henriques, £4.

6.8X Redraft each of the accounts given in your answer to 6.6X as three-column accounts.

CHAPTER 7

The trial balance

Learning objectives

After you have studied this chapter you should be able to:

- understand why the trial balance totals should equal one another
- draw up a trial balance from a given set of accounts
- appreciate that some kinds of errors can be made but the trial balance totals will still equal one another
- understand what steps to take if the trial balance doesn't balance.

7.1 Introduction

A trial balance is a list of account titles and their balances in the ledgers on a specific date. The trial balance lists the name of each account together with the balance shown in either the debit or credit columns. Since every debit entry in double entry book-keeping should have a corresponding credit entry then provided no errors have occurred, the two columns should agree when totalled.

It is important to note that the trial balance is not part of the double entry system; it is merely a list of balances drawn up to check the arithmetical accuracy of the book-keeping entries. It does, however, serve two purposes:

1 it checks the accuracy of the double entry transactions
2 it facilitates the preparation of the final accounts of the business (this topic is covered in Part 2 of this book).

7.2 Total debit entries = total credit entries

Using the double entry system of book-keeping it has been shown that:

- for each debit entry there is a credit entry
- for each credit entry there is a debit entry.

All the items recorded in all the accounts on the debit side should equal *in total* all the items recorded on the credit side of the accounts. We need to check that for each debit entry there is also a credit entry. In order to do so, we prepare a trial balance which may be drawn up at the end of a period.

A type of trial balance could be drawn up by listing all the accounts and then entering the total of all the debit entries in each account in one column and the total of all the credit entries in each account into another column. Finally, the two columns of figures would be added up to ensure they are equal. Using the worked exercise in Section 4.9, this trial balance would be:

Trial Balance as at 31 May 2006	Dr £	Cr £
Purchases	309	
Sales		255
Returns outwards		15
Returns inwards	16	
D Small	68	68
A Lyon & Son		141
D Hughes	60	60
M Spencer	45	16
Cash	210	153
	708	708

7.3 Total debit balances = total credit balances

The method described in Section 7.2 is not the usual method of drawing up a trial balance, but it is the easiest to understand at first. Usually, a trial balance is a list of balances only, arranged according to whether they are debit balances or credit balances. If the trial balance in Section 7.2 had been drawn up using the normal balances method, it would appear as below.

Trial Balance as at 31 May 2006	Dr £	Cr £
Purchases	309	
Sales		255
Returns outwards		15
Returns inwards	16	
A Lyon & Son		141
M Spencer	29	
Cash	57	
	411	411

Here, the two sides also 'balance'. The sums of £68 in D Small's account, £60 in D Hughes' account, £16 in M Spencer's account and £153 in the cash account have, however, been cancelled out from each side of these accounts by taking only the *balances* instead of the *totals*. As equal amounts have been cancelled from each side, £297 in all, the new totals should still equal one another, as in fact they do at £411.

This form of trial balance is the easiest to extract when there are more than a few transactions during the period and it is the one accountants use. As mentioned in the introduction to this chapter, the main purposes of preparing a trial balance is to ensure that no errors have been made and to facilitate the preparation of the final accounts. The final accounts consist of a 'profit and loss account' which shows how much profit the business has earned in a period. The balance sheet shows what the assets and liabilities of a business are at the end of a period. Both these financial statement are dealt with in Part 2 of the book.

7.4 A worked example

The following accounts, for K Potter, have been entered up for May 2006 and balanced off. Note the entries used to 'balance off' the accounts have been highlighted.

K Potter's Books:
Bank Account

Dr					Cr
2006		£	2006		£
May 1	Capital	9,000	May 21	Machinery	550
May 30	T Monk	300	May 29	T Wood	860
			May 31	Balance c/d	7,890
		9,300			9,300
June 1	Balance b/d	7,890			

Cash Account

Dr					Cr
2006		£	2006		£
May 5	Sales	180	May 30	K Young	170
May 12	Sales	210	May 31	Balance c/d	220
		390			390
June 1	Balance b/d	220			

T Wood Account

Dr					Cr
2006		£	2006		£
May 6	Returns outwards	40	May 2	Purchases	900
May 29	Bank	860			
		900			900

K Young Account

Dr					Cr
2006		£	2006		£
May 28	Returns outwards	80	May 3	Purchases	250
May 30	Cash	170	May 18	Purchases	190
May 31	Balance c/d	190			
		440			440
			June 1	Balance b/d	190

T Monk Account

Dr					Cr
2006		£	2006		£
May 10	Sales	590	May 23	Returns inwards	140
			May 30	Bank	300
			May 31	Balance c/d	150
		590			590
June 1	Balance b/d	150			

C Howe Account

Dr					Cr
2006		£	2006		£
May 22	Sales	220	May 25	Returns inwards	10
			May 31	Balance c/d	210
		220			220
June 1	Balance b/d	210			

AB Ltd Account

Dr			Cr
	2006		£
	May 31	Machinery	2,700

Capital Account

Dr			Cr
	2006		£
	May 1	Bank	9,000

Purchases Account

Dr					Cr
2006		£	2006		£
May 2	T Wood	900	May 31	Balance c/d	1,340
May 3	K Young	250			
May 18	K Young	190			
		1,340			1,340
June 1	Balance b/d	1,340			

Sales Account

Dr				Cr
2006	£	2006		£
May 31 Balance c/d	1,200	May 5 Cash		180
		May 10 T Monk		590
		May 12 Cash		210
		May 22 C Howe		220
	1,200			1,200
		June 1 Balance b/d		1,200

Returns Inwards Account

Dr			Cr
2006	£	2006	£
May 23 T Monk	140	May 31 Balance c/d	150
May 25 C Howe	10		
	150		150
June 1 Balance b/d	150		

Returns Outwards Account

Dr			Cr
2006	£	2006	£
May 31 Balance c/d	120	May 6 T Wood	40
		May 28 K Young	80
	120		120
		June 1 Balance b/d	120

Machinery Account

Dr			Cr
2006	£	2006	£
May 21 Bank	550	May 31 Balance c/d	3,250
May 31 AB Ltd	2,700		
	3,250		3,250
June 1 Balance b/d	3,250		

After each account has been balanced off, a trial balance can then be prepared as follows:

K Potter Trial Balance as at 31 May 2006		
	Dr £	Cr £
Bank	7,890	
Cash	220	
K Young		190
T Monk	150	
C Howe	210	
AB Ltd		2,700
Capital		9,000
Purchases	1,340	
Sales		1,200
Returns inwards	150	
Returns outwards		120
Machinery	3,250	
	13,210	13,210

7.5 Trial balance and errors

Students new to accounting often assume that when a trial balance 'balances', the entries in the accounts must be correct. *This, however, may not be true*. It means that certain types of error have not been made, but there are several types of error that will not affect the balancing of a trial balance, such as omitting a transaction altogether. Another example might be a credit sale of £87 to a customer that is inadvertently debited to the sales account instead of being credited; the customer's account then being credited instead of being debited. Since both the debit and the credit entries are of the same amount then this will not affect the agreement of the trial balance.

Examples of the errors which would be revealed, provided there are no compensating errors which cancel them out, are addition errors, using one figure for the debit entry and another figure for the credit entry, entering only one aspect of a transaction, and so on. These will be considered in greater detail in later chapters.

7.6 Steps to take if the trial balance doesn't balance

If the trial balance does not balance, i.e. the two totals are different, then this is evidence that one or more errors have been made in either the double entry book-keeping or in the preparation of the trial balance itself. In this case, the following eight steps should be taken to locate the error(s):

1 If the trial balance is badly written and contains many alterations, then rewrite it.
2 Add up again each side of the trial balance. If you added the numbers 'upwards' the first time, then start at the top and work 'downwards' the second time, and vice versa.

3 Find the amount of the discrepancy and then check in the accounts for a transaction of this amount and, if located, ensure that the double entry has been carried out correctly.

4 Halve the amount of the discrepancy. Check to see whether there is a transaction for this amount and, if located, ensure the double entry has been carried out correctly. This type of error may have occurred if an item had been entered on the wrong side of the trial balance.

5 If the amount of the discrepancy is divisible by nine, this indicates that when the figure was originally entered it may have had digits transposed, for example £63 entered in error as £36, or £27 entered as £72.

6 Check that the balance on each account has been correctly calculated and entered onto the trial balance in the right column using the correct amount.

7 Ensure that every outstanding balance from all the ledgers and the cash book have been included in the trial balance and tick each balance after ensuring it is entered correctly.

8 If the error has still not been identified, then the error must be sought in the accounts themselves. It may be necessary to check all the entries from the date of the last trial balance.

7.7 Multiple-choice self-test questions

A growing practice of examining boards is to set multiple-choice questions in Accounting. This type of question certainly gives an examiner the opportunity to cover large parts of the syllabus briefly but in detail. Students who omit to study areas of the syllabus will be caught out by an examiner's use of multiple-choice questions. No longer will it be possible to say that it is highly probable that a certain topic will not be tested – the examiner can easily cover it with a multiple-choice question.

We have deliberately set blocks of multiple-choice questions at given places in this textbook, rather than a few at the end of each chapter. Such questions are relatively easy to answer a few minutes after reading the chapter, and so by asking the questions later your powers of recall and understanding are far better tested. It also gives you practice at answering a few questions in one block, as in an examination.

Each multiple-choice question has: a 'stem', namely that part which poses the problem; a 'key', which is the one correct answer; and a number of 'distractors', i.e. incorrect answers. The key plus the distractors are known as the 'options'. If you do not know the answer you should guess. You may be right by chance, or you may remember something subconsciously. In any event, unless the examiner warns otherwise, he will expect you to guess if you don't know the answer.

You should now attempt Set 1 in Appendix C, which contains 20 multiple-choice questions.

Chapter summary

● A trial balance is a list of account titles and their balances in the ledger at a specific date which is prepared to check the arithmetical accuracy of the book-keeping entries.

- A trial balance also assists in the preparation of the financial statements.
- A worked example of a trial balance is shown.
- The balancing of a trial balance does not always indicate that no errors have been made since certain errors can be made and the trial balance will still agree.
- What steps to take if a trial balance does not balance.

Exercises

7.1   You are required to enter the following transactions for the month of May 2005, for a small electrical retailer. Balance the accounts off and extract a trial balance as at 31 May 2005.

2005
May   1   Started in business with capital of £2,500, which was paid into the bank
May   2   Bought goods on credit from the following: D Ellis £540; C Mendez £87; K Gibson £76
May   4   Sold goods on credit to: C Bailey £430; B Hughes £62; H Spencer £176
May   6   Paid rent by cash, £120
May   8   Sold goods for cash, £500
May   9   C Bailey paid us £250 by cheque on account
May 10   H Spencer paid us £150 on account by cheque
May 12   We paid the following by cheque: K Gibson £76; D Ellis £370 on account
May 15   Bought stationery for cash, £60
May 18   Bought goods on credit from: D Ellis £145; C Mendez £234
May 19   Paid rent by cash, £120
May 25   Sold goods on credit to: C Bailey £90; B Hughes £110; H Spencer £128
May 31   Paid C Mendez £87 by cheque.

7.2   Enter up the books from the following details of a Do-it-yourself Shop for the month of March, and extract a trial balance as at 31 March 2006.

2006
March   1   Started business with £8,000 in the bank
March   2   Bought goods on credit from the following persons: K Henriques £76; M Hyatt £27; T Braham £560
March   5   Cash sales, £870
March   6   Paid wages in cash, £140
March   7   Sold goods on credit to: H Elliott £35; L Lane £42; J Carlton £72
March   9   Bought goods for cash, £46
March 10   Bought goods on credit from: M Hyatt £57; T Braham £98
March 12   Paid wages in cash, £140
March 13   Sold goods on credit to: L Lane £32; J Carlton £23
March 15   Bought shop fixtures on credit from Betta Ltd, £500
March 17   Paid M Hyatt by cheque, £84
March 18   We returned goods to T Braham, £20
March 21   Paid Betta Ltd a cheque for £500
March 24   J Carlton paid us his account by cheque, £95
March 27   We returned goods to K Henriques, £24
March 30   J King lent us £600 by cash
March 31   Bought a motor van paying by cheque, £4,000.

7.3X Record the following transactions in the books of C Hilton. Balance off the accounts and extract a trial balance as at 30 June 2006.

2006
June 1 C Hilton started in business with £9,000 in cash
June 2 Paid £8,000 of the cash into a bank account
June 4 Paid rent for shop £300 by cheque
June 6 Bought goods on credit from Moorlands & Co. £675; J Swain £312; B Merton £225
June 12 Sold goods for cash, £450
June 13 Bought fixtures, paying by cheque, £230
June 15 Sold goods on credit T Green £180; K Wood £367; P Brown £256
June 18 Sold goods for cash, £220
June 20 Paid Moorlands & Co by cheque £675 and B Merton £225
June 21 Returned goods to J Swain £112 and paid the outstanding balance on their account by cheque
June 24 Bought goods on credit from Moorlands & Co £220 and J Swain £92
June 26 Paid wages in cash, £366
June 27 Cash drawings, £200
June 29 Bought motor van, paying by cheque, £4,000
June 30 Sold goods on credit to T Green £300; K Wood £50; P Brown £60
June 30 Received cheques from the following: T Green £180 and K Wood £367

7.4X You are required to enter the following transactions in the necessary accounts for April 2006 of a home furnishing business. At the end of the month balance off the accounts and prepare a trial balance.

2006
April 1 Started in business with £15,000 in the bank
April 3 Bought goods on credit from: Bowman Furnishers £320; Howe Homes £460; W Hunt £1,800; J Bond £620
April 7 Cash sales, £480
April 9 Paid rent by cheque, £500
April 11 Paid rates by cheque, £190
April 12 Sold goods on credit to: L Clark £480; K Allen £96; R Gee £1,170
April 14 Paid wages in cash, £400
April 17 We returned faulty goods to: Bowman Furnishers £28; J Bond £60
April 20 Bought goods on credit from: J Bond £220; W Hunt £270; Bowman Furnishers £240
April 23 Goods were returned to us from: K Allen £20; L Clark £40
April 25 Bought motor car on credit from Bates Motors, £5,000
April 26 Cash sales, £175
April 27 We paid the following by cheque: Bowman Furnishers £532; Howe Homes £460; W Hunt £2,070
April 28 Bought secondhand motor van, £3,000 paid by cheque
April 29 Bought stationery and paid in cash, £56
April 30 Received cheques from: L Clark £440; K Allen £76
April 30 Paid Bates Motors by cheque, £5,000.

7.5   Correct and balance the following trial balance.

Trial balance of P Brown as at 31 May 2006		
	Dr	Cr
	£	£
Capital		20,000
Drawings	7,000	
General expenses		500
Sales	38,500	
Purchases		29,000
Debtors		6,800
Creditors	9,000	
Bank balance (Dr)	15,100	
Cash		200
Plant and equipment		5,000
Heating and lighting		1,500
Rent	2,400	

7.6   Reconstruct the trial balance after making the necessary corrections.

Trial balance of S Higton as at 30 June 2007		
	Dr	Cr
	£	£
Capital	19,956	
Sales		119,439
Stationery	1,200	
General expenses	2,745	
Motor expenses		4,476
Cash at bank	1,950	
Stock 1 July 2006	7,668	
Wages and salaries		9,492
Rent and rates	10,500	
Office equipment	6,000	
Purchases	81,753	
Heating and lighting		2,208
Rent received	2,139	
Debtors	10,353	
Drawings		4,200
Creditors		10,230
Motor vehicle	7,500	
Interest received	1,725	
Insurance		3,444
	153,489	153,489

7.7X From the following list of balances, prepare a trial balance as at 31 December 2007 for Ms Anita Hall:

	£
Plant and machinery	21,450
Motor vehicles	26,000
Premises	80,000
Wages	42,840
Purchases	119,856
Sales	179,744
Rent received	3,360
Telephone, printing and stationery	3,600
Creditors	27,200
Debtors	30,440
Bank overdraft	2,216
Capital	131,250
Drawings	10,680
General expenses	3,584
Lighting and heating	2,960
Motor expenses	2,360

Part 2

The financial statements of a business

8 An introduction to the trading and profit and loss account

9 The balance sheet

10 Financial statements: further considerations

11 Accounting concepts

This part of the book is concerned with preparing, from double entry records, the financial statements of sole traders.

CHAPTER 8

An introduction to the trading and profit and loss account

Learning objectives

After you have studied this chapter you should be able to:
- understand why profit/losses are calculated
- calculate the cost of goods sold, gross profit and net profit
- close off sales, purchases and relevant expense accounts at the end of the period, using double entry, by transferring the balances to the trading and profit and loss account
- transfer the net profit and drawings to the capital account at the end of the period
- prepare a trading and profit and loss account from a trial balance
- recognise that an adjustment is needed for the stock of unsold goods at the end of a period
- understand that after drawing up the trading and profit and loss account all remaining balances are required for preparation of the balance sheet.

8.1 Purpose of the trading and profit and loss account

The main reason why people set up a business is to make profits of course, if they are not successful they will incur losses. To calculate how much profit or loss has been made over a period of time, a **trading and profit and loss account** is prepared. Normally, all businesses prepare a trading and profit and loss account at least once a year; the account could be prepared for a shorter period if required.

The main purpose of a trading and profit and loss account is for the owners to see how profitably the business is being run. It is also used for other purposes; for instance, it will be used as a basis for calculating the owners' UK income tax liability under self-assessment requirements.

8.2 Uses of the trading and profit and loss account

One of the most important uses of the trading and profit and loss account is the comparison of the results achieved with those of past periods. When doing this, it is essential for traders to calculate two sorts of profit. These are:

Gross profit: (calculated in the Trading Account)	This is the excess of sales over the **cost of goods sold** in the period.
Net profit: (calculated in the Profit and Loss Account)	This is what is left of the gross profit after all other expenses have been deducted.

It would be possible to have one account called a **trading account**, and another called a **profit and loss account**. Normally they are combined together to form one account called the **trading and profit and loss account**.

8.3 Horizontal and vertical format for the trading and profit and loss account

In Section 8.5, we will look at trading and profit and loss accounts drawn up using the horizontal style. The left-hand side is the debit side, whilst the right-hand side is the credit side of the accounts. These accounts can therefore be seen as part of the double entry system, and students should be able to understand why each item is shown as a debit or a credit in them.

In Section 8.9, we will see how the trading and profit and loss account can be shown using a vertical style.

8.4 Preparation of a trading and profit and loss account

Exhibit 8.1

K Wade Trial Balance as at 31 December 2006		
	Dr £	Cr £
Sales		9,650
Purchases	7,150	
General expenses	550	
Fixtures and fittings	1,840	
Debtors	1,460	
Creditors		1,180
Capital		2,800
Drawings	1,750	
Bank	820	
Cash	60	
	13,630	13,630

Before drawing up a trading and profit and loss account, you should first obtain the trial balance. This contains nearly all the information needed. (Later on in this book you will see that certain adjustments have to be made, but we will ignore these at this stage.)

Set out in Exhibit 8.1 is the trial balance for K Wade, made up to the end of his first year's trading. This information is needed to prepare his trading and profit and loss account for the year ended 31 December 2006. For now, we will assume that K Wade has no closing stock at 31 December 2006.

To calculate gross profit

Remember that:

> **Sales – Cost of Goods Sold = Gross Profit**

We could in fact calculate this by simply using arithmetic. However, we must remember that we are using double entry methods. The answer will be the same whether normal arithmetic or proper double entry methods are used. To enable you to see fully how the calculations are performed using double entry, we will show the balances for sales and purchases, as in Exhibit 8.1, and how the entries are made to transfer these items into the calculations within the trading account.

The following steps should be carried out:

Step 1   Transfer the credit balance of the sales account to the credit of the trading account portion of the trading and profit and loss account.

> Debit: sales account
> Credit: trading account.

Step 2   Transfer the debit balance of the purchases account to the debit of the trading account.

> Debit: trading account
> Credit: purchases account.

Remember that, in this case, there is no stock of unsold goods. This means that purchases = cost of goods sold.

Step 3   If sales are greater than the cost of goods sold, the difference is gross profit. (If not, the answer would be a **gross loss**.) We will carry this gross profit figure from the trading account part down to the profit and loss part.

The double entry for gross profit is:

> Debit: trading account
> Credit: profit and loss account.

The above transfers are shown below in Exhibit 8.2 for Exhibit 8.1.

Exhibit 8.2

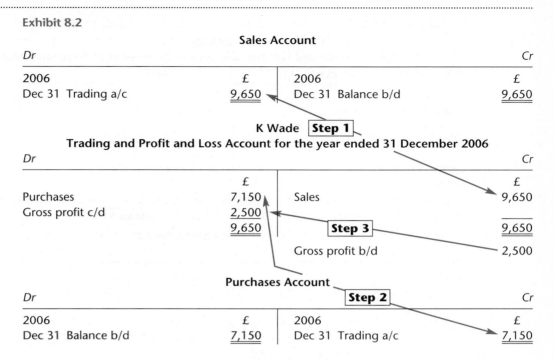

Sales Account

Dr				Cr
2006	£	2006		£
Dec 31 Trading a/c	9,650	Dec 31 Balance b/d		9,650

K Wade Step 1

Trading and Profit and Loss Account for the year ended 31 December 2006

Dr			Cr
	£		£
Purchases	7,150	Sales	9,650
Gross profit c/d	2,500		
	9,650	Step 3	9,650
		Gross profit b/d	2,500

Purchases Account

Dr		Step 2		Cr
2006	£	2006		£
Dec 31 Balance b/d	7,150	Dec 31 Trading a/c		7,150

Notice that, after the trading account has been completed, there are no balances remaining in the sales and purchases accounts. They are now said to be 'closed'.

To calculate net profit and record it

Remember that:

> Gross Profit – Expenses = Net Profit

Remember also (from Chapter 5) that:

> Old Capital + Net Profit = New Capital

Double entry needed to carry out these calculations:

Step 1   Transfer the debit balances on expenses accounts to the debit of the profit and loss account.

> Debit: profit and loss account
> Credit: expenses accounts.

Step 2   Transfer the net profit, when found, to the capital account to show the increase in capital.

> Debit: profit and loss account
> Credit: capital account.

The results are shown in Exhibit 8.3.

Exhibit 8.3

K Wade
Trading and Profit and Loss Account for the Year ended 31 December 2006

Dr   Cr

	£		£
Purchases	7,150	Sales	9,650
Gross profit c/d	2,500		
	9,650		9,650
General expenses	550	Gross profit b/d	2,500
Net profit	1,950		
	2,500		2,500

Step 1

General Expenses Account

Dr   Cr

2006	£	2006	£
Dec 31 Balance b/d	550	Dec 31 Profit and loss a/c	550

Capital Account

Dr   Step 2   Cr

		2006	£
		Dec 31 Balance b/d	2,800
		Dec 31 Net profit	1,950
			4,750

Note: See Section 8.5 for completion of this account.

8.5 Completion of capital account

You have seen that we credit the capital account with the amount of net profit. We have, therefore, recorded the increase in capital.

In the trial balance, Exhibit 8.1, we can see that there are drawings of £1,750. **Drawings** means withdrawals of capital.

After entering the net profit in the capital account we can now complete the account. To do this we transfer the drawings to the capital account. Thus:

Debit: capital account
Credit: drawings account.

The completed capital and drawings accounts are as follows:

Drawings Account

Dr   Cr

2006	£	2006	£
Dec 31 Balance b/d	1,750	Dec 31 Capital	1,750

Capital Account

Dr					Cr
2006		£	2006		£
Dec 31 Drawings		1,750	Dec 31 Balance b/d		2,800
Dec 31 Balance c/d		3,000	Dec 31 Net profit		1,950
		4,750			4,750
			2004		
			Jan 1 Balance b/d		3,000

8.6 Stock of unsold goods at end of period

We have already seen that gross profit is calculated as follows:

> **Sales – Cost of Goods Sold = Gross Profit**

However, purchases only equals cost of goods sold if there is no stock at the end of a period. We can calculate cost of goods sold as follows:

What we bought in this period:	Purchases
Less Goods bought but not sold in this period:	Closing Stock
	= Cost of Goods Sold

Remember, we are concerned here with the trading and profit and loss account of a business, as drawn up in its first year of trading when there is no opening stock. In Section 10.5 we will look at the later years of a business.

Now let us look at the preparation of a trading and profit and loss account for B Swift. His trial balance is shown as Exhibit 8.4 and was drawn up after his first year of trading:

Exhibit 8.4

B Swift Trial Balance as at 31 December 2005		
	Dr £	Cr £
Sales		3,850
Purchases	2,900	
Rent	240	
Lighting	150	
General expenses	60	
Fixtures and fittings	500	
Debtors	680	
Creditors		910
Bank	1,510	
Cash	20	
Drawings	700	
Capital		2,000
	6,760	6,760

Note: On 31 December 2005, at the close of trading, B Swift had goods costing £300 that were unsold.

The cost of goods sold figure will be:

	£
Purchases	2,900
Less Closing stock	300
Cost of goods sold	2,600

The gross profit will be:

	£
Sales	3,850
Less Cost of goods sold	2,600
Gross profit	1,250

The net profit will be:

	£	£
Gross profit		1,250
Less Expenses		
Rent	240	
Lighting	150	
General expenses	60	
		450
Net profit		800

We will now see this shown in double entry form:

Sales Account

Dr			Cr
2005	£	2005	£
Dec 31 Trading a/c	3,850	Dec 31 Balance b/d	3,850

Purchases Account

Dr			Cr
2005	£	2005	£
Dec 31 Balance b/d	2,900	Dec 31 Trading a/c	2,900

Rent Account

Dr			Cr
2005	£	2005	£
Dec 31 Balance b/d	240	Dec 31 Profit and loss a/c	240

Lighting Account

Dr				Cr
2005	£	2005		£
Dec 31 Balance b/d	150	Dec 31 Profit and loss a/c		150

General Expenses Account

Dr				Cr
2005	£	2005		£
Dec 31 Balance b/d	60	Dec 31 Profit and loss a/c		60

To record the stock we have entered the following:

> Debit: stock account
> Credit: trading account.

This yields the accounts shown in Exhibit 8.5.

Exhibit 8.5

Stock Account

Dr			Cr
2005	£		
Dec 31 Trading a/c	300 ◄		

B Swift
Trading and Profit and Loss Account
for the year ended 31 December 2005

2005	£	2005	£
Purchases	2,900	Sales	3,850
Gross profit c/d	1,250	Closing stock	300 ◄
	4,150		4,150
Rent	240	Gross profit b/d	1,250
Lighting	150		
General expenses	60		
Net profit	800		
	1,250		1,250

The figures shown in Exhibit 8.5 mean that there is now a balance on the stock account. We had to record it there because at 31 December 2005 we had an asset, namely £300 of stock, but there was no record of that fact in our books. We have now brought our records up to date by showing the stock in our accounts.

8.7 The capital account

The capital account for B Swift can now be completed, thus:

Capital Account

Dr				Cr
2005	£	2005		£
Dec 31 Drawings	700	Jan 1 Cash		2,000
Dec 31 Balance c/d	2,100	Dec 31 Net profit from profit		
		and loss a/c		800
	2,800			2,800
		2006		
		Jan 1 Balance b/d		2,100

Drawings Account

Dr			Cr
2005	£	2005	£
Dec 31 Balance b/d	700	Dec 31 Capital	700

8.8 The vertical style for trading and profit and loss accounts

The trading and profit and loss account shown above is written in the *horizontal* format to demonstrate how the double entry system works. However, the trading and profit and loss account is more often shown in the *vertical* format, and it is this format that we will use in future in this book. You may none the less wish to carry on preparing the horizontal format trading and profit and loss account before drawing up the vertical format, until you are sure you understand how to double enter directly into the vertical format.

The trading and profit and loss account of B Swift, in the vertical format, is shown below:

B Swift
Trading and Profit and Loss Account for the year ended 31 December 2005

	£	£
Sales		3,850
Less Cost of goods sold		
Purchases	2,900	
Less Closing stock	300	
		2,600
Gross profit		1,250
Less Expenses		
Rent	240	
Lighting	150	
General expenses	60	
		450
Net profit		800

8.9   The balances still in our books

Taking Exhibit 8.4, but including the adjustment for closing stock of £300, we can now see which balances still exist. We can do this by drawing up a trial balance as it would appear once the trading and profit and loss account has been completed. We will show it as Exhibit 8.6.

The following accounts have been closed in this process:

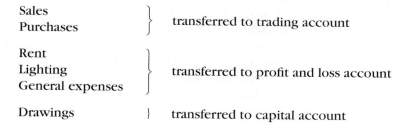

The balances still in our books

Exhibit 8.6

B Swift		
Trial Balance as at 31 December 2005		
(after Trading and Profit and Loss Accounts completed)		
	Dr	Cr
	£	£
Fixtures and fittings	500	
Debtors	680	
Creditors		910
Stock	300	
Bank	1,510	
Cash	20	
Capital		2,100
	3,010	3,010

The one account that was not in the original trial balance was the stock account. It was not brought into our books until the trading account was prepared. These balances will be used by us when we look at the balance sheets in the next chapter. They are also carried forward to the next accounting period.

Chapter summary

● The trading and profit and loss account is prepared to show how much profit a business makes or alternatively what losses they may incur.

- One of the main uses of the trading and profit and loss account is to provide information on the profit/losses made in the period and compare these figures with previous year's results.
- How to calculate the cost of goods sold, gross profit and net profit.
- How to close off the sales, purchases and relevant expense accounts at the end of a period and post the entries to the trading and profit and loss account.
- How to transfer the net profit and drawings to the capital account at the end of a period.
- How to treat stock of unsold goods at the end of a period.
- The preparation of the trading and profit and loss account from a trial balance using both the horizontal and vertical methods of presentation.
- Any balances still remaining in the books of account after preparation of the trading and profit and loss account represent assets, liabilities and capital. These balances are entered into the Balance Sheet (see the next chapter) and then carried forward to the next accounting period.

Exercises

Note: *All answers should show the vertical layout of the trading and profit and loss accounts.*

8.1 From the following details of I Simpson, draw up her trading and profit and loss account using the vertical style for the year ended 31 December 2006, this being her first year of trading:

Year to 31 December 2006	£
Purchases	24,190
Sales	38,220
Rent	4,170
Wages and salaries	5,390
Postage and stationery	840
Electricity expenses	710
General expenses	370

Note: At 31 December 2006, the stock was valued (at cost) at £4,310.

8.2X From the following details of C Newman, draw up his trading and profit and loss account using the vertical style for his first year of trading for the year ended 31 December 2007.

Year to 31 December 2007:	£
Rent	4,990
Motor expenses	2,370
Sundry expenses	410
Travel expenses	600
Office expenses	720
Sales	57,090
Purchases	42,910

Note: Stock at 31 December 2007 amounted in value to £8,220.

8.3 From the following trial balance of G Singh, extracted after one year's trading, prepare the trading and profit and loss account for the year ended 31 December 2006. A balance sheet is not required.

G Singh
Trial Balance as at 31 December 2006

	Dr £	Cr £
Sales		73,848
Purchases	58,516	
Wages	8,600	
Motor expenses	2,080	
Rates	2,680	
Insurance	444	
General expenses	420	
Premises	20,000	
Motor vehicle	12,000	
Debtors	7,800	
Creditors		6,418
Cash at bank	6,616	
Cash in hand	160	
Drawings	8,950	
Capital		48,000
	128,266	128,266

Stock at 31 December 2006 was valued at £10,192.

(Retain your answer – it will be used later in Exercise 9.1.)

8.4X   From the following trial balance of R Cairns after his first year's trading, you are required to draw up a trading and profit and loss account for the year ended 30 June 2006.

R Cairns
Trial Balance as at 30 June 2006

	Dr £	Cr £
Sales		99,082
Purchases	71,409	
Rates	2,000	
Printing and stationery	562	
Electricity	1,266	
Wages	9,492	
Insurance	605	
Premises	145,000	
Computer equipment	8,000	
Debtors	9,498	
Sundry expenses	1,518	
Creditors		3,618
Cash at bank	6,541	
Drawings	12,200	
Motor vehicle	16,500	
Motor expenses	3,109	
Capital		185,000
	287,700	287,700

Stock at 30 June 2006 was valued at £11,498.

(Retain your answer – it will be used later in Exercise 9.2X.)

8.5 Mrs P Stewart commenced trading as a card and gift shop with a capital of £6,855 on 1 April 2007. At the end of her first year's trading on 31 March 2008, she was able to identify from her accounting records that she had received £24,765 sales in the year. These sales had cost her £13,545 to purchase, and she had £2,345 cards and gifts, at cost, in stock on 31 March 2008. In the year she had also spent £2,100 on staff wages, and drawn personal cash of £5,500. Other overhead costs incurred were:

	£
Rent and rates	1,580
Electricity	565
Motor expenses	845
Insurance	345
General expenses	245

On 31 March 2008, Mrs P Stewart had cash in hand of £135, a bank balance of £2,675, and owed £3,285 to creditors. Mrs Stewart's business owned a car, which had a value of £5,875 at 31 March 2008. She had also bought shelving and fixtures and fittings in the year to the value of £1,495.

You are required to draw up the trading and profit and loss account for the first year's trading.

(*Exam hint*: Before you attempt to draw up the trading and profit and loss account, it would be a good idea to extract the trial balance at 31 March 2008 from the information given.) The closing stock figure should be shown as a note at the foot of the trial balance.
(Keep your answer – it will be used later in Exercise 9.3.)

8.6X Miss R Burgess has just completed her first year of trading for the year ended 30 April 2008, as a manufacturer of model railway accessories. Her initial capital was £9,025. At 30 April 2008, she was owed £5,600 by customers, and owed £4,825 to suppliers. She calculated that she had stock in hand, at cost, at the year end of £7,670, and her bank account was overdrawn by £2,560. The petty cash float held £25 at 30 April 2008.

From her records, she calculated her income and expenditure for the year ended 30 April 2008 as:

	£
Sales	56,540
Purchases	34,315
Rent of factory	6,000
Drawings	10,000
Motor expenses	1,735
Insurance	345
General expenses	780
Salaries	7,550

Miss R Burgess had plant and equipment to the value of £3,750 and a van worth £2,850 at 30 April 2008.

You are required to draw up the trading and profit and loss account for the first year's trading.
(Keep your answer – it will be used later in Exercise 9.5X.)

8.7X A business has been trading for one year. Extract a trading and profit and loss account for the year ended 30 June 2006 for M Kent. The trial balance as at 30 June 2006 is as follows:

M Kent Trial Balance as at 30 June 2006		
	Dr £	Cr £
Rent and rates	1,560	
Insurance	305	
Lighting expenses	516	
Motor expenses	1,960	
Salaries and wages	4,850	
Sales		35,600
Purchases	30,970	
Trade expense	806	
Motor van	3,500	
Creditors		3,250
Debtors	6,810	
Shop fixtures	3,960	
Shop buildings	28,000	
Cash at bank	1,134	
Drawings	6,278	
Capital		51,799
	90,649	90,649

Stock at 30 June 2006 was £9,960.

(Keep your answer – it will be used later in Exercise 9.6X.)

CHAPTER 9

The balance sheet

Learning objectives

After you have studied this chapter you should be able to:

● define a balance sheet
● understand that a balance sheet is prepared from the remaining balances in the trial balance after preparation of the trading and profit and loss accounts
● explain why a balance sheet is not part of the double entry system
● explain the meaning of the terms fixed assets, current assets, current liability and long-term liability
● prepare a balance sheet using the vertical method of presentation
● understand the importance of the term net current assets/working capital
● know which items appear in the owner's capital account.

9.1 Definition and content of a balance sheet

A **balance sheet** is a financial statement setting out the book values of assets, liabilities and capital 'as at' a particular point in time. In simple terms a balance sheet shows what a business '**owns**' and what it '**owes**' at a specific date.

Details of the assets, liabilities and capital have to be found in the records of the business and then written out as a balance sheet. It is easy to find these details as they consist of all the balances remaining in the records once the trading and profit and loss account for the period have been completed. All balances remaining have to be assets, liabilities or capital since the other balances should have been closed off when the trading and profit and loss account was completed.

9.2 Preparing a balance sheet

Let us look at Exhibit 9.1, the trial balance of B Swift (from Exhibit 8.6) as on 31 December 2005 after the trading and profit and loss account had been prepared.

Exhibit 9.1

B Swift Trial Balance as at 31 December 2005 (after Trading and Profit and Loss Accounts completed)		
	Dr £	Cr £
Fixtures and fittings	500	
Debtors	680	
Creditors		910
Stock	300	
Bank	1,510	
Cash	20	
Capital		2,100
	3,010	3,010

We can now draw up a balance sheet as at 31 December 2005, and this is shown in Exhibit 9.2. The layout is discussed further in Section 9.4.

Exhibit 9.2

B Swift
Balance Sheet as at 31 December 2005

	£	£
Fixed assets		
Fixtures and fittings		500
Current assets		
Stock	300	
Debtors	680	
Cash at bank	1,510	
Cash in hand	20	
	2,510	
Less Current liabilities		
Creditors	910	
Net current assets		1,600
Long-term liabilities		
Long-term loan		
Net assets		–
		2,100
Financed by:		
Capital account		
Cash introduced		2,000
Add net profit for the year		800
		2,800
Less Drawings		700
		2,100

9.3 No double entry in balance sheets

It may seem strange to you to learn that balance sheets are *not* part of the double entry system.

If accounts are drawn such as the cash account, rent account, sales account, trading and profit and loss account, and so on, we are writing up part of the double entry system. We make entries on the debit and credit sides of these accounts.

In preparing a balance sheet, we do not enter anything in the various accounts. We do not actually transfer the fixtures balance or the stock balance, or any of the others, to the balance sheet. All that we do is to list the balances for assets, capital and liabilities so as to form a balance sheet. This means that none of these accounts have been closed off. *Nothing is entered in the accounts.*

When the next accounting period starts, these accounts are still open containing balances. As a result of business transactions, entries are then made in these accounts to add to, or deduct from, the amounts shown in the accounts using normal double entry.

If you see the word 'account' you will know that it is part of the double entry system, and it will include debit and credit entries. If the word 'account' cannot be used, it is not part of double entry. For instance:

Trial balance:	A list of balances to see whether the records are correct.
Balance sheet:	A list of balances arranged according to whether they are assets, capital or liabilities.

9.4 Balance sheet layout

You would not expect to go into a department store and see goods for sale all mixed up and not laid out properly; you would expect that the goods would be displayed so that you could easily find them. Similarly, in balance sheets we do not want the items shown in a random order; we want them displayed so that useful information can easily be seen.

For users of the accounts, such as bank managers, accountants and investors, conformity of layout is needed in order to make a comparison of balance sheets easier. The standard layout is shown in Exhibit 9.2 and examined in more detail below.

Assets

Assets are shown under two headings, namely fixed assets and current assets.

Fixed assets

Fixed assets are assets that:

● are expected to be of use to the business for a long time
● are to be used in the business, and
● were not bought only for the purposes of resale.

Examples are buildings, machinery, motor vehicles, fixtures and fittings.

Fixed assets are listed first in the balance sheet starting with those that the business will keep the longest, down to assets with the shortest life expectancy. For instance:

Fixed Assets
1 Land and buildings
2 Fixtures and fittings
3 Machinery
4 Motor vehicles

Current assets

Current assets are assets that are likely to change in the near future and usually within twelve months of the balance sheet date. They include stock of goods for resale at a profit, amounts owed by debtors, cash at bank and any cash in hand. These are listed starting with the asset that is least likely to be turned into cash, finishing with cash itself. The accepted order is listed as:

Current assets
1 Stock
2 Debtors
3 Cash at bank
4 Cash in hand

Liabilities

There are two categories of liabilities, current liabilities and long-term liabilities.

Current liabilities

Current liabilities are liabilities due for repayment in the short term, usually within one year. Examples are bank overdrafts, amounts due to creditors for the supply of goods for resale.

Current liabilities are deducted from the current assets, as shown in Exhibit 9.2, to give the **net current assets** or **working capital**. This figure is very important in accounting since it shows the amount of resources the business has in the form of readily available cash to meet everyday running expenses.

Long-term liabilities

Long-term liabilities are liabilities not due for repayment in the near future. Examples are bank loans, loans from others such as friends or relatives and mortgages. Long-term liabilities are deducted from the total figure of assets plus the net current assets as illustrated in Exhibit 9.2.

Capital account

This is the proprietor's or partner's account with the business. It will start with the balance brought forward from the previous accounting period, to which is added any personal cash introduced into the business and the net profit made by the business in this accounting period. Deducted from the capital account will be amounts drawn from the business and any loss made by the business. The final balance on the capital account should equal the net assets or net liabilities figure – and hence the balance sheet balances. Exhibit 9.3 gives the standard format.

Exhibit 9.3

Capital Account		
	£	£
Balance b/d		X
Add Cash introduced		X
Net profit for the period		X
		X
Less Drawings	X	
Net loss for the period	X	
		X
		X

It is important to note that the balance sheet shows the position of the business at one point in time: the balance sheet date, i.e. 'as at 31 December 2006'. It is like taking a snapshot of the business at one moment in time. On the other hand the trading and profit and loss account shows the profit/loss of that business for a period of time (normally a year), i.e. 'for the year ended 31 December 2006'.

Chapter summary

- A balance sheet is a financial statement which lists the book values of assets, liabilities and capital 'as at' a specific date. It shows what a business 'owns' and 'owes' at a particular point in time.
- The balance sheet is prepared from the remaining balances in the trial balance after the trading and profit and loss account has been completed.
- The balance sheet is *not* part of the double entry system.
- Most balance sheets are set out using the vertical method of presentation which shows the assets divided into two categories namely fixed assets and current assets followed by current liabilities, long-term liabilities and capital.
- The term 'fixed assets' means assets of a more permanent nature such as land and building, equipment and cars that are owned by the business. These are listed in the balance sheet in descending order with the most permanent asset shown first.
- The term 'current assets' refers to assets that are likely to change within one year for example stock, debtors, cash at bank and cash in hand. These are listed in order of liquidity with the least liquid of the assets shown first, i.e. stock and the most liquid asset shown at the bottom, i.e. cash in hand.
- The term *net current assets* or *working capital* is an important figure in accounting since it represents the amount of readily available resources available for paying everyday running expenses.
- The capital account contains money invested by the owner of the business plus the net profit for the period less amounts taken out by the owner in the form of 'drawings'. If there is no net profit then a net loss will have been incurred.

Exercises

9.1 Complete exercise 8.3 by drawing up a balance sheet as at 31 December 2006 for G Singh.

9.2X Complete exercise 8.4X by drawing up a balance sheet as at 30 June 2006 for R Cairns.

9.3 Complete exercise 8.5 by drawing up a balance sheet as at 31 March 2008 for Mrs P Stewart.

9.4 Miss V Holland had been trading for a number of years as a cheese retailer, making up accounts each year to 30 June. As at 30 June 2008 she was able to extract the following information from her accounting records and has asked you as her accountant to draw up the balance sheet at that date:

(*a*) She owed amounts to businesses that had supplied her with cheese, totalling £4,565

(*b*) She was owed £2,375 by a customer who bought goods on credit

(*c*) She had cash in hand of £150

(*d*) Her bank account was overdrawn by £1,785

(*e*) She had stock of cheese unsold totalling £1,465

(*f*) She had a van that was used for deliveries and that was valued at £3,400 on 30 June 2008

(*g*) She had equipment valued at £2,885 at the year end

(*h*) She had introduced £2,000 of her own money in the year, when she was nearing her overdraft limit

(*i*) The business made a net profit of £2,525 in the year to 30 June 2008

(*j*) Miss V Holland drew £50 each week, for the whole year, and had no other drawings from the business

(*k*) The business had a loan from V Holland's mother for £2,000. This was not due to be repaid until the year 2012.

9.5X Complete exercise 8.6X by drawing up a balance sheet as at 30 April 2008 for Miss R Burgess.

9.6X Complete exercise 8.7X by drawing up a balance sheet as at 30 June 2006 for M Kent.

CHAPTER 10

Financial statements: further considerations

Learning objectives

After you have studied this chapter you should be able to:

- record returns inwards and returns outwards in the trading and profit and loss account
- understand that carriage inwards on goods purchased is treated as part of the cost of goods sold
- realise that carriage outwards is an expense to be entered in the profit and loss account
- adjust financial statements properly for both the opening and closing stocks of the period
- explain why the cost of putting goods into a saleable condition should be charged to the trading account.

10.1 Returns inwards and returns outwards

When firms deal with the purchase and sale of goods it is inevitable that there are occasions when goods have to be returned by the purchaser to the supplier because they are damaged, faulty or perhaps not to the specification ordered. The goods will be returned to the supplier accompanied by a returns note which gives details of the goods being returned and the reason together with details of the order number, date etc.

Returns outwards (also called purchases returns)

When a business returns goods to a supplier for one of the above-mentioned reasons they are known as **returns outwards** or **purchases returns**. The book-keeping entries are as follows:

> Debit: supplier's account (i.e. the creditor)
> Credit: the returns outwards (or purchases returns) account.

The returns outwards account is kept separate from the purchases account to enable a check to be made on the amount of goods being returned.

Returns inwards (also called sales returns)

If goods are returned by a customer (debtor) then they are referred to as **returns inwards** or **sales returns**. The book-keeping entries would be as shown below:

Debit: returns inwards (or sales returns) account
Credit: customer's (debtors') account.

The returns inwards are again kept separate from the sales account to enable a check to be made on the amount of goods being returned to the firm.

10.2 Dealing with returns in the trading account

In Chapter 8 the returns inwards and returns outwards accounts were deliberately omitted so that the first sight of the trading and profit and loss accounts would not be too difficult. Since a large number of firms will return goods to their suppliers (returns outwards), and have goods returned to them (returns inwards), then these returns must be taken into consideration when calculating the gross profit.

In the trading account the returns inwards and returns outwards are dealt with as follows:

● returns inwards should be deducted from **sales**
● returns outwards should be deducted from **purchases**.

Suppose that in Exhibit 8.1 the trial balance of K Wade, rather than simply containing a sales account balance of £9,650 and a purchases account balance of £7,150 the balances showing stock movement had been:

K Wade
Trial Balance as at 31 December 2006 (extract)

	Dr £	Cr £
Sales		10,000
Purchases	7,350	
Returns Inwards	350	
Returns outwards		200

If we compare the two trial balances, i.e. the one shown in Exhibit 8.1 and the one shown above, the gross profit amount will be exactly the same. Sales in the original example were £9,650, whilst in the above example the returns inwards is deducted from sales as follows:

	£
Sales	10,000
Less Returns Inwards	350
Net Sales	9,650

Purchases were originally shown as £7,150 but in the above example returns out-wards will need to be deducted from purchases to ascertain the amount of goods retained by the firm as shown below:

	£
Purchases	7,350
Less Returns Outwards	200
Net Purchases	7,150

The trading account using the figures from the above example will now appear as in Exhibit 10.1.

Exhibit 10.1

K Wade
Trading and Profit and Loss Account for the year ended 31 December 2006

	£	£
Sales		10,000
Less Returns inwards		350
		9,650
Less Cost of goods sold		
Purchases	7,350	
Less Returns outwards	200	7,150
Gross profit		2,500

The gross profit in the above example is £2,500 which is exactly the same amount as shown in Exhibit 8.3. You will notice that the trading and profit and loss account prepared in Exhibit 8.3 was prepared using the horizontal method. The trading and profit and loss account shown above in Exhibit 10.1 has been presented using the vertical method of presentation which will be used on all further examples in this book.

Student hint:
Many students have difficulty deciding whether returns inwards should be deducted from sales or purchases figures and vice versa. The same applies to the returns out-wards figure. The following illustration shows that the returns are always deducted from the figure on the opposite side so forming a 'cross' on the trial balance:

K Wade
Trial Balance as at 31 December 2006 (extract)

	Dr £	Cr £
Sales		10,000
Purchases	7,350	
Returns inwards	350	
Returns outwards		200

10.3 Carriage

When a firm buys goods from a supplier the cost of delivering or transporting the goods also has to be paid. In accountancy terms this cost of transport is often referred to as 'carriage'. Carriage charges for transporting goods purchased into a firm is known as '**carriage inwards**', whereas, carriage charges for the delivery of goods to a firm's customers is known as '**carriage outwards**'.

Carriage inwards

When goods are purchased, the cost of carriage inwards may be included as part of the price, or, alternatively, the firm may have to pay for it separately. Suppose the firm was buying exactly the same goods from different suppliers. One supplier might sell them for £100 and not charge anything for carriage. Another supplier might sell the goods for £95, but you would have to pay £5 to a courier for carriage inwards, i.e. a total of £100. In both cases the goods cost £100. Therefore, to keep the cost of buying goods on the same basis carriage inwards is *always* added to the cost of purchases in the trading account.

Carriage outwards

Carriage outwards is the cost of delivering the goods to the firm's customers. It is an expense and not part of the selling price of the goods. Carriage outwards is always charged as an expense in the profit and loss account.

10.4 Dealing with carriage in the trading and profit and loss account

Suppose that in the illustration shown earlier of K Wade the goods had been bought for the same total figure of £7,350 but, in fact, £7,200 was the figure for purchases and £150 for carriage inwards. Let us also assume that part of the general expenses figure of £550, in Exhibit 8.1 was, in fact, carriage outward amounting to £400.

The trial balance would appear as in Exhibit 10.2.

Exhibit 10.2

K Wade Trial Balance as at 31 December 2006 (extract)		
	Dr £	Cr £
Sales		10,000
Purchases	7,200	
Returns inwards	350	
Returns outwards		200
Carriage inwards	150	
Carriage outwards	400	
General expenses	150	

The trading and profit and loss account would then be shown in Exhibit 10.3.

Exhibit 10.3

K Wade Trading and Profit and Loss Account for the year ended 31 December 2006		
	£	£
Sales		10,000
Less Returns inwards		350
		9,650
Less Cost of goods sold		
Purchases	7,200	
Less Returns outwards	200	
	7,000	
Carriage inwards	150	7,150
Gross profit		2,500
Less Expenses:		
General expenses	150	
Carriage outwards	400	550
Net profit		1,950

It can be seen that the three versions of K Wade's trial balance have all been concerned with the same overall amount of goods bought and sold by the business, at the same overall prices. Therefore, in each case, the same gross profit of £2,500 is shown. The net profit of £1,950 also remains the same.

Before you proceed further you are advised to attempt Exercises 10.1 and 10.2X.

10.5 The second year of a business

Following on from Exhibit 9.2 in the last chapter, we assume that B Swift carries on his business for another year. He then extracts a trial balance as on 31 December 2006 as shown as Exhibit 10.4. Closing stock as at that date was valued at £550.

Exhibit 10.4

B Swift Trial Balance as at 31 December 2006		
	Dr £	Cr £
Sales		6,700
Purchases	4,260	
Lighting	190	
Rent	240	
Wages: store assistant	520	
General expenses	70	
Carriage outwards	110	
Shop premises	2,000	
Fixtures and fittings	750	
Debtors	1,200	
Creditors		900
Bank	120	
Cash	40	
Loan from J Marsh		1,000
Drawings	900	
Capital		2,100
Stock (at 1 January 2005)	300	
	10,700	10,700

Adjustments needed for stock

Previously we have prepared the accounts for new businesses only. When a business starts it has no stock brought forward. B Swift started his new business on 1 January 2005 so his first year of trading ended on 31 December 2005 when he had a closing stock of £300. Therefore, when preparing his trading and profit and loss account for that year we are only concerned with the closing stock figure of £300. When we prepare the trading and profit and loss account for the second year, we can now see the difference.

In the trading and profit and loss account for the first year of trading, i.e. the year ended 31 December 2005, only one stock figure appears; that is the closing stock £300. This figure of closing stock for the year ended 31 December 2005 becomes the opening stock for the second year of trading and will be entered into the trading account in Swift's second year of trading. Therefore, both opening and closing stock figures are shown in the trading and profit and loss account for the year ended 31 December 2006.

The stock figure shown in the trial balance given in Exhibit 10.4 is that brought forward from the previous year on 31 December 2005; it is, therefore, the opening stock. The closing stock at 31 December 2006 can only be found by stocktaking, assume that it amounts to £550.

The opening and closing stock account figures for Swift for the two years can now be summarised as follows:

Trading Account for period ⟶	Year to 31 December 2005	Year to 31 December 2006
Opening stock 1.1.2005	None	
Closing stock 31.12.2005	£300	
Opening stock 1.1.2006		£300
Closing stock 31.12.2006		£550

Double entry for stock

To enable you to understand the double entry aspect of stock, both the stock account and the trading account for B Swift for the year ended 31 December 2006 are shown below:

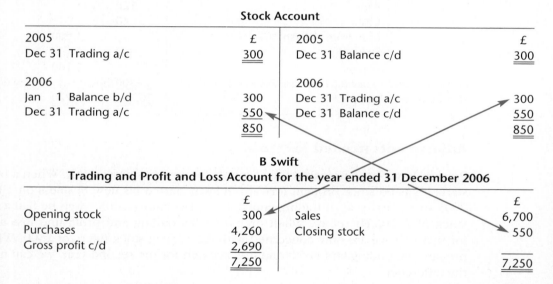

Stock Account

2005	£	2005	£
Dec 31 Trading a/c	300	Dec 31 Balance c/d	300
2006		2006	
Jan 1 Balance b/d	300	Dec 31 Trading a/c	300
Dec 31 Trading a/c	550	Dec 31 Balance c/d	550
	850		850

B Swift
Trading and Profit and Loss Account for the year ended 31 December 2006

	£		£
Opening stock	300	Sales	6,700
Purchases	4,260	Closing stock	550
Gross profit c/d	2,690		
	7,250		7,250

The stock at 31 December 2006 is £550 and had not been entered into the accounts previously. The entries above show how this has been recorded using double entry:

Debit: stock account £550
Credit: trading account £550.

Calculation of cost of goods sold

Let us now calculate the cost of goods sold for B Swift for the year ended 31 December 2006:

	£
Stock of goods at start of the year	300
Add Purchases	4,260
Total goods available for sale	4,560
Less What remains at the end of the year:	
(i.e. closing stock)	550
Therefore the cost of goods that have been sold	4,010

The gross profit can now be found by taking into consideration the effect the closing stock has on the gross profit. Remember that sales less cost of goods sold equals gross profit therefore:

	£
Sales	6,700
Less Cost of goods sold (see above)	4,010
Gross Profit	2,690

Now the trading and profit and loss account and balance sheet can be drawn up as shown in Exhibits 10.5 and 10.6.

Exhibit 10.5

B Swift Trading and Profit and Loss Account for the year ended 31 December 2006		
	£	£
Sales		6,700
Less Cost of goods sold		
Opening stock	300	
Add Purchases	4,260	
	4,560	
Less Closing stock	550	
		4,010
Gross profit		2,690
Less Expenses		
Wages	520	
Carriage outwards	110	
Lighting expenses	190	
Rent	240	
General expenses	70	
		1,130
Net profit		1,560

Exhibit 10.6

B Swift Balance Sheet as at 31 December 2006		
	£	£
Fixed assets		
Shop premises		2,000
Fixtures and fittings		750
		2,750
Current assets		
Stock	550	
Debtors	1,200	
Cash at bank	120	
Cash in hand	40	
	1,910	
Less Current liabilities		
Creditors	900	
Net current assets		1,010
		3,760
Long-term liabilities		
Loan from J Marsh		1,000
Net assets		2,760
Financed by		
Capital account		
Balance at 1 January 2006		2,100
Add Net profit for the year		1,210
		3,310
Less Drawings		550
		2,760

10.6 Financial statements

The term **financial statements** is often used to mean collectively the trading and profit and loss account and the balance sheet which are produced at the end of a trading period. They used to be referred to as **final accounts** but this term can be quite misleading since none of the financial statements are really 'accounts' in the book-keeping sense. Many people do, however, still refer to them as the 'final accounts' or just simply 'the accounts' of a business.

10.7 Other expenses in the trading account

The costs of putting goods into a saleable condition should be charged in the trading account. In the case of a trader these are relatively few. An example might be a trader who sells clocks packed in boxes. If he bought the clocks from one source and the boxes from another source, both of these items would be charged in the trading account as purchases. In addition, if a person is paid wages to pack the clocks, then such wages would be charged in the trading account. The wages of shop assistants who sold the clocks would be charged in the profit and loss account. The wages of the person packing the clocks would be the only wages in this instance concerned with 'putting the goods into a saleable condition'.

For goods imported from abroad it is usual to find that the costs of import duty, marine insurance and freight charges are also treated as part of the cost of goods sold and are, therefore, debited to the trading account.

10.8 Losses incurred by a business

So far, we have looked at the situation in which both a gross profit and a net profit have been made by a business. This will not always be the case in every business. For all kinds of reasons, such as poor trading conditions, bad management, or unexpected increases in expenses, the business may trade at a loss for a given period.

We will look at two cases, A Barnes, who made a gross profit but a net loss for the year, and K Jackson, who made both a gross loss and a net loss. The details for the trading and profit and loss accounts for the year ended 31 December 2005 for Barnes and Jackson are as follows:

	A Barnes £	K Jackson £
Opening stock 1 January 2005	3,500	9,200
Sales	21,000	33,000
Purchases	15,000	29,800
Closing stock 31 December 2005	2,200	4,800
Other expenses	6,300	3,900

The trading and profit and loss accounts for each business can now be prepared, see Exhibits 10.7 and 10.8.

Exhibit 10.7

A Barnes
Trading and Profit and Loss Account
for the year ended 31 December 2005

	£	£
Sales		21,000
Less Cost of goods sold		
Opening stock	3,500	
Add Purchases	15,000	
	18,500	
Less Closing stock	2,200	16,300
Gross profit		4,700
Less Other expenses		6,300
Net loss		1,600

In the above example of A Barnes a gross profit of £4,700 was made but since expenses of £6,300 were greater than that the final result is a net loss of £1,600.

Exhibit 10.8

K Jackson
Trading and Profit and Loss Account
for the year ended 31 December 2005

	£	£
Sales		33,000
Less Cost of goods sold		
Opening stock	9,200	
Add Purchases	29,800	
	39,000	
Less Closing stock	4,800	34,200
Gross loss		1,200
Add Other expenses		3,900
Net loss		5,100

In the above example of K Jackson a gross loss of £1,200 occurred since the cost of goods sold amounted to £34,200 whilst sales were only £33,000. Added to this gross loss of £1,200 were the expenses of £3,900 for the period and a resultant net loss of £5,100.

Recording losses in the capital account

If a net loss occurs then it will be recorded in the owner's capital account as follows:

> Debit: capital account
> Credit: profit and loss account.

10.9 Step-by-step guide to preparing financial statements (preliminary level)

Many students have difficulty in the preparation of the financial statements and in remembering the layout. The following step-by-step guide should help you in their preparation:

Preparing the financial statements

1 Before starting the exercise, rule lines connecting each item. This avoids selecting a wrong figure that is easily done under the stress of an examination.
2 Decide which section of the financial statement each item should be entered *before* you start, i.e. trading account, profit and loss account section or the balance sheet. On the left-hand side of the trial balance use the following abbreviations to identify where each item should be entered:
 ● T for trading account
 ● P/L for profit and loss account
 ● BS for the balance sheet

3 An *almost* inviolable rule:
- Each item displayed in the trial balance must only be entered *once* in the final accounts.
- Any item below a trial balance exercise should be dealt with *twice* (i.e. in the exercises following notice the closing stock figure is shown under the totals of the trial balance).

Dealing with adjustments in financial statements

1 Returns inwards and returns outwards:
    (a) returns inwards – deduct from sales in the trading account
    (b) returns outwards – deduct from purchases in the trading account.
2 Carriage inwards and carriage outwards:
    (a) carriage inwards – add to purchases in the trading account
    (b) carriage outwards – charge as an expense in the profit and loss account.

Note: In Appendix B you will find a model layout of the trading and profit and loss account and balance sheet of a sole trader. Further step-by-step instructions in the preparation of the financial statements are also shown in Chapter 28, Other adjustments for financial statements.

Chapter summary

- The returns inwards should always be deducted from the sales and the returns outwards deducted from the purchases; both are shown in the trading account.
- The name 'carriage' means the cost of transport.
- Carriage inwards is the cost of transporting the goods purchased 'into' the firm and, as such, is always *added* to the cost of purchases in the trading account.
- Carriage outwards is the cost of delivering the goods sold to the customers and is shown as an expense in the profit and loss account.
- When a new business first starts it has no opening stock; however, at the end of the first year of trading stocktaking is carried out to ascertain the amount of stock unsold, the closing stock.
- The closing stock of one year becomes the opening stock of the next year.
- A stock account is updated to record the closing stock figure and to carry forward the balance from one period to the next.
- When preparing a trading account for the first year of business only the closing stock figure is shown since there is no opening stock.
- In the second year of business both the opening and closing stock figures are shown in the trading account.
- The calculation of the figure for *cost of goods sold* is shown which appears under this heading in the trading account.
- The preparation of the trading and profit and loss account is shown including adjustments for returns inwards, returns outwards, carriage inwards, and both opening and closing stocks in the trading account. Carriage outwards is shown as an expense in the profit and loss account.

- A balance sheet is shown indicating the entry of the closing stock figure under the 'current asset' section.
- Any expenses incurred with getting the goods into a saleable condition are charged in the trading account.
- How to prepare a trading and profit and loss account if either a gross loss or net loss occurs.

Exercises

10.1   From the following details, prepare the trading account for the year ended 31 December 2007 for T Clarke.

		£
Carriage inwards		670
Sales		38,742
Purchases		26,409
Stocks of goods:	1 January 2007	6,924
	31 December 2007	7,489

10.2X   The following details for the year ended 31 March 2006 are available. Prepare the trading account for that year for M Parkin.

		£
Stocks:	31 March 2005	16,492
	31 March 2006	18,504
Purchases		36,905
Carriage inwards		1,122
Sales		54,600

10.3   Prepare the trading and profit and loss account for the year ended 31 December 2006, in respect of T Mann, from the following details:

		£
Returns inwards		490
Returns outwards		560
Purchases		31,000
Sales		52,790
Stocks of goods:	1 January 2006	5,690
	31 December 2006	4,230
Carriage inwards		1,700
Salaries and wages		5,010
Rent		1,460
Motor expenses		3,120
General expenses		420
Carriage outwards		790

10.4X A trading and profit and loss account for the year ended 31 December 2006 is to be prepared for K Lake from the following:

	£
Carriage outwards	490
Carriage inwards	210
Returns inwards	1,500
Returns outwards	1,580
Salaries and wages	6,250
Rent	1,750
Sundry expenses	360
Sales	99,500
Purchases	64,570
Stocks of goods: 1 January 2006	18,280
31 December 2006	17,360

10.5 From the following trial balance of S Makin, draw up a trading and profit and loss account for the year ended 30 September 2006, and balance sheet as at that date.

	Dr	Cr
	£	£
Stock 1 October 2005	2,368	
Carriage outwards	200	
Carriage inwards	310	
Returns inwards	205	
Returns outwards		322
Purchases	11,874	
Sales		18,600
Salaries and wages	3,862	
Rent and rates	304	
Insurance	78	
Motor expenses	664	
Office expenses	216	
Lighting and heating expenses	166	
General expenses	314	
Premises	15,000	
Motor vehicles	1,800	
Fixtures and fittings	350	
Debtors	3,896	
Creditors		1,731
Cash at bank	482	
Drawings	1,200	
Capital		22,636
	43,289	43,289

Stock at 30 September 2006 was £2,946.

10.6X The trial balance shown below was extracted from the books of J Collins on 31 March 2007. Prepare the trading and profit and loss account for the year ended 31 March 2007 and a balance sheet as at that date using the trial balance and the note regarding stock.

J Collins
Trial Balance as at 31 March 2007

	Dr £	Cr £
Sales		74,400
Purchases	46,224	
Stock 1 April 2006	15,104	
Carriage outwards	1,304	
Carriage inwards	936	
Salaries and wages	11,788	
Printing and stationery	810	
Telephone	756	
Travel expenses	490	
Rent	1,824	
Rates	1,080	
Sundry expenses	2,808	
Computer equipment	9,600	
Fixtures and fittings	2,400	
Debtors	18,308	
Creditors		12,180
Cash at bank	15,504	
Cash in hand	480	
Drawings	8,540	
Capital		51,376
	137,956	137,956

Stock at 31 March 2007 was £19,992.

10.7X G Bowyer manufactures sportswear, and for the year ended 31 October 2006 his sales were £76,540. He also paid carriage outwards of £4,275 to transport the sportswear to customers.

The materials purchased in the year amounted to £33,325, with an additional amount paid for carriage inwards of £2,715. Bowyer had stock of £8,255 on 1 November 2005, and of £7,985 on 31 October 2006. He was owed £6,285 by customers, and owed £4,825 to suppliers on 31 October 2006. His bank balance was overdrawn by £3,335, and he had equipment valued at £11,125 and a van valued at £2,225 on that date.

His overheads for the year ended 31 October 2006 were:

	£
Rent and rates	6,000
Motor expenses	3,110
Salaries	7,450
Telephone	495
Insurance	500
General expenses	750

He drew £3,675 in the year to 31 October 2006 and had a balance brought forward on his capital account on 1 November 2005 of £5,485.

You are required to draw up, in the vertical format, the trading and profit and loss account for the year ended 31 October 2006, and a balance sheet for G Bowyer at that date.

10.8 The following is the trial balance of J Smailes as at 31 March 2007. Draw up a set of final accounts for the year ended 31 March 2007 in vertical format.

	Dr	Cr
	£	£
Stock 1 April 2006	18,160	
Sales		92,340
Purchases	69,185	
Carriage inwards	420	
Carriage outwards	1,570	
Returns outwards		640
Wages and salaries	10,240	
Rent and rates	3,015	
Communication expenses	624	
Commissions payable	216	
Insurance	405	
Sundry expenses	318	
Buildings	20,000	
Debtors	14,320	
Creditors		8,160
Fixtures	2,850	
Cash at bank	2,970	
Cash in hand	115	
Loan from K Ball		10,000
Drawings	7,620	
Capital		40,888
	152,028	152,028

Stock at 31 March 2007 was £22,390.

10.9X   L Stokes drew up the following trial balance as at 30 September 2006. You are required to draft trading and profit and loss accounts for the year to 30 September 2006 and a balance sheet as at that date in vertical format.

	Dr	Cr
	£	£
Loan from P Owens		5,000
Capital		25,955
Drawings	8,420	
Cash at bank	3,115	
Cash in hand	295	
Debtors	12,300	
Creditors		9,370
Stock 30 September 2005	23,910	
Motor van	4,100	
Office equipment	6,250	
Sales		130,900
Purchases	92,100	
Returns inwards	550	
Carriage inwards	215	
Returns outwards		307
Carriage outwards	309	
Motor expenses	1,630	
Rent	2,970	
Telephone charges	405	
Wages and salaries	12,810	
Insurance	492	
Office expenses	1,377	
Sundry expenses	284	
	171,532	171,532

Stock at 30 September 2006 was £27,475.

CHAPTER 11

Accounting concepts

Learning objectives

After you have studied this chapter you should be able to:

- appreciate the assumptions that are made when recording accounting data
- explain why one set of accounts is used for several different purposes
- understand what is meant by objectivity and subjectivity
- explain the basic concepts of accounting
- explain how the further overriding concepts of materiality, going concern, prudence, realisation, consistency and substance over form affect the recording and adjustments of data
- understand the importance of confidentiality.

11.1 Introduction

In your studies of book-keeping and accounting so far, and the previous chapters in this book, concentration has been placed mainly on the recording of financial transactions in the books of account. Recording of these transactions has been based on certain *assumptions* which have deliberately not been discussed in detail previously. The reason for leaving this discussion until now is because it is much easier to look at them with a greater understanding *after* basic double entry has been covered and you have knowledge of the final accounts of a business. These assumptions are known as the 'accounting concepts'.

The trading and profit and loss accounts and balance sheets shown in the previous chapters were drawn up for the owner of the business. As shown later in the book, businesses are owned by more than just one person and the financial statements for those businesses are for the use of all owners.

An owner of a business may not be the only person to see the financial statements. The owners may wish to show a copy to the bank manager if they wish to borrow money. The Inspector of Taxes will also require a copy for the calculation of taxes. Then there may be other interested parties, such as prospective investors, suppliers, customers and so on.

11.2   One set of financial statements for all purposes

If it had always been the custom to draft different kinds of financial statements for different purposes, so that one set could be given to your banker, another set to a prospective purchaser of a business and so on, then accounting would be different from what it is today. However, copies of the same set of financial statements are given to all the different people.

This means that a banker, a prospective buyer of the business, an owner and all the other people with an interest see the same trading and profit and loss account and balance sheet. The interests of each stakeholder may be different, each one using the financial statements for their own particular purpose. For example the bank manager would like to know how much the assets would sell for if the business ceased trading. They would then see what the possibility would be of the bank obtaining repayment of its loan or overdraft. Others would also like to see the information in the way that is most useful to them. However, only one set of financial statements is normally available for all these different stakeholders. Thus trading and profit and loss accounts and balance sheets are used for many different purposes. For them to be of any use, the different parties have to agree to the way in which they are drawn up.

Assume that you are in a class of students and that you have the problem of valuing your assets that consists of ten textbooks. The first value you decide is based upon how much you could sell them for. Your own guess is £50, but the other members of your class may suggest they should be valued at anything from £30 to £60.

Suppose that you now decide to put a value on their use to you. You may well think that the use of these textbooks will enable you to pass your examinations and so you will get a good job. Another person may have the opposite idea concerning the use of the textbooks. The use value placed on the textbooks by others in the class will be quite different. Again, your value may be higher than those of some of your colleagues and lower than others.

Finally, you decide to value them by reference to cost. You examine the receipts for the books which show that you paid a total of £90 for them. The rest of the class may then agree that the cost valuation is a fair and equitable means of assessing their value.

This is, in fact, the means used to value the assets of a business and is referred to as the historical cost concept.

11.3   Objectivity and subjectivity

It is especially important in accounting that the procedures or methods used are agreed and understood by everyone. This approach is said to be **objective**. In the above example of the textbooks the amount eventually agreed upon to value the asset of books was the cost price, known as the historical cost concept, thus this method of valuation is said to be objective. Valuing assets at their cost price means that you are adhering to the facts and everyone knows where the value came from and you are not using your own judgement to arrive at a valuation.

When the approach is **subjective**, it means you wish to use your own judgement or method of valuation, even though no one else may agree to it. In the example of the textbooks the value of the books depended upon the importance of them to the user. To the person wishing to use them to obtain qualifications to help them in their career they may be of more value than to someone using them to fill up a shelf in their bookcase.

The desire to provide the same set of accounts for many different parties, and thus to provide a measure that gains their consensus of opinion, means that objectivity is sought in financial accounting. If you are able to understand this desire for objectivity, then many of the apparent contradictions can be understood because it is often at the heart of the financial accounting methods in use at the present time.

Financial accounting seeks objectivity and, of course, it must have rules which lay down the way in which the activities of the business are recorded. These rules are known as **accounting concepts**.

11.4 Basic accounting concepts

Over the years, accounting systems have developed more for practical reasons than for theoretical ones. Consequently, several basic procedures have evolved that form the basic rules of accounting. As mentioned above, these are often referred to as accounting concepts.

A concept may be defined as an idea. Thus, an accounting concept is an assumption that underlies the preparation of the financial statements of the organisation. There are several accounting concepts that are followed when preparing the financial accounts of a business – all of which you may be required to know when taking an examination. These are as follows:

The historical cost concept

The need for this has already been described in the example of valuing textbooks. It means that assets are normally shown at cost price and this is the basis for valuation of the asset.

The money measurement concept

Accounting is concerned only with these facts:

- it can be measured in money, and
- most people will agree to the 'monetary' value of the transaction.

This means that accounting can never tell you everything about a business. For example, accounting does not show the following:

(i)   whether the firm has good or bad managers
(ii)   that there are serious problems with the workforce
(iii) that a rival product is about to take away many of its best customers
(iv) that the government is about to pass a law that will cost the business extra expense in future.

The reason that (i) to (iv) above, or similar items, are not recorded is that it would be impossible to work out a money value for them that most people would agree to.

Some people think that accounting tells you everything you want to know, but the above shows that this is not true.

Business entity concept

The concept implies that the affairs of a business are to be treated as being quite separate from the personal activities of its owner(s). The items recorded in the books of the business, are, therefore, restricted to the transactions of the business. No matter what activities the proprietor(s) are involved in outside the business, they are completely disregarded in the books kept by the business.

The only time the personal resources of the proprietor(s) affect the firm's accounting records is when they introduce new capital into the business or take drawings from it.

The dual aspect concept

This states that there are two aspects of Accounting, one represented by the assets of a business and the other by the claims against them. The concept states that these two aspects are always equal to each other. In other words:

$$\text{Assets} = \text{Capital} + \text{Liabilities}$$

Double entry is the name given to the method of recording the transactions for the **dual aspect concept**.

11.5 Other important accounting concepts

There are several other important accounting concepts which have become accepted by the commercial world when preparing financial statements for a business. These concepts have been used for many years without being formally imposed on the accounting profession.

Such is the importance of these concepts that the Companies Act 1985, required that they be used as a basis for drawing-up financial statements. The following concepts are enforced by this Act.

Going concern concept

This concept implies that the business will continue to operate for the foreseeable future. In other words, it is assumed that the business will continue for a long period of time.

Consistency

Even if we do everything already listed under concepts and conventions, there will still be quite a few different ways in which items could be recorded. Each firm should try to choose the methods that give the most reliable picture of the business.

This cannot be done if one method is used in one year and another method in the next year, and so on. Constantly changing the methods would lead to misleading profits being calculated from the accounting records. Therefore the convention of 'consistency' is used. This convention says that when a firm has fixed a method for the accounting treatment of an item, it will enter all similar items in exactly the same way in following years.

However, it does not mean that the firm has to follow the method until the firm closes down. A firm can change the method used, but such a change is not taken without due consideration. When such a change occurs and the profits calculated in that year are affected by a material amount, then either in the profit and loss account itself or in one of the reports with it, the effect of the change should be stated.

Prudence

Very often, accountants have to use their judgement to decide which figure they will take for an item. Suppose a debt has been owing for quite a long time and no one knows whether it will be paid. Should the accountant be an optimist in thinking that it will be paid, or be more pessimistic?

It is the accountant's duty to see that people get the proper facts about a business. They should make certain that assets are not valued too highly. Similarly, liabilities should not be shown at values too low. Otherwise, people might inadvisedly lend money to a firm, which they would not do so had the proper facts been known.

The accountant should always be on the side of caution, and this is known as 'prudence'. The prudence convention means that, normally, accountants will take the figure that will understate rather than overstate the profit. Thus, they should choose the figure that will cause the capital of the firm to be shown at a lower amount rather than at a higher one. They will also normally make sure that all losses are recorded in the books, but profits should not be anticipated by recording them before they are realised.

Realisation

This concept holds the view that profit can only be taken into account when realisation has occurred – in other words, until it is reasonably certain of being earned. Profit is normally said to be earned when:

● goods or services are provided for the buyer
● the buyer accepts liability to pay for the goods or services
● the monetary value of the goods or services has been established
● the buyer will be in a situation to be able to pay for the goods or services.

Notice that it is not the time

● when the order is received, or
● when the customer pays for the goods.

However, it is only when you can be reasonably certain as to how much will be received that you can recognise profits or gains.

The accruals concept

This concept says that net profit is the difference between revenues and expenses incurred in generating those revenues, i.e.

$$\text{Revenues} - \text{Expenses} = \text{Net Profit}$$

Determining the expenses used up to obtain the revenues is referred to as *matching* expenses against revenues; that is why this concept is also called the **matching concept**. The key to the application of the concept is that all income and charges relating to the financial period to which the financial statements relate should be taken into account without regard to the date of the receipt or payment.

Sales are *revenues* when the goods are sold and *not* when the money is received, which can be in a later period. Purchases are *expenses* when goods are bought, not when they are paid for. As we shall see in a later chapter items such as rent, insurance, motor expenses and so on are treated as expenses when they are incurred, not when they are paid for. Adjustments are made when preparing financial statements for expenses owing and those paid in advance.

By showing the actual expenses 'incurred' in a period matched against revenues earned in the same period, a correct figure of net profit will be shown in the profit and loss account.

You need to know and understand the above concepts when taking an examination.

Separate determination concept

This concept refers to the accounting procedure to be used when dealing with potential gains and potential losses. You do not need to know about this concept until later in your accounting studies.

Substance over form

This concept is a requirement of Financial Reporting Standard FRS 5. The legal form of a transaction can differ from its real substance and where this happens accounting should show the transaction in accordance with its real substance which is basically how the transaction affects the economic situation of the firm. This means that accounting, in this instance, will not reflect the exact legal position concerning that transaction. An example would be when a business rented a car under a lease that allowed it to purchase the car at the end of three years for £1. The substance of the agreement is hire purchase, but the form is rental. It should be treated as if it were a hire purchase.

11.6 Materiality

This convention is applied to try to stop you wasting time and effort doing completely unnecessary work. Accounting does not serve a useful purpose if the effort of recording a transaction in a certain way is not worthwhile. As an example, if a box of paperclips was bought, it would be used over a period of time and this cost is gradually used up every time someone uses a paperclip. It is possible to record this as an expense every time it happens, but obviously the price of a box of paperclips is so little that it is not worth recording it in this way. You should not waste your time in the unnecessary recording of trivial items.

The box of paperclips is not a 'material' item, and it would therefore be charged as an expense in the period in which it was bought even though it could last for more than one accounting period. Similarly, the purchase of a cheap metal waste-bin would also be charged as an expense in the period it was bought because it is not a material item, even though it may last 20 years. It would not be worth calculating depreciation on it. A lorry, on the other hand, would be deemed to be a material item. We then calculate the depreciation to be charged in each period, with the cost consumed in each period of its use. Depreciation is dealt with in Chapters 25 and 26.

You can see that small amounts are not material, while larger amounts are material. The question is, at what figure does an item become material? There is no fixed rule for this; firms make all sorts of rules to say what is material and what is not, and there is no law that says what these should be.

What is material and what is not depends upon judgement. A firm may decide that all items under £100 should be treated as expenses in the period in which they were bought, even though they may be in use in the firm for the following ten years. Another firm – especially a large one – may put the limit at £1,000. Different limits may even be set for different types of items. The size and type of firm will also affect the decisions as to what is material, and what is not.

11.7 The assumption of the stability of monetary measures

Earlier in the chapter we saw how accounting uses the historical cost concept which states that the asset is normally shown at its cost price. This means that accounting statements can be misleading, because assets will be bought at different times at the prices then ruling, and the figures will be totalled up to show the value of the assets in cost terms.

For instance, suppose that you bought a building 20 years ago for £20,000. You now decide to buy an identical additional building, but the price has risen to £40,000. You buy it, and the buildings account now shows buildings at a figure of £60,000. One building is in the currency of 20 years ago, while the other is at today's currency value. The figure of £60,000 spent in total is historically correct but cannot be used for much else.

When we look at final accounts, we must understand such problems. There are ways of adjusting accounts to make the figures more useful, but these are not in your syllabus. You will have to study them if you take accounting examinations at an advanced level.

11.8 Confidentiality

Although it is not a concept of accounting, employees who work in the financial department of an organisation, and those who have access to its financial information, should recognise that this information is confidential. It should not be disclosed to anyone within the organisation except those authorised to receive it.

It should only be disclosed 'outside' the organisation to such bodies as the Inland Revenue or Customs and Excise, as required by government legislation.

The organisation's auditors will also require access to the financial records in order to prepare its financial statements.

Chapter summary

- A business prepares one set of financial statements that has to serve many purposes.
- How the need for general agreement on accounting issues has led to the development of concepts and conventions that govern accounting.
- What is meant by the terms 'objectivity' and 'subjectivity'.
- The basic accounting concepts used by organisations when preparing their financial statement.
- How other important concepts, recognised under the Companies Act 1985, are also used when preparing financial statements. These include going concern, consistency, prudence and realisation, accruals, separate determination and substance over form.
- The importance of materiality.
- The assumption that monetary measures remain stable.
- Understand the importance of confidentiality.

Exercises

11.1 Which accounting concept is used in each of the following accounting treatments? Explain.

(a) The cost of a tape dispenser has been charged to an expense account, although in fact it could still be in use in ten years' time.

(b) A sole proprietor has sold his private house, but has not recorded anything about it in the business records.

(c) A debt has been written off as a bad debt even though there is still a chance that the debtor eventually may be able to pay it.

(d) A machine has been bought for an exceedingly low figure, and it has been entered in the asset account at that figure even though it is worth more.

(e) An expert says that the value of the management team to the company is worth well over a million pounds, yet nothing is entered for it in the books.

(f) A motor van broke down in December 2007. The repair bill for it was not paid until 2008 yet it has been treated as a 2007 expense.

(g) A customer saw a carpet in 2007 and said he might well buy it. He phoned in 2008 and asked for the carpet to be delivered. The item was not treated as a sale in 2007 but was treated as a sale in 2008.

(h) The final day of the financial year saw the passing of a law that would render trading in our sort of goods illegal, and the business will have to close. The accountant says that our stock figure cannot be shown at cost in the balance sheet.

(i) We have been told that we cannot show our asset of motor cars at cost in one year and at cost plus the price increase the next year when the manufacturer increases prices of all cars, which also includes our unsold stock.

(j) We have shown all items of machinery costing less than £100 as machinery operating expenses.

11.2X When preparing the final accounts of your company, name the accounting concepts you should follow to deal with each of the following:

(*a*) Electricity consumed during the accounting period is still unpaid at the year end.

(*b*) The owner of the company has invested her private assets in the company.

(*c*) A debtor who owes the company a large amount has been declared bankrupt, and the outstanding amount due to the company is now considered to be irrecoverable.

(*d*) The company has suffered substantial losses in the past few years, and it is extremely uncertain whether the company can continue to operate next year.

11.3X Accounting concepts and conventions are used in preparing financial statements of a business.

(*a*) Briefly explain any three of the following concepts:
  (i)   Going concern
  (ii) Accruals
  (iii) Consistency
  (iv) Prudence.

(*b*) Objectivity is important in analysing and preparing accounting information. Explain the term 'objectivity', giving an example as to how it might be applied.

11.4 Explain briefly what you understand by the 'historical cost concept'. Give an advantage in using the cost method of valuation.

Part 3

Books of original entry

This part is concerned with the books and journals into which transactions are first entered, together with chapters on the banking system, capital and revenue expenditure, and VAT.

Books of original entry and ledgers

Learning objectives

After you have studied this chapter you should be able to:

- understand the need for books of original entry
- explain what each book of original entry is used for
- appreciate how the books of original entry are used alongside the ledgers
- distinguish between personal and impersonal accounts
- distinguish between the different types of ledgers
- understand the use of the general (nominal) ledger and private ledger.

12.1 The growth of the business

When a business is very small, then all the double entry account can be kept in one book, which we call a 'ledger'. Once the business expands it would be impossible to use just one book, as the large number of pages needed for the numerous transactions would mean that the book would be too big to handle. Also, suppose that there were several book-keepers; they could not all do their work properly if there was only one ledger.

The answer to this problem is for us to use more books. When we do this we put similar types of transactions together and have a book for each type. The different types of books used to record transactions will now be discussed.

12.2 Books of original entry

These are books in which the transaction is first entered. There are separate books for different types of transaction, as follows:

- **Sales day book*** (also called sales journal) – a book used for listing sales invoices; it gives details of the date of the sale, to whom and the amount of the sale. Sales day books may also contain analysis columns to give details of the amount charged for the goods, the VAT charged and, finally, the total amount due. Columnar sales day books may also be extended to analyse sales between different goods, departments and so on. Refer to Chapter 22.

- **Purchases day book*** (also called purchases journal) – this is similar to the sales day book, but contains lists of purchase invoices received from suppliers of goods or services. The purchases day book may also contain analysis columns depending upon the accounting system.
- **Returns inwards day book*** (also called returns inwards journal) – this is used to list any returns made by customers. This will lead to a credit note being issued to them.
- **Returns outwards day book*** (also returns outwards journal) – this is used to record returns to suppliers.
- **Cash book** – this is another book of original entry used to enter cash and bank receipts and payments. The cash book provides a record of the business's bank account and also provides details of the amount of cash in hand. It is both a book of original entry and part of the double entry system as it contains the balances of both cash in hand and cash at bank.
- **Petty cash book** – a cash book used for making small (petty) payments, details of which are entered from petty cash vouchers supported if possible by a receipt.
- **The journal** – this is used to record items that are much less common and sometimes complicated and are not recorded in any other book of original entry. All the above books are covered fully in later chapters in the book.

*Note: Most students may find it less confusing if 'day book' is used rather than 'journal' when referring to the sales, purchases, returns inwards and returns outwards day books, so as not to confuse these books with 'the journal' which is used for much less common transactions. The name 'day books' will be used in the remainder of this book but students must be aware that examination bodies may use either term.

12.3 Using more than one ledger

Once the details from the source documents (invoices, credit notes etc.) have been entered into the books of original entry, then the next stage of the book-keeping procedure is to show the effect of the transactions: this is done by transferring (posting) the details to the various ledgers using the double entry system. One of the main reasons for keeping various ledgers is to allow different members of staff the ability to record transactions at the same time. If only one ledger were available this would not be possible.

12.4 Types of ledgers

The different types of ledger that most businesses use are:

- **sales ledger** – contains records of customers' personal accounts
- **purchases ledger** – contains records of suppliers' personal accounts
- **general ledger** – contains the remaining double entry accounts, such as assets, capital, income, expenses (can also be called nominal ledger).

12.5 Diagram of the books commonly used

The various books used in accounting are shown in linked diagram form shown in Exhibit 12.1.

Exhibit 12.1

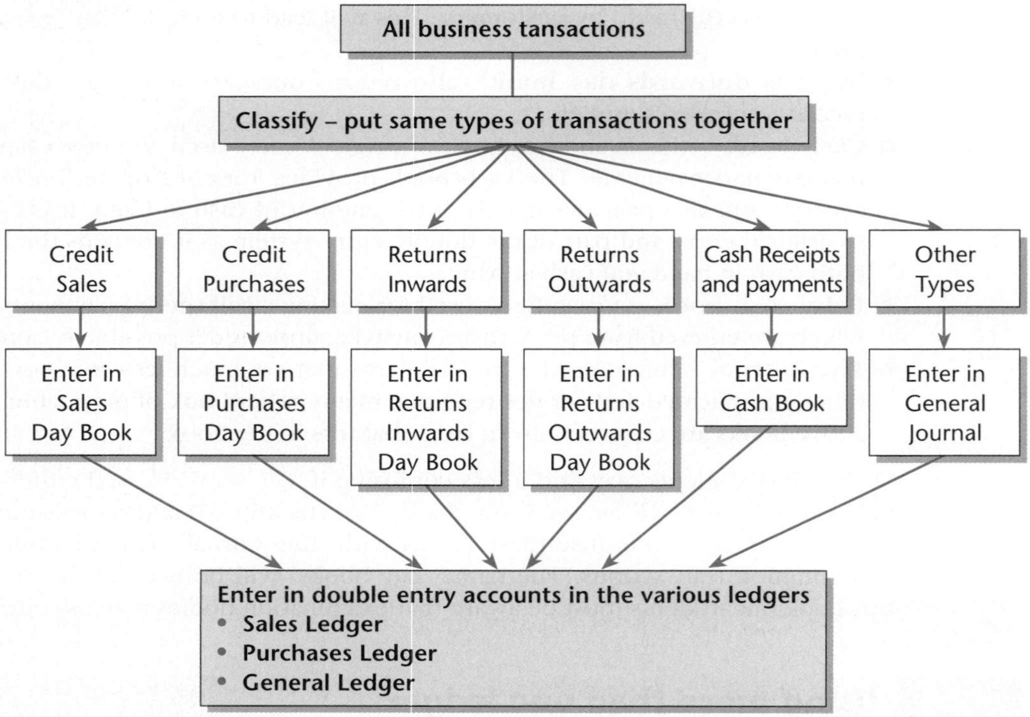

12.6 Types of accounts

Accounts are divided into 'personal accounts' and 'impersonal accounts'.

Personal accounts are accounts that deal with people and firms – in other words, the debtors and creditors. The debtors being people or firms who owe money to the firm and whose accounts are maintained in the sales ledger. Creditors are people or firms to whom money is owed by the firm, their accounts are kept in the purchase ledger.

Impersonal accounts are divided into 'real' and 'nominal' accounts:

- **real accounts** are those which deal with possessions of the business, for example, buildings, machinery, computer equipment, stock etc.
- **nominal accounts** are those in which expenses and income are recorded, for example, sales, purchases, wages, electricity, motor expenses, etc.

The diagram shown in Exhibit 12.2 illustrates these accounts.

Exhibit 12.2

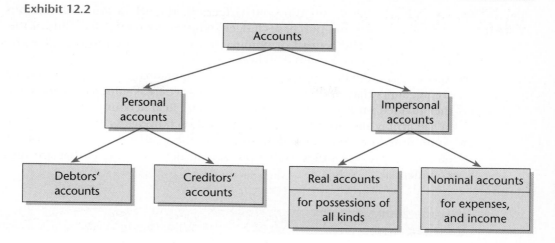

12.7 General (nominal) and private ledgers

The ledger in which the impersonal accounts are kept is known as the **general** or **nominal ledger**. In order to ensure privacy for the proprietor(s), the capital, drawings and other similar accounts are sometimes kept in a **private ledger**. This prevents office staff from seeing details of items which the proprietors want to keep confidential.

12.8 The use of computers in accounting

So far, it has been assumed that all book-keeping procedures are carried out using manual systems. But nowadays many businesses use computer systems, especially when dealing with large numbers of transactions. Computers are used for recording information in the same way as manual systems; thus, throughout the book the accounting terms of 'book' or 'journal' will be referred to for their use in either system.

Chapter summary

- As the business expands so does the requirement of additional books to record the accounting transactions.
- Books of original entry are where a transaction is entered first from the source document, i.e. invoice, credit note etc.
- There are various books of original entry, sales and purchases day books, returns inwards and returns outwards day book and the journal.
- The cash book is both a book of original entry and also a ledger account since it contains the balance of cash in hand and cash at bank. The petty cash book is also a book of original entry for small incidental expenses. It also contains the balance of the petty cash float.

- The business also uses different ledgers to record various transactions. These include the sales and purchases ledgers which contain the accounts of the debtors and creditors. The general or nominal ledger is also used to record such items as assets, capital, income and expenses.
- Accounts are divided into 'personal' and 'impersonal' accounts. Personal accounts are accounts that deal with people or firms whereas impersonal accounts are further divided into real and nominal accounts. Real accounts deal with possessions of the firm whilst nominal accounts record such things as expenses and income.
- Some firms use a private ledger to record the capital and drawings of the proprietor(s) to prevent office staff from seeing details of items that are regarded as confidential.

Exercises

12.1   For each of the following types of transactions, state the book of original entry, and the ledger and type of account, in which you would enter the transaction:

(*a*) Sales invoice
(*b*) Bank receipt
(*c*) Purchase invoice
(*d*) Bank payment
(*e*) Sales credit note
(*f*) Returns inwards
(*g*) Purchases credit note
(*h*) Closing stock.

12.2X   (*a*) State which document(s) would be entered into the following books of original entry:
    (i)   Purchases day book
    (ii)   Returns inwards day book
    (iii) Cash book
    (iv)   Sales day book
    (v)   Returns outwards day book.
(*b*) Distinguish between personal and impersonal accounts.

12.3   Show, by placing **one** tick in the appropriate column, whether each of the following accounts is personal, nominal or real. Account (a) has been completed as an example.

Name of Account	Personal	Nominal	Real
(*a*) Stock			✓
(*b*) Wages			
(*c*) Bank			
(*d*) Debtor			
(*e*) Office equipment			
(*f*) Purchases			
(*g*) Rent received			

NEAB (GCSE)

12.4X A table is shown below which lists some source documents. The table has spaces to show where entries will be made in an accounting system arising from these documents. Complete the table. As an example the entries have been made in the first line.
Note: ignore VAT.

Item	Source document	Subsidiary book	Account debited	Account credited
Example	**Invoice for stock**	*Purchases journal*	*Purchases*	*Creditor*
(*a*)	Cash receipt for rent paid			
(*b*)	Paying-in slip counterfoil for amount received from debtor			
(*c*)	Credit note received from supplier			

Southern Examining Group AQA

Please note that this question is NOT from the live examinations for the current specification.

Banking transactions

After you have studied this chapter you should be able to:

- understand the various means offered by the banking system of transferring money
- know how a business uses a particular option
- understand the basic procedure of operation of each method of transferring money
- know the reasons why a business uses a certain method.

13.1 Introduction

The trading activity, in which all businesses are engaged, involves the transfer of money as goods and/or services are bought and sold.

The banking system has changed dramatically over the last few years and there are now a number of different ways in which money can be transferred between businesses.

13.2 Transferring money

This can be received or paid by a business or organisation by various methods, including the following:

- cash
- cheques
- debit cards
- credit cards
- bank giro credit transfer
- BACS – this is the Bankers' Automated Clearing Service
- standing order
- direct debits
- paying-in slips.

13.3 Cash

Receiving cash

Cash is still used extensively in the retail business by customers purchasing goods. Security is a major problem in a number of ways for the business receiving the cash as shown below:

- it must be counted and checked to ensure that it corresponds with any documentation showing the amount to be received
- it must be stored safely and taken to the bank as soon as possible
- counterfeit money can be in circulation and detection equipment could be needed to prevent this type of fraud
- there should be regular internal checks to ensure that the persons handling cash are honest and funds do not go astray.

Most cash sales are made where electronic cash tills are in operation and these issue receipts automatically. The receipts should be kept by customers, not only as proof of payment, but, as evidence of the purchase should the goods have to be returned if faulty or unsuitable. A till receipt is shown in Exhibit 13.1.

Exhibit 13.1 Receipt for a cash sale

```
Name of store _____          MILO'S SUPERSTORE
                                                   MANCHESTER

VAT registration number _____          VAT No. 212 5212 78

                                                      RECEIPT

                                               Superjet travel game        17.50
Goods bought _____           Bulendo magic tricks        11.25
                                               Junior chess set             9.12
Total price due _____          3 items: TOTAL             37.87
Cash given _____          CASH                       40.00
Change to be given _____           CHANGE                      2.13

                                               Please keep receipt for refunds or queries

Location of cash till _____          Cash till No. 5
Date/time/reference number of transaction __   14/12/2003      11.58      1216 44/16
```

Cash that needs to be banked will be detailed on a paying-in slip – this is described in Section 13.10.

Paying by cash

When payments are made by a business it is safer and easier to use a non-cash method such as cheques or the BACS system (this is described in Section 13.7). Many firms who employ weekly paid staff still pay wages in cash and this method involves all the security problems which have been discussed previously. However, small value purchases can be made using the petty cash system. This is described in Chapter 17.

13.4 Cheques

Receiving cheques

Most customers who have received goods and/or services pay for them by cheque. These customers will have established a credit account with the business after credit worthiness checks have been carried out.

Cheques received from these well-established credit account customers should be carefully examined for the following:

- that the cheque is drawn payable to the receiver
- that the correct amount is stated both in words and in figures
- that the cheque is dated and is not out of date or postdated
- that the cheque has been properly signed.

If any of these factors are not in order the cheque will have to be returned to the drawer for amendment or for a new cheque to be issued. Cheques sent by post will not be accompanied by bank guarantee cards. It is not a legal requirement to issue a receipt for payment by cheque since the cheque is evidence of such payment. In spite of this many businesses do issue receipts.

When casual customers purchase goods and pay for them by cheque the business will only accept such payment when the cheque is supported by a **bank guarantee/ debit card**. The card company that has issued the card will guarantee to pay the cheque amount due. These cards usually have a cheque guarantee limit of £100. Cheques received by the business should be paid into the bank as soon as possible using paying-in slips.

Paying by cheque

When a business pays by cheque for goods or services it must be signed by an authorised signatory. The person signing the cheque for the business must have the approval of the company. The bank will also have previously been notified of the name of this person and will have carried out checks to verify this person's identity. They are legally bound to carry out this procedure to prevent fraud and to counter money-laundering activities. Larger businesses will usually insist on at least two authorised signatories to ensure proper payments are made.

It is vital that the business's account has sufficient money in it to cover the amounts paid otherwise the bank will not process the cheque.

The person writing the cheque and using it for payment is known as the **drawer**. The person to whom the cheque is paid is known as the **payee** and the **drawee** is the bank. A completed cheque is shown in Exhibit 13.2.

Exhibit 13.2

Sort Code

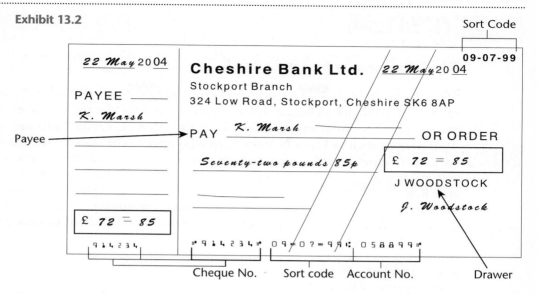

The completed cheque shows that J Woodstock, the drawer, is paying K Marsh, the sum of £72.85 on 22 May 2004. The counterfoil, at the left-hand side of the cheque, is also completed and retained by J Woodstock as a record of the transaction. It will be used to enter the details in the cash book which is covered in a later chapter.

Security of cheques

All cheques used by businesses will be crossed with two diagonal lines pre-printed on the face of the cheque as shown in Exhibit 13.2. This ensures that it must be paid into a bank account, building society account or saving account. The bank will ensure that it is paid into the payee's account if the words 'A/c Payee Only' are written between the diagonal lines.

Cheque clearing

It is important to understand how cheques paid from one person's bank account pass into another person's bank account. This process is shown below with reference to the cheque in Exhibit 13.2.

2004

May 22　J Woodstock, in Stockport, sends the cheque to K Marsh, who lives in Leeds. Woodstock enters the payment in his cash book.

May 23　Cheque received by Marsh. He banks it the same day in his bank account at Barclays Bank in Leeds. Marsh shows the cheque in his cash book as being received and banked on 23 May.

May 24　Barclays in London receive the cheque. They exchange it with the head office of the Cheshire Bank in London. The Cheshire Bank send the cheque to their Stockport branch.

May 25　The Stockport branch of the Cheshire Bank examine the cheque. If there is nothing wrong with it, the cheque can now be debited by the bank to J Woodstock's account.

13.5 Credit cards

Receiving money by credit card

Credit cards are a method for customers to purchase goods without needing to pay by cash or make out a cheque. They can also be used when the customer wishes to make a purchase by telephone, fax or via the internet. Credit cards are issued by organisations such as Visa and Mastercard who operate the system. The business will have an electronic card acceptance point in which the customer's card is inserted and information from it is fed to a computer. The customer's records are checked and, if approved, the proposed purchase value will be accepted. The business bank account will be credited with the purchase sum automatically.

When customers are remote from the business they will have to provide the following information:

- card number – 16 digit
- expiry date of the card
- name printed on the card.

Again the purchase sum is transferred automatically to the business and the customer's account with the company is charged.

Paying by credit card

Some organisations provide business credit cards to their staff usually to pay for such things as hotel accommodation, travel expenses, etc.

When these are used the charge will be made to the business, not to the person who has used the card. The business will set limits of expenditure on the card and will require copy vouchers and any other form of receipt to be handed in regularly. These will then be compared with the monthly account received from the credit card company.

13.6 Bank giro credit transfer

This is a safe and convenient way of receiving and paying money. Money paid by this method will be received directly into the business's bank account and the sums received will be shown on their bank statement.

Paying by this method requires the business to prepare the payments in the usual way but in addition prepares a list and bank giro credit slips detailing each payee's banking details and the amount due. The list and slips are then sent to the bank with one cheque to cover all the payments. These will be automatically sent to the various bank accounts through a centralised system.

This form of money transfer is still in use but larger organisations have adopted the BACS system.

13.7 BACS (Bankers' Automated Clearing Service)

The service enables the business to receive money due to it and to make payments. BACS is a company owned by the Bank of England, the high street banks and some building societies, which offers a computerised payment transfer system that organisations may use to pay not only wages and salaries but also creditors, dividends, grants, pensions, etc.

Processing the transfers is a three-day cycle. Information is stored by the BACS system to enable payments to be made on pre-set days, such as salary payments.

It is important to note that a remittance advice should be sent to the supplier when using BACS. Failing this the supplier will not know that the payment has been made until they receive their bank statement. They may also have difficulty in tracing the identity of the business paying the amount.

When the business receives payment from their customers they will also need a remittance advice from the customer for exactly the same reason as explained above and to know which invoices have been covered by the payment.

13.8 Standing order

A person may make a regular payment from their bank account, or receive a regular amount into their account by standing order. This is a straightforward method of making regular fixed payments over which the payer has full control. The steps necessary to make payments by a standing order are as follows:

- **payer** instructs the bank in writing to pay a certain amount, on a particular day to a specific organisation
- Bank makes payment via the computer banking system.

The payer can instruct the bank to cease or amend the payment at any time by giving written notification.

13.9 Direct debit

This has become a common method of paying both fixed and variable amounts of money. Many businesses offer discounts on payment since they are so anxious for their customers to use this method. The system of operation is as follows:

- the proposed receiver (**payee**) of the money sends a mandate to the payer
- **payer** completes the mandate and returns it to the payee
- payee sends the mandate to the payer's bank who will arrange to send the money to the payee's bank via the computer banking system.

The amounts that the payer has authorised to be withdrawn from their own account can vary as the payee makes changes. Typical examples of variations are usually increases in insurance premiums, business rates and loan repayments. It is normal for the payee to advise the payer of such increases.

Payees prefer this method of regular payment since they have control over them and should the payer wish to cancel a direct debit they have to do so through the payee. While this method of payment is convenient for both parties, the payer should exercise great care in giving permission for the setting up of direct debits.

13.10 Paying-in slips

A paying-in slip is prepared when the business wants to pay money into its current account. Details of cash and cheques, that are to be paid into the bank, are entered on the slip. The completed slip, cash and cheques are then taken to the bank. Normally a business deals with one particular branch of its bank but the bank giro credit shown in Exhibit 13.3 can be used to pay money into its account at any branch of any bank.

Exhibit 13.3

Face of paying-in slip

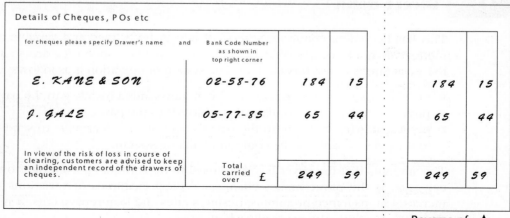

Counterfoil retained by Woodstock

Paying-in slip and cash and cheques handed in to bank

Reverse side of paying-in slip

Reverse of counterfoil

Chapter summary

- The trading activity is emphasised as meaning the sale of goods and/or services between organisations.
- Fundamental to the trading activity is the receipt and payment of money.
- Transferring money in the business can be carried out in various ways: cash, cheque, debit cards, credit cards, bank giro credit transfer, BACS, standing order and direct debits.
- Each of the above methods is discussed and reasons given as to why a business might use a particular method(s).
- Paying-in slips are described since they can be used to deposit both cash and cheques into a bank account.

Exercises

13.1 Businesses in the retail sector are highly likely to receive cash from their customers in payment for goods/services. State what steps a business should take in the handling, storage and transfer of cash to a bank.

13.2 State briefly what other non-cash methods are available to businesses in both receiving and paying out money.

13.3 BACS is an organisation formed to handle the transfer of money between businesses. State the full name of BACS and briefly describe how the organisation carries out this function.

13.4 Morridge Products Ltd receives a cheque which has the normal crossing but, in addition, the words 'A/c payee only' have been written between the lines. Explain how a bank would process this cheque.

13.5X Direct debits are a convenient method of making payments. Explain how the system operates and say what the advantages are for the payer and payee.

13.6X The cheque below has been received today.

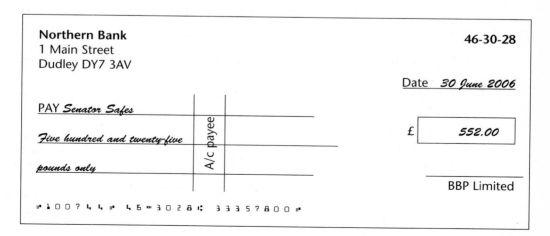

    (*a*) Give *three* reasons why the cheque will not be honoured by the bank.

    (*b*) What is the branch sort code number on the cheque?

    (*c*) What document would you expect to be sent with a cheque in payment of an account?

AAT

13.7 Howard Photographics banks with The Central Bank and has recently sent a cheque to a supplier, Ben Brown Ltd. **Give the name of the drawer, the drawee and the payee**.

    (*a*) The drawer

    (*b*) The drawee

    (*c*) The payee.

AAT

CHAPTER 14

Cash books

Learning objectives

After you have studied this chapter you should be able to:

- enter data into two and three column cash books
- balance off the cash book at the end of a period
- use folio columns for cross-referencing purposes
- enter 'contra' items in the cash book
- understand and complete entries for discounts allowed and discounts received both in the cash book, and at the end of a period, in the discount accounts in the general ledger
- understand and be able to enter transactions into an analytical cash book.

14.1 Introduction

The cash book consists of the cash account and the bank account put together in one book. Initially, we showed these two accounts on different pages of the ledger; now it is easier to put the two sets of account columns together. This means that we can record all money received and paid out on a particular date on the same page.

In the cash book, the debit column for cash is put next to the debit column for bank. The credit column for cash is put next to the credit column for bank.

14.2 Drawing up a cash book

We can now look at a cash account and a bank account (in Exhibit 14.1) as they would appear if they had been kept separately. Then, in Exhibit 14.2, they are shown as if the transactions had, instead, been kept in a cash book.

The bank column contains details of the payments made by cheque and direct transfer from the bank account and of the money received and paid into the bank account. The bank will have a copy of the account in its own books.

Periodically the bank sends a copy of the account in its books to the firm, this document is known as the **bank statement**. When the firm receives the bank statement, it will check it against the bank column in its own cash book to ensure that there are no errors.

Exhibit 14.1

Cash Account

Dr					Cr
2006		£	2006		£
Aug 2	T Moore	33	Aug 8	Rent	20
Aug 5	K Charles	25	Aug 12	C Potts	19
Aug 15	F Hughes	37	Aug 28	Wages	25
Aug 30	H Howe	18	Aug 31	Balance c/d	49
		113			113
Sept 1	Balance b/d	49			

Bank Account

Dr					Cr
2006		£	2006		£
Aug 1	Capital	1,000	Aug 7	Rates	105
Aug 3	W P Ltd	244	Aug 12	F Small Ltd	95
Aug 16	K Noone	408	Aug 26	K French	268
Aug 30	H Sanders	20	Aug 31	Balance c/d	1,204
		1,672			1,672
Sept 1	Balance b/d	1,204			

Exhibit 14.2

Cash Book

Dr		Cash £	Bank £			Cash £	Bank £
2006				2006			
Aug	1 Capital		1,000	Aug 7	Rates		105
"	2 T Moore	33		" 8	Rent	20	
"	3 W P Ltd		244	" 12	C Potts	19	
"	5 K Charles	25		" 12	F Small Ltd		95
"	15 F Hughes	37		" 26	K French		268
"	16 K Noone		408	" 28	Wages	25	
"	30 H Sanders		20	" 31	Balance c/d	49	1,204
"	30 H Howe	18					
		113	1,672			113	1,672
Sept	1 Balances b/d	49	1,204				

'MONEY IN'   'MONEY OUT'

14.3 Cash paid into the bank

In Exhibit 14.2 the payments into the bank were cheques received by the firm, which were banked immediately. We must now consider cash being paid into the bank.

1 Let us look at the position when a customer pays his account in cash, and later a part of this cash is paid into the bank. The receipt of the cash is debited to the cash column on the date received, the credit entry being in the customer's personal account. The cash banked has the following effect, needing action as shown:

Effect	Action
(a) Asset of cash is decreased	Credit the asset account, i.e. the cash account that is represented by the cash column in the cash book.
(b) Asset of bank is increased	Debit the asset account, i.e. the bank account that is represented by the bank column in the cash book.

Now let us look at an example:

Example 1: A cash receipt of £100 from M Davies on 1 August 2006, later followed by the banking on 3 August of £80 of this amount, would appear in the cash book as follows:

Cash Book							
Dr							Cr
	Cash £	Bank £				Cash £	Bank £
2006				2006			
Aug 1 M Davies	100			Aug 3 Bank		80	
Aug 3 Cash		80					

The details column shows entries against each item stating the name of the account in which the completion of double entry has taken place. Against the cash payment of £80 appears the word 'bank', meaning that the debit £80 is to be found in the bank column, and the opposite applies.

2 Where the whole of the cash received is banked immediately, the receipt can be treated in exactly the same manner as a cheque received, i.e. it can be entered directly in the bank column.

3 If the firm requires cash, it may withdraw cash from the bank. This is done by making out a cheque to pay itself a certain amount in cash. The bank will give cash in exchange for the cheque.

The twofold effect and the action required may be shown:

Effect	Action
(a) Asset of bank is decreased	Credit the asset account, i.e. the bank column in the cash book.
(b) Asset of cash is increased	Debit the asset account, i.e. the cash column in the cash book.

This can be shown in the following example:

Example 2: A withdrawal of £75 cash on 1 June 2006 from the bank would appear in the cash book thus:

Cash Book						
Dr						*Cr*
	Cash £	*Bank* £			*Cash* £	*Bank* £
2006			2006			
June 1 Bank	75		June 1 Cash			75

Both the debit and credit entries for this item are in the same book. When this happens it is known as a **contra** item.

14.4   The use of folio columns

As already illustrated the 'details column' in an account contains the name of the account in which the other part of the double entry has been entered. Anyone looking through the books should, therefore, be able to find the other half of the double entry in the ledgers. However, when many books are being used, just to mention the name of the other account may not be enough information to find the other account quickly. More information is needed, and this is given by using **folio columns**.

In each account and in each book being used, a folio column is added, always shown on the left of the money columns. In this column, the name of the other book and the number of the page in the other book where the other part of the double entry was made is stated against each and every entry. The double entry must be completed before the folio columns are filled in.

An entry for receipt of cash from C Kelly whose account was on page 45 of the sales ledger, and the cash recorded on page 37 of the cash book, would have the following folio column entries:

● in the cash book, the folio column entry would be SL 45
● in the sales ledger, the folio column entry would be CB 37.

Note how each of the titles of the books is abbreviated so that it can fit into the space available in the folio column. Each of any contra items (transfers between bank and cash) being shown on the same page of the cash book and would use the letter 'C' (for 'contra') in the folio column. There is no need to also include a page number in this case. The act of using one book as a means of entering transactions into the accounts, in order to complete the double entry, is known as **posting** the items.

14.5   Advantages of folio columns

The advantages of using folio columns are as follows:

● As described above in Section 14.4 folio entries speed up the process of finding the other side of the double entry in the ledgers.
● By going through the folio columns to ensure they have all been completed will assist in detecting any item that has not been posted.

14.6 Example of a cash book with folio columns

The following transactions are written up in the form of a cash book. The folio columns are filled in as though double entry had been completed to other accounts.

2007		£
Sept	1 Proprietor puts capital into a bank account for the business	940
Sept	2 Received cheque from M Boon	115
Sept	4 Cash sales	102
Sept	6 Paid rent by cash	35
Sept	7 Banked £50 of the cash held by the firm	50
Sept	15 Cash sales paid direct into the bank	40
Sept	23 Paid cheque to S Wills	277
Sept	29 Withdrew cash from bank for business use	120
Sept	30 Paid wages in cash	118

Cash Book									
Dr									Cr
		Folio	Cash £	Bank £			Folio	Cash £	Bank £
2007					2007				
Sept	1 Capital	GL 1		940	Sept	6 Rent	GL 65	35	
"	2 M Boon	SL 98		115	"	7 Bank	C	50	
"	4 Sales	GL 87	102		"	23 S Wills	PL 23		277
"	7 Cash	C		50	"	29 Cash	C		120
"	15 Sales	GL 87		40	"	30 Wages	GL 39	118	
"	29 Bank	C	120		"	30 Balances	c/d	19	748
			222	1,145				222	1,145
Oct	1 Balances	b/d	19	748					

The abbreviations used in the folio column are as follows: GL = General Ledger; SL = Sales Ledger; C = Contra; PL = Purchases Ledger.

14.7 Cash discounts

Businesses prefer it if customers pay their accounts quickly. A firm may accept a smaller sum in full settlement if payment is made within a certain period of time. The amount of the reduction of the sum to be paid is known as a **cash discount**. The term 'cash discount' thus refers to the allowance given for quick payment. It is still called a cash discount even if the account is paid by cheque or by direct transfer into the bank account.

The rate of cash discount is usually stated as a percentage. Full details of the percentage allowed, and the period within which payment is to be made, are quoted on all sales documents by the selling company. A typical period during which a discount may be allowed is one month from the date of the original transaction.

14.8 Discounts allowed and discounts received

A firm may have two types of cash discounts in its books. These are:

- **Discounts allowed** – cash discounts allowed by a firm to its customers when they pay their accounts quickly.
- **Discounts received** – cash discounts received by a firm from its suppliers when it pays their accounts quickly.

We can now see the effect of discounts by looking at two examples.

Example 1: W Clarke owed us £100. He pays on 2 September 2007 by cash within the time limit laid down, and the firm allows him 5 per cent cash discount. So he will pay £100 − £5 = £95 in full settlement of his account.

Effect	Action
1 Of cash: Cash is increased by £95. Asset of debtors is decreased by £95.	Debit: Cash Account, i.e. enter £95 in debit column of cash book. Credit: W Clarke £95.
2 Of discounts: Asset of debtors is decreased by £5. (After the cash was paid there remained a balance of £5. As the account has been paid this asset must now be cancelled.) Expenses of discounts allowed increased by £5.	Credit: W Clarke £5. Debit: Discounts allowed account £5.

This means that W. Clarke's debt of £100 has now been shown as fully settled, and exactly how the settlement took place has also been shown.

Example 2: The firm owed S Small £400. It pays him on 3 September 2007 by cheque within the time limit laid down by him and he allows 2½ per cent cash discount. Thus the firm will pay £400 − £10 = £390 in full settlement of the account.

Effect	Action
1 Of cheque: Asset of bank is reduced by £390. Liability of creditors is reduced by £390.	Credit: Bank, i.e. enter in credit bank column, £390. Debit: S Small's account £390.
2 Of discounts: Liability of creditors is reduced by £10. (After the cheque was paid, the balance of £10 remained. As the account has been paid, the liability must now be cancelled.) Revenue of discounts received increased by £10.	Debit: S Small's account £10. Credit: Discounts received account £10.

The accounts in the firm's books would appear thus:

Cash Book (*page 32*)

Dr								Cr
	Folio	Cash	Bank		Folio	Cash	Bank
2007		£	£	2007		£	£
Sept 2 W Clarke	SL 12	95		Sept 3 S Small	PL 75		390

Discounts Received Account (General Ledger *page 18*)

Dr						Cr
	Folio	£	2007		Folio	£
			Sept 2 S Small		PL 75	10

Discounts Allowed Account (General Ledger *page 17*)

Dr					Cr
	Folio	£		Folio	£
2007					
Sept 2 W Clarke	SL 12	5			

W Clarke Account (Sales Ledger *page 12*)

Dr						Cr
2005	Folio	£	2005		Folio	£
Sept 1 Balance	b/d	100	Sept 2 Cash		CB 32	95
			Sept 2 Discount		GL 17	5
		100				100

S Small Account (Purchases Ledger *page 75*)

Dr						Cr
2007	Folio	£	2007		Folio	£
Sept 3 Bank	CB 32	390	Sept 1 Balance		b/d	400
Sept 3 Discounts	GL 18	10				
		400				400

It is accounting custom to enter the word 'Discount' in the personal accounts, not stating whether it is a discount received or a discount allowed.

14.9 Discount columns in the cash book

The discounts allowed account and the discounts received account are in the general ledger, along with all the other revenue and expense accounts. It has already been stated that every effort should be made to avoid too much reference to the general ledger.

In the case of discounts, this is done by adding an extra column on each side of the cash book in which the amounts of discounts are entered. Discounts received are entered in the discounts column on the credit side of the cash book, and discounts allowed in the discounts column on the debit side of the cash book.

The cash book, if completed for the two examples so far dealt with, would appear thus:

Cash Book									*(page 32)*
2007	Folio	Discount £	Cash £	Bank £	2007	Folio	Discount £	Cash £	Bank £
Sept 2 W Clarke	SL 12	5	95		Sept 3 S Small	PL 75	10		390

There is no alteration to the method of showing discounts in the personal accounts.

To make entries in the discount accounts

Total of discounts column on receipts side of cash book } Enter on debit side of Discounts Allowed Account

Total of discounts column on payments side of cash book } Enter on credit side of Discounts Received Account

14.10 A worked example

The following is an example of a three-column cash book for the whole of a month, showing the ultimate transfer of the totals of the discounts columns to the discount accounts.

		£
2006		
May 1	Balances brought down from April:	
	Cash Balance	29
	Bank Balance	654
	Debtors accounts:	
	B King	120
	N Campbell	280
	D Shand	40
	Creditors accounts:	
	U Barrow	60
	A Allen	440
	R Long	100
May 2	B King pays us by cheque, having deducted 2$\frac{1}{2}$ per cent cash discount £3	117
May 8	We pay R Long his account by cheque, deducting 5 per cent cash discount £5	95
May 11	We withdrew £100 cash from the bank for business use	100
May 16	N Campbell pays us his account by cheque, deducting 2$\frac{1}{2}$ per cent discount £7	273
May 25	We paid wages in cash	92
May 28	D Shand pays us in cash after having deducted 2$\frac{1}{2}$ per cent cash discount	38
May 29	We pay U Barrow by cheque less 5 per cent cash discount £3	427
May 30	We pay A Allen by cheque less 2$\frac{1}{2}$ per cent cash discount £11	

Cash Book									(page 64)
Dr									Cr
	Folio	Discount	Cash	Bank		Folio	Discount	Cash	Bank
2006		£	£	£	2006		£	£	£
May 1					May 8				
Balances	b/d		29	654	R Long	PL 58	5		95
May 2					May 11				
B King	SL 13	3		117	Cash	C			100
May 11					May 25				
Bank	C		100		Wages	GL 77		92	
May 16					May 29				
N Campbell	SL 84	7		273	U Barrow	PL 15	3		57
May 28					May 30				
D Shand	SL 91	2	38		A Allen	PL 98	11		429
					May 31				
					Balances	c/d		75	363
		12	167	1,044			19	167	1,044
Jun 1									
Balances	b/d		75	363					

Sales Ledger

B King Account

Page 13

Dr						Cr
2006		Folio	£	2006	Folio	£
May 1 Balance		b/d	120	May 2 Bank	CB 64	117
				May 2 Discount	CB 64	3
			120			120

N Campbell Account

Page 84

Dr						Cr
2006		Folio	£	2006	Folio	£
May 1 Balance		b/d	280	May 16 Bank	CB 64	273
				May 16 Discount	CB 64	7
			280			280

D Shand Account

Page 91

Dr						Cr
2006		Folio	£	2006	Folio	£
May 1 Balance		b/d	40	May 28 Cash	CB 64	38
				May 28 Discount	CB 64	2
			40			40

Purchases Ledger

U Barrow Account

Page 15

Dr						Cr
2006		Folio	£	2006	Folio	£
May 29 Bank		CB 64	57	May 1 Balance	b/d	60
May 29 Discount		CB 64	3			
			60			60

R Long Account

Page 58

Dr						Cr
2006		Folio	£	2006	Folio	£
May 8 Bank		CB 64	95	May 1 Balance	b/d	100
May 8 Discount		CB 64	5			
			100			100

A Allen Account

Page 98

Dr						Cr
2006		Folio	£	2006	Folio	£
May 30 Bank		CB 64	429	May 1 Balance	b/d	440
May 30 Discount		CB 64	11			
			440			440

General Ledger

Wages Account

Page 77

Dr						Cr
2006		Folio	£		Folio	£
May 25 Cash		CB 64	92			

Discounts Received Account

Page 88

Dr						Cr
		Folio	£	2006	Folio	£
				May 31 Cash book	CB 64	19

Discounts Allowed Account

Page 90

Dr						Cr
2006		Folio	£		Folio	£
May 31 Cash book		CB 64	12			

Is the above method of entering discounts correct? You can easily check. See the following:

Discounts in Ledger Accounts	Debits		Credits	
		£		
Discounts received	U Barrow	3	Discounts	
	R Long	5	Received	
	A Allen	11	Account	£19
		19		
				£
Discounts allowed	Discounts		B King	3
	Allowed		N Campbell	7
	Account	£12	D Shand	2
				12

You can see that proper double entry has been carried out. Equal amounts, in total, have been entered on each side of the accounts.

14.11 Bank overdrafts and the cash book

A firm may borrow money from a bank by means of a bank overdraft. This means that the firm is allowed to pay more out of the bank account, by paying out cheques, than the total amount placed in the account.

Up to this point the bank balances have all been money at the bank, and so they have all been assets, i.e. debit balances. When the account is overdrawn, the firm owes money to the bank and so the account is a liability and the balance becomes a credit one.

Taking the cash book shown, suppose that the amount payable to A Allen was £1,429 instead of £429. Thus the amount in the bank account, £1,044, is exceeded by the amount withdrawn. The cash book would appear as follows:

		Cash Book							
Dr									Cr
		Discount	Cash	Bank			Discount	Cash	Bank
2006		£	£	£	2006		£	£	£
May 1	Balances b/d		29	654	May 8	R Long	5		95
" 2	B King	3		117	" 11	Cash			100
" 11	Bank		100		" 25	Wages		92	
" 16	N Campbell	7		273	" 29	U Barrow	3		57
" 28	D Shand	2	38		" 30	A Allen	11		1,429
" 31	Balance c/d			637	" 31	Balance c/d		75	
		12	167	1,681			19	167	1,681
Jun 1	Balance b/d		75		Jun 1	Balance b/d			637

On a balance sheet, a bank overdraft will be shown as an item included under the heading Current Liabilities.

14.12 Analytical cash book

Many businesses use an analytical cash book in a similar way to the analytical petty cash book. This has several advantages.

One advantage is that it enables the business to have the use of a VAT (Value Added Tax) column to record payments/receipts of VAT. At the end of each month, the VAT columns are added up and the totals transferred to the VAT account in the general ledger. This VAT column is especially useful if the business buys and sells goods and/or services for immediate payment. The topic of value added tax will be dealt with more fully in Chapter 16.

Another advantage is that it allows for analysis of, say sales or purchases. In the example below, Whitehead's Electrical Co wants to monitor the sales and profit margins of its various lines. The owner of Whitehead's uses four analysis columns:

- Electrical goods
- 'White' goods (e.g. washing machines, which are usually white)
- Sundry sales
- VAT.

Payments from the cash book are analysed in a similar way.

Some businesses have a separate sales ledger and purchase ledger, which are self-balancing by the use of control accounts. Analysis columns are used in an analytical cash book to record monies received from debtors or paid to creditors. At the end of each month, the columns are added up and the totals are posted to the respective sales and purchase ledger control accounts.

There is no set format for the number and names of the columns used in an analytical cash book; it is up to the organisation to adapt the cash book to meet its own requirements.

A worked example

Whitehead's Electrical Co is an independent electrical shop that sells television sets, radios and videos, as well as washing machines, dryers, fridges, etc. In order to monitor sales and profit margins, Mr Whitehead operates a columnar cash book, as follows.

Receipts
These are split between four main headings, namely:

- Electrical goods
- 'White' goods
- Sundry sales
- VAT.

Payments

The payments side of the cash book has headings as follows:

- VAT
- Electrical purchases
- White goods purchases
- Wages and salaries
- General overheads.

During October 2006, the following transactions took place:

2006

Oct 1 Balance of cash in hand £64.92
Balance at bank £416.17

2 Bought radios from Shaws Ltd,
£187.36 plus VAT of £32.78 paid by cheque.

4 Sold goods as follows:
– Washing machine £360.00 plus VAT of £63
to K Walters who paid by cheque
– Video to S Worrall who paid by cheque £330.00 plus
VAT of £57.75
Both cheques were paid into the bank.
– Sundry cash sales, plugs, etc., £27.50 including
VAT of £4.10

7 Paid postage £76.30 by cheque.

7 Paid wages £245. Drew cash from bank for this purpose.

10 Sold goods as follows:

Mrs J White – Colour TV	£550	(including VAT £81.92)
Dr V Ford – Fridge	£180	(including VAT £26.81)
Mr J Summers – Dryer	£225.50	(including VAT £33.59)

Cheques were received in respect of the above and duly banked.

12 Cash sales: radio, £80.00 (including VAT £11.91).

14 Purchased the following goods from Allan's Ltd,
and paid by cheque. This totalled £2,056.25.

Fridges	£450.00 plus VAT £78.75
Televisions	£1,300.00 plus VAT £227.50

14 Paid wages £245.00. Drew cash from bank.

18 Cash sale, one fridge £163.50 (including VAT £24.35).

20 Paid cash for petrol £20.00 (including VAT £2.98).

23 Paid wages £252.00. Drew cash from bank.

24 Sold TV and video to J Pratt £964.67
(including VAT £143.67). He paid by cheque.

26 Bought electrical clocks and radios from B Mason
for £327.50 (including VAT £48.78). Paid by cheque.

30 Sundry cash sales paid direct into the bank £367.00 (including VAT £54.66).

31 Paid rent £200.00 in cash.

Cash Book (debit side only)

Dr CB1

Date	Details	Folio	VAT	Electrical sales	White goods sales	Sundry sales	Cash	Bank
			£	£	£	£	£	
2006								
Oct 1	Balance b/d						64.92	416.17
4	K Walters		63.00		360.00			423.00
"	S Worrall		57.75	330.00				387.75
	Cash sales		4.10			23.40	27.50	
10	Mrs J White		81.92	468.08				550.00
"	Dr V Ford		26.81		153.19			180.00
"	Mr J Summers		33.59		191.91			225.50
12	Cash sales		11.91	68.09			80.00	
18	"		24.35		139.15		163.50	
24	J Pratt		143.67	821.00				964.67
30	Cash sales		54.66			312.34		367.00
			501.76	1,687.17	844.25	335.74	335.92	3,514.09
Nov 1	Balance b/d						115.92	91.90
			GL1	GL2	GL3	GL4		

Cash Book (credit side only)

Cr CB1

Date	Details	Folio	VAT	Electrical purchases	White goods purchases	Wages and salaries	General overheads	Cash	Bank
			£	£	£	£	£	£	£
2006									
Oct 2	Shaws Ltd		32.78	187.36					220.14
7	Postage						76.30		76.30
7	Wages					245.00			245.00
14	Allan's Ltd		306.25	1,300.00	450.00				2,056.25
"	Wages					245.00			245.00
20	Petrol		2.98				17.02	20.00	
23	Wages					252.00			252.00
26	B Mason		48.78	278.72					327.50
31	Rent						200.00	200.00	
31	Balance c/d							115.92	91.90
			390.79	1,766.08	450.00	742.00	293.32	335.92	3,514.09
			GL1						

Full coverage of the treatment of discounts allowed and discounts received in final accounts is shown in Chapter 28.

Chapter summary

- A cash book is made up of a cash account and a bank account put together into one book.
- Entries made on the debit side of the cash book are in respect of monies received via cash, cheque or bank transfer. The money comes 'into' the business and are therefore entered on the debit 'in' side of the cash book.
- Entries made on the credit side of the cash book are in respect of monies paid out via cash, cheque or bank transfer. Money is paid 'out' of the business so entries are made on the 'out' side of the account.
- Folio columns are used in the cash book so that items may easily be traced to other accounts in the ledgers and to provide assurance that the double entries have been completed.
- Cash discounts are given to encourage prompt payment of outstanding accounts. The discount is referred to as cash discount irrespective of whether the account is settled by cash, cheque or bank transfer.
- Discount allowed is the amount of discount allowed by a firm to its customers when their accounts are settled promptly and within the time limit.
- Discount received is when the firm's suppliers allow them to deduct discount if they pay the account within the stated terms of trade.
- Discounts allowed and received are entered into the appropriate column in the cash book, totalled at the end of the period, and the amount transferred to the discount accounts in the general ledger.
- Should the balance at the bank go into an overdraft position then the balance brought down will appear on the credit side of the cash book.
- Some businesses use analytical cash books to enable the organisation to have the use of various columns for analysing information specific to their needs.

Exercises

14.1   A two-column cash book is to be written up from the following, carrying the balances down to the following month:

2004
Jan   1   Started business with £4,000 in the bank
Jan   2   Paid for fixtures by cheque, £660
Jan   4   Cash sales £225: Paid rent by cash, £140
Jan   6   T Thomas paid us by cheque, £188
Jan   8   Cash sales paid direct into the bank, £308
Jan 10   J King paid us in cash, £300
Jan 12   Paid wages in cash, £275
Jan 14   J Walters lent us £500 paying by cheque
Jan 15   Withdrew £200 from the bank for business use
Jan 20   Bought stationery paying by cash, £60
Jan 22   We paid J French by cheque, £166
Jan 28   Cash drawings £100
Jan 30   J Scott paid us by cheque, £277
Jan 31   Cash sales £66.

14.2 You work for Stott & Co, a medium-sized clothes manufacturer, whose offices and works are situated in Derby. As book-keeper to the firm, one of your main duties is to enter up the cash book on a regular basis.

Required:

From the information given below, enter up the transactions for May 2005, balance off at the end of the month, and bring the balances down.

			£
May	1	Balances b/d	
		Cash in hand	14.72
		Bank (overdrawn)	820.54
May	2	Bought stationery by cash	10.00
May	3	Banked cheques received from:	
		P Wrench	432.36
		R Whitworth	634.34
		J Summers	341.00
May	6	South West Rail Ltd, cheque for travel expenses of company	
		secretary to London	37.50
May	9	Paid the following accounts by cheque,	
		Fabulous Fabrics Ltd	450.80
		Mellors Manufacturing Co	348.32
May	12	Received from cash sale	76.00
May	14	Paid employees PAYE and NI to the Inland Revenue, by cheque	221.30
May	17	Received cheque from Trentam Traders	32.81
May	20	Foreign currency drawn from bank for director's visit to Italy	250.00
		Bank charges re currency	3.20
May	24	Received cash from sale of goods	350.00
May	26	Cash to bank	300.00
May	27	Salaries by cheque	5,720.00
May	31	Received cheques from the following:	
		J Summers	1,231.00
		Bradnop Manufacturing Co	725.00
		Taylors	2,330.50

(NVQ Level 2)

14.3X As a trainee accounts clerk at Jepsons & Co you have as one of your tasks the job of entering-up the firm's cash book at the end of each month.

Required:

From the details listed below, enter up the cash book for February 2006, balance off at the end of the month, and bring the balances down.

2006			£
Feb	1	Balances brought down from January	
		Cash in hand	76.32
		Cash at bank	2,376.50
Feb	2	Paid electricity bill by cheque	156.00
Feb	4	Paid motor expenses by cash	15.00
Feb	6	Received cheques from the following debtors:	
		D Hill	300.00
		A Jackson	275.00
		H Wardle	93.20

		£
Feb 7	Paid for stationery by cash	3.70
Feb 10	Sold goods for cash	57.10
Feb 12	Paid for purchases from Palmer & Sons by cheque	723.50
Feb 14	Received loan by cheque from D Whitman	500.00
Feb 16	Paid Wright Brothers for repairs to office machinery by cheque	86.20
Feb 17	The proprietor, Stan Jepson, took cash for his own use.	50.00
	He asks you to pay his personal telephone bill by cheque	
	to the post office	140.60
Feb 22	J Smith paid his account by cheque	217.00
Feb 23	Petrol bill paid by cash	21.00
Feb 26	Received cheque for sale of goods	53.00
Feb 27	Bought new photocopier from Bronsons of Manchester	
	and paid by cheque	899.00
Feb 28	Paid monthly salaries by cheque	2,400.00

14.4 Enter up a three-column cash book from the details following. Balance off at the end of the month, and show the relevant discount accounts as they would appear in the general ledger.

2004

May 1 Started business with £6,000 in the bank
May 1 Bought fixtures paying by cheque, £950
May 2 Bought goods paying by cheque, £1,240
May 3 Cash sales £407
May 4 Paid rent in cash, £200
May 5 N Morgan paid us his account of £220 by a cheque for £210, we allowed him £10 discount
May 7 Paid S Thompson & Co £80 owing to them by means of a cheque £76, they allowed us £4 discount
May 9 We received a cheque for £380 from S Cooper, discount having been allowed £20
May 12 Paid rates by cheque, £410
May 14 L Curtis pays us a cheque for £115
May 16 Paid M Monroe his account of £120 by cash £114, having deducted £6 cash discount
May 20 P Exeter pays us a cheque for £78, having deducted £2 cash discount
May 31 Cash sales paid direct into the bank, £88.

14.5 From the following details, write up a three-column cash book, balance off at the end of the month, and show the relevant discount accounts as they would appear in the general ledger.

2006

Mar 1 Balances brought forward:
      Cash in hand £211
      Cash at bank £3,984
Mar 2 We paid each of the following accounts by cheque, in each case we deducted a 5 per cent discount: T Adams £80; C Bibby £260; D Clarke £440
Mar 4 C Potts pays us a cheque for £98
Mar 6 Cash sales paid direct into the bank, £49
Mar 7 Paid insurance by cash, £65
Mar 9 The following persons pay us their accounts by cheque, in each case they deducted a discount of 2½ per cent: R Smiley £160; J Turner £640; R Pimlott £520
Mar 12 Paid motor expenses by cash, £100
Mar 18 Cash sales, £98
Mar 21 Paid salaries by cheque, £120

Mar 23 Paid rent by cash, £60

Mar 28 Received a cheque for £500 being a loan from R Godfrey

Mar 31 Paid for stationery by cheque, £27.

14.6X You are to write up a three-column cash book for M Pinero from the details that follow. Then balance off at the end of the month and show the discount accounts in the general ledger.

2006

May   1 Balances brought forward:

Cash in hand £58

Bank overdraft £1,470

May   2 M Pinero pays further capital into the bank, £1,000

May   3 Bought office fixtures by cheque, £780

May   4 Cash sales, £220

May   5 Banked cash, £200

May   6 We paid the following by cheque, in each case deducting 2½ per cent cash discount: B Barnes £80; T Horton £240; T Jacklin £400

May   8 Cash sales, £500

May 12 Paid motor expenses in cash, £77

May 15 Cash withdrawn from the bank, £400

May 16 Cash drawings, £120

May 18 The following firms paid us their accounts by cheque, in each case deducting a 5 per cent discount: L Graham £80; B Crenshaw £140; H Green £220

May 20 Salaries paid in cash, £210

May 22 T Weiskopf paid us his account in cash, £204

May 26 Paid insurance by cheque, £150

May 28 We banked all the cash in our possession except for £20 in the cash till

May 31 Bought motor van, paying by cheque, £4,920.

CHAPTER 15

Bank reconciliation statements

Learning objectives

After you have studied this chapter you should be able to:

- understand the reason for preparing bank reconciliation statements
- reconcile cash book balances with bank statement balances
- understand how bank overdrafts affect the reconciliation process
- make necessary entries in the account for dishonoured cheques.

15.1 The purpose of bank reconciliation statements

At the end of each month the cash book will be brought up to date and balanced off. Shortly afterwards we will receive a bank statement from the bank showing the record of payments made into and out of the business's bank account. The bank balance shown in the cash book will now be compared with the bank statement. It might be expected that the cash book balance would be the same but in practice, this is unlikely. The difference may be caused by quite valid reasons and are usually due to the varying dates that the business and the bank record monies paid into and out of their particular account. It is possible that errors have been made by the business or bank and these will have to be identified and corrected.

A **bank reconciliation statement** will now need to be prepared to find the reasons for the difference. Reconciliation, in accounting terms, simply means 'an explanation of the differences'.

15.2 An example of a bank reconciliation statement

Let us assume that we have just written up our cash book. We call at the bank on 30 June 2006 and get from the bank manager a copy of our bank statement. On our return we tick off in our cash book and on the bank statement the items that are similar. A copy of our cash book (bank column only) and of our bank statement are now shown as Exhibit 15.1.

Exhibit 15.1

Cash Book (bank columns only)

Dr					Cr
2006		£	2006		£
June 1 Balance b/f		80	June 27 I Gordon ✓		35
June 28 D Jones ✓		100	June 29 B Tyrell		40
		___	June 30 Balance c/d		105
		180			180
July 1 Balance b/d		105			

Bank Statement

	Dr	Cr	Balance	
2006	£	£	£	
June 26 Balance b/f ✓			80	Cr
June 28 Banking ✓		100	180	Cr
June 30 I Gordon ✓	35		145	Cr

By comparing the cash book and the bank statement, it can be seen that the only item that was not in both of these was the cheque payment to B Tyrell for £40 in the cash book. The reason why this was entered in the cash book but does not appear on the bank statement is simply one of timing. The cheque had been posted to B Tyrell on 29 June, but there had not been time for it to be banked by Tyrell and passed through the banking system. Such a cheque is called an **unpresented cheque** because it has not yet been presented at the drawer's bank.

To prove that the balances are not different because of errors, even though they show different figures, a bank reconciliation statement is drawn up. This is given in Exhibit 15.2.

Exhibit 15.2

Bank Reconciliation Statement as at 30 June 2006

	£
Balance in hand as per cash book	105
Add unpresented cheque: Tyrell	40
Balance in hand as per bank statement	145

It would have been possible for the bank reconciliation statement to have started with the bank statement balance:

Bank Reconciliation Statement as at 30 June 2006

	£
Balance in hand as per bank statement	145
Less unpresented cheque: Tyrell	40
Balance in hand as per cash book	105

You should notice that the bank account is shown as a debit balance in the firm's cash book because, to the firm, it is an asset. In the bank's books the bank account is shown as a credit balance because this is a liability of the bank to the firm.

15.3 Some reasons for differences in balances

We can now look at a more complicated example in Exhibit 15.3. Similar items in both cash book and bank statement are shown ticked.

Exhibit 15.3

Cash Book

Dr						Cr
2006			£	2006		£
Dec 27	Total b/f		2,000	Dec 27 Total b/f		1,600
Dec 29	J Potter	✓	60	Dec 28 J Jacobs	✓	105
Dec 31	M Johnson (B)		220	Dec 30 M Chatwood (A)		15
				Dec 31 Balance c/d		560
			2,280			2,280
2007						
Jan 1	Balance b/d		560			

Bank Statement

2006		Dr £	Cr £	Balance £
Dec 27 Balance b/f				400 Cr
Dec 29 Cheque	✓		60	460 Cr
Dec 30 J Jacobs	✓	105		355 Cr
Dec 30 Credit transfers: L Shaw (C)			70	425 Cr
Dec 30 Bank charges (D)		20		405 Cr

The balance brought forward in the bank statement £400 is the same figure as that in the cash book, i.e. totals b/f £2,000 − £1,600 = £400. However, items (A) and (B) are in the cash book only, and (C) and (D) are on the bank statement only. We can now examine these in detail:

(A) This is a cheque recently sent by us to Mr Chatwood. It has neither yet passed through the banking system nor been presented to our bank, and it is therefore an **unpresented cheque**.

(B) This is a cheque banked by us on our visit to the bank when we collected the copy of our bank statement. As we handed this banking item over the counter at the same time as the bank clerk gave us our bank statement, naturally it has not yet been entered on the statement.

(C) A customer, L Shaw, has paid his account by instructing his bank to pay us direct through the banking system, instead of paying by cheque. Such a transaction is usually called a **credit transfer**.

(D) The bank has charged us for the services given in keeping a bank account for us. It did not send us a bill; it simply takes the money from our account by debiting it and reducing the amount of our balance.

Having taken into account the above differences the bank reconciliation statement can now be prepared. As mentioned earlier there are two ways in which a bank reconciliation statement can be prepared. You can start with the balance as shown in the cash book (see first example shown below) or, alternatively, you can start with the balance as shown on the bank statement in the second example. Examining bodies may ask for either method of presentation so ensure you know exactly which method is required before attempting the question.

Bank Reconciliation Statement as at 31 December 2006

	£	£
Balance in hand as per cash book		560
Add Unpresented cheque – M Chatwood	15	
Credit transfers	70	
		85
		645
Less Bank charges	20	
Bank lodgement not yet entered on bank statement	220	
		240
Balance in hand as per bank statement		405

A bank reconciliation statement starting with the bank statement balance appears thus:

Bank Reconciliation Statement as at 31 December 2006

	£	£
Balance in hand as per bank statement		405
Add Bank charges	20	
Bank lodgement not yet entered on bank statement	220	
		240
		645
Less Unpresented cheque – M Chatwood	15	
Traders credit transfers	70	
		85
Balance in hand as per bank statement		560

15.4 Writing up the cash book before attempting a reconciliation

The easiest way to do a reconciliation is to complete the cash book first. All items on the bank statement will then be in the cash book. This means that the only differences will be items in the cash book but not on the bank statement. At the same time, any errors found in the cash book by such a check can be corrected.

Although this would be the normal way to proceed before actually drawing up a bank reconciliation statement, it is possible that an examiner will ask you not to do it this way. If, in Exhibit 15.3 the cash book had been written up before the bank reconciliation statement was drawn up, then the cash book and the reconciliation statement would have appeared as follows in Exhibit 15.4.

Exhibit 15.4

Cash Book

Dr					Cr
2006		£	2006		£
Dec 27	Total b/fwd	2,000	Dec 27	Total b/fwd	1,600
Dec 29	J Potter	60	Dec 28	J Jacobs	105
Dec 31	M Johnson	220	Dec 30	M Chatwood	15
Dec 31	Credit transfers:		Dec 31	Bank charges*	20
	L Shaw*	70	Dec 31	Balance c/d	610
		2,350			2,350
2007					
Jan 1	Balance b/d	610			

*Adding items that appear in the bank statement but not in the cashbook.

Bank Reconciliation Statement as on 31 December 2006

	£
Balance in hand as per cash book	610
Add Unpresented cheque – M Chatwood	15
	625
Less Bank lodgement not yet entered on bank statement	220
Balance in hand as per bank statement	405

15.5 Bank overdrafts

When there is a bank overdraft (shown by a credit balance in the cash book), the adjustments needed for reconciliation work are opposite to those needed for a debit balance.

Exhibit 15.5 shows a cash book, and a bank statement, showing an overdraft. Only the cheque for G Cumberbatch (A) £106 and the cheque paid to J Kelly (B) £63 need adjusting. Work through the reconciliation statement in Exhibit 15.5 and then compare the reconciliation statements in Exhibits 15.4 and 15.5.

Exhibit 15.5

Cash Book (bank columns only)

Dr					Cr
2006		£	2006		£
Dec 5	I Howe	308	Dec 1	Balance b/f	709
Dec 24	L Mason	120	Dec 9	P Davies	140
Dec 29	K King	124	Dec 27	J Kelly (B)	63
Dec 31	G Cumberbatch (A)	106	Dec 29	United Trust	77
Dec 31	Balance c/f	380	Dec 31	Bank charges	49
		1,038			1,038
			2007		
			Jan 1	Balance b/f	380

Bank Statement

2006		Dr £	Cr £	Balance £
Dec 1 Balance b/f				709 O/D
Dec 5 Cheque			308	401 O/D
Dec 14 P Davies		140		541 O/D
Dec 24 Cheque			120	421 O/D
Dec 29 K King: Credit transfer			124	297 O/D
Dec 29 United Trust: Standing order		77		374 O/D
Dec 31 Bank charges		49		423 O/D

Note: On a bank statement an overdraft is often shown with the letters O/D following the amount; or else it is shown as a debit balance, indicated by the letters DR after the amount.

Bank Reconciliation Statement as at 31 December 2006

	£
Overdraft as per cash book	380
Add Bank lodgements not on bank statement	106
	486
Less Unpresented cheque	63
Overdraft per bank statement	423

Now compare the reconciliation statements in Exhibits 15.4 and 15.5. This comparison reveals the following:

	Exhibit 15.4 Balances	Exhibit 15.5 Overdrafts
Balance/Overdraft per cash book	XXXX	XXXX
Adjustments		
Unpresented cheque	PLUS	LESS
Banking not entered	LESS	PLUS
Balance/Overdraft per bank statement	XXXX	XXXX

Adjustments are, therefore, made in the opposite way when there is an overdraft.

15.6 Dishonoured cheques

When a cheque is received from a customer and paid into the bank, it is recorded on the debit side of the cash book. It is also shown on the bank statement as a deposit to the bank. However, at a later date, it may be found that the customer's bank will not pay us the amount due on the cheque. The cheque is therefore worthless. It is known as a **dishonoured cheque**.

There are several possible reasons for this. As an example, let us suppose that K King gave us a cheque for £5,000 on 20 May 2006. We banked it, but on 25 May 2006 our bank returned the cheque to us. Typical reasons are:

● King had put £5,000 in figures on the cheque, but had written it in words as five thousand five hundred pounds. You will have to give the cheque back to King for amendment or reissue.

- King had put the year 2005 on the cheque instead of 2006. Normally, cheques are considered 'stale' six months after the date on the cheque; in other words, the banks will not pay cheques over six months' old.
- King simply did not have sufficient funds in his bank account. Suppose he had previously only got a £2,000 balance and yet he has given us a cheque for £5,000. His bank has not allowed him to have an overdraft. In such a case the cheque would be dishonoured. The bank would write on the cheque 'refer to drawer', and we would have to get in touch with King to see what he was going to do to settle his bill.

In all of these cases the bank would show the original banking as being cancelled, by showing the cheque paid out of our bank account. As soon as this happens, they will notify us. We will then also show the cheque being cancelled by a credit in the cash book. We will then debit that amount to this account.

When King originally paid his account, our records would appear as:

K King Account

Dr				Cr
2006	£	2006		£
May 1 Balance b/d	5,000	May 20 Bank		5,000

Bank Account

Dr			Cr
2006	£		
May 20 K King	5,000		

After our recording the dishonoured cheque, the records will appear as:

K King Account

Dr			Cr
2006	£	2006	£
May 1 Balance b/d	5,000	May 20 Bank	5,000
May 25 Bank: cheque dishonoured	5,000		

Bank Account

Dr			Cr
2006	£	2006	£
May 20 K King	5,000	May 25 K King: cheque dishonoured	5,000

In other words, King is once again shown as owing us £5,000.

15.7 Some other reasons for differences in balances

As you will recall from Chapter 13, Banking transactions, both standing orders and direct debits can be set up to move money regularly out of one bank account and into another. As far as bank reconciliation statements are concerned, both of these types of payments will have passed through the bank account but will have not been entered in the cash book.

Chapter summary

- The purpose of preparing a bank reconciliation statement is to find the reasons for the differences in the balance as shown in the cash book with that shown on the bank statement.
- By preparing a bank reconciliation statement errors may be identified in either the cash book or the bank statement and be corrected.
- The differences in balances may be caused by quite valid reasons and are usually due to the varying dates that the business and the bank record monies paid into and out of their particular account.
- It is easier to write up the cash book first before preparing a bank reconciliation statement since the only differences will be items in the cash book but not on the bank statement.
- If the account is showing a bank overdraft then preparing a bank reconciliation statement is the opposite to when there is a balance in the account.
- If a business receives a cheque from a customer which ultimately 'bounces', i.e. there are insufficient funds in the account for the cheque to be paid, then it is known as a 'dishonoured cheque'.
- How to make the appropriate entries in the account to record a dishonoured cheque.

Exercises

15.1 On 2 December Berry Sports received the bank statement as at 30 November 2006.

(*a*) check the items on the bank statement against the items in the cash book
(*b*) write out and update the cash book as needed
(*c*) total the cash book and clearly show the balance carried down
(*d*) prepare a bank reconciliation statement as at 30 November 2006.

<table>
<tr><td colspan="5" align="center">MIDWAY BANK plc</td></tr>
<tr><td>To: Berry Sports</td><td colspan="2" align="center">Account No: 45619822</td><td colspan="2" align="right">30 November 2006</td></tr>
<tr><td></td><td colspan="2" align="center">STATEMENT OF ACCOUNT</td><td></td><td></td></tr>
<tr><td>Date</td><td>Details</td><td>Paid out</td><td>Paid in</td><td>Balance</td></tr>
<tr><td>2006</td><td></td><td>£</td><td>£</td><td>£</td></tr>
<tr><td>1 Nov</td><td>Balance b/f</td><td></td><td></td><td>9,000C</td></tr>
<tr><td>5 Nov</td><td>Cheque No 625109</td><td>6,300</td><td></td><td>2,700C</td></tr>
<tr><td>5 Nov</td><td>Credit</td><td></td><td>10,000</td><td>12,700C</td></tr>
<tr><td>8 Nov</td><td>Bank Giro Credit
    B. Green</td><td></td><td>3,500</td><td>16,200C</td></tr>
<tr><td>11 Nov</td><td>Cheque No 625110</td><td>1,100</td><td></td><td>15,100C</td></tr>
<tr><td>15 Nov</td><td>Direct Debit
    LBO Limited</td><td>1,300</td><td></td><td>13,800C</td></tr>
<tr><td>20 Nov</td><td>Bank charges</td><td>29</td><td></td><td>13,771C</td></tr>
<tr><td>25 Nov</td><td>Direct Debit
    HB Services</td><td>1,800</td><td></td><td>11,971C</td></tr>
<tr><td colspan="5">D = Debit   C = Credit</td></tr>
</table>

Cash Book

Date 2006	Details	Bank £	Date 2006	Cheque number	Details	Bank £
1 Nov	Balance b/f	9,000	1 Nov	625109	R B Lawley	6,300
5 Nov	L Burger	10,000	5 Nov	625110	B&B Limited	1,100
22 Nov	D Smith	1,396	22 Nov	625111	M Parkes	300
			22 Nov	625112	Richards Limited	9,667

AAT

15.2X   The following are extracts from the cash book and bank statement of Preston & Co

Cash Book

Dr				Cr
2007	£	2007		£
Dec 1 Balance b/d	8,700	Dec 6 S Little		1,745
Dec 7 T J Blake	440	Dec 14 L Jones		165
Dec 20 P Dyson	365	Dec 21 E Fraser		575
Dec 30 A Veale	945	Dec 31 Balance c/d		9,155
Dec 31 K Woodburn	300			
Dec 31 N May	890			
	11,640			11,640

Bank Statement

2007	Dr £	Cr £	Balance £
Dec 1 Balance b/d			8,700
Dec 9 Cheque		440	9,140
Dec 10 S Little	1,745		7,395
Dec 19 L Jones	165		7,230
Dec 20 Cheque		365	7,595
Dec 26 Credit transfer: P Todd		270	7,865
Dec 31 Bank Charges	110		7,755

You are required to:

(*a*) write up the cash book and state the new balance on 31 December 2007

(*b*) prepare a bank reconciliation statement as on 31 December 2007.

15.3 The bank statement for James Baxter for the month of March 2006 is as follows:

Bank Statement

2006		Dr £	Cr £	Balance £
Mar 1	Balance b/d			2,598 O/D
8	L Young	61		2,659 O/D
16	Cheque		122	2,537 O/D
20	A Duffy	104		2,641 O/D
21	Cheque		167	2,474 O/D
31	Credit Transfer: A May		929	1,545 O/D
31	Standing Order: Oak plc	100		1,645 O/D
31	Bank Charges	28		1,673 O/D

The Cash Book for March 2006 is shown below:

Cash Book

Dr			£	Cr			£
2006				2006			
Mar 16	N Morris		122	Mar 1	Balance b/d		2,598
" 21	P Fraser		167	" 6	L Young		61
" 31	Southern Elect. Co		160	" 30	A Duffy		104
" 31	Balance c/d		2,804	" 30	C Clark		490
			3,253				3,253

You are required to:

(a) write the cash book up to date

(b) draw up a bank reconciliation statement as at 31 March 2006.

15.4X Following is the cash book (bank columns) of E Flynn for December 2007:

Cash Book

Dr		£	Cr		£
2007			2007		
Dec 6	J Hall	155	Dec 1	Balance b/d	3,872
Dec 20	C Walters	189	Dec 10	P Wood	206
Dec 31	P Miller	211	Dec 19	M Roberts	315
Dec 31	Balance c/d	3,922	Dec 29	P Phillips	84
		4,477			4,477

The bank statement for the month is:

2007	Dr £	Cr £	Balance £
Dec 1 Balance			3,872 O/D
Dec 6 Cheque		155	3,717 O/D
Dec 13 P Wood	206		3,923 O/D
Dec 20 Cheque		189	3,734 O/D
Dec 22 M Roberts	315		4,049 O/D
Dec 30 Mercantile: Standing order	200		4,249 O/D
Dec 31 K Saunders: Trader's credit		180	4,069 O/D
Dec 31 Bank charges	65		4,134 O/D

You are required to:
(a) write the cash book up to date to take the necessary items into account
(b) draw up a bank reconciliation statement as on 31 December 2007.

15.5 On 31 December 2006 the bank columns of K Talbot's cash book showed a balance of £4,500. The bank statement as at 31 December 2006 showed a credit balance of £8,850 on the account. You checked the bank statement with the cash book and found that the following had not been entered in the cash book:

(i)   A standing order to RB Insurance for £600 had been paid by the bank.
(ii) Bank interest receivable of £720 had not been entered into the account.
(iii) Bank charges of £90 had been made.
(iv) A credit transfer of £780 from KB Ltd had been paid direct into the account.
(v)   Talbot's deposit account balance of £4,200 had been transferred into her bank current account.
(vi) A returned cheque of £210, dishonoured by C Hill, had been entered on the bank statement.

You also found that two cheques, payable to L Young £750 and K Clark £870, had been entered in the cash book but had not been presented for payment. In addition, a cheque for £2,070 had been paid into the bank on 31 December 2006 but had not been credited on the bank statement until 2 January 2007.

Required:
(a) Starting with the cash book debit balance of £4,500, write the cash book up to date.
(b) Draw up a bank reconciliation statement as on 31 December 2006.

15.6X   On 28 June Senator Safes received the following bank statement as at 24 June 2006.

SOUTH BANK plc				
High Street, Webley, W36 OKW				
To: Senator Safes	Account No: 721982716			24 June 2006
STATEMENT OF ACCOUNT				
Date	Details	Paid out	Paid in	Balance
2006		£	£	£
3 June	Balance b/f			7,000C
5 June	Cheque No 326705	300		6,700C
5 June	Cheque No 326710	6,900		200D
5 June	Cheque No 326711	300		500D
10 June	Bank Giro Credit			
	C Maguire		9,100	8,600C
11 June	Cheque No 326713	76		8,524C
14 June	Direct Debit			
	Bamber Limited	1,300		7,224C
20 June	Direct Debit			
	Webley MBC	100		7,124C
24 June	Bank charges	52		7,072C
D = Debit C = Credit				

The cash book as at 28 June 2006 is shown below.

Cash Book

Date 2006	Details	Bank £	Date 2006	Cheque No	Details	Bank £
1 June	Balance b/f	6,700	1 June	326710	B Groom Limited	6,900
26 June	P Kramer	3,100	1 June	326711	KKD Limited	300
26 June	L Jones	82	6 June	326712	F Bolton	250
			7 June	326713	Leigh & Company	76

(a) check the items on the bank statement against the items in the cash book
(b) write out the cash book and update as needed
(c) total the cash book and clearly show the balance carried down
(d) prepare a bank reconciliation statement as at 28 June 2006.

AAT

15.7X   Cunningham & Co is an old-established firm of accountants in Huddersfield. You have been employed as book-keeper to the company to assist the senior partner, Mr Cunningham, with the accounting records and day-to-day routine duties. The company's policies when dealing with both payments and receipts is extremely strict. All cash and cheques received are to be banked immediately. Any payments over £10 must be made by cheque. Small cash payments are all paid by the petty cash system.

One of your tasks is to enter the company's cash book and reconcile this with the bank statement. This task must be carried out on a weekly basis.

Required:

(*a*) Having obtained the company's cheque book and paying-in book (Exhibits 15.6 and 15.7), enter up the cash book (bank columns only) for the week commencing 3 November 2006. Unfortunately, on that date the company was overdrawn by £2,356.00.

(*b*) Balance up the cash book at the end of the week and bring the balance down.

(*c*) From the bank statement (Exhibit 15.8) you are required to prepare:

    (i)   The corrected cash book balance as at 10 November 2006

    (ii) A bank reconciliation statement as at 10 November 2006.

(NVQ Level 2)

Exhibit 15.6 **Details of cheque book stubs – Cunningham & Co**

Date 3 Nov 2006	Date 3 Nov 2006	Date 4 Nov 2006
Payee Post Office Stamps	Payee The Law Society	Payee Bayleys Office Supplies
Amount £ 146.50	Amount £ 121.80	Amount £ 94.10
001763	001764	001765

Date 5 Nov 2006	Date 6 Nov 2006	Date 10 Nov 2006
Payee Lower Bents Garage (Petrol A/c – Sept)	Payee Wages	Payee Petty Cashier (Restoring imprest)
Amount £ 450.15	Amount £ 489.20	Amount £ 46.00
001766	001767	001768

Exhibit 15.7 Details from paying-in book – Cunningham & Co

Date	3 Nov 2006
A/c	Cunningham & Co
Cash	
Cheques	Mrs Stoddard £540.00
£	540.00

Date	5 Nov 2006
A/c	Cunningham & Co
Cash	Bent Garage £221.00 P Ralphs £53.00
Cheques	Gardeners £1500.00
£	1774.00

Date	6 Nov 2006
A/c	Cunningham & Co
Cash	Mr Prince £130.50
Cheques	Stephens & Smith £523.10
£	653.60

Date	7 Nov 2006
A/c	Cunningham & Co
Cash	
Cheques	Rileys (Printers) & Co £759.00
£	759.00

Date	7 Nov 2006
A/c	Cunningham & Co
Cash	Brindle Bros £165.50
Cheques	Robert Andrews Ltd £325.00
£	490.50

Exhibit 15.8 Bank Statement – Cunningham & Co

TUDOR BANK	CONFIDENTIAL
High Street Huddersfield	**Account:** Cunningham & Co Chestergate Huddersfield
Account No: 0012770123	Sheet No: 67 Date: 8 November 2006

2006		Dr	Cr	Balance	
Nov 3 Balance b/d				2,356.00	O/D
4 Cheque	001763	146.50		2,502.50	O/D
3 Deposit			540.00	1,962.50	O/D
5 Deposit			1,774.00	188.50	O/D
6 S/O Noble Insurance		62.00		250.50	O/D
6 Cheque	001767	489.20		739.70	O/D
6 Deposit			653.60	86.10	O/D
7 Deposit			759.00	672.90	
7 Bank charges		22.45		650.45	
7 Cheque	001765	94.10		556.35	

15.8X The following are extracts from the cash book and bank statement of Noshin Choudhary for the month of February 2002.

Cash Book (Bank columns only) – N Choudhary

Dr		£	2002		Cr £
2002		£			£
Feb 1	Balance b/d	2200	Feb 10	J Fairhurst	157
8	P Burlace	98	16	B Shaw	243
18	P Burlace	140	28	T Rungren	130
28	J Garcia	124	28	Balance c/d	2,032
		2,562			2,562

N Choudhary Bank Statement as at 28 February 2002

2002	Debit £	Credit £	Balance £
Feb 1 Balance b/d			2,200
8 Cheque		98	2,298
13 J Fairhurst	157		2,141
18 Cheque		140	2,281
20 B Shaw	243		2,038
26 Standing order	42		1,996
28 Bank charges	26		1,970
28 Credit transfer		91	2,061

Using the above information:

(*a*) bring the cash book up to date to show a corrected bank balance

(*b*) prepare a statement reconciling the *corrected* cash book balance with the bank statement.

NEAB (GCSE)

CHAPTER 16

Value added tax

Learning objectives

After you have studied this chapter you should be able to:

- understand how the value added tax (VAT) system operates in the UK
- distinguish between standard-rated, zero-rated, exempted and partially exempt businesses
- prepare sales invoices including charges for VAT
- record VAT transactions in all the necessary books of account
- complete a VAT return form.

16.1 Introduction

This chapter looks at the accounting requirements when a tax is levied on sales by the government. The system in operation in the United Kingdom is called value added tax (VAT). Students studying in the UK will be examined on their knowledge and understanding of this system. For students studying in other countries, it is important to be familiar with the appropriate sales tax in operation and also advisable to seek the advice of a teacher or lecturer.

Value added tax (VAT) is a tax on turnover, not on profits. It is described as an 'indirect' tax, and ultimately the tax is paid by the final consumer of the goods or services. VAT is administered in the United Kingdom by HM Customs and Excise.

16.2 The scope of VAT

VAT is charged on the supply of most goods or services by a VAT registered trader. A VAT-registered trader may be a sole proprietor, a partnership or a limited company.

Not all goods and services are subject to VAT. Some goods and services are **zero-rated**. This means that VAT is charged at the rate of zero per cent. Examples of zero-rated supplies are:

- food for human consumption
- books and periodicals
- clothing and footwear for young children.

Some goods and services are **exempt** from VAT. This means that such supplies are outside the scope of VAT, and VAT cannot be charged. Examples of exempt supplies are:

- financial services
- postal services provided by the Post Office
- education.

It is very important to differentiate between zero-rated and exempt supplies, as we will see later.

16.3 The rate of VAT

The rate of VAT is decided by Parliament through the Finance Acts, which are passed each year after the budget(s). The rates at the publication of this book were:

- all zero-rated goods and services   0%
- fuel and power for domestic or charity use only   5%
- all other standard rated supplies   17.5%

The VAT charged *by* a business on its supplies (**outputs**) is called **output VAT**, and is payable by the business to HM Customs and Excise. The VAT charged *to* a business on its purchases and expenses (**inputs**), is called **input VAT** and is reclaimable by the business from HM Customs and Excise (HM C&E).

16.4 Example: how the VAT system works

A toymaker manufactures toys from scraps of material and sells them to a wholesaler for £200 plus VAT. The wholesaler sells these toys to a chain of retailers for £300 plus VAT, who in turn retail the toys in their shops for £400 plus VAT. VAT accounting per unit is as follows:

(i)   The toymaker accounts for VAT as follows:

	Net (£)	VAT (£) @ 17.5%
Sale of toys	200.00	35.00
Cost	–	–
VAT payable to HM C&E		35.00

(ii)   The wholesaler accounts for VAT as follows:

	Net (£)	VAT (£) @ 17.5%
Sale of toys	300.00	52.50
Cost of toys	200.00	35.00
VAT payable to HM C&E		17.50

(iii)   The retailer accounts for VAT as follows:

	Net (£)	VAT (£) @ 17.5%
Sale of toys	400.00	70.00
Cost of toys	300.00	52.50
VAT payable to HM C&E		17.50

It will be seen that the total output VAT paid to HM Customs and Excise is £70.00, as charged by the retailer to its customers. The VAT, however, has been paid to HM Customs and Excise at various stages in the distribution of the toys, as follows:

	£
Toymaker	35.00
Wholesaler	17.50
Retailer	17.50
	70.00

16.5 Zero-rated supplies

In Section 16.2, we introduced the concept of zero-rated supplies. The important matter to note is that items are charged to VAT at 0 per cent, which is a rate of VAT. In some EU countries, supplies that are zero-rated in the UK are charged to VAT at that country's VAT rate.

As the supplies are sold at a rate of VAT, (albeit 0 per cent), any input VAT incurred, relating to the business, can all be reclaimed.

Example 1: A book dealer sells £100,000 worth of books in a year and, during that year, purchases book shelving for £10,000 plus VAT.

The VAT reclaimable is therefore:

	Net (£)	VAT (£) @ 17.5%
Sales	100,000	Nil
Purchases	10,000	1,750
VAT reclaimable		1,750

16.6 Exempt supplies

In Section 16.2 we introduced the concept of exempt supplies. There are two types of exempt supplies:

- supplies of specifically exempted items, such as those stated in Section 16.2
- all supplies of goods and services by non-VAT-registered businesses, for example exempt businesses such as banks and insurance companies, and businesses that do not need to register because their annual turnover is below the VAT registration limit (currently £56,000), they don't need to register unless they want to. They can also deregister if their turnover falls below a certain level (currently £54,000).

The important matter to note is that input VAT directly attributable to exempt supplies or to non-VAT registered businesses cannot be reclaimed from HM Customs and Excise.

Example 2: An insurance company sells £100,000 worth of insurance, and purchases furniture for its office for £10,000 plus VAT.

This business cannot reclaim the £1,750 input VAT on the furniture as it does not have any vatable supplies. The total amount paid for the furniture, £11,750, will be the cost to the business. Contrast this situation with the zero-rated supplier in Example 1 above, which was able to reclaim £1,750.

16.7 Partly exempt traders

Some VAT-registered traders will sell some goods that are exempt from VAT and some that are either standard-rated or zero-rated. These businesses may reclaim part of the input VAT paid by them, but not all of it. The rules are complicated, but in essence the input VAT reclaimable will be proportionate to the standard- and zero-rated percentage of the business's total annual turnover.

16.8 Different methods of accounting for VAT

How VAT appears in the ledger accounts and in the financial statements depends on which of the following categories businesses fall into:

- **Businesses that can recover VAT paid** – all businesses except exempted firms do not incur VAT as an expense. They either:
  - obtain a refund of the VAT they have paid in the case of a zero-rated business, or
  - collect VAT from their customers, deduct the VAT paid on goods and services bought by them and simply remit the balance owing to HM Customs and Excise as in standard-rated businesses.
- **Businesses that cannot recover VAT paid** – this applies to all businesses that are treated as exempted businesses and are unable to obtain refunds for any tax paid (refer to Section 16.6).

The following section outlines the double entry requirements for recording VAT in the above categories.

16.9 Book-keeping entries for businesses that can recover VAT paid

Standard-rated businesses

Value added tax and sales invoices

These businesses will have to add VAT to the value of the sales invoice. It must be pointed out that this is based on the amount of the invoice *after* any trade discount has been deducted. Exhibit 16.1 is an invoice drawn up from the following details. On 2 March 2006, W Frank & Co, Hayburn Road, Stockport, sold the following goods to R Bainbridge Ltd, 267 Star Road, Colchester. Bainbridge's Order Number was A/4/559, for the following items:

> 220 Rolls T56 Black Tape at £6 per 10 rolls
> 600 Sheets R64 Polythene at £10 per 100 sheets
> 7,000 Blank Perspex B49 Markers at £20 per 1,000.

All of these goods are subject to VAT at the rate of 17.5 per cent. A trade discount of 25 per cent is given by Frank & Co. The sales invoice is numbered 8851.

Exhibit 16.1

W Frank & Co
Hayburn Road
Stockport SK2 5DB

INVOICE No 8851

Date/tax point: 2 March 2006

To: R Bainbridge
      267 Star Road
      Colchester CO1 1BT

Your order no: A/4/559
Account no: F/1896

	£
200 Rolls T56 Black Tape @ £6 per 10 rolls	120
600 Sheets R64 Polythene @ £10 per 100 sheets	60
7,000 Blank Perspex B49 Markers @ £20 per 1,000	140
	320
Less Trade Discount 25%	80
	240
Add VAT 17.5%	42
	282

VAT Registration No: 469 2154 42

The sales day book will normally have an extra column for the VAT contents of the sales invoice (*see* Chapter 22). This is needed to make it easier to account for VAT. The entry of several sales invoices in the sales day book and in the ledger accounts can now be examined for our sample case.

W Frank & Co sold the following goods during the month of March 2006:

	Total of invoice, after trade discount deducted but before VAT added	VAT 17.5%
2006	£	£
March 2 R Bainbridge Ltd (*see* Exhibit 16.1)	240	42
March 10 S Lange & Son	200	35
March 17 K Bishop	160	28
March 31 R Andrews & Associates	80	14

Sales Day Book					*Page 58*
	Invoice No	*Folio*	*Total*	*Net*	*VAT*
2006			£	£	£
March 2 R Bainbridge Ltd	8851	SL 77	282	240	42
March 10 S Lange & Son	8852	SL 119	235	200	35
March 17 K Bishop	8853	SL 185	188	160	28
March 31 R Andrews & Associates	8854	SL 221	94	80	14
Transferred to General Ledger			799	680	119
				GL 76	GL 90

Now that the sales day book has been written up, the next task is to enter the amounts of the invoices in the individual customer's accounts in the sales ledger. These are simply charged with the full amounts of the invoices, including VAT.

As an instance of this, K Bishop will be shown as owing £188. When she pays her account she will pay £188. It will then be the responsibility of W Frank & Co to ensure that the figure of £28 VAT in respect of this item is included in the total cheque payable to HM Customs and Excise.

Sales Ledger

R Bainbridge Ltd

Dr				Page 77 Cr
2006	Folio	£		
March 2 Sales	SB 58	282		

S Lange & Son

Dr				Page 119 Cr
2006	Folio	£		
March 10 Sales	SB 58	235		

K Bishop

Dr				Page 185 Cr
2006	Folio	£		
March 17 Sales	SB 58	188		

R Andrews & Associates

Dr				Page 221 Cr
2006	Folio	£		
March 31 Sales	SB 58	94		

In total, therefore, the personal accounts have been debited with £799, this being the total of the amounts that the customers will have to pay. The actual sales of the firm are not £799; the amount that is actually sales is £680, the other £119 being simply the VAT that W Frank & Co are collecting on behalf of the Government.

The double entry is made in the general ledger thus:

● credit the sales account with the sales content only, i.e. £680
● credit the VAT account with the VAT content only, i.e. £119.

These are shown as:

General Ledger

Sales

Dr				Page 76 Cr
	2006		Folio	£
	March 31 Credit Sales for the month		SB 58	680

		2006	Folio	£
Dr				Cr
		March 31 Sales Book: VAT	SB 58	119

Value Added Tax — *Page 90*

Value added tax and purchases

In the case of a taxable firm, the firm will have to add VAT to its sales invoices, but it will *also* be able to get a refund of the VAT it pays on its purchases.

Instead of paying VAT to HM Customs and Excise and then claiming a refund of the VAT on purchases, the firm can offset the amount paid as VAT on purchases against the amount payable as VAT on sales. This means that only the difference has to be paid to HM Customs and Excise. It is shown as:

	£
(a) Output VAT collected on sales invoices	xxx
(b) Less Input VAT already paid on purchases	xxx
(c) Net amount to be paid to HM Customs and Excise	xxx

In certain fairly rare circumstances (a) may be less than (b). If that were to be the case, then it would be HM Customs and Excise that would refund the difference (c) to the firm. Such a settlement between the firm and HM Customs and Excise will take place at least every three months.

The recording of purchases in the purchases day book and purchases ledger follows a similar method to that of sales, but with the personal accounts being credited instead of debited. We can now look at the records of purchases for W Frank & Co, whose sales have been dealt with in Exhibit 16.1. The firm made the following purchases for March 2006:

	Total invoice, after trade discount deducted but before VAT added	VAT 17.5%
2006	£	£
March 1 E Lyal Ltd (*see* Exhibit 16.2)	200	35
March 11 P Portsmouth & Co	280	49
March 24 J Davidson	40	7
March 29 B Cofie & Son Ltd	80	14

Before looking at the recording of these in the purchases records, compare the first entry for E Lyal Ltd with Exhibit 16.2 to ensure that the correct amounts have been shown.

Exhibit 16.2

<table>
<tr><td colspan="2" align="center">E Lyal Ltd
College Avenue
St Albans
Hertfordshire ST2 4JA</td></tr>
<tr><td colspan="2" align="center">INVOICE No K 453/A</td></tr>
<tr><td>Date/tax point: 1/3/2006
Your order no BB/667</td><td></td></tr>
<tr><td>To: W Frank & Co
      Hayburn Road
      Stockport</td><td>Terms: Strictly net 30 days
VAT Reg. No: 236 4054 56</td></tr>
</table>

	£
50 metres of BYC plastic 1 metre wide x £3.60 per metre	180
1,200 metal tags 500mm x 10p each	120
	300
Less Trade Discount at 33⅓%	100
	200
Add VAT 17.5%	35
	235

The purchases day book can now be entered up.

Purchases Day Book				Page 38
	Folio	Total £	Net £	VAT £
2006				
March 1 E Lyal Ltd	PL 15	235	200	35
March 11 P Portsmouth & Co	PL 70	329	280	49
March 24 J Davidson	PL 114	47	40	7
March 29 B Cofie & Son Ltd	PL 166	94	80	14
Transferred to General Ledger		705	GL 54 600	GL 90 105

These transactions are entered in the purchases ledger. Once again, there is no need for the VAT to be shown as separate amounts in the accounts of the suppliers.

Purchases Ledger

E Lyal Ltd   Page 15

Dr   Cr

		2006	Folio	£
		March 1 Purchases	PB 38	235

P Portsmouth & Co   Page 70

Dr   Cr

		2006	Folio	£
		March 11 Purchases	PB 38	329

	J Davidson		Page 114
Dr			Cr
	2006	Folio	£
	March 24 Purchases	PB 38	47

	B Cofie & Son Ltd		Page 166
Dr			Cr
	2006	Folio	£
	March 29 Purchases	PB 38	94

The personal accounts have been credited with a total of £705, this being the total of the amounts which W Frank & Co will have to pay to them. The actual cost of purchases is not, however, £705. You can see that the correct amount is £600. The other £105 is the VAT that the various firms are collecting for HM Customs and Excise. This amount is also the figure for VAT that is reclaimable from HM Customs and Excise by W Frank & Co.

The debit entry in the purchases account is, therefore, £600, as this is the actual cost of the goods to the firm. The other £105 is entered on the debit side of the VAT account. Notice that there is already a credit of £119 in the VAT account in respect of the VAT added to sales.

General Ledger
Purchases

				Page 54
Dr				Cr
2006	Folio	£		
March 31 Credit Purchases				
for the month	PB 38	600		

Value Added Tax

						Page 90
Dr						Cr
2006	Folio	£	2006		Folio	£
March 31 Purchases Day			March 31 Sales Day			
Book: VAT	PB 38	105	Book: VAT		SB 38	119
March 31 Balance c/d		14				
		119				119
			April 1 Balance b/d			14

In the final accounts of W Frank & Co, the following entries would be made:

(*a*) trading account for the month ended 31 March 2006:
- debited with £600 as a transfer from the purchases account
- credited with £680 as a transfer from the sales account.

(*b*) balance sheet as at 31 March 2006:
- balance of £14 (credit) on the VAT account would be shown as a current liability, as it represents the amount owing to HM Customs and Excise for VAT.

Zero-rated businesses

These businesses:

(*a*) Do not have to add VAT onto their sales invoices, as their rate of VAT is zero or nil.

(*b*) They can, however, reclaim from HM Customs and Excise any VAT paid on goods or services bought.

Accordingly, because of (*a*) no VAT is entered in the sales day book; VAT on sales does not exist. Because of (*b*) the purchases day book and purchases ledger will appear exactly in the same manner as for taxable firms, as already shown in the case of W Frank & Co. The VAT account will only have debits in it, being the VAT on purchases. Any balance on this account will be shown in the balance sheet as a debtor.

16.10   VAT and cash discounts

Where a cash discount is offered for speedy payment, VAT is calculated on an amount represented by the value of the invoice less such a discount. Even if the cash discount is lost because of late payment, the VAT will not change.

Exhibit 16.3 shows an example of such a sales invoice, assuming a cash discount offered of 2.5 per cent and a VAT rate at 17.5 per cent.

Exhibit 16.3

ATC Ltd
18 High Street
London WC2E 9AN

INVOICE No ZT 48910

VAT Reg No: 313 5924 71
Date/tax point: 11 May 2007
Your order no: TS/778

To: R Noble
      Belsize Road
      Edgeley
      Stockport

	£
500 paper dispensers @ £20 each	10,000
Less Trade Discount @ 20%	2,000
	8,000
Add VAT 17.5%	1,365*
	9,365

---

*The VAT has been calculated on the net price of £8,000 *less* the cash discount 2.5 per cent, i.e. £7,800. Then the VAT at 17.5% on £7,800 is calculated as £1,365.

16.11 Book-keeping entries for businesses that cannot get refunds of VAT paid

As these businesses do not add VAT on to the value of their sales invoices, there is obviously no entry for VAT in the sales day book or the sales ledger. They do not get a refund of VAT on purchases. This means that there will not be a VAT account; all that will happen is that VAT paid is included as part of the cost of the goods bought.

Assume that the only purchase made in a month was of goods for £120 + VAT £21 from D Oswald. The entries relating to it will appear as:

Purchases Day Book

Page 11

2007		Folio	£
May 16 D Oswald Ltd		PL 14	<u>141</u>
			<u><u>141</u></u>
			GL 17

Purchases Ledger
D Oswald Ltd

Dr   *Page 14*
         Cr

	2007	Folio	£
	May 16 D Oswald Ltd	PB 11	141

General Ledger
Purchases

Dr   *Page 17*
         Cr

2007	Folio	£	2007		£
May 31 Credit Purchases for the month	PB 11	<u>141</u>	May 31 Transfer to Trading Account		<u>141</u>

Trading Account for the month ended 31 May 2007 (extract)

	£	£
Sales		
Less **Cost of goods sold**		XXX
Purchases	141	

16.12 VAT included in gross amount

You will often know only the gross amount of an item. This figure will, in fact, be made up of the net amount plus VAT. To find the amount of VAT that has been added to the net amount, a formula capable of being used with any rate of VAT is:

$$\frac{\% \text{ rate of VAT}}{100 + \% \text{ Rate of VAT}} \times \text{Gross Amount} = \text{VAT in £}$$

Suppose that the gross amount of sales was £940 and the rate of VAT was 17.5 per cent. Finding the amount of VAT and the net amount before VAT was added using the formula yields:

$$\text{VAT} = \frac{17.5}{100 + 17.5} \times £940 = \frac{17.5}{117.5} \times £940 = 140.$$

Therefore, the net amount was £800, which, with VAT £140 added, becomes £940 gross.

16.13 VAT on items other than sales and purchases

VAT is not just paid on purchases. It is also payable on many items of expense and on the purchase of fixed assets.

Businesses that *can* get refunds of VAT paid will not include VAT as part of the cost of the expense or fixed asset. Firms that *cannot* get refunds of VAT paid will include the VAT cost as part of the expense or fixed asset. For example, two firms buying similar items would treat the following items as shown:

	Firm that can reclaim VAT		Firm that cannot reclaim VAT	
Buys Machinery £200 + VAT £35	Debit Machinery	£200	Debit Machinery	£235
	Debit VAT Account	£35		
Buys Stationery £160 + VAT £28	Debit Stationery	£160	Debit Stationery	£188
	Debit VAT Account	£28		

16.14 VAT owing

VAT owing by or to the business can be included with debtors or creditors, as the case may be. There is no need to show the amount(s) owing as separate items.

16.15 Relief from VAT on bad debts

It is possible to claim relief on any debt that is more than six months old and has been written off in the accounts. Should the debt later be paid, the VAT refunded will then have to be paid back to HM Customs and Excise.

16.16 Purchase of cars

Normally, the VAT paid on a car bought for a business is not reclaimable.

16.17 VAT records

All VAT records must be retained by a business for a period of six years.

16.18 Columnar day books and VAT

The use of columns for VAT in both sales and purchases analysis books is demonstrated in Chapter 22.

16.19 VAT return forms

At the end of each VAT accounting period, a form VAT 100 has to be filled in and sent to HM Customs and Excise. The most important part of the form is concerned with columns 1–9, which are shown in Exhibit 16.4. For illustration, we have assumed a VAT rate of 10 per cent.

Exhibit 16.4

		£	
VAT due in this period on **sales** and other outputs	1	8,750	–
VAT due in this period on **acquisitions** from other **EC Member States**	2	–	–
Total VAT due (**the sum of boxes 1** and **2**)	3	8,750	–
VAT reclaimed in this period on **purchases** and other inputs (including acquisitions from the EC)	4	6,250	–
Net VAT to be paid to Customs or reclaimed by you (difference between boxes 3 and 4)	5	2,500	–
Total value of **sales** and all other outputs excluding any VAT, **Include your box 8 figure**	6	97,500	–
Total value of **purchases** and all other inputs excluding any VAT. **Include your box 9 figure**	7	71,900	–
Total value of all supplies of goods and related services, excluding any VAT, to other **EC Member States**	8	10,000	–
Total value of all **acquisitions** of goods and related services, excluding any VAT, from other **EC Member States**	9	1,450	–

The contents of the columns on form VAT 100 are now explained:

1 We have added £8,750 VAT on to our sales invoices for the period.
2 This column would show the VAT due (but not paid) on all goods and related services acquired in this period from other EC member states. In this case there were no such transactions.
3 Total of columns 1 and 2.
4 We have made purchases and incurred expenses during the period, on which we have been charged £6,250 VAT.
5 As we have collected £8,750 VAT from our customers, but only incurred £6,250 on all purchases and expenses, we therefore owe HM Customs and Excise £2,500, i.e. £8,750 – £6,250.
6 Our total value of sales for the period was £97,500.
7 Our total value of purchases and expenses was £71,900, but some of these expenses were not subject to a charge for VAT.
8 Of the sales included under item 6, £10,000 of it was to other countries within the European Community. VAT was not charged on these sales.
9 Of the total purchases under item 7 £1,450 was from other countries within the European Community.

Only columns 1, 3, 4 and 5 actually refer to accounting for VAT. The other columns are for statistical purposes so that the UK government can assess the performance of the economy and similar matters.

16.20 VAT on goods taken for private use

If a trader takes some goods out of his own business stock for his own private use, the trader should be charged with any VAT due on these goods.

For instance, suppose that Smith, a furniture dealer, takes a table and chairs out of stock for permanent use in his own home. The cost to the business has been (cost price + value added tax). Therefore the proprietor's drawing should be charged with both the cost price of goods plus the VAT.

The double entry needed, assuming goods taken of £1,000 + VAT at 10 per cent, would therefore be:

Drawings:	Debit	£1,100
Purchases:	Credit	£1,000
VAT account:	Credit	£100

There can be complicating circumstances, outside the scope of this book, that might influence the amount of VAT to be charged on such drawings.

Chapter summary

- Value added tax (VAT) is a tax levied on sales by the UK government. It is described as an 'indirect tax' and ultimately the tax is paid by the final consumer of the goods or services.
- VAT is administered in the UK by HM Customs and Excise.
- There are currently three rates of VAT, namely 0 per cent, 5 per cent and 17.5 per cent.
- The way in which the VAT system operates is explained whereby VAT is paid at various stages in the distribution chain.
- Businesses may be classified as standard-rated, zero-rated, exempt or partially exempt.
- The book-keeping entries for the recording of VAT in the books of account is shown for the various types of business.
- When preparing sales invoices the trade discount is deducted before VAT is added on.
- If a business allows cash discount for prompt payment the VAT is calculated on the sales value less any cash discount offered. If the cash discount is lost because of late payment the VAT will not change.
- VAT may also be charged on items of expense and the purchase of fixed assets. The book-keeping entries vary depending upon whether the firm is able to reclaim the VAT paid or not.
- At the end of a particular quarter a VAT return form is completed and sent to HM Customs and Excise together with any payment due. Alternatively, there may be a refund due.

Exercises

16.1 On 1 May 2005, D Wilson Ltd, 1 Hawk Green Road, Stockport, sold the following goods on credit to G Christie & Son, The Golf Shop, Hole-in-One Lane, Marple, Cheshire:

Order No A/496
3 sets of 'Boy Michael' golf clubs at £240 per set.
150 Watson golf balls at £8 per 10 balls.
4 Faldo golf bags at £30 per bag.
Trade discount is given at the rate of 33$\frac{1}{3}$%.
All goods are subject to VAT at 17.5%.

Required:
(a) Prepare the sales invoice to be sent to G Christie & Son. The invoice number will be 10586.
(b) Show the entries in the personal ledgers of D Wilson Ltd and G Christie & Son.

16.2 The following sales have been made by S Thompson Ltd during the month of June 2006. All the figures are shown 'net' after deducting trade discount, but before adding VAT at the rate of 17.5 per cent.

2006

August   1 to M Sinclair & Co   £160
        "   8 to M Brown & Associates   £240
        "   19 to A Axton Ltd   £80
        "   31 to T Christie   £40

You are required to enter up the sales day book, sales ledger and general ledger in respect of the above items for the month.

16.3   The following sales and purchases were made by R Colman Ltd during the month of May 2005:

	Net	VAT added
2005	£	£
May 1 Sold goods on credit to B Davies & Co	160	28
" 4 Sold goods on credit to C Grant Ltd	200	35
" 10 Bought goods on credit from:		
– G Cooper & Son	400	70
– J Wayne Ltd	240	42
" 14 Bought goods on credit from B Lugosi	40	7
" 16 Sold goods on credit to C Grant Ltd	120	21
" 23 Bought goods on credit from S Hayward	40	7
" 31 Sold goods on credit to B Karloff	80	14

Enter up the sales and purchases day books, sales and purchases ledgers, and the general ledger for the month of May 2005. Carry the balance down on the VAT account.

16.4X   On 1 March 2005, C Black, Curzon Road, Stockport, sold the following goods on credit to J Booth, 89 Andrew Lane, Stockport, under Order No 1697:

20,000 coils sealing tape   @ £4.70 per 1,000 coils
40,000 sheets A5 paper   @ £4.50 per 1,000 sheets
30,000 sheets A4 paper   @ £4.20 per 1,000 sheets
All goods are subject to VAT at 17.5%.

Required:
(*a*) Prepare the sales invoice to be sent to J Booth.
(*b*) Show the entries in the personal ledgers of J Booth and C Black.

16.5   Comart Supplies Ltd recently purchased from Ace Import Ltd 10 printers originally priced at £200 each. A 10-per-cent trade discount was negotiated, together with a 5 per cent cash discount if payment was made within 14 days. Calculate the following:

(*a*) the total of the trade discount
(*b*) the total of the cash discount
(*c*) the total of the VAT.

AAT (part of Central Assessment)

16.6   A manufacturer sells a product to a wholesaler for £200 plus VAT of £35. The wholesaler sells the same product to a retailer for £280 plus VAT of £49. The retailer then sells the product to a customer for £320 plus VAT of £56. What is the amount of VAT collectable by HM Customs and Excise?

AAT (part of Central Assessment)

16.7   (*a*) Should the total of the VAT column in the petty cash book be debited or credited to the VAT account in the general ledger?

(*b*) For what period of time must VAT records be retained?

(*c*) MMS Textiles Ltd is a VAT-registered firm. Should it charge VAT on goods supplied to a customer that is not VAT-registered?

(*d*) What book-keeping entries would be necessary to record a cash refund of £94 (inclusive of VAT) to a customer?

AAT (part of Central Assessment)

16.8X   Bloomers Ltd purchases 40 glass crystal vases for £7.50 each plus VAT. The vases are then all sold to a hotel gift shop for £517 inclusive of VAT. How much is owed by Bloomers to HM Customs and Excise in respect of the vases?

AAT (part of Central Assessment)

Petty cash and the imprest system

After you have studied this chapter you should be able to:

- understand why organisations use a petty cash book
- recognise the need for a petty cash voucher
- understand the imprest system
- make entries in a petty cash book
- post the appropriate amounts from the petty cash book to the various accounts in the general ledger at the end of the period.

17.1 Introduction to petty cash

All types of organisations from very small ones to large businesses usually incur small items of expenditure. The type of expenditure incurred would be such items as the purchase of postage stamps or perhaps the posting of a parcel to a customer, travel expenses, cleaning materials and stationery. The items purchased are usually paid for in cash by a member of staff, on behalf of the organisation, who then seeks reimbursement of the amount spent. A petty cash book is used to record these transactions. Larger amounts of expenditure will be paid for by cheque and recorded in the cash book as discussed in Chapter 14.

The petty cash book is a book of original entry since items are entered here first and it also acts as a ledger account for the cash in hand at any point of time.

17.2 Petty cash voucher

When a person incurs expenditure on behalf of the organisation they need to complete a **petty cash voucher** in order to reclaim the amount of money spent.

This will show details of the expense incurred together with a receipt (if possible), the amount spent including VAT and signed by the person making the claim. The petty cash voucher will then need to be authorised for payment. Often the petty cashier is able to authorise payments up to a specific limit, for example £25.00, with any amount above that usually being authorised by a manager or accountant.

When the petty cash voucher is entered into the petty cash book it will be numbered for future reference purposes and then filed. An example of a petty cash voucher is shown below in Exhibit 17.1.

Exhibit 17.1

| Petty Cash Voucher | No. | *1* |
| | Date | *2 May 2006* |

Description	Amount
	£ p
Stationery	*14 10*
(including VAT £2.10)	

| Signature | *Ken Boardman* |
| Authorised | *Sandra Ashford* |

17.3   The imprest system

The **imprest system** is where the cashier gives the petty cashier enough cash to meet the needs of the following period. At the end of the period, the cashier finds out the amounts spent by the petty cashier, and tops up the petty cashier's cash by an amount equal to that spent. The petty cash in hand should then be equal to the original amount with which the period was started. Exhibit 17.2 shows an example of this method.

Exhibit 17.2

		£
Period 1	The cashier gives the petty cashier	100
	The petty cashier pays out in the period	78
	Petty cash now in hand	22
	The cashier now gives the petty cashier the amount spent	78
	Petty cash in hand at the end of period 1	100
Period 2	The petty cashier pays out in the period	84
	Petty cash now in hand	16
	The cashier now gives the petty cashier the amount spent	84
	Petty cash in hand end of period 2	100

It may be necessary to increase the fixed sum, often called the **cash float**, to be held at the start of each period. In the above case, if we had wanted to increase the float at the end of the second period to £120, then the cashier would have given the petty cashier an extra £20, i.e. £84 + £20 = £104.

Advantages of using the petty cash imprest system

- A junior member of the accounts department, usually called the petty cashier, can be given the task of operating the system thus allowing the cashier to concentrate on other areas of work.
- Small items of expenditure incurred by the organisation are entered into the petty cash book and only the totals at the end of the period are posted to the appropriate accounts in the general ledger. Thus eliminating the main cash book and ledger accounts of numerous transactions.
- The imprest system enables the cash to be checked at any time since the amount paid out, represented by the petty cash vouchers, and the cash in hand should equal the float at the beginning of the period.

17.4 Worked example of an analytical petty cash book

A small company offering secretarial services to local businesses incurs the following items of expenditure during May 2006. The items shown in Exhibit 17.3 will initially require entering in the petty cash book.

Exhibit 17.3

2006
May 1 The petty cashier received a cash float of £200.00 from the cashier
May 2 Stationery £14.10 including VAT £2.10 (see petty cash voucher no.1)
May 4 Postage stamps, £22.00
May 6 Tea and coffee for office visitors, £8.00
May 9 Travel expenses, £16.00
May 10 Computer disks, £12.80 including VAT £1.91
May 12 Postage on parcel, £3.60
May 15 Office cleaner, £25.00
May 22 Milk for office, £4.20
May 25 Received £6.00 from Anita Kerr, office manager, for personal photocopying*
May 27 Office cleaner, £25.00
May 27 Cleaning materials, £4.40 plus VAT 77p, total spent £5.17
May 31 Travel expenses, £23.00
May 31 The cashier reimbursed the petty cashier with the amount spent during the month.

Each of the above items will have had a petty cash voucher completed by the person who had incurred the expenditure on behalf of the business. For illustration purposes just one petty voucher is shown, petty cash voucher no. 1, see previous Exhibit 17.1.

*Receipts

Occasionally, a member of staff may wish to purchase stamps from the petty cashier or perhaps have some photocopying done for their own personal use. In these cases the petty cashier will issue a receipt to the staff member for the amount received. For example, see Exhibit 17.4.

Exhibit 17.4

```
                          RECEIPT
     Received from:    Anita Kerr        Date: 25 May 2006
     The sum of:       Six pounds only   No.   26


                                     £     p
                      Cheque          –     –
                      Cash            6    00
                                      6    00


     Re:   Photocopying

                                          Kim Patel
                                          WITH THANKS
```

The above items of expenditure and the receipt are entered in the petty cash book as illustrated in Exhibit 17.5.

Exhibit 17.5

Petty Cash Book   (page 31)

Receipts £ p	Date	Details	Voucher Number	Total £ p	VAT £ p	Postage £ p	Cleaning £ p	Travel Expenses £ p	Stationery £ p	Sundry Expenses £ p
	2006									
200.00	May 1	Cash	CB 19							
	May 2	Stationery	1	14.10	2.10				12.00	
	May 4	Postage stamps	2	22.00		22.00				
	May 6	Tea, coffee	3	8.00						8.00
	May 9	Travel expenses	4	16.00				16.00		
	May 10	Computer disks	5	12.80	1.91				10.89	
	May 12	Postage on parcel	6	3.60		3.60				
	May 15	Office cleaner	7	25.00			25.00			
	May 22	Milk	8	4.20						4.20
6.00	May 25	Anita Kerr								
		Photo-copying	26							
	May 27	Office cleaner	9	25.00			25.00			
	May 27	Cleaning materials	10	5.17	0.77		4.40			
	May 31	Travel expenses	11	23.00				23.00		
				158.87	4.78	25.60	54.40	39.00	22.89	12.20
	May 31	Balance	c/d	47.13	GL 17	GL 19	GL 29	GL 44	GL 56	GL 60
206.00				206.00						
47.13	June 1	Balance	b/d							
152.87	June 1	Cash	CB 22							

Entering the petty cash book

On 1 May the petty cashier received £200.00 cash from the main cashier. This is the amount of the float for the period of May.

The cashier would enter this item on the credit side of the cash book, the money comes 'OUT' of the bank. The debit entry is now shown on the 'Receipts' side of the petty cash book, the money comes 'INTO' the petty cash. Note the folio reference 'CB 19' (Cash Book page 19) is also entered to cross-reference the entry.

Each petty cash voucher is then entered in date order as follows:

- Enter the date.
- Enter the details of each payment.
- A voucher number is then given to each petty cash voucher and entered on the voucher itself and in the 'voucher number' column.
- The total amount of the expenditure incurred is then entered in the 'total' column.
- The expenditure is then analysed into an appropriate expense column.
- If VAT has been incurred then the VAT amount is entered in the 'VAT' column and the remaining expense in the appropriate column. For example, the petty cash voucher shown in Exhibit 17.1 is for stationery amounting to £14.10. In the total column £14.10 is entered, £2.10 is then entered in the VAT column and the cost of the stationery £12.00 is then entered in the stationery column.

Any money received from the sale of sundry items to a member of staff, as in the case of Anita Kerr who had some personal photocopying, then the receipt of the cash is entered into the 'receipts' column, in this example £6.00. The date, details and receipt number are also entered in the appropriate columns.

The petty cash book now requires balancing off at the end of the month as follows:

- Add up the 'total' column.
- Add up each of the expense columns. The total of all the expense columns added together should now equal the amount shown in the 'total' column.
  In Exhibit 17.5 this would be:

	£ p
VAT	4.78
Postage	25.60
Cleaning	54.40
Travel expenses	39.00
Stationery	22.89
Sundry expenses	12.20
Total	158.87

- The petty cashier now needs to calculate the amount of money needed to restore the imprest to £200.00 for the beginning of the next period. This is as follows:

	£ p
Amount of float at beginning of May	200.00
Money received during month	
Anita Kerr – Photocopying	6.00
	206.00
Less Amount spent (see above)	158.87
Cash in hand at 31 May 2006	47.13
Amount of float	200.00
Less Cash in hand at 31 May 2006	47.13
Cash required to restore the imprest	152.87

- The balance of cash in hand at 31 May 2006 £47.13 is now entered into the petty cash book and shown as 'balance c/d', £47.13 (*see* Exhibit 17.5).
- The 'receipts' and 'total' columns are now added up and should equal each other, i.e. £206.00. These totals should be shown on the same line and both double underlined.
- The 'Balance b/d' on 1 June, £47.13, is now entered in the receipts column and underneath that entry the amount received from the cashier to restore the imprest £152.87 is also entered.

The double entry for each of the expense columns is now carried out:

- The total of each expense column is debited to the expense account in the general ledger.
- The folio number of each general ledger account is entered under each of the expense columns in the petty cash book. This enables cross-referencing and also means that the double entry to the ledger account had been completed.

The double entry for all the items in Exhibit 17.5 appears as Exhibit 17.6.

Exhibit 17.6

Cash Book (Bank column only)   *Page 19*

Dr   *Cr*

	2006	Folio	£
	May 1 Petty Cash	PCB 31	200.00
	June 1 Petty Cash	PCB 31	152.87

General Ledger

VAT Account   *Page 17*

Dr   *Cr*

2006	Folio	£	
May 31 Petty Cash	PCB 31	4.78	

Postages Account   *Page 19*

Dr   *Cr*

2006	Folio	£	
May 31 Petty Cash	PCB 31	25.60	

Cleaning Account   *Page 29*

Dr   *Cr*

2006	Folio	£	
May 31 Petty Cash	PCB 31	54.40	

Travel Expenses Account   *Page 44*

Dr   *Cr*

2006	Folio	£	
May 31 Petty Cash	PCB 31	39.00	

Dr		*Stationery Account*		*Page 56* Cr
2006	*Folio*	£		
May 31 Petty Cash	PCB 31	22.89		

Dr		*Sundry Expenses Account*		*Page 60* Cr
2006	*Folio*	£		
May 31 Petty Cash	PCB 31	12.20		

Paying creditors from petty cash

Occasionally a creditor may be paid their account out of the petty cash. If this arises then the book-keeping entries would be to record the payment in the petty cash book, using a column headed 'ledger accounts', then post the item to the debit side of the creditor's account in the purchase ledger. This transaction is very rare and would only occur where the item to be paid was small, or if a refund was made out of petty cash to a customer who may have overpaid their account.

17.5 Bank cash book

In a firm with both a cash book and a petty cash book, the cash book is often known as a **bank cash book**. This means that *all* cash payments are entered in the petty cash book, and the bank cash book will contain *only* bank columns and discount columns. When this arrangement is in operation, any cash sales will be paid directly into the bank.

Chapter summary

- The petty cash book is used to record transactions involving small items of expenditure incurred by a member of staff on behalf of the organisation.
- Claims for reimbursement of monies paid out are usually made on a petty cash voucher. The voucher should be completed with all the relevant details together with receipt (if possible), duly signed and authorised.
- The imprest system is used by many organisations to operate the petty cash system. Here an amount of money called a 'float' is given to the petty cashier at the start of a period. At the end of the period the amount spent by the petty cashier is reimbursed by the cashier to restore the imprest to its original amount.
- The advantages of using a petty cash system is that it enables a junior member of staff to be appointed petty cashier so allowing the cashier or accountant to concentrate on other areas of work.
- Using the petty cash book saves both the cash book and the ledger account from containing many small items of expenditure.
- The imprest system enables the cash to be checked at any time.

- Entries made into the petty cash book include not only petty cash vouchers for expenses incurred on behalf of the business but also receipts of money that may have been received in respect of sundry sales to staff members.
- The petty cash book is totalled, balanced off and the double entry completed with postings to the ledger accounts in the general ledger.
- The name of the cash book is sometimes called a bank cash book when it only contains bank columns. Cash sales having been banked direct and the petty cash book used for small sundry cash items.

Exercises

17.1 You are employed as accounts clerk for Kitchen Designs who operate their petty cash using the imprest system. At the beginning of the month there was £18.52 left in the petty cash box from the previous month and the cashier has just given you £131.48 to restore the imprest to £150.

The following are details of the petty cash vouchers that have been authorised for payment by the cashier for June 2007, together with a receipt for cash received.

2007		£
June	1 Window cleaner	10.00
June	3 Postage stamps	7.60
June	4 Petrol (including VAT of £5.60)	37.60
June	6 Stationery (including VAT of £1.45)	9.75
June	10 Sold stamps to Jean Ford £2.00 (receipt no. 8)	
June	14 Office cleaner	20.00
June	16 Parcel postage	1.35
June	19 Magazine for reception (no VAT)	3.00
June	21 Computer disks (including VAT £1.05)	7.95
June	23 Petrol (including VAT £2.10)	14.10
June	27 Refreshments for clients (no VAT)	4.20
June	29 Office cleaner	20.00

Required:

(*a*) Enter the balance brought down and the cash received to restore the imprest in the petty cash book on 1 June 2007. The petty cash book page number to use is 47.

(*b*) Enter the above transactions into the petty cash book using the following analysis columns, VAT, postage, cleaning, motor expenses, stationery and sundry expenses. The next petty cash voucher number is 32.

(*c*) Total and balance the petty cash book on 30 June and bring down the balance on 1 July. Show the amount of cash received from the cashier to restore the imprest to £150.

17.2X Singh's Estate Agents operates their petty cash system on a fortnightly basis using the imprest system with a float of £100. On 15 October 2006 there was an opening balance of £23.40 in the petty cash box. The following transactions took place during the period commencing 15 October 2006.

2006	£
Oct 15 Received amount from cashier to restore the imprest	
Oct 16 Envelopes and files (including VAT of £1.66)	11.66
Oct 17 Tea, coffee and milk (for clients no VAT)	7.40
Oct 18 Special delivery postage charges	8.60

	£
2006	
Oct 20 Office cleaner	20.00
Oct 20 Cleaning materials (including VAT 63p)	4.23
Oct 23 Received £3.50 from M Lloyd for sale of stationery (receipt no. 78)	
Oct 23 Postage stamps	7.00
Oct 25 Travel expenses	16.42
Oct 27 Flowers for reception (including VAT 74p)	4.99
Oct 28 Photocopying paper (including VAT £1.40)	9.40
Oct 31 Received cash to restore imprest	

Required:

(a) Enter the balance brought down and the cash received to restore the imprest on 15 October 2006 in the petty cash book page 33.

(b) Enter the above transactions into the petty cash book using the following analysis columns, VAT, postage, cleaning, travel expenses, stationery and sundry expenses. The next petty cash voucher number is 80.

(c) Total and balance the petty cash book on 31 October and bring down the balance on 1 November. Show the amount of cash received from the cashier to restore the imprest to £100.

17.3X   Jane Porter has recently introduced a petty cash book using the imprest system. The monthly imprest is £100. On 1 March 2005 the balance of petty cash in hand was £15.20 and on this day the imprest was restored when cash for the appropriate amount was given to the petty cash clerk.

During March the following petty cash vouchers were prepared:

Voucher Number	Date	Details
187	March 5	Travel expenses £8.90
188	March 8	Postage £4.75
189	March 11	Visitor's train fare £14.50
190	March 17	Stationery £14.40 *plus* VAT at 17.5%
191	March 23	Registration fee on parcel £8.84
192	March 27	Stationery items totalling £21.15 *including* VAT at 17.5%

Tasks:

(a) Enter the above petty cash vouchers into a petty cash book using the following analysis columns, travel expenses, postage, stationery and VAT. Total the analysis columns on 31 March. Balance the petty cash book on 31 March and bring down the balance.

(b) List the main items of information that should be found on a petty cash voucher.

(c) Explain why it is important for the petty cash clerk to keep all petty cash vouchers.

Southern Examining Group AQA

Please note that this question is NOT from the live examinations for the current specification.

17.4   You work for S Dickinson (Estate Agents) as a receptionist, although some of your duties include administration tasks and dealing with the firm's petty cash, which is operated using the imprest system. A float of £120 is used by the firm for petty cash and this is given to you on 1 March.

Required:

(a) From the following petty cash vouchers (Exhibit 17.7), you are required to enter them in the petty cash book using analysis columns as you think appropriate. Balance off at the end of the month and obtain cash to restore the imprest from Ms Dickinson.

Exhibit 17.7

No	1

Petty Cash Voucher

Date _2/3/2009_

For what required	Amount	
	£	p
Postage Stamps	6	50
	6	50

Signature _A. Bond_
Passed by _SMD_

No	2

Petty Cash Voucher

Date _3rd March 2009_

For what required	Amount	
	£	p
Second-class rail fare to Stourbridge	23	—
	23	—

Signature _G. Jones_
Passed by _SMD_

No	3

Petty Cash Voucher

Date _7th March 2009_

For what required	Amount	
	£	p
Parcel Post to London	4	—
	4	—

Signature _A. Bond_
Passed by _SMD_

No	4

Petty Cash Voucher

Date _9th March 2009_

For what required	Amount	
	£	p
Window cleaning	8	—
	8	—

Signature _C. Cotton_
Passed by _SMD_

No	5

Petty Cash Voucher

Date _12th March 2009_

For what required	Amount	
	£	p
Envelopes	2	64
VAT		46
	3	10

Signature _A. Bond_
Passed by _SMD_

No	6

Petty Cash Voucher

Date _14th March 2009_

For what required	Amount	
	£	p
Tea etc (Hospitality)	6	40
	6	40

Signature _A. Bond_
Passed by _SMD_

Exhibit 17.7 (continued)

No	7

Petty Cash Voucher

Date _16th March 2009_

For what required	Amount	
	£	p
Petrol (including VAT)	10	—
	10	—

Signature _G. Jones_

Passed by _SMD_

No	8

Petty Cash Voucher

Date _19th March 2009_

For what required	Amount	
	£	p
Computer Discs	11	06
VAT @ 17.5%	1	94
	13	—

Signature _S. Dickinson_

Passed by _SMD_

No	9

Petty Cash Voucher

Date _20 March 2009_

For what required	Amount	
	£	p
Dusters & Polish	1	47
17.5% VAT		26
	1	73

Signature _J. Pratt_

Passed by _SMD_

No	10

Petty Cash Voucher

Date _23 March 2009_

For what required	Amount	
	£	p
Postage Stamps	2	40
	2	40

Signature _A. Bond_

Passed by _SMD_

No	11

Petty Cash Voucher

Date _27th March 2009_

For what required	Amount	
	£	p
Payment of creditors:- J. Cheetham (A/c No C44)	7	30
	7	30

Signature _S. Dickinson_

Passed by _SMD_

No	12

Petty Cash Voucher

Date _31st March 2009_

For what required	Amount	
	£	p
Magazines, Newspapers etc. (for reception)	6	40
	6	40

Signature _A. Bond_

Passed by _SMD_

(b) Post the petty cash expense columns to the accounts in the general ledger and enter the cash obtained to restore the imprest in the cash book.

(c) What are the advantages to using the imprest system? Draft a short memo outlining these to Ms Dickinson.

(NVQ Level 2)

17.5X You are employed as junior accountant's assistant of Morridge Products Ltd and one of your main tasks is that of petty cashier. The company uses an analytical petty cash book with columns for travelling expenses, postage, stationery, cleaning, sundry expenses and VAT, and they operate the imprest system.

Required:

(a) On 1 January 2006 the company's accountant, Mr Brammer, restores the petty cash float to £100 and gives you the petty cash vouchers shown in Exhibit 17.8. You are required to enter them in the petty cash book, balance off the book at the end of January, and obtain reimbursement from Mr Brammer to restore the imprest.

(b) Mr Brammer is anxious for you to become involved with all the financial aspects of the business and would like you to complete the book-keeping entries by posting the totals of the 'petty cash analysis columns' to the relevant accounts in the general ledger.

(c) Unfortunately, you have to go in hospital for a few days and will probably be absent from work for a couple of weeks. Mr Brammer asks you to write out a set of instructions in note form on the operation of the petty cash book as Jenny Cadwaller, his secretary, will be taking over in your absence. Ensure the instructions are clear, concise and easy to follow.

(NVQ Level 2)

Exhibit 17.8

No	1

Petty Cash Voucher

Date _1st Jan 2006_

For what required	Amount	
	£	p
Travelling Expenses to Crewe	5	36
	5	36

Signature _Jim Steadman_
Passed by _G Brammer_

No	2

Petty Cash Voucher

Date _5 Jan 2006_

For what required	Amount	
	£	p
Office Cleaning	10	—
	10	—

Signature _A. Duffy_
Passed by _G. Brammer_

No	3

Petty Cash Voucher

Date _9 Jan 2006_

For what required	Amount	
	£	p
Parcel to Northampton	1	98
	1	98

Signature _Tom Finikin_
Passed by _G Brammer_

No	4

Petty Cash Voucher

Date _10 Jan 2006_

For what required	Amount	
	£	p
Milk & Coffee for Office	6	50
	6	50

Signature _J. Cadwaller_
Passed by _G. Brammer_

No	5

Petty Cash Voucher

Date _12 Jan 2006_

For what required	Amount	
	£	p
Air-mail Stationery	7	15
VAT	1	25
	8	40

Signature _J. Cadwaller_
Passed by _G. Brammer_

No	6

Petty Cash Voucher

Date _15 Jan 2006_

For what required	Amount	
	£	p
Light Bulbs & 3 plugs.	3	64
VAT		64
	4	28

Signature _Tom Finikin_
Passed by _G Brammer_

Exhibit 17.8 *(continued)*

No	7

Petty Cash Voucher

Date   *21 Jan 2006*

For what required	Amount	
	£	p
Office cleaning	20	—
	20	—

Signature   *A. Duffy*
Passed by   *G Brammer*

No	8

Petty Cash Voucher

Date   *22 Jan 2006*

For what required	Amount	
	£	p
1 Ream Copier Paper	4	30
+ VAT		75
	5	05

Signature   *J. Cadwaller*
Passed by   *G. Brammer*

No	9

Petty Cash Voucher

Date   *24 Jan 2006*

For what required	Amount	
	£	p
Car Allowance: Manchester – Visiting Customer	15	—
	15	—

Signature   *J. Steadman*
Passed by   *G. Brammer*

No	10

Petty Cash Voucher

Date   *24 Jan 2006*

For what required	Amount	
	£	p
Financial Times & Economist for Reception	2	10
	2	10

Signature   *J. Cadwaller*
Passed by   *G Brammer*

No	11

Petty Cash Voucher

Date   *30 Jan 2006*

For what required	Amount	
	£	p
Milk	1	50
	1	50

Signature   *P. Fisher*
Passed by   *G. Brammer*

No	12

Petty Cash Voucher

Date   *31 Jan 2006*

For what required	Amount	
	£	p
First Class Stamps	4	80
	4	80

Signature   *J. Cadwaller*
Passed by   *G. Brammer*

17.6X (*a*) Why do some businesses keep a petty cash book as well as a cash book?

(*b*) List *three* items of information that must appear on a petty cash voucher.

(*c*) Give *one* reason why many businesses use the imprest system for recording petty cash.

(*d*) Jenny Clare keeps her petty cash book on the imprest system, the imprest being £50. For the month of February 2004, her petty cash transactions were as follows:

		£
Feb 1	Petty cash balance	10.50
2	Petty cashier presented vouchers to cashier and obtained cash to restore the imprest	39.50
5	Bought petrol	10.00
8	Bought envelopes	2.50
12	Paid to Mary Kenny, a creditor	3.16
15	Paid bus fares	0.85
20	Bought book of ten first class stamps at 26p each	2.60
24	Received cash for personal telephone call	0.90
27	Bought petrol	15.00

(i) Enter the above transactions in a petty cash book with analysis columns for Travelling Expenses, Postage and Stationery, and Ledger Accounts. Then balance the petty cash book at 28 February, bringing down the balance on 1 March.

(ii) On 1 March Jenny Clare received an amount of cash from the cashier to restore the imprest. Enter this transaction in the petty cash book.

(*e*) Open the ledger accounts to complete the double entry for the following:

(i) the petty cash analysis columns headed *Postage and Stationery* and *Travelling Expenses*;

(ii) the transactions dated 12 and 24 February 2004.

NEAB (GCSE)

Capital and revenue expenditures

After you have studied this chapter you should be able to:

- distinguish between expenditure that is capital in nature and that which is revenue
- understand that some expenditure is part capital expenditure and part revenue expenditure
- realise the effect on the final accounts, and the profits shown there, if revenue expenditure is wrongly treated as being capital expenditure, and vice versa.

18.1 Introduction

This chapter will deal with the distinction between capital and revenue expenditure and show the importance of careful classification, which can ultimately affect the recorded profits and the balance sheet valuations of a business.

18.2 Capital expenditure

Capital expenditure is expenditure on the purchase of fixed assets or of additions to existing fixed assets. Fixed assets, you will remember from Chapter 9 are those assets that have an expected life of greater than one year and are used in the business to enable it to generate income and, ultimately, profit. Examples include:

- premises, land and buildings
- machinery, plant and equipment
- office and computer equipment
- furniture and fittings.

Additions to existing fixed assets should also be classified as capital expenditure, and examples include:

- purchasing a scanner for the computer
- adding extra storage capacity to a mainframe computer
- expenses incurred in updating machinery to increase production
- additional shelving and fittings in a retail store.

It is important to include the following items of expenditure when fixed assets are purchased:

- the cost of acquiring the fixed assets
- the cost of delivery of the assets to the firm
- legal costs of buying premises, land and buildings
- installation costs
- architects' fees for building plans and for supervising the construction of buildings
- demolition costs to remove obsolete buildings before new work can begin.

18.3 Revenue expenditure

Revenue expenditure is expenditure that does not increase the value of fixed assets but is incurred in the day-to-day running expenses of the business.

The difference from capital expenditure can be seen when considering the cost of running a motor vehicle for a business. The expenditure incurred in acquiring the motor vehicle is classed as capital expenditure, while the cost of the petrol used to run the vehicle is revenue expenditure. This is because the revenue expenditure is used up in a few days and does not add to the value of the fixed asset.

18.4 Difference between capital and revenue expenditure

The difference between capital and revenue expenditure can be seen more generally in the following table (Exhibit 18.1). Revenue expenditure is the day-to-day running expense of the business and, as such, is chargeable to the trading and profit and loss account. Capital expenditure, in contrast, results in an increase in the fixed assets shown in the balance sheet.

Exhibit 18.1

Capital	Revenue
Premises purchased	Rent of premises
Legal charges for conveyancing	Legal charges for debt collection
New machinery	Repairs to machinery
Installations of machinery	Electricity costs of using machinery
Additions to assets	Maintenance of assets
Motor vehicles	Current Road Fund Tax
Delivery charges on new assets	Carriage on purchases and sales
Extension costs of new offices	Redecorating existing offices
Cost of adding air-conditioning to room	Interest on loan to purchase air-conditioning

18.5 Joint expenditure

In certain cases, an item of expenditure will need dividing between capital and revenue expenditure. Suppose a builder was engaged to carry out some work on your premises, the total bill being £30,000. If one-third of this was for repair work and two-thirds for improvements, then £10,000 should be charged to the profit and loss account as revenue expenditure, and £20,000 should be identified as capital expenditure and added to the value of the firm's premises and shown as such in the balance sheet.

18.6 Incorrect treatment of expenditure

If one of the following occurs:

● capital expenditure is incorrectly treated as revenue expenditure, or
● revenue expenditure is incorrectly treated as capital expenditure,

then both the balance sheet figures and trading and profit and loss account figures will be incorrect. This means that the net profit figure will also be incorrect.

If capital expenditure is incorrectly posted to revenue expenditure – for example, if the purchase of a photocopier is posted in error to the stationery account instead of the office equipment account – then:

> **Net profit** would be understated, *and*
> **Balance sheet** values would not include the value of the asset.

If revenue expenditure is incorrectly posted to capital expenditure – for example if stationery is posted to office equipment instead of the stationery account – then:

> **Net profit** would be overstated, *and*
> **Balance sheet** values would be over-valued.

If the expenditure affects items in the trading account, then the **gross profit** figure will also be incorrect.

18.7 Treatment of loan interest

If money is borrowed to finance the purchase of a fixed asset, then interest will have to be paid on the loan. The loan interest, however, is *not* a cost of acquiring the asset but is simply a cost of financing its acquisition. This means that loan interest is revenue expenditure and *not* capital expenditure, and should be charged to the profit and loss account.

18.8 Capital and revenue receipts

When an item of capital expenditure is sold, the receipt is called a capital receipt. Suppose a motor van is bought for £10,000, and sold five years later for £2,000. The £10,000 was treated as capital expenditure; the £2,000 received is treated as a capital receipt.

Revenue receipts are sales or other revenue items, such as rent receivable or commissions receivable.

Chapter summary

- The distinction between capital and revenue expenditure is explained and how important it is to classify items carefully since this can ultimately affect the recording of profits and the balance sheet valuations of a business.
- Capital expenditure is money spent on the purchase of fixed assets or additions to existing assets. They are usually purchased to be retained in the business to enable it to generate profits.
- Revenue expenditure is money spent on day-to-day running expenses of the business.
- Some items are both capital and revenue expenditure and the costs involved need to be apportioned carefully.
- If capital expenditure or revenue expenditure is mistaken one for the other, then either gross or net profit (or both) will be incorrectly stated. The value of the assets in the balance sheet will also be affected.
- It is also important to classify capital receipts, i.e. the sale of a fixed asset, from revenue receipts which are accounted for from sales or other revenue items.

Exercises

18.1 Newton Data Systems specialises in providing computer services to small commercial businesses.

You are required to state whether the following transactions should be classified as capital or revenue expenditure, giving reasons for your choice:

(*a*) Salaries of the computer operators.
(*b*) Purchase of new computer for use in the office.
(*c*) Purchase of computer printout paper.
(*d*) Insurance of all the company's computer hardware.
(*e*) Cost of adding additional storage capacity to a mainframe computer to be used by the company.
(*f*) Cost of providing additional security to the company's offices.

18.2 Cairns Engineering Company extracted the following information from their financial records:

	£
(*a*) New stationery and brochures	411
(*b*) Purchase of new pickup truck	18,000
(*c*) Purchase of new lathe	5,200
(*d*) Delivery cost of new lathe	200
(*e*) Electricty (including new wiring £1,800, part of premises improvement)	3,900
(*f*) Wages (including wages of two of Cairn's employees for improvement work on Cairns premises, amount involved £20,000)	65,000

You are required to:
- State whether each of the items listed above are capital or revenue expenditure and state how much the company has spent on each category for the year.
- Briefly explain the difference between capital and revenue expenditure.

18.3X (*a*) Star Fashions Ltd, which manufactures children's clothing, is planning to purchase a new cutting machine costing £20,000. Would the following items of expenditure be classed as capital or revenue expenditure?
  (i)   The purchase price of the cutting machine.
  (ii) The cost of installing the machine.
  (iii) The significant cost of initial training for the staff to operate the new machine.
  (iv) The cost of future repairs and maintenance of the machine.
(*b*) If capital expenditure is treated as revenue expenditure, then:
  (i)   How would the total expenses and the net profit for the period be affected?
  (ii) What effect would the error have on the value of the fixed assets in the balance sheet?

18.4 T Taylor has drawn up his final accounts for the year ended 31 December 2008. On examining them, you find that:

(*a*) Taylor has debited the cost of office equipment £311 to the purchases account.
(*b*) Taylor has debited the cost of repairing office equipment £290 to the motor repairs account.
(*c*) Sale of a building for £10,000 has been credited to the sales account.
(*d*) Repayment of a loan £500 has been debited to the loan interest account.

From his figures he had calculated gross profit as £95,620 and net profit as £28,910.
 Ignoring any adjustments for depreciation, calculate revised figures of gross and net profits after taking (*a*) to (*d*) into account.

18.5X S Simpson has calculated her gross profit for the year to 30 June 2006 as £129,450 and her net profit as £77,270. You find that Simpson's books show:

(*a*) Sale of a motor vehicle for £4,100 has been credited to the sales account.
(*b*) Fixtures, bought for £750, have been debited to the repairs account.
(*c*) Receipt of a loan for £6,000 has been credited to the sales account.
(*d*) Repairs to motor vehicles £379 have been debited to the general expenses account.

Ignoring any adjustments for depreciation, calculate the revised figures of gross and net profits.

18.6X A business has incorrectly charged some of its expenditure in its final accounts. The incorrect figures shown were as follows:

(*a*) Gross profit £216,290
(*b*) Net profit £110,160
(*c*) Fixed assets £190,000
(*d*) Current assets £77,600.

Required:
You are to show, for each of the following, the effects on the calculations of (*a*) gross profit, (*b*) net profit, (*c*) fixed assets in the balance sheet and (*d*) current assets in the balance sheet. (Ignore depreciation.)

(i)   Motor van costing £5,500 debited to motor expenses account.
(ii) Carriage outwards £77 debited to fixtures account.
(iii) Rent £2,000 debited to buildings account.
(iv) Machinery £6,000 debited to fixtures account.
(v)   Office equipment £790 debited to purchases account.
(vi) Discounts allowed £2,380 debited to machinery account.

18.7X (a) For each of the following transactions place *one* tick (✓) in the appropriate column to indicate whether the item is an example of capital expenditure, revenue expenditure, revenue receipt or capital receipt.

Transaction (i) is done as an example for you.

Transaction	Capital expenditure	Capital receipt	Revenue expenditure	Revenue receipt
(i) Purchase of goods for resale			✓	
(ii) Rent received for office sub-let				
(iii) Purchase of stationery for office use				
(iv) Sale of old equipment no longer required				
(v) Cost of building an extension to premises				
(vi) Sale of stock				
(vii) Repairs to existing premises				

(b) How should items of capital expenditure be treated when preparing final accounts?

NEAB (GCSE)

The sales day book, sales ledger, related documentation and other considerations

Learning objectives

After you have studied this chapter you should be able to:

- distinguish between a cash sale and a credit sale and the way each are recorded in the books of account
- prepare a sales invoice and appreciate the need for copy invoices
- enter invoices into the sales day book and post transactions to the appropriate accounts in the sales ledger and general ledger
- explain the difference between trade discount and cash discounts and understand the treatment of each in the books of account
- appreciate documentation used in the sale of goods
- understand the importance of internal control
- understand terms and abbreviations used in trading activity
- appreciate the need for credit control over debtors.

19.1 Introduction

In Chapter 12, Books of original entry and ledgers, we discussed the growth of a business. As a business expands additional accounting record books are required to enable the system of recording transactions to be made easier and more efficient. You may remember that a 'book of original entry' is where a transaction is first recorded. All transactions that are entered into the book-keeping system originate from a 'source document' such as an invoice, credit note, cheque book stub, paying-in slip and so on. In the next four chapters we will be looking at invoices and credit notes that are raised when goods or services are sold to customers and perhaps returned if a problem arises with the goods when a credit note would be issued.

In Chapter 16, Value added tax, it was shown that certain types of goods and/or services sold are subject to VAT, others were zero-rated and some exempt. Businesses were also categorised into standard-rated, exempt, partly exempt and zero-rated businesses. In this and the next two chapters we will assume that the sales and purchases are not subject to VAT to enable you to understand the book-keeping entries more easily. In Chapter 22, Analytical sales and purchases day books, you will learn how to account for VAT on sales and purchases.

19.2   Cash sales

When goods are purchased by a customer who pays for them immediately by cash then there is no necessity to enter the sale of these goods into the sales day book or the sales ledger since the customer is not in debt to the business. Keeping details of these customers' names and addresses is, therefore, not needed.

19.3   Credit sales

In many businesses most of the sales will be made on credit rather than for cash. In fact, the sales of some businesses or organisations will consist entirely of credit sales.

For each credit sale the supplier will send a document to the buyer showing details and prices of the goods sold. This document is known as a sales invoice to the supplier and a purchase invoice to the buyer. An example of an invoice was shown in Chapter 16 in Exhibit 16.1; a further example is now shown in Exhibit 19.1.

Exhibit 19.1

Your Purchase Order 10/A/980		J Blake
Invoice No: 16554	**INVOICE**	7 Over Warehouse Leicester LE1 2AP
To: D Poole & Co		1 September 2005
Deansgate Restaurant		
45 Charles Street		
Manchester M1 5ZN		

Quantity and description	Per unit	Total
	£	£
21 cases Cape Glory Pears	20	420
5 cartons Kay's Flour	4	20
6 cases Joy's Sauce	20	120
		560
Terms: 1¼% cash discount if paid within one month		

Most businesses have individually designed invoices but inevitably they follow a generally accepted accounting format. All invoices will be numbered and contain the names and addresses of both the supplier and the customer. In Exhibit 19.1 the supplier is J Blake and the customer is D Poole & Co.

19.4   Copies of sales invoices

Once the goods have been despatched to the buyer a **sales invoice** is made out by the supplier. The top copy of the sales invoice is sent to the buyer, further copies are retained by the supplier for use within the organisation. For example, one copy is usually sent to the accounts department to enable the sale of goods on credit to be recorded in the sales day book and sales ledger, another copy may be passed to the sales department and so on.

19.5 Entering credit sales into the sales day book

As mentioned above, a copy of the sales invoice is passed to the accounts department where the supplier enters this into the sales day book. This book is merely a list, showing the following:

● date of sale
● name of customer to whom the goods have been sold
● invoice number
● final amount of invoice.

There is no need to show details of the goods sold in the sales day book. This can be found by looking at copy invoices.

Exhibit 19.2 shows a **sales day book**, which illustrates how the invoices are entered starting with the entry of the invoice shown in Exhibit 19.1. Assume that the entries are on page 26 of the day book.

Exhibit 19.2

Sales Day Book		*(page 26)*
	Invoice No	*Amount* *£*
2005		
Sept 1 D Poole & Co	16554	560
8 T Cockburn	16555	1,640
28 C Carter	16556	220
30 D Stevens & Co	16557	1,100
		3,520

19.6 Posting credit sales to the sales ledger

Instead of having one ledger for all accounts, a sales ledger is used for recording credit sale transactions.

1 The credit sales are now posted, one by one, to the **debit** side of each customer's account in the sales ledger.
2 At the end of each period, the total of the credit sales is posted to the **credit** of the sales account in the general ledger.

It may be easier to use 'IN' and 'OUT', as shown in Chapter 3, to post these transactions; i.e. the goods sold go 'into' each individual customer's account and they come 'out' of the sales account. This is now illustrated in Exhibit 19.3.

Exhibit 19.3 Posting Credit Sales

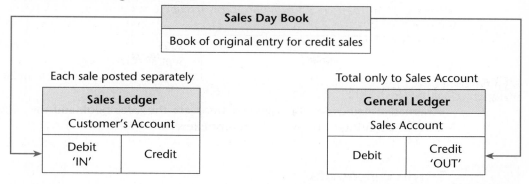

19.7 An example of posting credit sales

The sales day book in Exhibit 19.2 is now shown again. This time posting is made to the sales ledger and the general ledger. Notice the completion of the folio columns with the reference numbers.

Sales Day Book			(page 26)
	Invoice No	Folio	Amount £
2005			
Sept 1 D Poole & Co	16554	SL 12	560
8 T Cockburn	16555	SL 39	1,640
28 C Carter	16556	SL 125	220
30 D Stevens & Co	16557	SL 249	1,100
Transferred to Sales Account		GL 44	3,520

Sales Ledger
D Poole & Co Account (page 12)

Dr				Cr
2005	Folio	£		
Sept 1 Sales	SB 26	560		

T Cockburn Account (page 39)

Dr				Cr
2005	Folio	£		
Sept 8 Sales	SB 26	1,640		

C Carter Account (page 125)

Dr				Cr
2005	Folio	£		
Sept 28 Sales	SB 26	220		

D Stevens & Co Account (page 249)

Dr				Cr
2005	Folio	£		
Sept 30 Sales	SB 26	1,100		

General Ledger

Sales Account   *(page 44)*

Dr   Cr

	2005	Folio	£
	Sept 30 Credit Sales		
	for the month	SB 26	3,520

Alternative names for the sales day book are the sales book and the sales journal. Before you continue, you should attempt Exercise 19.1.

19.8 Trade discounts

Suppose you are the proprietor of a business. You are selling to three different kinds of customers:

1 traders who buy many goods from you
2 traders who buy only a few items from you
3 direct to the general public.

The traders themselves have to sell the goods to the general public in their own areas. They have to make a profit, so they will want to pay you less than the retail price.

The traders who buy in large quantities will not want to pay as much as traders who buy in small quantities. You want to attract large customers, and so you are happy to sell to them at a lower price.

This means that your selling prices are at three levels:

1 to traders buying large quantities
2 to traders buying small quantities
3 to the general public.

So that your staff do not need three different price lists, all goods are shown on your price lists at the same price. However, a reduction (discount), called a **trade discount** is given to traders 1 and 2. An example illustrating this is shown in Exhibit 19.4.

Exhibit 19.4

You are selling a particular make of food mixing machine. The retail price is £200. Traders **1** are given 25 per cent trade discount, traders **2**, 20 per cent and the general public who pay the full retail price. The prices paid by each type of customer would be:

		Trader 1 £		Trader 2 £	General public 3 £
Retail price		200		200	200
Less Trade discount	(25%)	50	(20%)	40	nil
Price to be paid by customer		150		160	200

Exhibit 19.5 is an invoice for goods supplied by R Grant (Catering Supplies) to D Poole & Co. The items supplied by R Grant (Catering Supplies) are the same as supplied by J Blake – see Exhibit 19.1; however, you will notice that R Grant (Catering Supplies) uses **trade discounts** to encourage customers to buy from him.

By comparing Exhibits 19.1 and 19.5 you can see that the prices paid by D Poole & Co were the same. It is simply the method of calculating the price that is different.

Exhibit 19.5

INVOICE

R GRANT (CATERING SUPPLIES)
HIGHER SIDE PRESTON PR1 2NL

Telephone: (01703) 33122
Fax: (01703) 22331

D Poole & Co
Deansgate Restaurant
45 Charles Street
Manchester M1 5ZN

Invoice No 30756
Account No P/4298
Date: 1 September 2005

Your Purchase Order 11/A/G80

Quantity	Per unit	Total
	£	£
21 cases Cape Glory Pears	25	525
5 cartons Kay's Flour	5	25
6 cases Joy's Sauce	25	150
		700
Less 20% Trade Discount		140
		560

19.9 Trade discounts and cash discounts compared

As trade discount is simply a way of calculating sales prices, no entry for a trade discount should be made in the double entry records nor in the sales day book.

The recording of Exhibit 19.5 in R Grant's (Catering Supplies) sales day book and D Poole's personal account will appear thus:

Sales Day Book			(page 87)
	Invoice No	Folio	Amount
2005			£
Sept 2 D Poole & Co	30756	SL 32	560

Sales Ledger
D Poole & Co Account (page 32)

Dr				Cr
2005	Folio	£		
Sept 2 Sales	SB 87	560		

To compare with cash discounts:

● trade discounts are not shown in double entry accounts
● cash discounts *are* shown in double entry accounts.

19.10 Other documentation

Each firm will have its own system of making out documents. All but the very smallest organisations will have their documents prepared via computer.

The sales invoice is the document from which the book-keeping records are prepared. There will usually be several other documents prepared at the same time, so that the firm may properly organise the sending of the goods and ensuring that they are safely received. These extra documents may be as set out next.

Advice note

Advice notes will be sent to the customer before the goods are dispatched. This means that the customer will know that the goods are on the way and when they should arrive. If the goods do not arrive within a reasonable time, the customer will notify the seller so that enquiries may be made with the carrier to establish what has happened to the goods.

The document will look something like that shown in Exhibit 19.6. Compare it with the invoice sent out as Exhibit 19.5.

Exhibit 19.6

ADVICE NOTE	R GRANT (CATERING SUPPLIES) Higher Side Preston PR1 2NL	No 178554 Tel (01703) 33122 Fax (01703) 22331
30 August 2005		

J. Jones, Head Buyer
D Poole & Co
Deansgate Restaurant
45 Charles Street
Manchester M1 5ZN

Your order No 11/A/G80
Despatch details: 27 cases and 5 cartons

Quantity	Cat No	Description	Price
21 cases	M566	Cape Glory Pears	£25 each
5 cartons	K776	Kay's Flour	£5 each
6 cases	J865	Joy's Sauce	£25 each
			All less 20%

Delivery to:
   D Poole & Co, Warehouse 2,
   Longmills Trading Estate, Manchester M14 2TT

Delivery note

When goods are sent out, they usually have a delivery note to accompany them. This means that the customer can check immediately, and easily, what goods are being received. Very often, a copy will be retained by the carrier, with the customer having to sign to say that the goods have been received as stated on the note.

In connection with the goods shown on the advice note in Exhibit 19.6 a delivery note may appear as in Exhibit 19.7.

Exhibit 19.7

DELIVERY NOTE	R GRANT (CATERING SUPPLIES)	No 194431
	Higher Side	
	Preston	Tel (01703) 33122
11 September 2005	PR1 2NL	Fax (01703) 22331

J. Jones, Head Buyer
D Poole & Co
Deansgate Restaurant
45 Charles Street
Manchester M1 5ZN

Order No 11/A/G80
Despatch details: 27 cases, 5 cartons by road

Quantity	Cat No	Details
21 cases	M566	Cape Glory Pears
5 cartons	K776	Kay's Flour
6 cases	J865	Joy's Sauce

Delivery to: Warehouse 2, Longmills Trading Estate,
Manchester M14 2TT

Received 27 cases and 5 cartons

Signed   ....

On behalf of   ....

Other documents

Each firm may vary in the type and number of documents used. Some of these other documents may be:

● *Dispatch notes* These will resemble delivery notes, and are used by the despatch department.
● *Acknowledgement letters* These may be sent to customers to show that their orders have been received, and whether delivery will be made as per the order.

19.11 Manufacturer's recommended retail price

Looking at an item displayed in a shop window, you will frequently see something like the following:

Wide Screen TV:	Manufacturer's Recommended Retail Price	£500
	Less discount of 20 per cent	£100
	You pay only	£400

Very often the manufacturer's recommended retail price is a figure above what the manufacturer would expect the public to pay for its product. Probably, in the case shown, the manufacturer would have expected the public to pay around £400 for its product.

The inflated figure used for the 'manufacturer's recommended retail price' is simply a sales gimmick. Most people like to feel they are getting a bargain. The salesmen know that someone would usually prefer to get '20 per cent off' and pay £400, rather than for the price simply be shown as £400 with no mention of a discount.

19.12   Credit control

Any organisation that sells goods on credit should keep a close check to ensure that debtors pay their accounts on time. If this is not done properly, the amount of debtors can grow to a level that will make the business short of cash. Businesses that grow too short of cash will fail, no matter how profitable they may be.

The following four procedures should be carried out:

1 For each debtor, a credit limit should be set and the debtor should not be allowed to owe more than this limit. The amount of the limit will depend on the circumstances. Such things as the size of the customer's firm and the amount of business done with it, as well as its past record of payments, will help in choosing the limit figure. Credit rating agencies may be used to assess the credit worthiness of customers before credit is granted.
2 As soon as the payment date has been reached, check to see whether payment has been made or not. Failure to pay on time may mean you refuse to supply any more goods unless payment is made quickly.
3 Where payment is not forthcoming, after investigation it may be necessary to take legal action to sue the customer for the debt. This will depend on the circumstances.
4 It is important that customers are made aware of what will happen if they do not pay their account by the due date.

19.13   Internal checks

When sales invoices are being made out, they should be scrutinised very carefully. A system is usually set up so that each stage of the preparation of the invoice is checked by someone other than the person whose job it is to send out the invoice. If this was not done, it would be possible for someone inside a firm to send out an invoice, as an instance, at a price less than the true price. Any difference could then be split between that person and someone outside the firm. If an invoice should have been sent to Ivor Twister & Co for £2,000, but the invoice clerk deliberately made it out for £200, then, if there was no cross-check, the difference of £1,800 could be split between the invoice clerk and Ivor Twister & Co.

Similarly, outside firms could send invoices for goods that were never received by the firm. This might be in collaboration with an employee within the firm, but there are firms sending false invoices that rely on the firms receiving them being inefficient and paying for items never received. There have certainly been firms sending invoices for such items as advertisements that have never been published. The cashier of the firm receiving the invoice, if the firm is an inefficient one, might possibly think that someone in the firm had authorised the advertisements and would pay the bill. Besides these cases, there are, of course, genuine errors, and these should also be detected.

A system therefore needs to be set up whereby the invoices have to be subject to scrutiny, at each stage, by someone other than the person who sends out the invoices or is responsible for paying them. Naturally, in a small firm – simply because the number of office staff might be few – this cross-check may be in the hands of only one person other than the person who will pay it.

A similar sort of check will be made in respect of sales invoices being sent out.

19.14 Factoring

One of the problems that face many businesses is the time taken by debtors to pay their accounts. Few businesses have so much cash available to them that they do not mind how long the debtor takes to pay. It is a fact that many businesses that become bankrupt do so, not because the business is not making profits, but because the business has run out of cash funds. Once that happens, the confidence factor in business evaporates, and the business then finds that very few people will supply it with goods, and it also cannot pay its employees. Closure of the firm then generally happens fairly quickly.

In the case of debtors, the cash problem may be alleviated by using the services of a financial intermediary called a 'factor'. **Factoring** is a financial service designed to improve the cash flow of healthy, growing companies, enabling them to make better use of management time and the money tied up in trade credit to customers. In essence, factors provide their clients with three closely integrated services, covering sales accounting and collection, credit management (which can include protection against bad debts), and the availability of finance against sales invoices.

19.15 Slip system

Some organisations avoid using day books by using the **slip system**. This involves putting information such as lists of invoices in 'slip' form, which can then be entered directly into the ledger accounts. The entry into the appropriate day book is thus eliminated.

For instance, banks use the slip system, whereby a customer makes out a paying-in slip to pay money into his or her account, and the slip is then used to enter the details of the transaction and become the documentary evidence.

Nowadays, with most organisations using computerised accounting systems, invoices tend to be collated into batches prior to entry. The invoices are then entered directly onto the system and the total checked, with the slip, prior to processing the invoices by computer.

The advantages of the slip system are that:

● it is easy to operate
● it is quicker than using day books
● it minimizes the risk of error, i.e. batch totals should be verified before processing when using a computerised system of accounting.

The disadvantages are:

● if invoices are lost, this can cause problems
● fraud is made easier to get away with
● it is not easy to analyse items, e.g. sales of different kinds of goods.

19.16　Abbreviations

Business documents frequently contain abbreviations and terms of trade, the most common of which are as follows:

● **Carriage paid** Another word for carriage is transport costs. Thus 'carriage paid' indicates that the cost of transport has been included in the cost of the goods.
● **COD** This abbreviation stands for 'cash on delivery' and means that the goods must be paid for on delivery.
● **E & OE** On some invoices and other documents you will see the initials 'E & OE' printed at the bottom of the invoice. This abbreviation stands for 'errors and omissions excepted'. Basically, this is a warning that there may possibly be errors or omissions, which could mean that the figures shown are incorrect, and that the recipient should check the figures carefully before taking any action concerning them.
● **Ex works** An indication that the price of the goods does not include delivery costs.
● **Net monthly** This phrase frequently appears at the foot of an invoice and means that the full amount of the invoice is due for payment within one month of the date of the invoice.

Chapter summary

● When goods/services are sold for cash it is not necessary to enter the details into the sales day book and sales ledger since the customer is not in debt to the business.
● When goods/services are sold on credit then an invoice will need to be prepared and sent to the buyer. This document is known as a sales invoice to the supplier and a purchase invoice to the buyer. Several copies of the invoice are usually made to enable the accounts staff to record the sale in the books of account, other copies may be required for internal use.
● Sales invoices are a 'source document' and are entered into the sales day book which is a book of original entry. They are then posted to each individual customer's account in the sales ledger. At the end of the period total sales will be posted to the sales account in the general ledger.

- Trade discount is a discount or reduction given to a customer when calculating the price of goods. No entry is made of trade discount in the accounting records.
- Other documentation involved in the selling process include an advice note, delivery note, dispatch note and acknowledgement letters.
- The importance of credit control to ensure that the business maintains a healthy cash flow.
- Other areas that are important include the checking of invoices prior to entry into the books of account and before payment is made.
- Factoring is offered to businesses to help improve their cash flow. This involves 'selling' its debtors to a factoring company who then become responsible for collecting debts as they become due. The company retains a percentage of the amount collected for their services.
- An alternative to entering items into the sales day book would be to use the slip system.

Exercises

19.1 You are to enter up the sales day book from the following details. Post the items to the relevant accounts in the sales ledger and then show the transfer to the sales account in the general ledger.

2006
Mar 1	Credit sales to J Gordon	£187
Mar 3	Credit sales to G Abrahams	£166
Mar 6	Credit sales to V White	£12
Mar 10	Credit sales to J Gordon	£55
Mar 17	Credit sales to F Williams	£289
Mar 19	Credit sales to C Richards	£66
Mar 27	Credit sales to V Wood	£28
Mar 31	Credit sales to L Simes	£78

19.2X Enter up the sales day book from the following, then post the items to the relevant accounts in the sales ledger. Show the transfer to the sales account in the general ledger.

2006
May 1	Credit sales to J Johnson	£305
May 3	Credit sales to T Royes	£164
May 5	Credit sales to B Howe	£45
May 7	Credit sales to M Lee	£100
May 16	Credit sales to J Jakes	£308
May 23	Credit sales to A Vinden	£212
May 30	Credit sales to J Samuels	£1,296

19.3   During April 2006 the following credit sales were made by Dabell's Stationery Supplies Ltd:

Date	Debtor	Invoice no.	Amount
			£
1 April	Fisher & Co	6265	1,459
3 April	Elder (Office Supplies)	6266	73
5 April	Haigh (Mfr) Ltd	6267	56
11 April	Ardern & Co (Solicitors)	6268	1,598
15 April	I Rafiq	6269	540
20 April	Royle's Business Systems	6270	2,456
22 April	Fisher & Co	6271	23
22 April	Ardern & Co (Solicitors)	6272	345
25 April	Elder (Office Supplies)	6273	71
27 April	Haigh (Mfr) Ltd	6274	176

Required:

(*a*) Draw up a sales day book and enter the above invoices into the day book for the month of April 2006. The next sales day book page no. is 26.

(*b*) The sales ledger showed the following balances at 1 April 2006.

Customer	Amount outstanding	Sales ledger ref.
	£	
Ardern & Co (Solicitors)	472	SL1
Elder (Office Supplies)	75	SL2
Fisher & Co	231	SL3
Haigh (Mfr) Ltd	1,267	SL4
I Rafiq	330	SL5
Royle's Business Systems	750	SL6

Open an account for each of the firm's customers in the sales ledger and enter the balances outstanding on 1 April 2006.

(*c*) Post the sales invoices for the month of April to the appropriate ledger account in the sales ledger.

(*d*) During April the firm received cheques from Fisher & Co for £231, I Rafiq for £330 and £1,000 on account from Haigh (Mfr) Ltd. Post the cheques to the customer's accounts in the sales ledger.

(*e*) Balance each account off at the end of April and draw up a list of outstanding debtors.

19.4X   Morton's Garage is situated on the outskirts of Macclesfield and sells petrol and accessories in addition to carrying out repairs and maintenance on vehicles. At 1 January 2006 Morton's sales ledger showed the following balances on their customers' accounts:

	£	
C Crawford	1,078	Dr
S Brocklehurst	563	Dr
L Price & Partners	321	Dr
D Woolham & Co	146	Dr

During January 2006 the garage issued the following invoices in respect of credit sales of petrol, accessories and repairs.

2006	Invoice no.	Name	Amount
			£
2 Jan	37542	D Woolham & Co	230
6 Jan	37543	C Crawford	345
7 Jan	37544	S Brocklehurst	1,980
9 Jan	37545	L Price & Partners	523
13 Jan	37546	D Woolham & Co	56
18 Jan	37547	L Price & Partners	200
21 Jan	37548	C Crawford	340
24 Jan	37549	C Crawford	45
29 Jan	37550	S Brocklehurst	845
31 Jan	37551	L Price & Partners	721

On 31 January 2006 the garage proprietor, Mr Morton, received cheques from the following customers, who settled their account for the previous month:

Customer	Amount of cheque
	£
C Crawford	1,078
L Price & Partners	321
D Woolham & Co	146

Required:

Carry out the following tasks using your own reference numbers:

(a) Draw up a sales day book and enter the above invoices into the day book and total it for the month of January 2006.

(b) Open an account for each customer and enter the balances as at 1 January 2006. Post the sales from the day book to each account and the amounts received.

(c) Balance the customers' accounts at 31 January 2006 and bring down the balances.

(d) Post the total sales to the sales account in the general ledger.

19.5 Why is it important to ensure that sales invoices are thoroughly checked before being sent out to customers?

19.6 What is meant by the term 'factoring'?

CHAPTER 20

The purchases day book, purchases ledger and related documentation

Learning objectives

After you have studied this chapter you should be able to:

- prepare a purchase order
- enter purchase invoices into the purchases day book
- post the purchases day book to the purchase ledger
- authorise and code invoices for payment.

20.1 Purchase orders

When a business or organisation decides to buy goods or engage the services of another company, it usually issues a **purchase order**. Such a document contains the following information:

- name and address of supplier
- purchase order number
- date of order
- details of the goods or services ordered, including part numbers or catalogue references
- quantity required
- delivery date
- authorised signature of a senior member of the company such as the buyer.

Each purchase order is normally raised by the customer's purchasing office and then sent to the supplier. Once it has been accepted by the supplier a formal contract will exist between the two parties. An example of a purchase order is shown in Exhibit 20.1.

Exhibit 20.1 Purchase order

PURCHASE ORDER

Stoke Engineering Co Ltd
Blythe End Works
Stoke-on-Trent

Telephone: 01782 923116
Fax: 01782 923431
VAT Reg No: 964 7688 21

Order No: ST 6032
Date: 12 March 2006

Morridge Products Ltd
Moor Top Lane
Leek

Please supply the following:

120 off	Suspension arm	Part No B402	£38.50 each
60 off	Axle Shaft	Part No B424	£27.65 each
120 off	Backplate	Part No B432	£43.20 each

Delivery required: by end April 2006 to our works.
If there are any queries regarding this order please contact the undersigned immediately.

Signed *A Barton*
        Buyer

20.2 Purchase invoices

When organisations purchase goods or services from suppliers on credit they are sent a purchase invoice detailing the goods or services and their price.

In the previous chapter, Exhibit 19.1 showed an invoice raised by J Blake, the supplier, and sent to D Poole & Co, the buyer. The invoice is common to both parties since it details the goods supplied and the amount outstanding.

1 In the books of D Poole & Co it is a **purchase invoice**.
2 In the books of J Blake it is a **sales invoice**.

20.3 Making entries into the purchases day book

Upon receipt of the purchase invoice for goods and services supplied on credit, the purchaser enters the details in his purchase day book. This book is merely a list showing the following:

- date of purchase
- name of supplier from whom the goods were purchased
- reference number of the invoice
- final amount of invoice.

There is no need to show details of the goods bought in the purchases day book; this can be found by looking at the invoices themselves. Exhibit 20.2 is an example of a purchases day book.

Exhibit 20.2

Purchases Day Book			(page 49)
	Invoice No	Folio	Amount £
2006			
Sept 2 R Simpson	9/101		670
8 B Hamilton	9/102		1,380
19 C Brown	9/103		120
30 K Gabriel	9/104		510
			2,680

The purchases day book is often known also as the purchases book or the purchases journal.

20.4   Posting credit purchases to the purchases ledger

We now have a separate purchases ledger. The double entry is as follows:

● The credit purchases are posted one by one, to the **credit** of each supplier's account in the purchases ledger.
● At the end of each period, the total of the credit purchases is posted to the **debit** of the purchases account in the general ledger.

Again, you may find it easier to use 'IN' and 'OUT', as discussed in Chapters 3 and 19; i.e. the goods purchased come from each supplier and therefore their accounts are entered on the 'OUT' side. The total purchases for the period are then entered on the 'IN' side of the purchases account since the goods are coming 'IN' to us. This is illustrated in Exhibit 20.3.

Exhibit 20.3 Posting Credit Purchases

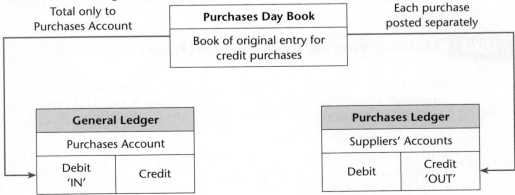

20.5 A worked example of posting credit purchases

The purchases day book in Exhibit 20.2 is shown again below. This time, posting is made to the purchases ledger and the general ledger. Notice the completion of the folio columns.

Purchases Day Book			(page 49)
2006	Invoice No	Folio	Amount £
Sept 2 R Simpson	9/101	PL 16	670
8 B Hamilton	9/102	PL 29	1,380
19 C Brown	9/103	PL 55	120
30 K Gabriel	9/104	PL 89	510
Transferred to purchases account		GL 63	2,680

Purchases Ledger

R Simpson Account

Dr (page 16) Cr

	2006	Folio	£
	Sept 2 Purchases	PB 49	670

B Hamilton Account

Dr (page 29) Cr

	2006	Folio	£
	Sept 8 Purchases	PB 49	1,380

C Brown Account

Dr (page 55) Cr

	2006	Folio	£
	Sept 19 Purchases	PB 49	120

K Gabriel Account

Dr (page 89) Cr

	2006	Folio	£
	Sept 30 Purchases	PB 49	510

General Ledger

Purchases Account

Dr (page 63) Cr

2006	Folio	£	
Sept 30 Credit purchases for the month	PB 49	2,680	

20.6 Authorisation and coding of invoices

Authorisation of purchase invoices

When purchase invoices are received from various suppliers of goods or services, it is important to check the invoices for accuracy in the calculations and to ensure that the goods invoiced have been received and agree with the relevant purchase order and specifications.

On receipt, each purchase invoice should be numbered, recorded and stamped with an appropriate rubber stamp (*see* Exhibit 20.4), to enable the invoice to be checked and coded.

Exhibit 20.4

Invoice no	
Purchase order no	
Goods received	
Extensions	
Passed for payment	
Code	

Coding of invoices

After stamping, it is necessary to perform the **coding of invoices**. Each invoice should be sent to the department responsible for ordering the goods, the invoice should be checked and, if everything is satisfactory, it is coded, passed for payment by a department head and returned to the accounts department for entry into the books of account and, ultimately, payment.

Organisations using computer accounting systems need to give unique numbers to all their various accounts so that the computer can recognise them instantly:

● *Purchases Ledger* Suppliers are given account numbers – for example:

	Account number
Blackshaws	0207
Harvey Construction Ltd	0243
Morridge Products	0275
Travis and Humphreys	0284

● *Sales Ledger* Customers' account numbers may be thus:

	Account number
Heath Manufacturing Ltd	1084
Office Supplies Ltd	1095
Seddon & Sons	1098
Yeoman's Supplies	1099

● *General Ledger* Examples of account codes are as follows:

	Account number
Capital account	4003
Motor expenses account	4022
Printing and stationery account	4074
Sales account	4098

A register of code numbers allocated to specific accounts must be maintained and updated as necessary. This register may be a manual one or held on the computer system.

Chapter summary

● An organisation uses a document called a purchase order when ordering goods or services from a supplier.
● When organisations purchase goods or services from suppliers they are sent a purchase invoice detailing the goods or services and their price. The invoice is used by both buyer and seller, to the buyer it is a purchase invoice and to the seller a sales invoice.
● Only invoices relating to goods bought on credit are entered into the purchases day book which is merely a list showing details of each credit purchase, i.e. the date of purchase, name of supplier, reference number and amount due.
● Each purchase invoice is then posted to the individual customer's account in the purchases ledger.
● At the end of the period, usually a month, the total purchases are posted to the purchases account in the general ledger.
● Many organisations have a system of coding the invoices prior to entry into the books of account. Part of this process involves authorising the invoice for payment.

Exercises

20.1 B Mann has the following purchases for the month of May 2006:

2006
May 1 From K King: 4 radios at £30 each, 3 music centres at £160 each. Less 25 per cent trade discount.
May 3 From A Bell: 2 washing machines at £200 each, 5 vacuum cleaners at £60 each, 2 dish dryers at £150 each. Less 20 per cent trade discount.
May 15 From J Kelly: 1 music centre at £300 each, 2 washing machines at £250 each. Less 25 per cent trade discount.
May 20 From B Powell: 6 radios at £70 each, less $33^{1}/_{3}$ per cent trade discount.
May 30 From B Lewis: 4 dish dryers at £200 each, less 20 per cent trade discount.

Required:
(*a*) Enter up the purchases day book for the month.
(*b*) Post the transactions to the suppliers' accounts, use your own folio references.
(*c*) Transfer the total to the purchases account in the general ledger.

20.2X   A Rowland has the following purchases for the month of June 2006:

2006
June   2   From C Lee: 2 sets golf clubs at £250 each, 5 footballs at £20 each.
              Less 25 per cent trade discount.
June 11   From M Elliott: 6 cricket bats at £20 each, 6 ice skates at £30 each, 4 rugby balls at
              £25 each. Less 25 per cent trade discount.
June 18   From B Wood: 6 sets golf trophies at £100 each, 4 sets golf clubs at £300 each. Less
              $33\frac{1}{3}$ per cent trade discount.
June 25   From B Parkinson: 5 cricket bats at £40 each. Less 25 per cent trade discount.
June 30   From N Francis: 8 goal posts at £70 each. Less 25 per cent trade discount.

Required:
(*a*) Enter up the purchases day book for the month.
(*b*) Post the items to the suppliers' accounts, use your own folio references.
(*c*) Transfer the total to the purchases account in the general ledger.

20.3   You are employed as accounts assistant for a catering company, Surprise Desserts, that specialises in making desserts for sale to local restaurants, hotels and shops. During July 2006 the following purchases invoices are received.

2006		£	Invoice no.
July 1	Barton Foods Ltd	78.50	201
July 3	Henmore Eggs	56.26	202
July 8	Barton Foods Ltd	101.30	203
July 10	Fernley & Co	98.00	204
July 12	Henmore Eggs	48.20	205
July 14	Bridge Catering Co	142.00	206
July 19	Ruffoni Creams	132.82	207
July 23	Fernley & Co	43.20	208
July 25	Ace Packaging Co	217.75	209
July 31	Henmore Eggs	62.60	210

Required:
(*a*) Draw up a purchases day book, enter the invoices and total it up at the end of the month.
(*b*) Open accounts for each of the suppliers, use your own folio numbers and post the
        invoices to the suppliers' accounts in the purchase ledger.
(*c*) Post the totals to the purchases account in the general ledger.

20.4X   (*a*) As accounts assistant for a builders' merchants you are responsible for approving invoices
                prior to payment at the end of each month. List the steps you would take in authorising
                an invoice for payment.
        (*b*) The company has recently purchased four concrete mixers which are shown in the catalogue at £260 less 25 per cent trade discount and a further 2.5 per cent cash discount if
                the invoice is settled within 7 days. Assuming the invoice is paid within 7 days what is the
                total amount the firm would have to pay for the concrete mixers? Ignore VAT.

20.5X   You are employed as a sales assistant for a small company, Wilshaws Ltd, who sell farm supplies. As the company employs the minimum administrative staff, one of your duties is to look
after the purchases ledger. This task involves entering the invoices received from suppliers
into the day book and posting to the relevant creditors' accounts in the ledger.

Wilshaw's purchase invoices received for November 2006 are as follows:

Date	Supplier	Our Inv No	Total
2006			£
Nov 1	Bould & Co	SR2103	104.26
Nov 3	Hambleton's	SR2104	140.57
Nov 7	Farm Supplies Co	SR2105	448.12
Nov 10	Worthington's Ltd	SR2106	169.91
Nov 12	Sigley Bros	SR2107	47.00
Nov 15	Hambleton's	SR2108	259.09
Nov 20	Harlow's Mfr	SR2109	84.96
Nov 20	Bould & Co	SR2110	29.14
Nov 25	Clark & Robinson	SR2111	61.63
Nov 30	T Adams Ltd	SR2112	233.83

Required:

(*a*) Draw up a purchase day book, enter the invoices, and total up at the end of the month.

(*b*) Open accounts for each of the suppliers, using your own folio numbers, and post the invoices to the suppliers' accounts in the purchases ledger.

(*c*) Post the totals to the purchases account in the general ledger.

CHAPTER 21

The returns day books and documentation

Learning objectives

After you have studied this chapter you should be able to:

● enter credit notes in the returns inwards day book

● post entries from the returns inwards day book to the appropriate customers' accounts in the sales ledger and the returns inwards account in the general ledger

● enter debit notes in the returns outwards day book

● post entries from the returns outwards day book to the appropriate suppliers' accounts in the purchase ledger and the returns outwards account in the general ledger

● understand the reason for keeping the returns inwards and returns outwards day books

● understand the use of statements

● reconcile ledger accounts with suppliers' statements.

21.1 Returns inwards and credit notes

Customers may return goods to the supplier if they are faulty, damaged or not suitable for their requirements, where the consignment is incomplete when compared with the delivery note, or where an overcharge has been made. When this happens, the supplier will make an allowance to correct the situation. Occasionally, a customer may decide to keep the goods but will expect a reduction in price as compensation.

Since customers will have been sent an invoice at the same time as the goods were delivered, they will be in debt to the supplier for the value of the goods. When a supplier makes an allowance for goods that have been returned, or a reduction in price has been agreed, the supplier will issue a **credit note** to the customer. It is called a credit note since the customer's account will be credited with the amount of the allowance, thereby showing a reduction in the amount owed by the customer. This procedure involving credit notes is necessary so that the various books of account that are maintained by the supplier and customer do, in fact, reflect the correct amount owed.

Exhibit 21.1 shows an example of a credit note – and note that credit notes are usually printed in red to distinguish them from invoices.

Exhibit 21.1

CREDIT NOTE		
R GRANT (CATERING SUPPLIES)		
HIGHER SIDE PRESTON PR1 2NL		

	Telephone:	(01703) 33122
	Fax:	(01703) 22331

D Poole & Co
Deansgate Restaurant
45 Charles Street
Manchester M1 5ZN

Credit Note No 0/37
Account No P/4298
Date: 8 September 2006

Quantity	Per unit	Total
	£	£
2 cases Cape Glory Pears	25	50
Less 20% Trade Discount		10
		40

21.2 Returns inwards day book

Credit notes are listed in a returns inwards day book. This is then used for posting the items, as follows:

- *Sales ledger* Credit the amount of credit notes, one by one, to the accounts of the customers in the sales ledger.
- *General ledger* At the end of the period, the total of the returns inwards day book is posted to the debit of the returns inwards account.

Again, you may find it easier to use 'IN' and 'OUT' as discussed previously; i.e. goods returned to us are entered on the 'IN' side of the returns inwards account since the goods are coming 'IN' to us, and on the 'OUT' side of the individual customers' accounts.

Alternative names in use for the returns inwards day book are the returns inwards journal or the sales returns day book.

21.3 Example of a returns inwards day book

An example of a returns inwards day book showing the items posted to the sales ledger and the general ledger is now shown:

Returns Inwards Day Book			(page 10)
	Note No	Folio	Amount £
2006			
Sept 8 D Poole & Co	9/37	SL 12	40
17 A Brewster	9/38	SL 58	120
19 C Vickers	9/39	SL 99	290
29 M Nelson	9/40	SL 112	160
Transferred to returns inwards account		GL 114	610

Sales Ledger
D Poole & Co Account   (page 12)

Dr   Cr

			2006	Folio	£
			Sept 8 Returns inwards	RI 10	40

A Brewster Account   (page 58)

Dr   Cr

			2006	Folio	£
			Sept 17 Returns inwards	RI 10	120

C Vickers Account   (page 99)

Dr   Cr

			2006	Folio	£
			Sept 19 Returns inwards	RI 10	290

M Nelson Account   (page 112)

Dr   Cr

			2006	Folio	£
			Sept 29 Returns inwards	RI 10	160

General Ledger
Returns Inwards Account   (page 114)

Dr   Cr

2006	Folio	£			
Sept 30 Returns for					
the month	RI 10	610			

21.4   Returns outwards and debit notes

If the supplier agrees, goods bought previously may be returned. When this happens, a **debit note** is sent to the supplier giving details of the goods and the reason for their return.

Also, an allowance might be given by the supplier for any faults in the goods. Here also, a debit note should be sent to the supplier.

Exhibit 21.2 shows an example of a debit note.

Exhibit 21.2

DEBIT NOTE		

R GRANT (CATERING SUPPLIES)
HIGHER SIDE PRESTON PR1 2NL

	Telephone:	(01703) 33122
	Fax:	(01703) 22331

B Hamilton Food Supplies
20 Fourth Street
Kidderminster
KD2 4PP

Debit Note No 9/34
Account No H/3752
Date: 11 September 2006

Quantity	Per unit	Total
	£	£
4 cases Canadian Salmon	60	240
Less 25% Trade Discount		60
		180
Returned damaged in transit		

21.5 Returns outwards day book

Debit notes are listed in a returns outwards day book. This is then used for posting the items, as follows:

- *Purchases ledger*   Debit the amounts of debit notes, one by one, to the accounts of the suppliers in the purchases ledger.
- *General ledger*   At the end of the period, the total of the returns outwards day book is posted to the credit of the returns outwards account.

Using 'IN' and 'OUT', the entries would be as follows: the goods returned by us to the supplier go 'IN' to the suppliers' accounts and come 'OUT' of the returns outwards account.

Other names in use for the returns outwards day book are the returns outwards journal or the purchases returns day book.

21.6 A worked example of a returns outwards day book

An example of a returns outwards day book, showing the items posted to the purchases ledger and the general ledger, is now shown.

Returns Outwards Day Book			(page 7)
	Note No	Folio	Amount £
2006			
Sept 11 B Hamilton	9/34	PL 29	180
16 B Rose	9/35	PL 46	100
28 C Blake	9/36	PL 55	30
30 S Saunders	9/37	PL 87	360
Transferred to returns outwards account		GL 116	670

Purchases Ledger
B Hamilton Account (page 29)

Dr   Cr

2006	Folio	£	
Sept 11 Returns outwards	RO 7	180	

B Rose Account (page 46)

Dr   Cr

2006	Folio	£	
Sept 16 Returns outwards	RO 7	100	

C Blake Account (page 55)

Dr   Cr

2006	Folio	£	
Sept 28 Returns outwards	RO 7	30	

S Saunders Account (page 87)

Dr   Cr

2006	Folio	£	
Sept 30 Returns outwards	RO 7	360	

General Ledger
Returns Outwards Account (page 116)

Dr   Cr

			2006	Folio	£
			Sept 30 Returns for the month	RO 7	670

21.7 Double entry and returns

Exhibit 21.3 shows how double entry is made for both returns inwards and returns outwards.

Exhibit 21.3 Posting returns inwards and returns outwards

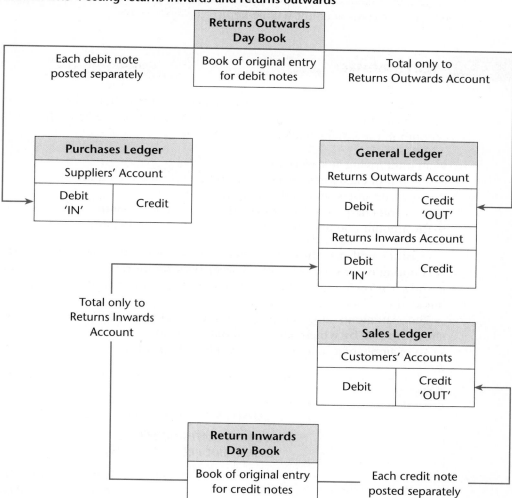

Note that full coverage of the treatment of returns inwards and returns outwards in the final accounts has already been shown in Chapter 10 (Sections 10.1 and 10.2).

21.8 Reasons for keeping separate returns accounts

It might be thought that the returns inwards could have been debited to the sales account rather than to a separate returns inwards account. This, however, would have meant that it would only be the net figure of sales that appeared in the trading account.

It is important for the owners of a business to check on how much in sales is being returned. This may show that too many faulty goods are being sold, thus needing to be returned. This would involve the business in a lot of unnecessary costs, such as carriage outwards, packing expenses and so on. Showing the figures separately will highlight an excessive amount of returns.

Similar considerations will apply with returns outwards, and therefore a separate returns outwards account will be kept.

21.9 Statements

At the end of each month a **statement of account** should be sent to each debtor that owes money on the last day of that month. It is really a copy of the debtor's account in the seller's books. It should show:

- amount owing at start of month
- amount of each sales invoice sent to them during the month
- any credit notes sent to them during the month
- cash and cheques received from them during the month
- the amount due from the debtor at the end of the month.

Debtors will use these statements to see whether the accounts in their own accounting records agrees with their account in our records. If in our books a debtor is shown as owing £798 then, depending on items in transit between us, the debtors books should show us as a creditor for £798.

The statements also act as a reminder to debtors that money is owed, and will show the date by which payment should be made.

An example of a statement is shown in Exhibit 21.4.

Exhibit 21.4

STATEMENT OF ACCOUNT

R GRANT (CATERING SUPPLIES)
HIGHER SIDE PRESTON PR1 2NL

Telephone: (01703) 33122
Fax: (01703) 22331

Accounts Department
D Poole & Co
Deansgate Restaurant
45 Charles Street
Manchester M1 5ZN

Date: 30 September 2006

Date	Details	Debit	Credit	Balance
2006		£	£	£
Sept 1	Balance b/f			880
Sept 2	Invoice 30956	560		1,440
Sept 3	Returns 9/37		40	1,400
Sept 25	Bank		880	520
Sept 30	Balance owing c/f			<u>520</u>

All accounts due and payable within one month

21.10 Reconciliation of our ledger accounts with suppliers' statements

Because of differences in timing, the balance on a supplier's statement on a certain date can differ from the balance on that supplier's account in our purchases ledger. This is similar to the fact that a bank statement balance may differ from the cash book balance. In similar fashion, a reconciliation statement may also be necessary. This can now be shown through the example given as Exhibit 21.5.

Exhibit 21.5

(a) Our Purchases Ledger

C Young Ltd Account

Dr					Cr
2006		£	2006		£
Jan 10	Bank	1,550	Jan 1	Balance b/d	1,550
Jan 29	Returns (i)	116	Jan 6	Purchases	885
Jan 31	Balance c/d	1,679	Jan 18	Purchases	910
		3,345			3,345
			Feb 1	Balance b/d	1,679

(b) Supplier's statement

C Young Ltd
Market Place, Leeds

STATEMENT

Account Name: A Hall Ltd
Account Number: H93

Date: 31 January 2006

	Debit	Credit	Balance
2006	£	£	£
Jan 1 Balance			1,550 Dr
Jan 4 Invoice No 3250	885		2,435 Dr
Jan 13 Payment received		1,550	885 Dr
Jan 18 Invoice No 3731	910		1,795 Dr
Jan 31 Invoice No 3894	425		2,220 Dr

Comparing our purchases ledger account with the supplier's statement, two differences can be seen:

(i) We sent returns £116 to C Young Ltd, but they had not received them and recorded them in their books by the end of January.

(ii) Our supplier sent goods to A Hall Ltd (our company), but we had not received them and had not entered the £425 in our books by the end of January.

A reconciliation statement can be drawn up by us, A Hall Ltd, as on 31 January 2006.

Reconciliation of Supplier's Statement
C Young Ltd as on 31 January 2006

		£	£
Balance per our purchases ledger			1,679
Add Purchases not received by us	(ii)	425	
Returns not received by supplier	(i)	116	
			541
Balance per supplier's statement			2,220

21.11 Sales and purchases via credit cards

As discussed in Chapter 13, Section 13.5 Credit cards, banks, building societies and other financial organisations issue credit cards to their customers.

The holder of a credit card purchases items or services without giving cash or cheques, but simply signs a special voucher used by the store or selling organisation. Later on – usually several weeks later – the credit card holder pays the organisation for which they hold the card (e.g. Visa) for all or part of their previous month's expenditure. The sellers of the goods or services then present the vouchers to the credit card company, and the total of the vouchers less commission is paid to them by that credit card company.

In effect, the sales are 'cash sales' so far as the purchasers are concerned: they have seen goods (or obtained services) and have received them, and in their eyes they have paid for them by using their credit card. Such sales are very rarely sales to anyone other than the general public, as compared with sales to professionals in a specific trade.

Once a customer has received the goods or services from the seller, he or she does not need to be entered in the sales ledger as a debtor. All the selling company is then interested in, from a recording point of view, is collecting the money from the credit card company.

The double entry needed is:

- Sale of items via credit cards: Dr: Credit card company
  Cr: Cash sales
- Receipt of money from credit card company: Dr: Bank
  Cr: Credit card company
- Commission charged by credit card company: Dr: Selling expenses
  Cr: Credit card company

Chapter summary

- A credit note is a document issued by a supplier and sent to a purchaser showing details of an allowance made in respect of unsatisfactory goods or services.
- Credit notes are entered into a returns inwards day book. The total returns for the month are posted to the **debit side** of the returns inwards account in the general ledger. Each transaction is also posted to the **credit side** of the individual customers' accounts in the sales ledger.

- A useful hint: goods returned to us are entered on the 'IN' side of the returns inwards account and on the 'OUT' side of the individual customers' accounts.
- A debit note is a document sent to a supplier claiming an agreed allowance for unsatisfactory goods or services.
- Debit notes are entered into a returns outwards day book. Each transaction is then posted to the **debit side** of the individual suppliers' accounts in the purchase ledger. The total returns for the month are posted to the **credit side** of the returns outwards account in the general ledger.
- A useful hint: the goods returned by us to the supplier go 'IN' to the suppliers' accounts and come 'OUT' of the returns outwards account.
- To keep a note of the number of returns being made it is important to have separate accounts for returns inwards and returns outwards.
- Statements are issued by suppliers and sent to their customers, i.e. their debtors, requesting payment of amounts due. The debtor uses the statement to check the suppliers' records against their own and if correct will make payment against the statement.
- Statements are also used to reconcile the records of the supplier to those of the customer. Differences are identified and if errors or discrepancies have arisen then amendments can be made.

Exercises

21.1 You are to enter up the purchases day book and the returns outwards day book from the following details, then post the items to the relevant accounts in the purchases ledger, and then show the transfers to the general ledger at the end of the month.

2007

May   1 Credit purchase from H Lloyd, £119
May   4 Credit purchases from the following: D Scott £98; A Simpson £114; A Williams £25; S Wood £56
May   7 Goods returned by us to the following: H Lloyd £16; D Scott £14
May 10 Credit purchase from A Simpson, £59
May 18 Credit purchases from the following: M White £89; J Wong £67; H Miller £196; H Lewis £119
May 25 Goods returned by us to the following: J Wong £5; A Simpson £11
May 31 Credit purchases from: A Williams £56; C Cooper £98.

21.2X Enter up the sales day book and the returns inwards day book from the following details. Then post to the customer's accounts and show the transfers to the general ledger.

2007

June   1 Credit sales to: A Simes £188; P Tulloch £60; J Flynn £77; B Lopez £88
June   6 Credit sales to: M Howells £114; S Thompson £118; J Flynn £66
June 10 Goods returned to us by: A Simes £12; B Lopez £17
June 20 Credit sales to M Barrow, £970
June 24 Goods returned to us by S Thompson, £5
June 30 Credit sales to M Parkin, £91.

21.3 Framework Ltd is a small company which specialises in framing pictures, photographs, certificates, etc. At the beginning of the new financial year 1 January 2007 the following balances appeared in the ledgers:

Sales Ledger

	£
J Forbes (Fancy Gifts)	745 Dr
J Goodwin & Co	276 Dr
L & P Moss	390 Dr

Purchases Ledger

	£
M & P Fitzsimons	800 Cr
L Horne	450 Cr
M Ward & Sons	245 Cr

During January 2007 the following transactions took place:

Jan 2 Purchased goods from L Horne, £650
Jan 3 Purchased goods from M Ward & Sons, £334
Jan 11 Sold goods to J Goodwin & Co, £328
Jan 12 Received credit note from L Horne, £42, in respect of goods returned as unsuitable
Jan 22 Purchased goods from M & P Fitzsimons, £756
Jan 23 Sold goods to J Forbes (Fancy Gifts), £1,234
Jan 27 Sold goods to L & P Moss, £2,500
Jan 28 Received credit note from M & P Fitzsimons, £200

On 31 January the company received a cheque from J Forbes (Fancy Gifts) for £745 and a cheque for £200 on account from L & P Moss.

On the same date the company paid cheques to M & P Fitzsimons £500 on account and M Ward & Sons £245.

Required:
(*a*) Open personal accounts for the debtors and creditors and enter the outstanding balances at 1 January 2007.
(*b*) Post the above transactions to the accounts in the sales and purchases ledgers.
(*c*) Balance off the accounts at 31 January and bring the balances down.

Note: Day books and postings to the general ledger are not required.

21.4X You are employed as an accounts clerk for Elder's Printing Co, 36 High Street, Shrewsbury SH4 8JK. One of your tasks is to prepare statements of account which are sent out to customers at the end of each month. Two of the customers' accounts are shown below.

Sales Ledger

Dr	*D Hammond Ltd Account*			*Cr*
2007		£	2007	£
Jan 1 Balance b/d		1,403	Jan 7 Bank	1,380
Jan 3 Sales		177	Jan 12 Credit note	23
Jan 10 Sales		527		
Jan 25 Sales		200		

Dr	*Alex Richards Ltd Account*			*Cr*
2007		£	2007	£
Jan 1 Balance b/d		346	Jan 7 Bank	292
Jan 7 Sales		27	Jan 7 Discount	8
Jan 9 Sales		521	Jan 12 Credit note	46
Jan 27 Sales		400		
Jan 31 Sales		53		

The addresses of the above customers are as follows:

D Hammond Ltd Bay House Heath Road Shrewsbury SH7 3KL	Alex Richards Ltd Unit 12 Greenways Industrial Estate Chester CE21 9HU

Required:

(*a*) Balance each of the above accounts off, and state the amount owing by each of the customers.

(*b*) Draft a statement of account to be sent to each customer.

21.5X Vantage Products is one of your suppliers. Its account in your ledger is as follows:

Vantage Products

2006		£	2006		£
Oct 12	Purchase returns	75	Oct 1	Balance b/d	1,625
28	Bank	1,570	8	Purchases	1,050
28	Discount	55	19	Purchases	1,675
30	Purchase returns	105			
31	Balance c/d	2,545			
		4,350			4,350
			Nov 1	Balance b/d	2,545

On 2 November, the following statement of account is received from Vantage Products:

Vantage Products: Statement

2006	Debit £	Credit £	Balance £
Oct 1 Balance			3,175
3 Bank		1,500	1,675
3 Discount		50	1,625
8 Sales	1,050		2,675
15 Returns inwards		75	2,600
19 Sales	1,675		4,275
28 Sales	1,550		5,825

You are required to do the following:

(*a*) Prepare a reconciliation statement, *starting with the balance in your books of £2,545*, to explain the difference between the balance in your ledger and the closing balance on the statement of account.

(*b*) If the outstanding balance in your ledger on 1 November was settled less a 2½% discount:
   (i) state the amount of discount
   (ii) state the amount of the cheque.

OCR

CHAPTER 22

Analytical sales and purchases day books

Learning objectives

After you have studied this chapter you should be able to:

- enter invoices into analytical sales and purchases day books
- post transactions from analytical sales and purchases day books to the personal accounts in the sales and purchases ledgers
- post totals from the analytical day books to the general ledger.

22.1 Introduction

In Chapters 19 and 20, the sales and purchases day books were shown using only one total column for the value of the goods sold or purchased. Often goods are subject to VAT, as discussed in Chapter 16. In that chapter you will have noticed that additional columns were used to take account of the VAT, as shown in the sales day book in Exhibit 16.1 and the Purchases Day Book in Exhibit 16.2.

In addition to accounting for VAT, many businesses find it useful to analyse their sales and purchases between different types of goods bought and sold, or perhaps between different departments. For example, a coffee shop may sell refreshments and gifts and wish to ascertain the profit on the two different sales areas. In this example it would be advantageous to analyse both sales and purchases to reflect the goods/services bought or sold in each area. The purchases day book could be ruled as follows:

Purchases Day Book						
Date	Details	Folio	Total	VAT	Gifts	Food
			£	£	£	£

22.2 Entering sales invoices into an analytical sales day book

When a business requires additional information from its records, the books can easily be adapted to meet particular needs.

Let us consider a retail computer shop that sells hardware and software to the public, local businesses and schools. The proprietor, Mr Harlow, wishes to monitor the sales of each of these lines separately. Exhibit 22.1 shows an example of Mr Harlow's **analytical sales day book**.

Exhibit 22.1

	Sales Day Book					(page 7)
Date	Details	Folio	Total	VAT	Software	Hardware
			£	£	£	£
April 1	Mount Hey School	SL 1	705	105		600
3	Ashby Marketing	SL 2	564	84	480	
15	Davenport Manufacturing	SL 3	4,700	700		4,000
20	St James College	SL 4	23,500	3,500		20,000
			29,469	4,389	480	24,600
				GL 3	GL 1	GL 2

22.3 Posting credit sales

Each sale now has to be posted to the individual debtors accounts in the sales ledger, as follows:

(i) The total of each sales invoice (i.e. the net price of the goods plus VAT) is posted to each individual debtors account on the debit side, since the goods are going 'into' their account.

(ii) At the end of the period, the sales day book is added up and the totals posted on the credit, or 'OUT', side of the following accounts:
- sales of software account
- sales of hardware account
- VAT account.

The results are shown below:

Sales Ledger
Mount Hey School   *SL 1*

Dr   Cr

	Folio	£			
April 1 Sales	SB 7	705			

Ashby Marketing Co   *SL 2*

Dr				Cr
	Folio	*£*		
April 3 Sales	SB 7	564		

Davenport Manufacturing Co   *SL 3*

Dr				Cr
	Folio	*£*		
April 15 Sales	SB 7	4,700		

St James College   *SL 4*

Dr				Cr
	Folio	*£*		
April 20 Sales	SB 7	23,500		

General Ledger

Sale of Software   *GL 1*

Dr				Cr
		April 30 Credit sales	*Folio*	*£*
		for April	SB 7	480

Sale of Hardware   *GL 2*

Dr				Cr
		April 30 Credit sales	*Folio*	*£*
		for April	SB 7	24,600

VAT   *GL 3*

Dr				Cr
		April 30 VAT on credit	*Folio*	*£*
		sales for April	SB 7	4,389

22.4 Entering purchase invoices into an analytical purchases day book

Another business might wish to monitor its purchases that might include goods for resale and business expenses such as electricity, motor expenses, etc. The example shown in Exhibit 22.2 illustrates how a business could analyse its purchase invoices using an **analytical purchases day book.**

Exhibit 22.2

			Purchases Day Book				(page 3)
Date	Details	Folio	Total	VAT	Goods	Motor Exp	Stationery
			£	£	£	£	£
Nov 1	Bould & Co	PL 1	4,230	630	3,600		
10	Sigley's (Stat)	PL 2	47	7			40
17	T Adams Ltd	PL 3	940	140	800		
30	Robinson's Garage	PL 4	188	28		160	
			5,405	805	4,400	160	40
				GL 3	GL 1	GL 2	GL 3

22.5 Posting credit purchases

Each purchase now has to be posted to the individual creditors' accounts in the purchase ledger, as follows:

(i) The *total* of each purchase invoice (i.e. the net price of the goods, plus VAT) is posted to each individual creditor's account on the *credit* side, since the goods are coming 'OUT' of their accounts.

(ii) At the end of the period, the purchases day book is added up and the totals are posted on the *debit*, or 'IN', side of the following accounts:
- purchases account
- motor expenses account
- stationery account
- VAT account.

Purchases Ledger

Bould & Co   PL 1

Dr				Cr
			Folio	£
	Nov 1 Purchases		PB 3	4,230

Sigley's Stationers   PL 2

Dr				Cr
			Folio	£
	Nov 10 Purchases		PB 3	47

T Adams Ltd   PL 3

Dr				Cr
			Folio	£
	Nov 17 Purchases		PB 3	940

Robinson's Garage   PL 4

Dr				Cr
			Folio	£
	Nov 30 Purchases		PB 3	188

General Ledger

Purchases GL 1

Dr				Cr
	Folio	£		
Nov 30 Credit purchases for November	PB 3	4,400		

Motor Expenses GL 2

Dr				Cr
	Folio	£		
Nov 30 Purchases day book	PB 3	160		

Stationery GL 3

Dr				Cr
	Folio	£		
Nov 30 Purchases day book	PB 3	40		

VAT GL 4

Dr				Cr
	Folio	£		
Nov 30 Purchases day book	PB 3	805		

22.6   Advantages of analysis books

The advantages of analysis books are that businesses can be provided with exactly the information that they need, at the time when they want it. Different firms have different needs, and they therefore analyse their books in different ways.

Analysis books enable firms to do such things as:

- calculate the profit or loss made by each part of a business
- draw up control accounts for the sales and purchases ledgers (*see* Chapter 23)
- keep a check on the sales of each type of goods
- keep a check on goods sold in different locations, departments or sections
- identify purchasers of each type of good offered for sale.

22.7   Books as collection points

We can see that the various sales and purchases day books, and the ones for returns, are simply collection points for data to be entered in the accounts of the double entry system. There is nothing in law that says that, for instance, a sales day book has to be written up.

It would be possible to use a firm's sales invoices to enter the debits in the customer's personal accounts. The sales invoices would then be held in a file until the end of the month, when they would then be added up. The total would be entered to the credit of the sales account in the general ledger.

Chapter summary

- Many organisations use analytical day books for entering sales and purchases invoices, they are books of original entry.
- Analytical day books are especially useful for the recording of VAT since the day book contains several analysis columns allowing the VAT content of an invoice to be recorded. The additional columns enable further analysis to be made, for example, recording sales for different sections of the business or different types of expenditure in the purchases day book.
- Invoices are entered and analysed according to the type of sale or expense at the time the transaction is recorded.
- The total amount of the invoice (i.e. the amount of the goods plus the VAT) is posted to the individual debtors' or creditors' account.
- At the end of the month the total of the VAT column and other columns, appropriately analysed, will be posted to the accounts in the general ledger.
- There are many advantages of using analytical day books.

Exercises

22.1 The Curtain Design Company sells both ready-made and custom-made curtains to local hotels, nursing homes and the public. It operates an analytical sales day book, where it analyses the sales into sales of ready-made curtains and custom-made curtains.

The following invoices were sent during November 2006. All goods are subject to VAT at 17.5 per cent.

Date	Customer	Ready-made £	Custom-made £
Nov 1	Jarvis Arms Hotel		2,300
Nov 8	Springs Nursing Home	1,000	
Nov 15	J P Morten	220	
Nov 17	Queen's Hotel		1,500
Nov 30	W Blackshaw	90	

You are required to:
(a) record the above transactions in an analytical sales day book
(b) post the invoices to the personal accounts in the sales ledger
(c) post the totals to the appropriate accounts in the general ledger.

22.2 The Hall Engineering Company manufactures small engineering components for the motor-car industry. It operates an analytical purchases day book, in which the purchases invoices are recorded.

During May 2006, the following invoices were received. All goods are subject to VAT at 17.5 per cent.

			£
May 1	Black's Engineering Co	Engineering goods	520
May 3	Ace Printing Co	Printing catalogues	145
May 24	Morgan's Garage	Petrol Account	120
May 26	Martin's Foundry	Engineering parts	700
May 28	Office Supplies	Stationery	126
May 29	Black's Engineering Co	Engineering parts	220

Required:

(*a*) Enter the purchase invoices in an analytical purchases day book using the following analysis columns:

- Engineering parts
- Printing and stationery
- Motor expenses
- VAT.

(*b*) Post the transactions to the personal accounts in the purchases ledger.

(*c*) Post the totals to the appropriate accounts in the general ledger.

22.3 Smart Campers supplies an extensive range of camping equipment and accessories. It has three branches, situated at Horsforth, Moortown and Otley. Sales day books are kept at Head Office and are compiled from information received from branches.

During the month of May 2006, credit sales were as follows. All sales are subject to VAT at 10 per cent.

2 May	Outdoor Centre
	Moortown branch
	12 Flair cools boxes at £15.90 each
	6 Camping stoves at £29.95 each
	All less trade discount 20%

8 May	Premier Leisure
	Horsforth branch
	10 Explorer rucksacks at £34.99 each
	Less trade discount 20%
	12 Trekker ridge tents at £59.95 each
	Less trade discount 15%

16 May	Airedale Sport
	Otley branch
	8 Palma cool bags at £7.85 each
	15 Flair cool boxes at £15.90
	All less trade discount 20%

28 May	Empire Products
	Moortown branch
	14 Dome tents at £47.90 each
	8 trekker ridge tents at £59.95 each
	All less trade discount 15%

You are required to draw up a sales day book with analysis columns as follows: Total, Horsforth, Moortown, Otley, and VAT. Once that has been done, enter the above transactions for May 2006.

OCR

22.4X Adel Garden Centre divides its purchases of stock into two main departments: Outdoor Furniture and Garden Tools. Credit purchases during the month of October 2006 were as set out below, with VAT at 10 per cent to be included on all transactions.

2 October	Oakland Supplies
	6 steel spades at £18.75 each
	8 garden forks at £10.50 each
	Less trade discount 20%

14 October	Airedale Products
	4 patio furniture sets at £49.60 each
	Less trade discount 15%

22 October	Oakland Supplies
	6 garden tool sets at £34.90 each
	4 garden forks at £10.50 each
	Less trade discount 20%
	8 sun loungers at £39.95 each
	Less trade discount 25%

20 October	Airedale Products
	1 patio furniture set invoiced on 14 October was returned because it was damaged. A credit note was issued.

28 October	Oakland Supplies
	2 garden tool sets were returned because they were faulty. A credit note was issued.

You are required to do the following:

(*a*) Draw up a purchases day book and purchases returns day book with analysis columns for Total, Outdoor Furniture, Garden Tools and VAT. Enter the date, name of supplier and the amounts of money into the appropriate columns. (Details of invoices are NOT required in the day books.)

(*b*) Total the day books.

(*c*) Write up the purchases ledger accounts from the day books, and balance the accounts at the end of the month.

OCR

Control accounts

After you have studied this chapter you should be able to:

● understand the need for control accounts
● prepare a sales ledger control account
● prepare a purchase ledger control account
● know the sources of information for control accounts
● understand the double entry aspect of control accounts
● appreciate the advantages of control accounts
● understand the meaning and use of memorandum accounts.

23.1 Need for control accounts

Where a business is small all the accounts may be contained in one ledger and at the end of the accounting period a trial balance could easily be drawn up as a test of the arithmetical accuracy of the accounts. However, it must be remembered that certain errors may not be revealed by the trial balance (refer to Chapter 7). If the trial balance totals disagree, the books could easily and quickly be checked to find the errors.

However, as the business grows the accounting requirements also expand and the work has to be divided up into various separate ledgers and, consequently, errors are not as easily identifiable. The error or errors could be very difficult to find and it may be necessary to check every item in every ledger. Therefore, what is required is a type of trial balance for each ledger, and this requirement is met by the **control account**. Thus it is only the ledgers where the control accounts do not balance that need detailed checking to locate any errors. This is summarised in Exhibit 23.1.

Exhibit 23.1

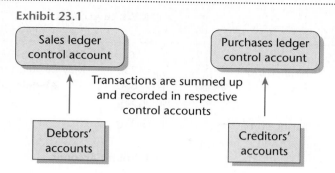

23.2 Principle of control accounts

The principle on which the control account is based is simple, and is as follows. If the opening balance of an account is known, together with the information of the additions and deductions entered in the account, the closing balance can be calculated.

This idea can be applied to a complete ledger. Suppose that there were only four accounts in the sales ledger, and for the month of May 2007, the accounts were as laid out below.

Sales Ledger
T Allen Account

Dr					Cr
2007		£	2007		£
May 1	Balance b/d	850	May 7	Bank	820
" 4	Sales	900	" 7	Discounts allowed	30
" 30	Sales	350	" 31	Balance c/d	1,250
		2,100			2,100
Jun 1	Balance b/d	1,250			

P May Account

Dr					Cr
2007		£	2007		£
May 1	Balance b/d	1,500	May 9	Returns inwards	200
" 28	Sales	400	" 14	Bank	900
			" 14	Discounts allowed	20
			" 31	Balance c/d	780
		1,900			1,900
Jun 1	Balance b/d	780			

K White Account

Dr					Cr
2007		£	2007		£
May 1 Balance b/d		750	May 20 Returns inwards		110
" 15 Sales		600	" 31 Balance c/d		1,240
		1,350			1,350
Jun 1 Balance b/d		1,240			

C Young Account

Dr					Cr
2007		£	2007		£
May 1 Balance b/d		450	May 28 Bad debts		450

A control account, in this case a *sales ledger* control account, would consist only of the totals of each of the items in the sales ledger. Let us therefore first list the totals for each type of item.

May 1 Balances b/d:	£850 + £1,500 + £750 + £450 = £3,550
Sales in May:	£900 + £350 + £400 + £600 = £2,250
Cheques received in May:	£820 + £900 = £1,720
Discounts allowed in May:	£30 + £20 = £50
Returns inwards in May:	£200 + £110 = £310
Bad debts written off in May:	£450

Now, looking at the totals only, it is possible to draw up a sales ledger control account. Debits are shown as usual on the left-hand side, and credits on the right-hand side. Thus:

Sales Ledger Control Account

Dr					Cr
2007		£	2007		£
May 1 Balance b/d		3,550	May 31 Bank		1,720
" 31 Sales for the month		2,250	" 31 Discounts allowed		50
			" 31 Returns inwards		310
			" 31 Bad debts		450
			" 31 Balances c/d (A)		?
		5,800			5,800
Jun 1 Balances b/d (B)		?			

From your studies so far of double entry, you should be able to see that the Balance c/d (A) is the figure needed to balance the account, i.e. the difference between the two sides. It works out to be £3,270.

We can now look at the ledger and see if that is correct. The balances are £1,250 + £780 + £1,240 = £3,270. As this has now proved to be correct, the figure of £3,270 can be shown in the sales ledger control account as the balances carried down (A) and the balances brought down (B).

In the above very simple example, there were only four ledger accounts. Suppose instead that there were 400 – or 4,000 or 40,000 – ledger accounts. In these cases, the information concerning the totals of each type of item cannot be obtained so easily.

Remember that the main purpose of a control account is to act as a check on the accuracy of the entries in the ledgers. The total of a list of all the balances extracted from the ledger should equal the balance on the control account. If not, a mistake, or even many mistakes, may have been made and will have to be found.

23.3 Information for control accounts

The following tables show where information is obtained from in order to draw up control accounts.

Sales Ledger Control	Source
1 Opening debtors	List of debtors' balances drawn up at the end of the previous period.
2 Credit sales	Total from sales day book.
3 Returns inwards	Total of returns inwards day book.
4 Cheques received	Cash book: Bank column on received side. All transactions of credit sales extracted.
5 Cash received	Cash book: Cash column on received side. All transactions of cash sales extracted.
6 Discounts allowed	Total of discounts allowed column in the cash book.
7 Closing debtors	List of debtors' balances drawn up at the end of the period.

Purchases Ledger Control	Source
1 Opening creditors	List of creditors' balances drawn up at the end of the previous period.
2 Credit purchases	Total from purchases day book.
3 Returns outwards	Total of returns outwards day book.
4 Cheques paid	Cash book: Bank column on payments side. All transactions of credit purchases extracted.
5 Cash paid	Cash book: Cash column on payments side. All transactions of cash purchases extracted.
6 Discounts received	Total of discounts received column in the cash book.
7 Closing creditors	List of creditors' balances drawn up at the end of the period.

23.4 Form of control accounts

It is usual to find control accounts in the same format as an account with the totals of the debit entries in the sales and purchases ledgers on the left-hand side of the control account, and the totals of the various credit entries in the ledgers on the right-hand side of the control account.

This can also be shown in the form of two diagrams. Exhibit 23.2 shows how information is used to construct a sales ledger control account for the month of May 2006, and Exhibit 23.3 illustrates the construction of a purchases ledger control account for May 2006. The letters A, B, C and so on refer to the information used in the control accounts.

Exhibit 23.2 Sales ledger control account – source of data

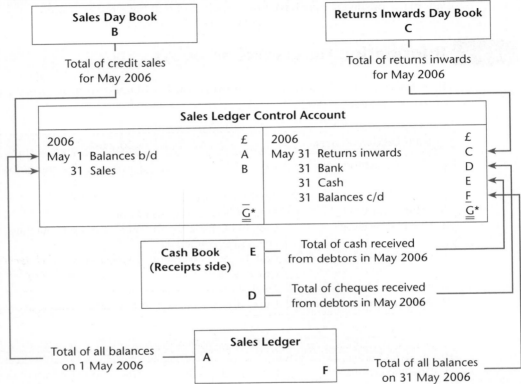

* G: If the two totals labelled G are not equal to each other, then there is an error somewhere in the books.

Exhibit 23.3 Purchases ledger control account – source of data

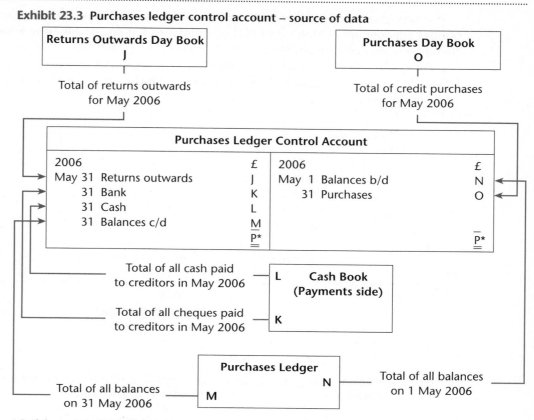

* P: If the two totals labelled P are not equal to each other, then there is an error somewhere in the books.

Exhibit 23.4 shows an example of a sales ledger control account for a sales ledger in which all the entries are arithmetically correct.

Exhibit 23.4

Sales ledger	£
Debit balances on 1 January 2006	1,894
Total credit sales for the month	10,290
Cheques received from customers in the month	7,284
Cash received from customers in the month	1,236
Returns inwards from customers during the month	296
Debit balances on 31 January as extracted from the sales ledger	3,368

Sales Ledger Control Account

Dr				Cr
2006	£	2006		£
Jan 1 Balances b/d	1,894	Jan 31 Bank		7,284
31 Sales	10,290	31 Cash		1,236
		31 Returns inwards		296
		31 Balances c/d		3,368
	12,184			12,184

We have proved the ledger to be arithmetically correct, because the totals of the control account equal each other. If the totals were not equal, then this would prove that there is an error somewhere.

Exhibit 23.5 shows an example where an error is found to exist in a purchases ledger. The ledger will have to be checked in detail, the error found, and the control account then corrected.

Exhibit 23.5

Purchases ledger	£
Credit balances on 1 January 2006	3,890
Cheques paid to suppliers during the month	3,620
Returns outwards to suppliers in the month	95
Bought from suppliers in the month	4,936
Credit balances on 31 January as extracted from the purchases ledger	5,151

Purchases Ledger Control Account

Dr		£			Cr £
2006			2006		
Jan 31 Bank		3,620	Jan 1 Balances b/d		3,890
31 Returns outwards		95	31 Purchases		4,936
31 Balances c/d		5,151			
		8,866*			8,826*

* As can be seen from the totals at the bottom of the control account, there is a £40 (£8,866 − £8,826) error in the purchases ledger. We will have to check that ledger in detail to find the error.

Notice that a double line does not appear under the totals figures. We will not finalise the account (and double-rule it) until the error is traced and corrected.

23.5 Other transfers

Transfers to bad debt accounts will have to be recorded in the sales ledger control account because they involve entries in the sales ledgers.

Similarly, a contra account, whereby the same firm is both a supplier and a customer and inter-indebtedness is set off, will also need entering in the control accounts. An example of this follows:

(i)   The firm has sold A Hughes £600 goods on 1 May
(ii) Hughes has supplied the firm with £880 goods on 12 May
(iii) The £600 owing by Hughes is set off against £880 owing to him on 30 May
(iv) This leaves £280 owing to Hughes on 31 May

Sales Ledger

Dr		A Hughes		Cr
		£		
May 1 Sales	(i)	600		

Purchases Ledger

Dr   A Hughes   Cr

			£
	May 12 Purchases	(ii)	880

The set-off now takes place:

Sales Ledger

Dr   A Hughes   Cr

			£				£
May 1 Sales	(i)		600	May 30 Set-off Purchases ledger	(iii)		600

Purchases Ledger

Dr   A Hughes   Cr

			£				£
May 30 Set-off: Sales ledger	(iii)		600	May 12 Purchases	(ii)		880
May 31 Balance c/d	(iv)		280				
			880				880
				Jun 1 Balance b/d	(iv)		280

The transfer of the £600 will appear on the credit side of the sales ledger control account and on the debit side of the purchases ledger control account.

Students often find it difficult to work out which side of each control account contra items (set-offs) are shown. Think of it as cash received and cash paid, for the entries go on the same sides of the control accounts as these items. Thus a contra item will appear on the credit side of the sales ledger control account (the same side as cash received from debtors) and will appear on the debit side of the purchases ledger control account (the same side as cash paid to creditors would appear). Remember this and you won't get it wrong.

23.6   A more complicated example

Exhibit 23.6 shows a worked example of a more complicated control account. You will see that there are sometimes credit balances in the sales ledger as well as debit balances. Suppose, for instance, that we sold £500 goods to W Young, she then paid in full for them, and then afterwards she returned £40 goods to us. This would leave a credit balance of £40 on the account, whereas usually the balances in the sales ledger are debit balances.

There may also be reason to write off a debt as bad where a business finds it impossible to collect the debt. If this happens, the double entry would be as follows:

> Debit: bad debts account
> Credit: individual debtors' accounts.

Ultimately, the bad debts account would be credited and the profit and loss account would be debited (*see* Chapter 27). If the business uses control accounts, then the sales ledger control account would also be credited, as shown in Exhibit 23.6.

Exhibit 23.6

2006		£
Aug 1	Sales ledger – debit balances	3,816
Aug 1	Sales ledger – credit balances	22
Aug 31	Transactions for the month:	
	Cash received	104
	Cheques received	6,239
	Sales	7,090
	Bad debts written off	306
	Discounts allowed	298
	Returns inwards	664
	Cash refunded to a customer who had overpaid his account	37
	Dishonoured cheques	29
	Interest charged by us on overdue debt	50
	At the end of the month:	
	Sales ledger – debit balances	3,429
	Sales ledger – credit balances	40

Sales Ledger Control Account

Dr		£			Cr £
2006			2006		
Aug 1	Balances b/d	3,816	Aug 1	Balances b/d	22
Aug 31	Sales	7,090	Aug 31	Cash	104
	Cash refunded	37		Bank	6,239
	Bank: dishonoured			Bad debts	306
	cheques	29		Discounts allowed	298
	Interest on debt	50		Returns inwards	664
	Balances c/d	40		Balances c/d	3,429
		11,062			11,062

23.7 Control accounts and double entry

When a business operates control accounts, it has to decide where the control accounts should be kept within the book-keeping system. There are two options:

● the control accounts within the double entry system
● control accounts as memorandum accounts.

These two options are discussed next.

Control accounts within the double entry system

In order to maintain the control accounts within the general ledger, the control account becomes part of the double entry system and the individual debtors and creditors accounts become memorandum accounts (*see* Exhibit 23.7).

Exhibit 23.7 **Control Account as part of a double entry system**

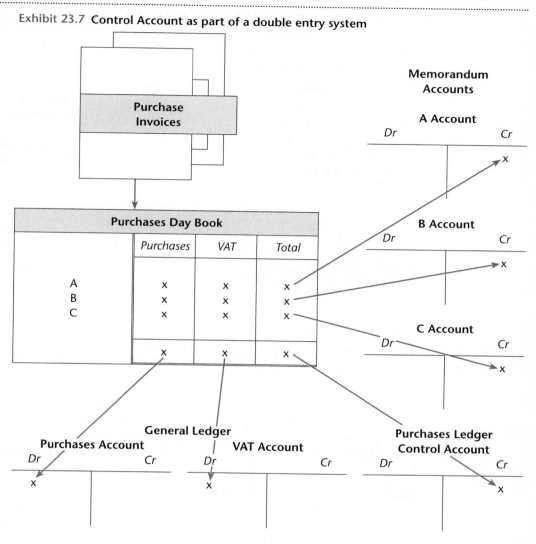

In Exhibit 23.7, the balance of outstanding creditors is taken from the control account and included in the trial balance at the end of the month or year end, as required. In this case, the personal accounts of the creditors (i.e. A Account, B Account, C Account, etc.) are not part of the double entry and are referred to as **memorandum accounts**. It is, however, important to balance the memorandum accounts periodically with the sales and purchases ledger control accounts so that errors can be located and corrected. The same procedure would apply to the sales.

Control accounts as memorandum accounts

In order to maintain the control accounts in the sales and purchases ledgers, the control accounts become memorandum accounts. Using this method, the debtors' and creditors' personal accounts are included in the double entry system via the sales and purchases ledgers, while the control account becomes the memorandum account.

Exhibit 23.8 illustrates this procedure with the purchase ledger. The sales would be similar.

Exhibit 23.8 Control Account as a Memorandum Account

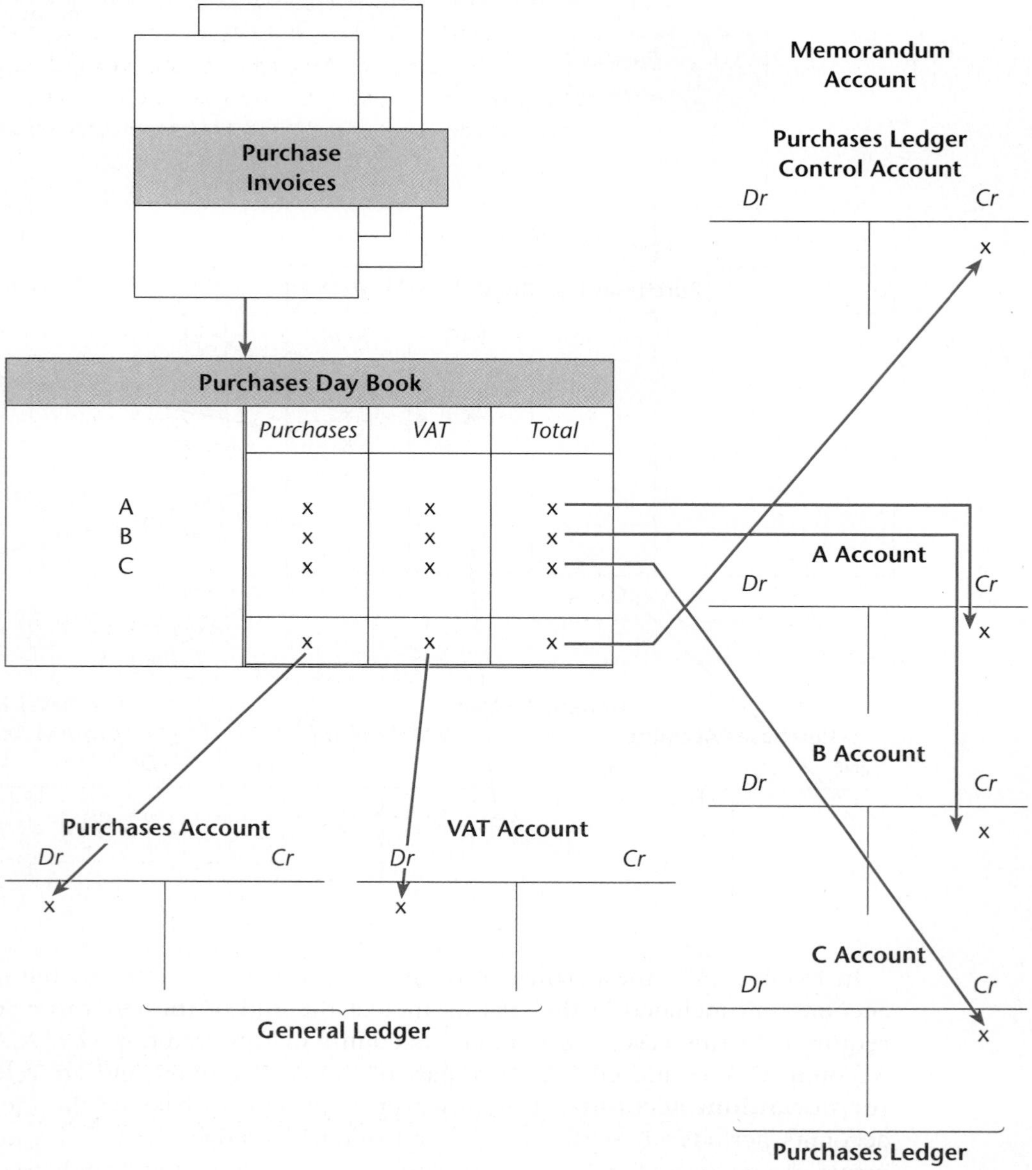

23.8 Other advantages of control accounts

Control accounts have merits other than that of locating errors. Normally the control accounts are under the charge of a responsible official, and fraud is made more difficult because any attempted fraudulent transfers will have to pass the scrutiny of this person.

For management purposes the balances on the control accounts can always be taken to equal debtors and creditors without waiting for an extraction of individual balances. Management control is thereby aided because the speed at which information is obtained is one of the prerequisites of efficient control.

23.9 Other sources of information for control accounts

With a large organisation there may well be more than one sales ledger or purchase ledger. The accounts in the sales ledger may be divided up in ways such as:

- *Alphabetically* – thus we may have three sales ledgers, split: A–F, G–O and P–Z.
- *Geographically* – this could be split: Europe, Far East, Africa, Australasia, North and South America.

For each ledger we must therefore have a separate control account.

Note that many students become confused when making postings to control accounts. You might find it useful to remember that when posting entries to control accounts the entry goes on the same side as it would in the personal account. Another useful hint can also be applied when entering 'contra' or 'set-off' items: here, think of the contra or set-off as *cash* and enter the item where you would normally enter cash on the respective control account (as mentioned previously in Section 23.5).

Chapter summary

- As a business expands it becomes increasingly difficult to trace any error(s) that may have occurred. Tracing an error may involve checking every item in every ledger which is very time consuming. Therefore, what is needed is a type of trial balance for each ledger and this requirement is met by the control account.
- Control accounts are prepared usually at the end of each month or period. The account contains the total of the various individual personal account balances which are held in subsidiary ledgers such as the 'sales ledger' or 'purchase ledger'. By comparing the balance on the control account with the total outstanding balances in a subsidiary ledger the arithmetical accuracy can be checked. Errors can more easily be located and rectified.
- Control accounts contain information gathered from the various accounting books including, sales and purchase day books, returns inwards and returns outwards day books and cash book. These items are entered into the control accounts in 'total', i.e. total credit sales for the month, total monies received from the debtors for the month and so on.
- Transfers from one ledger to another may be called 'contra entries' or sometimes 'set-offs'. Remember to enter these on the same side in the control account as you would normally enter cash either received or paid.
- If the sales ledger control account and the purchase ledger control account are maintained in the general ledger, then they are part of the double entry system and the sales ledger accounts and purchases ledger accounts (i.e. the personal accounts) are classed as 'memorandum accounts'.

- If, however, the sales ledger and purchases ledger are part of the double entry system, then the control accounts are classed as 'memorandum accounts'.
- Control accounts act as an aid to management.
- Finally, remember that when making entries into the control accounts the entry goes on exactly the same side as it would in the personal accounts. Think of 'contra items' or 'set-offs' as cash and enter them on the same side you would normally enter cash on the respective control account.

Exercises

23.1 You are required to prepare a sales ledger control account from the following:

2007		£
May 1 Sales ledger balances		4,560
Total of entries for May:		
Sales day book		10,870
Returns inwards day book		460
Cheques and cash received from customers		9,615
Discounts allowed		305
May 31 Sales ledger balances		5,050

23.2 You are to prepare a sales ledger control account from the following. Deduce the closing figure for the sales ledger balance as at 31 March 2007.

2007		£
Mar 1 Sales ledger balances		6,708
Totals for March:		
Discounts allowed		300
Cash and cheques received from debtors		8,970
Sales day book		11,500
Bad debts written off		115
Returns inwards day book		210
Mar 31 Sales ledger balances		?

23.3X Draw up a purchases ledger control account from the following:

2006		£
June 1 Purchases ledger balances		3,890
Totals for June:		
Purchases day book		5,640
Returns outwards day book		315
Cash and cheques paid to creditors		5,230
Discounts received		110
June 30 Purchases ledger balances		?

23.4X The following is a summary of sales activities during the month of November.

	£
Balance of debtors at 1 November 2006	220,617
Goods sold on credit	99,300
Money received from credit customers	109,262
Sales returns from credit customers	2,000
Journal credit to correct an error	550

(*a*) Prepare a debtors control account from the above details. Show clearly the balance carried down at 30 November 2006, and brought down at 1 December 2006.

The following closing balances were in the Subsidiary (Sales) Ledger on 30 November.

Robertson Mechanics	£15,016	Dr
Parkes and Company	£52,109	Dr
JJP Limited	£13,200	Dr
Components Limited	£42,982	Dr
OKK Parts	£44,798	Dr
Stevens Limited	£550	Dr
Mechanics Supplies	£40,000	Dr

(*b*) Reconcile the balances shown above with the debtors control account balance you have calculated in part (*a*).

	£
Debtors control account balance as at 30 November 2006	
Total of Subsidiary (Sales) Ledger accounts as at 30 November 2006	_____
Difference	======

(*c*) What may have caused the difference you calculated in part (*b*) above?

Association of Accounting Technicians

23.5X Draw up a sales ledger control account from the following.

2006		£
Apr 1	Debit balances	4,960
	Credit balances	120
	Totals for April:	
	Sales journal	8,470
	Cash and cheques received from debtors	7,695
	Discounts allowed	245
	Debit balances in the sales ledger set off against credit balances in the purchases ledger	77
Apr 30	Debit balances	?
	Credit balances	46

23.6 On 1 January 2006, the balances on Shery Tatupu's sales ledger were as follows:

	£	
L Barker	62	Cr
D Blackhurst	1,466	Dr
H Brackenbridge	58	Cr

During the three months ended 31 March 2006, the following transactions took place:

	Credit sales £	Cash sales £	Sales returns £	Payments received on account by cheque £	Discount allowed by cheque £
L Barker	18,642	946	–	15,023	142
D Blackhurst	16,428	–	88	16,009	–
H Brackenbridge	19,886	887	–	17,332	227

You are required to:
(*a*) write up the sales ledger accounts for the quarter ended 31 March 2006
(*b*) prepare the sales ledger control account for the quarter ended 31 March 2006
(*c*) reconcile the control account balance with the ledger account balances.

City & Guilds Pitman qualifications

23.7X On 1 September 2005, the balances on Neil Weeke's Purchase Ledger were as follows:

	£	
D Betts	3,240	Cr
S Haughton	2,228	Cr
M Cassidy	44	Dr

During the month of September 2005, the following transactions took place:

	Cash purchases £	Credit purchases £	Purchase returns £	Payments by cheque £	Discount received £
D Betts	340	6,430	860	9,650	255
S Haughton	180	4,667	328	5,108	187
M Cassidy	–	4,387	–	3,600	–

You are required to:
(*a*) write up the purchase ledger accounts for the month ended 30 September 2005
(*b*) prepare the purchase ledger control account for the month ended 30 September 2005
(*c*) reconcile the control account balance with the ledger account balances.

City & Guilds Pitman qualifications

CHAPTER 24

The journal

Learning objectives

After you have studied this chapter you should be able to:
- identify the journal as an original book of entry
- use the journal for entering a range of different transactions
- post items from the journal to the ledgers
- describe and explain the accounting cycle.

24.1 Main books of original entry

We have seen in earlier chapters that most transactions are entered in one of the following books of original entry:

- cash book
- sales day book
- purchases day book
- returns inwards day book
- returns outwards day book.

Each of the above books contains particular forms of transactions; for example, the sales day book contains details of all credit sales. To trace any of the transactions entered in the above five books would be relatively easy since it is known which book of original entry contains which item.

24.2 The journal: a book of original entry

Other items that are not entered into one of the above books of original entry are much less common and sometimes more complicated. It would be easy for a book-keeper to forget details of these transactions or perhaps the book-keeper may leave the company making it impossible at a later date to understand such book-keeping entries.

It is, therefore, important to record such transactions in a form of diary to relate to entries being made in the double entry accounts. The book used to record these transactions is called the **journal** and contains the following details for each transaction:

● the date
● the name of the account(s) to be debited and credited and the amount(s)
● a description and explanation of the transaction (this is called a **narrative**)
● a reference number for the source of the document giving proof of the transaction.

By recording the transaction in the journal there is less chance of further errors occurring by ensuring that the item is recorded properly and posted in the appropriate double entry accounts. Without such a record in the journal fraudulent transactions could occur more easily. Despite these advantages many businesses do not use a journal.

24.3 Typical uses of the journal

Some of the main uses of the journal are listed below. It must not be thought that this is a fully detailed list.

● the purchase and sale of fixed assets on credit
● writing off bad debts
● the correction of errors
● opening entries, the entries needed to open a new set of books
● other items.

The layout of the journal can be shown as follows:

The Journal

Date		Folio	Dr	Cr
	The name of the account to be debited.			
	The name of the account to be credited.			
	The narrative.			

It can be seen that on the first line the name of the account to be *debited* is entered while the second line gives the account to be *credited*. The name of the account to be credited is indented slightly and not shown directly under the name of the account to be debited, because this makes it easier to distinguish between the debit and credit items.

It should be remembered that the journal is not a double entry account; it is a form of diary, and entering an item in the journal is not the same as recording an item in an account. Once the journal entry has been made, the entry into the double entry accounts can be made.

Examples of the uses of the journal are given more fully in Sections 24.5 to 24.8.

24.4 Journal entries and examination questions

If you were to ask examiners about what types of book-keeping and accounting questions are most often answered badly, they would certainly include 'Questions involving journal entries'. This is not because questions about journal entries are actually more difficult than other types, but rather that many students seem to get some sort of a mental block when dealing with them.

It appears that this difficulty arises because students often think in terms of the debits and credits in accounts. Instead, they should think of the journal simply as a form of written instruction stating which account is to be debited and which account is to be credited, with a description of the transaction involved.

To try to help you avoid this sort of problem with journal entries, we will first show what the entries are in the accounts, and then write up the journal for those entries. We will now look at a few examples, which include folio numbers.

24.5 Purchase and sale on credit of fixed assets

Example 1: A machine was bought on credit from Toolmakers for £550 on 1 July 2007. From what you have learned in earlier chapters, you will know that the double entry accounts would be as follows:

Machinery *(Folio GL 1)*

2007	Folio	£	
Jul 1 Toolmakers	PL 55	550	

Toolmakers *(Folio PL 55)*

		2007	Folio	£
		Jul 1 Machinery	GL 1	550

Now we have to record these entries in the journal. Remember, the journal is simply a kind of diary, not in account form but in ordinary written form. It says which account has been debited, which account has been credited, and then gives a narrative that simply describes the nature of the transaction.

For the transaction above, the journal entry will appear as follows:

The Journal

Date	Details	Folio	Dr	Cr
2007			£	£
Jul 1	Machinery	GL 1	550	
	Toolmakers	PL 55		550
	Purchase of milling machine on credit, purchases invoice no 7/159			

Example 2: Sale of stationery no longer required, for £300 on credit to K King on 2 July 2007. Here again, it is not difficult to work out what entries are needed in the double entry accounts. They are as follows:

K King *(Folio SL 79)*

2007	Folio	£	
Jul 2 Stationery	GL 51	300	

Stationery *(Folio GL 51)*

	2007	Folio	£
	Jul 2 K King	SL 79	300

These are shown in journal form as follows:

The Journal

Date	Details	Folio	Dr	Cr
2007			£	£
Jul 2	K King	SL 79	300	
	Stationery	GL 51		300
	Sale of some stationery not now needed –			
	see letter ref: CT 568			

24.6 Writing off bad debts

Example 3: A debt of £78 owing to us from H Mander is written off as a bad debt on 31 August 2007. As the debt is now of no value, we have to stop showing it as an asset. This means that we will need to credit H Mander's account to cancel the amount out of his account. A bad debt is an expense, and so we will debit the amount to the bad debts account.

In double entry form this is shown as:

Bad debts *(Folio GL 16)*

2007	Folio	£	
Aug 31 H Mander	SL 99	78	

H Mander *(Folio SL 99)*

2007	Folio	£	2007	Folio	£
Aug 1 Balance	b/d	78	Aug 31 Bad debts	GL 16	78

The journal entry showing the same transaction would be as follows:

The Journal

Date	Details	Folio	Dr	Cr
2007			£	£
Aug 31	Bad debts	GL 16	78	
	H Mander	SL 99		78
	Debt written off as bad. See letter in file 7/8906			

24.7 Opening entries

Example 4: J Brew, after being in business for some years without keeping proper records, now decides to keep a double entry set of books. On 1 July 2006, he establishes that his assets and liabilities are as follows:

- *Assets*: Motor van £840, Fixtures £700, Stock £390,
  Debtors – B Young £95, D Blake £45,
  Bank £80, Cash £20.
- *Liabilities*: Creditors – M Quinn £129, C Walters £41.

The assets therefore total (£840 + £700 + £390 + £95 + £45 + £80 + £20) = £2,170; and the liabilities total (£129 + £41) = £170. The capital in the business consists of assets minus liabilities, which in Brew's case is (£2,170 − £170) = £2,000.

We must start the writing up of the books on 1 July 2006. To do this:

1 Open asset accounts, one for each asset. Each opening asset is shown as a debit balance.
2 Open liability accounts, one for each liability. Each opening liability is shown as a credit balance.
3 Open an account for the capital. Show it as a credit balance.
4 Record steps 1–3 in the journal.

Exhibit 24.1 shows the journal and the opening entries in the double entry accounts.

Exhibit 24.1

The Journal *Page 5*

Date	Details	Folio	Dr	Cr
2006			£	£
July 1	Motor van	GL 1	840	
	Fixtures	GL 2	700	
	Stock	GL 3	390	
	Debtors – B Young	SL 1	95	
	D Blake	SL 2	45	
	Bank	CB 1	80	
	Cash	CB 1	20	
	Creditors – M Quinn	PL 1		129
	C Walters	PL 2		41
	Capital	GL 4		2,000
	Assets and liabilities at the date entered to open the books		2,170	2,170

General Ledger
Motor Van Account

Dr					Cr
					Page 1
2006		Folio	£		
July 1	Balance	J 5	840		

	Fixtures Account			Page 2
Dr				Cr

2006		Folio	£
July 1 Balance		J 5	700

	Stock Account			Page 3
Dr				Cr

2006		Folio	£
July 1 Balance		J 5	390

	Capital Account			Page 4
Dr				Cr

				2006		Folio	£
				July 1 Balance		J 5	2,000

Sales Ledger
B Young Account

			Page 1
Dr			Cr

2006		Folio	£
July 1 Balance		J 5	95

D Blake

			Page 2
Dr			Cr

2006		Folio	£
July 1 Balance		J 5	45

Purchases Ledger
M Quinn Account

			Page 1
Dr			Cr

				2006		Folio	£
				July 1 Balance		J 5	129

C Walters Account

			Page 2
Dr			Cr

				2006		Folio	£
				July 1 Balance		J 5	41

Cash Book
Cash Bank

				Page 1
Dr				Cr

2006		Folio	£	£
July 1 Balances		J 5	20	80

Once the opening balances have been recorded in the books, the day-to-day transactions are entered in the normal way. Opening entries are needed only *once* in the life of the business.

24.8   Other items

Items other than those already described in Sections 24.5 to 24.7 can be of many kinds and it is impossible to write out a complete list. Correction of errors is explained in Chapters 31 and 32. Several other examples are now shown:

Example 5: K Young, a debtor, owes £2,000 on 1 July 2006. He is unable to pay his account in cash, but offers a motor car in full settlement of the debt. The offer is accepted on 5 July 2006.

The personal account is now no longer owed and therefore needs to be credited. On the other hand, the firm now has an extra asset, a motor car, and therefore the motor car account needs to be debited.

The double entry records are therefore:

K Young   *(SL 333)*

2006		*Folio*	£	2006		*Folio*	£
July 1	Balance	b/d	2,000	July 5	Motor car	GL 171	2,000

Motor Car   *(GL 171)*

2006		*Folio*	£				
July 5	K Young	SL 333	2,000				

This is shown in the journal as follows:

The Journal

		Folio	*Dr*	*Cr*
2006			£	£
July 5	Motor car	GL 171	2,000	
	K Young	SL 333		2,000
	Accepted motor car in full settlement of debt			
	per letter dated 5/7/2006			

Example 6: T Jones is a creditor. On 10 July 2006 his business is taken over by A Lee, to whom the debt of £150 is to be paid. Here, one creditor is being exchanged for another. The action needed is to cancel the amount owing to T Jones by debiting his account, and to show it owing to A Lee by opening an account for A Lee and crediting it.

The double entry records are therefore thus:

T Jones   *(SL 92)*

2006		*Folio*	£	2006		*Folio*	£
July 10	A Lee	SL 44	150	July 1	Balance	b/d	150

A Lee   *(SL 44)*

				2006		*Folio*	£
				July 10	T Jones	SL 92	150

The journal entries are thus:

The Journal

	Folio	Dr	Cr
2006		£	£
July 10 T Jones	SL 92	150	
A Lee	SL 244		150
Transfer of indebtedness as per letter ref G/1335			

***Example* 7**: We had previously bought an office photocopier for £1,310. It has been found to be faulty, and on 12 July 2006 we return it to the supplier, RS Ltd. An allowance of £1,310 is agreed, so we no longer owe the supplier for it.

The double entry records are therefore thus:

RS Ltd   *(PL 124)*

2006	Folio	£	2006	Folio	£
July 12 Office machinery	GL 288	1,310	July 1 Balance	b/d	1,310

Office machinery   *(GL 288)*

2006	Folio	£	2006	Folio	£
July 1 Balance	b/d	1,310	Jul 12 RS Ltd	PL 124	1,310

The journal entries are thus:

The Journal

	Folio	Dr	Cr
2006		£	£
July 12 RS Ltd	PL 124	1,310	
Office machinery	GL 288		1,310
Faulty photocopier returned to supplier.			
Full allowance given. See letter 10/7/2006			

24.9   Examination guidance

Later on in your studies, you may find that some of the journal entries become rather more complicated than those you have seen so far. The best plan for nearly all students would be to follow this advice during examinations:

● On your examination answer paper, write a heading entitled 'Workings'. Then under that show the double entry accounts.
● Now put a heading entitled 'Answer', and show the answer in the form of the journal, as shown in this chapter.

If you are already confident about dealing with these questions and you feel that you can manage them without showing your workings, then you may wish to leave out your workings from your answer.

If the question asks for 'journal entries' you must *not* fall into the trap of just showing the double entry accounts, as you could get no marks at all even though your double entry records are correct. The examiner wants to see the *journal* entries, and you must show them as your answer.

24.10   The accounting cycle

Each accounting period sees a cycle of recording transactions, being completed when the trading and profit and loss account and the balance sheet are prepared. The **accounting cycle** through which all accounting transactions pass can be shown in the form of a diagram. Exhibit 24.2 shows the accounting cycle for a profit-making organisation.

Exhibit 24.2 The accounting cycle for a profit-making organisation

Source documents

Where original information is to be found

- Sales and purchases invoices
- Debit and credit notes for returns
- Bank paying-in slips and cheque counterfoils
- Receipts for cash paid out and received
- Correspondence containing other financial information

Original entry

What happens to it

Classified and then entered in books of prime entry:
- Sales and purchases day books
- Returns inwards and outwards day books
- Cash books*
- The journal

Double entry

How the dual aspect of each transaction is recorded

Double entry accounts

General ledger	Sales ledger	Purchases ledger	Cash books*
Real and nominal accounts	Debtors' accounts	Creditors' accounts	Cash book and petty cash book

(*Note: Cash books fulfil both roles of books of prime entry and double entry accounts)

Check arithmetic

Checking the arithmetical accuracy of double entry accounts

Trial balance

Profit or loss

Calculation of profit or loss for the accounting period

Trading and profit and loss account

Closing financial position

Financial statement showing liabilities, assets and capital at the end of the accounting period

Balance sheet

Each accounting period will see the same cycle performed. The connection between one period and the next are the balances remaining on the balance sheet, each of which is carried forward to start the next period's recording.

24.11 Multiple-choice questions

Now attempt Set No. 2 of the multiple-choice questions in Appendix C. This set contains 35 questions.

Chapter summary

● The journal is an original book of entry and is used to record rare or exceptional transactions that do not appear in the other books of original entry.
● Typical uses of the journal include the purchase and sale of fixed assets, writing off bad debts, correction of errors and opening entries.
● When preparing a journal entry the date is entered first followed by the name of the account to be debited and amount, this is followed by entering the name of the account to be credited, slightly indented, and the amount. Finally, a narrative, giving a brief description of the transaction is written.
● Since many students have problems answering examination questions involving journal entries it is recommended that they prepare 'a working section' to show the double entry aspect prior to preparing the journal entry which usually forms the 'Answer' to the question.
● The accounting cycle shows the period in which a business operates in its financial year. It involves recording all the trading activities from source documents in the day books, posting to the various ledgers and the preparation of the financial statements.

Exercises

24.1   Show the journal entries to record the following:

2007
Jan   1 Bought computer on credit from Data Systems for £4,000
Jan   5 Goods taken from the business for own use, £120. The goods were not paid for by the proprietor
Jan   8 A debt of £220 owing to us by J Oddy is written off as a bad debt
Jan 15 Bought a motor vehicle from Smithy Garage paying by cheque, £15,500
Jan 29 J Street owes us £250. She is unable to pay her debt and we agree to take some filing cabinets valued at £250 from her to cancel the debt.

Narratives are not required.

24.2X   Show the journal entries for April 2007 necessary to record the following items:

(*a*) Apr   1 Bought fixtures on credit from J Harper, £1,809
(*b*) Apr   4 We take £500 goods out of the business stock without paying for them

(c) Apr   9 £28 worth of the goods taken by us on 4 April are returned back into stock by us. We do not take any money for the return of the goods

(d) Apr 12 K Lamb owes us £500. He is unable to pay his debt. We agree to take some office equipment from him at the value and so cancel the debt

(e) Apr 18 Some of the fixtures bought from J Harper, £65 worth, are found to be unsuitable and are returned to him for full allowance

(f) Apr 24 A debt owing to us by J Brown of £68 is written off as a bad debt

(g) Apr 30 Office equipment bought on credit from Super Offices for £2,190.

24.3   (a) J Green's financial position at 1 May 2008 is as follows:

		£
Bank		2,910
Cash		160
Equipment		5,900
Premises		25,000
Creditors:	R Smith	890
	T Thomas	610
Debtors:	J Carnegie	540
Loan from:	J Higgins	4,000

You are required to show the opening entries needed to open a double entry set of books for Green as at 1 May 2008. Then open up the necessary accounts in J Green's ledger to record the above, as well as the succeeding transactions.

(b) During May 2008, Green's transactions were as follows:

2008
May   2 Bought goods from T Thomas on credit, £2,100
May   5 Paid R Smith on account by cheque, £500
May 12 Repaid J Higgins by cheque, £1,000
May 24 Sold goods to J Carnegie on credit, £2,220
May 31 Total cash sales for the month £8,560, of which £8,000 banked on 31 May
May 31 J Carnegie returned goods to us, £400
May 31 Paid loan interest to Higgins by cheque, £200.

You are required to post all accounts and to extract a trial balance as at 31 May 2008, but only the cash book needs balancing down. Note that the sales, purchases and returns day books are *not* needed.

24.4X   M Maxwell is in business as a trader. During February 2006, the following transactions took place:

February
  3 Purchased a motor vehicle from J Saunders costing £5,000 paying 50% of the total cost by cheque with the remainder due in 6 months.
  8 Purchased fixtures and fittings on credit from J McNulty. List price £200 less trade discount of 15%.
  9 M Maxwell put a further £10,000 into the business, 25% went into cash and the remainder into the firm's bank account.
 10 A Robinson, a debtor owing £250 was declared bankrupt. M Maxwell received 10% of the amount outstanding by cheque. The remainder to be written off to bad debts.
 16 It was found that the £5,000 paid for the motor vehicle purchased on 3 February included Road Fund Licence valued at £150.

22 An account of £50 for petrol for M Maxwell's private car had been posted to the firm's Motor Expenses Account.

24 Rent received of £125 had been posted to the Commissions Received Account.

24 Purchased a piece of machinery on credit from C Mattey. The list price was £6,000 but a trade discount of 20% was allowed.

26 The machine, purchased on 24 February, had chipped paintwork. Maxwell kept it but Mattey agreed to a credit of £100.

You are required to enter these transactions (including cash) into the journal, giving suitable brief narratives.

OCR

Part 4

Adjustments for financial statements

This part is concerned with the adjustments that are needed and the use of the extended trial balance in preparing the financial statements.

Methods of depreciation

25.1 Introduction

In Chapter 18 we considered the distinction between capital and revenue expenditure. Capital expenditure involves the purchase of fixed assets. This chapter covers the need for charging depreciation on these assets and the causes of depreciation.

The methods of calculating depreciation usually involve either the straight line or reducing balance method.

The double entry aspect of recording transactions showing the purchase of fixed assets, charges for depreciation and the disposal of assets will be shown in the following Chapter 26.

25.2 Depreciation of fixed assets

Fixed assets are those assets of material value that are:

- of long life, and
- to be used in the business, and
- not bought with the intention of being resold.

However, fixed assets such as machinery, motor vehicles, fixtures and even buildings do not last for ever. If the amount received (if any) on disposal is deducted from the cost of buying them, the difference is called **depreciation**.

The only time that depreciation can be calculated accurately is when the fixed asset is finally disposed of, and the difference between the cost to its owner and the amount received on disposal is then calculated. If a motor vehicle were to be bought for £10,000 and sold five years later for £2,000, then the amount of depreciation is £10,000 − £2,000 = £8,000.

25.3   Depreciation as an expense

Depreciation is part of the original cost of a fixed asset consumed during its period of use by a firm. It is an expense for services consumed, in the same way as expenses for items such as wages, rent or electricity. Since depreciation is an expense, it will have to be charged to the profit and loss account and will, therefore, reduce net profit.

You can see that the only real difference between the cost of depreciation for a motor vehicle and the cost of petrol for the motor vehicle is that the petrol cost is used up in a day or two, whereas the cost of depreciation for the motor vehicle is spread over several years. Both are costs to the business.

25.4   Causes of depreciation

The principal causes of depreciation are:

● physical deterioration
● economic factors
● the time factor
● depletion.

These are described in greater detail below.

Physical depreciation

Physical depreciation can come in two basic forms:

● *Wear and tear* When a motor vehicle, or machinery, or fixtures and fittings are used, they eventually wear out. Some last many years, but others last only a few. This is even true of buildings, although some may last for a very long time.
● *Erosion, rust, rot and decay* Land may be eroded or wasted away by the action of wind, rain, sun or the other elements of nature. Similarly, the metals in motor vehicles or machinery will rust away. Wood will rot eventually. Decay is a process, which will be present due to the elements of nature and the a lack of proper attention.

Economic factors

Economic factors may be said to be the reasons for an asset being put out of use even though it is in good physical condition. The two main factors are usually **obsolescence** and **inadequacy**, described further thus:

● *Obsolescence* This is the process of becoming out of date. For instance, over the years there has been great progress in the development of synthesisers and electronic devices used by leading commercial musicians. The old equipment will therefore have become obsolete, and much of it will have been taken out of use by such musicians. This does not mean that the equipment is worn out. Other people may well buy the old equipment and use it, possibly because they cannot afford to buy new up-to-date equipment.
● *Inadequacy* This arises when an asset is no longer used because of the growth and change in the size of the firm. For instance, a small ferryboat that is operated

by a firm at a coastal resort will become entirely inadequate when the resort becomes more popular. Then it will be found that it would be more efficient and economical to operate a larger ferryboat, and so the smaller boat will be taken out of use by the firm. In this case, it does not mean that the ferryboat is no longer in good working order; it may be sold to a firm at a smaller resort.

Both obsolescence and inadequacy do not necessarily mean that the asset is destroyed. It is merely put out of use by the firm, and another firm will often buy it. For example, many of the aeroplanes no longer used by the large airlines are bought by smaller airlines.

The time factor

Obviously time is needed for wear and tear, erosion, and for obsolescence and inadequacy to take place. However, there are fixed assets to which the time factor is connected in a different way. These are assets that have a legal life fixed in terms of years.

For instance, you may agree to rent some buildings for ten years. Such an agreement is normally called a **lease**. When a lease expires, it is worth nothing to you as it has finished; whatever you paid for the lease is now of no value.

A similar asset is where you buy a patent with complete rights, so that only you are able to produce something using that patent. When the patent's time has expired, it then has no value. The usual length of life of a patent is 16 years.

Instead of using the term depreciation, the term **amortisation** is often used for these assets.

Depletion

Other assets are of a 'wasting' character, perhaps due to the extraction of raw materials from them. The materials are then either used by the firm to make something else, or are sold in their raw state to other firms. Natural resources such as mines, quarries and oil wells come under this heading.

To provide for the consumption of an asset of a wasting character is called provision for **depletion**.

25.5 Land and buildings

Prior to the accounting regulation known as SSAP 12, which applied after 1977, freehold and long leasehold properties were very rarely subject to a charge for depreciation. It was contended that, as property values tended to rise instead of fall, it was inappropriate to charge depreciation.

However, SSAP 12 requires that depreciation be charged over the property's useful life, with the exception that freehold land will not normally require a provision for depreciation. This is because land does not normally depreciate. Buildings do, however, eventually fall into disrepair or become obsolete and must be subject to a charge for depreciation each year. When a revaluation of property takes place, the depreciation charge must be on the revalued figure.

Many of the accounting standards have over the last few years been replaced with what are known as Financial Reporting Standards. In 1999, SSAP 12, was replaced by Financial Reporting Standard 15 (FRS 15) that repeated the requirements of the original standard. However, the new FRS dealt with the problem of the distinction between the cost of freehold land and the cost of the buildings upon it, by insisting that each cost should be separated. Since accounting standards are outside the scope of this text book the above reference to these are for note only. This topic is dealt with fully in *Business Accounting 1* by Frank Wood and Alan Sangster.

25.6 Appreciation

At this stage, readers may well begin to ask themselves about the assets that increase (appreciate) in value. The answer to this is that normal accounting procedure would be to ignore any such **appreciation**, as to bring appreciation into account would be to contravene both the historical cost concept and the prudence concept (as discussed in Chapter 11). However, one of the problems when SSAP 12 was introduced was that the UK was in the middle of a property boom when businesses could see the market value of their properties rising. At the same time, they were being instructed by the accounting standard to charge their profit and loss account with depreciation that represented a fall in the value of the property over the period. Not surprisingly, this didn't make sense. Therefore, SSAP 12 allowed fixed assets to be revalued and for depreciation to then be calculated on the basis of the revalued amount. FRS 15 also permits this to be done.

25.7 Provision for depreciation as an allocation of cost

Depreciation in total over the life of an asset can be calculated quite simply as cost less amount receivable when the asset is put out of use by the firm. If the item is bought and sold within one accounting period, then the depreciation for that period is charged as a revenue expense in arriving at that period's net profit. The difficulties start when the asset is used for more than one accounting period, and an attempt has to be made to charge each period with the depreciation for that period.

Even though depreciation provisions are now regarded as allocating cost to each accounting period (except for accounting for inflation), it does not follow that there is any 'true' method of performing even this task. All that can be said is that the cost should be allocated over the life of the asset in such a way as to charge it as equitably as possible to the periods in which the asset is used.

The difficulties involved are considerable, and some of them are now listed.

- Apart from a few assets, such as a lease, how accurately can a firm assess an asset's useful life? Even a lease may be put out of use if the premises leased have become inadequate.
- How does one measure 'use'? A car owned by a firm for two years may have been driven one year by a very careful driver and another year by a reckless driver. The standard of driving will affect the motor car and also the amount of cash receivable on its disposal. How should such a firm apportion the car's depreciation costs?

- There are other expenses beside depreciation, such as repairs and maintenance of the fixed asset. As both of these affect the rate and amount of depreciation, should they not also affect the depreciation provision calculations?
- How can a firm possibly know the amount receivable in a number of years' time when the asset is put out of use?

These are only some of the difficulties. Therefore, the methods of calculating provisions for depreciation are mainly accounting customs.

25.8 Methods of calculating depreciation charges

The two main methods in use for calculating depreciation charges are the **straight line method** and the **reducing balance method**. Most accountants think that, although other methods may be needed in certain cases, the straight line method is the one that is generally most suitable. Both methods are now described.

Straight line method

By this method, the number of years of use is estimated. The cost is then divided by the number of years, to give the depreciation charge each year.

For instance, if a lorry was bought for £22,000 and we thought we would keep it for four years and then sell it for £2,000, the depreciation to be charged would be:

$$\frac{\text{Cost (£22,000)} - \text{Disposal value (£2,000)}}{\text{Number of years use (4)}} = \frac{£20,000}{4}$$

= £5,000 depreciation each year for four years.

If, after four years, the lorry would have had no disposal value, the charge for depreciation would have been:

$$\frac{\text{Cost (£22,000)}}{\text{Number of years use (4)}} = \frac{£22,000}{4}$$

= £5,500 depreciation each year for four years.

Reducing balance method

By this method a fixed percentage for depreciation is deducted from the cost in the first year. In the second or later years the same percentage is taken of the reduced balance (i.e. cost *less* depreciation already charged). This method is also known as the 'diminishing balance' method.

For instance, if a machine is bought for £10,000 and depreciation is to be charged at 20 per cent, the calculations for the first three years would be as follows:

	£
Cost	10,000
First year: depreciation (20% of £10,000)	2,000
	8,000
Second year: depreciation (20% of £8,000)	1,600
	6,400
Third year: depreciation (20% of £6,400)	1,280
Net book value at the end of the third year	5,120

Note that **net book value** means the cost of a fixed asset with depreciation deducted. It is sometimes simply known as 'book value'.

Using this method means that much larger amounts are charged in the earlier years of use as compared with the latter years of use. It is often said that repairs and upkeep in the early years will not cost as much as when the asset becomes old. This means that:

In the early years		In the later years
A higher charge for depreciation + A lower charge for repairs and upkeep	will tend to be fairly equal to	A lower charge for depreciation + A higher charge for repairs and upkeep

The worked example in Section 25.9 gives a comparison of the calculations using the two methods, if the same cost applies for the two methods.

25.9 A worked example

A firm has just bought a machine for £8,000. It will be kept in use for four years, and then it will be disposed of for an estimated amount of £500. The firm's management asks for a comparison of the amounts charged as depreciation using both methods.

For the straight line method, a figure of (£8,000 − £500) ÷ 4 = £7,500 ÷ 4 = £1,875 per annum is to be used. For the reducing balance method a percentage figure of 50 per cent will be used.

	Method 1 Straight Line £		Method 2 Reducing Balance £
Cost	8,000		8,000
Depreciation: year 1	1,875	(50% of £8,000)	4,000
	6,125		4,000
Depreciation: year 2	1,875	(50% of £4,000)	2,000
	4,250		2,000
Depreciation: year 3	1,875	(50% of £2,000)	1,000
	2,375		1,000
Depreciation: year 4	1,875	(50% of £1,000)	500
Disposal value	500		500

This illustrates the fact that using the reducing balance method there is a much higher charge for depreciation in the early years, and lower charges in the later years.

Other methods

There are many more methods of calculating depreciation but they are outside the scope of this volume. Special methods are often used in particular industries, where there are circumstances which are peculiar to that industry.

25.10 Depreciation provisions and assets bought or sold

There are two main methods of calculating depreciation provisions for assets bought or sold during an accounting period.

1 Ignore the dates during the year that the assets were bought or sold and merely calculate a full period's depreciation on the assets in use at the end of the period. Thus, assets sold during the accounting period will have no provision made for depreciation for that last period irrespective of how many months they were in use. Conversely, assets bought during the period will have a full period of depreciation provision charged even though they may not have been owned throughout the whole period.

2 Provide for depreciation made on the basis of one month's ownership equals one month's depreciation. Fractions of months are usually ignored. This is obviously a more precise method than method 1.

The first method is the one normally used in practice. However, for examination purposes, where the dates on which the assets are bought and sold are shown, you should use method 2. If no such dates are given then, obviously, method 1 is the one to use. Often the question will indicate which method to use so it is important to read the instructions carefully before attempting your answer.

Chapter summary

- Depreciation is charged on fixed assets in use during an accounting period.
- Fixed assets are defined as those assets of material value that are intended to be used in the business over a period of time and have not been bought with the intention of resale.
- Depreciation is an expense of the business and as such is charged to the profit and loss account.
- The main causes of depreciation are physical deterioration, economic factors, the time factor and depletion.
- The increase in value over the cost of an asset, usually land and buildings, is called appreciation.
- The straight line method is where an equal amount of depreciation is charged each year.
- The reducing balance method is where a fixed percentage for depreciation is taken from the cost of the asset in the first year. In the second and later years the same percentage is taken from the reduced balance (i.e. cost *less* depreciation already charged).

Exercises

25.1 K Richardson runs a small manufacturing business and purchases a new machine for £40,000. It has an estimated life of five years and a scrap value of £5,000. Richardson is not sure whether to use the straight line or reducing method of depreciation for the purpose of calculating depreciation on the machine.

You are required to calculate the depreciation on the machine using both methods, showing clearly the balance remaining in the machine account at the end of the five years for each method. Assume that 40 per cent per annum is to be used for the reducing balance method.

25.2 A printing press cost £37,500 and will be kept for four years when it will be traded in at an estimated value of £15,360. Show the calculations of the figures for depreciation (to the nearest £) for each of the four years using:

(*a*) the straight line method, and
(*b*) the reducing balance method, using a depreciation rate of 20 per cent.

25.3X A motor vehicle costs £19,200 and will be kept for four years, and then sold for an estimated value of £1,200. Calculate the depreciation for each year using:

(*a*) the reducing balance method, using a depreciation rate of 50 per cent, and
(*b*) the straight line method.

25.4X A photocopier costs £5,120. It will be kept for five years, and then sold at an estimated figure of £1,215. Show the calculations of the figures for depreciation for each year using:

(*a*) the straight line method, and
(*b*) the reducing balance method, using a depreciation rate of 25 per cent.

25.5X A tractor cost £72,900 and has an estimated life of five years after which it will be traded in at an estimated value of £9,600. Show your calculations of the amount of depreciation each year using:

(*a*) the reducing balance method at a rate of $33^{1}/_{3}$ per cent, and
(*b*) the straight line method.

25.6 A dumper is bought for £6,000. It will last for three years and will then be sold back to the supplier for £3,072. Show the depreciation calculations for each year using:

(*a*) the reducing balance method with a rate of 20 per cent, and
(*b*) the straight line method.

25.7X From the following information, which shows the depreciation for the first two years of use for two assets, you are required to answer the questions set out below.

	Machinery £	Fixtures £
Cost Year 1	8,000	3,600
Year 1 Depreciation	1,600	900
	6,400	2,700
Year 2 Depreciation	1,600	675
	4,800	2,025

(*a*) Which type of depreciation method is used for each asset?
(*b*) What will be the book value of each of the assets after four years of use?
(*c*) If, instead of the method used, the machinery had been depreciated by the alternative method but using the same percentage rate, what would have been the book value after four years? (Calculate your answer to the nearest £.)

25.8X   Harry Green is the owner of HG Computers, a business that buys and sells computer equipment whose financial year end is 31 October 2005. As book-keeper to the company you have just prepared the trial balance which you pass to Harry Green. Harry looks at the figures in the trial balance and tells you that he:

- sees that there is an account called 'Computer equipment at cost';
- understands that he has several computers that he uses to run the business;
- hopes to keep these computers for about three years;
- thought that all his computers were treated as stock.

Task:

Write a memo to Harry Green explaining why computers used by the business would not be classified as stock.

AAT

CHAPTER 26

Double entry records for depreciation and the disposal of assets

Learning objectives

After you have studied this chapter you should be able to:

- incorporate depreciation calculations into the accounting records
- record the disposal of fixed assets and the adjustments needed to the provision for depreciation accounts.

26.1 Recording depreciation

Looking back a number of years, the charge for depreciation was always shown in the fixed asset accounts; this method has now fallen into disuse. In the method used today, the fixed assets accounts show the assets at cost price, the depreciation being shown separately accumulating in a **'provision for depreciation account'**.

The following example illustrates the accounting records.

A business purchases a stamping machine for use in the firm's workshop for £2,000 (ignore VAT) on 1 January 2005. The company uses the reducing balance method of depreciation using a rate of 20 per cent per annum. The financial year end is 31 December. The records for the first three years are shown in Exhibit 26.1. Notice that no entry is made in the asset account for depreciation. This means that the fixed asset accounts will normally be shown at cost price.

The double entry for depreciation is:

- debit the profit and loss account
- credit the provision for depreciation account.

Exhibit 26.1

Machinery

Dr		£		Cr £
2005			2005	
Jan 1	Cash	2,000	Dec 31 Balance c/d	2,000
2006			2006	
Jan 1	Balance b/d	2,000	Dec 31 Balance c/d	2,000
2007			2007	
Jan 1	Balance b/d	2,000	Dec 31 Balance c/d	2,000
2008				
Jan 1	Balance b/d	2,000		

Provision for Depreciation – Machinery Account

Dr		£			Cr £
2005			2005		
Dec 31	Balance c/d	400	Dec 31	Profit and loss a/c	400
2006			2006		
Dec 31	Balance c/d	720	Jan 1	Balance b/d	400
			Dec 31	Profit and loss a/c	320
		720			720
2007			2007		
Dec 31	Balance c/d	976	Jan 1	Balance b/d	720
			Dec 31	Profit and loss a/c	256
		976			976
			2008		
			Jan 1	Balance b/d	976

Profit and Loss account (extracts) for the year ended 31 December

		£
2005	Depreciation	400
2006	Depreciation	320
2007	Depreciation	256

Now, the balance on the Machinery Account is shown on the balance sheet at the end of each year, less the balance on the Provision for Depreciation Account.

Balance Sheet (extracts) as at 31 December

	Cost	Total depreciation	Net book value
	£	£	£
2005			
Machinery	2,000	400	1,600
2006			
Machinery	2,000	720	1,280
2007			
Machinery	2,000	976	1,024

Another example can now be given in Exhibit 26.2. This is of a business with financial years ending 30 June. A motor car is bought on 1 July 2006 for £8,000. Another car is bought on 1 July 2007 for £11,000. Each car is expected to be in use for five years, and the disposal value of the first car is expected to be £500 and of the second car £1,000. The method of depreciation to be used is the straight line method. The first two years' accounts are shown in the Exhibit.

Exhibit 26.2

Motor Cars Account

Dr					Cr
2006		£	2007		£
Jul 1	Bank	8,000	Jun 30 Balance c/d		8,000
2007			2008		
Jul 1	Balance b/d	8,000	Jun 30 Balance c/d		19,000
Jul 1	Bank	11,000			
		19,000			19,000
2008					
Jul 1	Balance b/d	19,000			

Provision for Depreciation – Motor Cars Account

Dr				Cr
2007		£	2007	£
Jun 30 Balance c/d		1,500	Jun 30 Profit and loss a/c	1,500
			Jul 1 Balance b/d	1,500
2008			2008	
Jun 30 Balance c/d		5,000	Jun 30 Profit and loss a/c	3,500
		5,000		5,000
			Jul 1 Balance b/d	5,000

Profit and Loss Account for the year ended 30 June (extracts)

		£
2007	Depreciation	1,500
2008	Depreciation	3,500

Balance Sheet (extract) as at 30 June 2007

	Cost	Total depreciation	Net book value
	£	£	£
Motor car	8,000	1,500	6,500

Balance Sheet (extract) as at 30 June 2008

	Cost	Total depreciation	Net book value
	£	£	£
Motor cars	19,000	5,000	14,000

The disposal of a fixed asset

Reason for accounting entries

Upon the sale of an asset, we will want to delete it from our accounts. This means that the cost of that asset needs to be taken out of the asset account. In addition, the depreciation of the asset that has been sold will have to be taken out of the depreciation provision. Finally, the profit or loss on sale, if any, will have to be calculated.

When we charge depreciation on a fixed asset, we are having to make estimates. We cannot be absolutely certain how long we will keep an asset in use, nor can we be certain at the date of purchase how much the asset will be sold for on disposal. Nor will we always estimate correctly. This means that when the asset is disposed of, the cash received for it is usually different from our original estimate.

Accounting entries needed

On the sale of a fixed asset, the following entries are needed (for instance, let us assume the sale of machinery):

(A) Transfer the cost price of the asset sold to an Assets Disposal Account (in this case a Machinery Disposals Account).	Debit Machinery Disposals Account. Credit Machinery Account.
(B) Transfer the depreciation already charged to the Assets Disposal Account.	Debit Provision for Depreciation – Machinery Account. Credit Machinery Disposals Account.
(C) For remittance received on disposal.	Debit Cash Book. Credit Machinery Disposals Account.
(D) Transfer balance (difference) on Machinery Disposals Account to the Profit and Loss Account.	
(i) If the difference is on the debit side of the Disposals Account, it is a *profit* on sale.	Debit Machinery Disposals Account. Credit Profit and Loss Account.
(ii) If the difference is on the credit side of the Disposal Account, it is a *loss* on sale.	Debit Profit and Loss Account. Credit Machinery Disposals Account.

These entries can be illustrated by looking at those needed if the machinery already shown in Exhibit 26.1 was sold. The records to 31 December 2007 show that the cost of the machine was £2,000 and a total of £976 has been written off as depreciation, leaving a net book value of (£2,000 − £976) = £1,024. If, therefore, the machine is sold on 2 January 2008 for *more than* £1,024, a profit on sale will be made; if, on the other hand, the machine is sold for *less than* £1,024, then a loss on disposal will be incurred.

Exhibit 26.3 shows the entries needed when the machine has been sold for £1,070 and a small profit on sale has been made. Exhibit 26.4 shows the entries where the machine has been sold for £950, thus incurring a loss on the sale. In both cases the sale is on 2 January 2008 and no depreciation is charged for the two days' ownership in 2008. The letters (A) to (D) in Exhibits 26.3 and 26.4 are references to the table of instructions shown above.

Exhibit 26.3

Machinery Account

Dr						Cr
2005		£	2008			£
Jan 1	Cash	2,000	Jan 2	Machinery disposals	(A)	2,000

Provision for Depreciation: Machinery Account

Dr					Cr
2008		£	2008		£
Jan 2	Machinery disposals (B)	976	Jan 1	Balance b/d	976

Machinery Disposals Account

Dr							Cr
2008			£	2008			£
Jan 2	Machinery	(A)	2,000	Jan 2	Cash	(C)	1,070
Dec 31	Profit and			2	Provision for		
	loss a/c	(D)	46		depreciation	(B)	976
			2,046				2,046

Profit and Loss Account for the year ended 31 December 2008

			£
Gross Profit			xxx
Add Profit on sale of machinery		(D)	46

Exhibit 26.4

Machinery Account

Dr						Cr
2005		£	2008			£
Jan 1	Cash	2,000	Jan 2	Machinery disposals	(A)	2,000

Provision for Depreciation: Machinery Account

Dr					Cr
2008		£	2008		£
Jan 2	Machinery disposals (B)	976	Jan 1	Balance b/d	976

Machinery Disposals Account

Dr							Cr
2008			£	2008			£
Jan 2	Machinery	(A)	2,000	Jan 2	Cash	(C)	950
				2	Provision for		
					depreciation	(B)	976
				Dec 31	Profit and loss	(D)	74
			2,000				2,000

287

Profit and Loss Account for the year ended 31 December 2008

		£
Gross Profit		xxx
Less Loss on sale of machinery	(D)	74

In this chapter, all unnecessary difficulties have been avoided. For instance, all assets have been bought, or sold, on the first day of a financial year. Exactly what happens when assets are sold or bought part way through the year is dealt with in *Business Accounting 1* by Frank Wood and Alan Sangster.

26.3 Depreciation provisions and the replacement of assets

Making a provision for depreciation does not mean that money is invested somewhere to finance the replacement of the asset when it is put out of use. It is simply a book-keeping entry, and the end result is that lower net profits are shown because the provisions have been charged to the profit and loss account.

It is not surprising to find that people who have not studied accounting misunderstand the situation. They often think that a provision is the same as money kept somewhere with which to replace the asset eventually.

On the other hand, lower net profits may also mean lower drawings by the owner(s) of the business. If this is the case, then there will be more money in the bank with which to replace the asset. However, there is no guarantee that lower profits mean lower drawings.

Note: A step-by-step guide dealing with depreciation in final accounts is shown in Chapter 28, Section 28.14.

Chapter summary

- Although depreciation used to be charged to the asset account this method is now outdated and only used by a small number of businesses.
- The method used today shows the fixed asset at cost price in the appropriate asset account. Any depreciation charge is shown separately and accumulating in a 'Provision for depreciation account'.
- The depreciation charge for the period is then debited to the Profit and Loss Account.
- In the balance sheet the asset is shown at cost price, less the accumulated depreciation so giving the 'Net book value' of the asset.
- On disposal of a fixed asset the book-keeping entries will involve a new account, i.e. 'asset disposal account'. It is then necessary to transfer the cost price of the asset, the accumulated depreciation and the cash received to this account when the asset is sold. The balancing figure in the asset disposal account may be either a profit or loss on disposal.
- If there is a profit on disposal this will then be added to the gross profit in the profit and loss account.
- If there is a loss on disposal this will be charged as an expense in the profit and loss account.

Exercises

26.1 A White, an exporter, bought a new car for his business on 1 January 2005 for £12,500. He decided to write off depreciation at the rate of 20 per cent, using the reducing balance method.
Show the following for each of the financial years ended 31 December 2005, 2006 and 2007.

(a) motor cars account
(b) provision for depreciation account
(c) extracts from the profit and loss accounts
(d) extracts from the balance sheets.

26.2X H Slater, a jewellery manufacturer, purchased a new machine for £18,000 on 1 November 2007. Her business year end is 31 October, but she cannot decide which method of depreciation she should use in respect of the machine – the straight line method or the reducing balance method.

Required:
In order to assist her in making a decision, draw up the machinery account and the provision for depreciation account for the three years from 1 November 2007 using:

(a) the straight line method
(b) the reducing balance method.

Each account must indicate which method is being used, and each account should be balanced at the end of each of the three years. In both cases the rate of depreciation is to be 10 per cent, and calculations should be made to the nearest £.

(c) Also show the extracts from the profit and loss accounts and balance sheets for each of the three years.

26.3 On 1 January 2005, which was the first day of a financial year, T Young bought networked computer hardware for £9,500. It is to be depreciated by the straight line method at the rate of 20 per cent, ignoring salvage value. On 1 January 2008 the system was sold for £4,250.
Show the following for the complete period of ownership.

(a) The computer account.
(b) The provision for depreciation.
(c) The computer disposal account.
(d) The extracts from profit and loss accounts for four years.
(e) The extracts from three years' balance sheets – 2005, 2006 and 2007.

26.4 Show the relevant disposal account for each of the following cases, including the transfers to the profit and loss account.

(a) Motor vehicle: cost £12,000; depreciated £9,700 to date of sale; sold for £1,850.
(b) Machinery: cost £27,900; depreciated £19,400 to date of sale; sold for £11,270.
(c) Fixtures: cost £8,420; depreciated £7,135 to date of sale; sold for £50.
(d) Buildings: cost £200,000; depreciated straight line 5 per cent on cost for 11 years to date of sale; sold for £149,000.

26.5X Wai Lan Chung owns a Chinese restaurant. The business's fixed assets include some kitchen equipment which cost £38,000 when it was purchased on 1 January 2004.
It was decided that kitchen equipment should be depreciated using the straight line method. It was estimated that the equipment has a useful life of five years and a likely scrap value of £2,000. Depreciation is recorded in the accounts on 31 December each year.

On 28 March 2006 some of the kitchen equipment was sold for cash £520. The equipment had cost £4,400 on 1 January 2004; at date of sale the equipment had a net book value of £2,000.

Tasks:

(*a*) Give *one* cause of depreciation.

(*b*) Explain why it is important for businesses to make an annual charge for depreciation of fixed assets.

(*c*) Prepare the disposal account recording the profit or loss on the sale of the kitchen equipment.

Southern Examining Group AQA

Please note that this question is NOT from the live examinations for the current specification.

26.6X   (*a*) What is meant by the term depreciation?

(*b*) Which accounting concept is being ignored if a business changes the method of charging depreciation each year?

(*c*) Name *two* methods of charging depreciation provision.

(*d*) The accountant for a business recommends that, because of the size of the organisation, all items of machinery less than £500 should be treated as revenue expenditure. What accounting concept or convention is being applied in this example?

(*e*) A business whose financial year ends on 31 December each year purchased a delivery van by cheque for £20,000 on 1 January 2006. Depreciation is to be charged on delivery vans at 20% p.a. on cost. The delivery van was sold on 30 June 2008 for a cheque of £13,000. Depreciation is not charged in the year of disposal. Show the *relevant entries* in *each* of the following accounts for the years ended 31 December 2006, 2007 and 2008:

   (i)   delivery van account

   (ii) provision for depreciation account

   (iii) delivery van disposal account

   (iv) profit and loss account.

NEAB (GCSE)

CHAPTER 27

Bad debts and provisions for doubtful debts

Learning objectives

After you have studied this chapter, you should be able to:

- understand how bad debts are written off
- understand why provisions for doubtful debts are made
- make the accounting entries necessary for recording a provision for doubtful debts
- make the accounting entries for increasing or reducing the provision for doubtful debts
- make all the entries in respect of the provision for doubtful debts in the profit and loss account and balance sheet
- make accounting entries in respect of bad debts recovered.

27.1 Bad debts

If a firm finds that it is impossible to collect a debt, then that debt should be written off as a **bad debt**. This could happen if the debtor is suffering a loss in the business, or may even have gone bankrupt and is thus unable to pay the debt. A bad debt is, therefore, an expense on the firm that is owed the money.

An example of debts being written off as bad is shown next.

Example 1: We sold £50 goods to K Leeming on 5 January 2005, but that firm became bankrupt. On 16 February 2005 we sold £240 goods to T Young. Young managed to pay £200 on 17 May 2005, but it became obvious that he would never be able to pay the final £40.

When drawing up our final accounts to 31 December 2005, we decided to write these off as bad debts. The accounting entries are shown in the table below.

Accounting entries	Explanation
Debit: Bad debts account	To transfer the amount of unpaid debt to the bad debts account
Credit: Debtor's account	To reduce the liability of the debtor who is unable to settle the debt
Debit: Profit and loss account	To record the amount of bad debts of the period concerned
Credit: Bad debts account	To transfer the amount of bad debts to profit and loss account

The accounts would appear as follows:

K Leeming Account

Dr   Cr

2005		£	2005		£
Jan 5	Sales	50	Dec 31	Bad debts	50

T Young Account

Dr   Cr

2005		£	2005		£
Feb 16	Sales	240	May 17	Cash	200
			Dec 31	Bad debts	40
		240			240

Bad Debts Account

Dr   Cr

2005		£	2005		£
Dec 31	K Lee	50	Dec 31	Profit and loss a/c	90
Dec 31	T Young	40			
		90			90

Profit and Loss Account for the year ended 31 December 2005 (extract)

	£	
Gross profit		xxx
Less Expenses:		
Bad debts	90	90

27.2   Provisions for doubtful debts

Let us look, as an example, at the accounts of K Clark, who started in business on 1 January 2005 and has just completed his first year of trading on 31 December 2005.

He has sold goods for £50,000 and they cost him £36,000, so his gross profit was (£50,000 − £36,000) = £14,000. However, included in the £50,000 sales was a credit sale to C Yates for £250. C Yates has died, leaving no money, and he had not paid his account. The £250 debt is therefore a bad debt and should be charged in the profit and loss account as an expense.

Beside that debt, a credit sale of £550 on 1 December 2005 to L Hall is unlikely to get paid. Clark cannot yet be certain about this, but he has been told by others that Hall had not paid his debts to other businesses. As Clark had given three months' credit to Hall, the debt is not repayable until 28 February 2006. However, the final accounts for the year 2005 are to be drawn up in January 2006 at the request of the bank. Clark cannot wait until after 28 February 2006 to see whether the debt of £550 owing by Hall will be a bad debt.

What, therefore, can Clark do? When he shows the bank his final accounts, he wants to achieve the following objectives:

(*a*) to charge as expenses in the profit and loss account for the year 2005 an amount representing sales of that year for which he will never be paid
(*b*) to show in the balance sheet as correct a figure as possible for the true value of debtors at the balance sheet date.

He can carry out (*a*) above by writing off Yates' debt of £250 and then charging it as an expense in his profit and loss account.

For (*b*) he cannot yet write off Hall's debt of £550 as a bad debt because he is not certain about it being a bad debt. If he does nothing about it, the debtors shown on the balance sheet will include a debt that is probably of no value. The debtors on 31 December 2005, after deducting Yates' £250 bad debt, amount to £10,000.

The answer to this is as shown in Exhibit 27.1.

Exhibit 27.1

K Clark
Trading and Profit and Loss Account
for the year ended 31 December 2005

	£	£
Sales		50,000
Less Cost of goods sold:		36,000
Gross profit		14,000
Less Expenses:		
Other expenses	5,000	
Bad debts	250	
Provision for doubtful debts	550	
		5,800
Net profit		8,200

K Clark
Balance Sheet as at 31 December 2005 (extracts)

	£	£
Debtors	10,000	
Less Provision for doubtful debts	550	
		9,450

Exactly how we will do the double entry for this is explained in Section 27.4 following. What we have achieved so far is to show bad debts and **provision for doubtful debts** as an expense in the year when the sales were made. The debtors are also shown at probably what is their true value.

27.3 Provisions for doubtful debts: estimating provisions

The estimates of provisions for doubtful debts can be made thus:

- by looking into each debt, and estimating which ones will be bad debts
- by estimating, on the basis of experience, what percentage of the debts will result in bad debts.

It is well known that the longer a debt is owing, the more likely it will become a bad debt. Some firms draw up an ageing debtors schedule, showing how long debts have been owing. Older debtors need higher percentage estimates of bad debts than newer debtors. Exhibit 27.2 gives an example of such an ageing schedule.

Exhibit 27.2 Ageing Schedule for Doubtful Debts

Period debt owing	Amount	Estimated percentage doubtful	Provision for doubtful debts
	£		£
Less than one month	5,000	1	50
1 month to 2 months	3,000	3	90
2 months to 3 months	800	4	32
3 months to 1 year	200	5	10
Over 1 year	160	20	32
	9,160		214

In the above example the calculation of the provision for doubtful debts has been specifically detailed. Many businesses do not go to this level of detail; instead they apply a percentage based upon the experience that has been established within the business over a number of years. For example, they may decide to use 5 per cent of the debtors figure as a provision for doubtful debts.

27.4 Accounting entries for provisions for doubtful debts

When a decision has been taken as to the amount of provision to be made, then the accounting entries needed for the provision relate to the year in which provision is *first* made, as follows:

- debit: profit and loss account with the amount of provision
- credit: provision for doubtful debts account.

Let us look at an example that shows the entries needed for a provision for doubtful debts.

Example 2: As at 31 December 2003, the debtors' figure for a firm amounted to £10,000 after writing off £422 of definite bad debts. It is estimated that 2 per cent of debts (i.e. £10,000 × 2% = £200) will prove to be bad debts, and it is decided to make a provision for these. The accounts would appear as follows:

Profit and Loss Account for the year ended 31 December 2003 (extracts)

	£	£
Gross profit		xxx
Less Expenses:		
Bad debts	422	
Provision for doubtful debts	200	622

Provision for Doubtful Debts Account

Dr					*Cr*
2003		£	2003		£
Dec 31 Balance c/d		200	Dec 31 Profit and loss a/c		200
			2004		
			Jan 1 Balance b/d		200

In the balance sheet, the balance on the provision for doubtful debts will be deducted from the total of debtors, thus:

Balance Sheet (extracts) 31 December 2003

Current assets	£	£
Debtors	10,000	
Less Provision for doubtful debts	200	9,800

27.5 Increasing the provision

Taking the same example as shown in Example 2 above, let us suppose that at the end of the following year, on 31 December 2004, the doubtful debts provision needed to be increased because the provision could be kept at 2 per cent but the debtors had risen to £12,000. Not included in the figure of £12,000 debtors is £884 in respect of debts that had already been written off as bad debts during the year. A provision of £200 had been brought forward from the *previous* year, but we now want a total provision of £240 (i.e. 2 per cent of £12,000). All that is needed is a provision for an extra £40.

The double entry will be:

● debit: profit and loss account
● credit: provision for doubtful debts account,

and the relevant accounts will look as set out below.

Profit and Loss Account (extracts) for the year ended 31 December 2004

	£	£
Gross profit		xxx
Less Expenses:		
Bad debts	884	
Provision for doubtful debts	40	

Provision for Doubtful Debts Account

Dr					Cr
2004		£	2004		£
Dec 31 Balance c/d		240	Jan 1 Balance b/d		200
			Dec 31 Profit and loss a/c		40
		240			240
			2005		
			Jan 1 Balance b/d		240

Balance Sheet as at 31 December 2004 (extracts)

	£	£
Current Assets		
Debtors	12,000	
Less Provision for doubtful debts	240	11,760

27.6 Reducing the provision

The provision is shown as a credit balance. To reduce it, we would need a debit entry in the provision account. The credit would be in the profit and loss account. Again, using Example 2 above, let us assume that on 31 December 2005 the debtors figure had fallen to £10,500 but the provision remained at 2 per cent, i.e. £210 (£10,500 × 2%). As the provision had previously been £240, it now needs a reduction of £30. Bad debts of £616 had already been written off during the year and are not included in the debtors figure of £10,500.

The double entry is:

● debit: provision for doubtful debts account
● credit: profit and loss account,

and the relevant accounts look thus:

Profit and Loss Account (extracts) for the year ended 31 December 2005

	£	£
Gross profit		xxx
Add Reduction in provision for doubtful debts		30
		xxx
Less Expenses:		
Bad debts	616	616

Provision for Doubtful Debts Account

Dr				Cr
2005		£	2005	£
Dec 31 Profit and loss a/c		30	Jan 1 Balance b/d	240
Dec 31 Balance c/d		210		
		240		240
			2006	
			Jan 1 Balance b/d	210

Balance Sheet as at 31 December 2005 (extracts)

	£	£
Current Assets		
Debtors	10,500	
Less Provision for doubtful debts	210	10,290

The main points that you have to remember about provisions for doubtful debts are:

● *Year 1 – provision first made:* (a) debit profit and loss account with full provision
  (b) show in balance sheet as a deduction from debtors.

● *Later years:* (a) only the increase, or decrease, in the provision is shown in the profit and loss account, as follows:
  – *to increase*: debit the profit and loss account, and credit the provision for doubtful debts account.
  – *to decrease*: credit the profit and loss account, and debit the provision for doubtful debts account.
  (b) the balance sheet will show the amended figure of the provision as a deduction from debtors.

27.7 A worked example

Let us now look at a comprehensive example.

Example 3: A business started on 1 January 2002 and its financial year end is 31 December. A table of debtors, the bad debts written off and the estimated doubtful debts at the rate of 2 per cent of debtors at the end of each year, as well as the double entry accounts and the extracts from the final accounts, follow as Exhibit 27.3.

Exhibit 27.3

Year to 31 December	Debtors at end of year (after bad debts written off)	Bad debts written off during year	Debts thought at end of year to be impossible to collect: 2% of debtors
	£	£	£
2002	6,000	423	120 (2% of £6,000)
2003	7,000	510	140 (2% of £7,000)
2004	7,750	604	155 (2% of £7,750)
2005	6,500	610	130 (2% of £6,500)

Provision for Doubtful Debts Account

Dr		£		Cr £
2002			2002	£
Dec 31	Balance c/d	120	Dec 31 Profit and loss a/c	120
2003			2003	
Dec 31	Balance c/d	140	Jan 1 Balance b/d	120
			Dec 31 Profit and loss a/c	20
		140		140
2004			2004	
Dec 31	Balance c/d	155	Jan 1 Balance b/d	140
			Dec 31 Profit and loss a/c	15
		155		155
2005			2005	
Dec 31	Profit and loss a/c	25	Jan 1 Balance b/d	155
Dec 31	Balance c/d	130		
		155		155
			2006	
			Jan 1 Balance b/d	130

Bad Debts Account

Dr		£		Cr £
2002			2002	£
Dec 31	Debtors	423	Dec 31 Profit and loss a/c	423
2003			2003	
Dec 31	Debtors	510	Dec 31 Profit and loss a/c	510
2004			2004	
Dec 31	Debtors	604	Dec 31 Profit and loss a/c	604
2005			2005	
Dec 31	Debtors	610	Dec 31 Profit and loss a/c	610

Profit and Loss Account(s) (extracts) for the year ended

		£	£
Gross profit for 2002, 2003, 2004			xxx
2002	*Less* Expenses:		
	Bad debts	423	
	Provision for doubtful debts (increase)	120	543
2003	*Less* Expenses:		
	Bad debts	510	
	Provision for doubtful debts (increase)	20	530
2004	*Less* Expenses:		
	Bad debts	604	
	Provision for doubtful debts (increase)	15	619
2005	Gross profit for 2005		xxx
	Add Reduction in provision for doubtful debts		25
			xxx
	Less Bad debts		610
			xxx

Balance Sheet (extracts) as at 31 December

		£	£
2002	Debtors	6,000	
	Less Provision for doubtful debts	120	5,880
2003	Debtors	7,000	
	Less Provision for doubtful debts	140	6,860
2004	Debtors	7,750	
	Less Provision for doubtful debts	155	7,595
2005	Debtors	6,500	
	Less Provision for doubtful debts	130	6,370

27.8 Bad debts recovered

It is not uncommon for a *debt written off* in previous years to be *recovered* in later years. When this occurs, the book-keeping procedures are such that, first, you should reinstate the debt by making the following entries:

● debit: debtor's account
● credit: bad debts recovered account.

The reason for reinstating the debt in the ledger account of the debtor is to have a detailed history of the account as a guide for granting credit in the future. By the time a debt is written off as bad, it will be recorded in the debtors' ledger account. Thus, when such a debt is recovered, it must also be shown in the debtors' ledger account.

When cash or a cheque is later received from the debtor in settlement of the account or part thereof, other book-keeping entries are necessary:

● debit: cash/bank with the amount received
● credit: debtor's account with the amount received.

At the end of the financial year, the credit balance on the bad debts recovered account will be transferred to either the bad debts account or direct to the credit side of the profit and loss account. The net effect of either of these entries is the same, since the bad debts account will be transferred to the profit and loss account at the end of the financial year. In other words, the net profit will be the same no matter which method is used.

Note: A step-by-step guide to dealing with bad debts and provision for and debts in final accounts is shown in Chapter 28, Section 28.14.

Chapter summary

● If a debt is unlikely to be paid then it is known as a bad debt.
● When the debt has been outstanding for a length of time the business usually decides to write if off. The debt is debited to the bad debts account and the customer's account is credited. The bad debt account is later credited and the profit and loss account debited where it is charged as an expense.

- A provision for doubtful debts is created in case some of the outstanding debts are not paid. The provision is charged to the profit and loss account and then deducted from the debtors in the balance sheet, thereby showing a realistic figure of the debts owed and what payment the business expects to receive.
- The provision for doubtful debts is calculated after any bad debts have been written off and deducted from the outstanding debtors.
- The provision for doubtful debts can be adjusted if the debtors at the end of the financial year either increase or decrease.
- To increase the provision debit the profit and loss account and credit the provision for doubtful debts account with the amount of the increase.
- To reduce the provision debit the provision for doubtful debts account and credit the profit and loss account with the amount of the reduction.
- A debt that has previously been written off but is subsequently paid by the debtors is known as a bad debt recovered.

Exercises

27.1 Data Computer Services commences in business on 1 January 2006, and during its first year of trading the following debts are found to be bad and the firm decided to write them off as bad:

2006		
April 30	H Gordon	£1,110
August 31	D Bellamy Ltd	£640
October 31	J Alderton	£120

On 31 December 2006, the schedule of remaining debtors, amounting in total to £68,500, is examined, and it is decided to make a provision for bad debts of £2,200.

You are required to show:

(a) the bad debts account and the provision for doubtful debts account
(b) the charge to the profit and loss account
(c) the relevant extracts from the balance sheet as at 31 December 2006.

27.2 A business started on 1 January 2004, and its financial year end is 31 December.

Date: 31 Dec	Total debtors	Profit and loss	Dr/Cr	Final figure for Balance Sheet
2004	7,000			
2005	8,000			
2006	6,000			
2007	7,000			

The table shows the figure for debtors appearing in a trader's books on 31 December of each year from 2004 to 2007. The provision for doubtful debts is to be 1 per cent of debtors from 31 December 2004. Complete the table indicating the amount to be debited or credited to the profit and loss accounts for the year ended on each 31 December, and the amount for the final figure of debtors to appear in the balance sheet on each date.

27.3X   A business started on 1 January 2005 and its financial year end is 31 December annually. The table shows the debtors, the bad debts written off and the estimated doubtful debts at the end of year.

Year to 31 December	Debtors at end of year (after bad debts written off)	Bad debts written off during the year	Debts thought at end of year to be unlikely to collect
2005	12,000	298	100
2006	15,000	386	130
2007	14,000	344	115
2008	18,000	477	150

Show the Bad Debts Account and Provision for Doubtful Debts Account, as well as the extracts from the profit and loss account for each year and the balance sheet extracts.

27.4   Emford & Co was advised to create a provision for doubtful debts at the end of the business's accounting year, 31 December 2004. It was decided to use a rate of 5 per cent based on trade debtors which totalled £18,600 at that date.

A year later, on 31 December 2005, when trade debtors totalled £19,240, the provision for doubtful debts was maintained at the same rate.

During 2006 the business experienced far fewer bad debts than had been expected and so on 31 December 2006 the rate was reduced to 2.5 per cent. Trade debtors at this date totalled £20,400.

Task:
Complete the following table.

Date	Amount of provision for doubtful debts £	Amount of adjustment to existing provision £	Write either 'increase' or 'decrease' to indicate the effect on the *profit* for the year
31 December 2004			
31 December 2005			
31 December 2006			

Southern Examining Group AQA

Please note that this question is NOT from the live examinations for the current specification.

27.5X   From the details below, write up the accounts shown in the ledger of C Bedford Ltd, a wholesaler, for the year ended 31 December 2008. You should show clearly the amounts transferred to the profit and loss account. Information of relevance is as follows:

● At 1 January 2008, T Strange owed C Bedford Ltd £2,000. On 30 November 2008, C Bedford Ltd is notified that T Strange has been declared bankrupt and Bedford receives a cheque for 25p for each £1 owed. The balance owing by T Strange is written off as a bad debt.

● C Bedford Ltd also maintains a provision for doubtful debts equivalent to 1% of outstanding debts at the end of the year. On 1 January 2008 the balance on this account is £500. At 31 December 2008 C Bedford is owed £52,000 by debtors.

NEAB (GCSE)

27.6X (*a*) On 1 January 2004, there was a balance of £2,500 in the provision for bad debts account and it was decided to maintain the provision at 5% of the debtors at the end of each year. The debtors on 31 December each year were as follows:

	£
2004	60,000
2005	40,000
2006	40,000

You are required to show the accounting entries for the three years ended 31 December 2004, 2005 and 2006 as follows:
(i)   the provision for doubtful debts account
(ii) the profit and loss account
(iii) the balance sheet extract.

(*b*) Explain the difference between bad debts and a provision for doubtful debts.

(*c*) As more and more businesses are experiencing difficulty collecting debts they find it important to create a provision for doubtful debts to provide for such a contingency. What is the purpose of creating such a provision, and which accounting concept covers this area.

CHAPTER 28

Other adjustments for financial statements

Learning objectives

After you have studied this chapter you should be able to:

- understand why it is necessary to adjust expense accounts for amounts owing or paid in advance
- adjust expense accounts for amounts owing (accruals) and paid in advance (prepayments)
- adjust revenue accounts for amounts owing at the end of a period
- show accruals, prepayments and revenue debtors in the balance sheet
- ascertain the amounts of expenses and revenue that should be shown in the profit and loss account after making adjustments for accruals and prepayments
- enter up the necessary account for goods taken for own use
- prepare financial statements for service sector organisations
- understand what is meant by goodwill and distinguish between various kinds of capital
- enter discounts allowed and received in the financial statements
- prepare financial statements, incorporating the above mentioned adjustments, for a sole trader using the fully worked example and step-by-step guide.

28.1 The final accounts so far

The trading and profit and loss account that has been considered until now has taken sales for a period and deducted *all* the expenses for that period, resulting in either a net profit or net loss.

So far, it has been assumed that the expenses incurred have belonged exactly to the period of the trading and profit and loss account. If, for example, the trading and profit and loss account for the year ended 31 December 2005 was being drawn up, then the rent paid as shown in the trial balance was exactly that due for 2005. There was no rent owing at the beginning of 2005 nor any owing at the end of 2005, nor had any rent been paid in advance. It is easier to consider a simple example at first to understand the principles of final accounts.

28.2 Adjustments needed for expenses owing or paid in advance

Not all businesses pay their rent exactly on time and, indeed, some businesses prefer to pay for their rent in advance. The following examples will illustrate the adjustments necessary if expenses are either owing, or paid in advance, at the end of a financial period.

Two firms rent their premises for £1,200 per year.

1 Firm A pays £1,000 during the year and owes £200 rent at the end of the year:

Rent expense used up during the year = £1,200
Rent actually paid in the year   = £1,000.

2 Firm B pays £1,300 during the year, including £100 in advance for the following year:

Rent expense used up during the year = £1,200
Rent actually paid for in the year   = £1,300.

A profit and loss account for the 12 months needs 12 months' rent as an expense (= £1,200). This means that in the above two examples the double entry accounts will have to be adjusted.

In all the examples following in this chapter, the trading and profit and loss accounts are for the period ended 31 December 2005.

28.3 Accrued expenses (i.e. expenses owing)

Assume that rent of £1,000 per year is payable at the end of every three months but that the rent is not always paid on time. Details are given in the table below.

Amount	Rent due	Rent paid
£250	31 March 2005	31 March 2005
£250	30 June 2005	2 July 2005
£250	30 September 2005	4 October 2005
£250	31 December 2005	5 January 2006

The rent account appears thus:

Rent Account

Dr				Cr
2005		£		
Mar 31	Cash	250		
Jul 2	"	250		
Oct 4	"	250		

The rent paid on 5 January 2006 will appear in the books of the year 2006 as part of the double entry.

The expense for 2005 is obviously £1,000 as that is the year's rent, and this is the amount needed to be transferred to the profit and loss account. But if £1,000 was put on the credit side of the rent account (the debit being in the profit and loss account), the account would not balance. We would have £1,000 on the credit side of the account and only £750 on the debit side.

To make the account balance, the £250 rent owing for 2005 but paid in 2006 must be carried down to 2006 as a credit balance because it is a liability on 31 December 2005. Instead of rent owing, it could be called rent accrued (or just simply an **accrual**). The completed account can now be shown, thus:

Rent Account

Dr		£			Cr £
2005			2005		
Mar 31	Cash	250	Dec 31	Profit and loss	1,000
Jul 2	"	250			
Oct 4	"	250			
Dec 31	Accrued c/d	250			
		1,000			1,000
			2006		
			Jan 1	Accrued b/d	250

The balance c/d has been described as 'accrued c/d', rather than as a balance. This is to explain what the balance is for; it is for an **accrued expense**.

28.4 Prepaid expenses

Insurance for a firm is at the rate of £840 a year, starting from 1 January 2005. The firm has agreed to pay this at the rate of £210 every three months. However, payments were not made at the correct times. Details were:

Amount	Insurance due	Insurance paid
£210	31 March 2005	£210 28 February 2005
£210	30 June 2005	£420 31 August 2005
£210	30 September 2005	
£210	31 December 2005	£420 18 November 2005

The insurance account for the year ended 31 December 2005 will be shown in the books as:

Insurance Account

Dr		£	Cr
2005			
Feb 28	Bank	210	
Aug 31	"	420	
Nov 18	"	420	

The last payment shown of £420 is not just for 2005; it can be split as £210 for the three months to 31 December 2005 and £210 for the three months ended 31 March 2006. For a period of 12 months the cost of insurance is £840 and this is, therefore, the figure needing to be transferred to the profit and loss account.

If this figure of £840 is entered, then the amount needed to balance the account will be £210 and at 31 December 2005 there is a benefit of a further £210 paid for but not used up – an asset that needs carrying forward as such to 2006, i.e. as a debit balance. It is a **prepaid expense**. The account can now be completed as follows:

Insurance Account

Dr				Cr
2005		£	2005	£
Feb 28 Bank		210	Dec 31 Profit and loss	840
Aug 31 "		420		
Nov 18 "		420	Dec 31 Prepaid c/d	210
		1,050		1,050
2006				
Jan 1 Prepaid b/d		210		

Prepayment happens when items other than purchases are bought for use in the business and they are not fully used up in the period. For instance, packing materials and stationery items are normally not entirely used up over the period in which they are bought, there being a stock in hand at the end of the accounting period. This stock is, therefore, a form of prepayment and needs carrying down to the following period in which it will be used. This can be seen in the following example:

Year ended 31 December 2005:
Packing materials bought in the year £2,200
Stock of packing materials in hand as at 31 December 2005 £400.

Looking at the example, it can be seen that in 2005 the packing materials used up will have been (£2,200 − £400) = £1,800. We will still have a stock of £400 packing materials at 31 December 2005, to be carried forward to 2006 as an asset balance (debit balance). Thus:

Packing Materials Account

Dr		Cr	
2005	£	2005	£
Dec 31 Bank	2,200	Dec 31 Profit and loss	1,800
		Dec 31 Stock c/d	400
	2,200		2,200
2006			
Jan 1 Stock b/d	400		

The stock of packing materials is not added to the stock of unsold goods in hand in the balance sheet, but it is added to the other prepayments of expenses.

28.5 Revenue owing at the end of period

The revenue owing for sales is already shown in the books. These are the debit balances on our customers' accounts, i.e. debtors. There may be other kinds of revenue, all of which have not been received by the end of the period – e.g. rent receivable. An example now follows.

A firm's warehouse is larger than it needs to be. The firm rents part of it to another firm for £800 per annum. Details for the year ended 31 December are as shown in the table below.

Amount	Rent due	Rent received
£200	31 March 2005	4 April 2005
£200	30 June 2005	6 July 2005
£200	30 September 2005	9 October 2005
£200	31 December 2005	7 January 2006

The account for 2005 will appear as follows:

Rent Receivable Account

Dr		Cr
	2005	£
	Apr 4 Bank	200
	Jul 6 Bank	200
	Oct 9 Bank	200

The rent received of £200 on 7 January 2006 will be entered in the books in 2006 (not shown).

Any rent paid by the firm would be charged as a debit to the profit and loss account. Any rent received, being the opposite, is transferred to the credit of the profit and loss account, as it is a revenue.

The amount to be transferred for 2005 is that earned for the 12 months, i.e. £800. The rent received account is completed by carrying down the balance owing as a debit balance to 2006. The £200 owing is an asset on 31 December 2005.

The rent receivable account can now be completed:

Rent Receivable Account

Dr		Cr	
2005	£	2005	£
Dec 31 Profit and loss	800	Apr 4 Bank	200
		Jul 6 Bank	200
		Oct 9 Bank	200
		Dec 31 Accrued c/d	200
	800		800
2006			
Jan 1 Accrued b/d	200		

28.6 Expenses and revenue account balances and the balance sheet

In all the cases listed dealing with adjustments in the final accounts, there will still be a balance on each account after the preparation of the trading and profit and loss accounts. All such balances remaining should appear in the balance sheet. The only question left is where and how they should be shown.

The amounts owing for expenses are usually added together and shown as one figure. These could be called 'expense creditors', 'expenses owing' or 'accrued expenses'. The item would appear under current liabilities because it is for expenses that have to be discharged in the near future.

Items prepaid are also added together and called 'prepayments', 'prepaid expenses' or 'payments in advance'. They are shown next under the debtors. Amounts owing for rents receivable or other revenue owing are usually added to debtors.

The balance sheet in respect of the accounts so far seen in this chapter would appear thus:

Balance Sheet as at 31 December 2005

	£	£	£
Current assets			
Stock		xxx	
Debtors		200	
Prepayments (210 + 400)		610	
Bank		xxx	
Cash		xxx	
		x,xxx	
Less Current liabilities			
Trade creditors	xxx		
Accrued expenses	250	xxx	
Net current assets			xxx

28.7 Expenses and revenue accounts covering more than one period

Students are often asked to draw up an expense or revenue account for a full year where there are amounts owing or prepaid at both the beginning and end of a year. We can now see how this is done.

Example 1: The following details are available:

(A) On 31 December 2004, three months' rent of £3,000 is owing.
(B) The rent chargeable per year is £12,000.
(C) The following payments are made in the year 2005: 6 January £3,000; 4 April £3,000; 7 July £3,000; 18 October £3,000.
(D) The final three months rent for 2005 is still owing.

Now we can look at the completed rent account. The letters (A) to (D) give reference to the details above.

Rent Account

Dr							Cr
2005			£	2005			£
Jan 6	Bank	(C)	3,000	Jan 5	Owing b/d	(A)	3,000
Apr 4	Bank	(C)	3,000	Dec 31	Profit and loss	(B)	12,000
Jul 7	Bank	(C)	3,000				
Oct 18	Bank	(C)	3,000				
Dec 31	Accrued c/d	(D)	3,000				
			15,000				15,000
				2006			
				Jan 1	Accrued b/d		3,000

Example 2: The following details are available:

(A) On 31 December 2004, packing materials in hand amount in value to £1,850.
(B) During the year to 31 December 2005, £27,480 is paid for packing materials.
(C) There are no stocks of packing materials on 31 December 2005.
(D) On 31 December 2005, we still owed £2,750 for packing materials already received and used.

The packing materials account will appear thus:

Packing Materials Account

Dr					Cr
2005			£	2005	£
Jan 1	Stocks b/d	(A)	1,850	Dec 31 Profit and loss	32,080
Dec 31	Bank	(B)	27,480		
Dec 31	Owing c/d	(D)	2,750		
			32,080		32,080
				2006	
				Jan 1 Owing b/d	2,750

The figure of £32,080 is the difference on the account, and is transferred to the profit and loss account. We can prove it is correct through the following:

	£	£
Stock at start of year		1,850
Add Bought and used:		
Paid for	27,480	
Still owed for	2,750	30,230
Cost of packing materials used in the year		32,080

Example 3: Where different expenses are put together in one account, it can get even more confusing. Let us look at where rent and rates are joined together. Here are the details for the year ended 31 December 2005:

(A) Rent is payable of £6,000 per annum.

(B) Rates of £4,000 per annum are payable by instalments.

(C) At 1 January 2005, rent £1,000 has been prepaid in 2004.

(D) On 1 January 2005 rates are owed of £400.

(E) During 2005, rent of £4,500 is paid.

(F) During 2005, rates of £5,000 were paid.

(G) On 31 December 2005, rent £500 is owing.

(H) On 31 December 2005, rates of £600 have been prepaid.

A combined rent and rates account is to be drawn up for the year 2005 showing the transfer to the profit and loss account, and balances are to be carried down to 2006. Thus:

Rent and Rates Account

Dr							Cr
2005				£	2005		£
Jan 1	Rent prepaid b/d	(C)		1,000	Jan 1 Rates owing b/d (D)		400
Dec 31	Bank: rent	(E)		4,500	Dec 31 Profit & loss a/c (A)+(B)		10,000
Dec 31	Bank: rates	(F)		5,000			
Dec 31	Rent owing c/d	(G)		500	Dec 31 Rates prepaid c/d (H)		600
				11,000			11,000
2006					2006		
Jan 1	Rates prepaid b/d	(H)		600	Jan 1 Rent owing b/d (G)		500

28.8 Goods for own use

Traders will often take items out of their business stocks for their own use, without paying for them. There is nothing wrong about this, but an entry should be made to record the event. This is done as follows:

● credit the purchases account, to reduce cost of goods available for sale
● debit the drawings account, to show that the proprietor has taken the goods for private use.

In the United Kingdom, an adjustment may be needed for value added tax. If goods supplied to a trader's customers have VAT added to their price, then any such goods taken for own use will need such an adjustment. This is because the VAT regulations state that VAT should be added to the cost of goods taken. The double entry for the VAT content would be:

● debit the drawings account
● credit VAT account.

Adjustments may also be needed for other private items. For instance, if a trader's private insurance had been incorrectly charged to the insurance account, then the correction would be:

● credit the insurance account
● debit the drawings account.

28.9 Goodwill

When starting in business, we could start from nothing. At that time we would have no customers at all. Over the years we might work hard, and then have a lot of customers who would buy or trade with us year after year.

As an alternative way of starting up, we might buy an existing business. We would need to look at it carefully and put a value on the items in the business. These are (say):

	£
Premises	50,000
Equipment	20,000
Stock	12,000
	82,000

But the owner wants £100,000 for the business, an extra £18,000. He says it is worth £18,000 extra because he has made the business into a very good one, with many customers. Most of the customers trade continually with him.

We agree to pay the extra £18,000. This extra amount is known as **goodwill**. And we do this because we will get many customers immediately – it might take us many years to do this if we start from nothing.

In the balance sheet, we will show goodwill as an **intangible fixed asset** – that is, an asset that cannot be physically seen or touched.

28.10 Distinctions between various kinds of capital

The capital account represents the claim of the proprietor against the assets of a business at a point in time. The word 'capital' is, however, often used in a specific sense. The main uses are listed below.

Capital invested

This means the actual amount of money, or money's worth, brought into a business by its proprietor from his or her outside interests. The amount of capital invested is not disturbed by the amounts of profits made by the business or any losses incurred.

Capital employed

The term **capital employed** has many meanings but basically it means the amount of money that is being used (or 'employed') in the business. If, therefore, all the assets were added up in value and the liabilities of the business deducted, the answer would be that the difference is the amount of money employed in the business (i.e. the net assets).

Another way of looking at the calculation of capital employed is to take the balance of the capital account and add this to any long-term loan. The result will be the same as the net assets, i.e. the capital employed.

Working capital (net current assets)

The difference between the current assets and current liabilities is often referred to as **working capital** or 'net current assets'. This amount represents the money that is available to pay the running expenses of the business and, ideally, the current assets should exceed the current liabilities twice over, i.e. in the ratio 2 : 1. In simple terms it means that, for every £1 owed, the business should be able to raise £2.

28.11 Financial statements in the services sector

All the accounts considered so far have been accounts for businesses that trade in some sort of goods. To enable the business to ascertain the amount of gross profit made on selling the goods, a trading account has been drawn up. There are, however, many organisations that do not deal in goods but instead supply customers with a 'service'. These will include professional firms such as accountants, solicitors, doctors, estate agents, management consultants and advertising agencies. Also firms that provide such services as window cleaning, gardening, hairdressing, repairs and maintenance to washing machines, computer repairs, leisure and health clubs and so on. Since they do not deal in 'goods' there is no need for trading accounts to be drawn up; a profit and loss account, together with a balance sheet, is prepared instead.

The first item in the profit and loss account will be the revenue which might be called 'fees', 'charges', 'accounts rendered', 'takings' etc., depending on the nature of the organisation. Any other item of income will also be added, e.g. rent receivable. Following this, the expenses incurred in running the business will be deducted to arrive at the net profit or loss.

An example of the profit and loss account of a solicitor is illustrated below in Exhibit 28.1.

Exhibit 28.1

E B Brown, Solicitor
Profit and Loss Account for the year ended 31 December 2006

	£	£
Revenue:		
Fees charged		87,500
Insurance commissions		1,300
		88,800
Less Expenses:		
Wages and salaries	29,470	
Rent and rates	11,290	
Office expenses	3,140	
Motor expenses	2,115	
General expenses	1,975	
Depreciation	2,720	50,710
Net profit		38,090

28.12 Treatment of discounts allowed and discounts received in final accounts

In Chapter 14 we dealt with recording cash discounts in the cash book and ledgers and you will recall that such a discount could be either 'discounts allowed', which represents a reduction given to our customers for prompt payment of their account or 'discounts received' when the reduction is given by a supplier to us when we pay their account within a specified period.

Using the example below of D Marston (Exhibit 28.2) let us assume that the discount allowed amounted to £310 and the discount received totalled £510. These items would appear in the trading and profit and loss account as follows:

Exhibit 28.2

Trading and Profit and Loss Account of D Marston
for the year ended 31 December 2006

	£	£
Gross profit		30,500
Less Expenses		
Discounts allowed	310	
Other expenses	10,000	10,310
		20,190
Add Income		
Discounts received		510
Net profit		20,700

28.13 Worked example of the financial statements for a sole trader

We have now covered all the adjustments that may be necessary before preparing the financial statements for a business. The adjustments covered are depreciation, from Chapter 26, writing off bad debts and the provision for doubtful debts from Chapter 27, and in this chapter we have dealt with accruals, prepayments, discounts allowed and received. You may also recall that Chapter 10 dealt with closing stock and returns inwards and outwards and carriage inwards and outwards.

Shown in Exhibit 28.3 is a fully worked example that includes all the items mentioned above and in Section 28.14 you will find another step-by-step guide that deals with these rather tricky adjustments; remember there is also a step-by-step guide to preparing financial statements, preliminary level, in Chapter 10, Section 10.9.

Exhibit 28.3

G Lea, a sole trader, extracted the following trial balance from his books for the year ended 31 March 2006.

G Lea
Trial Balance as at 31 March 2006

	Dr £	Cr £
Purchases and sales	224,000	419,700
Stock 1 April 2005	51,600	
Capital 1 April 2005		72,000
Bank overdraft		43,500
Cash	900	
Carriage inwards	4,600	
Discounts	14,400	9,300
Returns inwards	8,100	
Returns outwards		5,700
Carriage outwards	21,600	
Rent and insurance	17,400	
Provision for doubtful debts		6,600
Office equipment	20,000	
Delivery vans	27,000	
Debtors and creditors	119,100	61,200
Drawings	28,800	
Bad debts written off	400	
Wages and salaries	89,000	
General office expenses	4,500	
Provision for depreciation		
Office equipment		8,000
Delivery vans		5,400
	631,400	631,400

Notes:
(1) Stock 31 March 2006 was valued at £42,900
(2) Wages and salaries accrued £2,100 and office expenses owing £200 at 31 March 2006
(3) Rent prepaid 31 March 2006 was £1,800
(4) Increase the provision for doubtful debts to £8,100
(5) Provide for depreciation on the office equipment at 20 per cent per annum using the straight line method.
(6) Provide for depreciation on the delivery vans at 20 per cent per annum using the reducing balance method.

You are required to prepare the trading and profit and loss account for the year ended 31 March 2006 together with a balance sheet as at that date.

G Lea
Trading and Profit and Loss Account for the year ended 31 March 2006

		£	£
Sales			419,700
Less Returns inwards			8,100
			411,600
Less Cost of goods sold			
Opening stock		51,600	
Add Purchases	224,000		
Add Carriage inwards	4,600		
	228,600		
Less Returns outwards	5,700	222,900	
		274,500	
Less Closing stock		42,900	231,600
Gross Profit			180,000
Add Discounts received	(G)		9,300
			189,300
Less Expenses			
Wages and salaries (89,000 + 2,100)	(C)	91,100	
Discounts allowed	(F)	14,400	
Carriage outwards		21,600	
Rent and insurance (17,400 – 1,800)	(A)	15,600	
Bad debts written off	(N)	400	
General office expenses (4,500 + 200)	(D)	4,700	
Increase in provision for doubtful debts (8,100 – 6,600)	(L)	1,500	
Depreciation:			
Office equipment	(H)	4,000	
Delivery vans	(J)	4,320	157,620
Net Profit			31,680

G Lea
Balance Sheet as at 31 March 2006

Fixed Assets			Cost	Total Depreciation	Net Book Value
			£	£	£
Office equipment	(I)		20,000	12,000	8,000
Delivery vans	(K)		27,000	9,720	17,280
			47,000	21,720	25,280
Current Assets					
Stock			42,900		
Debtors		119,100			
Less Provision for doubtful debts	(M)	8,100	111,000		
Prepaid expenses	(B)		1,800		
Cash in hand			900	156,600	
Less Current Liabilities					
Creditors			61,200		
Bank overdraft			43,500		
Expenses owing (2,100 + 200)	(E)		2,300	107,000	
Net Current Assets					49,600
					74,880
Financed by:					
Capital					72,000
Add Net Profit					31,680
					103,680
Less Drawings					28,800
					74,800

28.14 Step-by-step guide dealing with further adjustments to financial statements

Note: The letters (A) to (N) shown after each adjustment can be cross referenced to the Trading and Profit and Loss Account and Balance Sheet of G Lea.

1 Prepayments (amounts paid in advance)
In the financial statements
(*a*) If a trial balance is provided in a question then ensure that you *deduct* the amount of the prepayment from the appropriate expense account and put the resultant figure in the profit and loss account. Ensure that only the expenses incurred for that particular period are charged against the profits for that period. Refer to the worked example, note (3) rent prepaid £1,800. This amount should be deducted from the rent in the trial balance, i.e. £17,400 − £1,800 = £15,600, this figure should be entered as an expense in the profit and loss account (A).

(*b*) In the balance sheet show the amount of the *prepayment* in the current assets section directly under the debtors, i.e. Prepaid expenses £1,800 (B).

2 Accruals (amount owing)

In the financial statements

(*a*) If a trial balance is provided in a question then *add* the amount of the accrual to the appropriate expense account and put this figure in the profit and loss account. Refer to the worked example, note (2) wages and salaries accrued £2,100 and office expenses owing £200. These figures should be added as follows:

Wages and salaries   £89,000 + £2,100 = £91,100
General office expenses   £4,500 + £200   = £4,700

The amounts to be charged as expenses to the profit and loss account are thus, wages and salaries £91,100 (C) and general office expenses £4,700 (D).

(*b*) In the balance sheet show the amount of the *accrual* under the heading current liabilities section directly under the creditors, i.e. Expenses owing £2,100 + £200 = £2,300 (E).

3 Discounts allowed and received

Discount allowed

Charge as an expense in the profit and loss account. Refer to the worked example where the discount allowed £14,400 has been charged as an expense (F).

Discount received

Add as income in the profit and loss account directly underneath the gross profit figure. Again, refer to the worked example where there is discount received of £9,300 that has been added as income (G).

4 Depreciation

Straight line method (Refer to the worked example, note 5)

(*a*) Find the cost price of the office equipment   £20,000

(*b*) Using percentage given   20 per cent
      calculate 20 per cent of £20,000   = £4,000
      then

(*c*) Charge £4,000 as an expense in the profit and loss account (H).

(*d*) In the balance sheet, deduct *total* depreciation £4,000 from this year plus depreciation deducted in previous years £8,000* = £12,000 from the cost price of the asset to give you the net book value of the asset £20,000 – £12,000 = £8,000. Enter each of these figures in the appropriate columns in the balance sheet (I). (*See trial balance credit side).

Reducing balance method (Refer to the worked example, note 6)

(*a*) Find the cost price of the delivery vans   £27,000

(*b*) Find the total amount of depreciation to date
      (refer to trial balance credit side)   £5,400

(*c*) Find the difference (£27,000 – £5,400)   £21,600

(*d*) Using percentage given   20 per cent
      calculate 20 per cent × £21,600   = £4,320
      then

(*e*) Charge £4,320 as an expense in the profit and loss account (J).

(*f*) In the balance sheet, deduct *total* depreciation £4,320 from this year plus depreciation deducted in previous years £5,400* = £9,720 from the cost price of the asset to give you the net book value of the asset £27,000 – £9,720 = £17,280. Enter these figures in the appropriate columns in the balance sheet (K). (*See trial balance credit side.)

5 Provision for doubtful debts

Creating a provision

(*a*) If a provision is to be created for the first time look in the question for details of the amount to be set aside. Let us assume in our worked example that a provision had been created in 2005 amounting to £6,600.

(*b*) The *provision for doubtful debts £6,600* would have been charged to the profit and loss account as an expense in 2005.

(*c*) In the balance sheet, the *provision for doubtful debts £6,600* would have been deducted from the debtors. The debtors are to be found under the heading of current assets.

Increasing the provision

(*a*) Refer to your question and ascertain the new provision, in our example the new provision is £8,100 for this year (see note 4).

(*b*) Find last year's provision, using our example the figure is £6,600 (this figure can be found in the trial balance, credit side).

(*c*) Charge the difference between the new and old provision, £8,100 – £6,600 = £1,500 to the profit and loss account (L).

(*d*) In the balance sheet, deduct the *new provision £8,100* from the debtors (M).

Reducing the provision

(*a*) Refer to your question and ascertain the new provision. Using our worked example we will assume that in 2007 it was decided to reduce the provision to £5,000.

(*b*) Find the old provision, again using our example this would be £8,100.

(*c*) Take the difference between the old and the new provision, £8,100 – £5,000 = £3,100 then add this amount as income in the profit and loss account.

(*d*) Deduct the *new provision for doubtful debts £5,000* from the debtors in the balance sheet.

6 Bad debts

Simply write them off as an expense in the profit and loss account. In our example you will see that bad debts written off are £400, this is shown as an expense in the profit and loss account (N).

Note: A model layout of the financial statements of a sole trader is shown in Appendix B.

Chapter summary

- It is important to ensure that expenses incurred in a particular period are charged against the profit for that period whether or not they have been paid. In the same way revenue earned in a period should be included as income for that period irrespective of whether the money has been received or is still owed.
- Items owing are called 'accruals', items paid in advance are called 'prepayments'.
- Adjustments need to be made in the expense and revenue accounts to ensure that expenses incurred or revenue due for the period are included in that year's financial statements.
- Expenses owing (accruals) are shown in the balance sheet under the heading of current liabilities whilst expenses prepaid (prepayments) are shown under current assets. Amounts owing for rents receivable or other revenue due is usually added to the debtors.

- If the owner of a business takes goods for his or her own use without paying for them then an adjustment is made by crediting the purchases account and debiting the drawings account, plus an adjustment for VAT if appropriate.
- Goodwill is the extra amount paid for an existing business above the value of its other assets.
- There are various forms of 'capital' used in a business; capital invested, capital employed and working capital.
- A fully worked example of the financial statements for a sole trader, including all adjustments, is illustrated using the step-by-step guide.

Exercises

28.1 The first financial year's trading of C Homer ended on 31 December 2008. You are required to present ledger accounts showing the amount transferred to the profit and loss account in respect of the following items:

(a) Rent: paid in 2008 amounted to £1,600; owing at 31 December 2008, £400.

(b) Insurance: paid in 2008 amounted to £900. Of the amount paid £265 was in respect of insurance for 2009.

(c) Motor expenses: paid in 2008, £7,215; owing at 31 December 2008, £166.

(d) Rates: paid six months' rates on 1 January 2008, £750; on 1 July 2008 paid nine months' rates for the period 31 March 2009, £1,125.

(e) K Whalley rented part of the buildings from C Homer for £400 per month from 1 January 2008. On 15 April 2008 he paid C Homer £2,000 and on 15 December 2008 he paid £4,400. Show these transactions in C Homer's accounts.

28.2 The following accounts are from T Norton's books during his first year of trading to 31 December 2005.

(a) General expenses: paid in 2005, £615; still owing at 31 December 2005, £56.

(b) Telephone: paid in 2005, £980; owing at 31 December 2005, £117.

(c) Norton received commission from the sale of goods. In 2005 he received £3,056 and was owed a further £175 on 31 December 2005.

(d) Carriage outwards: paid in 2005, £666; still owing at 31 December 2005, £122.

(e) Insurance: paid 1 January 2005 for nine months' insurance, £1,080; paid 1 October 2005 the sum of £1,080 for insurance to 30 June 2006.

Show the ledger accounts balanced off at the end of the year, showing balances carried down and the amounts transferred to the final accounts for the year 2005.

28.3X T Dale's financial year ended on 30 June 2004. Write up the ledger accounts, showing the transfer to the final accounts.

(a) Stationery: paid for the year to 30 June 2004, £855; stocks of stationery at 30 June 2003, £290; at 30 June 2004, £345.

(b) General expenses: paid for the year to 30 June 2004, £590; owing at 30 June 2003, £64; owing at 30 June 2004, £90.

(c) Rent and rates (combined account): paid in the year to 30 June 2004, £3,890; rent owing at 30 June 2003, £160; rent paid in advance at 30 June 2004, £250; rates owing at 30 June 2003, £205; rates owing at 30 June 2004, £360.

(*d*) Motor expenses: paid in the year to 30 June 2004, £4,750; owing as at 30 June 2003, £180; owing as at 30 June 2004, £375.

(*e*) Dale earned commission from the sales of goods. Received for the year to 30 June 2004, £850; owing at 30 June 2003, £80; owing at 30 June 2004, £145.

28.4 The following balances were part of the trial balance of C Cainen on 31 December 2008:

	Dr	Cr
	£	£
Stock at 1 January 2008	2,050	
Sales		18,590
Purchases	11,170	
Rent	640	
Wages and salaries	2,140	
Insurance	590	
Bad debts	270	
Telephone	300	
General expenses	180	

On 31 December 2008 you ascertain that:

(*a*) the rent for four months of 2009, £160, has been paid in 2008
(*b*) £290 is owing for wages and salaries
(*c*) insurance has been prepaid £190
(*d*) a telephone bill of £110 is owed
(*e*) stock is valued at £3,910.

Draw up Cainen's trading and profit and loss account for the year ended 31 December 2008.

28.5X The following were part of the trial balance of K Tyler on 31 December 2007:

	Dr	Cr
	£	£
Stock at 1 January 2007	8,620	
Sales		54,190
Purchases	30,560	
Returns inwards	200	
Wages and salaries	4,960	
Motor expenses	2,120	
Rent and rates	1,200	
Discounts allowed	290	
Lighting expenses	580	
Computer running expenses	1,210	
General expenses	360	

Given the information that follows, you are to draw up a trading and profit and loss account for the year ended 31 December 2007.

(*a*) stock on 31 December 2007 is £12,120
(*b*) items prepaid: rates £160; computer running expenses £140
(*c*) items owing: wages £510; lighting expenses £170
(*d*) £700 is to be charged as depreciation of motor vehicles.

28.6 From the following trial balance of J Sears, a store owner, prepare a trading and profit and loss account for the year ended 31 December 2007 and a balance sheet as at that date, taking into consideration the adjustments shown below:

Trial Balance as at 31 December 2007

	Dr £	Cr £
Sales		80,000
Purchases	70,000	
Returns inwards	1,000	
Returns outwards		1,240
Stock at 1 January 2007	20,000	
Provision for bad debts		160
Wages and salaries	7,200	
Telephone	200	
Store fittings	8,000	
Motor van	6,000	
Debtors and creditors*	1,960	1,400
Bad debts	40	
Capital		35,800
Bank balance	600	
Drawings	3,600	
	118,600	118,600

Adjustments:

(a) closing stock at 31 December 2007 is £24,000
(b) accrued wages £450
(c) telephone prepaid £20
(d) provision for bad debts to be increased to 10 per cent of debtors
(e) depreciation on store fittings £800, and motor van £1,200.

Note: *Sometimes, in examinations, two items will be shown on the same line. The examiner is testing to see whether the student knows which of the figures relate to the account titles. In Exercises 28.6 and 28.7X the item 'Debtors and creditors' is shown on the same line.

28.7X The following trial balance was extracted from the records of L Robinson, a trader, as at 31 December 2006:

	Dr	Cr
	£	£
Discounts allowed	410	
Discounts received		506
Carriage inwards	309	
Carriage outwards	218	
Returns inwards	1,384	
Returns outwards		810
Sales		120,320
Purchases	84,290	
Stock at 31 December 2005	30,816	
Motor expenses	4,917	
Repairs to premises	1,383	
Salaries and wages	16,184	
Sundry expenses	807	
Rates and insurance	2,896	
Premises at cost	40,000	
Motor vehicles at cost	11,160	
Provision for depreciation – motors as at 31 December 2006		3,860
Debtors and creditors*	31,640	24,320
Cash at bank	4,956	
Cash in hand	48	
Drawings	8,736	
Capital		50,994
Loan from P Hall (repayable 2008)		40,000
Bad debts	1,314	
Provision for doubtful debts as at 31 December 2006		658
	241,468	241,468

*Note: See footnote to exercise 28.6 for an explanation of why two figures are on one line.

The following matters are to be taken into account at 31 December 2006:

(a) stock £36,420
(b) expenses owing: sundry expenses £62; motor expenses £33
(c) prepayment: rates £166
(d) provision for doubtful debts to be reduced to £580
(e) depreciation for motor vehicles to be £2,100 for the year
(f) part of the premises were let to a tenant, who owed £250 at 31 December 2006
(g) loan interest owing to P Hall £4,000.

Draw up a trading and profit and loss account for the year ended 31 December 2006 and a balance sheet as at that date.

28.8 Freddy Tuilagi is a baker. His trial balance as at 30 September is as follows:

	Dr	Cr
	£	£
Motor van (at cost)	7,000	
Discount received		230
Bank		50
Opening stock	850	
General expenses	610	
Provision for depreciation: Equipment		2,000
Drawings	1,400	
Sales		30,490
Cash	30	
Creditors		845
Purchases	13,725	
Wages	3,880	
Advertising	420	
Telephone	160	
Equipment (at cost)	17,000	
Capital		11,460
	45,075	45,075

The following additional information is available at 30 September:

(1) Stock at cost amounted to £960.
(2) Over the year Freddy Tuilagi took purchases for his own use, at cost £320.
(3) The advertising was prepaid by £46.
(4) Depreciation is to be provided for as follows
   - Equipment 30 per cent reducing (diminishing) balance method
   - Motor van 15 per cent straight line (on cost) method.
(5) Discounts received of £80 have not yet been entered in the books.

Required:

(a) Prepare Freddie Tuigali's trading, profit and loss account for the year ended 30 September.
(b) Prepare Freddie Tuigali's balance sheet as at 30 September.

City & Guilds Pitman qualifications

28.9X Ben Axtell owns a sports shop. His business's financial year ended on 31 March 2005. The trading account for the year ended on that date has been prepared. The following information was gathered from the business's accounting records in order that the other year end financial statements could be prepared.

	£
Gross profit	56,738
Rent of shop premises	9,340
Business rates	4,070
Wages of shop assistants	19,360
Discounts received	133
Trade creditors	4,839
Stock in trade, 31 March 2005	32,980
Maintenance and servicing charges	740
Cash at bank	3,354
Advertising	1,450
Light and heat	1,740
Capital on 1 April 2004	32,056
Insurance	580
Drawings	17,240
Loan from Kay French	8,000
Loan interest	1,212
Shop furniture, fittings and equipment	
at cost	14,000
provision for depreciation, 1 April 2004	4,300

Additional information:

● Business rates, £320, were outstanding on 31 March 2005.
● Advertising costs, £414, were paid by cheque on 30 March 2005. This transaction was omitted from the accounting records.
● Insurance premiums, £65, were prepaid at 31 March 2005.
● The shop furniture, fittings and equipment should be depreciated by 15 per cent per annum using the straight line method.
● The loan from Kay French is due to be repaid in 2009.

Tasks:
(*a*) Prepare the profit and loss account for the year ended 31 March 2005.
(*b*) Prepare a balance sheet as at 31 March 2005. The balance sheet should show clearly the subtotal for working capital.
(*c*) Show how the following accounts should appear in the ledger:
    (i) business rates;
    (ii) insurance.

Note: the accounts should show the figures given in the list above, and any entries arising from the additional information including the transfer of the correct amount to the profit and loss account.

Balance the accounts and bring down the balances.

Southern Examining Group

Please note that this question is NOT from the live examinations for the current specification.

CHAPTER 29

Extended trial balance

Learning objectives

After you have studied this chapter you should be able to:

- enter balances from the general ledger and other records on the extended trial balance
- deal with adjustments, including accruals and prepayments, and enter them correctly on the extended trial balance
- enter the closing stock valuation on the extended trial balance
- deal with other adjustments such as depreciation and provision for doubtful debts and enter them on the extended trial balance
- deal with any errors and discrepancies and enter them on the extended trial balance
- extend the extended trial balance entries into appropriate columns of adjustments, profit and loss account and balance sheet and total them correctly.

29.1 Introduction

As already mentioned in Chapter 7, a **trial balance** is a list of all balances on the double entry (the ledgers) accounts and the cash book at a particular point in time. The main purpose of the trial balance is to ensure that the books 'balance' and, if any errors are identified, to make the necessary corrections. Another important function of the trial balance is to provide the balances to be used in preparation of the financial statements of the business, the trading and profit and loss account and the balance sheet.

29.2 The extended trial balance

The extended trial balance is often referred to as a 'worksheet' which provides a useful aid where a large number of adjustments are needed prior to the preparation of the financial statements. The extended trial balance is drawn up on specially preprinted stationery on which suitable columns are printed. Exhibit 29.1 shows an example of an extended trial balance. You may wish to photocopy this format and use it when carrying out some of the student activities at the end of the chapter.

Exhibit 29.1 Format for an extended trial balance

Description	Ledger Balances		Adjustments		Profit and Loss		Balance Sheet	
	Dr	Cr	Dr	Cr	Dr	Cr	Dr	Cr
	£	£	£	£	£	£	£	£

It should be noted, however, that some examining bodies may require a slightly different format which needs more columns. It is advisable to find out in which format the examining body, whose syllabus you are studying, require the extended trial balance to be shown.

29.3 Preparing the extended trial balance

Once the trial balance has been drawn up and balanced off correctly, the next task is to implement the following adjustments:

- accruals and prepayments
- include the closing stock valuation
- make provision for depreciation and provision for doubtful debts
- correct any errors.

29.4 A worked example

In Exhibit 29.2 you will find the trial balance which was extracted from the books of D Simpson, a retailer, at 31 December 2005.

Exhibit 29.2

Trial Balance of D Simpson as at 31 December 2005

	£	£
Purchases	138,872	
Sales		202,460
Carriage inwards	490	
Carriage outwards	1,406	
Returns inwards and outwards	424	2,280
Stock 1 January 2005	9,820	
Wages and salaries	29,950	
Rent	11,000	
Rates and insurance	3,900	
Heating and lighting	1,254	
Motor vehicle	9,000	
Motor expenses	2,500	
Capital 1 January 2005		37,896
Bank overdraft		5,638
Fixtures and fittings	6,400	
Drawings	27,900	
Debtors	23,200	
Creditors		17,842
	266,116	266,116

Notes:
(a) Rent owing amounted to £1,000 as at 31 December 2005.
(b) Rates paid in advance amounted to £500.
(c) Closing stock was valued at £12,042 as at 31 December 2005.
(d) Depreciate the motor vehicle at 20% using the straight line method.
     [Note: Fixtures and fittings are not to be depreciated in this example.]
(e) Provide for the creation of a provision for doubtful debts amounting to 2% of the debtors.

You are required to:

1 Prepare an extended trial balance at 31 December 2005.
2 Prepare a trading and profit and loss account for the year ended 31 December 2005 and a balance sheet as at that date.

Since many students have difficulty in preparing extended trial balances the above example will be carried out using the 'step-by-step guide' shown below.

Step-by-step guide

Step 1

First of all draw up a trial balance in the usual way (refer to Chapter 7, Exhibit 7.3). Remember:

Debit Balances are Assets or Expenses
and
Credit Balances are Liabilities, Capital or Income

If there have been no errors then the two sides should agree. Refer to Exhibit 29.3 and note that the balances have now been entered on the ETB under the heading 'ledger balances'.

Step 2

Deal with the adjustments at the bottom of the trial balance.
Note: Each item must be dealt with twice to comply with the double entry rules.
Adjustments fall into four categories:

1 accruals
2 prepayments
3 closing stock valuation
4 other adjustments:
    depreciation provision
    provision for doubtful debts
    correction of errors

When dealing with adjustments think double entry, i.e.

which account should be debited
and
which account should be credited

When entering the adjustment on the extended trial balance first of all look to see if there is already an 'Account' for the transaction and, if so, use it. If not, then open an account at the foot of the extended trial balance. (This is illustrated in the following examples.)

Step 3

Deal with accruals and prepayments.

1 Accruals (amounts owing)

For example, referring to Exhibit 29.2(a) rent owing amounts to £1,000, which is entered as follows:

> Debit   Rent Account £1,000
> Credit   Accruals – Rent £1,000 (as this item is a liability).

This transaction is now shown in Exhibit 29.3 below as '(a)' under the 'Adjustments' column – see the debit entry of £1,000 next to the 'Rent Account' and the credit entry of £1,000 entered below the totals of the trial balance under the heading 'Accruals – Rent'.

2 Prepayments (amounts paid in advance)

Exhibit 29.2(b) shows a rates prepayment of £500, which is entered as follows:

> Debit   Prepayments – rates £500
> Credit   Rates account £500.

This again is shown in Exhibit 29.3(b) under the Adjustments column – see the debit entry of £500 entered below the totals of the trial balance under the heading 'Prepayment – rates £500' and the corresponding credit entry shown next to the 'rates account'.

3 Dealing with the closing stock valuation

At the end of the financial year a business usually undertakes a valuation of the stock. Exhibit 29.2(c) shows a closing stock of £12,042, which is entered as follows:

> Debit   Stock account (to be shown in the balance sheet as an asset)
> Credit   Stock account (shown in the profit and loss account as a deduction from the cost of goods sold calculation).

This is shown in Exhibit 29.3(c) under the trial balance totals is the Adjustments column.

4 Dealing with other adjustments

Depreciation provision   Exhibit 29.2(d) requires provision for depreciation of 20 per cent on motor vehicles using the straight line method. Motor vehicles cost £9,000, therefore, 20 per cent of cost equals £1,800 depreciation to be charged against the profit and loss account. This transaction is entered on the extended trial balance under the Adjustments column, see note (d) as follows:

> Debit   Depreciation of motor vehicle £1,800 (amount to be charged to profit and loss account)
> Credit   Depreciation provision of motor vehicle £1,800 (amount to be shown as a deduction from the value of the asset in the balance sheet).

Provision for doubtful debts   Exhibit 29.2(e) requires the creation of a provision for doubtful debts amounting to 2 per cent of the debtors figure of £23,200 which amounts to £464. The entry in the extended trial balance will appear in the adjustments column – note (e) as follows:

> Debit   Creation of provision for doubtful debts £464 (this amount to be charged in the profit and loss account)
> Credit   Provision for doubtful debts £464 (this amount to be shown as deduction from the debtors in the balance sheet).

Correction of errors To keep the worked example as straightforward as possible, no errors require correcting in Exhibit 29.2. This topic will be covered later in this chapter.

Step 4

The next step is to add up both parts of the adjustments column. Providing the adjustments have been carried out correctly, the two columns should agree – in other words, the adjustments column acts rather like a mini trial balance.

Step 5

It is now necessary to add/subtract the figures *across* the extended trial balance and enter the *total* in either the profit and loss account or balance sheet column. This step requires a certain amount of skill from the students since they must be fully conversant with the position of each balance figure in the financial statements. A useful hint is to carry out this identification *before* starting the analysis by entering either of the following immediately before the description column (*see* Exhibit 29.3), namely:

> PL   Profit and loss account
> BS   Balance sheet

to indicate which analysis column to use.

It is important to note when carrying out the analysis that if the balance is shown as a debit balance in the ledger balance column then it will appear as a debit balance in either the profit and loss account column or the balance sheet column. The same thing applies to the credit balances, which will appear in either the profit and loss account column or balance sheet column as a credit balance. Whilst carrying out the analysis, any figures appearing in the adjustments column must be taken into consideration; for example, referring to Exhibit 29.3(a), the balance of rent will be analysed as:

> Rent £11,000 plus £1,000 (owing) = £12,000

This will be analysed into the profit and loss account column as a debit balance of £12,000.

Note: Refer to Exhibit 29.3 where this task has been carried out.

A further example can also be seen in Exhibit 29.3(b) where the prepayment of rates £500 will be analysed as follows:

Rates and Insurance	£3,900
Less amount paid in advance	500
	£3,400

The amount to be shown in the profit and loss account column will be £3,400 debit balance.

Exhibit 29.3 D Simpson – extended trial balance at 31 December 2005

	Description	Ledger Balances Dr £	Ledger Balances Cr £	Adjustments Dr £	Adjustments Cr £	Profit and Loss Dr £	Profit and Loss Cr £	Balance Sheet Dr £	Balance Sheet Cr £
PL	Purchases	138,872				138,872			
PL	Sales		202,460				202,460		
PL	Carriage inwards	490				490			
PL	Carriage outwards	1,406				1,406			
PL	Returns inwards and outwards	424	2,280			424	2,280		
PL	Stock 1 January 2005	9,820				9,820			
PL	Wages and salaries	29,950				29,950			
PL	Rent	11,000		(a) 1,000		12,000			
PL	Rates and insurance	3,900			(b) 500	3,400			
PL	Heating and lighting	1,254				1,254			
BS	Motor vehicle	9,000						9,000	
PL	Motor expenses	2,500				2,500			
BS	Capital 1 January 2005		37,896						37,896
BS	Bank overdraft		5,638						5,638
BS	Fixtures and fittings	6,400						6,400	
BS	Drawings	27,900						27,900	
BS	Debtors	23,200						23,200	
BS	Creditors		17,842						17,842
		266,116	266,116						
BS	Accrual – Rent				(a) 1,000				1,000
BS	Prepayment – Rates			(b) 500				500	
BS	Stock 31 December 2005			(c) 12,042				12,042	
PL	Stock 31 December 2005				(c) 12,042		12,042		
PL	Depreciation – Motor vehicle			(d) 1,800		1,800			
BS	Depreciation – Provision for motor vehicle				(d) 1,800				1,800
PL	Provision for doubtful debts			(e) 464		464			
BS	Provision for doubtful debts				(e) 464				464
				15,806	15,806				
				(Step 4)					
	Net profit (Step 6)					14,402			14,402
						216,782	216,782	79,042	79,042
								(Step 7)	

Step 6

Add up the profit and loss account columns. The difference between the two figures will represent a profit or loss for the period. In our example of D Simpson the difference between these two columns is £14,402, representing a net profit. This figure will now be entered on the extended trial balance as net profit £14,402, a *debit entry* in the profit and loss account column.

The corresponding *credit entry* will appear as under the balance sheet columns.

Step 7

The only remaining task to carry out is to add up the balance sheet column totals and, provided all transactions have been carried out correctly, the totals should agree.

Note: Refer to Exhibit 29.3 where you can see that the extended trial balance balances with a total of £79,042.

The trading and profit and loss account and balance sheet of D Simpson for the year ended 31 December 2005 is shown in Exhibit 29.4.

Exhibit 29.4

D Simpson
Trading and Profit and Loss Account
for the year ended 31 December 2005

	£	£	£
Sales		202,460	
Less Returns inwards		424	202,036
Less Cost of goods sold:			
Opening stock		9,820	
Purchases		138,872	
Carriage inwards		490	
		149,182	
Less Returns outwards	2,280		
Closing stock	12,042	14,322	134,860
Gross profit			67,176
Less Expenses:			
Carriage outwards		1,406	
Wages and salaries		29,950	
Rent (11,000 + 1,000)		12,000	
Rates and insurance (3,900 – 500)		3,400	
Heating and lighting		1,254	
Motor expenses		2,500	
Depreciation – Motor vehicle		1,800	
Creation of provision for doubtful debts		464	52,774
Net profit			14,402

D Simpson
Balance Sheet as at 31 December 2005

		Cost £	Total Dep'n £	Net Book Value £
Fixed assets:				
Fixtures and fittings		6,400	–	6,400
Motor vehicles		9,000	1,800	7,200
		15,400	1,800	13,600
Current assets:				
Stock		12,042		
Debtors	23,200			
Less Provision for doubtful debts	464	22,736		
Prepayments		500	35,278	
Less Current liabilities:				
Bank overdraft		5,638		
Creditors		17,842		
Accruals		1,000	24,480	
Net current assets				10,798
				24,398
Financed by:				
Capital: Balance 1 January 2005				37,896
Add Net profit for the year				14,402
				52,298
Less Drawings				27,900
				24,398

29.5 **Other considerations**

In the above example of D Simpson the transactions involving depreciation and provision for bad debts was kept as straightforward as possible to avoid complications. However, assuming it is the next accounting period of D Simpson, the following adjustments will now be shown:

1 Depreciate the motor vehicle by 20 per cent using the straight line method (for the second year).
2 Increase the provision for bad debts to £550.
3 Write off a bad debt amounting to £100.

1 Depreciate the motor vehicle by 20 per cent using the straight line method

First of all the amount of depreciation to be charged against the profit and loss account needs to be calculated. As the method of depreciation to be used is the straight line method, the amount of depreciation will be the same each year, namely, 20 per cent of £9,000 = £1,800. This amount is then entered on the extended trial balance as follows:

D Simpson
Extended Trial Balance (extract) as at 31 December 2006

Description	Ledger balances		Adjustments		Profit and loss		Balance sheet	
	Dr £	Cr £	Dr £	Cr £	Dr £	Cr £	Dr £	Cr £
Motor vehicle	9,000						9,000	
Provision for depreciation Motor vehicle*		1,800		1,800				3,600
Depreciation of motor vehicle			1,800		1,800			

The above example shows that the motor vehicle remains a debit balance of £9,000 which appears in the balance sheet column as a debit (an asset). The provision for depreciation of motor vehicle* appears under the ledger balances column as £1,800, representing the amount of depreciation charged for the first year. To this figure another £1,800 is added representing the depreciation for this year showing a total of depreciation to date of £3,600. This is shown as a credit balance in the balance sheet column of the extended trial balance.

When the balance sheet is prepared it will appear as follows:

D Simpson
Balance Sheet (extract) as at 31 December 2006

	Cost	Total dep'n	Net book value
	£	£	£
Fixed assets			
Motor vehicle	9,000	3,600	5,400

The remaining debit balance of depreciation of motor vehicle £1,800 will be charged in the profit and loss account. This is shown in the extended trial balance under the profit and loss account column as a debit balance (see above in the extended trial balance extract).

2 Increase the provision for doubtful debts to £550

In the accounts for the year ended 31 December 2005, D Simpson created a provision for bad debts equal to 2 per cent of the debtors which amounted to £464 (this is illustrated in the extract from extended trial balance below).

In the year to 31 December 2006 it was decided to increase the provision to £550, representing an increase of £86 (£550 *less* £464). To record this increase the following entries need to be made:

- Show the increase of provision for doubtful debts of £86 as a debit entry in the adjustments column to be charged in the profit and loss account.
- Increase the existing 'provision for doubtful debts account' by £86 to £550; this will be shown as a credit entry in the adjustments column of the extended trial balance. This figure is then extended to the balance sheet column as £550 (credit entry).

This can now be seen in the following extract from the extended trial balance.

D Simpson
Extended Trial Balance (extract) as at 31 December 2006

Description	Ledger balances		Adjustments		Profit and loss		Balance sheet	
	Dr £	*Cr* £	*Dr* £	*Cr* £	*Dr* £	*Cr* £	*Dr* £	*Cr* £
Provision for bad debts		464		86				550
Increase in provision for bad debts			86		86			

3 Write off a bad debt amounting to £100

After the preparation of the draft accounts one of the firm's debtors was reported to have been declared bankrupt. The balance on the debtor's account was £100 and it was decided to write the debt off as bad.

This would be entered on the extended trial balance as follows:

D Simpson
Extended Trial Balance (extract) as at 31 December 2006

Description	Ledger balances		Adjustments		Profit and loss		Balance sheet	
	Dr £	*Cr* £	*Dr* £	*Cr* £	*Dr* £	*Cr* £	*Dr* £	*Cr* £
Debtors (say)	26,000			100			25,900	
Bad debts			100		100			

The above entries show that the debtors, which we have assumed are £26,000 for this year ended 2006, have been reduced by £100 and will appear in the balance sheet as £25,900. The bad debt will also be charged to the profit and loss account. This is shown as a debit entry in both the adjustments column and the profit and loss account column.

29.6 A more complicated example

Exhibit 29.5 shows a worked example of a more complicated extended trial balance.

Exhibit 29.5

J Blake is a sole trader. He extracted the following list of balances from the books of his business on 31 March 2005:

	Dr £	Cr £
Sales		80,650
Purchases	45,380	
Returns inwards	510	
Returns outwards		930
Discounts allowed	1,120	
Discounts received		390
Stock at 1 April 2004	12,460	
Motor van, at cost	12,500	
Office equipment	9,600	
Provision for depreciation of motor van 1 April 2004		3,800
Provision for depreciation of office equipment 1 April 2004		2,150
Salaries and wages	17,620	
Motor van running expenses	3,910	
Sundry expenses	1,140	
Rent and rates	3,200	
Bad debts	375	
Provision for doubtful debts 1 April 2004		320
Debtors	12,870	
Creditors		9,100
Bank	8,040	
Cash	60	
Drawings	7,000	
Capital		38,445
	135,785	135,785

This additional information is available at 31 March 2005:

(*a*) Stock was valued at £20,100.

(*b*) Salaries and wages of £490 are to be accrued.

(*c*) The following have been prepaid: rent and rates £790.

(*d*) An additional £270 is to be written off as bad debts, and the provision for doubtful debts is to be adjusted to 2 per cent of debtors after writing off bad debts.

(*e*) Goods taken by Blake for his private use during the year amounted at cost to £370. No record of this has yet been made in the books.

(*f*) Depreciation is to be written off as follows: motor van £2,000; office equipment at 15 per cent using the straight line method.

Exhibit 29.6 J Blake – extended trial balance at 31 March 2005

	Description	Ledger Balances Dr £	Ledger Balances Cr £	Adjustments Dr £	Adjustments Cr £	Profit and Loss Dr £	Profit and Loss Cr £	Balance Sheet Dr £	Balance Sheet Cr £
PL	Sales		80,650				80,650		
PL	Purchases	45,380				45,010			
PL	Returns inwards/Returns outwards	510	930		370	510	930		
PL	Discounts	1,120	390			1,120	390		
PL	Stock at 1 April 2004	12,460				12,460			
BS	Motor van, at cost	12,500						12,500	
BS	Office equipment, at cost	9,600						9,600	
BS	Provision for dep'n – Motor van 1.4.2004		3,800		2,000				5,800
BS	Provision for dep'n – Office equip. 1.4.2004		2,150		1,440				3,590
PL	Salaries and wages	17,620		490		18,110			
PL	Motor van running expenses	3,910				3,910			
PL	Sundry expenses	1,140				1,140			
PL	Rent and rates	3,200			790	2,410			
PL	Bad debts	375		270		645			
BS	Provision for bad debts 1.4.2004		320	68					252
BS	Debtors	12,870			270			12,600	
BS	Creditors		9,100						9,100
BS	Bank	8,040						8,040	
BS	Cash	60						60	
BS	Drawings	7,000		370				7,370	
BS	Capital		38,445						38,445
		135,785	135,785						
BS	Accrual – Salaries and wages				490				490
BS	Prepayment – Rent and rates			790				790	
BS	Stock – 31 March 2005			20,100				20,100	
PL	Stock – 31 March 2005				20,100		20,100		
PL	Depreciation – Motor van			2,000		2,000			
PL	Depreciation – Office equipment			1,440		1,440			
PL	Reduction in provision for bad debts				68		68		
				25,528	25,528				
BS	Net profit (balancing figure)					13,383			13,383
						102,138	102,138	71,060	71,060

You are required to:

1 Prepare an extended trial balance as at 31 March 2005.
2 Prepare a trading and profit and loss account for the year ended 31 March 2005 and a balance sheet as at that date.

Remember to follow the 'Step-by-step guide' to assist you in following the workings of Exhibit 29.5 and note the order of dealing with the 'adjustments':

- accruals and prepayments
- deal with the closing stock valuation
- make provision for depreciation and provision for doubtful debts
- other adjustments
  - writing off the bad debt (refer back to Section 29.5(3) and Chaper 27)
  - goods taken for own use (see the worked example, Exhibit 29.6).

The extended trial balance of J Blake is now shown in Exhibit 29.6 and the trading and profit and loss account and balance sheet is shown in Exhibit 29.7 as follows:

Exhibit 29.7

J Blake
Trading and Profit and Loss Account for the year ended 31 March 2005

	£	£	£
Sales		80,650	
Less Returns inwards		510	80,140
Less Cost of goods sold:			
Opening stock		12,460	
Add Purchases (45,380 – 370 own use)	45,010		
Less Returns outwards	930	44,080	
		56,540	
Less Closing stock		20,100	36,440
Gross profit			43,700
Add Income:			
Discount received		390	
Reduction in provision for bad debts			
(320 – 2% of (12,870 – 270))		68	458
			44,158
Less Expenses:			
Discounts allowed		1,120	
Salaries and wages (17,620 + 490)		18,110	
Motor van running expenses		3,910	
Rent and rates (3,200 – 790)		2,410	
Sundry expenses		1,140	
Bad debts (375 + 270)		645	
Depreciation: Motor van		2,000	
Office equipment		1,440	30,775
Net profit			13,383

J Blake
Balance Sheet as at 31 March 2005

		Cost	Total dep'n	Net book value
		£	£	£
Fixed assets:				
Office equipment		9,600	3,590	6,010
Motor van		12,500	5,800	6,700
		22,100	9,390	12,710
Current assets:				
Stock		20,100		
Debtors (12,870 – 270)	12,600			
Less Provision for bad debts	252	12,348		
Prepayments		790		
Cash at bank		8,040		
Cash in hand		60	41,338	
Less Current liabilities				
Creditors	9,100			
Accruals	490	9,590		
Net current assets				31,748
				44,458
Financed by:				
Capital				38,445
Add Net profit				13,383
				51,828
Less Drawings (7,000 + 370 goods for own use)				7,370
				44,458

Chapter summary

- The extended trial balance is often referred to as a 'worksheet' since it provides a useful aid where a large number of adjustments are needed prior to the preparation of the financial statements.
- Initially a trial balance is prepared in the usual way with debit balances consisting of assets or expenses and credit balances being liabilities, capital or income.
- At the end of the financial year there are often several adjustments to be made. These consist of accruals and prepayments, closing stock valuation and making provisions for depreciation and doubtful debts.
- It is important to remember that each adjustment must be recorded *twice* on the extended trial balance, one being a debit entry the other the credit entry.
- A careful systematic approach must be applied when entering items in the extended trial balance. Each category must be entered one step at a time, i.e. accruals, prepayments, dealing with the closing stock valuation and then other adjustments.
- It is important to ensure that the 'adjustment columns' add up correctly, rather like a mini-trial balance.

● The next step is to add/subtract the figures across the extended trial balance entering the total in either the profit and loss or balance sheet columns. The balancing figure in the profit and loss columns represents the *profit* or *loss* for the period which is also entered in the balance sheet columns. All columns are then added up with each section agreeing.

Exercises

Note: A blank worksheet for preparing extended trial balance exercises is given in Appendix B.

29.1　Reconstruct the trial balance after making the necessary corrections.

S Dickinson
Trial Balance as at 30 September 2005

	Dr £	Cr £
Capital	59,868	
Motor vehicles	22,500	
Computer equipment	18,000	
Debtors	31,059	
Creditors		30,690
Purchases	245,259	
Sales		358,317
Wages and salaries		38,476
Motor expenses		3,428
Printing and stationery	3,600	
General expenses	8,235	
Cash at bank	5,850	
Stock 1 October 2004	23,004	
Rent and rates	31,500	
Heating and lighting		6,624
Interest received	6,417	
Insurance		10,332
Rent received	5,175	
Drawings		12,600
	460,467	460,467

29.2　From the following list of balances taken from the books of G Brammer you are required to draw up a trial balance as at 31 December 2005.

	£
Capital	100,000
Premises	66,250
Motor vehicle	17,000
Office equipment	2,438
Wages	19,637
Purchases	37,455
Sales	56,170
Commission received	1,050
Electricity	925
Telephone	1,125
Motor expenses	1,500
Printing, stationery and advertising	2,050
Creditors	8,500
Debtors	12,012
General expenses	2,371
Bank overdraft	3,505
Drawings	6,462

29.3X From the list of balances from the accounts of Fraser & Co, you are required to prepare a trial balance as at 31 December 2006.

Fraser & Co
List of Outstanding Balances as at 31 December 2006

	£
Purchases	334,500
Sales	511,050
Returns inwards	10,050
Returns outwards	8,400
Stock 1 January 2006	33,000
Discount allowed	6,900
Discount received	8,250
Wages and salaries	55,750
Carriage inwards	2,100
Carriage outwards	3,300
Printing and stationery	4,200
Electricity	7,300
Motor expenses	18,250
Telephone	3,100
General expenses	2,900
Debtors	51,000
Creditors	32,400
Bad debts written off	1,650
Provision for doubtful debts at 31 December 2006	675
Cash in hand	1,200
Bank overdraft	35,100
Capital	57,825
Property	75,000
Plant and equipment	96,000
Provision for depreciation at 31 December 2006	
Property	15,000
Plant and equipment	37,500

29.4 The following is a list of balances extracted from the books of J Steadman, a sole trader, as at 31 January 2006.

J Steadman
List of Balances as at 31 January 2006

	£
Capital	58,260
Equipment	11,250
Furniture and fittings	6,000
Motor vehicles	17,370
Sales	96,030
Purchases	59,220
Cash at bank	750
General expenses	1,800
Wages	17,820
Rent, rates and insurance	7,650
Heating and lighting	2,100
Debtors	24,000
Creditors	10,800
Stock 1 February 2005	17,130

The following additional information is available as at 31 January 2006:

(*a*) Wages unpaid amounted to £351.
(*b*) Insurance paid in advance £600.
(*c*) Closing stock was valued at £14,730.

You are required to take the above adjustments into account and prepare the figures for the final accounts for J Steadman for the year ended 31 January 2006, using the extended trial balance.

Note: Remember to use the blank extended trial balance worksheet in Appendix B.

29.5X The following is a list of balances taken from the ledgers of Rigby & Co as at 31 July 2006, the end of the financial year.

Rigby & Co
List of Balances as at 31 July 2006

	£
Stock at 1 August 2005	29,150
Purchases	243,800
Sales	509,450
Returns inwards	3,805
Returns outwards	2,655
Discounts allowed	6,620
Discounts received	5,750
Wages and salaries	76,500
Lighting and heating	9,250
Telephone, stationery and advertising	13,600
Motor expenses	10,500
General expenses	3,005
Rates and insurance	15,000
Motor vehicles:	
At cost	20,000
Accumulated depreciation	5,000
Fixtures and fittings:	
At cost	22,100
Accumulated depreciation	9,945
Creditors	21,900
Debtors	31,700
Drawings	22,325
Cash in hand	995
Cash at bank	10,985
Capital	114,635
Land and buildings	150,000

The following additional information is available as at 31 July 2006:

(*a*) Motor expenses owing £200.

(*b*) Insurance paid in advance £3,500.

(*c*) Closing stock was valued at £30,700.

(*d*) Depreciate motor vehicles at 25 per cent and fixtures and fittings at 15 per cent per annum using the straight line method.

You are required to take the above adjustments into account and prepare the figures for the final accounts of Rigby & Co for the year ended 31 July 2006, using the extended trial balance.

29.6 Amanda Carver is the proprietor of Automania, a business which supplies car parts to garages to use in servicing and repair work.

At the end of the financial year, on 30 April 2005, the balances were extracted from the general ledger and have been entered onto a trial balance, as shown below:

Automania
Trial Balance as at 30 April 2005

Description	Ledger balances	
	Dr	Cr
	£	£
Capital		135,000
Drawings	42,150	
Rent	17,300	
Purchases	606,600	
Sales		857,300
Sales returns	2,400	
Purchases returns		1,260
Salaries and wages	136,970	
Motor vehicles (M.V.) at cost	60,800	
Provision for depreciation (M.V.)		16,740
Fixtures and fittings (F&F) at cost	40,380	
Provision for depreciation (F&F)		21,600
Bank		3,170
Cash	2,100	
Lighting and heating	4,700	
VAT		9,200
Stock at 1 May 2004	116,100	
Bad debts	1,410	
Provision for doubtful debts		1,050
Debtors control account	56,850	
Creditors control account		50,550
Sundry expenses	6,810	
Insurance	1,300	
Accruals		
Prepayments		
Depreciation		
Provision for doubtful debts – Adjustment		
Closing stock – Profit and loss		
Closing stock – Balance sheet		
	1,095,870	1,095,870

The following adjustments need to be taken into account as at 30 April 2005:

(*a*) Rent payable by the business is as follows:
  ● For the period to 31 July 2004 – £1,500 per month
  ● From 1 August 2004   – £1,600 per month

(*b*) The insurance balance includes £100 paid for the period 1 May 2005 to 31 May 2005.

(*c*) Depreciation is to be calculated as follows:
  ● Motor vehicles   – 20 per cent per annum straight line method
  ● Fixtures and fittings – 10 per cent per annum reducing balance method

(*d*) The provision for doubtful debts is to be adjusted to a figure representing 2 per cent of debtors.

(e) Stock has been valued at cost on 30 April 2005 at £119,360. However, this figure includes old stock, the details of which are as follows:
- Cost price of old stock — £3,660
- Net realisable value of old stock – £2,060

Also included is a badly damaged car door which was to have been sold for £80 but will now have to be scrapped. The cost price of the door was £60.

(f) A credit note received from a supplier on 5 April 2005 for goods returned was filed away with no entries having been made. The credit note has now been discovered and is for £200 net plus £35 VAT.

Required:

(i) Make appropriate entries in the adjustments columns of the extended trial balance taking account of the above information. Show all workings.

(ii) Complete the extended trial balance showing clearly the profit or loss made by Automania for the year ended 30 April 2005.

Note: Use a photocopy of the blank extended trial balance form in Appendix B for your answer.

Association of Accounting Technicians (Amended)

29.7X Helen Grant is the owner of Road Runner, a business that buys and sells car tyres.

- The financial year end is 30 April 2005.
- You are employed to assist with the book-keeping.
- The business uses a manual system consisting of a general ledger, a sales ledger and a purchase ledger.
- Double entry takes place in the general ledger. Individual accounts of debtors and creditors are kept in memorandum accounts.
- You use a purchases day book and a sales day book. Totals from the day books are transferred into the general ledger.

At the end of the financial year on 30 April 2005, the following balances were taken from the general ledger.

	£
Sales	689,250
Purchases	414,875
Stock at 1 May 2004	69,376
Salaries and wages	115,654
General expenses	82,440
Shop fittings at cost	48,140
Provision for depreciation, shop fittings	17,890
Computer equipment at cost	12,900
Provision for depreciation, computer equipment	7,460
Debtors control account	58,200
Creditors control account	45,320
Bad debts	1,850
Provision for doubtful debts	2,010
Bank (debit balance)	4,658
Cash	550
VAT (credit balance)	13,500
Discount allowed	8,740
Discount received	3,658
Drawings	22,000
Bank deposit account	20,000
Capital	80,295

The following adjustments need to be made for the year ended 30 April 2005.

(*a*) Stock was valued at cost on 30 April 2005 at £58,450.
(*b*) Depreciation needs to be provided as follows:
  ● Shop fittings – 10 per cent per annum straight line method
  ● Computer equipment – 25 per cent per annum reducing balance method.
(*c*) General expenses include insurance of £2,400, which was paid for the year ended 31 October 2005.
(*d*) The provision for doubtful debts should be adjusted to 2.5 per cent of the debtors.
(*e*) £2,000 is owed in wages on 30 April 2005.
(*f*) The bank deposit account was opened on 1 November 2004. Interest is paid at a fixed rate of 6 per cent per annum.

Tasks:

1 Using the blank extended trial form on page 507 (Appendix B) enter the balances into the trial balance and total both columns, before taking into account the additional information.
2 Prepare journal entries to record the above adjustments; dates and narratives are not required.
3 Make appropriate entries in the adjustment columns of the extended trial balance taking account of all the journal entries.
4 Complete the extended trial balance showing clearly the profit or loss made by Helen Grant.

Association of Accounting Technicians (Amended)

CHAPTER 30

Stock valuation

Learning objectives

After you have studied this chapter you should be able to:

- understand that there can be more than one way of valuing stock
- calculate the value of stock using three different methods
- understand how the closing stock valuation affects the profit figures
- adjust stock valuations, where necessary, by a reduction to net realisable value
- adjust stock valuations in respect of goods on sale or return
- understand the importance of the final stock valuation figure that appears in the balance sheet and maintaining appropriate stock levels.

30.1 Different valuations of stock

Stock is the name given to goods purchased for re-sale; it can also include work in progress and raw materials, which you will learn about later in Chapter 35, Manufacturing accounts.

Most people would assume that there can only be one figure for the valuation of stock. This is, however, untrue. This chapter will examine how the valuation of stock can be calculated using different figures.

Assume that a firm has just completed its first financial year and is about to value stock on hand at cost price. The firm has only dealt with one type of goods. A record of the transactions is now shown below in Exhibit 30.1.

Exhibit 30.1

Bought				Sold			
2005			£	2005			£
January	10	at £30 each	300	May	8	for £50 each	400
April	10	at £34 each	340	November	24	for £60 each	1,440
October	20	at £40 each	800				
	40		1,440		32		1,840

The balance of stock on hand at 31 December 2005 is 8 units. The total figure of purchases is £1,440 and that of sales is £1,840. The trading account for the first year of trading can now be completed if the closing stock is brought into the calculations.

But what value do we put on each of the 8 units left in stock at the end of the year? If all of the units bought during the year had cost £30 each, then the closing stock would be 8 × £30 = £240. However, we have bought goods at different prices. This means that the valuation depends on which goods are taken for this calculation: the units at £30, or those at £34, or yet others at £40.

Many firms do not know exactly whether they have sold all the oldest units before they sell new units. For instance, a firm selling spanners may not know whether the oldest spanners had been sold before the newest spanners.

The stock valuation will, therefore, be based on an accounting custom, and not on the facts of exactly which units were still in stock at the year end. The three main methods of doing this are now shown.

30.2 First in, first out method

This is usually known as **FIFO**, the first letters of each word. The method says that, as far as the accounts are concerned, the first goods to be received are the first to be issued. Using the figures in Exhibit 30.1, we can now calculate the closing figure of stock as follows:

2005	Received	Issued	Stock	£	£
Jan	10 × £30 each		10 × £30		300
April	10 × £34 each		10 × £30 10 × £34	300 340	640
May		8 × £30 each	2 × £30 10 × £34	60 340	400
Oct	20 × £40 each		2 × £30 10 × £34 20 × £40	60 340 800	1,200
Nov		2 × £30 each 10 × £34 each 12 × £40 each	8 × £40		320

The closing stock at 31 December 2005 is therefore valued at £320 using the FIFO method.

30.3 Last in, first out method

This is usually known as **LIFO**. As each issue of goods is made, the goods are said to be from the last batch received before that date. Where there is not enough left of the last batch, then the balance of goods needed is said to come from the previous batch still unsold.

From the information shown in Exhibit 30.1, the calculation under this basis can now be shown.

2005	Received	Issued	Stock	£	£
Jan	10 × £30 each		10 × £30		300
April	10 × £34 each		10 × £30 10 × £34	300 340	640
May		8 × £34 each	10 × £30 2 × £34	300 68	368
Oct	20 × £40 each		10 × £30 2 × £34 20 × £40	300 68 800	1,168
Nov		20 × £40 each 2 × £34 each 2 × £30 each	8 × £30		240

The closing stock at 31 December 2005 is therefore valued at £240 using the LIFO method.

30.4 Average cost method (AVCO)

Using the **AVCO** method, with each receipt of goods the average cost for each item of stock is recalculated. Further issues of goods are then at that figure, until another receipt of goods means that another recalculation is needed.

From the information in Exhibit 30.1, the calculation can be shown thus:

2005	Received	Issued	Average cost per unit of stock held	Number of units in stock	Total value of stock
			£		£
January	10 × £30		30	10	300
April	10 × £34		32*	20	640
May		8 × £32	32	12	384
October	20 × £40		37**	32	1,184
November		24 × £37	37	8	296

Note: *In April, the average cost is calculated as follows:
stock 10 × £30 = £300 + stock received (10 × £34) £340 = total £640.
20 units in stock, so the average is £640 ÷ 20 = £32.

**In October, the average is calculated as follows:
stock 12 × £32 = £384 + stock received (20 × £40) £800 = £1,184.
32 units in stock, so the average is £1,184 ÷ 32 = £37.

The closing stock at 31 December 2005 is therefore valued at £296 using the AVCO method.

30.5 Stock valuation and the calculation of profits

Using the figures from Exhibit 30.1, with stock valuations shown by the three methods of FIFO, LIFO, and AVCO, the trading accounts would appear as set out in the table.

Trading Account for the year ended 31 December 2005

	FIFO		LIFO		AVCO	
	£	£	£	£	£	£
Sales		1,840		1,840		1,840
Less Cost of sales						
Purchases	1,440		1,440		1,440	
Less Closing stock	320	1,120	240	1,200	296	1,144
Gross Profit		720		640		696

As can be seen from the table above, different methods of stock valuation will mean that different profits are shown.

30.6 Reduction to net realisable value

The **net realisable value** of stock is calculated as follows:

Saleable value *less* any expenses needed
to complete the item or get it in a condition
to be sold = **Net realisable value**.

The concept of prudence is used when stock is valued. Stock should not be over-valued; otherwise, profits shown will be too high. Therefore, if the net realisable value of stock is less than the cost of the stock, prudence dictates that the figure to be taken for the final accounts is that of net realisable value.

Example 1: An item of stock was purchased at cost price £300. Unfortunately, the item was damaged in the warehouse and the cost of repair and repainting amounted to £50 after which it was estimated it could be sold for £200. The item would be valued as follows:

Saleable value £200 less cost of repair and repainting £50 = Net realisable value of £150.

30.7 Goods on sale or return

Goods received on sale or return

Sometimes we may receive goods from a supplier on a **sale or return** basis. This means that we do not have to pay for the goods until we sell them. If we do not sell them we have to return them to our supplier.

This means that the goods do not belong to us. If we have some goods on sale or return at the stocktaking date, they should not be included in our stock valuation.

Goods sent to our customers on sale or return

We may send goods on a sale or return basis to our customers. The stock will belong to us until it is sold. At our stocktaking date, any goods held by our customers on sale or return should be included in our stock valuation.

30.8 Stocktaking and the balance sheet date

Students often think that all the counting and valuing of stock is done on the last day of the accounting period. This might be true in a small business, but it is often impossible in larger businesses. There may be too many items of stock to do it so quickly.

This means that stocktaking may take place over a period of days. To get the figure of the stock valuation as on the last day of the accounting period, we will have to make adjustments. Exhibit 30.2 gives an example of such calculations.

Exhibit 30.2

Lee Ltd has a financial year that ends on 31 December 2007. The stocktaking is not in fact done until 8 January 2008. When the items in stock on that date are priced out, it is found that the stock value amounts to £28,850. The following information is available about transactions between 31 December 2007 and 8 January 2008.

(a) Purchases since 31 December 2007 amounted to £2,370 at cost.
(b) Returns inwards since 31 December 2007 were £350 at selling price.
(c) Sales since 31 December 2007 amounted to £3,800 at selling price.
(d) The selling price is always cost price + 25 per cent.

Lee Ltd
Computation of stock as on 31 December 2007

	£	£	£
Stock (at cost)			28,850
Add Items which were in stock on 31 December 2007 (at cost)			
Sales		3,800	
Less Profit content (20 per cent of selling price)*		760	3,040
			31,890
Less Items which were not in stock on 31 December 2007 (at cost)			
Returns inwards	350		
Less Profit content (20 per cent of selling price)*	70	280	
Purchases (at cost)		2,370	2,650
Stock in hand as on 31 December 2007			29,240

Note: *Stock is at cost (or net realisable value) and not at selling price. As this calculation has a sales figure in it, which includes profit, we must deduct the profit part to get to the cost price. This is true also for returns inwards.

At one time it was very rare for auditors to attend at stocktaking time as observers. The professional accounting bodies now encourage auditors to be present if at all possible.

30.9 Stock levels

One of the most common faults found in the running of a business is that too high a level of stock is maintained. A considerable number of firms that have problems with a shortage of finance will find that they can help matters by having a sensible look at the amounts of stock they hold. It would be a very rare firm indeed which, if they had not investigated the matter previously, could not manage to let parts of their stock run down. As this would save spending cash on items not really necessary, this cash could be better utilised elsewhere.

Chapter summary

● There are three methods of valuing stock namely: first in, first out (FIFO), last in, first out (LIFO) and the average cost method (AVCO).
● Each of the above methods gives a different closing stock valuation that subsequently affects the profit figure. The lower the closing stock figure the lower the profit whilst the higher the closing stock figure the higher the profit.
● Net realisable value is the sales value of goods less expenses before sale.
● When a business supplies goods to a customer on sale or return they belong to the supplier until such time as the customer decides they wish to purchase them and an order is placed.
● It may be necessary to make adjustments to the final stock figure which appears in the balance sheet depending upon when the physical stock take has taken place.
● It is important that businesses do not maintain a high level of stock since this means funds are tied up and could cause a cash flow problem.

Exercises

30.1 (a) From the following figures, calculate the closing stock in trade that would be shown using (i) FIFO, (ii) LIFO, (iii) AVCO methods.

2007	Bought	2007	Sold
January	24 at £10 each	June	30 at £16 each
April	16 at £12.50 each	November	34 at £18 each
October	30 at £13 each		

(b) Draw up trading accounts for 2007 using each of the three methods for stock valuation.

30.2X (a) From the following figures, calculate the closing stock-in-trade that would be shown using (i) FIFO, (ii) LIFO, (iii) AVCO methods.

2006	Bought	2006	Sold
January	30 at £12 each	July	24 at £15.50 each
May	30 at £14 each	November	16 at £18 each

(b) Draw up trading accounts for 2006 using each of the three methods for stock valuation.

30.3 DC Ltd, whose financial year end was 31 December 2006, does not take a stock check until 8 January 2007, when it is shown to be £50,850 at cost. It is then established that:

(a) a calculation of 1,000 items at £1.60 was shown as £160

(b) during the period from the year end to 8 January 2007, no purchases were made but sales of £500 were made. The profit margin is 20 per cent

(c) some goods costing £560 had a net realisable value of £425

(d) one stock sheet has been added up to be £2,499. The total should have been £4,299.

Calculate the correct figure of stock on 31 December 2006.

30.4X You are valuing stock at your business as it was at 31 December 2007. The actual date on which the stock was counted was 7 January 2008. The stock sheets show a total of £85,980 at cost as on that date. You are to adjust this figure to find out the stock as at 31 December 2007. The rate of gross profit is 25 per cent on selling price.

On further scrutiny you find:

(a) goods received after 1 January and for which invoices bear the date of January amount to £3,987

(b) one of the stock sheets has been added up to give a total of £4,897 instead of £4,798

(c) goods selling at £480 have been sent to a customer on 'sale or return' during December – these had not been sold by the customer but they had been omitted from the stock figures

(d) an item of 360 units priced at £1.60 each has been extended on the stock sheets as £420

(e) goods amounting to £98 have been returned to suppliers during the first week of January.

30.5X (a) If the closing stock of a business had been mistakenly overvalued by £5,000 and the error has gone unnoticed, what would be the effect of the error on:
  (i) this year's profit?
  (ii) next year's profit?

(b) A company that sells videos and electrical goods values its closing stock at £72,050 (cost price) at 30 June 2006. However, it has found that this figure includes the following:
  (i) Five videos that had cost £300 each have now been replaced by an improved model. In order to sell these obsolete models, it is thought that they will have to be sold at £250 each.
  (ii) A hi-fi system that cost £500 has been damaged and it is estimated that repairs will cost £100 before it can be sold.

Calculate the value of the closing stock after taking into the account the above adjustments.

30.6 On 30 November 2007, the last day of its financial year, The Pine Warehouse made a cash sale of some pine tables and chairs. These had originally cost £1,000 and were sold for £1,500. Although the sale was immediately recorded in the accounts of the business and the cash had been paid at the time of the sale, the customer asked for delivery to take place on 22 December 2007. The tables and chairs were therefore still in stock at the financial year end. The proprietor of the business, Pat Hall, has suggested that the tables and chairs should be included in the valuation of the closing stock at the selling price of £1,500. Pat Hall comments to you: 'This seems to be in accordance with the prudence concept since profits can be recognised once they are realised.'

You are required to write a memo to Pat Hall stating whether or not you agree with the proposed accounting treatment for the tables and chairs. Clearly explain the reasons for your answer.

AAT Central Assessment

30.7X (*a*) You are required to value the closing stock, after taking into account the necessary adjustments, in the following separate situations:

(i) Closing stock was valued at cost at £43,795. However, this figure includes two items, cost price £175 each, which have been damaged in storage. It has been estimated that if a total of £35 was spent on repairing them, they could be sold for £140 each.

(ii) The value of the closing stock had been valued at cost on 31 October 2007 at £107,300. However, this includes some discontinued kitchen cabinets the details of which are as follows:

Cost	£2,300
Normal selling price	£3,500
Net realisable value	£1,800

(*b*) Stock has always been valued by Electronics World Ltd on a FIFO basis and this includes the closing stock figure of £198,650 as at 31 May 2007. It has been suggested that the closing stock figure should now be recalculated on a LIFO basis.

(i) Assuming that the prices of electronic goods have been gradually rising throughout the year, would the change suggested increase profit for the year ended 31 May 2007, decrease profit or would profit remain the same?

(ii) Which accounting concept states that the company should not normally change its basis for valuing stock unless it has very good reasons for doing so?

AAT Central Assessment

Errors and their effect on accounting records

After you have studied this chapter you should be able to:

- appreciate that every transaction should be entered twice in the accounts, once on the debit side and once on the credit side on an account
- understand that there are two types of error, those that effect the agreement of the trial balance and those that do not
- appreciate that errors are usually identified after a period of time has elapsed
- distinguish between the different kinds of errors
- correct errors using the journal.

31.1 Introduction

So far you have learnt that each accounting transaction requires two entries:

- one entry must be on the debit side of an account, and
- one entry must be on the credit side on an account.

At the end of an accounting period each account is balanced up and a trial balance drawn up to check the arithmetical accuracy of the book-keeping entries. Provided that every item has been entered correctly, the two sides of the trial balance should equal each other, i.e.

> Total debit balances = Total credit balances

However, it is inevitable that errors will occur when data are entered into the books of account. There are two main classifications of errors:

- those that affect the balancing of the trial balance
- those that do not affect the balancing of the trial balance.

Errors affecting trial balance agreement

These errors result in the total of the debit columns in the trial balance *not* being the same as the total of the credit column. Suppose we correctly entered cash received of £103 from H Lee, our debtor, in the cash book as shown below:

Cash Book (debit side only)

	Cash	Bank	
2005 May 1 H Lee	£ 103	£	

However, when posting this item to H Lee's account we entered the amount received on the credit side as £13, see below:

Sales ledger

Dr		H Lee Account			Cr
			2005		£
			May 1 Cash		13

When the trial balance is drawn up the totals will be different by (£103 − £13) = £90. This effect will arise in every case where a debit entry does not equal a credit entry for a transaction. Correction of these types of errors is covered in Chapter 32.

Errors not affecting trial balance agreement

Although the trial balance totals agree, complete accuracy cannot be guaranteed. Certain errors can still be made which do not affect the balancing of the trial balance, i.e. the trial balance would still appear to balance even though certain errors have occurred. The errors that lead to this situation are listed below:

● **errors of commission**
● **errors of principle**
● **errors of original entry**
● **errors of omission**
● **compensating errors**
● **complete reversal of entries**.

In Sections 31.3 to 31.8, to follow, each of the above errors are illustrated together with the journal entries required to correct the error.

31.2 Correction of errors

Most errors are discovered after a period of time has elapsed. Once identified they need to be corrected properly via the journal and not by crossing out items or tearing a page out of a ledger or even using correcting fluid. If the latter was permitted then there is more risk of fraudulent transactions taking place.

Corrections are recorded in the journal which, as already mention in Chapter 24, is a book of original entry. By entering them in the journal a permanent record is made for future reference.

Since many students have difficulty with journal entries you may remember from Chapter 24 that it is often useful to think 'double entry' before entering the details in the journal. In other words, think where the transaction has been entered in the double entry accounts and then where the entry should have been made; this then gives you the basis for preparing the journal entry. Work through the following sections with this in mind.

31.3 Errors of commission

An **error of commission** arises when a correct amount is entered in the books, but in the wrong person's account.

Example 1: D Long paid us £50 by cheque on 18 May 2005. The transaction is correctly entered in the cash book, but it was entered by mistake in the account for D Longman. This means that there had been both a debit of £50 and a credit of £50. It has appeared in the personal account as:

D Longman Account

Dr			Cr
		2005	£
		May 18 Bank	50

The error was found on 31 May 2005. This will now have to be corrected and requires two entries:

Accounting entries	Explanation
Debit D Longman's account	To cancel out the error on the credit side of that account
Credit D Long's account	To enter the amount in the correct account

The accounts will now appear thus:

D Longman Account

Dr	£	Cr	£
2005		2005	
May 31 D Long:			
Error corrected	50	May 18 Bank	50

D Long Account

Dr	£	Cr	£
2005		2005	
		May 31 Cash entered in error in	
May 1 Balance b/d	50	D Longman's account	50

The journal

The ways by which errors have been corrected should all be entered in the journal. The correction has already been shown above in double entry. In fact, the journal entries should be made before completing the double entry accounts for the transaction. For teaching purposes only in this chapter, the journal entries are shown last.

The journal entry will be thus:

The Journal	Dr	Cr
	£	£
2005	50	
May 31 D Longman		50
D Long		
Cheque received . . . entered in wrong		
personal account, now corrected.		

31.4 Errors of principle

An **error of principle** is where a transaction is entered in the wrong type of account. For instance, the purchase of a fixed asset should be debited to a fixed asset account. If in error it is debited to an expense account, then it has been entered in the wrong type of account.

Example 2: The purchase of a motor car for £5,500 by cheque on 14 May 2005 has been debited in error to a motor expenses account. In the cash book it is shown correctly. This means that there has been both a debit of £5,500 and a credit of £5,500.

It will have appeared in the expense account as:

Motor Expenses Account

Dr			Cr
2005	£		
May 14 Bank	5,500		

The error is detected on 31 May 2005 and is corrected. To do so, two entries are needed:

Accounting entry	Explanation
Debit Motor Car account	To put the amount in the correct account
Credit Motor Expenses account	To cancel the error previously made in the Motor Expenses account

The accounts then are corrected thus:

Motor Expenses Account

Dr				Cr
2005	£	2005		£
May 14 Bank	5,500	May 31 Motor car error corrected		5,500

Motor Car Account

Dr			Cr
2005	£		
May 31 Bank: entered originally in			
Motor expenses	5,500		

The journal

The journal entries to correct the error will be shown as:

The Journal		Dr	Cr
		£	£
2005			
May 31 Motor car		5,500	
Motor expenses			5,500
Correction of error whereby purchase of motor car was debited to motor expenses account.			

31.5 Errors of original entry

An **error of original entry** occurs where an original amount is incorrect and is then entered in double entry.

Example 3: Sales of £150 to T Higgins on 13 May 2005 have been entered as both a debit and a credit of £130. The accounts would appear thus:

T Higgins Account

Dr			Cr
2005	£		
May 13 Sales	130		

Sales Account

Dr			Cr
		2005	£
		May 31 Sales day book	
		(part of total)	130

The error is found on 31 May 2005. The entries to correct it are now shown:

T Higgins Account

Dr			Cr
2005	£		
May 13 Sales	130		
May 31 Sales: error	20		

Sales Account

Dr			Cr
		2005	£
		May 31 Sales day book	130
		May 31 T Higgins:	
		error corrected	20

The journal

To correct the error, the journal entries will be:

The Journal		Dr	Cr
		£	£
2005			
May 31 T Higgins		20	
Sales account			20
Correction of error. Sales of £150			
had been incorrectly entered as £130.			

31.6 Errors of omission

Errors of omission are where transactions are not entered into the books at all.

Example 4: We purchased goods from T Hope for £250 on 13 May 2005 but did not enter the transaction in the accounts. So there were nil debits and nil credits. We found the error on 31 May 2005. The entries to correct it will be thus:

Purchases Account

Dr			Cr
2005	£		
May 13 T Hope:			
error corrected	250		

T Hope Account

Dr			Cr
		2005	£
		May 31 Purchases:	
		error corrected	250

The journal

The journal entries to correct the error will be:

The Journal		Dr	Cr
		£	£
2005			
May 31 Purchases		250	
T Hope			250
Correction of error. Purchase omitted			
from books.			

31.7 Compensating errors

These errors are where they cancel each other out.

Example 5: Let us take a case where incorrect totals had purchases of £7,900 and sales of £9,900. The purchases day book adds up to be £100 too much. In the same period, the sales day book also adds up to be £100 too much.

If these were the only errors in our books, the trial balance totals would equal each other. Both totals would be wrong – they would both be £100 too much – but they would be equal. In this case, the accounts would have appeared as follows:

Purchases Account

Dr			Cr
2005	£		
May 13 Purchases	7,900		

Sales Account

Dr			Cr
		2005	£
		May 31 Sales	9,900

When corrected, the accounts will appear as:

Purchases Account

Dr			Cr
2005	£	2005	£
May 13 Purchases	7,900	May 31 The Journal:	
		error corrected	100

Sales Account

Dr			Cr
2005	£	2005	£
May 31 The Journal:		May 31 Sales	9,900
error corrected	100		

The journal

Journal entries to correct these two errors will be thus:

The Journal		Dr	Cr
2005		£	£
May 31 Sales account		100	
Purchases account			100
Correction of compensating errors.			
Totals of both purchases and sales day books			
incorrectly added up to £100 too much.			

31.8 Complete reversal of entries

This error is where the correct amounts are entered in the correct accounts, but each item is shown on the wrong side of each account.

Example 6: We pay a cheque for £200 on 28 May 2005 to D Charles. We enter it as follows in accounts with the letter (A). There has, therefore, been both a debit and a credit of £200.

Cash Book (A)

Dr					Cr
	Cash £	Bank £		Cash £	Bank £
2005					
May 28 D Charles		200			

D Charles (A)

Dr			Cr
		2005	£
		May 28 Bank	200

This is incorrect. It should have been debit D Charles Account £200, credit Bank £200. Both items have been entered in the correct accounts, but each is on the wrong side of its account.

The way to correct this is more difficult to understand than with other errors. Let us look at how the items would have appeared if we had done it correctly in the first place. We will show the letter (B) behind the account names.

Cash Book (B)

Dr					Cr
	Cash £	Bank £		Cash £	Bank £
			2005		200
			May 28 D Charles		

D Charles (B)

Dr			Cr
2005		£	
May 28 Bank		200	

We found the error on May 31 and it was corrected as follows:

1 First we have to cancel the error. This would mean entering these amounts:

    Dr: D Charles   £200
    Cr: Bank   £200

2 Then we have to enter up the transaction:

    Dr: D Charles   £200
    Cr: Bank   £200

Altogether then, the entries to correct the error are twice the amounts first entered.

When corrected, the accounts appear as follows, marked (C).

Cash Book (C)

Dr						Cr
	Cash £	Bank £			Cash £	Bank £
2005 May 8 D Charles		200	2005 May 31 D Charles: error corrected			400

D Charles (C)

Dr			Cr
2005 May 28 Bank: error corrected	£ 400	2005 May 28 Bank	£ 200

You can see that accounts (C) give the same final answer as accounts (B).

			£	£
(B)	*Dr:*	D Charles	200	
	Cr:	Bank		200
(C)	*Dr:*	D Charles (£400 − £200)	200	
	Cr:	Bank (£400 − £200)		200

The journal

Journal entries. These would be shown as follows:

The Journal		
	Dr	*Cr*
2005	£	£
May 31 D Charles	400	
Bank		400
Payment of £200 on 28 May 2005 to		
D Charles incorrectly credited to his account,		
and debited to bank. Error now corrected.		

31.9 Casting

You will often notice the use of the expression **casting**, which means adding up. **Overcasting** means incorrectly adding up a column of figures to give an answer that is *greater* than it should be. **Undercasting** means incorrectly adding up a column of figures to give an answer that is *less* than it should be.

Chapter summary

● Periodically businesses balance their accounts and prepare a trial balance to check the arithmetical accuracy of the book-keeping entries. However, agreement in the trial balance does not necessarily mean that no errors have occurred.

- There are two types of errors: those that affect the balancing of the trial balance and those that do not.
- Errors that can occur and yet the trial balance still agree are errors of commission, principle, original entry, omission, compensating and complete reversal of entries.
- Once identified the errors are corrected by using the journal. However, it is sometimes easier for students to carry out the double entry first followed by the journal entry. In normal circumstances you would prepare the journal entry first followed by postings to the appropriate ledger accounts.
- The term 'casting' refers to figures that are added up. Overcasting means adding figures up to an amount greater than they should be, whereas, undercasting means adding a column of figures up to less than it should be.

Exercises

31.1 Show the journal entries necessary to correct the following errors:

(a) A sale of goods £678 to J Harkness had been entered in J Harker's account.

(b) The purchase of a machine on credit from L Pearson for £4,390 had been completely omitted from our books.

(c) The purchase of a motor vehicle for £3,800 had been entered in error in the motor expenses account.

(d) A sale of £221 to E Fletcher had been entered in the books – both debit and credit – as £212.

(e) Commission received £257 had been entered in error in the sales account.

31.2X Show the journal entries needed to correct the following errors:

(a) Purchases £699 on credit from K Webb had been entered in H Weld's account.

(b) A cheque of £189 paid for advertisements had been entered in the cash column of the cash book instead of in the bank column.

(c) Sale of goods £443 on credit to B Maxim had been entered in error in B Gunn's account.

(d) Purchase of goods on credit from K Innes £89 entered in two places in error as £99.

(e) Cash paid to H Mersey £89 has been entered on the debit side of the cash book and the credit side of H Mersey's account.

31.3 The following errors have been made in the accounting records of Berry Sports:

(a) £110 has been debited to the rent account instead of the rates account.

(b) Purchases returns valued at £300 have been debited to the purchases returns account and credited to the creditors control account.

(c) £2,000 has been debited to the insurance accounts and credited to the bank account instead of the correct amount of £200.

Record the journal entries in the main (general) ledger to correct the above.
Narratives are not required.

Association of Accounting Technicians

31.4 The following errors have been made in the main (general) ledger of Senator Safes:

(a) £300 has been debited to the miscellaneous expenses account instead of the rates account.

(b) Purchases returns have been entered in the accounting records as £706 instead of £607 (ignore VAT).

(c) A credit customer, Leeson and Company, has ceased trading. The amount outstanding on its account of £800 plus VAT has been written off as a bad debt in the subsidiary (sales) ledger only, but the net amount and VAT should also have been written off.

Record the journal entries necessary in the main (general) ledger to correct the errors shown above. Narratives are not required.

Association of Accounting Technicians

31.5X The following errors have been made in the main (general) ledger of McGee Autos:

(a) £25 has been credited to the discounts received account instead of to the interest received account.

(b) The total of the sales day book has been posted incorrectly as £51,010 instead of the correct amount of £50,101 (ignore VAT).

(c) A payment of £100 to settle a hotel bill has been incorrectly credited to the hotel expenses account and debited to the bank account.

Record the journal entries needed in the main (general) ledger to correct the errors shown above. Dates and narratives are not required.

Association of Accounting Technicians

31.6X John Granger is the owner of a business of a retail business trading in car accessories. John has been told that he ought to prepare a trial balance at regular intervals. However, he has doubts about the value of trial balances.

(a) Explain *two* benefits that can arise from the preparation of a trial balance.

(b) Point out the limitations of this accounting technique.

(c) Provide an example of a situation which illustrates the limitations of a trial balance.

Assessment and Qualifications Alliance (AQA)

31.7X D Singh, a retail trader, has a lot still to learn about accounting but has managed to draw up the following trial balance from his business records.

	£	£
Stock 1 April 2007		21,400
Stock 31 March 2008	15,600	
Discounts allowed		620
Discounts received	900	
Purchases	188,000	
Returns outwards	2,800	
Sales		264,200
Returns inwards	2,200	
Buildings at cost	140,000	
Provision for depreciation of buildings	7,000	
Motor vehicles at cost	30,000	
Provision for depreciation of motor vehicles	9,000	
Capital: D Singh		169,200
Bank	14,200	
Debtors		22,600
Provision for doubtful debts	1,920	
Creditors	15,200	
General expenses	33,200	
Drawings	18,000	
	478,020	478,020

Required:

(*a*) Prepare a corrected trial balance as at 31 March 2008.

(*b*) After the preparation of the corrected trial balance, but before drawing up the final accounts, the following items were discovered:

    (i)   A credit note for £148 had been received from FH Ltd. This was in respect of goods returned by Singh in December 2007. No entry was made in the books.

    (ii) No entry has been made in the books in respect of £333 goods taken for own use.

    (iii) A payment by a debtor, T Hall, of £168 has been credited in error to T Hallworth's account.

    (iv) Free samples sent to a customer, L Shah, have been charged to him as though they were sales for £88.

    (v) A discount allowed to K Young of £64 was found to be incorrect. It should have been £94.

Show the journal entries needed for items (i) to (v) above.

Suspense accounts and errors

32.1 Introduction

In the previous chapter errors that did not affect the balancing of the trial balance were discussed. However, there are many errors which occur that do affect the balancing of the trial balance, for example:

- incorrect additions in any account
- making an entry on only one side of the accounts – e.g. a debit but no credit, or a credit but no debit
- entering a different amount on the debit side from the amount on the credit side.

32.2 Suspense accounts

If a trial balance does not balance it is important that errors are located and corrected as soon as possible. When they cannot be found, then the trial balance totals should be made to agree with each other by inserting the amount of the difference between the two sides in a **suspense account**. This occurs in Exhibit 32.1 where there is a difference of £40.

Exhibit 32.1

Trial Balance as at 31 December 2005

	Dr £	Cr £
Totals after all the accounts have been listed	100,000	99,960
Suspense account		40
	100,000	100,000

To make the two totals the same, a figure of £40 for the suspense account has been shown on the credit side. A suspense account is opened and the £40 difference is also shown there on the credit side.

Suspense Account

Dr		Cr
	2005	£
	Dec 31 Difference per trial balance	40

32.3 Suspense account and the balance sheet

If the errors are not found before the financial statements are prepared, the suspense account balance will be included in the balance sheet. Where the balance is a credit balance, it should be included under current liabilities on the balance sheet. When the balance is a debit balance, it should be shown under current assets on the balance sheet. Large errors should always be found before the financial statements are drawn up.

32.4 Correction of errors

When errors are found, they must be corrected using double entry. Each correction must be described by an entry in the journal.

One error only

We will look at two examples:

Example 1: Assume that the error of £40 as shown in Exhibit 32.1 is found in the following year on 31 March 2006, the error being that the sales account was undercast by £40. The action taken to correct this is:

● Debit the suspense account to close it: £40.
● Credit the sales account to show item where it should have been: £40.

The accounts now appear as Exhibit 32.2.

Exhibit 32.2

Suspense Account

Dr					Cr
2006		£	2005		£
			Dec 31 Difference per		
Mar 31 Sales		40	trial balance		40

Sales Account

Dr					Cr
			2006		£
			Mar 31 Suspense		40

This can be shown in journal form as follows:

The Journal

	Dr	Cr
2006	£	£
Mar 31 Suspense	40	
Sales		40
Correction of undercasting of sales by £40		
in last year's accounts.		

Example 2: The trial balance on 31 December 2006 shows a difference of £168. It was a shortage on the debit side. A suspense account is opened and the difference of £168 is entered on the debit side.

On 31 May 2007 the error is found. We had made a payment of £168 to D Miguel to close his account. It was correctly entered in the cash book, but it was not entered in Miguel's account.

To correct the error, the account of D Miguel is debited with £168, as it should have been in 2006, and the suspense account is credited with £168 so that the account can be closed. The accounts and journal entry now appear as in Exhibit 32.3.

Exhibit 32.3

D Miguel Account

Dr					Cr
2007		£	2007		£
May 31 Bank		168	Jan 1 Balance b/d		168

Suspense Account

Dr					Cr
2007		£	2007		£
May 31 Difference					
per trial balance		168	May 31 D Miguel		168

The Journal

	Dr	Cr
2007	£	£
May 31 D Miguel	168	
Suspense		168
Correction of non-entry of payment last year		
in D Miguel's account.		

More than one error

We can now look at an example where the suspense account difference has been caused by more than one error.

Example 3: A trial balance at 31 December 2007 shows a difference of £77, being a shortage on the debit side. A suspense account is opened, and the difference of £77 is entered on the debit side of the account.

On 28 February 2008 all the errors from the previous year were found:

(*a*) A cheque of £150 paid to L Kent had been correctly entered in the cash book, but had not been entered in Kent's account.
(*b*) The purchases account has been undercast by £20.
(*c*) A cheque of £93 received from K Sand has been correctly entered in the cash book but has not been entered in Sand's account.

These three errors have resulted in a net error of £77, shown by a debit of £77 on the debit side of the suspense account.

These are corrected by:

● making correcting entries in the accounts for (*a*), (*b*) and (*c*)
● recording the double entry for these items in the suspense account.

L Kent Account

Dr			Cr
2008	£		
Feb 28 Suspense (*a*)	150		

Purchases Account

Dr			Cr
2008	£		
Feb 28 Suspense (*b*)	20		

K Sand Account

Dr			Cr
		2008	£
		Feb 28 Suspense (*c*)	93

Suspense Account

Dr   Cr

2008	£	2008	£
Jan 1 Balance b/d	77	Feb 28 L Kent (*a*)	150
Feb 28 K Sand (*c*)	93	Feb 28 Purchases (*b*)	20
	170		170

The Journal

	Dr	Cr
2008	£	£
Feb 28 L Kent	150	
Suspense		150
Cheque paid omitted from Kent's account		
Feb 28 Purchases	20	
Suspense		20
Undercasting of purchases by £20 in		
last year's accounts		
Feb 28 Suspense	93	
K Sand		93
Cheque received omitted from Sand's		
account		

Only those errors that make the trial balance totals different from each other have to be corrected via the suspense account.

32.5 The effect of errors on profits

Some of the errors will have meant that the calculation of original profits will be wrong. Other errors will have no effect upon profits. We will use Exhibit 32.4 to illustrate the different kinds of errors. Exhibit 32.4 shows a set of accounts in which errors have been made.

Exhibit 32.4

K Davis
Trading and Profit and Loss Account for the year ended 31 December 2005

		£	£
Sales	(A)		8,250
Less Cost of goods sold			
Opening stock		500	
Purchases	(B)	6,100	
		6,600	
Less Closing stock		700	
			5,900
Gross profit			2,350
Less Expenses			
Rent	(C)	200	
Insurance	(D)	120	
Lighting		180	
Depreciation		250	
			750
Net profit			1,600

K Davis
Balance Sheet as at 31 December 2005

		£ Cost	£ Depreciation	£
Fixed assets				
Fixtures and fittings		2,200	800	1,400
Current assets				
Stock		700		
Debtors	(E)	600		
Cash at bank		340		
Suspense	(G)	60	1,700	
Current liabilities				
Creditors	(F)	600	600	
Net current assets				1,100
Net assets				2,500
Financed by				
Capital Account				
Balance as at 1 January 2005				1,800
Add Net profit for the year				1,600
				3,400
Less Drawings				(900)
				2,500

Errors that *do not* affect profit calculations

If an error affects items only in the balance sheet, then the original calculated profit will not need altering. The example below shows this:

Example 4: Assume that in Exhibit 32.4 the £60 debit balance on the suspense account shown in the balance sheet was because, on 1 November 2005, we paid £60 to a creditor T Monk and it was correctly entered in the cash book, but it was not entered anywhere else. The error was found on 1 June 2006.

We can see that when this error is corrected, only two items in the final accounts will have to be altered. These are (F) Creditors, which will have to be reduced by £60, and (G) Suspense account, which will now be cancelled and not shown in the balance sheet. This means that neither the trading account nor the profit and loss account have been affected. The profit as shown for 2005 is correct, but the balance sheet is incorrect.

The double entry records needed are as follows:

T Monk

	£		£
2006		2006	
June 1 Suspense (Correction)	60	Jan 1 Balance b/d	60

Suspense Account

	£		£
2006		2006	
Jan 1 Balance b/d (Difference			
in last year's trial balance)	60	June 1 T Monk	60

The journal entries to correct it will be thus:

The Journal

	Dr	Cr
	£	£
2006		
June 1 T Monk	60	
Suspense account		60
Payment to T Monk on 1 November 2005		
not entered in his account.		
Correction now made.		

Errors that *do* affect profit calculations

If the error is in one of the numbers labelled (A), (B), (C) or (D) shown in the trading and profit and loss account, then the original profit will need altering. Example 5 shows this:

Example 5: Assume that in Exhibit 32.4 the £60 debit balance was because the rent account (C) was added up incorrectly: it should be shown as £260 instead of £200. The error was found on 1 June 2006. The journal entries to correct it are:

The Journal

	Dr	Cr
	£	£
2006		
June 1 Rent	60	
Suspense		60
Correction of rent undercast last year.		

Rent last year should have been increased by £60. This would have reduced net profit by £60. A statement of corrected profit for the year is now shown.

K Davis
Statement of Corrected Net Profit for the year ended 31 December 2005

	£
	1,600
Net profit per the accounts	
Less Rent understated	60
	1,540

Where there have been several errors

Example 6: If in Exhibit 32.4 there had been four errors found in the accounts of K Davis on 31 March 2006, their correction can now be seen. Assume that the net difference had also been £60, with the four errors as:

	£
(A) Sales overcast by	70
(B) A credit purchase from C Hall of £59 was entered in the books, debit and credit entries, as	95
(D) Insurance undercast by	40
(E) Cash received from a debtor, L Young entered in the cash book only	50

Error (A) affected the profits: both gross and net profit were shown £70 too much because of this error. It also affected the Suspense account (G).

Error (B) showed purchases too high by (£95 − £59) = £36. This means that gross and net profits were shown £36 too little. The other item affected is (F) Creditors, which is shown as being £36 too much. This error does not affect (G) Suspense account.

Error (D) needs insurance increasing by £40. This will reduce the net profit by £40. It also affects the Suspense account (G).

Error (E) does not affect the profits at all. It affects only items in the balance sheet, namely (E) Debtors and (G) Suspense.

The entries in the ledger accounts are as follows:

General Ledger		Sales		
2006	£			
Mar 31 Suspense (Correction) (A)	70			

General Ledger		Purchases		
		2006		£
		Mar 31 C Hall (Correction) (B)		36

Purchases Ledger		C Hall		
2006	£			
Mar 31 Purchases (Correction) (B)	36			

General Ledger		Insurance		
2006	£			
Mar 31 Suspense (Correction) (D)	40			

Sales Ledger		L Young		
		2006		£
		Mar 31 Suspense (Correction) (E)		50

The entries in the suspense account and the journal entries will be as follows:

General Ledger   **Suspense Account**

2006		£	2006		£
Jan 1 Balance b/d		60	Mar 31 Sales	(A)	70
Mar 31 L Young	(E)	50	" 31 Insurance	(D)	40
		110			110

The Journal

		Dr	Cr
2006		£	£
(A) Mar 31 Sales		70	
Suspense			70
Sales overcast of £70 in 2005.			
(B) Mar 31 C Hall		36	
Purchases*			36
Credit purchase of £59 entered both as			
debit and credit as £95 in 2005.			
(D) Mar 31 Insurance		40	
Suspense			40
Insurance expense undercast by £40 in 2005.			
(E) Mar 31 Suspense		50	
L Young			50
Cash received omitted from L Young's account in 2005.			

Note: *In (B), the correction of the understatement of purchases does not pass through the Suspense account.

Now we can calculate the corrected net profit for the year 2005. Only items (A), (B) and (D) affect figures in the trading and profit and loss account. These are the only adjustments to be made to profit.

K Davis
Statement of corrected Net Profit for the year ended 31 December 2006

		£	£
Net profit per the accounts			1,600
Add Purchases overstated	(B)		36
			1,636
Less Sales overcast	(A)	70	
Insurance undercast	(D)	40	110
Corrected net profit for the year			1,526

32.6   Limitations of trial balances

In this and the previous chapter, you have seen various kinds of errors. Those in Chapter 31 were not revealed by trial balance totals being unequal. This shows a serious limitation in depending completely on the trial balance as an absolute check on the accuracy of the entries in the books of account. To refresh your memory, the kinds of errors not disclosed by a trial balance are:

● errors of commission
● errors of principle
● errors of original entry
● errors of omission
● compensating errors
● complete reversal of entries.

Even when the balances in a trial balance agree, there can be very large errors of various kinds, which may mean that profits have been wrongly calculated and that the balance sheet is incorrect. This current chapter has demonstrated these kinds of errors, where they have resulted in a difference being put into a suspense account until the error(s) have been found.

A very small amount in a suspense account could hide very large errors. For instance, a £50 credit in a suspense account could eventually be found to be either of the following:

● Sales overcast £10,000, debtors total overcast £10,050. If the errors are not found, then both the gross and net profits will be overstated by £10,000 and the figure of debtors in the balance sheet overstated by £10,050.
● Rent expense undercast by £2,000, total of creditors undercast by £1,950. In this case the net profit will be shown at £2,000 more than it should be, while creditors in the balance sheet will be understated by £1,950.

This shows that there is always a possibility of serious errors occurring without it being obvious at first sight.

Every attempt should be made to find errors. Opening a suspense account should be done only if all other efforts have failed.

32.7   Suspense accounts: examinations and business

Examinations

Unless it is part of a question, *do not* make your balance sheet totals agree by using a suspense account. The same applies to trial balances. Examiners are very likely to penalise you for including a suspense account when it should not be required.

Business

When preparing financial statements for a business every effort should be made to ensure that trial balance and balance sheet balance. However, if all else fails it may be necessary to open a suspense account and hopefully the error(s) may subsequently be located and posted to the suspense account, as shown in this chapter, and the balance eliminated.

Chapter summary

- If the totals in the trial balance do not agree it may be necessary to open a suspense account and enter the difference into the account until the error(s) can be located.
- In the unlikely event that the error(s) are not found when the balance sheet is prepared it may be necessary to include the suspense account. If the suspense account shows a credit balance then it should be entered under the current liabilities whereas a debit balance would be shown under current assets.
- Any errors found should be corrected using a journal and subsequently posted to the appropriate double entry accounts. If the error affects the suspense account then the posting should be made to that account.
- Some errors may affect the gross profit and net profit calculations and adjustments have to be made to these profit figures.
- Other errors that do not affect the profit calculations may affect a figure in the balance sheet. If this is the case then the figure in the balance sheet will require amending.
- Whilst the balancing of the trial balance is seen to ensure that the book-keeping entries have been carried out correctly the trial balance does have limitations in that certain errors occur which are not revealed by the trial balance agreement.

Exercises

32.1 On 31 March 2005 the following items are to be corrected via the journal. Show the corrections. Narratives are not required.

(a) T Thomas, a customer, had paid us a cheque for £900 to settle his debt. The cheque has now been returned to us marked 'Dishonoured'.

(b) We had allowed C Charles, a debtor, a cash discount of £35. Because of a dispute with her, we have now disallowed the cash discount.

(c) Office equipment bought for £6,000 has been debited to motor vehicles account.

(d) The copy sales invoice of sales to J Graham £715 was lost, and therefore was completely omitted from our books.

(e) Cash drawings of £210 have been correctly entered in the cash book, but have been credited to the wages account.

32.2 Jaspa West wishes to record the following in his books of account:

1 A cash receipt of £55 for rent has been recorded as a debit entry in the rent received account. The cash book entry had been correctly made. This matter should be corrected.

2 A debt of £150 owing by Mary Beagle will not be received and is to be written of as a bad debt.

3 The sales account has been overcast by £350. Therefore, this needs to be corrected.

4 A motor vehicle, costing £3,500, has been purchased on credit from C Williams.

5 A provision for bad debts of £225 is to be created.

Required:

(*a*) Write up the journal entries to record the above transactions.

(*b*) Give two examples of book-keeping errors which would not be revealed by the trial balance.

City & Guilds Pitman qualifications

32.3X John Laundau has just extracted a trial balance at 30 August, the end of his financial year. The debit side was greater than the credit side by £520 and a suspense account was opened for that amount. The auditors subsequently found the following errors:

1 £200 cash received from the sale of an old computer has been credited to the rent received account.
2 A payment of £100 for water entered in the cash book had not been entered in the water account.
3 The sales account had been undercast by £260.
4 A private purchase of a £1,000 computer had been included in the computer account.
5 Sale of goods to Lynne Beagle had been correctly entered in the sales account as £2,150 but had been entered in the personal account as £2,510.
6 No provision against doubtful debts had been created. This should have been 3 per cent of the end of year total debtors of £7,000.

Required:

(*a*) Make appropriate journal entries, with narrative, to rectify the errors.

(*b*) Show how the suspense account would be cleared by the appropriate entries.

City & Guilds Pitman qualifications

32.4 H Logan extracted a trial balance as at 31 December 2005. He was unable to balance it, but as he urgently needed his accounts for tax purposes, he opened a suspense account and entered £705 debit balance in it.

The following year he found the errors now listed:

(*a*) The returns inwards day book had been undercast by £100.
(*b*) Drawings of £80 had been debited to wages account.
(*c*) Carriage inwards £75 had been debited to carriage outwards.
(*d*) A payment of bank charges £270 had not been posted to the expense account.
(*e*) A sale of goods £385 to K Abbott on 30 December 2005 had not been entered at all.
(*f*) Discounts allowed of £218 had been credited to the discounts allowed account.
(*g*) A rent rebate of £200 had been entered in the cash book but not posted elsewhere.
(*h*) The purchases day book had carried forward a figure of £24,798 when it should have been £24,897.

Required:

1 Show the journal entries needed to correct the errors. Narratives are not required.
2 Show the suspense account balanced off.
3 If the original incorrect gross profit was shown as £129,487 and the original net profit was shown as £77,220 calculate the corrected figures for gross and net profits after the above items have been corrected.

32.5 The following trial balance was extracted by K Woodburn from her books as at 30 June 2008. She is unable to get the totals to agree.

Trial Balance as at 30 June 2008

	Dr £	Cr £
Sales		87,050
Purchases	62,400	
Discounts allowed and received	305	410
Salaries and wages	3,168	
General expenses	595	
Fixtures	10,000	
Stock 1 July 2007	12,490	
Debtors and creditors	8,120	5,045
Bank	6,790	
Drawings	4,520	
Capital		17,017
Suspense	1,134	
	109,522	109,522

The following errors are found:

(i)   Sales journal overcast by £350.
(ii) Discounts allowed undercast by £100.
(iii) Fixtures, bought for £850, have been entered in the cash book but not in the fixtures account.
(iv) Credit purchase of £166 was entered in the purchases journal only, but not in the creditor's account.
(v)   Cheque payment to a creditor of £490 had been debited to the drawings account in error.

You are required to:
(a) draw up the suspense account to record the corrections
(b) redraft the trial balance after all corrections have been made.

32.6X T Sawyer extracted the following trial balance from his books. He could not get the totals to agree with each other.

Trial Balance as at 31 December 2007

	Dr £	Cr £
Capital		25,621
Drawings	13,690	
Sales		94,630
Purchases	60,375	
Returns inwards and outwards	1,210	1,109
Wages and salaries	14,371	
Sundry expenses	598	
Stock 1.1.2007	8,792	
Debtors and creditors	11,370	4,290
Loan from J Chandler		5,000
Equipment	16,000	
Bank	5,790	
Suspense		1,546
	132,196	132,196

The following errors are discovered:

(i) Purchases journal was overcast by £258.
(ii) A repayment of loan £2,000 was debited in error to the wages account.
(iii) A cheque payment for equipment £1,500 has been entered in the equipment account but not in the cash book.
(iv) Returns outwards £168 have been entered in the returns journal but not in the creditor's account.
(v) Sundry expenses £44 have been entered in the cash book but not in the sundry expenses account.

You are required to:
(*a*) draw up the suspense account, showing corrections
(*b*) redraft the trial balance after all corrections have been made.

32.7 The trial balance of Philip Hogan as at 31 December 2006 does not balance. The difference of £5,400 has been credited to a suspense account. The following errors were subsequently discovered:

(*a*) The sales day book is undercast by £3,000.
(*b*) Purchases received from Dawson & Co, amounting to £1,147, had been received on 31 December 2006, and included in the closing stock at that date. Unfortunately, the invoice had not been entered in the purchases day book.
(*c*) Motor repairs of £585 have been charged to the motor vehicles account.
(*d*) Credit sales of £675 made to J Greenway have been debited to the account of J Green.
(*e*) A payment of £425 in respect of electricity has been debited to the electricity account as £575.
(*f*) A cheque for £2,250 received from Teape Ltd, a debtor, has been correctly entered in the cash book but no entry has been made in Teape's account.

Required:
(i) Show the journal entries, including narratives, to correct the above errors, (ii) Write up the suspense account after correction of the above errors.

32.8X A trial balance does not balance and a suspense account has been opened with a credit balance of £510. The following errors are then discovered.

(i) Cash purchases of £450 were recorded in both the cash book and ledger as £540.
(ii) The total of the motor expenses account was undercast by £70.
(iii) Cash received from a debtor £150 is entered in the cash book only.
(iv) The sales account was undercast by £350.
(v) The insurance account was overcast by £80.

Required:
(*a*) Show the journal entries to correct the errors.
(*b*) Write up the suspense account showing correction of the errors.
(*c*) The net profit figure originally calculated for the year ended 31 December 2008 was £12,250. Calculate the corrected net profit figure.

NEAB (AQA) (GCSE)

This part is concerned with the accounting procedures that have to be followed with different forms of organisations. It also includes a chapter outlining the basic ratios that are used for analysis and interpretation of accounts.

Single entry and incomplete records

Learning objectives

After you have studied this chapter you should be able to:

- understand why it is sometimes not appropriate to use a double entry book-keeping system
- deduce the figure of profits where only the increase in capital and details of drawings are known
- draw up a trading and profit and loss account and balance sheet from records not kept in a double entry system
- deduce the figures of sales and purchases from incomplete records.

33.1 Why double entry is not used

It would be impractical to expect every small shopkeeper, market stall or other small business to record its finances using a full double entry system. First of all, a large number of the owners of such firms would not know how to write up double entry records, even if they wanted to. It is more likely that they would enter details of a transaction once only, using a single entry system. Also, many of them would fail to record every transaction, resulting in incomplete records.

It is, perhaps, only fair to remember that accounting is supposed to be an aid to management; it is not something to be done as an end in itself. Therefore, many small firms, especially retail shops, can have all the information they want by merely keeping a cash book and having some form of record, not necessarily in double entry form, of their debtors and creditors.

The profits, however, will still need to be calculated in some way. This could be for the purpose of calculating income tax payable. How can profits be calculated if the book-keeping records are inadequate or incomplete?

33.2 Profit as an increase in capital

Probably the way to start is to recall that, unless there has been an introduction of extra cash or resources into the firm, the only way that capital can be increased is by making profits. Therefore, profits can be found by comparing capital at the end of the last period with that at the end of this period.

Let us look at a firm where capital at the end of 2004 is £2,000. During 2005 there have been no drawings, and no extra capital has been brought in by the owner. At the end of 2005 the capital is £3,000. Then:

$$\begin{array}{ccc} & \text{This year's} & \text{Last year's} \\ & \text{capital} & \text{capital} \\ \text{Net profit} = & £3,000 \quad - & £2,000 \quad = £1,000 \end{array}$$

If on the other hand the drawings had been £700, the profits must have been £1,700, calculated thus:

$$\begin{array}{ccccc} \text{Last year's Capital} & + & \text{Profits} & - & \text{Drawings} = \text{This year's Capital} \\ £2,000 & + & ? & - & £700 \quad = \quad £3,000 \end{array}$$

We can see that £1,700 profits was the figure needed to complete the formula, filling in the missing figure by normal arithmetical deduction:

$$£2,000 + £1,700 - £700 = £3,000$$

Exhibit 33.1 shows the calculation of profit where insufficient information is available to draft a trading and profit and loss account, only information of assets and liabilities being known.

Exhibit 33.1

H Taylor has not kept proper book-keeping records, but he has kept notes in diary form of the transactions of his business. He is able to give you details of his assets and liabilities as at 31 December 2005 and at 31 December 2006 as follows:

At 31 December 2005	Assets:	Motor van	£1,000
		Fixtures	£700
		Stock	£850
		Debtors	£950
		Bank	£1,100
		Cash	£100
	Liabilities:	Creditors	£200
		Loan from J Ogden	£600
At 31 December 2006	Assets:	Motor van (after depreciation)	£800
		Fixtures (after depreciation)	£630
		Stock	£990
		Debtors	£1,240
		Bank	£1,700
		Cash	£200
	Liabilities:	Creditors	£300
		Loan from J Ogden	£400
	Drawings were £900		

First of all a **statement of affairs** is drawn up as at 31 December 2005. This is the name given to what would have been called a balance sheet if it had been drawn up from a set of records. The capital is the difference between the assets and liabilities.

H Taylor
Statement of Affairs as at 31 December 2005

	£	£
Fixed assets		
Motor van		1,000
Fixtures		700
		1,700
Current assets		
Stock	850	
Debtors	950	
Bank	1,100	
Cash	100	
	3,000	
Less Current liabilities		
Creditors	200	
Net current assets		2,800
		4,500
Less Long-term liability		
Loan from J Ogden		600
		3,900
Financed by		
Capital (difference)		3,900

A statement of affairs is now drafted up as at the end of 2006. The formula of opening capital + profit − drawings = closing capital is then used to deduce the figure of profit.

H Taylor
Statement of Affairs as at 31 December 2006

	£	£
Fixed assets		
Motor van		800
Fixtures		630
		1,430
Current assets		
Stock	990	
Debtors	1,240	
Bank	1,700	
Cash	200	
	4,130	
Less Current liabilities		
Creditors	300	
Net current assets		3,830
		5,260
Less Long-term liability		
Loan from J Ogden		400
		4,860
Financed by		
Capital balance at 1.1.2006		3,900
Add Net profit	(C)	?
	(B)	?
		900
Less Drawings	(A)	?

Deduction of net profit   Opening capital + net profit − drawings = closing capital. Find the missing figures (A), (B) and (C) by deduction:

(A) is the figure needed to make the balance sheet totals equal, i.e. £4,860;
(B) is therefore £4,860 + £900 = £5,760;
(C) is therefore £5,760 − £3,900 = £1,860.

To check:

Capital		3,900
Add Net profit	(C)	1,860
	(B)	5,760
Less Drawings		900
	(A)	4,860

Obviously, this method of calculating profit is very unsatisfactory as it is much more informative when a trading and profit and loss account can be drawn up. Therefore, whenever possible, the 'comparison of capital' method of ascertaining profit should be avoided and financial statements drawn up from the available records.

It is important to realise that a business would have exactly the same trading and profit and loss account and balance sheet whether the managers kept their books by single entry or double entry. As shown previously, the double entry system uses the trial balance in preparing the final accounts, whereas the single entry system will have to arrive at the same answer by different means.

33.3   Drawing up the final accounts

The following example shows the various steps for drawing up the financial statements from a single entry set of records.

The accountant for J Frank's shop has been given the following information for the year ended 31 December 2005:

(*a*) The sales are mostly on a credit basis. No record of sales has been made, but £10,000 has been received, £9,500 by cheque and £500 by cash, from persons to whom goods have been sold.
(*b*) Amount paid by cheque to suppliers during the year = £7,200.
(*c*) Expenses paid during the year: by cheque, rent £200, general expenses £180; by cash, rent £50.
(*d*) J Frank took £10 cash per week (for 52 weeks) as drawings.
(*e*) Other information is available:

	At 31.12.2004	At 31.12.2005
	£	£
Debtors	1,100	1,320
Creditors for goods	400	650
Rent owing	–	50
Bank balance	1,130	3,050
Cash balance	80	10
Stock	1,590	1,700

(f) The only fixed asset consists of fixtures that were valued at 31 December 2004 at £800. These are to be depreciated at 10 per cent per annum.

Step-by-step guide

Step 1

First, draw up a statement of affairs on the closing day of the last accounting period. This is shown thus:

All of these opening figures are then taken into account when drawing up the final accounts for 2005.

J Frank
Statement of Affairs as at 31 December 2004

	£	£
Fixed Assets		
Fixtures		800
Current Assets		
Stock	1,590	
Debtors	1,100	
Bank	1,130	
Cash	80	
	3,900	
Less Current Liabilities		
Creditors	400	
Net current assets		3,500
		4,300
Financed by		
Capital (difference)		4,300
		4,300

Step 2

Next, a cash and bank summary, showing the totals of each separate item plus opening and closing balances, is drawn up. Thus:

Dr	Cash	Bank		Cash	Bank Cr
	£	£		£	£
Balances 31.12.2004	80	1,130	Suppliers		7,200
Receipts from debtors	500	9,500	Rent	50	200
			General Expenses		180
			Drawings	520	
			Balances 31.12.2005	10	3,050
	580	10,630		580	10,630

Step 3

Calculate the figures for purchases and sales to be shown in the trading account. Remember that the figures needed are the same as those which would have been found if double entry records had been kept.

Purchases

In double entry, purchases means the goods that have been bought in the period, irrespective of whether or not they have been paid for during the period. The figure of payments to suppliers must therefore be adjusted to find the figure for purchases. In our example we have:

	£
Paid during the year	7,200
Less Payments made, but which were for goods which were purchased in a previous year (creditors 31.12.2004)	400
	6,800
Add Purchases made in this year, but for which payment has not yet been made (creditors 31.12.2005)	650
Goods bought in this year, i.e. purchases	7,450

The same answer could have been obtained if the information had been shown in the form of a total creditors account, the figure for purchases being the amount required to make the account totals agree:

Total Creditors' Account

Dr				Cr
	£			£
Cash paid to suppliers	7,200	Balances b/f		400
Balances c/d	650	Purchases (missing figure)		7,450
	7,850			7,850

Sales

The sales figure will only equal receipts where all the sales are for cash. Therefore, the receipts figures need adjusting to find sales. This can only be done by constructing a total debtors' account, the sales figure being the one needed to make the totals agree.

Total Debtors' Account

Dr				Cr
	£			£
Balances b/f	1,100	Receipts: Cash		500
		Cheque		9,500
Sales (missing figure)	10,220	Balances c/d		1,320
	11,320			11,320

The above accounts are exactly the same as the creditors and debtors control accounts, described in Chapter 23.

Step 4

Expenses

Where there are no accruals or prepayments either at the beginning or end of the accounting period, then expenses paid will equal the expenses used up during the period. These figures will be charged to the trading and profit and loss account.

In contrast, where such prepayments or accruals exist, then an expense account should be drawn up for that particular item. When all known items have been entered, the missing figure will be the expenses to be charged for the accounting period.

In our example, only the rent account needs to be drawn up:

Rent Account

Dr			Cr
	£		£
Cheques	200	Rent (missing figure)	300
Cash	50		
Accrued c/d	50		
	300		300

Alternatively, the rent for the year can be found using the following calculation:

Accrual – Rent

		£
Paid:	Bank	200
	Cash	50
		250
Add: Owing 31.12.05		50
Rent for the year		**300**

Step 5

Check to see if any depreciation needs to be charged to the profit and loss account. In our example, Section 33.3 (*f*), it states that the fixtures are valued at £800 and should be depreciated at 10 per cent per annum. Therefore, depreciation charge for the year is 10 per cent of £800 = £80; this amount should be charged to the profit and loss account. In the balance sheet remember to deduct the depreciation from the fixtures, i.e. £800 − £80 = £720 to give you the net book value of the asset.

Now prepare the financial statements using all the information given in the details and the figures you have calculated.

J Frank
Trading and Profit and Loss Account for the year ended 31 December 2005

	£	£
Sales (Step 3)		10,220
Less Cost of goods sold		
Stock at 1.1.2005	1,590	
Add Purchases (Step 3)	7,450	
	9,040	
Less Stock at 31.12.2005	1,700	7,340
Gross profit		2,880
Less Expenses		
Rent (Step 4)	300	
General expenses	180	
Depreciation: Fixtures	80	560
Net profit		2,320

Balance Sheet as at 31 December 2005

	£	£	£
Fixed Assets			
Fixtures at 1.1.2005		800	
Less Depreciation (Step 5)		80	720
Current Assets			
Stock		1,700	
Debtors		1,320	
Bank (Step 2)		3,050	
Cash (Step 2)		10	
		6,080	
Less Current Liabilities			
Creditors	650		
Rent owing	50	700	
Net current assets			5,380
			6,100
Financed by			
Capital (Step 1)			
Balance 1.1.2005 (per opening statement of affairs)			4,300
Add Net profit			2,320
			6,620
Less Drawings			520
			6,100

Note: A step-by-step guide to incomplete records is given in Section 33.7 at the end of this chapter.

33.4 Incomplete records and missing figures

In practice, part of the information relating to cash receipts or payments is often missing. If the missing information is in respect of one type of payment, then it is normal to assume that the missing figure is the amount required to make both totals agree in the cash column of the cash and bank summary. This does not happen with bank items since another copy of the bank statement can always be obtained from the bank.

Exhibit 33.2 shows an example when the drawings figure is unknown; Exhibit 33.3 is an example where the receipts from debtors had not been recorded.

Exhibit 33.2

The following information on cash and bank receipts and payments is available:

	Cash	Bank
	£	£
Cash paid into the bank during the year	5,500	
Receipts from debtors	7,250	800
Paid to suppliers	320	4,930
Drawings during the year	?	–
Expenses paid	150	900
Balances at 1.1.2005	35	1,200
Balances at 31.12.2005	50	1,670

	Cash	Bank			Cash	Bank
Dr						Cr
	£	£			£	£
Balances 1.1.2005	35	1,200	Bankings	C	5,500	
Received from debtors	7,250	800	Suppliers		320	4,930
Bankings	C		5,500	Expenses		150	900
			Drawings			?
			Balances 31.12.2005		50	1,670
	7,285	7,500			7,285	7,500

The amount needed to make the two sides of the cash columns agree is £1,265. Therefore, this is taken as the figure of drawings.

Exhibit 33.3

Information of cash and bank transactions is available as follows:

	Cash	Bank
	£	£
Receipts from debtors	?	6,080
Cash withdrawn from the bank for business use (this is the amount which is used besides cash receipts from debtors to pay drawings and expenses)		920
Paid to suppliers		5,800
Expenses paid	640	230
Drawings	1,180	315
Balances at 1.1.2006	40	1,560
Balances at 31.12.2006	70	375

	Cash	Bank		Cash	Bank
Dr					Cr
	£	£		£	£
Balances 1.1.2006	40	1,560	Suppliers		5,800
Received from debtors	?	6,080	Expenses	640	230
Withdrawn from Bank C	920		Withdrawn from Bank C		920
			Drawings	1,180	315
			Balances 31.12.2006	70	375
	1,890	7,640		1,890	7,640

Receipts from debtors is, therefore, the amount needed to make each side of the cash column agree, namely £930.

It must be emphasised that balancing figures are acceptable only when all the other figures have been verified. Should, for instance, a cash expense be omitted when cash received from debtors is being calculated, then this would result in an understatement not only of expenses but also ultimately of sales.

33.5 Where there are two missing pieces of information

If both cash drawings and cash receipts from debtors were not known, it would not be possible to deduce both of these figures. The only course available would be to estimate whichever figure was more capable of being accurately assessed, use this as a known figure, and deduce the other figure. However, this is a most unsatisfactory position as both of the figures are no more than pure estimates, the accuracy of one relying entirely upon the accuracy of the other.

33.6 Cash sales and purchases for cash

Where there are cash sales as well as sales on credit terms, then the cash sales must be added to sales on credit to give the total sales for the year. This total figure of sales will be the one shown in the trading account.

Similarly, purchases for cash will need adding to credit purchases to give the figure of total purchases for the trading account.

33.7 Step-by-step guide to incomplete records

Note: You may find it useful to use this guide when studying the example in Section 33.3 the accounts of J Frank.

Step 1

Prepare a statement of affairs on the closing day of the *last* accounting period to ascertain the initial *opening capital*. Remember to include the cash and bank balances. (In our example the opening capital is £4,300.)

Step 2

Either draw up and balance a cash and bank summary or, if a cash and bank summary is shown, it may only be necessary to balance off the account. Remember to include the *final cash and bank balances in the final balance sheet*. (In our example the balances at 31 December 2005 are cash £10 and bank £3,050.)

Step 3

Calculate the figures for purchases and sales to be shown in the trading account. Remember that there are *two ways* that this may be achieved: either as a calculation or by using double entry 'T' accounts. (In our example the purchases are £7,450 and the sales £10,220.)

Step 4

Calculate the figures for expenses. If there are no accruals or prepayments either at the beginning or end of the accounting period, the expenses paid will equal the expenses used up during the period. If, however, there *are* accruals and prepayments, then it will be necessary to make adjustments; again, this may be carried out as a calculation or by using 'T' accounts. (In our example there is an 'accrual for rent' therefore it is necessary to calculate the rent for the year using either of the aforementioned methods, the figure for the year is £300.) Remember that 'accounting for prepaid expenses' has been shown in Chapter 28, Section 28.4.

Step 5 Depreciation

Check to see if you need to take account of any depreciation before preparing the financial statements. The amount of depreciation may be given or, alternatively, you may have to compare the value of each asset at the beginning of the period with that at the end of the period – the difference being *depreciation*. (In our example under section (*f*) we are told the value of the fixed asset of 'fixtures' is £800 and they are to be depreciated at 10 per cent per annum. Thus 10 per cent of £800 = £80 depreciation which has been charged to the profit and loss account and shown as a deduction from the fixtures in the balance sheet.)

Remember to check to see if there are any additions to assets and, if so, ensure that you include them on the balance sheet and depreciate them as indicated above.

Finally, prepare the financial statements:

- trading and profit and loss account, and
- balance sheet.

Chapter summary

- In many small businesses it may not be practical to use a full double entry accounting system; instead single entry is used.
- Where there are no proper accounts kept possibly the only way to ascertain the amount of profit is to compare the capital account at the beginning and end of an accounting period. Provided no additional funds have been invested in the business or drawings taken out then the difference must be either profit or loss.
- A statement of affairs is often prepared to ascertain the capital of the proprietor. This statement shows the value of the assets and liabilities at a specific date and by using the accounting equation the capital can be found.
- Using the step-by-step method the financial statements can be prepared from records not kept by the double entry system of book-keeping (refer to Section 33.7).
- Where there are missing figures it is possible to deduce the figure by careful analysis of data available and process of elimination.

Exercises

33.1 The following figures have been extracted from the records of K Rogers, who does not keep a full record of his transactions on the double entry system:

			£
1 November	2005	Debtors	2,760
1 November	2005	Creditors	1,080
1 November	2005	Stock	2,010
31 October	2006	Debtors	3,090
31 October	2006	Creditors	1,320
31 October	2006	Stock	2,160

All goods were sold on credit and all purchases were made on credit. During the year ended 31 October 2006, cash received from debtors amounted to £14,610, whereas cash paid to creditors amounted to £9,390.

Required:

(*a*) Calculate the amount of sales and purchases for the year ended 31 October 2006.

(*b*) Draw up the trading account for the year ended 31 October 2006.

33.2X The following figures for a business are available:

			£
1 June	2007	Stock	11,590
1 June	2007	Creditors	3,410
1 June	2007	Debtors	5,670
31 May	2008	Stock	13,425
31 May	2008	Creditors	4,126
31 May	2008	Debtors	6,108
Year to 31 May 2008:			
Received from debtors			45,112
Paid to creditors			29,375

All goods were bought or sold on credit.

Required:

Draw up the trading account for the year 31 May 2008, deducing any figures that might be needed.

33.3 On 1 July 2005, D Lewinski commenced business with £6,000 in his bank account. After trading for a full year, he ascertained that his position on 30 June 2006 was as follows:

	£		£
Plant	3,600	Fixtures	360
Creditors	720	Bank balance	600
Debtors	930	Stock-in-trade	1,350
Cash in hand	135	Drawings	1,600

You are required to:

(*a*) calculate D Lewinski's capital at 30 June 2006

(*b*) prepare D Lewinski's balance sheet at 30 June 2006 (assuming a profit of £1,855), set out in such a manner as to show clearly the totals normally shown in a balance sheet.

33.4 J Marcano is a dealer who has not kept proper books of account. At 31 August 2006 her state of affairs was as follows.

	£
Cash	115
Bank balance	2,209
Fixtures	3,500
Stock	16,740
Debtors	11,890
Creditors	9,952
Motor van (at valuation)	3,500

During the year to 31 August 2007, her drawings amounted to £7,560. Winnings from the national lottery of £12,800 were put into the business. Extra fixtures were bought for £2,000. At 31 August 2007 Marcano's assets and liabilities were: cash £84; bank overdraft, £165; stock, £24,891; creditors for goods £6,002; creditors for expenses £236; fixtures to be depreciated by £300; motor van to be valued at £2,800; debtors, £15,821; prepaid expenses, £72.

You are required to draw up a statement showing the profit or loss made by Marcano for the year ended 31 August 2007.

33.5X A Hanson is a sole trader who, although keeping very good records, does not operate a full double entry system. The following figures have been taken from his records:

	31 March 2008	31 March 2009
	£	£
Cash at bank	1,460	1,740
Office furniture	600	500
Stock	2,320	2,620
Cash in hand	60	80

Debtors on 31 March 2008 amounted to £2,980 and sales for the year ended 31 March 2009 to £11,520. During the year ended 31 March 2009, cash received from debtors amounted to £10,820.

Creditors on 31 March 2008 amounted to £1,880 and purchases for the year ended 31 March 2009 to £8,120. During the year ended 31 March 2009, cash paid to creditors amounted to £7,780.

During the year to 31 March 2009 no bad debts were incurred. Also during the same period, there was neither discounts allowed nor discounts received.

Required (with all calculations shown):
(a) Calculate debtors and creditors as at 31 March 2009.
(b) Calculate Hanson's capital as at 31 March 2008 and 31 March 2009.
(c) Calculate his net profit for the year ended 31 March 2009, allowing for the fact that during the year Hanson's drawings amounted to £2,540.

33.6 Leigh Osawa had not kept full accounting records. On 31 March 2005 he attempted to prepare his final accounts for his business but was unable to calculate the figure for total sales, rent and business rates for the year ended on that date.

The following information is available:

	Balance 1 April 2004	Balance 31 March 2005
	£	£
Trade debtors	23,460	28,270
Rent due	1,040	730
Business rates prepaid	390	440

The bank statements for the year ended 31 March 2005 reveal:

	£
Receipts from trade debtors	226,820
Payment for	
Rent	12,290
Business rates	4,680

It should be noted that trade debtors were allowed discounts of £280 during the year under review.

Set out detailed calculations of the amounts to be included in the final accounts for the year ended 31 March 2005 for:

(*a*) sales
(*b*) rent
(*c*) business rates.

Southern Examining Group AQA

Please note that this question is NOT from the live examinations for the current specification.

33.7X An accountant has prepared quarterly accounts for Linda Goodheart, who runs a small newsagent's shop. After he had prepared the accounts for the third quarter of the year to 31 July 2008, the trial balance was as follows:

	£	£
Fixtures and fittings, at cost	7,800	
Provision for depreciation of fixtures and fittings		1,600
Balance at bank	1,572	
Prepayment for shop expenses	250	
Trade creditors		11,980
Sundry debtors	11,156	
Capital account		20,632
Stock	13,434	
	34,212	34,212

Due to illness of her accountant, she has asked you to prepare the accounts for the final quarter of her financial year. Looking through the bank statements you have elicited this information:

	Quarter to *31/10/08*
Paid into bank:	
Cash sales	16,216
Receipts from debtors	22,860
Bank interest	47
Cheque from creditor, who had been overpaid	381
Amounts withdrawn –	
Purchases	34,886
Shop expenses	5,401
For personal use	3,000
Wages	440

You have also discovered that:

(i) all receipts and payments for the business go through the bank account
(ii) the business is owed £11,340 by customers at 31 October 2008
(iii) shop expenses are paid for at the time of purchase

(iv) sales produce a gross profit of 35 per cent
(v) fixtures and fittings are depreciated at the rate of 10 per cent p.a. on cost
(vi) the stock at 31 October 2008 is valued at £16,111.

You are required (showing all workings) to:
(*a*) produce a summary bank account for the quarter to 31 October 2008
(*b*) prepare the business profit and loss account for the period from 1 August to 31 October 2008
(*c*) prepare the balance sheet as at 31 October 2008.

OCR (Accounting Stage II)

33.8X Ruth Eridge has not kept proper accounting records for her business which opened on 1 April 2004. On that date she opened a business bank account with £30,000 of her private funds.
A summary of her bank account for the year ended 31 March 2005 is shown below:

	£		£
Capital introduced	30,000	Drawings	14,500
Cash sales	64,200	Purchase of fixed assets	25,000
		Payments to suppliers of stock	27,800
		Business expenses	18,100
		Balance at bank 31 March 2005	8,800
	94,200		94,200

On 31 March 2005:

● unsold stock was valued at £7,700
● there were business expenses of £200 prepaid
● fixed assets were to be depreciated by £4,000
● the amount owing to trade creditors was £3,200.

Tasks:
(*a*) Prepare the business's trading and profit and loss account for the year ended 31 March 2005.
(*b*) Ruth Eridge would like to expand her business but will need £25,000 to finance the expansion. Advise Ruth of *two* ways in which she could finance the expansion of the business. In each case explain the financial implications of your suggestion.

Southern Examining Group AQA

Please note that this question is NOT from the live examinations for the current specification.

Club accounts

34.1 Non-profit-making organisations

The organisations we have covered so far have all been profit-making businesses. However, there are other organisations whose objective is not to make a profit but instead provide facilities for their members to pursue a hobby, sporting activity or provide voluntary services. These clubs and associations do not have to prepare a trading and profit and loss account since they are not formed to carry on trading and make profits. Instead the financial statements prepared by them are either 'receipts and payments accounts' or 'income and expenditure accounts'.

34.2 Receipts and payments account

Receipts and payments accounts are usually prepared by the treasurer of the club or association. This account is a summary of the cash book for the period and if the organisation has no assets (other than cash) and no liabilities, a summary of the cash book tells the members all they need to know about the financial activities during a period. Exhibit 34.1 is an example of a receipts and payments account.

Exhibit 34.1

The Homers Running Club
Receipts and Payments Account for the year ended 31 December 2005

Receipts	£	Payments	£
Bank balance 1.1.2005	236	Groundsman's wages	728
Subscriptions received for 2005	1,148	Sports ground expenses	296
Rent received	116	Committee expenses	58
		Printing and stationery	33
		Bank balance 31.12.2005	385
	1,500		1,500

34.3   Income and expenditure accounts

When assets are owned, and/or there are liabilities, the receipts and payments account is not a good way of drawing up financial statements. Other than the cash received and paid out, it shows only the cash balances; the other assets and liabilities are not shown at all.

What is required is:

● a balance sheet, and
● an account showing whether the association's capital has increased.

The second of these two requirements is provided via an income and expenditure account. Such an account follows the same rules as trading and profit and loss accounts, the only differences being the terms used.

A comparison of terms used now follows:

Profit-making organisation	Non-profit organisation
1 Trading and profit and loss account	1 Income and expenditure account
2 Net profit	2 Surplus of income over expenditure
3 Net loss	3 Excess of expenditure over income

34.4   Profit or loss for a special purpose

Sometimes there are reasons why a non-profit-making organisation would want a profit and loss account. This is where something is done to make a profit. The profit is not to be kept, but used to pay for the main purpose of the organisation.

For instance, a football club may have discos or dances that people pay to attend. Any profit from these events helps to pay football expenses. For these discos and dances a trading and profit and loss account would be drawn up. Any profit (or loss) would be transferred to the income and expenditure account.

34.5 Accumulated fund

A sole trader or a partnership would have capital accounts. A non-profit-making organisation would instead have an **accumulated fund**. It is in effect the same as a capital account, for it is the difference between assets and liabilities.

For a sole trader or partnership:

> Capital = Assets – Liabilities

In a non-profit-making organisation:

> Accumulated Fund = Assets – Liabilities

34.6 Drawing up income and expenditure accounts

We can now look at the preparation of an income and expenditure account and a balance sheet of a club. A separate trading account is to be prepared for a bar, where food and alcohol are sold to make a profit.

Long Lane Football Club Trial Balance as at 31 December 2008		
	Dr £	Cr £
Sports equipment	8,500	
Club premises	29,600	
Subscriptions received		6,490
Wages of staff	4,750	
Furniture and fittings	5,260	
Rates and insurance	1,910	
General expenses	605	
Accumulated fund 1 January 2008		42,016
Donations received		360
Telephone and postage	448	
Bank	2,040	
Bar purchases	9,572	
Creditors for bar supplies		1,040
Bar sales		14,825
Bar stocks 1 January 2008	2,046	
	64,731	64,731

The following information is also available:

(i) Bar stocks at 31 December 2008 amount in value to £2,362.
(ii) There is a need to provide for depreciation: sports equipment £1,700; furniture and fittings £1,315.

The club's trading account will look thus:

Long Lane Football Club Bar
Trading Account for the year ended 31 December 2008

	£	£
Sales		14,825
Less Cost of goods sold		
Opening stock	2,046	
Purchases	9,572	
	11,618	
Closing stock	2,362	
		9,256
Gross profit		5,569

The result of the club bar operation is calculated separately. The gross profit/loss will then be incorporated into the club's income and expenditure account for calculation of the overall result, as shown below:

Income and Expenditure Account
for the year ended 31 December 2008

	£	£
Income		
Gross profit from bar		5,569
Subscriptions		6,490
Donations received		360
		12,419
Less Expenditure		
Wages to staff	4,750	
Rates and insurance	1,910	
Telephone and postage	448	
General expenses	605	
Depreciation: Furniture	1,315	
Sports equipment	1,700	
		10,728
Surplus of income over expenditure		1,691

Balance Sheet at 31 December 2008

	£	£	£
	Cost	Depreciation	Net book value
Fixed assets			
Club premises	29,600	–	29,600
Furniture and fittings	5,260	1,315	3,945
Sports equipment	8,500	1,700	6,800
	43,360	3,015	40,345
Current assets			
Bar stocks		2,362	
Cash at bank		2,040	
		4,402	

	£	£	£
Current liabilities			
Creditors for bar supplies		1,040	
Net current assets			3,362
Net assets			43,707
Accumulated fund			
Balance at 1 January 2008			42,016
Add Surplus of income over expenditure			1,691
			43,707

34.7 Subscriptions

No subscriptions owing

Where there are no **subscriptions** owing, or paid in advance, at the beginning and the end of a financial year, then the amount shown on the credit side of the subscriptions account can be transferred to the credit side of the income and expenditure account, as follows:

Dr		Subscriptions		Cr
2005	£	2005		£
Dec 31 Income & expenditure a/c	3,598	Dec 31 Bank (total received)		3,598

Income and Expenditure Account
for the year ended 31 December 2003 (extract)

Income:		£
Subscriptions		3,598

Subscriptions owing

On the other hand, there may be subscriptions owing at both the start and the end of the financial year. In a case where £325 was owing at the start of the year, a total of £5,668 was received during the year, and £554 was owing at the end of the year, then this would appear as follows:

Dr		Subscriptions		Cr
2005	£	2005		£
Jan 1 Owing b/d	325	Dec 31 Bank (total received)		5,668
Dec 31 Income & expenditure a/c		Dec 31 Balance c/d		554
(difference)	5,897			
	6,222			6,222

Income and Expenditure Account
for the year ended 31 December 2005 (extract)

Income:		£
Subscriptions		5,897

In the balance sheet, the subscription owing at the end of December 2005 would be shown under the heading of 'Current assets' as a debtor, as shown below:

Balance Sheet as at 31 December 2005 (extract)

	£
Current assets	
Stock	x,xxx
Debtors (xxx + 554)	xxx

Subscriptions owing and paid in advance

In the third case, at the start of the year there are both subscriptions owing from the previous year and also subscriptions paid in advance. In addition, there are also subscriptions paid in the current year for the next year (in advance) and subscriptions unpaid (owing) at the end of the current year. The example below concerns an amateur theatre organisation.

An amateur theatre organisation charges its members an annual subscription of £20 per member. It accrues for subscriptions owing at the end of each year and also adjusts for subscriptions received in advance. The following applies:

(A) On 1 January 2002, 18 members owed £360 for the year 2001.
(B) In December 2001, 4 members paid £80 for the year 2002.
(C) During the year 2002, the organisation received cash subscriptions of £7,420.

For 2001	£360
For 2002	£6,920
For 2003	£140
	£7,420

(D) At the close of 31 December 2002, 11 members had not paid their 2002 subscriptions.

These facts are translated into the accounts as set out below:

Subscriptions

Dr				Cr		
2002			£	2002		£
Jan 1 Owing b/d	(A)		360	Jan 1 Prepaid b/d	(B)	80
Dec 31 Income and expenditure a/c	*7,220			Dec 31 Bank	(C)	7,420
Dec 31 Prepaid c/d	(C)		140	Dec 31 Owing c/d	(D)	220
			7,720			7,720
2003				2003		
Jan 1 Owing b/d	(D)		220	Jan 1 Prepaid b/d	(C)	140

*The difference between the two sides of the account.

Income and Expenditure Account
for the year ended 31 December 2002 (extract)

	£
Income:	
Subscriptions	7,220

In this last case in the balance sheet as at 31 December 2002, the amounts owing for subscriptions (D), £220, will be shown under current assets as a debtor. The subscriptions (C) paid in advance for 2003 will appear as an item under current liabilities as subscriptions received in advance, £140, as shown below:

Balance Sheet as at 31 December 2002 (extract)

Current Assets	
Stock	xxx
Debtors (xxx + 220)	xx
Current Liabilities	
Subscriptions in advance	140

Note: Treasurers of clubs and societies are very much aware that if subscriptions are outstanding for a long time it is unlikely that they will ever be paid, the member may have lost interest or moved on to another organisation. Consequently, many clubs and indeed charities do not include unpaid subscriptions as an asset in the balance sheet.

34.8 Donations

Any **donations** received are shown as income in the year that they are received.

34.9 Entrance fees

New members often have to pay an entrance fee in the year that they join, in addition to the membership fee for that year. Entrance fees are normally included as income in the year that they are received.

34.10 Life membership

In some clubs and societies members can pay one amount for **life membership**, and they will never have to pay any more money. This membership will last for their lifetime. In this case, all of the money received from life membership should not be credited to the income and expenditure account of the year in which it is received.

In a club where members joined at age 20 and would probably be members for 40 years, then one-fortieth (2½ per cent) of the life membership fee should be credited in the income and expenditure account each year. The balance not transferred to the income and expenditure account would appear in the balance sheet as a long-term liability. This is because it is the liability of the club to allow the members to use the club for the rest of their lives without paying any more for membership.

On the other hand, a club especially for people over the age of 60 would transfer a much bigger share of the life membership fee paid to the income and expenditure account. This is because the number of years of future use of the club will be far less because people are already old when they join. It may be, in those circumstances, that 10 per cent of the life membership fee per year would be transferred to the credit of the income and expenditure account.

34.11 Treasurers' responsibilities

Treasurers of clubs or societies have a responsibility for maintaining proper accounting records in the same way as an accountant has when looking after the financial affairs of a business. It is important to ensure that any monies paid out by the treasurer have been properly authorised, especially when purchasing an item of capital expenditure (such as new sound equipment for a dramatic society). In such cases, the authorisation for purchase will more than likely have been approved at a committee meeting and noted in the minutes of the meeting. For smaller items of expenditure such as postages, telephone calls etc., the club or society's rules will provide the treasurer with the authority to make payments against receipted bills.

It is also important for the treasurer to keep all invoices, receipted accounts and any other documents as evidence against payments. Treasurers should also provide receipts for any monies received. All documents should be filed and available at the year end for the club's auditor to carry out an audit and for preparation of the club's year-end financial statements.

Chapter summary

- The main objective of non-profit-making organisations is to provide members with facilities to pursue a leisure activity and not to trade and make profits.
- The financial statements prepared for non-profit-making organisations may either be a 'receipts and payments account' or 'income and expenditure account'.
- A 'receipts and payments account' is very much like a cash book summary.
- An 'income and expenditure account' is very similar to a trading and profit and loss account except that the terminology used is different. A profit in the trading and profit and loss account is expressed as 'surplus of income over expenditure' in the 'income and expenditure account'. A loss would be referred to as 'excess of expenditure over income'.
- The 'accumulated fund' is basically the same as a capital account.
- Although clubs and societies are non-profit making sometimes activities are held to generate profits for the benefit of the organisation and its members.
- The treatment of members' subscriptions may involve subscriptions owing and/or paid in advance.
- Donations should be treated as income in the year in which they are received.
- Entrance fees are usually treated as income in the year in which the member joins the organisation.
- Life membership subscriptions should be spread over the anticipated length of membership which is usually decided by the club's committee or may be set out in the rules and regulations.
- Club treasurers carry an important role and, as such, are responsible for maintaining the organisation's accounting records and looking after their financial affairs.

Exercises

34.1 You are given the following details of the Horton Hockey Club for its year to 30 June 2006:

Payments:	£
Teams' travel expenses	1,598
Groundsman's wages	3,891
Postage and stationery	392
Rent of pitches and clubhouse	4,800
General expenses	419
Cost of prizes for raffles	624
Receipts:	
Subscriptions	8,570
Donations	1,500
Receipts from raffles	3,816

Cash and bank balances:	£
1 July 2005	2,715
30 June 2006	4,877

You also find out that members owe £160 subscriptions on 30 June 2006. On that date, the club owed £400 for rent and £75 for wages.

You are required to draw up:

(a) a receipts and payments account for the year ended 30 June 2006

(b) an income and expenditure account for the year ended 30 June 2006.

34.2X These are the financial details of the Superball Football Club for the year to 31 May 2006:

Payments:	£
Hire of transport	3,710
Ground maintenance costs	1,156
Groundsman's wages	5,214
Committee expenses	906
Costs of disco	1,112
Rent of ground	2,450
General expenses	814
Receipts:	
Members' subscriptions	8,124
Prize money for winning cup	1,000
Receipts from disco	3,149
Collections at matches	5,090

Cash and bank balances:	£
1 June 2005	905
31 May 2006	2,906

Members' subscriptions owing on 31 May 2005 amount to £160 and on 31 May 2006 to £94. On 31 May 2006 the rent had been prepaid £200, and owing were transport hire £90 and committee expenses £170.

You are required to draw up:

(a) a receipts and payments account for the year ended 31 May 2006

(b) an income and expenditure account for the year ended 31 May 2006.

34.3 The following receipts and payments account for the year ending 31 May 2008 was prepared by the treasurer of the Down Town Sports and Social Club.

Receipts	£	Payments	£
Balance at bank 1 June 2007	286	Purchases of new equipment	166
Subscriptions	135	Bar stocks purchased	397
Net proceeds of jumble sale	91	Hire of rooms	64
Net proceeds of dance	122	Wages of part-time staff	198
Sale of equipment	80	Balance at bank 31 May 2008	352
Bar takings	463		
	1,177		1,177

Notes:
(i) On 1 June 2007, the club's equipment was valued at £340. Included in this total, valued at £92, was the equipment sold during the year for £80.
(ii) Bar stocks were valued as follows: 31 May 2007, £88; 31 May 2008, £101. There were no creditors for bar supplies on either of these dates.
(iii) Allow £30 for depreciation of equipment during the year ending 31 May 2008. This is additional to the loss on equipment sold during the year.
(iv) No subscriptions were outstanding at 31 May 2007, but on 31 May 2008 subscriptions due but unpaid amounted to £14.

Required (with calculations shown):
(a) Calculate the accumulated fund of the club as at 1 June 2007.
(b) Draw up the income and expenditure account of the club for the year ending 31 May 2008.

34.4X The following trial balance was extracted from the books of the Upper Harbour Sports Club at the close of business on 31 March 2006:

	Dr £	Cr £
Club premises	13,500	
Sports equipment	5,100	
Bar purchases and sales	9,540	15,270
Bar stocks 1 April 2005	2,190	
Balance at bank	2,790	
Subscriptions received		8,640
Accumulated fund 1 April 2005		22,290
Salary of secretary	3,600	
Wages of staff	5,280	
Postage and telephone	870	
Office furniture	1,200	
Rates and insurance	1,230	
Cash in hand	60	
Sundry expenses	840	
	46,200	46,200

Notes:
(i) All bar purchases and sales are on a cash basis. Bar stocks at 31 March 2006 were £2,460.
(ii) No subscriptions have been paid in advance but subscriptions in arrears at 31 March 2006 amounted to £90.
(iii) Rates pre-paid at 31 March 2006: £60.
(iv) Provision for depreciation as follows: sports equipment £600; office furniture £120.

Required:

Prepare the bar trading account and the income and expenditure account of the club for the year ended 31 March 2006, together with a balance sheet as on that date. For this purpose, the wages of staff £5,280 should be shown in the income and expenditure account and not the bar trading account.

34.5 Amit Mall is the treasurer of the local tennis club. He needs to prepare some financial statements and has asked you to help.

The following information is available for the year ended 30 November 2005.

● The bank summary shows:

	£		£
Opening balance	850	Bar purchases	6,400
Subscriptions	33,000	Wages	25,500
Bar sales	8,700	General expenses	4,850
Bank loan	5,400	Purchase of land	12,000
Closing balance	800		
	48,750		48,750

● The year end balances are:

	30 November 2004	30 November 2005
	£	£
Stock of bar purchases	680	890
Creditors for bar purchases	1,000	540
Subscriptions in arrear	1,000	4,000
Accrual for general expenses	150	250

● 20 per cent of wages relate to the bar, 80 per cent to other activities
● 30 per cent of expenses relate to the bar, 70 per cent to other activities
● the loan was taken out on 1 January 2004 at a rate of interest of 8 per cent per annum
● the subscription is £100 per member per year.

Tasks:

1 Calculate the purchases made for the bar for the year ended 30 November 2005.
2 Calculate the net profit or loss made from the bar for the year ended 30 November 2005.
3 Calculate the total number of members who should have paid a subscription to the tennis club for the year ended 30 November 2005.
4 Calculate the surplus or deficit made by the tennis club for the year ended 30 November 2005.
5 List the assets and liabilities held by the tennis club on 30 November 2005.
6 The tennis club does not provide for depreciation of land. Briefly explain why.

Association of Accounting Technicians

34.6 The treasurer of a local amateur dramatic society is trying to ascertain the amount of subscriptions to transfer to the society's income and expenditure account for the year ended 31 December 2002 and asks for your help.

The following information is made available to you:

	2001	2002
	£	£
Subscriptions in arrears	235	185
Subscriptions in advance	220	140

In addition, you are told that the amount received from members during the year 2002 amounted to £2,600, all of which was banked immediately.

You are required to draw up the society's subscriptions account for the year ended 31 December 2002, showing clearly the amount of subscriptions to be transferred to the income and expenditure account.

34.7X Pat Hall is the treasurer of a local tennis club that has 420 members. The subscription details for the club are as follows:

Subscriptions for year to 31 December 2007 – £220 per member
Subscriptions for year to 31 December 2008 – £240 per member
Subscriptions for year to 31 December 2009 – £250 per member

On 31 December 2007, 6 members had prepaid their subscriptions for 2008. By 31 December 2008, 8 members will have prepaid their subscriptions for 2009. All other members have paid, and will continue to pay their subscriptions during the relevant year.

You are required (showing all your workings) to:
(a) calculate the subscriptions figure to be entered in the income and expenditure account for the year ended 31 December 2008
(b) calculate the total amount of money received for subscriptions during the year ended 31 December 2008.

Association of Accounting Technicians

34.8X Harry Green is the treasurer of his golf club.

● During the year ended 30 November 2005, the club received £110,000 in cash and cheques from members for annual subscriptions.
● The annual subscription is £50 per member.
● On 30 November 2004, four members were in arrears and two had paid in advance.
● On 30 November 2005, three members were in arrears and five had paid in advance.

Tasks:
(a) Prepare the subscription account, clearly showing the amount of subscriptions to be entered in the income and expenditure account for the year ended 30 November 2005.
(b) How many members does the golf club have?

Association of Accounting Technicians

34.9X The following items represented the assets and liabilities of the Torrevieja Club at 1 January 2006:

	£
Rent paid in advance	400
Cash at bank	800
Subscriptions in advance	1,200
Equipment	40,000
Lawn mower	600
Subscriptions in arrears	200
Insurance in arrears	100
Heating in advance	200

The Receipts and Payments Account for the year to 31 December 2006 reveals the following:

	£		£
Subscriptions	26,000	Purchase of lawn mower	1,100
Dinner and dance ticket sales	4,650	Soft drink purchases	3,600
Sale of existing lawn mower	700	Insurance	1,050
Soft drink sales	7,200	Rent	4,420
		Heating	1,450
		Dinner dance expenses	3,200

The following additional information is also available:

(i)   The club depreciates its lawn mowers by 15 per cent on those in existence at 31 December 2006.
(ii) Subscriptions in arrears at 31 December 2006 amounted to £750, whilst those in advance amounted to £590.
(iii) Unsold soft drinks at 31 December 2006 amounted to £1,400.
(iv) Dinner dance expenses in arrears at 31 December amounted to £160.
(v)   Insurance paid in advance at 31 December 2006 amounted to £180.

You are required to:

(a) calculate the club's accumulated fund at 1 January 2006
(b) prepare the club's income and expenditure account for the year ended 31 December 2006
(c) prepare the club's balance sheet as at 31 December 2006.

City & Guilds Pitman qualifications

CHAPTER 35

Manufacturing accounts

Learning objectives

After you have studied this chapter you should be able to:

- calculate prime cost and production costs of goods manufactured
- distinguish between stock of raw materials, work in progress and finished goods
- prepare a manufacturing account and appropriate trading and profit and loss accounts
- adjust the accounts in respect of work in progress.

35.1 Introduction to manufacturing accounts

So far the accounts dealt with have related to retailing businesses; we will now consider firms that are manufacturers. For these businesses a **manufacturing account** is prepared in addition to the trading and profit and loss account. Manufacturing accounts tend to be produced for internal use by the owners and managers and are rarely shown to other people outside the organisation.

The manufacturing account is prepared to show the production cost of making goods. As shown below these costs build up starting with the direct materials, direct labour and direct expenses to give us the prime cost. Indirect manufacturing costs are then added to give the production cost of manufacture. The *production cost* is then shown in the trading account (refer to Section 35.8).

35.2 Total cost of manufacturing

In a manufacturing firm the costs are divided into different types. These may be summarised in chart form as follows:

Total cost calculation

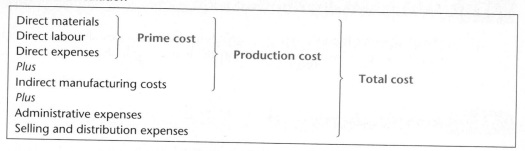

35.3   Direct and indirect costs

Referring to the chart in the previous section, you will see the word **direct** followed by a type of cost, and you will know that it has been possible to trace the costs of manufacturing an item. The total of all the **direct costs** is known as the **prime cost**. If a cost cannot easily be traced to the item being manufactured, then it is an indirect cost and will be included under the **indirect manufacturing costs** also known as factory overhead expenses. **Production cost** is the total of the prime cost plus the indirect manufacturing costs.

For example, the wages of a machine operator making a particular item will be direct labour. The wages of a foreman in charge of several people on different jobs will be indirect labour and will be part of the indirect manufacturing costs. Other examples of costs being direct costs would be:

● cost of raw materials including carriage inwards on those raw materials
● hire of special machinery for a job.

35.4   Indirect manufacturing costs

Indirect manufacturing costs are all those costs which occur in the factory or other places where production is being carried out but that cannot easily be traced to the items being manufactured. Examples are:

● wages of cleaning staff
● wages of crane drivers
● rent and business rates for the factory
● depreciation of plant and machinery
● costs of operating forklift trucks
● factory power and lighting.

35.5   Administration expenses

Administration expenses consist of such items as managers' salaries, legal and accountancy charges, the depreciation of office equipment, and secretarial salaries.

35.6 Selling and distribution expenses

Selling and distribution expenses are items such as sales staff salaries and commission, carriage outwards, depreciation of delivery vehicles, advertising, and display expenses.

35.7 Finance charges

Finance charges are those expenses incurred in providing finance facilities such as interest charged on a loan, bank charges and discounts allowed.

35.8 Format of financial statement

Manufacturing account section

This is debited with production cost of goods completed during the accounting period. It consists of:

● Direct material. This is found as follows:
  (i) opening stock of raw materials
  (ii) add the cost of purchases of raw materials plus carriage inwards charges
  (iii) less closing stock of raw materials
  (iv) this gives the cost of raw material consumed.
  To this figure add the following:
● Direct labour.
● Direct expenses.
  This now gives the figure of Prime cost.
  Now add:
● Indirect manufacturing costs such as indirect wages, factory rent, depreciation of plant and machinery etc.
● Add opening work in progress and deduct closing work in progress
  This now gives production cost of goods completed.

Thus, when completed, the manufacturing account shows the total production costs relating to the goods manufactured and available for sale during the accounting period. This figure is then transferred to the trading account section of the trading and profit and loss accounts.

Note: Many students are so used to deducting expenses such as wages, rent, depreciation etc., in profit and loss accounts that they can easily fall into the trap of *deducting* these instead of *adding* them in the manufacturing account. Remember we are building up the cost of manufacture so all costs are added.

Trading account section

This account includes:

- Production cost brought down from the manufacturing account.
- Opening and closing stocks of finished goods.
- Sales.

When completed, this account will disclose the gross profit. This figure will then be carried down to the profit and loss account section of the final accounts.

The Manufacturing Account and the Trading Account can be shown in the form of a diagram.

Manufacturing Account

	£
Production costs for the period:	
Direct materials	
Direct labour	xxx
Direct expenses	xxx
Indirect manufacturing costs	xxx
Production cost of goods completed c/d to trading account	xxx
	xxx

Trading Account

		£	£
Sales			xxx
Less Production cost of goods sold:			
Opening stock of finished goods	(A)	xxx	
Add Production costs of goods completed b/d		xxx	
		xxx	
Less Closing stock of finished goods	(B)	xxx	xxx
Gross profit			xxx

(A) is production costs of goods unsold in previous period.
(B) is production costs of goods unsold at end of the period.

Profit and loss account section

This section includes:

- Gross profit brought down from the trading account.
- All administration expenses.
- All selling and distribution expenses.
- All finance charges.

Since some of the charges usually found in the profit and loss account will have already been included in the manufacturing account only the remainder need charging to the profit and loss account.

When complete the profit and loss account will show the net profit.

35.9 A worked example of a manufacturing account

Exhibit 35.1 shows the necessary details for a manufacturing account. It has been assumed that there were no partly completed units (known as **work in progress**) either at the beginning or end of the period.

Exhibit 35.1
Details of production cost for the year ended 31 December 2007:

	£
1 January 2007, stock of raw materials	500
31 December 2007, stock of raw materials	700
Raw materials purchased	8,000
Manufacturing (direct) wages	21,000
Royalties	150
Indirect wages	9,000
Rent of factory – excluding administration and selling and distribution blocks	440
Depreciation of plant and machinery in factory	400
General indirect expenses	310

Manufacturing Account for the year ended 31 December 2007

	£	£
Stock of raw materials 1.1.2007		500
Add Purchases		8,000
		8,500
Less Stock of raw materials 31.12.2007		700
Cost of raw materials consumed		7,800
Manufacturing wages		21,000
Royalties		150
Prime cost		28,950
Indirect Manufacturing Costs		
Rent	440	
Indirect wages	9,000	
General expenses	310	
Depreciation of plant and machinery	400	10,150
Production cost of goods completed c/d		39,100

Sometimes, if a firm has produced less than its customers have demanded, the firm may well have bought an outside supply of finished goods. In this case, the trading account will have both a figure for purchases and for the production cost of goods completed.

35.10 Work in progress

The production cost to be carried down to the trading account is that of production cost of goods completed during the period. If items have not been completed, they cannot be sold. Therefore, they should not appear in the trading account.

For instance, if we have the following information, we can calculate the transfer to the trading account:

	£
Total production costs expended during the year	5,000
Production costs last year on goods not completed last year, but completed in this year (work in progress)	300
Production costs this year on goods which were not completed by the year end (work in progress)	440
The calculation is:	
Total production costs expended this year	5,000
Add Costs from last year, in respect of goods completed in this year (work in progress)	300
	5,300
Less Costs in this year, for goods to be completed next year (work in progress)	440
Production costs expended on goods completed this year	4,860

35.11 A worked example for a manufacturing account

Consider the case whose details are given in Exhibit 35.2.

Exhibit 35.2

	£
1 January 2007, Stock of raw materials	800
31 December 2007, Stock of raw materials	1,050
1 January 2007, Work in progress	350
31 December 2007, Work in progress	420
Year to 31 December 2007	
Wages: Direct	3,960
Indirect	2,550
Purchase of raw materials	8,700
Fuel and power	990
Direct expenses	140
Lubricants	300
Carriage inwards on raw materials	200
Rent of factory	720
Depreciation of factory plant and machinery	420
Internal transport expenses	180
Insurance of factory buildings and plant	150
General factory expenses	330

Manufacturing Account for the year ended 31 December 2007

	£	£
Stock of raw materials 1.1.2007		800
Add Purchases		8,700
Carriage inwards		200
		9,700
Less Stock of raw materials 31.12.2007		1,050
Cost of raw materials consumed		8,650
Direct wages		3,960
Direct expenses		140
Prime cost		12,750

Indirect Manufacturing Cost	£	£
Fuel and power	990	
Indirect wages	2,550	
Lubricants	300	
Rent	720	
Depreciation of plant	420	
Internal transport expenses	180	
Insurance	150	
General factory expenses	330	5,640
		18,390
Add Work in progress 1.1.2007		350
		18,740
Less Work in progress 31.12.2007		420
Production cost of goods completed c/d		18,320

The trading account is concerned with finished goods. If in Exhibit 35.2 there had been £3,500 stock of finished goods at 1 January 2007 and £4,400 at 31 December 2007, and the sales of finished goods amounted to £25,000, then the trading account would appear thus:

Trading Account for the year 31 December 2007

	£	£
Sales		25,000
Less Cost of goods sold		
Stock of finished goods 1.1.2007	3,500	
Add Production cost of goods completed b/d	18,320	
	21,820	
Less Stock of finished goods 31.12.2007	4,400	17,420
Gross profit c/d		7,580

The profit and loss account is then constructed in the normal way.

35.12 Apportionment of expenses

Quite often, expenses will have to be split between:

- Indirect manufacturing costs: to be charged in the manufacturing account section

- Administration expenses:
- Selling and distribution expenses: to be charged in the profit and loss account section
- Financial charges:

An instance of this could be the rent expense. If the rent is paid separately for each part of the organisation, then it is easy to charge the rent to each sort of expense. However, only one figure of rent might be paid, without any indication as to how much is for the factory part, how much is for the selling and distribution part and that for the administration buildings.

How the rent expense will be apportioned in the latter case will depend on circumstances, but will use the most equitable way of doing it. A range of methods may be used, including ones based upon:

● floor area
● property valuations of each part of the buildings and land.

35.13 Full set of final accounts: worked example

A complete worked example is now given. Note that in the profit and loss account the expenses have been separated to show whether they are administration expenses, selling and distribution expenses, or financial charges.

The trial balance in Exhibit 35.3 has been extracted from the books of J Jarvis, Toy Manufacturer, as on 31 December 2007.

Exhibit 35.3

J Jarvis
Trial Balance as at 31 December 2007

	Dr £	Cr £
Stock of raw materials 1.1.2007	2,100	
Stock of finished goods 1.1.2007	3,890	
Work in progress 1.1.2007	1,350	
Wages (direct £18,000; factory indirect £14,500)	32,500	
Royalties	700	
Carriage inwards (on raw materials)	350	
Purchases of raw materials	37,000	
Productive machinery (cost £28,000)	23,000	
Accounting machinery (cost £2,000)	1,200	
General factory expenses	3,100	
Lighting	750	
Factory power	1,370	
Administrative salaries	4,400	
Salesmen's salaries	3,000	
Commission on sales	1,150	
Rent	1,200	
Insurance	420	
General administration expenses	1,340	
Bank charges	230	
Discounts allowed	480	
Carriage outwards	590	
Sales		100,000
Debtors and creditors	14,230	12,500
Bank	5,680	
Cash	150	
Drawings	2,000	
Capital as at 1.1.2007		29,680
	142,180	142,180

Notes at 31.12.2007:
(i)   Stock of raw materials £2,400; stock of finished goods £4,000; work in progress £1,500.
(ii) Lighting, rent and insurance are to be apportioned: factory five-sixths, administration one-sixth.
(iii) Depreciation on productive and accounting machinery is at 10 per cent per annum on cost.

J Jarvis
Manufacturing, Trading and Profit and Loss Account
for the year ended 31 December 2007

	£	£	£
Stock of raw materials 1.1.2007			2,100
Add Purchases			37,000
Carriage inwards			350
			39,450
Less Stock raw materials 31.12.2007			2,400
Cost of raw materials consumed			37,050
Direct labour			18,000
Royalties			700
Prime cost			55,750
Indirect Manufacturing Cost			
General factory expenses		3,100	
Lighting ⁵⁄₆ths		625	
Power		1,370	
Rent ⁵⁄₆ths		1,000	
Insurance ⁵⁄₆ths		350	
Depreciation of plant		2,800	
Indirect labour		14,500	23,745
			79,495
Add Work in progress 1.1.2007			1,350
			80,845
Less Work in progress 31.12.2007			1,500
Production cost of goods completed c/d			79,345
Sales			100,000
Less Cost of goods sold			
Stock of finished goods 1.1.2007		3,890	
Add Production cost of goods completed		79,345	
		83,235	
Less Stock of finished goods 31.12.2007		4,000	79,235
Gross profit			20,765
Administration Expenses			
Administrative salaries	4,400		
Rent ¹⁄₆th	200		
Insurance ¹⁄₆th	70		
General expenses	1,340		
Lighting ¹⁄₆th	125		
Depreciation of accounting machinery	200	6,335	
Selling and Distribution Expenses			
Sales representatives' salaries	3,000		
Commission on sales	1,150		
Carriage outwards	590	4,740	
Financial Charges			
Bank charges	230		
Discounts allowed	480	710	11,785
Net profit			8,980

J Jarvis
Balance Sheet as at 31 December 2007

	Cost	Total Depreciation	Net Book Value
	£	£	£
Fixed Assets			
Productive machinery	28,000	7,800	20,200
Accounting machinery	2,000	1,000	1,000
	30,000	8,800	21,200
Current Assets			
Stock:			
Raw materials	2,400		
Finished goods	4,000		
Work in progress	1,500		
Debtors	14,230		
Bank	5,680		
Cash	150	27,960	
Less Current Liabilities			
Creditors	12,500	12,500	
Net current assets			15,460
			36,660
Financed by			
Capital			
Balance as at 1.1.2007			29,680
Add Net profit			8,980
			38,660
Less Drawings			2,000
			36,660

Note: Students often find the preparation of manufacturing accounts difficult to grasp and may find it useful to remember the following areas in which they could easily make a mistake:

1 Remember to *add* any item appearing under the heading of 'Indirect Manufacturing Costs', i.e. rent, wages, depreciation, power and lighting etc.
2 In the trading account 'Cost of Goods Sold' section ensure you use the '**Production cost of goods completed**' i.e. £79,345 and *not* the **purchases** figure.
3 In the balance sheet, under current assets, be sure to include all three closing stocks if applicable to your question, i.e.
    (i)   stock of raw materials
    (ii)   stock of work in progress
    (iii) stock of finished goods.

Chapter summary

● Where a firm makes goods rather then buying them ready made then the cost of production is found by drawing up a manufacturing account.
● The cost of producing an item is made up of direct materials, direct labour and direct expenses to give us the '**prime cost**'. To this figure is added any indirect manufacturing costs, plus the opening stock of work in progress less closing stock of work in progress to find the '**production cost of goods completed**'.

- Direct costs are those costs that can be traced to the item being manufactured.
- Indirect manufacturing costs are those costs relating to the manufacture of an item that cannot be easily traced, for example, a foreman's wages. Also called 'indirect costs'.
- Where an organisation manufactures its own goods then the financial statements consist of a manufacturing account which gives the production cost of goods completed, the trading account showing gross profit and the profit and loss account showing net profit.
- It is important to adjust the manufacturing account for any work in progress at the start and end of the accounting period.
- Be careful to watch out for the areas likely to cause errors when preparing financial statements of a manufacturing organisation.

Exercises

35.1 From the following information, prepare the manufacturing and trading account of E Smith for the year ended 31 March 2006.

	£
Stocks at 1 April 2005:	
Finished goods	6,724
Raw materials	2,400
Work in progress	955
Carriage on purchases (raw materials)	321
Sales	69,830
Purchases of raw materials	21,340
Manufacturing wages	13,280
Factory power	6,220
Other manufacturing expenses	1,430
Factory rent and rates	2,300
Stocks at 31 March 2006	
Raw materials	2,620
Work in progress	870
Finished goods	7,230

35.2X From the following details, you are to draw up a manufacturing, trading and profit and loss account of P Lucas for the year ended 30 September 2006.

	30.9.2005	30.9.2006
	£	£
Stocks of raw materials, at cost	8,460	10,970
Work in progress	3,070	2,460
Finished goods stock	12,380	14,570

	£
For the year:	
Raw materials purchased	38,720
Manufacturing wages	20,970
Factory expenses	12,650
Depreciation:	
Plant and machinery	7,560
Delivery vans	3,040
Office equipment	807

	£
Factory power	6,120
Advertising	5,080
Office and administration expenses	5,910
Sales representatives' salaries and expenses	6,420
Delivery van expenses	5,890
Sales	134,610
Carriage inwards	2,720

35.3 The Oldport Manufacturing Co's financial year ended on 30 April 2005. The following list includes some of the balances in the business's book at that date.

	£
Stocks 1 May 2004	
Finished goods	27,900
Raw materials	31,550
Wages	
Direct manufacturing	67,525
Indirect manufacturing	24,390
Office	38,440
Purchases of raw materials	98,560
Factory rent and rates	22,400
Stocks 30 April 2005	
Finished goods	31,280
Raw materials	34,585

Tasks:

(*a*) Set out a detailed calculation of the company's prime cost. Select appropriate items from the information provided.

(*b*) Explain what is meant by the term 'variable costs'. Illustrate your answer with *one* example of a variable cost.

Southern Examining Group AQA

Please note that this question is NOT from the live examinations for the current specification.

35.4 CCC Ltd makes ornaments, which it sells in wooden cases. The following information is made available to you in respect of the year ended 31 December 2005:

	1 Jan 2005	31 Dec 2005
	£	£
Raw materials	4,500	5,800
Wooden cases	2,250	1,920
Work-in-progress	1,250	1,900

The activities for the year ended 31 December 2005 were:

	£
Raw materials purchased	8,800
Purchases of wooden cases	2,250
Carriage outwards	210
Carriage inwards on raw materials	390
Wages	22,500
Salary of factory manager	1,650
Factory power	1,820
Factory rates	910
Lighting	600
Administration expenses	2,400
Salesmen's salaries	5,950

The firm completely finished the manufacture of 1,000 ornaments. All ornaments were sold immediately on completion for £80 each. In addition:

- Factory plant was valued at £100,000 on 1 January 2005. It depreciates by 20 per cent for 2005.
- 80 per cent of the wages are for productive workers, and 20 per cent for factory overheads.
- 50 per cent of the lighting is for the factory.

Required:

(a) Draw up a manufacturing account to disclose:
- (i) cost of raw materials used
- (ii) cost of wooden cases used
- (iii) prime cost
- (iv) factory overheads
- (v) cost of production.

(b) Draft the trading and profit and loss account for the year ended 31 December 2005.

(c) Ascertain the production cost of each boxed ornament.

(d) Calculate the gross profit on each boxed ornament sold.

35.5X The following balances have been extracted from the books of Tan Guat Hoon as at 31 August 2007:

	£
Stock at 1 September 2006	
Raw materials	16,300
Work in progress	21,200
Finished goods	43,100
Provision for doubtful debts at 1 September 2006	1,460
Purchases of raw materials	71,200
Returns of raw materials	700
Sales	187,300
Discounts allowed	640
Discounts received	700
Production wages	21,300
Office salaries	11,300
Production equipment (cost £60,000)	29,400
Office equipment (at cost)	5,400
Carriage on raw materials	930
Rent and rates	8,000
Heat and light	1,100
Insurance	500

The following information is also relevant at 31 August 2007:

(i) Closing stocks are:

- Raw materials £15,800
- Work in progress £20,100
- Finished goods £36,400.

(ii) The following amounts remain outstanding:

- Rent and rates £500
- Heat and light £220
- Production wages £2,600.

(iii)   £100 insurance has been prepaid.
(iv)   Three-quarters of insurance relates to the factory and the remainder to the office.
(v)   Two-thirds of heat and light relates to the factory and the remainder to the office.
(vi)   Eighty per cent of rent and rates relates to the factory and the remainder to the office.
(vii)   The provision for doubtful debts is to be reduced to £1,010.
(viii)   Depreciation is to be provided:

- on production equipment at 30 per cent reducing (diminishing) balance basis
- on office equipment at 40 per cent on cost.

You are required to:
(a)   prepare a Manufacturing Account for the year ended 31 August 2007
(b)   prepare a Trading, Profit and Loss Account for the year ended 31 August 2007.

City & Guilds Pitman qualifications

35.6X   Toybox Products Ltd manufactures wooden toys for younger children. The following information is available about the company's financial year ended 30 April 2004.

	£
Direct wages	226,450
Indirect factory power	37,720
Sales of finished goods	545,800
Factory insurance	13,240
Purchases of raw materials	104,850
Returns inwards (finished goods)	3,620
Depreciation of factory plant and machinery	33,800
Indirect factory wages and salaries	24,390
Stocks at 1 May 2003	
Raw materials	11,250
Finished goods	21,480
Stocks at 30 April 2004	
Raw materials	14,740
Finished goods	26,260

Tasks:
(a)   Prepare the company's manufacturing account for the year ended 30 April 2004. The account should show subtotals for:
-   raw materials consumed
-   prime cost
-   total factory overheads.
(b)   Prepare a trading account for the year ended 30 April 2004.

The company's directors had been hoping to expand the company. However, during recent months sales have decreased because of increasing competition.

Tasks:
(c)   Explain *three* ways in which it might be possible to overcome competition and increase sales.
(d)   Recommend *two* ways in which the company could finance an expansion programme. In each case explain the effect of the recommendation on the company's cash resources.

Southern Examining Group AQA

Please note that this question is NOT from the live examinations for the current specification.

Partnership accounts

36.1 The need for partnerships

So far, we have mainly considered businesses owned by only one person. Businesses set up to make a profit can often have more than one owner and there are various reasons for multiple ownership:

- The capital required is more than one person can provide.
- The experience or ability required to manage the business cannot be found in one person alone.
- Many people want to share management instead of doing everything on their own.
- Very often partners will be members of the same family.

There are two types of multiple ownership; partnerships and limited companies. This chapter deals only with partnerships, limited companies are dealt with in Chapter 37.

36.2 Nature of a partnership

A partnership has the following characteristics:

1 It is formed to make profits.
2 It must obey the law as given in the Partnership Act 1890. If there is a limited partner, as described in Section 36.3, the Limited Partnerships Act of 1907 must also be complied with.

3 Normally, there can be a minimum of two and a maximum of twenty partners. Exceptions are banks, where there cannot be more than ten partners; also, there is no maximum limit for firms of accountants, solicitors, stock exchange members or other professional bodies receiving the approval of the relevant government body for this purpose.

4 Each partner (except for limited partners, described below) must pay his or her share of any debts that the partnership is unable to pay; they are personally liable. If necessary, partners could be forced to sell their private possessions to pay their share of any debts. This can be said to be 'unlimited' liability.

36.3 Limited partners

A partnership may be unlimited as previously discussed or limited. In a **limited partnership** there must be at least one partner who is not limited. All limited partnerships must be registered with the Registrar of Companies. Limited partners are not liable for the debts as in 36.2 (4) above. The following characteristics are found in limited partnerships:

1 Their liability for the debts of the partnership is limited to the capital they have invested in the partnership. They can lose that capital, but they cannot be asked for any more money to pay the debts unless they break the regulations relating to the involvement in the partnership (2 and 3 below).
2 The partners are not allowed to take out or receive back any part of their contribution to the partnership during its lifetime.
3 They are not allowed to take part in the management of the partnership business.
4 All the partners cannot be limited partners as mentioned above; there must be at least one partner with unlimited liability.

36.4 Partnership agreements

Agreements in writing are not necessary for partnerships. However, it is better if a proper written **partnership agreement** is drawn up by a lawyer or accountant, for where there is such a written agreement there will be fewer problems between partners. A written agreement means less confusion about what has been agreed.

36.5 Content of partnership agreements

The written agreement can contain as much, or as little, as the partners want. The law does not say what it must contain. The usual accounting contents are:

1 The capital to be contributed by each partner.
2 The ratio in which profits (or losses) are to be shared.
3 The rate of interest, if any, to be paid on capital before the profits are shared.
4 The rate of interest, if any, to be charged on partners' drawings.
5 Salaries to be paid to partners.
6 Performance-related payments to partners.

7 Arrangement for the admission of a new partner.

8 Procedures to be carried out when a partner retires or dies.

Points 1 to 6 in the list above are now examined. Points 7 and 8 are outside the scope of this book but are covered in *Business Accounting 1* by Frank Wood and Alan Sangster.

1 Capital contributions

Partners need not contribute equal amounts of capital. What matters is how much capital each partner *agrees* to contribute.

2 Profit (or loss) sharing ratios

Partners can agree to share profits/losses in any ratio or any way that they may wish. However, it is often thought by students that profits should be shared in the same ratio as that in which capital is contributed. For example, suppose the capitals were Allen £2,000 and Beet £1,000; many people would share the profits in the ratio of two-thirds to one-third, even though the work to be done by each partner is similar. A look at the division of the first few years' profits on such a basis would be:

Years	1	2	3	4	5	Total
	£	£	£	£	£	£
Net profits	1,800	2,400	3,000	3,000	3,600	
Shared:						
Allen $^2/_3$	1,200	1,600	2,000	2,000	2,400	9,200
Beet $^1/_3$	600	800	1,000	1,000	1,200	4,600

It can be seen from the above table that Allen would receive £9,200, or £4,600 more than Beet. To treat each partner fairly, the difference between the two shares of profit in this case, as the duties of the partners are the same, should be adequate to compensate Allen for putting extra capital into the firm. It is clear that £4,600 extra profits is far more than adequate for this purpose, as Allen only put in an extra £1,000 as capital.

Consider, too, the position of capital-ratio sharing of profits if one partner put in £99,000 and the other put in £1,000 as capital.

To overcome the difficulty of compensating for the investment of extra capital, the concept of interest on capital was devised.

3 Interest on capital

If the work to be done by each partner is of equal value but the capital contributed is unequal, it is reasonable to grant **interest on the partners' capital** input. This interest is treated as a deduction prior to the calculation of profits and the latter's distribution according to the profit-sharing ratio. The rate of interest is a matter of agreement between the partners, but it should equal the return that they would have received if they had invested the capital elsewhere.

Taking Allen and Beet's firm again, but sharing the profits equally after charging 5 per cent per annum interest on capital, the division of profits would become:

Years	1	2	3	4	5		Total
	£	£	£	£	£		£
Net profits	1,800	2,400	3,000	3,000	3,600		
Interest on capital							
Allen	100	100	100	100	100	=	500
Beet	50	50	50	50	50	=	250
Remainder shared:							
Allen $^1/_2$	825	1,125	1,425	1,425	1,725		= 6,525
Beet $^1/_2$	825	1,125	1,425	1,425	1,725		= 6,525

Summary	Allen	Beet
	£	£
Interest on capital	500	250
Balance of profits	6,525	6,525
	7,025	6,775

4 Interest on drawings

It is clearly in the best interests of the firm that cash is withdrawn from the firm by the partners in accordance with the two basic principles of: (*a*) as little as possible, and (*b*) as late as possible. The more cash that is left in the firm, the more expansion can be financed, the greater the economies of having ample cash to take advantage of bargains and of not missing cash discounts because cash is not available, and so on.

To deter the partners from taking out cash unnecessarily, the concept can be used of charging the partners **interest on each withdrawal**, calculated from the date of withdrawal to the end of the financial year. The amount charged to them helps to swell the profits divisible between the partners. The rate of interest should be sufficient to achieve this without being too harsh.

Suppose that Allen and Beet have decided to charge interest on drawings at 5 per cent per annum, and that their year end is 31 December. The following drawings are made:

Allen

Drawings		*Interest*		£
1 January	£100	5% of £100 for 1 year	=	5
1 March	£240	5% of £240 for 10 months	=	10
1 May	£120	5% of £120 for 8 months	=	4
1 July	£240	5% of £240 for 6 months	=	6
1 October	£ 80	5% of £80 for 3 months	=	1
		Interest charged to Allen	=	26

Beet

Drawings		*Interest*		£
1 January	£ 60	5% of £60 for 1 year	=	3
1 August	£480	5% of £480 for 5 months	=	10
1 December	£240	5% of £240 for 1 month	=	1
		Interest charged to Beet	=	14

The interest charged to each partner would vary depending on when and how much money was taken out as drawings.

5 Salaries to partners

One partner may have more responsibility or tasks than others. As a reward for this and rather than change the profit and loss sharing ratio, that **partner may have a salary**, which is deducted before sharing the balance of profits.

6 Performance-related payments to partners

Partners may agree that commission or performance-related bonuses should be payable to some or all the partners in a way that is linked to their individual performance. As with salaries, these would be deducted before sharing the balance of profits.

36.6 An example of the distribution of profits

Taylor and Clarke have been in partnership for one year, sharing profits and losses in the ratio of Taylor three-fifths and Clarke two-fifths. They are entitled to 5 per cent per annum interest on capital, Taylor having put in £2,000 and Clarke £6,000. Clarke is to have a salary of £500. They charge interest on drawings, Taylor being charged £50 and Clarke £100. The net profit, before any distributions to the partners, amounts to £5,000 for the year ended 31 December 2005.

The results are shown in Exhibit 36.1.

Exhibit 36.1

	£	£	£
Net profit			5,000
Add Charged for interest on drawings:			
Taylor		50	
Clarke		100	
			150
			5,150
Less Salary: Clarke		500	
Interest on capital (@5%)			
Taylor	100		
Clarke	300		
		400	
			900
			4,250
Balance of profits shared:			
Taylor (three-fifths)		2,550	
Clarke (two-fifths)		1,700	4,250
			4,250

The £5,000 net profits have therefore been shared as follows:

	Taylor	Clarke
	£	£
Balance of profits	2,550	1,700
Interest on capital	100	300
Salary	–	500
	2,650	2,500
Less Interest on drawings	50	100
	2,600	2,400

£5,000

36.7 The financial statements

If the sales, stock and expenses of a partnership were exactly the same as that of a sole trader, then the trading and profit and loss account would be identical with that as prepared for the sole trader. However, a partnership would have an extra section shown under the profit and loss account. This section is called the profit and loss **appropriation account**, and it is in this account that the distribution of profits is shown. The heading to the trading and profit and loss account does not include the words 'appropriation account'. It is purely an accounting custom not to include it in the heading.

The trading and profit and loss account of Taylor and Clarke from the details given would appear as shown in Exhibit 36.2.

Exhibit 36.2

Taylor and Clarke
Trading and Profit and Loss Account
for the year ended 31 December 2005

(Trading Account – same as for sole trader)
(Profit and Loss Account – same as for sole trader)
Profit and loss appropriation account

	£	£	£
Net profit			5,000
Interest on drawings:			
Taylor		50	
Clarke		100	150
			5,150
Less:			
Interest on capital:			
Taylor	100		
Clarke	300	400	
Salary		500	900
			4,250
Balance of profits shared:			
Taylor (three-fifths)		2,550	
Clarke (two-fifths)		1,700	4,250
			4,250

36.8 Fixed and fluctuating capital accounts

There is a choice available in partnership accounts. Partnerships can operate either fixed capital accounts plus current accounts, or fluctuating capital accounts. Each option is described below, with a final comment on which is generally preferable.

Fixed capital accounts plus current accounts

With **fixed capital accounts**, the capital account for each partner remains year by year at the figure of capital put into the firm by the partners. The profits, interest on capital, and the salaries to which the partner may be entitled are then credited to a separate current account for the partner, and the drawings and the interest on drawings are debited to it. The balance of the current account at the end of each financial year will then represent the amount of undrawn (or withdrawn) profits. A credit balance will be undrawn profits, while a debit balance will be drawings in excess of the profits to which the partner is entitled.

For Taylor and Clarke, capital and current accounts, assuming drawings of £2,000 each, will appear thus:

	Taylor		
Dr	Capital Account		Cr
		2005	£
		Jan 1 Bank	2,000

	Clarke		
Dr	Capital Account		Cr
		2005	£
		Jan 1 Bank	6,000

	Taylor		
Dr	Current Account		Cr
2005	£	2005	£
Dec 31 Cash: Drawings	2,000	Dec 31 Profit and loss	
Dec 31 Profit and loss		appropriation account:	
appropriation account:		Interest on capital	100
Interest on drawings	50	Share of profits	2,550
Dec 31 Balance c/d	600		
	2,650		2,650
		2006	
		Jan 1 Balance b/d	600

Clarke
Current Account

Dr		Cr	
2005	£	2005	£
Dec 31 Cash: Drawings	2,000	Dec 31 Profit and loss	
Dec 31 Profit and loss		appropriation account:	
appropriation account:		Interest on capital	300
Interest on drawings	100	Share of profits	1,700
Dec 31 Balance c/d	400	Salary	500
	2,500		2,500
		2006	
		Jan 1 Balance b/d	400

Notice that the salary of Clarke was not paid to him but was merely credited to his account. If in fact it was paid in addition to his drawings, the £500 cash paid would have been debited to the current account, changing the £400 credit balance into a £100 debit balance.

Examiners often ask for the capital accounts and current accounts to be shown in columnar form. For the previous accounts of Taylor and Clarke, these would appear as follows:

Capital Accounts

	Taylor	Clarke			Taylor	Clarke
	£	£	2005		£	£
			Jan 1 Bank		2,000	6,000

Current Accounts

	Taylor	Clarke			Taylor	Clarke
2005	£	£	2005		£	£
Dec 31 Cash: Drawings	2,000	2,000	Dec 31 Interest on capital		100	300
Dec 31 Interest on			Dec 31 Share of profits		2,550	1,700
drawings	50	100	Dec 31 Salary			500
Dec 31 Balances c/d	600	400				
	2,650	2,500			2,650	2,500
			2006			
			Jan 1 Balances b/d		600	400

Fluctuating capital accounts

In this arrangement of **fluctuating capital accounts** the distribution of profits would be credited to the capital account, and the drawings and interest on drawings is debited. Therefore, the balance on the capital account will change each year, i.e. it will fluctuate.

If fluctuating capital accounts had been kept for Taylor and Clarke, they would have appeared:

Taylor
Capital Account

Dr		£			Cr £
2005			2005		
Dec 31	Cash: Drawings	2,000	Jan 1	Bank	2,000
Dec 31	Profit and loss		Dec 31	Profit and loss	
	appropriation account:			appropriation account:	
	Interest on drawings	50		Interest on capital	100
Dec 31	Balance c/d	2,600		Share of profits	2,550
		4,650			4,650
			2006		
			Jan 1	Balance b/d	2,600

Clarke
Capital Account

Dr		£			Cr £
2005			2005		
Dec 31	Cash: Drawings	2,000	Jan 1	Bank	6,000
Dec 31	Profit and loss		Dec 31	Profit and loss	
	appropriation account:			appropriation account:	
	Interest on drawings	100		Interest on capital	300
Dec 31	Balance c/d	6,400		Salary	500
				Share of profits	1,700
		8,500			8,500
			2006		
			Jan 1	Balance b/d	6,400

Fixed capital accounts preferred

The keeping of fixed capital accounts plus current accounts is considered preferable to operating fluctuating capital accounts. When partners are taking out greater amounts than the share of the profits that they are entitled to, this is shown up by a debit balance on the current account and so acts as a warning.

36.9   Where no partnership agreement exists

Where no formal partnership agreement exists – either express or implied – section 24 of the Partnership Act 1890 governs the situation. The accounting content of this section states:

● Profits and losses are to be shared equally.
● There is to be no interest allowed on capital.
● No interest is to be charged on drawings.
● Salaries are not allowed.
● If a partner puts a sum of money into a firm in excess of the capital he or she has agreed to subscribe, that partner is entitled to interest at the rate of 5 per cent per annum on such an advance.

This section applies where there is no agreement. There may be an agreement not by a partnership deed but in a letter, or it may be implied by conduct – for instance, when a partner signs a balance sheet that shows profits shared in some ratio other than equally. Where a dispute arises as to whether agreement exists or not, and this cannot be resolved by the partners, only the courts will be competent to decide.

36.10 The balance sheet

The capital side of the balance sheet will appear as follows for our example. Note that figures in brackets, e.g. '(2,000)', is an accounting convention indicating a negative amount.

Balance Sheet as at 31 December 2005

	£ Taylor	£ Clarke	£ Total
Capital accounts			
Balance	2,000	6,000	8,000
Current accounts			
Interest on capital	100	300	
Share of profits	2,550	1,700	
Salary	–	500	
	2,650	2,500	
Less Drawings	(2,000)	(2,000)	
Interest on drawings	(50)	(100)	
	(2,050)	(2,100)	
	600	400	
			1,000

If one of the current accounts had finished in debit – for instance, if the current account of Clarke had finished up as £400 debit – the figure of £400 would appear in brackets and the balances would appear net in the totals column:

	Taylor	*Clarke*	
	£	£	£
Closing balance	600	(400)	200

If the net figure, e.g. the £200 just shown, turned out to be a debit figure, then this would be deducted from the total of the fixed capital accounts.

36.11 A fully worked exercise

We can now look at a fully worked exercise covering nearly all the main points shown in this chapter.

Luty and Minchin are in partnership. They share profits in the ratio: Luty three-fifths to Minchin two-fifths. The following trial balance was extracted as at 31 March 2004:

Trial balance as at 31 March 2004

	Dr £	Cr £
Office equipment at cost	6,500	
Motor vehicles at cost	9,200	
Provision for depreciation at 31.3.2003:		
Motor vehicles		3,680
Office equipment		1,950
Stock at 31 March 2003	24,970	
Debtors and creditors	20,960	16,275
Cash at bank	615	
Cash in hand	140	
Sales		90,370
Purchases	71,630	
Salaries	8,417	
Office expenses	1,370	
Discounts allowed	563	
Current accounts at 31.3.2003:		
Luty		1,379
Minchin		1,211
Capital accounts:		
Luty		27,000
Minchin		12,000
Drawings:		
Luty	5,500	
Minchin	4,000	
	153,865	153,865

A set of final accounts for the year ended 31 March 2004 for the partnership are to be drawn up. The following notes are applicable at 31 March 2004:

(i) Stock at 31 March 2004 was valued at £27,340.

(ii) Office expenses owing £110.

(iii) Provision for depreciation: motor vehicles 20 per cent of cost, office equipment 10 per cent of cost.

(iv) Charge interest on capital at 10 per cent.

(v) Charge interest on drawings: Luty £180; Minchin £210.

(vi) Charge £500 for salary for Minchin.

The final accounts then look as set out in Exhibit 36.3.

Exhibit 36.3

Luty and Minchin
Trading and Profit and Loss Account for the year ended 31 March 2004

	£	£	£
Sales			90,370
Less Cost of goods sold:			
Opening stock		24,970	
Add Purchases		71,630	
		96,600	
Less Closing stock		27,340	69,260
Gross profit			21,110
Less Expenses:			
Salaries*		8,417	
Office expenses (1,370 + 110)		1,480	
Discounts allowed		563	
Depreciation: Motor vehicles	1,840		
Office equipment	650	2,490	12,950
Net profit			8,160
Add Interest on drawings: Luty		180	
Minchin		210	390
			8,550
Less Interest on capital: Luty	2,700		
Minchin	1,200	3,900	
Less Salary: Minchin		500	4,400
			4,150
Balance of profits shared: Luty (three-fifths)		2,490	4,150
Minchin (two-fifths)		1,660	4,150
			4,150

Does not include partner's salary.

Luty and Minchin
Balance Sheet as at 31 March 2004

	Cost	Depreciation	NBV
Fixed Assets	£	£	£
Office equipment	6,500	2,600	3,900
Motor vehicles	9,200	5,520	3,680
	15,700	8,120	7,580
Current assets			
Stock		27,340	
Debtors		20,960	
Bank		615	
Cash		140	
		49,055	
Less Current Liabilities			
Creditors	16,275		
Expenses owing	110	16,385	
Net Current assets			32,670
			40,250

Capital accounts		Luty		Minchin	Total
Balance		27,000		12,000	39,000
Current accounts					
Balances 1.4.2003		1,379		1,211	
Add Interest on capital		2,700		1,200	
Add Salary				500	
Add Share of profits		2,490		1,660	
		6,569		4,571	
Less Drawings	5,500		4,000		
Less Interest on drawings	180	5,680	210	4,210	
Balances 31.3.2004		889		361	1,250
					40,250

Chapter summary

- Partnerships are formed with two or more partners carrying on in business with a view to making a profit.
- There are two types of partnership, unlimited and a limited partnership.
- Where there is a limited partnership there must be at least one unlimited partner within the partnership. Limited partnerships should be registered with the Registrar of Companies and the Limited Partnership Act 1907 must be complied with.
- Limited partners cannot withdraw any of the capital they invested in the partnership nor may they take part in the management of the partnership.
- It is advisable for all partnerships to draw up a Partnership Agreement detailing the accounting requirements of the partnership (Section 36.5).
- If there is no partnership agreement then the provisions of the Partnership Act 1890 will apply (Section 36.9).
- The partners may use either fixed or fluctuating capital accounts.
- The financial statements of a partnership are: trading and profit and loss account that has an additional section called the 'appropriation account' and balance sheet. The balance sheet will show the capital and current accounts of all the partners.

Exercises

36.1 Stead and Jackson are partners in a retail business in which they share profits and losses equally. The balance on the partners' capital and current accounts at the year end 31 December 2005 were as follows:

	Capital Account £	Current Account £
Stead	24,000	2,300 Cr
Jackson	16,000	3,500 Cr

During the year, Stead had drawings amounting to £15,000 and Jackson £19,000. Jackson was to receive a partnership salary of £5,000 for extra duties undertaken. The net profit of the partnership, before taking any of the above into account, was £45,000.

You are required to:

(a) draw up the appropriation account for the partnership for the year ended 31 December 2005

(b) show the partners' capital and current accounts.

36.2X Wain, Brown and Cairns own a garage, and the partners share profits and losses in the ratio of Wain 50 per cent, Brown 30 per cent and Cairns 20 per cent. Their financial year end is 31 March 2004 and the following details were extracted from their books on that date:

	Wain	Brown	Cairns
	£	£	£
Capital account balances	30,000	50,000	70,000
Current account balances	2,400 Cr	3,100 Cr	5,700 Cr
Partnership salaries	10,000	8,000	–
Drawings	12,000	15,050	14,980

The net profit for the year ended 31 March 2004 amounted to £60,000 before taking any of the above into account.

You are required to:

(a) prepare an appropriation account for the year ended 31 March 2004

(b) draw up the partners' capital and current accounts in columnar form for the year ended 31 March 2004.

36.3X The following balances were extracted from the books of Bradford and Taylor as at 31 December 2007:

	£
Capital accounts	
Bradford	40,000
Taylor	30,000
Current accounts	
Bradford	3,450 Cr
Taylor	2,680 Dr
Drawings	
Bradford	8,000
Taylor	12,000
Net profit for the year	44,775

The following information is also available from their partnership agreement:

(i)   The partners are entitled to receive 5 per cent interest on capital.

(ii) Taylor is to receive a partnership salary of £6,000.

(iii) Interest is to be charged on drawings as follows: Bradford £200; Taylor £125.

(iv) Bradford and Taylor are to share profits and losses in the ratio 3 : 2.

Required:

(a) Show the profit and loss appropriation account for the year ended 31 December 2007.

(b) Show the partners' capital and current accounts for the year ended 31 December 2007.

(c) Show how the profits and losses would be distributed and how much each partner would receive if there was no partnership agreement.

36.4 Simpson and Young are in partnership, sharing profits and losses in the ratio 3 : 2. At the close of business on 30 June 2005 the following trial balance was extracted from their books:

	Dr	Cr
	£	£
Premises at cost	28,000	
Motor vans (cost £16,000)	11,000	
Office equipment (cost £8,400)	5,600	
Stock 1 July 2004	18,000	
Purchases	184,980	
Sales		254,520
Wages and salaries	32,700	
Rent, rates and insurance	3,550	
Electricity	980	
Stationery and printing	420	
Motor expenses	3,480	
General office expenses	1,700	
Debtors and creditors	28,000	15,200
Capital accounts: Simpson		50,000
Young		20,000
Drawings: Simpson	10,000	
Young	5,000	
Current accounts: Simpson		640
Young		300
Cash at bank	7,250	
	340,660	340,660

Notes:
(i) Interest is to be allowed on capital accounts at the rate of 10 per cent per annum, and no interest is to be charged on drawings.
(ii) Rates prepaid at 30 June 2005 amount to £250.
(iii) Wages due at 30 June 2005 are £500.
(iv) Provision for depreciation is as follows: motor van at 20 per cent per annum on cost; office equipment at 10 per cent using the reducing balance method.
(v) Stock 30 June 2005 was valued at £19,000.

Required:
Prepare the trading and profit and loss appropriation account for the year ended 30 June 2005, and a balance sheet as at that date.

36.5X Kirkham and Keeling are in partnership, sharing profits and losses in the ratio of 3 : 2. Their partnership agreement also provides for interest on capital to be given to the partners at 10 per cent per annum, but no interest may be charged on drawings. The following trial balance was drawn up at the end of the financial year:

Trial Balance of Kirkham and Keeling as at 30 June 2005

	£	£
Premises	59,200	
Motor vehicles (cost £30,000)	24,000	
Computer equipment (cost £12,000 at 1.7.2003)	8,000	
Cash at bank	12,500	
Debtors	56,000	
Creditors		30,400
Sales		509,040
Purchases	369,960	
Stock 1 July 2004	36,000	

	£	£
Salaries	65,400	
Electricity	1,960	
Telephone	840	
Motor expenses	3,960	
Printing, stationery and advertising	3,000	
Rates and insurance	7,100	
General expenses	3,400	
Capital accounts: Kirkham		100,000
Keeling		40,000
Current accounts: Kirkham		1,280
Keeling		600
Drawings: Kirkham	20,000	
Keeling	10,000	
	681,320	681,320

Notes:
(i)   The closing stock has been valued at £38,000.
(ii) Insurance paid in advance at 30 June 2005 amounted to £1,000.
(iii) Motor expenses owing at 30 June 2005 amounted to £400.
(iv) You are to provide for depreciation on the motor vehicles at 20 per cent on cost. The computer equipment is expected to last three years from the date of purchase.

You are required to prepare the trading and profit and loss appropriation account for the year ended 30 June 2005 and a balance sheet as at that date.

36.6   Bhayani and Donnell are in partnership, sharing profits and losses in the ratio 2 : 1. The following trial balance was extracted after the preparation of their trading account for the year ended 31 December:

	Dr	Cr
	£	£
Provision for depreciation: Vehicles		3,000
Provision for depreciation: Fittings		2,000
Bank balance		950
Drawings: Bhayani	2,000	
Donnell	600	
Vehicles (at cost)	35,000	
Fittings (at cost)	12,000	
Premises (at cost)	20,000	
Rent received		500
Debtors and creditors	25,700	15,600
Current accounts: Bhayani	600	
Donnell	nil	nil
Provision for doubtful debts		950
Gross profit		32,000
Heating and lighting	1,400	
Wages and salaries	4,100	
Cash	600	
Capital accounts: Bhayani		35,000
Donnell		12,000
	102,000	102,000

At 31 December the following information needs to be taken into consideration:
(i)   The provision for doubtful debts is to be maintained at 3 per cent of debtors.
(ii) Rent received of £100 has been paid in advance.

(iii) A heating invoice of £100 has yet to be paid.

(iv) £200 of wages have been prepaid.

(v) Depreciation needs to be provided for on the following basis:
- vehicles at 10 per cent straight line method
- fittings at 15 per cent reducing (diminishing) balance method.

(vi) The partnership agreement provides for the following:
- interest on drawings is charged at 6 per cent per annum
- interest on capital is allowed at 8 per cent per annum
- Donnell is to receive a salary of £3,263.

You are required to:

(a) prepare the partnership profit and loss account for the year ended 31 December

(b) prepare the partnership appropriation account for the year ended 31 December

(c) prepare each partner's current account at 31 December

(d) prepare the partnership balance sheet as at 31 December.

City & Guilds Pitman qualifications

36.7X Jane Hanford and Kevin Pearson are partners in a travel agency. They share profits and losses equally. On 31 March 2005 the firm's final accounts were prepared. The following balances remained in the accounts.

	£
Cash at bank	3,460
Expenses due	240
Expenses prepaid	160
Furniture and equipment at net book value	45,000
Net profit for the year ended 31 March 2005	31,280
Trade creditors	6,300
Trade debtors	7,500
Capital accounts	
Jane Hanford	25,000
Kevin Pearson	20,000
Drawings for the year	
Jane Hanford	17,000
Kevin Pearson	13,000
Current account balances at 1 April 2004	
Jane Hanford	2,100
Kevin Pearson	1,200

From this information the partners' current accounts were prepared.

Current Accounts

	Jane Hanford £	Kevin Pearson £		Jane Hanford £	Kevin Pearson £
Drawings	17,000	13,000	Opening Balances	2,100	1,200
Balances c/f	740	3,840	Net Profit	15,640	15,640
	17,740	16,840		17,740	16,840

(a) Prepare the firm's balance sheet as at 31 March 2005.

(b) Jane and Kevin want to expand the business but they disagree how this should be financed. Jane thinks that they ought to get a loan from the bank. Kevin thinks they ought to take on a new partner who could provide additional finance. What method of finance do you think they should choose? Give reasons for your choice.

AQA

Limited company accounts

37.1 Introduction

This chapter looks at further ways of owning a business other than the arrangements of sole traders and partnerships. When a business needs to expand, additional capital will probably be needed, and forming a limited company makes it possible to raise more funds for the expansion.

37.2 Limited companies

Limited companies are formed because of the advantages they provide over the status of partnerships.

The previous chapter has stated the terms under which a partnership operates. Briefly, a partnership can have no more than 20 owners, not counting limited partners. In addition, if a partnership fails, a partner is responsible for the business assets and could lose all or part of privately owned assets. In contrast, a public limited company can have as many owners as it wants and each owner cannot lose more than the amount invested in the company. No private assets can be lost.

The law governing the preparation and publication of the final accounts of limited companies in the United Kingdom is contained in two Acts of Parliament. These are the Companies Acts of 1985 and 1989. Both Acts are in force for this purpose, the 1989 Act adding to and amending the 1985 Act.

37.3 | Limited liability

The capital of a limited company is divided into **shares**. These can be shares of 10p, 25p, £1, £5, £10, or any other amount per share. To become a member of a limited company – a **shareholder** – a person must buy one or more of the shares.

If a shareholder has paid in full for the shares, his liability is limited to those shares. If a company loses all its assets, all the shareholder can lose is his shares. He cannot be forced to pay anything out of his private money in respect of the company's losses. If a shareholder has only partly paid for the shares, he can be forced to pay the balance owing on the shares. Apart from that, he cannot be forced to pay out of his private money for the company's losses.

This is known as **limited liability** and the company is known as a **limited company**. You can see that these fit the need for organisations needing limited liability for their owners where it is also possible to have a large amount of capital.

37.4 | Public and private companies

There are two classes of company, the **public company** and the **private company**. In the United Kingdom, private companies far outnumber public companies.

In the Companies Acts, a public company is defined as one that fulfils the following conditions:

- Its Memorandum of Association (*see* Section 37.5 below) states that it is a public company, and has registered as such.
- It has an authorised share capital of at least £50,000.
- Minimum membership is two; there is no maximum.
- Its name must end with the words 'public limited company', or its abbreviation 'plc'.

A private company is usually – but not always – a smaller business, and may be formed by one or more persons. It is defined by the Companies Act as a company that is not a public company. The main differences between a private company and a public company are that a private company:

- can have an authorised capital of less than £50,000
- cannot offer its shares for subscription to the public at large (whereas public companies can).

37.5 | Legal status of a limited company

The most important feature of a limited company is its status in law as a 'separate legal entity'. This means that no matter how many individuals have bought its shares, it is treated in its dealings with the outside world as if it were a 'person' in its own right.

When a limited company is formed, it is required by law to raise two documents known as the Memorandum of Association and the Articles of Association. The first document sets down the details of the company and its objectives, while the Articles of Association state the regulations concerning the powers of the directors. These regulations are of the utmost importance when it is realised that the legal owners of the business, namely the shareholders, have entrusted the running of the company to the directors.

37.6 Company directors

A shareholder normally has the right to attend the general meetings of a company, and can vote at such meetings. Shareholders use their votes to appoint **directors** who manage the business on behalf of the shareholders.

At each **Annual General Meeting**, the financial statements for the year are given to the shareholders. The directors at the meeting have to give a report on the performance made by the company.

37.7 Share capital and dividends

The term 'share capital' refers to:

(*a*) **Authorised share capital** – the total of the share capital that the company would be allowed to issue (as stated in the Memorandum of Association); also called 'nominal capital'.

(*b*) **Issued share capital** – the amount of share capital actually issued to shareholders.

(*c*) **Called-up capital** – where only part of the amounts payable on each share has been asked for; the total amount requested on all the shares is known as the 'called-up capital'.

(*d*) **Uncalled capital** – the amount that is to be received in future, but which has not yet been requested.

(*e*) **Calls in arrear** – the amount for which payment has been requested (i.e. called for), but has not yet been paid by shareholders.

(*f*)**Paid-up capital** – the total of the amount of share capital that has been paid for by shareholders.

If all of the authorised share capital has been issued, then items (*a*) and (*b*) above are the same.

Example 1 below illustrates these different meanings.

Example 1: Better Enterprises Ltd was formed with the legal right to be able to issue 100,000 shares of £1 each. The company has actually issued 75,000 shares. None of the shares has yet been fully paid-up; so far the company has made calls of 80p (£0.80) per share. All of the calls have been paid by shareholders, except for £200 owing from one particular shareholder. On this basis, therefore:

(*a*) Authorised (or nominal) share capital is £100,000.
(*b*) Issued share capital is £75,000.
(*c*) Called-up capital is $(75,000 \times £0.80) = £60,000$.
(*d*) Calls in arrear amounted to £200.
(*e*) Paid-up capital is £60,000 less (*d*) £200 = £59,800.

When a company makes a profit, the directors will have to decide how this is to be used. They will probably retain part of the profit as reserves, which will be used to expand the business. The remaining part is likely to be used to reward the shareholders for investing in the company. This share of the profits is known as the **dividend**.

The dividend is usually shown as a percentage. A dividend of 10 per cent in Firm A on 500,000 ordinary shares of £1 each will amount to £50,000. A dividend of 6 per cent in Firm B on 200,000 ordinary shares of £2 each will amount to £24,000. A shareholder having 100 shares in each firm would receive £10 from Firm A and £12 from Firm B.

There are two main types of shares:

- **Preference shares** Preference shareholders get an agreed percentage rate of dividend before the ordinary shareholders receive anything.
- **Ordinary shares** Ordinary shareholders receive the remainder of the total profits available for dividends. There is no upper limit to the amounts of dividends they can receive.

For example, if a company had 10,000 5 per cent preference shares of £1 each and 20,000 ordinary shares of £1 each, then the dividends would be payable as in Exhibit 37.1.

Exhibit 37.1

Year	1	2	3	4	5
	£	£	£	£	£
Profits appropriated for dividends	900	1,300	1,600	3,100	2,000
Preference dividends	(5%) 500	500	500	500	500
Ordinary dividend	(2%) 400	(4%) 800	(5½%) 1,100	(13%) 2,600	(7½%) 1,500

It can be seen that preference shareholders receive a fixed amount of dividend each year, whilst the ordinary shareholders receive a variable amount depending on the performance of the company. The profit level in Year 4 was very good and the ordinary shareholders received a substantial 13 per cent dividend.

There are two main types of preference shares:

- non-cumulative shares
- cumulative shares.

The description of the shares refers to their differing rights for the payment of dividends, but you do not require further knowledge of these at this stage.

37.8 Debentures

The term **debenture** is used when a limited company receives money on loan, and certificates called 'debenture certificates' are issued to the lender. Interest will be paid to the holder of the debenture, the rate of interest being shown on the certificate. **Debenture interest** has to be paid irrespective of whether the company makes a profit. Debentures are, therefore, different from shares, where dividends depend on profits being made. They are often secured on the assets of the business.

37.9 Trading and profit and loss accounts

The trading and profit and loss accounts are drawn up in exactly the same way for both private and public companies.

The trading account of a limited company is no different from that of a sole trader or a partnership. However, some differences may be found in the profit and loss account. The two main expenses that would be found only in company accounts are directors' remuneration and any debenture interest.

Directors' remuneration

As directors exist only in companies, this type of expense is found only in company accounts.

Directors are, in legal terms, employees of the company, appointed by the shareholders. **Directors' remuneration** is charged to the main profit and loss account.

Debenture interest

The interest payable for the use of the money is an expense of the company and is payable whether profits are made or not. This means that debenture interest is charged as an expense in the profit and loss account itself. Contrast this with dividends, which are dependent on profits having been made (see above Sections 37.7 and 37.8).

37.10 The appropriation account

There is a section under the profit and loss account called the profit and loss appropriation account (*see* Section 36.7). The appropriation account shows how the net profits are to be appropriated, i.e. how the profits are to be used.

We may find any of the following in the appropriation account:

Credit side

(*a*) *Net profit for the year* This is the net profit brought down from the main profit and loss account.

(*b*) *Balance brought forward from last year* As you will see, all the profits may not be appropriated during a period. This will be the balance on the appropriation account, as brought forward from the previous year. They are usually called **retained profits**.

Debit side

(*c*) *Transfers to reserves* The directors may decide that some of the profits should not be included in the calculation of how much should be paid out as dividends. These profits are transferred to **reserve accounts**. There may be a specific reason for the transfer, such as a need to replace fixed assets; in this case an amount would be transferred to a fixed assets replacement reserve account. Alternatively, the reason may not be specific, and in this case an amount would be transferred to a general reserve account.

(d) *Amounts of goodwill written off* Any amounts written off as goodwill should be shown in the appropriation account and not in the main profit and loss account.

(e) *Amounts of **preliminary expenses** written off* When a company is formed, there are many kinds of expenses concerned with its formation. These include, for example, legal expenses and various government taxes. The amount of preliminary expenses can be written off and charged in the appropriation account.

(f) *Taxation payable on profits* As taxation is not in your syllabus, we will not examine it here.

(g) *Dividends* Out of the remainder of the profits, the directors propose what dividends should be paid.

(h) *Balance carried forward to next year* After the dividends have been proposed, there will probably be some profits that have not been appropriated. These retained profits will be carried forward to the following year.

Exhibit 37.2 shows the profit and loss appropriation account of a new business for its first three years of trading.

Exhibit 37.2
IDO Ltd has a share capital of 40,000 ordinary shares of £1 each and 20,000 5 per cent preference shares of £1 each.

● The net profits for the first three years of business ended 31 December are: 2004 £15,967; 2005 £17,864; 2006 £18,822.
● Transfers to reserves are made as follows: 2004 nil; 2005 general reserve £10,000; 2006, fixed assets replacement reserve £11,500.
● Dividends were proposed for each year on the preference shares and on the ordinary shares at: 2004 10 per cent; 2005 12.5 per cent; 2006 15 per cent.
● In 2006, £750 was written off as goodwill.

Thus we have:

IDO Ltd
Profit and Loss Appropriation Accounts
(1) For the year ended 31 December 2004

	£	£
Net profit b/d		15,967
Less: Appropriations:		
Proposed dividends:		
5% Preference dividend (£20,000 × 5%)	1,000	
Ordinary dividend (£40,000 × 10%)	4,000	5,000
Retained profits carried forward to next year		10,967

(2) For the year ended 31 December 2005

	£	£
Net profit b/d		17,864
Add Retained profits brought forward from last year		10,967
		28,831
Less Appropriations:		
Transfer to general reserve	10,000	
Proposed dividends:		
5% Preference dividend (£20,000 × 5%)	1,000	
Ordinary dividend (£40,000 × 12.5%)	5,000	16,000
Retained profits carried forward to next year		12,831

(3) For the year ended 31 December 2006

	£	£
Net profit b/d		18,822
Add Retained profits brought forward from last year		12,831
		31,653
Less Appropriations:		
Transfer to fixed assets replacement reserve	11,500	
Goodwill written off	750	
Proposed dividends:		
5% Preference dividend (£20,000 × 5%)	1,000	
Ordinary dividend (£40,000 × 15%)	6,000	19,250
Retained profits carried forward to next year		12,403

37.11 The balance sheet

Prior to the Companies Act 1981 in the United Kingdom, a company could, provided it disclosed the necessary information, draw up its balance sheet and profit and loss account for publication in any way that it wished. The 1981 Act, however, stopped such freedom of display, and laid down the precise details to be shown. These have been repeated in the Companies Acts of 1985 and 1989.

As many of the readers of this book will not be sitting UK examinations, they will not have to comply with the UK Companies Acts. We are, therefore, showing two specimen balance sheets containing the same facts:

1 Exhibit 37.3 is for students sitting examinations based on UK laws. The specimen shown does not contain all the possible items that could be shown, as this chapter is an introduction to the topic only. Students are advised to refer to *Business Accounting 1* and *2* for greater insight.
2 Exhibit 37.4 is for students sitting local overseas examinations not based on UK legislation.

Exhibit 37.3 (for students sitting examinations based on UK legislation)

Balance Sheet as at 31 December 2007
Letters in brackets (A) to (F) refer to the notes following the balance sheet

		£	£	£
Fixed assets				
Intangible assets	(A)			
Goodwill				10,000
Tangible assets	(B)			
Buildings			9,000	
Machinery			5,600	
Motor vehicles			2,400	17,000
				27,000
Current assets				
Stock		6,000		
Debtors		3,000		
Bank		4,000	13,000	
Creditors: Amounts falling due within one year	(C)			
Proposed dividend		1,000		
Creditors		5,000	6,000	
Net current assets	(D)			7,000
Total assets less current liabilities				34,000
Creditors: amounts falling due after more than one year	(E)			
Debenture loans				8,000
				26,000
Capital and reserves				
Called-up share capital	(F)			20,000
Other reserves				
General reserve				5,000
Profit and loss account				1,000
				26,000

Notes:

(A) Intangible assets are those not having a 'physical' existence; for instance, you can see and touch tangible assets under (B), i.e. buildings, machinery etc., but you cannot see and touch goodwill.

(B) Tangible fixed assets under a separate heading. Notice that figures are shown net of depreciation. In a note accompanying the accounts, the cost and depreciation on these assets would be given.

(C) Only items payable within one year go under this heading.

(D) The term 'net current assets' replaces the more familiar term of 'working capital'.

(E) These particular debentures are repayable several years hence. If they had been payable within one year, they would have been shown under (C).

(F) An analysis of share capital will be given in supplementary notes to the balance sheet.

Exhibit 37.4 **(for local overseas examinations)**

Balance Sheet as at 31 December 2007

		Cost	Depreciation to date (b)	Net
Fixed assets	(a)	£	£	£
Goodwill		15,000	5,000	10,000
Buildings		15,000	6,000	9,000
Machinery		8,000	2,400	5,600
Motor vehicles		4,000	1,600	2,400
		42,000	15,000	27,000
Current assets				
Stock			6,000	
Debtors			3,000	
Bank			4,000	
			13,000	
Less Current liabilities				
Proposed dividend		1,000		
Creditors		5,000	6,000	
Net current assets				7,000
				34,000
Debentures				
Six per cent debentures: repayable 2010				8,000
				26,000
Financed by:				
Share capital				
Authorised 30,000 shares of £1 each	(c)			30,000
Issued 20,000 ordinary shares of £1 each, fully paid	(d)			20,000
Reserves	(e)			
General reserve			5,000	
Profit and loss account			1,000	
				6,000
	(f)			26,000

Notes:

(a) Fixed assets should normally be shown either at cost or, alternatively, at some other valuation. In either case, the method chosen should be clearly stated.

(b) The total depreciation from date of purchase to the date of the balance sheet should be shown.

(c) The authorised share capital, where it is different from the issued share capital, is shown as a note.

(d) Where shares are only partly called up, then it is the amount actually called up that appears in the balance sheet and not the full amount.

(e) Reserves consist either of those unused profits remaining in the appropriation account, or those transferred to a reserve account appropriately title e.g. general reserve, fixed assets replacement reserve. At this point, all that needs to be said is that any account labelled as a reserve has originated by being charged as a debit in the appropriation account and credited to a reserve account with an appropriate title. These reserves are shown in the balance sheet after share capital under the heading of 'Reserves'.

(f) The share capital and reserves should be totalled so as to show the book value of all the shares in the company. Either the term 'shareholders' funds' or 'members' equity' is often given to the total of share capital plus reserves.

37.12   Investments

Where a company buys shares in another company as an investment, the investment is shown as an asset in the balance sheet. It is shown as a separate item in the accounts between the fixed assets and the current assets.

The market value of such investments is shown in the balance sheet as a note in brackets, e.g.

Balance Sheet (Extracts)

	£
Investments at cost (market value £10,000)	7,500

In the above case, the market value is above cost. If the market value falls below cost, then the difference is written off to the debit of the profit and loss appropriation account, so that the balance sheet will then show the investment at the written-down figure.

37.13   Revaluation of land and buildings

When there is a surplus on revaluation, the value of land and buildings in the balance sheet is shown at the higher figure. The amount of surplus cannot be used for the payment of cash dividends and is therefore shown as an addition to reserves in the balance sheet. It must be described as, for example, 'surplus on revaluation of land and buildings'.

37.14   Loan capital

The term **loan capital** includes money owing on debentures, and loans from banks and other sources not repayable in the near future.

37.15   A fully worked example of the financial statements

Two examples of a limited company's financial statements are now shown as Exhibits 37.5 and 37.6. They contain most types of accounts that will be found in a company final accounts. Exhibit 37.6 contains a more complicated example including preference shares and debentures.

Exhibit 37.5

The following trial balance is extracted from the books of an imaginary company called Ashford Ltd as at 31 December 2006:

Ashford Ltd
Trial Balance as at 31 December 2006

	Dr £	Cr £
Ordinary share capital		150,000
Premises at cost	97,500	
Equipment at cost	82,500	
Provision for depreciation on equipment as at 31.12.05		23,700
Purchases	302,547	
Sales		475,215
Wages and salaries	61,310	
Directors' remuneration	20,000	
General expenses	48,252	
Rates and insurance	6,450	
Electricity	2,324	
Bad debts	1,122	
Provision for doubtful debts 31.12.05		1,291
Debtors	32,676	
Creditors		26,240
Stock as at 1.1.06	38,534	
Bank	34,651	
Profit and loss account unappropriated profits as at 31.12.05		51,420
	727,866	727,866

The following adjustments are needed:

(i) The authorised and issued share capital is divided into 150,000 shares of £1 each.
(ii) Stock in trade at 31 December 2006 is valued at £43,713.
(iii) Wages and salaries due at 31 December 2006 amount to £872.
(iv) Rates and insurance paid in advance at 31 December 2006 amount to £450.
(v) A dividend of 10% is proposed for 2006 on the ordinary shares.
(vi) The provision for doubtful debts is to be increased to £1,407.
(vii) A depreciation charge is to be made on equipment at the rate of 10 per cent per annum on cost.
(viii) Transfer £10,000 to a general reserve account.

The financial statements will now be shown using a vertical form. The profit and loss account will be suitable for both those sitting UK examinations, and those sitting local overseas examinations; the balance sheets will be shown separately for both kinds of students.

Ashford Ltd
Trading and Profit and Loss and Appropriation Account
for the year ended 31 December 2006
(suitable for both UK and overseas examinations)

		£	£
Sales			475,215
Less Cost of goods sold:			
Opening stock		38,534	
Add Purchases		302,547	
		341,081	
Less Closing stock		43,713	297,368
Gross profit			177,847
Less Expenses:			
Salaries and wages (61,310 + 872)		62,182	
Directors' remuneration	(A)	20,000	
General expenses		48,252	
Rates and insurance (6,450 − 450)		6,000	
Electricity		2,324	
Bad debts		1,122	
Increase in provision for doubtful debts (1,407 − 1,291)		116	
Depreciation: Equipment		8,250	148,246
Net profit			29,601
Add Unappropriated profits brought forward from last year			51,420
			81,021
Less Appropriations:			
Transfer to general reserve		10,000	
Ordinary share dividends (10% of 150,000)	(B)	15,000	25,000
Unappropriated profits carried forward to next year			56,021

Notes:
(A) Directors' remuneration is shown as an expense in the profit and loss account.
(B) The dividend of 10 per cent is based on the issued ordinary share capital.

Ashford Ltd
Balance Sheet as at 31 December 2006
(based on UK legislation)

Fixed assets		£	£	£
Tangible assets	(A)			
Premises			97,500	
Equipment			50,550	148,050
Current assets				
Stock		43,713		
Debtors		31,719		
Bank		34,651	110,083	
Creditors: Amounts falling due within one year				
Creditors		27,112		
Proposed dividend		15,000	42,112	
Net current assets				67,971
Total assets less current liabilities				216,021

		£	£	£
Capital and reserves	(B)			
Called-up share capital				150,000
Reserves:				
General reserve			10,000	
Profit and loss account			56,021	66,021
				216,021

Notes:

(A) Notes to be given in an appendix as to cost, acquisitions and sales in the year and depreciation.

(B) 'Reserves' consist either of those unused profits remaining in the appropriation account, or those transferred to a reserve account appropriately titled (e.g. general reserve, fixed assets replacement reserve).

Ashford Ltd
Balance Sheet as at 31 December 2006
(for students sitting local overseas examinations)

	Cost	Depreciation to date	Net Book Value
Fixed assets	£	£	£
Premises	97,500		97,500
Equipment	82,500	31,950	50,550
	180,000	31,950	148,050
Current assets			
Stock	43,713		
Debtors	31,719		
Bank	34,651	110,083	
Less Current Liabilities			
Creditors	27,112		
Dividends owing	15,000	42,112	
Net current assets			67,971
			216,021

	Authorised	Issued	
Financed by:			
Share Capital	£	£	£
Ordinary shares	150,000	150,000	150,000
Reserves			
General Reserve		10,000	
Profit and Loss		56,021	66,021
			216,021

A more complicated worked example including preference shares, debentures and share premium account follows in Exhibit 37.6.

Exhibit 37.6

The following trial balance was extracted from the books of an imaginary company called Dyson Ltd as on 31 December 2005:

Dyson Ltd
Trial Balance as at 31 December 2005

	Dr £	Cr £
8% Preference share capital		35,000
Ordinary share capital		125,000
10% Debentures (repayable 2010)		20,000
Share premium		21,000
Profit and loss account 31.12.04		13,874
Equipment at cost	122,500	
Motor vehicles at cost	99,750	
Provision for depreciation: Equipment 1.1.05		29,400
Provision for depreciation: Motor vehicles 1.1.05		36,225
Stock 1.1.05	136,132	
Sales		418,250
Purchases	232,225	
Returns inwards	4,025	
General expenses	1,240	
Salaries and wages	46,260	
Directors' remuneration	18,750	
Rent, rates and insurance	18,095	
Motor expenses	4,361	
Debenture interest	1,000	
Bank	12,751	
Cash	630	
Debtors	94,115	
Creditors		93,085
	791,834	791,834

The following adjustments are needed:

(i)   Stock at 31.12.05 was £122,000.
(ii) Accrue rent £2,000.
(iii) Accrue debenture interest £1,000.
(iv) Depreciate the equipment at 10 per cent on cost and motor vehicles at 20 per cent on cost.
(v)   Transfer to general reserve £5,000.
(vi) It is proposed to pay the 8 per cent preference dividend and a 10 per cent dividend on the ordinary shares.
(vii) Authorised share capital is £35,000 in preference shares and £200,000 in £1 ordinary shares.

Dyson Ltd
Trading and Profit and Loss and Appropriation Account
for the year ended 31 December 2005
(suitable for both UK and overseas examinations)

		£	£
Sales			418,250
Less Returns inwards			4,025
			414,225
Less Cost of goods sold:			
Opening stock		136,132	
Add Purchases		232,225	
		368,357	
Less Closing stock		122,000	246,357
Gross profit			167,868
Less Expenses:			
Salaries and wages		46,260	
Rent, rates and insurance (18,095 + 2,000)		20,095	
Motor expenses		4,361	
General expenses		1,240	
Directors' remuneration	(A)	18,750	
Debenture interest (1,000 + 1,000)	(B)	2,000	
Depreciation:			
Equipment (10% × 122,500)		12,250	
Motor vehicles (20% × 99,750)		19,950	124,906
Net profit			42,962
Add Unappropriated profit brought forward from			
last year			13,874
			56,836
Less Appropriations			
Transfer to general reserve		5,000	
Preference share dividend (8% × 35,000)		2,800	
Ordinary share dividend (10% × 125,000)	(C)	12,500	20,300
Unappropriated profits carried forward to next year			36,536

Notes:

(A) Directors' remuneration is shown as an expense in the profit and loss account.

(B) Debenture interest is an expense to be shown in the profit and loss account.

(C) The final dividend of 10 per cent is based on the issued ordinary share capital and *not* on the author- ised ordinary share capital.

Dyson Ltd
Balance Sheet as at 31 December 2005
(based on UK legislation)

		£	£	£
Fixed assets				
Tangible assets	(A)			
Equipment			80,850	
Motor vehicles			43,575	124,425
Current assets				
Stock		122,000		
Debtors		94,115		
Bank		12,751		
Cash		630	229,496	
Creditors: Amounts falling due within one year				
Creditors (93,085 + 2,000)		95,085		
Proposed dividends: Preference shares		2,800		
Ordinary shares		12,500		
Debenture interest due		1,000	111,385	
Net current assets				118,111
				242,536
Creditors: Amounts falling due after more than one year				
10% Debentures				20,000
				222,536
Capital and reserves				
Called-up share capital				160,000
Share premium	(B)			21,000
General reserve				5,000
Profit and loss account				36,536
				222,536

Notes:

(A) Notes to be given in an appendix as to cost, acquisitions and sales in the year and depreciation.

(B) One reserve that is in fact not labelled with the word 'reserve' in its title is the **share premium account**. For various reasons (fully discussed in *Business Accounting 2*) shares can be issued for more than their face or nominal value. The excess of the price at which they are issued over the nominal value of the shares is credited to a share premium account. This is then shown with the other reserves in the balance sheet.

(C) 'Reserves' consist either of those unused profits remaining in the appropriation account, or those transferred to a reserve account appropriately titled (e.g. general reserve, fixed assets replacement reserve).

Dyson Ltd
Balance Sheet as at 31 December 2005
(for students sitting local overseas examinations)

	Cost	Dep'n to date	Net Book Value
	£	£	£
Fixed assets			
Equipment	122,500	41,650	80,850
Motor vehicles	99,750	56,175	43,575
	222,250	97,825	124,425
Current assets			
Stock	122,000		
Debtors	94,115		
Bank	12,751		
Cash	630	229,496	
Less Current liabilities			
Creditors (93,085 + 2,000)	95,085		
Dividends owing	15,300		
Debenture interest owing	1,000	111,385	
Net current assets			118,111
			242,536
Loan capital			
10% Debentures			20,000
			222,536

Financed by:	Authorised	Issued	
Share capital	£	£	£
Preference shares	35,000	35,000	
Ordinary shares	200,000	125,000	160,000
	235,000		
Reserves			
Share premium		21,000	
General reserve		5,000	
Profit and loss		36,536	62,536
			222,536

Chapter summary

- When more than one person wishes to own and run a business they can form either a partnership or limited company. The advantage of forming a limited company is the owners of the company have 'limited liability'. This means that the liability of the shareholders in a company is limited to any amount they have agreed to invest and their personal assets are safe if the company gets into financial difficulties.
- A public company is one that can issue its shares publicly and there is no maximun number of shareholders. It must also have an authorised capital of at least £50,000. A private company must issue its shares privately and can have an authorised capital of less than £50,000.
- Limited companies are a separate legal entity to the shareholders and as such it can sue and be sued in its own name.

- Companies hold an annual general meeting once a year at which the financial statements and annual report are submitted for approval by the shareholders who have a right to attend and vote at the meeting. Shareholders vote to appoint the directors who manage the business on behalf of the shareholders.
- Authorised share capital is the total amount of share capital or number of shares the company would be allowed to issue.
- Issued share capital is the amount of share capital actually issued to shareholders.
- There are two main types of shares: (1) preference shares – here the shareholders get an agreed percentage rate of dividend before the ordinary shareholders receive anything; (2) ordinary shares – the shareholders are entitled to a dividend after the preference shareholders have been paid their dividends. The amount they receive fluctuates depending on the profits available.
- A debenture is a loan to the company upon which a fixed rate of interest is paid annually. The interest must be paid even if the company makes a loss. Debentures are often secured on the assets of the business.
- The financial statements for a limited company consist of a trading and profit and loss account, which includes an appropriation section, and a balance sheet.
- Both debenture interest and directors' remuneration must be charged to the profit and loss account.
- Any unappropriated profits are carried forward to the next accounting period and must also be shown in the balance sheet. (Note: these can sometimes be referred to as 'retained profits' and 'profit and loss account balance'.)
- Reserve accounts contain appropriated profits that have been transferred for use in future years.
- Share premium is another class of reserve that arises when shares are issued above the face or nominal value. The extra amount received above the nominal value is credited to the share premium account.

Exercises

37.1   Draw up a balance sheet for LMT Ltd from the following as at 31 December 2004:

	£
Premises at cost	45,000
Machinery at cost	24,000
Fixtures at cost	12,000
Stock	18,000
Bank	6,000
Debtors	9,000
Depreciation to date:	
Premises	18,000
Machinery	7,200
Fixtures	4,800
Authorised share capital: Ordinary shares £1	60,000
Issued share capital: Fully paid	36,000
Debentures: 10 per cent	18,000
Proposed dividend owing	3,000
Creditors	9,000
General reserve	15,000
Profit and loss account (balancing figure, for you to ascertain)	?

37.2X C Blake Ltd has an authorised share capital of 90,000 ordinary shares of £1 each and 10,000 10 per cent preference shares of £1 each. The company's trial balance, extracted after one year of trading, was as follows on 31 December 2004:

	£
Net profit for the year to 31 December 2004	11,340
Debentures	30,000
Issued ordinary share capital, fully paid	60,000
Issued preference share capital, fully paid	10,000
Creditors	3,550
Debtors	4,120
Cash	2,160
Stock	8,800
Provision for doubtful debts	350
Provision for depreciation: Equipment	4,500
Equipment at cost	45,000
Premises at cost	50,000
Bank (use the balancing figure)	?

The directors decide to transfer £1,500 to the general reserve and to recommend a dividend of 12½ per cent on the ordinary shares. The preference dividend was not paid until after January 2005.

You are required to:
(a) draw up the appropriation account for the year ended 31 December 2004
(b) draft a balance sheet as at 31 December 2004.

37.3 CA Company Ltd, manufacturing agricultural implements, made a net profit of £210,000 for the year to 31 December 2006. Retained profits at 31 December 2005 amounted to £17,000. At the directors' meeting, the following appropriations were agreed:

	£
● to be transferred to general reserve:	30,000
● to be transferred to foreign exchange reserve:	16,000

It had also been agreed that a dividend of 10 per cent be proposed on the ordinary share capital. This amounted to 500,000 shares of £2 each. Preference share dividends of 10 per cent have been paid during the year on 250,000 preference shares of £1 each.

You are required to draw up the company's profit and loss appropriation account for the year ended 31 December 2006.

37.4 The trial balance extracted from the books of Chang Ltd at 31 December 2004 was as follows:

	£	£
Share capital		100,000
Unappropriated profits brought forward from last year		34,280
Freehold premises at cost	65,000	
Machinery at cost	55,000	
Provision for depreciation on machinery account as at 31 December 2003		15,800
Purchases	201,698	
Sales		316,810
General expenses	32,168	
Wages and salaries	54,207	
Rent	4,300	
Lighting expenses	1,549	
Bad debts	748	
Provision for doubtful debts as at 31 December 2003		861
Debtors	21,784	
Creditors		17,493
Stock in trade as at 31 December 2003	25,689	
Bank balance	23,101	
	485,244	485,244

You are given the following additional information:

(i) The authorised and issued share capital is divided into 100,000 shares of £1 each.
(ii) Stock in trade as at 31 December 2004 was £29,142.
(iii) Wages and salaries due at 31 December 2004 amounted to £581.
(iv) Rent paid in advance at 31 December 2004 amounted to £300.
(v) A dividend of £10,000 is proposed for 2004.
(vi) The provision for doubtful debts is to be increased to £938.
(vii) A depreciation charge is to be made on machinery at the rate of 10 per cent per annum at cost.

Required:
Draw up a trading and profit and loss account for the year ended 31 December 2004 and a balance sheet as at 31 December 2004.

37.5X On 30 September 2007, Reynolds Ltd had an authorised capital of £250,000, divided into 200,000 ordinary shares of £1 each and 50,000 7 per cent preference shares of £1 each. All the preference shares were issued and fully paid, while 150,000 of the ordinary shares were issued and fully paid. The company also had a balance on the general reserve account of £45,000 and a balance brought forward on the profit and loss account of £30,000.

During the year ended 30 September 2008, the company made a net profit of £70,000, out of which a transfer of £8,000 was made to the general reserve account. The directors had paid an interim dividend of 6p per share on the ordinary share capital and now propose to pay the preference dividend and a final dividend of 14p per share on the ordinary share capital.

From the information given above you are required to prepare for Reynolds Ltd:

(a) a profit and loss appropriation account for the year ended 30 September 2008
(b) the capital and reserves section of the balance sheet as at 30 September 2008.

37.6 Jaspa West Ltd has an authorised share capital of £300,000, divided into 200,000 ordinary shares of £1 each and 100,000 8 per cent preference shares of £1 each. The following balances remained in the accounts of the company after the preparation of the trading and profit and loss account for the year ended 31 December 2006:

	Dr	Cr
	£	£
Premises at cost	270,600	
Bank balance		21,400
Heating and lighting	3,800	
Provision for depreciation on machinery		18,400
Machinery at cost	72,600	
Preference share capital: fully paid		80,000
Ordinary share capital: fully paid		150,000
Profit and loss account balance: 1 January 2006		92,000
Debtors and creditors	80,000	37,000
Stock	56,000	
Wages and salaries		4,200
Net profit (for the year ended 31 December 2006)		80,000
	483,000	483,000

The directors have recommended:

- the creation of a general reserve, amounting to 40 per cent of the year's net profit
- an ordinary dividend of 4 per cent
- payment of the year's preference dividend.

You are required to:
(a) prepare the profit and loss appropriation account for the year ended 31 December 2006
(b) prepare the balance sheet as at 31 December 2006.

City & Guilds Pitman qualifications

37.7X Cityjag plc has an authorised capital of 500,000 £1 ordinary shares and 250,000 £1 (9 per cent) preference shares. The following balances remained in the books after the profit and loss account has been prepared for the year ended 31 December 2008:

	Dr	Cr
	£	£
140,000 £1 ordinary shares		140,000
90,000 £1 (9 per cent) Preference shares		90,000
Profit and loss account balance 1 January 2008		10,000
Premises at cost	180,000	
Motor vehicles at cost	90,200	
Fixtures and fittings at cost	45,000	
Provision for depreciation on motor vehicles		30,200
Provision for depreciation on fixtures and fittings		25,000
Trade debtors and trade creditors	7,700	9,000
Bank	8,500	
Expenses prepaid and owing	2,000	1,000
Stock at 31 December 2008	21,800	
General reserve		10,000
Net trading profit for the year ended 31 December 2008		40,000
	355,200	355,200

The directors of Cityjag plc have decided to transfer £20,000 to the general reserve; to recommend payment of the preference share dividend; and to recommend a dividend of 11 per cent on ordinary shares.

From the information given, you are required to prepare for Cityjag plc

(a) a profit and loss appropriation account for the year ended 31 December 2008

(b) a balance sheet as at 31 December 2008.

NEAB (GCSE)

37.8X Vivex plc's financial year ended on 31 March 2004. On this date the following balances remained in the company's books after the preparation of the profit and loss account.

	£,000
Fixed assets at net book value	9,600
Rent receivable due	60
Issued capital, £1 ordinary shares fully paid	7,000
Provision for doubtful debts	35
Trade debtors	695
Debenture interest due	40
Debentures (10 per cent)	800
Expenses prepaid	30
Share premium	1,200
Profit and loss account balance, 1 April 2003	386
Trade creditors	374
General reserve, 1 April 2003	500
Bank overdraft	76
Stock	823
Net profit for year	797

On 31 March 2004 the directors agreed that there should be a transfer of £300,000 to the general reserve. They proposed that shareholders should receive a dividend of 7.5p per share.

Tasks:

(a) Prepare the company's profit and loss appropriation account for the year ended 31 March 2004.

(b) List the company's current liabilities at 31 March 2004.

(c) Prepare an extract from the company's balance sheet as at 31 March 2004 showing issued capital, reserves and the total of the shareholders' funds.

The directors of the company are concerned because the return on capital employed has been declining during recent years.

(d) Advise the directors of *two* ways in which the return on capital employed could be improved.

Southern Examining Group AQA

Please note that this question is NOT from the live examinations for the current specification.

CHAPTER 38

Analysis and interpretation of accounts

Learning objectives

After you have studied this chapter you should be able to:
- understand the difference between mark-up and margin
- use accounting ratios to calculate missing figures in financial statements
- appreciate the importance of analysing financial statements for the benefit of internal and external parties
- calculate and analyse ratios on profitability, liquidity and efficiency to assess a businesses performance
- understand the term 'capital employed'
- appreciate and understand the importance of working capital.

38.1 Introduction

It has been noted in Chapter 33 that sole traders and small businesses may not use a full double entry system. It is more likely that they would enter details of a transaction only once, using a single entry system; they may also fail to record every transaction, resulting in incomplete records. The ratios, margin and mark-up can be used to calculate missing figures from incomplete records and to show the relationship between profit and selling price, and profit and cost price, respectively.

38.2 Mark-up and margin

The purchase cost, gross profit and selling price of goods or services may be shown as:

Cost price + Gross profit = Selling price

The gross profit when shown as a fraction or percentage of the **cost price** is known as the **mark-up**. The gross profit when shown as a fraction or percentage of the **selling price** is known as the **margin**.

The mark-up and margins can now be calculated using this example:

Cost price + Gross profit = Selling price

£4 + £1 = £5

Mark-up $= \dfrac{\text{Gross profit}}{\text{Cost price}}$ as a fraction, or if required as a percentage, multiply by 100:

$$£\frac{1}{4} = \frac{1}{4}, \text{ or } \frac{1}{4} \times 100 = 25 \text{ per cent}$$

Margin $= \dfrac{\text{Gross profit}}{\text{Selling price}}$ as a fraction, or if required as a percentage, multiply by 100:

$$£\frac{1}{5} = \frac{1}{5}, \text{ or } \frac{1}{5} \times 100 = 20 \text{ per cent}$$

Author's hint

Students often confuse the relationship between the selling price and profit (margin) and cost price and profit (mark-up). This can easily be remembered using the mnemonic 'Mrs Muc', as shown in Exhibit 38.1.

Exhibit 38.1

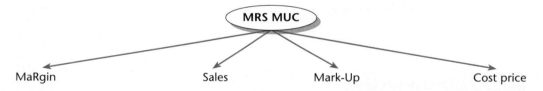

MaRgin   Sales   Mark-Up   Cost price

38.3 Calculating missing figures

We can use the ratios given in Section 38.2 to complete trading accounts where some of the figures are missing. For ease of illustrating this fact, all examples in this chapter:

● assume that all the goods in a firm have the same rate of mark-up
● ignore wastages and theft of goods.

Example 1: The following figures apply for the year 2006:

	£
Stock 1.1.2006	400
Stock 31.12.2006	600
Purchases	5,200

A uniform rate of mark-up of 20 per cent is applied.

Required: Find the gross profit and the sales figure.

Trading Account for the year ended 31 December 2006

	£	£
Sales		?
Less Cost of goods sold		
Stock 1.1.2006	400	
Add Purchases	5,200	
	5,600	
Less Stock 31.12.2006	600	
		5,000
Gross profit		?

Answer:

It is known that: Cost of goods sold + Gross profit = Sales

and you know that you can use
mark-up to find profit, because: Cost of goods sold + % mark-up = Sales

So: £5,000   +   20%   = Sales

So sales =   £5,000   +   £1,000   = £6,000

The trading account can now be completed as shown below:

Trading Account for the year ended 31 December 2006

	£	£
Sales		6,000
Less Cost of goods sold		
Stock 1.1.2006	400	
Add Purchases	5,200	
	5,600	
Less Stock 31.12.2006	600	5,000
Gross Profit		6,000

Example 2: Another firm has the following figures for 2005:

	£
Stock 1.1.2005	500
Stock 31.12.2005	800
Sales	6,400

A uniform rate of margin of 25 per cent is in use.

Required: Find the gross profit and the figure of purchases.

Trading Account for the year ended 31 December 2005

	£	£
Sales		6,400
Less Cost of goods sold		
Stock 1.1.2005	500	
Add Purchases	?	
	?	
Less Stock 31.12.2005	800	?
Gross profit		?

Answer:

$$\text{Cost of goods sold} + \text{Gross profit} = \text{Sales}$$

Rearranging items:

Sales	– Gross profit = Cost of goods sold
Sales	– 25% Margin = Cost of goods sold
£6,400	– £1,600 (25% × £6,000) = £4,800

Now the following figures are known:

	£	£
Cost of goods sold:		
Stock 1.1.2005	500	
Add Purchases (A)	?	
(B)	?	
Less Stock 31.12.2005	800	
		4,800

The two missing figures are found by normal arithmetical deduction:

(B) *less* £800	= £4,800
Therefore (B)	= £5,600

So that:

£500 opening stock + (A)	= £5,600
Therefore (A)	= £5,100

The completed trading account can now be shown:

Trading Account for the year ended 31 December 2005

	£	£
Sales		6,400
Less Cost of goods sold		
Stock 1.1.2005	500	
Add Purchases	5,100	
	5,600	
Less Stock 31.12.2005	800	4,800
Gross profit		1,600

This technique is found very useful by retail stores when estimating the amount to be bought if a certain sales target is to be achieved. Alternatively, stock levels or sales figures can be estimated given information as to purchases and opening stock figures.

38.4 The relationship between mark-up and margin

As both of these figures refer to the same profit but are expressed as a fraction or a percentage of different figures, there is a relationship between them. If one is known as a fraction, the other can soon be found.

If the mark-up is known, in order to find the margin you need to take the same numerator to be the numerator of the margin. Then, for the denominator of the margin, take the total of the mark-up's denominator *plus* the numerator. An example can now be shown:

Mark-up	Margin
$\dfrac{1}{4}$	$\dfrac{1}{4+1} = \dfrac{1}{5}$
$\dfrac{2}{11}$	$\dfrac{2}{11+2} = \dfrac{2}{13}$

If the margin is known, to find the mark-up take the same numerator to be the numerator of the mark-up. Then, for the denominator of the mark-up, take the figure of the margin's denominator *less* the numerator:

Margin	Mark-up
$\dfrac{1}{6}$	$\dfrac{1}{6-1} = \dfrac{1}{5}$
$\dfrac{3}{13}$	$\dfrac{3}{13-3} = \dfrac{3}{10}$

38.5 Interpretation of accounts

The whole purpose of recording and classifying financial information about a firm, and communicating this to the owners and managers in the form of the financial statements, is to assess the performance of the business. The information contained in the financial statements can be used to evaluate various aspects of the company by the use of accounting ratios.

For the ratios to be a reliable guide to performance, two criteria need to be applied:

● The financial statements used for calculating the current ratios must be *up to date.*
● Each ratio must be *compared* with the same ratio from the previous year's accounts or with those from a competitor's accounts.

The concept of comparison is crucial, since this identifies trends in the business and allows action to be taken.

The analysis of a business using accounting ratios is widely practised by both internal and external parties and the main ones are listed in Exhibit 38.2.

Exhibit 38.2

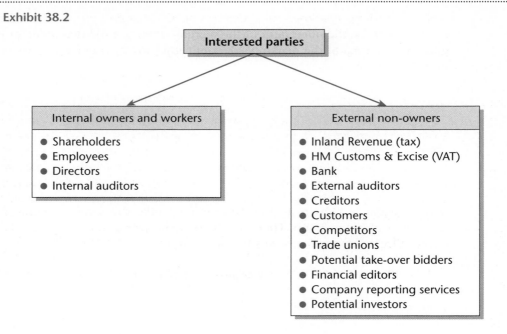

38.6 Profitability and liquidity

The two most important factors in the running of a business are, first, to see that it operates at a profit and, second, to organise it so that it can pay its creditors and expenses at the correct times. If either of these points is not covered effectively, it could mean that the business might have to be closed down.

The ability to pay one's debts as they fall due is known as having **liquidity**. The ability to make a profit is known as **profitability**, and the ratios commonly used to give valuable information on a business's performance are known as **profitability ratios**.

We will now consider the profitability ratios followed by the liquidity ratios.

38.7 Profitability ratios

The main ratios used to examine profitability are:

1 **Gross profit : sales ratio**
2 **Net profit : sales ratio**
3 **Expenses : sales ratio**
4 **Return on capital employed (ROCE) ratio**
5 **Stock turnover ratio.**

Each is examined in turn in the sections following.

1 Gross profit to sales ratio

This ratio is calculated as follows:

$$\frac{\text{Gross profit}}{\text{Sales}}$$

Normally, this is referred to as a percentage and is calculated thus:

$$\text{Gross profit as a percentage of sales} = \frac{\text{Gross profit}}{\text{Sales}} \times 100$$

The figures of sales and gross profit are found in the trading account. If the gross profit/sales percentage was 20 per cent, this would mean that for every £100 of sales, £20 gross profit was made before any expenses were paid.

This ratio measures how effectively a company has controlled its cost of goods and sold them at the right price to give maximum gross profit. If, however, there has been a change in this ratio from one period to another it may be attributed to one or more of the following:

● Cost of goods may have increased resulting in lower gross profit.
● Selling price of goods may have been reduced in order to sell more but targets have not been met. Alternatively, selling price could have been increased and less goods sold.
● Wastage or theft of goods.

2 Net profit to sales ratio

This ratio is calculated as follows:

$$\frac{\text{Net profit}}{\text{Sales}}$$

Normally, this is referred to as a percentage and is calculated thus:

$$\text{Net profit as a percentage of sales} = \frac{\text{Net profit}}{\text{Sales}} \times 100$$

Again the figure of sales can be found in the trading account whilst the net profit can be obtained from the profit and loss account. The net profit/sales percentage takes into account the expenses incurred and shows the amount of profit remaining. Changes in this ratio may be attributed to:

● the gross profit/sales percentage changing and/or
● the expenses changing.

Expenses need to be minimised to ensure a reasonable net profit is made.

3 Expenses to sales ratio

This ratio is calculated as follows:

$$\frac{\text{Expenses}}{\text{Sales}}$$

Normally, this is referred to as a percentage and is calculated as follows:

$$\text{Expenses as a percentage of sales} = \frac{\text{Expenses}}{\text{Sales}} \times 100$$

It is useful to compare the expenses/sales percentage with the previous results. If an increase was evident this would indicate an increase in the expenses of the business and would require further investigation by management. If the result remained stable or in fact had reduced this would indicate that expenses incurred in running the business had been carefully monitored.

4 Return on capital employed ratio (ROCE)

This ratio is calculated as follows:

$$\frac{\text{Net profit}}{\text{Capital employed}}$$

Normally, this is referred to as a percentage and is calculated as follows:

$$\text{Return of capital employed} = \frac{\text{Net profit}}{\text{Capital employed}} \times 100$$

It shows (as a percentage) the net profit made for each £100 of capital employed. The higher the ratio, the more profitable the firm. This is the most important ratio of all.

There has never been an agreed definition of the term 'capital employed'. Very often it has been taken to mean the average capital. For this, the opening capital for the period is added to the closing capital and then the total is divided by two. In an examination, use the method stated by the examiner. If you are given only the closing capital, use the closing capital figure.

In the following example, two businesses of sole traders (A) and (B) have made the same profits, but the capital employed in each case is different. From the balance sheets that follow, the return on capital employed is calculated using the average of the capital account as capital employed.

Balance Sheets	(A) £	(B) £
Fixed Assets + Current Assets − Current Liabilities	10,000	16,000
Capital Accounts:		
Opening balance	8,000	14,000
Add Net profits	3,600	3,600
	11,600	17,600
Less Drawings	1,600	1,600
	10,000	16,000

Return on capital employed is calculated thus for the two firms:

$$\text{(A)} \quad \frac{£3,600}{(£8,000 + £10,000) \div 2} \times 100\% = 40\%$$

$$\text{(B)} \quad \frac{£3,600}{(£14,000 + £16,000) \div 2} \times 100\% = 24\%$$

The ratio illustrates that what is important is not simply how much profit has been made but how well the capital has been employed. Business (A) has made far better use of its capital, achieving a return of £40 net profit for every £100 invested, whereas (B) has received a net profit of only £24 per £100.

In this case, only the accounts of sole traders have been dealt with, so that a straightforward example could be used. In Section 38.9 other meanings of 'capital employed' will be considered, when dealing with:

● sole traders who have received loans to help finance their businesses
● partnerships
● limited companies.

5 Stock turnover ratio

Every business should operate both to keep its stock to as low a figure as possible without losing profitability, and to sell its goods as quickly as possible. The stock turnover ratio measures how well the firm is managing to do these things. Any increase in stocks or slowdown in sales will show a lower ratio.

The ratio is calculated as follows:

$$\frac{\text{Cost of goods sold}}{\text{Average stock}} = \text{Stock turnover ratio}$$

If only the opening and closing stocks are known, the average stock is found by adding these two figures and dividing them by two (i.e. averaging them). That is the usual situation in examinations.

The higher this ratio, the more profitable the firm. Take the example of a product on which £5 gross profit is made on sales per unit. With stock turnover of 6 for this item, the firm would make a gross profit of $6 \times £5 = £30$. If the stock turnover ratio for it increased to 9, then $9 \times £5 = £45$ gross profit would be made.

38.8 Liquidity ratios

A business that has satisfactory liquidity (*see* Section 38.6 above) will have sufficient funds, normally referred to as 'working capital', to pay creditors at the required time. The ability to pay creditors on time is vital to ensure that good business relationships are maintained.

The ratios used to examine liquidity i.e. the **liquidity ratios** are:

1 **Current ratio (working capital ratio)**
2 **Acid test ratio (quick ratio)**
3 **Debtors : sales ratio**
4 **Creditors : purchases ratio.**

Each of the liquidity ratios stated can be compared period by period to see whether that particular aspect of liquidity is getting better or worse. In the case of the current ratio, it was often thought in the past that the ideal ratio should be around 2 : 1 and that, ideally, the acid test ratio should be in the region of 1 : 1 to 1.5 : 1. However, in recent years it has become recognised that such a fixed figure cannot possibly apply to every business, as the types and circumstances of businesses vary so widely.

1 Current ratio (or working capital ratio)

The current ratio measures current assets against current liabilities. It will compare assets that will be turned into cash within the next 12 months with any liabilities that will have to be paid within the same period. The current ratio is thus stated as:

$$\frac{\text{Current assets}}{\text{Current liabilities}}$$

If, therefore, the current assets are £125,000 and the current liabilities are £50,000, the current ratio will be:

$$\frac{£125,000}{£50,000} = 2.5 : 1, \text{ or } 2.5 \text{ times}$$

If the ratio increases by a large amount, the firm may have more current assets than it needs. If the ratio falls by a large amount, then perhaps too little is being kept as current assets.

2 Acid test ratio (or quick ratio)

To determine a further aspect of liquidity, the acid test ratio takes into account only those current assets that are cash or can be changed very quickly into cash. This will normally mean Cash + Bank + Debtors. You can see that this means exactly the same as current assets less stock. The acid test ratio may, therefore, be stated as:

$$\frac{\text{Current assets less stock}}{\text{Current liabilities}}$$

For instance, if the total of current assets is £40,000 and stock is £10,000, and the total of current liabilities is £20,000, then the ratio will be:

$$\frac{£40,000 - £10,000}{£20,000} = 1.5 : 1, \text{ or } 1.5 \text{ times}$$

This ratio shows whether there are enough liquid assets to be able to pay current liabilities quickly. It is dangerous if this ratio is allowed to fall to a very low figure. If suppliers and others cannot be paid on time, supplies to the firm may be reduced or even stopped completely. Eventually, the firm may not have enough stock to be able to sell properly. In that case, it may have to cease business.

3 Debtors to sales ratio

This ratio assesses how long it takes for debtors to pay what they owe. The calculation is made as follows:

$$\frac{\text{Debtors}}{\text{Sales for the year}} \times 12 = \frac{\text{number of months that debtors}}{\text{(on average) take to pay up}}$$

For example:

	(C)	(D)
Sales for the year	£240,000	£180,000
Debtors as per balance sheet	£60,000	£30,000

In firm (C), debtors therefore take three months on average to pay their accounts, calculated from:

$$\frac{£60,000}{£240,000} \times 12 = 3 \text{ months}$$

In firm (D), debtors therefore take two months on average to pay their accounts, given from:

$$\frac{£30,000}{£180,000} \times 12 = 2 \text{ months}$$

If the ratio is required to be shown in days instead of months, the formula should be multiplied by 365 instead of 12. The higher the ratio, the worse a firm is at getting its debtors to pay on time. The lower the ratio, the better it is at managing its debtors.

Firms should make certain that debtors pay their accounts on time. There are two main reasons for this. First, the longer a debt is owed, the more likely it will become a bad debt. Second, any payment of money can be used in the firm as soon as it is received, and so this increases profitability; it can help reduce expenses. For example, it would reduce a bank overdraft and therefore reduce the bank overdraft interest.

4 Creditors to purchases ratio

This ratio shows how long it takes a firm (on average) to pay its suppliers. The calculation is made as follows:

$$\frac{\text{Creditors}}{\text{Purchases for the year}} \times 12 = \frac{\text{Number of months it takes}}{\text{(on average) to pay up suppliers}}$$

For example:

	(E)	(F)
Purchases for the year	£120,000	£90,000
Creditors as per balance sheet	£40,000	£22,500

Firm (E) therefore takes four months' credit on average from its suppliers, i.e.

$$\frac{£40,000}{£120,000} \times 12 = 4 \text{ months}$$

Firm (F) takes on average three months to pay its suppliers, i.e.

$$\frac{£22,500}{£90,000} \times 12 = 3 \text{ months}$$

Taking longer to pay suppliers could be a good thing or a bad thing, depending upon circumstances. If so long is taken to pay that possible discounts are lost, or that suppliers refuse to supply again, then it would be undesirable. On the other hand, paying before it is necessary simply takes money out of the firm early without gaining any benefit.

38.9 Definition of capital employed in various circumstances

In Section 38.7 (4), it was pointed out that there is not one single agreed definition of the term 'capital employed'. In answering an exam question in this area, you must follow the examiner's instructions, if any are given; otherwise, state what basis you have used.

Sole proprietorships

'Capital employed' could mean any of the following:

- closing balance on capital account at the end of a financial period
- average of opening and closing balances on the capital account for the accounting period
- capital balances plus any long-term loans.

Partnerships

'Capital employed' could mean any of the following:

- closing balance on the fluctuating capital accounts at the end of a financial period
- average of opening and closing balances on the fluctuating capital accounts for an accounting period
- total of fixed capital accounts plus total of partners' current accounts at the end of a financial period
- average of opening and closing balances on the partners' capital and current accounts for an accounting period
- any of the above, plus long-term loans to the partnership.

Limited companies

Given the following details, different figures for capital employed may be used.

	£
(a) Ordinary share capital	100,000
(b) Preference share capital	40,000
(c) Total of different types of reserves including balance in profit and loss account	35,000
(d) Debentures	60,000

- To calculate return on ordinary shareholders' funds, it would be (a) £100,000 + (c) £35,000 = £135,000.
- To calculate return on total shareholders' fund, it would be (a) £100,000 + (b) £40,000 + (c) £35,000 = £175,000.
- To calculate return on total capital employed, i.e. including borrowed funds, it would be (a) £100,000 + (b) £40,000 + (c) £35,000 + (d) £60,000 = £235,000.

Any question involving return of capital employed for limited companies should be read very carefully indeed. Use the method suggested by the examiner. If no indication is given, use that of (*a*) + (*c*) above, but you must state what method you have used.

38.10 Definition of working capital

Working capital is the amount by which current assets exceed current liabilities. It is also known as 'net current assets'. (*See* Chapter 9.)

It is vital for businesses to have sufficient working capital to enable them to have funds available to pay everyday running expenses. Working capital tends to circulate through a business, as shown in the diagram in Exhibit 38.3. As it flows, profits are made as stock is sold to debtors; the quicker it is sold, the quicker the business makes profits.

Exhibit 38.3

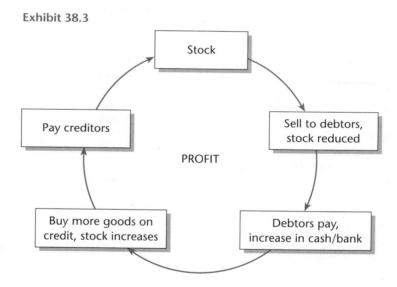

38.11 A fully worked example of calculating ratios

A fully worked example of calculating ratios and interpreting accounts is shown in Exhibit 38.4. Check all the calculations yourself and see whether your conclusions about the changes in the ratios agree with the author's.

Exhibit 38.4

The following are the final accounts for two similar types of retail stores:

Trading and Profit and Loss Accounts

	J £	J £	K £	K £
Sales		80,000		120,000
Less Cost of goods sold:				
Opening stock	25,000		22,500	
Add Purchases	50,000		91,000	
	75,000		113,500	
Less Closing stock	15,000	60,000	17,500	96,000
Gross profit		20,000		24,000
Less Depreciation	1,000		3,000	
Other expenses	9,000	10,000	6,000	9,000
Net profit		10,000		15,000

Balance Sheets

	J £	J £	K £	K £
Fixed Assets				
Equipment at cost	10,000		20,000	
Less Depreciation to date	8,000	2,000	6,000	14,000
Current Assets				
Stock	15,000		17,500	
Debtors	25,000		20,000	
Bank	5,000		2,500	
	45,000		40,000	
Less Current Liabilities				
Creditors	5,000		10,000	
Net current assets		40,000		30,000
		42,000		44,000
Financed by:				
Capital				
Balance at start of year		38,000		36,000
Add Net profit		10,000		15,000
		48,000		51,000
Less Drawings		6,000		7,000
		42,000		44,000

We will now calculate the following ratios (with all calculations shown correct to one decimal place):

(a) Gross profit as a percentage of sales
(b) Net profit as a percentage of sales
(c) Expenses as a percentage of sales
(d) Stock turnover ratio
(e) Rate of return of net profit on capital employed (use the average of the capital account for this purpose)
(f) Current ratio
(g) Quick ratio
(h) Debtors : Sales ratio
(i) Creditors : Purchases ratio

	J	K
(a) Gross profit as a % of sales	$\dfrac{£20,000}{£80,000} \times 100\% = 25\%$	$\dfrac{£24,000}{£120,000} \times 100\% = 20\%$
(b) Net profit as a % of sales	$\dfrac{£10,000}{£80,000} \times 100\% = 12.5\%$	$\dfrac{£15,000}{£120,000} \times 100\% = 12.5\%$
(c) Expenses as a % of sales	$\dfrac{£10,000}{£80,000} \times 100\% = 12.5\%$	$\dfrac{£9,000}{£120,000} \times 100\% = 7.5\%$
(d) Stockturn	$\dfrac{£60,000}{(£25,000 + £15,000) \div 2} = 3 \text{ times}$	$\dfrac{£96,000}{(£22,500 + £17,500) \div 2} = 4.8 \text{ times}$
(e) Rate of return on capital employed	$\dfrac{£10,000}{(£38,000 + £42,000) \div 2} \times 100\% = 25\%$	$\dfrac{£15,000}{(£36,000 + £44,000) \div 2} \times 100\% = 37.5\%$
(f) Current ratio	$\dfrac{£45,000}{£5,000} = 9 : 1$	$\dfrac{£40,000}{£10,000} = 4 : 1$
(g) Quick ratio	$\dfrac{£45,000 - £15,000}{£5,000} = 6 : 1$	$\dfrac{£40,000 - £17,500}{£10,000} = 2.25 : 1$
(h) Debtors : Sales ratio	$\dfrac{£25,000}{£80,000} \times 12 = 3.75 \text{ months}$	$\dfrac{£20,000}{£120,000} \times 12 = 2 \text{ months}$
(i) Creditors : Purchases ratio	$\dfrac{£5,000}{£50,000} \times 12 = 1.2 \text{ months}$	$\dfrac{£10,000}{£91,000} \times 12 = 1.3 \text{ months}$

Having calculated the ratios, we will now attempt briefly to see what we have learned from studying the accounts and the ratios. At this stage in your studies, we would not expect a very long analysis. Instead, you should know what your examiner would expect of you in the examination.

You should not just say that the ratios differ. You should try to see why the ratios are different. Show the examiner that you are looking at the ratios as though they belong to a business for which the ratios mean something. He will not give you any marks for this part of the question if you talk only about the arithmetic of the ratios.

Business K is more profitable, both in terms of actual net profits (£15,000 compared with £10,000), but also in terms of capital employed. K has managed to achieve a return of £37.50 for every £100 invested, i.e. 37.5 per cent. J has managed a lower return of 25 per cent.

The conclusions are only possible reasons because you must know more about the business before you can give a definite answer.

● Possibly K managed to sell far more merchandise because of lower prices, i.e. it took only 20 per cent margin as compared with J's 25 per cent margin.
● Maybe K made more efficient use of mechanised means in the business. Note that it has more equipment, and perhaps as a consequence it kept other expenses down to £6,000 as compared with J's £9,000.

- K did not have as much stock lying idle. K turned over stock 4.8 times in the year, as compared with 3 times for J.
- J's current ratio of 9 : 1 was far greater than normally needed. K kept it down to 4 : 1. J therefore had too much money lying idle.
- The acid test ratio for J was higher than necessary and followed a similar trend to that shown by the current ratio.
- One reason for the better current and acid test ratios for K was that debts were collected on a 2 months' average.
- J also paid creditors more quickly than K – but only slightly faster.

When all these factors are considered, it is clear that business K is being run much more efficiently and, consequently, more profitably.

38.12 Summary of the formulae appearing in this chapter

The formulae for this chapter are summarised in Exhibit 38.5.

Exhibit 38.5

Mark-up $= \dfrac{\text{Profit}}{\text{Cost price}}$ (or if required as a percentage, multiply by 100)

Margin $= \dfrac{\text{Profit}}{\text{Selling price}}$ (or if required as a percentage, multiply by 100)

Gross profit as a percentage of sales $= \dfrac{\text{Gross profit}}{\text{Sales}} \times 100$

Net profit as a percentage of sales $= \dfrac{\text{Net profit}}{\text{Sales}} \times 100$

Expenses as a percentage of sales $= \dfrac{\text{Expenses}}{\text{Sales}} \times 100$

Return on capital employed (ROCE) $= \dfrac{\text{Net profit}}{\text{Capital employed}} \times 100$

Stock turnover $= \dfrac{\text{Cost of goods sold}}{\text{Average stock}}$,

where average stock $= \dfrac{\text{Opening stock + closing stock}}{2}$

Current ratio (working captial ratio) $= \dfrac{\text{Current assets}}{\text{Current liabilities}}$

Acid test ratio (quick ratio) $= \dfrac{\text{Current assets – stock}}{\text{Current liabilities}}$

Debtors : Sales ratio = Number of months debtors (on average) take to pay

$= \dfrac{\text{Debtors}}{\text{Sales for the year}} \times 12$ Times a year

(If days instead of months are required, the formula should be multiplied by 365 instead of 12.)

Creditors : Purchases ratio = Number of months it takes (on average) to pay suppliers

$$= \frac{\text{Creditors}}{\text{Purchases for the year}} \times 12 \text{ Times a year}$$

(If days instead of months are required, the formula should be multiplied by 365 instead of 12.)

38.13 Multiple-choice questions

Now attempt Set No 3 of the multiple-choice questions in Appendix C, which contains 27 questions.

Chapter summary

- Both margin and mark-up are based upon the formula, cost price + gross profit = sales. When the gross profit is shown as a percentage of the cost price this gives us the **mark-up**. If the gross profit is shown as a percentage of the selling price this gives us the **margin**. Remember **Mrs MUC!**
- Mark-up and margin can be used to ascertain missing figures in incomplete records.
- Financial statements are analysed and interpreted for internal and external parties. It is important to remember that a ratio on its own is of no use at all. It must be compared with previous years' results or the results of a competitor to be meaningful.
- Profitability and liquidity are equally important factors when running a business.
- The use of the profitability ratios ensure owners of a business keep a careful check on figures such as cost of goods, sales, expenses, gross and net profits.
- Liquidity ratios measure the ability of a business to pay its debts as they fall due and ensure smooth cash flow.
- Working capital is found by deducting the total current assets from the total current liabilities.
- There are various methods of calculating capital employed depending upon the type of business, i.e. sole trader, partnership or limited company.

Note: In Appendix B you will find a worksheet that you can photocopy and use to answer questions on ratio analysis.

Exercises

38.1 (*a*) If an item costs £20 and is sold for £25, what are the mark-up and margin, expressed as percentages?

(*b*) If the mark-up on a unit is $33\frac{1}{3}$ per cent, what is the margin?

(*c*) If the margin is $16\frac{2}{3}$ per cent, what is the mark-up?

38.2X (*a*) If an item costs £60 and is sold for £90, what are the mark-up and margin, expressed as percentages?

(*b*) If the margin on a unit is 50 per cent, what is the mark-up?

(*c*) If the mark-up is 50 per cent, what is the margin?

38.3 K Young is a trader who marks up the selling price of his goods to 25 per cent above cost. His books give the following information at 31 July 2006:

	£
Stock as at 1 August 2005	4,936
Stock as at 31 July 2006	6,310
Sales for the year	30,000

You are required to create a trading account for Young showing:

(*a*) the cost of goods sold

(*b*) the value of purchases during the year

(*c*) the profit that Young made.

38.4 T Rigby produced from his trial balance as at 31 August 2006 the following information:

	£
Stock as at 1 September 2005	2,000
Purchases for the year	18,000

Rigby has a 'mark-up' of 50 per cent on 'cost of sales'.
His average stock during the year was valued at £4,000.

You are required to:

(*a*) calculate the closing stock for Rigby as at 31 August 2006

(*b*) prepare his trading account for the year ended 31 August 2006

(*c*) ascertain the total amount of expenses that Rigby *must not exceed* if he is to maintain a net profit on sales of 10 per cent.

38.5 The following accounts are of two companies that each sell sports goods:

Trading and Profit and Loss Accounts

	M Ltd		N Ltd	
	£	£	£	£
Sales		360,000		250,000
Less Cost of goods sold:				
Opening stock	120,000		60,000	
Add Purchases	268,000		191,500	
	388,000		251,500	
Less Closing stock	100,000	288,000	64,000	187,500
Gross profit		72,000		62,500
Less Expenses:				
Wages	8,000		11,300	
Directors' remuneration	12,000		13,000	
Other expenses	8,800	28,800	3,200	27,500
Net profit		43,200		35,000
Add Retained profits from last year		16,800		2,000
		60,000		37,000
Less Appropriations:				
General reserve	8,000		2,000	
Dividends	40,000	48,000	30,000	32,000
Retained profits carried to next year		12,000		5,000

Balance Sheets

	M Ltd		N Ltd	
	£	£	£	£
Fixed Assets:				
Fixtures at cost	200,000		180,000	
Less Depreciation to date	50,000	150,000	70,000	110,000
Motor vans at cost	80,000		120,000	
Less Depreciation to date	30,000	50,000	40,000	80,000
		200,000		190,000
Current Assets:				
Stock	100,000		64,000	
Debtors	60,000		62,500	
Bank	40,000		3,500	
	200,000		130,000	
Less Current Liabilities				
Creditors	50,000		65,000	
Net current assets		150,000		65,000
		350,000		255,000
Financed by:				
Issued share capital		300,000		200,000
General reserve		38,000		50,000
Profit and loss		12,000		5,000
		350,000		255,000

Required:

(*a*) Calculate the following ratios to one decimal place:
- (i)   current ratio
- (ii)   acid test ratio
- (iii) stockturn
- (iv)   debtors : sales ratio
- (v)   creditors : purchases ratio
- (vi)   gross profit as a percentage of sales
- (vii) net profit as a percentage of sales
- (viii) rate of return on shareholders' funds.

(*b*) Compare the results of the two companies, giving possible reasons for the different results.

38.6X   The owners of Hailstone company and Taylor company are having a friendly argument over the relative performance of their two similar businesses. The following information is available:

	Hailstone company	Taylor company
	£	£
Cash	4,000	100
Sales	200,000	200,000
Operating expenses	8,000	80,000
Closing stock	8,000	30,000
Debtors	3,000	33,000
Bank overdraft	nil	5,000
Opening stock	10,000	40,000
Capital employed	320,000	320,000
Creditors	7,500	50,000
Purchases	140,000	60,000

Required:

(*a*) For each company, calculate to one decimal place:

    (i)   gross profit margin

    (ii) stock turnover (use cost of goods sold divided by average stock)

    (iii) net profit margin

    (iv) return on capital employed

    (v) debtors collection period

    (vi) current ratio.

(*b*) Comment on the performance of each of the companies, using the ratios you have calculated.

City & Guilds Pitman qualifications

38.7X The following figures are extracted from the final accounts of a company for the year ended 31 December 2008:

	£
Opening stock	5,000
Purchases	32,000
Closing stock	7,000
Sales	60,000
Debtors	7,500

For the year ended 31 December 2008, calculate:

(*a*) cost of goods sold

(*b*) average stock

(*c*) rate of stock turnover

(*d*) debtors collection period.

For the year ended 31 December 2007, the following had been calculated.

- Rate of stock turnover (stockturn)   =   6 times p.a.
- Debtors collection period   =   31 days (1 month)

(*e*) With that additional information in mind, state which you think was the better year out of 2007 and 2008. Give *two* reasons to support your answer.

NEAB (GCSE)

Appendices

The Appendices provide ancillary information to aid understanding of the main narrative of the book. Test questions are also included.

Glossary of accounting terms

The chapter where the term first appears is shown at the end of each definition.

Account	The place in a ledger where all the transactions relating to a particular asset, liability or capital, expenses or revenue item are recorded. Accounts are part of the double entry book-keeping system. They are sometimes referred to as 'T accounts' or ledger accounts. (**3**)
Accounting	A skill or practice of maintaining accounts and preparing reports to aid the financial control and management of a business. (**1**)
Accounting concepts	The rules which lay down the way in which the activities of a business are recorded. (**11**)
Accounting cycle	The period in which a business operates its financial year. It involves recording all trading activities from source documents to the preparation of final accounts. (**24**)
Accounting equation	If a business starts trading it will require resources, expressed as: resources supplied by the owner = resources in the business or capital = assets – liabilities. (**2**)
Accrual	An accrued expense. An amount owing. (**28**)
Accrual concept	Where net profit is the difference between revenues and expenses. (**11**)
Accrued expense	An expense that has been incurred and the benefit received but that has not been paid for at the end of the accounting period. Also referred to as an accrual. (**28**)
Accumulated fund	A form of capital account for a non-profit-making organisation. (**34**)
Acid test ratio	A ratio comparing current assets less stock with current liabilities. Also known as the 'quick ratio'. (**38**)
Advice note	A note sent to a customer by the supplier prior to goods being despatched, advising of the goods to be despatched and the estimated date of delivery. (**19**)
Amortisation	A term used instead of depreciation when assets are used up simply because of the time factor. (**25**)
Analytical day book	Book of original entry in which sales and/or purchase invoices are entered. The book has various analysis columns, which are totalled at the end of the month and posted to the general ledger and control accounts. (**22**)

Annual General Meeting (AGM)	A meeting held every year to which all shareholders in a company are invited to attend. At the meeting, the latest set of final accounts is considered, together with the appointment or removal of directors and/or auditors. (37)
Appreciation	The increase in value over the cost of an asset, usually land and buildings. (25)
Appropriation account	An addition to the Profit and Loss Account of partnerships and companies. The appropriation account shows how profit earned is divided. In a partnership it is divided in accordance with the partnership deed or agreement. With a company it is apportioned to reserve accounts, provision for taxation and distributed as a dividend to the shareholders. (36)
Assets	Resources owned by the business. (2)
Authorised share capital	The total amount of share capital or number of shares which a company can have in issue at any given time. (37)
AVCO	A method by which the goods used are priced out at average cost. (30)
Bad debt	A debt owing to a business which is unlikely to be paid. (27)
Bad debt recovered	A debt, previously written off, that is subsequently paid by the debtor. (27)
Balance sheet	A statement showing the assets, capital and liabilities of a business. (2)
Balancing the account	Finding and entering the difference between the two sides of an account. (6)
Bank cash book	The cash book for other than petty cash. (14) and (17)
Bank giro credit transfers	Method used by businesses to pay creditors, wages and/or salaries. A bank giro credit list and slips containing information about each person or organisation to be paid and the amount payable are sent to the bank, together with one cheque to cover all the payments. The bank then automatically transfers the funds from the business's account to the account of each of the respective people or organisations. (13)
Bank guarantee/debit card	Used by customers when paying by cheque and this tells the seller that a bank or card company guarantees that payment will be made. (13)
Bank overdraft	What results when we have paid more out of our bank account than we have paid into it. (14)
Bank reconciliation statement	A calculation comparing the cash book balance with the bank statement balance. (15)
Bank statement	Copy of our current account given to us by our bank. (14)
Bankers' Automated Clearing Service (BACS)	Computerised payment transfer system that is a very popular way of paying creditors, wages and salaries. (13)
Book-keeping	The recording of accounting data. (1)
Books of original entry	Books where the first entry of a transaction is made. (12)
Business entity concept	Concerning only transactions that affect the firm, and ignoring the owner's private transactions. (11)

485

Called-up capital	Where only part of the amounts payable on each share have been asked for. The total amount requested on all the shares is known as the 'called-up capital'. (**37**)
Calls in arrear	The amount for which payment has been requested (i.e. called for), but has not yet been paid by shareholders. (**37**)
Capital	The total of resources supplied to a business by its owner. (**2**)
Capital employed	This term has many meanings, but basically it means the amount of money that is being used up (or 'employed') in the business. It is the balance of the capital account plus any long-term loan or, alternatively, the total net assets of the business. (**28**)
Capital expenditure	When a firm spends money to buy or add value to a fixed asset. (**18**)
Capital invested	The amount of money, or money's worth, brought into a business by its proprietor from outside. (**28**)
Capital reserve	Reserves which cannot be used for the payment of dividends. The two most common types of capital reserve are the Share Premium Account and Revaluation Reserve Account. (Capital reserves are outside the scope of this book.) (**37**)
Carriage inwards	Cost of transport of goods into a business. (**10**)
Carriage outwards	Cost of transport of goods to the customers of a business. (**10**)
Carriage paid	See Section 19.16. (**19**)
Cash book	Book of original entry for cash and bank receipts and payments. (**12**)
Cash discount	An allowance given for quick payment of an account owing. (**14**)
Cash float	The sum held as petty cash. (**17**)
Casting	Adding up figures. (**31**)
Cheque	A cash free method of transferring money using a form of standard format. It is used to instruct one's own bank to transfer money from one's own account to another person or business. (**13**)
COD	Literally 'Cash on delivery'. (**19**)
Coding of invoices	A process used, particularly in computerised accounting, to code the invoice to the supplier or purchaser, and also to the relevant account in the general ledger. (**20**)
Compensating error	Where two errors of equal amounts but on opposite sides of the accounts, cancel out each other. (**31**)
Conservatism	An older term for 'prudence'. (**11**)
Consistency	To keep the same method, except in special cases. (**11**)
Contra	A contra is where both the debit and credit entries are shown in the cash book. (**14**)
Control account	An account which checks the arithmetical accuracy of a ledger. (**23**)
Cost of goods sold	This is calculated as follows: Opening stock plus purchases during the period less the value of the stock at the end of the period (closing stock). (**8**)

Credit	The right-hand side of the accounts in double entry. (**3**)
Credit card	Issued by organisations such as Visa, Mastercard and involve electronic transfer of money to the seller by the credit card company who will bill the buyer for repayment. (**13**)
Credit note	A document sent to a customer showing allowance given by supplier in respect of unsatisfactory goods. (**21**)
Credit transfer	An amount paid by someone direct into our bank account. (**15**)
Creditor	A person to whom money is owed for goods or services. (**2**)
Creditors : purchases ratio	A ratio assessing how long it takes a business to pay its creditors. (**38**)
Current assets	Assets consisting of cash, goods for resale, or items having a shorter life. (**9**)
Current liabilities	Liabilities to be paid for in the near future. (**9**)
Current ratio	A ratio comparing current assets with current liabilities. Also known as the 'working capital' ratio. (**38**)
Debenture	Loan to a company. (**37**)
Debenture interest	An agreed percentage of interest paid to a debenture holder for lending a company money. (**37**)
Debit	The left-hand side of the accounts in double entry. (**3**)
Debit note	A document sent to a supplier showing allowance given for unsatisfactory goods. (**21**)
Debtor	A person who owes money to the business for goods or services supplied. (**2**)
Debtors : Sales ratio	A ratio assessing how long it takes debtors to pay a business. (**38**)
Delivery note	A note which accompanies goods being despatched, enabling the customer to check what goods have been received. The carrier often retains a copy and asks the customer to sign this to verify that the customer has received the goods. (**19**)
Depletion	The wasting away of an asset as it is used up. (**25**)
Depreciation	The part of the cost of the fixed asset consumed during its period of use by a firm. (**25**)
Direct costs	Costs which can be traced to the item being manufactured. (**35**)
Direct debit	Payment made out of payer's bank, direct to payee's bank, on *payee's* instructions. (**13**)
Directors	Officials appointed by shareholders to manage the company for them. (**37**)
Directors' remuneration	Directors are legally employees of the company and any pay they receive is called directors' remuneration. (**37**)
Discounts allowed	A reduction given to customers who pay their accounts within the time allowed. (**14**)
Discounts received	A reduction given to us by a supplier when we pay their account before the time allowed has elapsed. (**14**)

Dishonoured cheque	A cheque that is found to be worth nothing. (**15**)
Dividends	The amount given to shareholders as their share of the profits of the company. (**37**)
Donation	A monetary gift donated to the club or society, monies received should be shown as income in the year that they are received. (**34**)
Double entry book-keeping	A system where each transaction is entered twice, once on the debit side and once on the credit side. (**3**)
Drawee	The bank on which a cheque is drawn. (**13**)
Drawer	The person making out a cheque and using it for payment. (**13**)
Drawings	Cash or goods taken out of a business by the owner for private use. (**5**)
Dual aspect concept	Dealing with both aspects of a transaction. (**11**)
E & OE	See Section 19.16. (**19**)
Equity	Another name for the capital of the owner. Also described as 'net worth'. (**2**)
Error of commission	Where a correct amount is entered, but in the wrong person's account. (**31**)
Error of omission	Where a transaction is completely omitted from the books. (**31**)
Error of original entry	Where an item is entered, but both debit and credit entries are of the same incorrect amount. (**31**)
Error of principle	Where an item is entered in the wrong type of account, e.g. a fixed asset entered in an expense account. (**31**)
Ex works	An indication that the price of certain goods does not include delivery costs. (**19**)
Exempted businesses	Businesses that do not have to add VAT to the price of goods and services supplied by them, and that cannot obtain a refund of VAT paid on goods and services purchased by them. (**16**)
Exempt supplies	Supplies which are outside the scope of VAT and, therefore, VAT cannot be charged. (**16**)
Expenses	Costs of operating the business. (**5**)
Expenses : Sales ratio	A ratio which indicates whether costs are rising against sales or whether sales are falling against expenses. (**38**)
Extended trial balance	A trial balance with additional columns added to enable adjustments to be made prior to the preparation of the financial statements. The extended trial balance is often referred to as a 'worksheet'. (**29**)
Factoring	A system used by a business to improve its cash flow. This involves 'selling' its debtors to a factoring company, which is then responsible for collecting debts as they become due and which keeps a percentage of the money collected, usually around 10 per cent. (**19**)

Factory overhead costs	Refer to: Indirect manufacturing costs. (**35**)
FIFO	A method by which the first goods to be received are said to be the first to be sold. (**30**)
Final accounts	At the end of the accounting period or year a business usually prepares its final accounts, which includes the trading and profit and loss account and balance sheet. (**10**)
Financial statements	Formal documents produced by an organisation to show the financial status of the business at a particular time. These include the trading and profit and loss account and the balance sheet. (**1**)
Fixed assets	Assets bought which have a long life and are to be used in the business. (**9**)
Fixed capital accounts	Capital accounts which consist only of the original capital invested in the business. (**36**)
Fluctuating capital accounts	Capital accounts whose balances change from one period to the next. (**36**)
Folio columns	Columns used for entering reference numbers. (**14**)
General journal	Book of original entry for all items other than those for cash or goods. (**12**)
General ledger	All accounts other than those for customers and suppliers. (**12**)
Going concern concept	Where a business is assumed to continue for a long time. (**11**)
Goodwill	The extra amount paid for an existing firm above the value of its other assets. (**28**)
Gross loss	When the 'cost of goods sold' exceeds 'sales', then the business has incurred a gross loss. (**8**)
Gross profit	Found by deducting cost of goods sold from sales. (**8**)
Gross profit : sales ratio	A ratio which states gross profit as a percentage of sales; can indicate how effectively a business has controlled their cost of goods. (**38**)
Historical cost concept	The normal means of valuing the assets of a business based on their cost price. (**11**)
Impersonal accounts	All accounts other than debtors' and creditors' accounts. (**12**)
Imprest system	A system used for controlling expenditure of small cash items which are recorded in the petty cash book. A cash 'float' of a fixed amount is provided initially to the person responsible for operating the petty cash system. Any cash paid out during a particular period, i.e. a week, is reimbursed to the petty cashier so restoring the 'float' to its original sum. (**17**)
Inadequacy	When an asset is no longer used because of changes within an organisation due to growth, competition or product range changes. (**25**)

Income and expenditure account	An account for a non-profit-making organisation to find the surplus or loss made during a period. (**34**)
Incomplete records	Where only some transactions are recorded in the books of account, the missing information has to be obtained by other means. (**33**)
Indirect manufacturing costs	Costs which occur in a factory or other production facility but cannot be easily traced to the items being manufactured. (**35**)
Input tax	The VAT charged to a business on its purchases and expenses (inputs). (**16**)
Inputs	The value of goods and services purchased by a business. (**16**)
Intangible fixed asset	A fixed asset that cannot be physically seen or touched. (**28**)
Interest on capital	An amount, at an agreed rate of interest, that is credited to a partner based on the amount of capital contributed by him/her. (**36**)
Interest on drawings	An amount, at an agreed rate of interest, that is based on the drawings taken out and is debited to the partners. (**36**)
Investment property	Property purchased with the intent of making profit, usually by leasing it. (**25**)
Invoice	A document prepared by the seller and sent to the purchaser whenever a business buys goods or services on credit. It gives details of the supplier and the customer, the goods purchased and their price. (**19**)
Issued share capital	The amount of the authorised share capital of a company that has been issued to shareholders. (**37**)
Journal	A book of account used to record rare or exceptional transactions that should not appear in the other books of original entry in use. (**12**)
Lease	An agreement to rent property for a period of time. (**25**)
Liabilities	Total of money owed for assets supplied to the business. (**2**)
Life membership	Where members pay one amount for membership to last them their lifetime. (**34**)
LIFO	A method by which the goods sold are said to have come from the last lot of goods to be received. (**30**)
Limited company	An organisation owned by its shareholders, whose liability is limited to their share capital. (**37**)
Limited liability	The liability of shareholders, in a company, is limited to any amount they have agreed to invest. (**37**)
Limited partner	A partner whose liability is limited to the capital invested in the firm. (**36**)
Liquidity	The ability of a business to pay its debts as they fall due and to meet unexpected expenses within a reasonable settlement period. (**38**)

Liquidity ratios	Ratios that attempt to indicate the ability of a business to meet its debts as they become due and include current ratio and acid test ratio. (**38**)
Loan capital	Money owing by a company for debentures and for loans from banks and other sources that are not repayable in the near future. (**37**)
Long-term liabilities	Liabilities not having to be paid for in the near future. (**9**)
Loss	Result of selling goods for less than they have cost the business. (**5**)
Manufacturing account	An account in which production cost is calculated. (**35**)
Margin	Profit shown as a percentage or fraction of the selling price. (**38**)
Mark-up	Profit shown as a percentage or fraction of the cost price. (**38**)
Materiality	To record something in a special way only if the amount is not a small one. (**11**)
Memorandum account	An account which is not pat of the double-entry system. These may be the personal accounts of debtors or creditors where the control account is part of the double entry and the personal accounts are classified as 'memorandum accounts'. Alternatively, the sales and purchases ledgers may be part of the double entry and the control accounts classified as 'memorandum accounts'. (**23**)
Money measurement concept	Accounting is only concerned with the money measurement of things and where most people will agree to the monetary value of a transaction.
Narrative	A description and explanation of the transaction recorded in the journal. (**24**)
Net book value	The cost of a fixed asset with depreciation deducted, also known as 'book value'. (**25**)
Net current assets	The value of current assets less that of current liabilities. Also known as 'working capital'. (**9**)
Net monthly	See Section 19.13. (**19**)
Net profit	Gross profit less expenses. (**8**)
Net profit : sales ratio	A ratio that states net profit as a percentage of sales and brings expenses into the calculation. (**38**)
Net realisable value	The value of goods calculated as the selling price less expenses before sale. (**30**)
Net worth	See 'equity'. (**2**)
Nominal accounts	Accounts in which expenses, revenue and capital are recorded. (**12**)
Nominal ledger	Ledger for impersonal accounts (also called general ledger). (**12**)
Non-profit-making organisations	Clubs, associations and societies operated to provide a service or activity for members since their main purpose is not trading or profit making. (**34**)

Non-trading organisations	These include clubs, associations and other non-profit-making organisations that are normally run for the benefit of their members to engage in a particular activity. (**1**)
Objectivity	Using a method that everyone can agree to. (**11**)
Obsolescence	Becoming out of date. (**25**)
Opening entry	An entry needed to open a new set of books of account. (**24**)
Ordinary shares	Shares entitled to dividends after the preference shareholders have been paid their dividends. (**37**)
Output tax	The VAT charged by a business on its supplies (outputs). (**16**)
Outputs	The value of goods and services sold to a business. (**16**)
Overcasting	Incorrectly adding up a column of figures to give an answer which exceeds the correct total. (**31**)
Paid-up capital	The total of the amount of share capital that has been paid for by shareholders. (**37**)
Partly-exempt businesses	These will sell some goods that are exempt from VAT and some goods that are either standard-rated or zero-rated. They may reclaim part of the input VAT paid by them. (**16**)
Partnership	A group of more than two people and a maximum of twenty, who together are carrying on a particular business with a view to making profit. (**1**)
Partnership agreement	The contractual relationship, either written or verbal, between partners, which usually covers details such as how profits or losses should be shared and the relevant responsibilities of the partners. (**36**)
Partnership salaries	Agreed amounts payable to partners in respect of duties undertaken by them. (**36**)
Payee	The person to whom a cheque is paid. (**13**)
Paying-in slip	Form used for paying money into a bank account. (**13**)
Personal accounts	Accounts for both creditors and debtors. (**12**)
Petty cash book	A cash book used for making small (petty) payments. Payments are usually analysed and the totals of each column later posted to the various accounts in the general ledger. The source document used for entry into the petty cash book is a petty cash voucher. (**12**)
Petty cash voucher	The form used by anyone requesting payment for a small item of expenditure incurred on behalf of the business. The form gives details of the expense and should be signed and duly authorised. (**17**)
Posting	The act of using one book as a means of entering the transactions to another account. (**14**)
Preference shares	Shares that are entitled to an agreed rate of dividend before the ordinary shareholders receive anything. (**37**)

Preliminary expenses	All the costs that are incurred when a company is formed. (37)
Prepaid expense	An expense – usually a service – that has been paid for in one accounting period, the benefit of which will not be received until a subsequent period. It is a payment for an expense that has been paid for in advance. (28)
Prepayment	Also referred to as 'prepaid expense'. (28) (See above)
Prime cost	Direct materials plus labour plus direct expenses. (35)
Private ledger	Ledger for capital and drawings accounts. (12)
Private limited company	A legal entity with at least two shareholders, where the liability of the shareholders is limited to the amount of their investment. The public cannot subscribe for its shares. (1)
Production cost	Prime cost plus indirect manufacturing costs. (35)
Profit	The result when goods are sold for more than they cost. (If they are sold for less than they cost, then a *loss* is incurred.) (5)
Profit and loss account	Account in which net profit is calculated. (8)
Profitability	The effective operation of a business to make ongoing profits to ensure its long-term viability. (38)
Profitability ratios	Ratios that attempt to indicate the trend in a business's ability to make profit. These include gross profit and net profit to sales and return on capital employed. (38)
Provision for doubtful debts	An account showing the expected amounts of debtors, who at the balance sheet date, may not be able to pay their outstanding accounts. (27)
Provision for depreciation account	The account where depreciation is accumulated for balance sheet purposes. In the balance sheet the cost price of the asset is shown, less the depreciation to date, to give the net book value. (26)
Prudence or conservatism	To ensure that profit is not shown as being too high, or assets shown at too high a value. (11)
Public limited company	A legal entity with many shareholders since the public can subscribe for its shares. Shareholder liability is limited to the amount of their investment. (1)
Purchase invoice	A document received by purchaser showing details of goods bought and their prices. (20)
Purchase order	This is a document prepared by the purchaser and it contains details of the goods or services required by the purchaser. (20)
Purchases	Goods bought by the business for the purpose of selling them again. (4)
Purchases day book	Book of original entry for credit purchases. (12)
Purchases ledger	A ledger for suppliers' personal accounts. (12)
Quick ratio	Same as the acid test ratio. (38)

Real accounts	Accounts in which property of all kinds is recorded. (**12**)
Realisation concept	The point at which profit is treated as being earned. (**11**)
Receipt	A form acknowledging receipt of money for goods or services rendered. (**14**)
Receipts and payments account	A summary of the cash book of a non-profit-making organisation. (**34**)
Reducing balance method	Depreciation calculation which is at a lesser amount every following period. (**25**)
Reserve accounts	The transfer of apportioned profits to accounts for use in future years. (**37**)
Retained profits	Profits earned in a year but not paid out in dividends. (**37**)
Return on capital employed (ROCE) ratio	A ratio that shows the net profit made for each £100 of capital employed. (**38**)
Returns inwards	Goods returned to the business by its customers. (**4**)
Returns inwards day book	Book of original entry for goods returned by customers. (**12**)
Returns outwards	Goods returned by the business to its suppliers. (**4**)
Returns outwards day book	Book of original entry for goods returned to suppliers. (**12**)
Revenue expenditure	Expenses needed for the day-to-day running of the business. (**18**)
Revenue reserve	Reserves of a company which are available for distribution as a dividend. (**37**)
Revenues	Monetary value of goods and services supplied to the customers. (**5**)
Sale or return	Goods that do not belong to the person holding them. (**30**)
Sales	Goods sold by the business. (**4**)
Sales day book	Book of original entry for credit sales. (**12**)
Sales invoice	A document showing the details of goods sold and the prices of those goods. (**19**)
Sales ledger	A ledger for customers' personal accounts. (**12**)
Shareholder	An owner of shares in a company. (**37**)
Shares	The division of the capital of a limited company into parts. (**37**)
Share premium	The excess in price of an issued share over its nominal value. (**37**)
Single entry	Where transactions are only recorded once in the books of account. (**33**)
Slip system	This involves putting information, such as lists of invoices, in slip form which can then be entered directly into the ledger accounts, eliminating the need to enter them in the day books. Also used by banks whereby a customer makes out a paying-in slip to pay money into their account, the slip is used to enter details of the transaction. The slip is used as documentary evidence. (**19**)
Sole trader	A business owned by one person only. (**1**)

Standard-rated businesses	These will have to add VAT to the value of the sales invoice, but they can also claim back VAT paid on purchases. (16)
Standing order	Payment made out of payer's bank, direct to payee's bank, on the *payer's* instructions. (13)
Statement of account	This is normally sent to purchasers at the end of each month and it states the amount owing to the supplier at the end of that particular month. (21)
Statement of affairs	A statement from which the capital of the owner is deduced by estimating assets and liabilities. Then Capital = Assets *less* Liabilities. (33)
Stock	Unsold goods. (2)
Stock turnover (or stockturn) ratio	A ratio comparing the cost of goods sold to the average stock. It shows the number of times stock is sold in an accounting period. (38)
Straight line method	Depreciation calculation which remains at an equal amount each year. (25)
Subjectivity	Using a method which other people may not agree to. (11)
Subscriptions	Amounts paid by members of a club or society, usually on an annual basis, to enable them to participate in the activities of the organisation. (34)
Suspense account	Account showing balance equal to difference in trial balance. (32)
Total cost	Production cost plus administration, selling and distribution expenses. (35)
Trade discount	A reduction given to a customer when calculating the selling prices of goods. (19)
Trading account	Account in which gross profit is calculated. (8)
Trading and profit and loss account	Combined account in which both gross and net profits are calculated. (8)
Transaction	Events which change two items in the balance sheet. (3)
Trial balance	A list of all the balances in the books at a particular point in time. The balances are shown in debit and credit columns. These columns should balance provided no errors have occurred. (7)
Uncalled capital	The amount that is to be received in future, but which has not yet been requested. (37)
Undercasting	Incorrectly adding up a column of figures to give an answer which is less than the correct total. (31)
Unpresented cheque	A cheque which has been sent but has not yet gone through the bank account of the receiver of it. (15)
Value Added Tax (VAT)	A tax charged on the supply of most goods and services. The tax is borne by the final consumer of the goods or services, not by the business selling them to the consumer. VAT is administered by HM Customs and Excise. (16)

Work in progress	Items not completed at the end of a period. (**35**)
Working capital	The amount by which the current assets exceed the current liabilities. Also known as 'net current assets'. (**28**)
Working capital ratio	Same as the current ratio. (**38**)
Zero-rated businesses	Businesses that do not have to add VAT to goods and services supplied to others by them, but they can receive a refund of VAT paid on goods and services purchased by them. (**16**)
Zero-rated supplies	Goods or services where VAT is charged at the rate of 0%. (**16**)

Model layouts for financial statements and worksheets

Many students have difficulty remembering the layout of the financial statements of various businesses. In this appendix you will find suggested model layouts of the financial statements, which include the trading and profit and loss account and balance sheet for the following organisations:

- sole trader
- partnership – including the appropriation account
- limited company – including the appropriation account
- a manufacturing account.

Also included are suggested working sheets for answering questions on petty cash, ratio analysis and the extended trial balance. You may find it useful to photocopy the above documents and put them in your file for reference and to use when answering questions on these topics.

In this appendix you will find the following suggested model layouts of financial statements and worksheets; these are shown with column lines for ease of working:

- **Financial statements:**
  1 Sole trader
  2 Partnership
  3 Limited company
      Trading and profit and loss account suitable for both UK and overseas examinations
      Balance sheet based on UK legislation
      Balance sheet for local overseas examinations
  4 Manufacturing account
- **Worksheets:**
  5 Petty cash book
  6 Worksheet for accounting rations
  7 Worksheet for extended trial balance

1 Sole trader financial statements

Trading and Profit and Loss Account – Sole trader

Trading and Profit and Loss Account of . . . for the year ended . . .		
	£	£
Sales		xxx
Less Returns inwards		xx
		xxx (a)
Less Cost of goods sold		
Opening stock	x	
Add Purchases	x	
Add Carriage inwards	x	
	xx	
Less Returns outwards	x	
	xx	
Less Closing stock	x	xxx (b)
Gross profit (a) – (b)		xxx (c)
Less Expenses		
Bad debts (written off)	x	
Wages and salaries	x	
Rates	x	
Insurance	x	
Rent	x	
General expenses	x	
Postages	x	
Stationery	x	
Carriage outwards	x	
Discounts allowed	x	
Heating	x	
Electricity	x	
Depreciation	x	
Increase in provision for bad debts	x	xxx (d)
(c) – (d)		xxx (e)
Add income*		
Discounts + interest received	x	
Reductions in provision for bad debts	x	xx (f)
Net profit (e) + (f)		£xxx (g)

Trading Account — covers the section from Sales to Gross profit.

Profit and Loss Account — covers the section from Less Expenses to Net profit.

Note: Alternatively, the Income can be added to Gross Profit before deducting expenses.

Balance Sheet – Sole trader

Balance Sheet of . . . as at . . .			
	Cost (a)	Total depreciation (b)	Net book value (a) – (b)
Fixed assets	£	£	£
Premises	x	x	x
Motor vehicle	x	x	x
Office furniture	x	x	x
Office equipment	x	x	x
Machinery	x	x	x
	xx	xx	x (c)
Current assets			
Stock (closing)	x		
Debtors (*Less* Provision for bad debts)	x		
Prepayment	x		
Cash at bank	x		
Cash in hand	x	xx (d)	
Less Current liabilities			
Creditors	x		
Expenses owing	x		
Bank overdraft	x	xx (e)	
Net current assets (d) – (e)			xx (f)
(c) + (f)			xxx (g)
Less Long-term liabilities			
Long-term loan			x (h)
Net assets (g) – (h)			£xxx (i)
Financed by			
Capital			xxx
Add Profit			x
			xxx
Less Drawings			x
			£xxx (i)

2 Partnership – Financial Statements

Alan and Graham
Trading and Profit and Loss Account for the year ended . . .

	£	£	£
Trading Account – Same as sole trader			
Profit and Loss Account – Same as sole trader			
Profit and Loss Appropriation Account*			
Net Profit			xxx (a)
Add Interest charged on drawings			
Alan		x	
Graham		x	xx (b)
(a) + (b)			xxx (c)
Less Interest on capital			
Alan	x		
Graham	x	xx	
Salary			
Graham	x	x	xx (d)
(c) − (d)			xxx (e)
Share of Profits:			
Alan		xx	
Graham		xx	
			xxx (e)

Note: The Appropriation Account is usually shown under the general heading of Trading and Profit and Loss Account.

Alan and Graham
Balance Sheet as at . . .

	Alan	Graham	Total
Asset section of the balance sheet – Same as sole trader			
Extract showing Financed by section only			
Financed by:			
Capital Accounts			
Balance	xx	xx	xxx (a)
Current Accounts			
Balance b/d	xx	xx	
Add Share of profit	x	x	
Salary – Graham	–	x	
Interest on capital	x	x	
	xx	xx	
Less Drawings	(x)	(x)	
Interest on drawings	(x)	(x)	
	xx	xx	
			xxx (b)
(a) + (b) =			xxxx (c)

3 Limited company – Financial Statements

Name of Company . . . Limited
Trading and Profit and Loss Account for the year ended . . .

	£	£	£
Sales			xxx
Less Returns inwards			x
			xxx (a)
Less Cost of goods sold			
Opening stock		xxx	
Add Purchases	xxx		
Add Carriage inwards	xx		
	xxx		
Less Returns outwards	xx	xxx	
		xxx	
Less Closing stock		xx	xxx (b)
Gross Profit (a) – (b)			xxx (c)
Less Expenses:			
Salaries and wages	xx		
Directors' remuneration		xx	
General expenses		xx	
Rates and insurance	xx		
Motor expenses		xx	
Debenture interest	xx		
Bad debts written off	xx		
Depreciation – Motors	xx		
– Equipment		xx	xxx (d)
Net Profit (c) – (d)			xxx (e)
Add Retained profits from last year			xx (f)
(e) + (f)			xxx (g)
Less Appropriations:			
Transfers to general reserve		xx	
Interim dividends paid:			
Preference shares		xx	
Ordinary shares		xx	
Final dividends paid:			
Preference shares		xx	
Ordinary shares		xx	xxx (h)
Retained profits carried forward			xxx (i)
to next year (g) – (h)			

Note: The above Trading and Profit and Loss Account is suitable for both UK and overseas examinations. For internal use, not for publication.

Name of Company . . . Limited
Balance Sheet as at . . .

	£	£	£	
Fixed assets				
Intangible assets				
Goodwill			xx	(a)
Tangible assets (A)				
Premises		xxx		
Equipment		xxx		
Motors		xxx	xxx	(b)
(a) + (b)			xxx	(c)
Current assets				
Stock	xx			
Debtors	xx			
Bank	xx			
Cash	xx	xxx	(d)	
Creditors: amounts falling due within one year				
Creditors	xx			
Bank overdraft	xx			
Proposed dividends	xx			
Debenture interest due	xx	xxx	(e)	
Net Current assets (d) − (e)			xxx	(f)
Total assets less current liabilities (c) + (f)			xxx	(g)
Creditors: amounts falling due after more than one year				
Debentures			xxx	(h)
(g) − (h)			xxxx	(i)
Capital and reserves				
Called-up share capital (B)			xxxx	(j)
Reserves				
Share premium		xxx		
General reserve		xxx		
Profit and loss account		xxx	xxx	(k)
(j) + (k)			xxxx	(i)

Notes: Based on UK legislation

(A) Notes to be given in appendix as to cost, acquisitions and sales in the year and depreciation.

(B) 'Reserves' consist either of those unused profits remaining in the appropriation account, or those transferred to a reserve account appropriately titled (e.g. general reserve, fixed asset replacement reserve, etc.).

Name of Company . . . Limited
Balance Sheet as at . . .

	Cost £	Total Depreciation £	Net Book Value £
Fixed Assets			
Goodwill	xxx	x	xx
Buildings	xxx	x	xxx
Equipment	xxx	xx	xxx
	xxx	xx	xxx (a)
Current Assets			
Stock	xx		
Debtors	xx		
Bank	xx		
Cash	xx	xxx (b)	
Less Current Liabilities			
Creditors	xx		
Bank overdraft	xx		
Dividends owing	xx		
Debenture interest owing	xx	xxx (c)	
Net Current Assets (b) – (c)			xxx (d)
Total assets less current liabilities (a) + (d)			xxx (e)
Loan capital			
Debentures			xx (f)
(e) – (f)			xxx (g)
Financed by:		Authorised	Issued
Share capital			
Preference shares		xxx	xxx
Ordinary shares		xxx	xxx
		xxx	xxx (h)
Reserves			
Share premium		xxx	
General reserve		xxx	
Profit and loss		xxx	xxx (i)
(h) + (i)			xxx (g)

Note: (For students sitting local overseas examinations)

4 Manufacturing Account

Name of firm
Manufacturing Account for the year ended . . .

		£	£	
Stock of raw materials (opening)			xxx	
Add Purchases			xxx	
Add Carriage inwards			xxx	
			xxx	(a)
Less Stock of raw materials (closing)			xxx	(b)
Cost of raw materials consumed	(a) – (b)		xxx	(c)
Direct labour			xxx	(d)
Direct expenses				
Royalties			xx	(e)
Prime cost	(c) + (d) + (e)		xxx	(f)
Indirect manufacturing cost				
General factory overheads		xx		
Lighting		xx		
Power		xx		
Rent		xx		
Insurance		xx		
Indirect labour		xx		
Depreciation of plant		xx	xxx	(g)
	(f) + (g)		xxx	(h)
Add Work in progress (opening)			xx	(i)
	(h) + (i)		xxx	(j)
Less Work in progress (closing)			xx	(k)
Production cost of goods completed c/d	(j) – (k)		xxx	

Note: The Production cost of goods completed will be entered in the trading account, refer to Chapter 35.

5 Petty Cash Book

Receipts £	Date	Details	Voucher Number	Total £	VAT £	£	£	£	£	£

6 Accounting ratios – Calculation sheet

Profitability Ratios – Chapter 38, Section 38.7			
Ratio	Formula	Year 1	Year 2
1 Gross profit to sales %	$\dfrac{GP}{Sales} \times 100 = \%$		
2 Net profit to sales %	$\dfrac{NP}{Sales} \times 100 = \%$		
3 Expenses to sales %	$\dfrac{Expenses}{Sales} \times 100 = \%$		
4 Return on capital employed (ROCE)	$\dfrac{NP}{Capital\ Employed} \times 100 = \%$		
5 Stock turnover e.g. 5 times	$\dfrac{Cost\ of\ Goods\ Sold}{Average\ Stock} = X\ Times\ a\ year$		
Liquidity Ratios – Chapter 38, Section 38.8			
1 Current (or working capital ratio)	$\dfrac{Current\ Assets}{Current\ Liabilities} = X : 1$		
2 Acid test (or quick ratio)	$\dfrac{Current\ Assets - Stock}{Current\ Liabilities} = X : 1$		
3 Debtors to sales ratio (for months)	$\dfrac{Debtors}{Sales\ for\ year} \times 12 = X\ Months$		
or Debtors to sales ratio (for days)	$\dfrac{Debtors}{Sales\ for\ year} \times 365 = X\ Days$		
4 Creditors to purchases (for months)	$\dfrac{Creditors}{Purchases\ for\ year} \times 12 = X\ Months$		

7 Format for an extended worksheet

Description	Ledger Balances		Adjustments		Profit and Loss		Balance Sheet	
	Dr £	Cr £	Dr £	Cr £	Dr £	Cr £	Dr £	Cr £

Multiple-choice questions

Each multiple-choice question has four suggested answers, either letter (A), (B), (C) or (D). You should read each question and then decide which choice is best, either (A) or (B) or (C) or (D). Write down your answers on a separate piece of paper. You will then be able to repeat the set of questions later without having to try to ignore your previous answers.

When you have completed a set of questions, check your answers against those given in Appendix D.

Set No 1: Questions MC1–MC20

MC1 Which of the following statements is *in*correct?
(A) Assets − Liabilities = Capital
(B) Capital − Liabilities = Assets
(C) Assets = Capital + Liabilities
(D) Assets − Capital = Liabilities.

MC2 Which of the following is not an asset?
(A) Debtor
(B) Motor Vehicle
(C) Creditor
(D) Stock of Goods.

MC3 Which of the following is a liability?
(A) Cash balance
(B) Loan from J Owens
(C) Debtor
(D) Buildings.

MC4 Which of the following is *in*correct?

	Assets £	Liabilities £	Capital £
(A)	9,460	2,680	6,780
(B)	7,390	1,140	6,250
(C)	6,120	2,490	4,630
(D)	8,970	3,580	5,390

MC5   Which of the following statements is *in*correct?

		Effect upon	
		Assets	Liabilities
(A)	Paid creditor by cheque	− Bank	+ Creditors
(B)	Bought goods on credit	+ Stock	+ Creditors
(C)	Received cash from debtor	+ Cash	
		− Debtor	
(D)	Sold goods for Cash	+ Cash	
		− Stock	

MC6   Which of the following are correct?

	Accounts	To record	Entry in the account
(i)	Assets	a decrease	Debit
		an increase	Credit
(ii)	Capital	a decrease	Debit
		an increase	Credit
(iii)	Liabilities	a decrease	Debit
		an increase	Credit

   (A)   (i) and (ii)
   (B)   (i) and (iii)
   (C)   (ii) and (iii)
   (D)   None of them.

MC7   Which of the following are correct?

		Account to be debited	Account to be credited
(i)	Bought motor van by cheque	Motor van	Bank
(ii)	Paid a creditor, T Allen, by cheque	Cash	T Allen
(iii)	Loan repaid to C Kirk by cheque	Loan from Kirk	Bank
(iv)	Sold goods for cash	Sales	Cash

   (A)   (i) and (ii) only
   (B)   (ii) and (iii) only
   (C)   (iii) and (iv) only
   (D)   (i) and (iii) only.

MC8   Which of the following are *in*correct?

		Account to be debited	Account to be credited
(i)	Sold goods on credit to P Moore	P Moore	Sales
(ii)	Bought fixtures on credit from Furnishers Ltd	Fixtures	Furnishers Ltd
(iii)	Introduce more capital in cash	Capital	Cash
(iv)	A debtor, L Sellars, pays by cheque	Cash	L Sellars

   (A)   (iii) and (iv) only
   (B)   (ii) and (iii) only
   (C)   (i) and (iv) only
   (D)   (i) and (iii) only.

MC9 Which of the following should not be called 'sales'?
- (A) Goods sold, to be paid for in one month's time
- (B) Goods sold, cash being received immediately
- (C) Item previously included in purchases, now sold on credit
- (D) Sale of a motor lorry not now required.

MC10 Which of the following should not be called 'purchases'?
- (A) Items bought for the prime purpose of resale
- (B) Goods bought on credit
- (C) Office stationery purchased
- (D) Goods bought for cash.

MC11 Which of the following are *in*correct?

		Account to be debited	Account to be credited
(i)	B Ash returns goods to us	Returns Inwards	B Ash
(ii)	Goods bought on credit from L Thomas	L Thomas	Purchases
(iii)	Motor van bought on Credit from X L Garages	Purchases	X L Garages
(iv)	Goods sold for cash	Cash	Sales

- (A) (i) and (ii) only
- (B) (i) and (iii) only
- (C) (ii) and (iii) only
- (D) (iii) and (iv) only.

MC12 Of the following, which are correct?

		Account to be debited	Account to be credited
(i)	Surplus office furniture sold for cash	Cash	Sales
(ii)	We returned goods to F Ward	F Ward	Returns Inwards
(iii)	Goods bought for cash	Purchases	Cash
(iv)	Goods sold on credit to F Clarke	F Clarke	Sales

- (A) (i) and (ii) only
- (B) (iii) and (iv) only
- (C) (ii) and (iii) only
- (D) (ii) only.

MC13 What is the amount of capital, given the following information? Buildings £30,000, Stock £5,600, Bank £750, Creditors £2,200, Loan from K Noone £7,000:
- (A) £29,150
- (B) £36,350
- (C) £41,150
- (D) None of the above.

MC14 Which of these statements is *in*correct?
- (A) Profit is another word for capital
- (B) A loss decreases capital
- (C) Profit increases capital
- (D) Drawings decreases capital.

MC15 Which of the following are *in*correct?

		Account to be debited	Account to be credited
(i)	Paid insurance by cheque	Insurance	Bank
(ii)	Paid telephone bill by cash	Telephone	Cash
(iii)	Received refund of part of motor expenses by cheque	Cash	Motor Expenses
(iv)	Took cash out of business for personal use	Drawings	Capital

(A) (i) and (iii) only
(B) (ii) and (iv) only
(C) (iii) and (iv) only
(D) (iv) only.

MC16 Of the following, which are correct?

		Account to be debited	Account to be credited
(i)	Paid rent by cheque	Rent	Cash
(ii)	Received commission in cash	Commissions	Cash
(iii)	Introduced extra capital in cash	Cash	Capital
(iv)	Sold surplus stationery for cash	Cash	Stationery

(A) None of them
(B) (i) and (iv) only
(C) (ii) and (iii) only
(D) (iii) and (iv) only.

MC17 What is the balance on the following account on 30 June 2005?

Dr		£	N Garth		Cr
2005			2005		£
June 18 Bank		400	June 1 Purchases		870
June 22 Returns		44	June 15 Purchases		245
			June 29 Purchases		178

(A) A debit balance of £849
(B) A credit balance of £829
(C) A credit balance of £849
(D) There is a nil balance on the account.

MC18 What was the balance on the account of N Garth, in MC17, on 20 June 2005?
(A) A credit balance of £671
(B) A debit balance of £715
(C) A credit balance of £715
(D) A debit balance of £671.

MC19 Of the following, which *best* describes a trial balance?
(A) Is the final account in the books
(B) Shows all the asset balances
(C) Is a list of balances on the books
(D) Discloses the financial position of a business.

MC20 When should the trial balance totals differ?
- (A) Only when it is drawn up by the accountant
- (B) When drawn up before the profit and loss account is prepared
- (C) If drawn up half-way through the financial year
- (D) Never.

Set No 2: Questions MC21–MC55

MC21 Gross profit is:
- (A) Excess of cost of goods sold over sales
- (B) Purchases + Sales
- (C) Net profit less expenses
- (D) Excess of sales over cost of goods sold.

MC22 Net profit is calculated in the:
- (A) Trial balance
- (B) Trading account
- (C) Profit and loss account
- (D) Balance sheet.

MC23 The credit entry for net profit is shown in the:
- (A) Capital account
- (B) Profit and loss account
- (C) Balance sheet
- (D) Trading account.

MC24 The value of closing stock is found by:
- (A) Adding opening stock to purchases
- (B) Deducting purchases from sales
- (C) Looking in the stock account
- (D) Doing a stock-taking.

MC25 Which of the following are *not* part of the double entry system?
- (i) Trading account
- (ii) Balance sheet
- (iii) Trial balance
- (iv) Profit and loss account.

- (A) (i) and (ii)
- (B) (i) and (iii)
- (C) (ii) and (iii)
- (D) (ii) and (iv).

MC26 Which is the *best* definition of a balance sheet?
- (A) A list of balances after calculating net profit
- (B) A statement of all liabilities
- (C) A trial balance at a different date
- (D) A list of balances before calculating net profit.

MC27 The descending order in which current assets should be shown in the balance sheet are:
- (A) Debtors, Bank, Stock, Cash
- (B) Stock, Debtors, Bank, Cash
- (C) Stock, Debtors, Cash, Bank
- (D) Cash, Bank, Debtors, Stock.

MC28 Carriage inwards is charged to the trading account because:
- (A) It is not a balance sheet item
- (B) It is not part of motor expenses
- (C) Returns inwards also goes in the trading account
- (D) It is basically part of the cost of buying goods.

MC29 Given figures showing Sales £28,500, Opening stock £4,690, Closing stock £7,240, Carriage inwards £570 and Purchases £21,360, the cost of goods sold figure is:
- (A) £19,830
- (B) £19,380
- (C) £18,810
- (D) Another figure.

MC30 If someone owns a grocery store, which of the following are *not* capital expenditure?
- (i) Rent
- (ii) Motor van
- (iii) Fixtures
- (iv) Fire insurance.

- (A) (ii) and (iii)
- (B) (i) and (ii)
- (C) (i) and (iii)
- (D) (i) and (iv).

MC31 The purchases day book is *best* described as:
- (A) A list of purchases bought on credit
- (B) Containing suppliers' accounts
- (C) A list of purchases bought for cash
- (D) Part of the double entry system.

MC32 Customers' personal accounts are found in:
- (A) The private ledger
- (B) General ledger
- (C) Purchases ledger
- (D) Sales ledger.

MC33 Which of the following are *not* personal accounts?
- (i) Debtors
- (ii) Drawings
- (iii) Rent
- (iv) Creditors.

(A) (iii) only

(B) (i) and (ii) only

(C) (i) and (iv) only

(D) (ii) and (iii) only.

MC34 A debit balance of £500 in the cash columns of the cash book would mean:

(A) The book-keeper has made a mistake

(B) We have £500 cash in hand

(C) We have spent £500 cash more than we have received

(D) Someone has stolen £500 cash.

MC35 A sum of £200 withdrawn from the bank and placed in the cash till is entered:

(A) Debit bank column £200: Credit bank column £200

(B) Debit cash column £200: Credit bank column £200

(C) Debit bank column £200: Credit cash column £200

(D) Debit cash column £400: Credit cash column £400.

MC36 A contra item is where:

(A) Cash is banked before it has been paid out

(B) Where double entry is completed within the cash book

(C) Where the proprietor has repaid his capital in cash

(D) Where sales have been paid by cash.

MC37 An invoice shows a total of £3,200 less a $2^1/_2$-per-cent cash discount. If this was paid in time, the amount of the cheque paid would be for:

(A) £2,960

(B) £3,040

(C) £3,120

(D) £2,800.

MC38 The total of the discounts received column in the cash book is posted to:

(A) The credit of the discounts received account

(B) The credit of the discounts allowed account

(C) The debit of the discounts allowed account

(D) The debit of the discounts received account.

MC39 A bank overdraft is *best* described as:

(A) A firm wasting its money

(B) Having more receipts than payments

(C) A firm having bought too many goods

(D) A firm having paid more out of its bank account than it has put in it.

MC40 A cash discount is *best* described as a reduction in the sum to be paid:

(A) If goods are bought on credit and not for cash

(B) If either cheque or cash payment is made within an agreed period

(C) If cash is paid instead of cheques

(D) If trade discount is also deducted.

MC41 If a sales invoice shows 12 items of £250 each, less trade discount of 20 per cent and cash discount of 5 per cent, then the amount to be paid, if the payment is made within the credit period, will be for:
- (A) £2,440
- (B) £2,360
- (C) £2,280
- (D) £2,500.

MC42 The total of the sales day book is entered on:
- (A) The debit side of the sales day book
- (B) The credit side of the sales account in the general ledger
- (C) The debit side of the sales account in the general ledger
- (D) The debit side of the sales day book.

MC43 A trade discount is *best* described as:
- (A) A discount given if the invoice is paid
- (B) A discount given for cash payment
- (C) A discount given to suppliers
- (D) A discount given to traders.

MC44 The sales day book does *not* contain:
- (A) Credit sales made without deduction of trade discount
- (B) Credit sales made to overseas customers
- (C) Cash sales
- (D) Credit sales which eventually turn out to be bad debts.

MC45 The purchases day book consists of:
- (A) Cash purchases
- (B) Suppliers' ledger accounts
- (C) A list of purchases invoices
- (D) Payments for goods.

MC46 The total of the purchases day book is transferred to the:
- (A) Debit side of the purchases account
- (B) Credit side of the purchases day book
- (C) Debit side of the purchases day book
- (D) Debit side of the purchases ledger.

MC47 The balances in the purchases ledger are usually:
- (A) Credit balances
- (B) Contras
- (C) Nominal account balances
- (D) Debit balances.

MC48 Debit notes are entered in the:
- (A) Returns outwards day book
- (B) Returns inwards day book
- (C) Purchases account
- (D) Returns outwards account.

MC49 A statement of account:
- (A) Is used instead of an invoice
- (B) Means that customers need not keep accounts
- (C) Saves sending out invoices
- (D) Acts as a reminder to the purchaser of the amount owed.

MC50 Originally we bought 80 items at £60 each, less trade discount of 25 per cent. We now return 5 items, so we will issue a debit note amounting to:
- (A) £270
- (B) £240
- (C) £225
- (D) £220.

MC51 A cheque given to you by a customer and banked by you, but for which he has proved not to have enough funds to meet it, is known as:
- (A) A dishonoured cheque
- (B) A debit transfer
- (C) A standing order
- (D) A bank error.

MC52 Which of the following are not true? A bank reconciliation statement is:
- (i) Drawn up by the bank monthly
- (ii) Not part of the double entry system
- (iii) Part of the double entry system
- (iv) Drawn up by our cashier.

- (A) (i) and (ii)
- (B) (i) and (iii)
- (C) (ii) and (iv)
- (D) (iii) and (iv).

MC53 The journal is:
- (A) Part of the double entry system
- (B) A form of sales day book
- (C) A form of diary
- (D) A supplement to the balance sheet.

MC54 Given a desired cash float of £700, if £541 is spent in the period and the opening cash float has been £700, how much will be reimbursed at the end of the period?
- (A) £541
- (B) £700
- (C) £159
- (D) None of the above.

MC55 A petty cash book:
- (A) Is used only in limited companies
- (B) Is used when there is a bank overdraft
- (C) Is used for small cheque payments
- (D) Will keep down the number of entries in the general ledger.

Set No 3: Questions MC56–MC82

MC56 The straight line method of depreciation consists of:
- (A) Unequal amounts of depreciation each year
- (B) Increasing amounts of depreciation each year
- (C) Reducing amounts of depreciation each year
- (D) Equal amounts of depreciation each year.

MC57 Depreciation is:
- (A) The cost of a current asset wearing away
- (B) The cost of a replacement for a fixed asset
- (C) The salvage value of a fixed asset plus its original cost
- (D) The part of the cost of the fixed asset consumed during its period of use by the firm.

MC58 A firm bought a machine for £50,000. It is expected to be used for 6 years, then sold for £5,000. What is the annual amount of depreciation if the straight line method is used?
- (A) £7,000
- (B) £8,000
- (C) £7,500
- (D) £6,750.

MC59 When a separate provision for depreciation account is in use, then book-keeping entries for the year's depreciation are:
- (A) Debit profit and loss: Credit the balance sheet
- (B) Debit profit and loss: Credit asset account
- (C) Debit asset account: Credit provision for depreciation account
- (D) Debit profit and loss: Credit provision for depreciation account.

MC60 In a trial balance, the balance on the provision for depreciation account is:
- (A) Shown as a credit item
- (B) Not shown, as it is part of depreciation
- (C) Shown as a debit item
- (D) Sometimes shown as a credit, sometimes as a debit.

MC61 If a provision for depreciation account is not in use, then the entries for the year's depreciation would be:
- (A) Debit asset account, credit profit and loss account
- (B) Credit asset account, debit provision for depreciation account
- (C) Credit profit and loss account, debit provision for depreciation account
- (D) None of the above.

MC62 A provision for bad debts is created:
- (A) When debtors become bankrupt
- (B) When debtors cease to be in business
- (C) To provide for possible bad debts
- (D) To write off bad debts.

MC63 When final accounts are prepared, the bad debts account is closed by a transfer to the:
(A) Balance sheet
(B) Profit and loss account
(C) Trading account
(D) Provision for bad debts account.

MC64 These questions relate to the following assets and liabilities:

	£		£
Stock	1,000	Machinery	750
Cash at bank	750	Debtors	750
Cash in hand	50	Fixtures	250
Creditors	500	Motor vehicle	750
Capital	3,800		

(i) The balance sheet totals are (use the vertical presentation):
(A) £4,800. (B) £3,800. (C) £4,000. (D) £4,500.

(ii) Current liabilities are:
(A) £1,750. (B) £500. (C) £3,800. (D) £2,550.

(iii) Working capital is:
(A) £3,050. (B) £2,050. (C) £500. (D) £800.

Pitman Qualifications

MC65 If we take goods for own use, we should:
(A) Debit drawings account: Credit purchases account
(B) Debit purchases account: Credit drawings account
(C) Debit drawings account: Credit stock account
(D) Debit sales account: Credit stock account.

MC66 A debit balance brought down on a packing materials account means:
(A) We owe for packing materials
(B) We have no stock of packing materials
(C) We have lost money on packing materials
(D) We have a stock of packing materials unused.

MC67 A credit balance brought down on a rent account means:
(A) We owe that rent at that date
(B) We have paid that rent in advance at that date
(C) We have paid too much rent
(D) We have paid too little in rent.

MC68 Working capital is a term meaning:
(A) The amount of capital invested by the proprietor
(B) The excess of the current assets over the current liabilities
(C) The capital less drawings
(D) The total of fixed assets + current assets.

MC69 In the trading account, the returns inwards should be:
(A) Added to cost of goods sold
(B) Deducted from purchases
(C) Deducted from sales
(D) Added to sales.

MC70 If £750 was added to rent instead of being added to a fixed asset:
(A) Gross profit would not be affected
(B) Gross profit would be affected
(C) Both gross and net profits would be affected
(D) Just the balance sheet items would be affected.

MC71 Of the following, which should *not* be entered in the journal?
(i) Cash payments for wages
(ii) Bad debts written off
(iii) Credit purchases of goods
(iv) Sale of fixed assets.

(A) (i) and (ii)
(B) (i) and (iii)
(C) (ii) and (iii)
(D) (iii) and (iv).

MC72 Which of the following do *not* affect trial balance agreement?
(i) Purchases £585 from C Owens completely omitted from the books
(ii) Sales £99 to R Morgan entered in his account as £90
(iii) Rent account added up to be £100 too much
(iv) Error on sales invoice of £14 being entered in the books.

(A) (i) and (iv)
(B) (i) and (ii)
(C) (i) and (iii)
(D) (iii) and (iv).

MC73 Which of the following *are* errors of principle?
(i) Rent entered in buildings account
(ii) Purchases £150 completely omitted from books
(iii) Sale of machinery £500 entered in sales account
(iv) Cheque payment to R Kago entered only in cash book.

(A) (ii) and (iii)
(B) (iii) and (iv)
(C) (i) and (ii)
(D) (i) and (iii).

MC74 When trial balance totals do not agree, the difference is entered in:
(A) The balance account
(B) A suspense account
(C) An errors account
(D) The profit and loss account.

MC75 Which of these errors would be disclosed by the trial balance?
  (A) Error on a purchase invoice
  (B) Purchases from T Morgan entered in C Morgan's account
  (C) Carriage outwards debited to sales account
  (D) Overcast of total on sales account.

MC76 All these questions refer to the following trading and profit and loss account.

Trading Account and Profit and Loss Account				
			£	£
Sales				24,770
Less Returns inwards				270
				24,500
Less Cost of goods sold:				
Opening stock			700	
Add Purchases		18,615		
Less Returns outwards		280		
		18,335		
Add Carriage Inwards		320	18,655	
			19,355	
Less Closing Stock			980	18,375
Gross Profit				6,125
Less Expenses:				
Wages			1,420	
Rent (360 + 90)			450	
General expenses			220	
Carriage outwards			360	?
Net Profit				?

  (i)   The missing net profit figure should be:
         (A) £1,675.   (B) £21,675.   (C) £3,675.   (D) £4,675.
  (ii)   Total expenses were:
         (A) £210.   (B) £2,450.   (C) £810.   (D) £2,575.
  (iii) The cost of goods sold totalled:
         (A) £18,375.   (B) £19,500.   (C) £24,500.   (D) £24,770.
  (iv)   The expense item of Rent totalled:
         (A) £360.   (B) £270.   (C) £90.   (D) £450.
  (v)   The turnover is:
         (A) £24,770.   (B) £24,500.   (C) £19,355.   (D) £18,375.
  (vi)   The net cost of purchases is:
         (A) £18,615.   (B) £18,335.   (C) £18,655.   (D) £18,375.
  (vii) Purchases returned totalled:
         (A) £360.   (B) £320.   (C) £280.   (D) £270.
  (viii) Gross profit as a percentage on net sales is:
         (A) 20%.   (B) 30%.   (C) 25%.   (D) $33\frac{1}{3}$%.
  (ix)   Net profit as a percentage on net sales is:
         (A) 10%.   (B) 20%.   (C) 25%.   (D) 15%.

(x) The value of unsold goods was:

(A) £980.   (B) £24,500.   (C) £6,125.   (D) £19,355.

Pitman Qualifications

MC77 Answer the following questions using the following trial balance and the information given below:

Trial Balance as at 31 December

	£	£
Capital		5,600
Furniture and fittings	5,880	
Stock January 1	700	
Drawings	1,200	
Bank overdraft		1,260
Salaries	3,560	
General expenses	190	
Purchases/sales	4,020	9,840
Discount all'd/rec'd	150	130
Rent and rates	820	
Returns in/out	90	80
Trade debtors/creditors	1,500	1,070
Bad debt provision		130
	£18,110	£18,110

Notes:

(a) Salaries owing at 31 December – £140

(b) Rent and rates paid in advance – £220

(c) Depreciate furniture and fittings by 10% p.a.

(d) Closing stock valuation – £800

(e) Increase the bad debt provision to bring it up to 10% of debtors' balances.

(i) What will be the yearly depreciation charge?

(A) £5,292.   (B) £6,468.   (C) £588.   (D) £5,886.

(ii) What will be the salaries figure shown on the profit and loss account?

(A) £140.   (B) £3,700.   (C) £3,420.   (D) £3,560.

(iii) The rent and rates figure shown on the profit and loss account will be:

(A) £600.   (B) £820.   (C) £220.   (D) £1,040.

(iv) The new bad debt provision will be:

(A) £1,650.   (B) £1,450.   (C) £150.   (D) £110.

(v) What will be the gross profit on the trading account?

(A) £5,910.   (B) £5,830.   (C) £4,630.   (D) £4,430.

(vi) The net profit on the profit and loss account will be:

(A) £1,420.   (B) £792.   (C) £1,400.   (D) £812.

(vii) The book value of furniture and fittings on the balance sheet will be:

(A) £5,292.   (B) £6,000.   (C) £6,368.   (D) £5,880.

(viii) What will be the turnover for the year?

(A) £9,840.   (B) £3,840.   (C) £9,750.   (D) £4,640.

(ix) Using the adjusted sales figure, the stock turnover for the year will be:

(A) 10.   (B) 11.   (C) 12.   (D) None of these.

(x) What will be the capital figure at end of year?

(A) £4,100.   (B) £5,600.   (C) £5,192.   (D) £6,392.

Pitman Qualifications

MC78 Given last year's capital as £57,500, this year's capital as £64,300, and drawings as £11,800, then profit must have been:
- (A) £18,600
- (B) £18,100
- (C) £16,600
- (D) £19,600.

MC79 Given last year's capital as £74,500, closing capital as £46,200, and drawings of £13,400, then:
- (A) Profit for the year was £14,900
- (B) Loss for the year was £14,900
- (C) Loss for the year was £15,900
- (D) Profit for the year was £16,800.

MC80 Given this year's closing capital as £29,360, the year's net profit as £8,460 and drawings as £5,320, what was the capital at the beginning of the year?
- (A) £29,360
- (B) £26,220
- (C) £34,680
- (D) None of the above.

MC81 In a commercial firm, an 'accumulated fund' would be known as:
- (A) fixed assets
- (B) Total assets
- (C) Net current assets
- (D) Capital.

MC82 A receipts and payments account does not show:
- (A) Cheques paid out during the year
- (B) The accumulated fund
- (C) Receipts from sales of assets
- (D) Bank balances.

Answers to multiple-choice questions

Set 1

1	B	2	C	3	B	4	C	5	A
6	C	7	D	8	A	9	D	10	C
11	C	12	B	13	D	14	A	15	C
16	D	17	C	18	C	19	C	20	D

Set 2

21	D	22	C	23	A	24	D	25	C
26	A	27	B	28	D	29	B	30	D
31	A	32	D	33	D	34	B	35	B
36	B	37	C	38	A	39	D	40	B
41	C	42	B	43	D	44	C	45	C
46	A	47	A	48	A	49	D	50	C
51	A	52	B	53	C	54	A	55	D

Set 3

56	D	57	D	58	C	59	D	60	A
61	D	62	C	63	B	64 (i) B (ii) B (iii) B		65	A
66	D	67	A	68	B	69	C	70	A
71	B	72	A	73	D	74	B	75	D

76 (i) C (ii) B (iii) A (iv) D (v) B (vi) B (vii) C (viii) C (ix) D (x) A

77 (i) C (ii) B (iii) A (iv) C (v) A (vi) B (vii) A (viii) C (ix) D (x) D

78	A	79	B	80	B	81	D	82	B

APPENDIX E

Answers to exercises

*Set out in this Appendix are the answers to the Exercises at the end of each chapter, **excluding** those with suffix 'X' in the Exercise number.*

Chapter 1

No questions.

Chapter 2

2.1
(a) £26,373
(b) £62,486
(c) £77,100
(d) £986,763
(e) £10,265
(f) £404,903

2.3
(a) Asset
(b) Asset
(c) Liability
(d) Asset
(e) Liability
(f) Asset

2.5 Wrong:
Assets — Creditors, Loan from C Shaw
Liabilities — Debtors, Stock of Goods

2.7

	£
Assets	
Shop premises	50,000
Motor vehicle	10,000
Stock of goods	5,000
Cash at bank	7,000
Cash in hand	100
	72,100
Less Liabilities	
Loan from Uncle	30,000
Owed for stock	2,100
	32,100
CAPITAL INTRODUCED	40,000

2.9

Balance Sheet of T Lymer as at 31 December 2007

	£	£	£
Fixed assets:			
Office furniture			8,640
Delivery van			12,000
			20,640
Current assets:			
Stock	4,220		
Debtors	10,892		
Cash at Bank	11,722	26,834	
Less Current liabilities:			
Creditors	12,651	12,651	
Net current assets			14,183
			£34,823
Financed by:			
Capital			34,823
			£34,823

2.11

	Assets £	Capital £	Liabilities £
(a)	+400		+400
(b)	+500		+500
(c)	-50		-50
(d)	-330		-330
(e)	+5,000	+5,000	
(f)	+880		
	-880		
(g)	+45		
	-45		
(h)	+77		+77
	-77		

Chapter 3

3.1

	Account to be debited	Account to be credited
(a)	Motor van	Cash
(b)	Office machinery	J Grant & Son
(c)	Cash	Capital
(d)	Bank	J Beach
(e)	A Barrett	Cash

3.3

Bank

		£			£
(1)	Capital	2,500	(2)	Office F	150
			(5)	Motor van	600
			(15)	Planers Ltd	750
			(31)	Machinery	280

Capital

		£
(1)	Bank	2,500

Office Furniture

		£			£
(2)	Bank	150	(8)	J Walker & Sons	60

Machinery

		£
(3)	Planers Ltd	750
(31)	Bank	280

Cash

		£
(23)	J Walker	60

Planers Ltd

		£			£
(15)	Bank	750	(3)	Machinery	750

Motor Van

		£
(5)	Bank	600

J Walker & Sons

		£			£
(8)	Office F	60	(23)	Cash	60

3.5

A Burton

Capital Account

		£
(1)	Bank	15,000

Bank Account

		£			£
(1)	Capital	15,000	(3)	Motor vehicles	6,500
			(9)	Furniture	1,150
			(17)	Cash	200
			(25)	Computex Ltd	1,000
			(27)	Motor vehicles	2,450
			(31)	Computex Ltd	1,400

Furniture Account

		£
(9)	Bank	1,150
(19)	Cash	42
(29)	Cash	100

Computer Equipment Account

		£
(12)	Computex Ltd	2,400

Computex Ltd Account

		£			£
(25)	Bank	1,000	(12)	Computer equipment	2,400
(31)	Bank	1,400			

Cash Account

		£			£
(17)	Bank	200	(19)	Furniture	42
			(29)	Furniture	100

Motor Vehicles Account

		£
(3)	Bank	6,500
(27)	Bank	2,450

Chapter 4

4.1

	Account to be debited	Account to be credited
(a)	Purchases	P Hart
(b)	Cash	Sales
(c)	Motor vehicles	Morgan Motors
(d)	Purchases	Cohens Ltd
(e)	P Hart	Returns outwards
(f)	H Perkins	Sales
(g)	Bank	Sales
(h)	Cash	Office furniture
(i)	Returns inwards	H Perkins
(j)	Purchases	P Griffith

4.3

Paul Garner

Capital

		(1) Cash	4,000

Purchases

(2) Flynn Bros	1,230		
(4) Cash	345		
(20) Flynn Bros	450		

Sales

		(7) Cash	120
		(16) D Knott	600
		(23) Bateson's Ltd	570

Computer Equipment

(14) Bank	1,000		

Bateson's Ltd

(23) Sales	570	(30) Returns inwards	109

Returns Inwards

(30) Bateson's Ltd	109		

Cash

| (1) Capital | 4,000 | (4) Purchases | 345 |
| (7) Sales | 120 | (10) Bank | 3,500 |

Flynn Bros

| (25) Returns outwards | 75 | (2) Purchases | 1,230 |
| (27) Bank | 1,605 | (20) Purchases | 450 |

Bank

| (10) Cash | 3,500 | (14) Computer Equip | 1,000 |
| | | (27) Flynn Bros | 1,605 |

D Knott

(16) Sales	600		

Returns Outwards

		(25) Flynn Bros	75

4.4

Grace Andrews

Capital

| | | (1) Bank | 10,000 |
| | | (1) Cash | 100 |

Cash

| (1) Capital | 100 | (10) Office furniture | 65 |
| (30) Sales | 280 | | |

Shop Fittings

(3) Duffy & Son	1,900		

Barrett's Fashions

| (15) Returns outwards | 180 | (5) Purchases | 2,378 |
| | | (28) Purchases | 1,434 |

Office Furniture

(10) Cash	65		

Returns Outwards

		(15) Barrett's Fashions	180

Bank

(1) Capital	10,000	(9) Computer	1,020
(12) Sales	800	(22) Duffy & Son	1,900
(25) Sales	600	(30) Motor vehicles	4,750

Duffy & Son

(22) Bank	1,900	(3) Shop fittings	1,900

Purchases

| (5) Barrett's Fashions | 2,378 | | |
| (28) Barrett's Fashions | 1,434 | | |

Computer

(9) Bank	1,020		

Sales

		(12) Bank	800
		(25) Bank	600
		(30) Cash	280

Motor Vehicles

(30) Bank	4,750		

Chapter 5

5.1

	Account to be debited	Account to be credited
(a)	Rent	Cash
(b)	Purchases	Cash
(c)	Bank	Rates
(d)	General exps	Bank
(e)	Cash	Commissions recd
(f)	T Jones	Returns outwards
(g)	Cash	Sales
(h)	Office fixtures	Bank
(i)	Wages	Cash
(j)	Drawings	Cash

5.3

Bank

Jan 1	Capital	20,000	Jan 3	Rent	1,000
Jan 25	Sales	800	Jan 4	Motor van	5,000
			Jan 19	Insurance	220
			Jan 31	Electricity	78

Capital

			Jan 1	Bank	20,000

Rent

Jan 3	Bank	1,000

Motor Van

Jan 4	Bank	5,000

Cash

Jan 5	Sales	1,005	Jan 10	Motor expenses	75
			Jan 12	Wages	120
			Jan 31	Wages	135

Motor Expenses

Jan 10	Cash	75

Wages

Jan 12	Cash	120
Jan 31	Cash	135

Insurance

Jan 19	Bank	220

Electricity

Jan 31	Bank	78

Purchases

Jan 4	M Parkin	580
Jan 4	J Kane	2,400
Jan 17	M Parkin	670

Sales

			Jan 5	Cash	1,005
			Jan 25	Bank	800

M Parkin

			Jan 4	Purchases	580
			Jan 17	Purchases	670

J Kane

			Jan 4	Purchases	2,400

5.5

Bank

Jul 1	Capital	8,000	Jul 2	Rent	375
			Jul 3	Shop Fittings	800
			Jul 6	Insurance	130
			Jul 13	Printing & Stationery	120
			Jul 30	High Lane Motors	5,000

Capital

			Jul 1	Bank	8,000

Rent

Jul 2	Bank	375

Shop Fittings

Jul 3	Bank	800

Insurance

Jul 6	Bank	130

Chapter 6

6.1

D Binns

(1) Sales	1,035	(9) Returns inwards	60
		(25) Cash	450
		(31) Balance c/d	525
	1,035		1,035
(1) Balance b/d	525		

M Loute

(3) Sales	99	(31) Balance c/d	99
(1) Balance b/d	99		

C Cade

(1) Sales	450	(12) Bank	450

H Teate

(1) Sales	630	(9) Returns inwards	30
		(16) Bank	600
	630		630

J Watts

(3) Sales	627	(31) Balance c/d	762
(31) Sales	135		
	762		762
(1) Balance b/d	762		

6.2

G Birks

(11) Returns outwards	87	(2) Purchases	687
(27) Cash	300	(17) Purchases	120
(31) Balance c/d	420		
	807		807
		(1) Balance b/d	420

B Dixon

(21) Bank	1,320	(5) Purchases	1,320

T Potts

(11) Returns outwards	33	(2) Purchases	1,012
(31) Balance c/d	979		
	1,012		1,012
		(1) Balance b/d	979

A Weale

(31) Returns outwards	42	(2) Purchases	180
(31) Balance c/d	138		
	180		180
		(1) Balance b/d	138

K Lee

(31) Balance c/d	150	(5) Purchases	150
		(1) Balance b/d	150

Motor Van

Jul 7 High Lane Motors	5,000

Cash

Jul 11 Sales	1,500	Jul 15 Wages	200
Jul 21 Sales	780	Jul 25 Motor expenses	89
		Jul 31 Wages	300
		Jul 31 Stationery	45

Printing and Stationery

Jul 13 Bank	120
Jul 31 Cash	45

Wages

Jul 15 Cash	200
Jul 31 Cash	300

Motor Expenses

Jul 25 Cash	89

Purchases

Jul 5 A Jackson	450
Jul 5 D Hill	675
Jul 5 E Frudd	1,490
Jul 18 A Jackson	890

Sales

	Jul 11 Cash	1,500
	Jul 21 Cash	780

A Jackson

	Jul 5 Purchases	450
	Jul 18 Purchases	890

D Hill

	Jul 5 Purchases	675

E Frudd

	Jul 5 Purchases	1,490

High Lane Motors

Jul 30 Bank	5,000	Jul 7 Motor van	5,000

6.3

D Binns

	Dr £	Cr £	Balance £	
(1) Sales	1,035		1,035	Dr
(9) Returns inwards		60	975	Dr
(25) Cash		450	525	Dr

C Cade

	Dr £	Cr £	Balance £	
(1) Sales	450		450	Dr
(12) Bank		450	0	Dr

H Teate

	Dr £	Cr £	Balance £	
(1) Sales	630		630	Dr
(9) Returns inwards		30	600	Dr
(16) Bank		600	0	Dr

J Watts

	Dr £	Cr £	Balance £	
(3) Sales	627		627	Dr
(31) Sales	135		762	Dr

M Lowe

	Dr £	Cr £	Balance £	
(3) Sales	99		99	Dr

6.5

T Tickle

	£			£
(1) Sales	690		(14) Returns inwards	46
(31) Balance c/d	30		(25) Bank	674
	720			720

D Stott

	£			£
(19) Returns outwards	19		(3) Purchases	116
(23) Bank	97			
	116			116

J Rhodes

	£			£
(31) Balance c/d	98		(3) Purchases	98

J Ahmed

	£			£
(29) Cash	367		(11) Purchases	367

S Ames

	£			£
(1) Sales	330		(14) Returns inwards	45
(9) Sales	645		(30) Bank	500
			(31) Balance c/d	430
	975			975

D Owen

	£			£
(19) Returns outwards	36		(3) Purchases	347
(31) Balance c/d	446		(11) Purchases	135
	482			482

T Johnson

	£			£
(9) Sales	376		(31) Bank	376

Debtors   S Ames

Creditors   T Tickle
D Owen
J Rhodes

Chapter 7

7.1

Capital

				£
			May 1 Bank	2,500

Bank

	£			£
May 1 Capital	2,500		May 12 K Gibson	76
May 9 C Bailey	250		May 12 D Ellis	370
May 10 H Spencer	150		May 31 C Mendez	87
			May 31 Balance c/d	2,367
	2,900			2,900
Jun 1 Balance b/d	2,367			

Cash

Dr		£	Cr		£
May 8	Sales	500	May 6	Rent	120
			May 15	Stationery	60
			May 19	Rent	120
			May 31	Balance c/d	200
		500			500
Jun 1	Balance b/d	200			

Rent

Dr		£	Cr		£
May 6	Cash	120	May 31	Balance c/d	240
" 19	Cash	120			
		240			240
Jun 1	Balance b/d	240			

Stationery

Dr		£	Cr		£
May 15	Cash	60			

Purchases

Dr		£	Cr		£
May 2	D Ellis	540	May 31	Balance c/d	1,082
May 2	C Mendez	87			
May 2	K Gibson	76			
May 18	D Ellis	145			
May 18	C Mendez	234			
		1,082			1,082
Jun 1	Balance b/d	1,082			

Sales

Dr		£	Cr		£
May 31	Balance c/d	1,496	May 4	C Bailey	430
			May 4	B Hughes	62
			May 4	H Spencer	176
			May 8	Cash	500
			May 25	C Bailey	90
			May 25	B Hughes	110
			May 25	H Spencer	128
		1,496			1,496
			Jun 1	Balance b/d	1,496

H Spencer

Dr		£	Cr		£
May 4	Sales	176	May 10	Bank	150
May 25	Sales	128	May 31	Balance c/d	154
		304			304
Jun 1	Balance b/d	154			

D Ellis

Dr		£	Cr		£
May 12	Bank	370	May 2	Purchases	540
May 31	Balance c/d	315	May 18	Purchases	145
		685			685
			Jun 1	Balance b/d	315

C Mendez

Dr		£	Cr		£
May 31	Bank	87	May 2	Purchases	87
May 31	Balance c/d	234	May 18	Purchases	234
		321			321
			Jun 1	Balance b/d	234

K Gibson

Dr		£	Cr		£
May 12	Bank	76	May 2	Purchases	76

C Bailey

Dr		£	Cr		£
May 4	Sales	430	May 9	Bank	250
May 25	Sales	90	May 31	Balance c/d	270
		520			520
Jun 1	Balance b/d	270			

B Hughes

Dr		£	Cr		£
May 4	Sales	62	May 31	Balance c/d	172
May 25	Sales	110			
		172			172
Jun 1	Balance b/d	172			

Trial Balance as at 31 May 2005

	Dr £	Cr £
Capital		2,500
Bank	2,367	
Cash	200	
Rent	240	
Stationery	60	
Purchases	1,082	
Sales		1,496
H Spencer	154	
D Ellis		315
C Mendez		234
C Bailey	270	
B Hughes	172	
	4,545	4,545

7.2

Bank

Mar 1	Capital	8,000	Mar 17	M Hyatt	84
Mar 24	J Carlton	95	Mar 21	Betta Ltd	500
			Mar 31	Motor van	4,000
			Mar 31	Balance c/d	3,511
		8,095			8,095
Apr 1	Balance b/d	3,511			

Cash

Mar 5	Sales	870	Mar 6	Wages	140
Mar 30	J King (Loan)	600	Mar 9	Purchases	46
			Mar 12	Wages	140
			Mar 31	Balance c/d	1,144
		1,470			1,470
Apr 1	Balance b/d	1,144			

Capital

			Mar 1	Bank	8,000

Motor Van

Mar 31	Bank	4,000			

Returns Outwards

Mar 31	Balance c/d	44	Mar 18	T Braham	20
			Mar 27	K Henriques	24
		44			44
			Apr 1	Balance b/d	44

Wages

Mar 6	Cash	140	Mar 31	Balance c/d	280
Mar 12	Cash	140			
		280			280
Apr 1	Balance b/d	280			

Purchases

Mar 2	K Henriques	76	Mar 31	Balance c/d	864
Mar 2	M Hyatt	27			
Mar 2	T Braham	560			
Mar 9	Cash	46			
Mar 10	M Hyatt	57			
Mar 10	T Braham	98			
		864			864
Apr 1	Balance b/d	864			

Sales

Mar 31	Balance c/d	1,074	Mar 5	Cash	870
			Mar 7	H Elliott	35
			Mar 7	L Lane	42
			Mar 7	J Carlton	72
			Mar 13	L Lane	32
			Mar 13	J Carlton	23
		1,074			1,074
			Apr 1	Balance b/d	1,074

Shop Fixtures

Mar 15	Betta Ltd	500			

J King (Loan)

			Mar 30	Cash	600

H Elliott

Mar 7	Sales	35			

L Lane

Mar 7	Sales	42	Mar 31	Balance c/d	74
Mar 13	Sales	32			
		74			74
Apr 1	Balance b/d	74			

J Carlton

Mar 7	Sales	72	Mar 24	Bank	95
Mar 13	Sales	23			
		95			95

7.5

Trial Balance of P Brown as at 31 May 2006

	Dr £	Cr £
Capital		20,000
Drawings	7,000	
General expenses	500	
Sales		38,500
Purchases	29,000	
Debtors	6,800	
Creditors		9,000
Bank	15,100	
Cash	200	
Plant and equipment	5,000	
Heating and lighting	1,500	
Rent	2,400	
	67,500	67,500

7.6

Trial Balance of S Higton as at 30 June 2007

	Dr £	Cr £
Capital		19,956
Sales		119,439
Stationery	1,200	
General expenses	2,745	
Motor expenses	4,476	
Cash at bank	1,950	
Stock 1 July 2006	7,668	
Wages and salaries	9,492	
Rent and rates	10,500	
Office equipment	6,000	
Purchases	81,753	
Heating and lighting	2,208	
Rent received		2,139
Debtors	10,353	
Drawings	4,200	
Creditors		10,230
Motor vehicle	7,500	
Interest received		1,725
Insurance	3,444	
	153,489	153,489

K Henriques

Mar 27	Returns	24	Mar 2	Purchases	76
Mar 31	Balance c/d	52			
		76			76
			Apr 1	Balance b/d	52

M Hyatt

Mar 17	Bank	84	Mar 2	Purchases	27
			Mar 10	Purchases	57
		84			84

T Brabam

Mar 18	Returns	20	Mar 2	Purchases	560
Mar 31	Balance c/d	638	Mar 10	Purchases	98
		658			658
			Apr 1	Balance b/d	638

Betta Ltd

Mar 21	Bank	500	Mar 15	Shop Fixtures	500

Trial Balance as at 31 March 2006

	Dr £	Cr £
Bank	3,511	
Cash	1,144	
Capital		8,000
Motor van	4,000	
Returns outwards		44
Wages	280	
Purchases	864	
Sales		1,074
Shop fixtures	500	
J King (Loan)		600
H Elliott	35	
L Lane	74	
K Henriques		52
J Braham		638
	10,408	10,408

Chapter 8

8.1

L Simpson
Trading and Profit and Loss Account
for the year ended 31 December 2006

	£	£
Sales		38,220
Less Cost of goods sold:		
Purchases	24,190	
Less Closing stock	4,310	
		19,880
Gross profit		18,340
Less Expenses:		
Rent	4,170	
Wages and salaries	5,390	
Postage and stationery	840	
Electricity expenses	710	
General expenses	370	
		11,480
Net profit		6,860

8.3

G Singh
Trading and Profit and Loss Account
for the year ended 31 December 2006

	£	£
Sales		73,848
Less Cost of goods sold:		
Purchases	58,516	
Less Closing stock	10,192	
		48,324
Gross profit		25,524
Less Expenses:		
Wages	8,600	
Motor expenses	2,080	
Rates	2,680	
Insurance	444	
General expenses	420	
		14,224
Net profit		11,300

8.5

Mrs P Stewart
Trial Balance as at 31 March 2008

	Dr £	Cr £
Sales		24,765
Purchases	13,545	
Staff wages	2,100	
Drawings	5,500	
Rent and rates	1,580	
Electricity	565	
Motor expenses	845	
Insurance	345	
General expenses	245	
Cash in hand	135	
Cash at bank	2,675	
Creditors		3,285
Vehicle	5,875	
Fixtures and fittings	1,495	
Capital		6,855
	34,905	34,905

Closing stock £2,345

Mrs P Stewart
Trading and Profit and Loss Account
for the year ended 31 March 2008

	£	£
Sales		24,765
Less Cost of goods sold		
Purchases	13,545	
Less Closing stock	2,345	
		11,200
Gross profit		13,565
Less Overheads		
Staff wages	2,100	
Rent and rates	1,580	
Electricity	565	
Motor expenses	845	
Insurance	345	
General expenses	245	
		5,680
Net profit		7,885

Chapter 9

9.1

G Singh
Balance Sheet as at 31 December 2006

	£	£	£
Fixed Assets			
Premises			20,000
Motor vehicle			12,000
			32,000
Current Assets			
Stock		10,192	
Debtors		7,800	
Cash at bank		6,616	
Cash in hand		160	
		24,768	
Less Current Liabilities			
Creditors	6,418	6,418	
Net current assets			18,350
			50,350
Financed by			
Cash introduced			48,000
Add Net profit for the year			11,300
			59,300
Less Drawings			8,950
			50,350

9.3

Mrs P Stewart
Balance Sheet as at 31 March 2008

	£	£	£
Fixed Assets			
Fixtures and fittings			1,495
Motor car			5,875
			7,370
Current Assets			
Stock	2,345		
Debtors	–		
Bank	2,675		
Cash	135		
		5,155	
Less Current Liabilities			
Creditors	3,285	3,285	
Net current assets			1,870
Total net assets			9,240
Financed by			
Capital			6,855
Add Net profit			7,885
			14,740
Less Drawings			5,500
			9,240

9.4

Miss V Holland
Balance Sheet as at 30 June 2008

	£	£	£	£
Fixed Assets				
Equipment				2,885
Van				3,400
				6,285
Current Assets				
Stock in hand		1,465		
Trade debtors		2,375		
Cash in hand		150		
			3,990	
Current Liabilities				
Trade creditors		4,565		
Bank overdraft		1,785		
			6,350	
Net current liabilities				(2,360)
				3,925
Long-term Liabilities				
Loan from mother				2,000
Net assets				1,925
Financed by				
Capital account				
Cash introduced				2,000
Net profit				2,525
				4,525
Drawings				2,600
				1,925

Chapter 10

10.1

T Clarke
Trading Account for the year ended 31 December 2007

	£	£	£
Sales			38,742
Less cost of goods sold			
Opening stock		6,924	
Add Purchases		26,409	
Add Carriage inwards		670	
		34,003	
Less Closing stock		7,489	
			26,514
Gross profit			12,228

10.3

T Mann
Trading and Profit and Loss Account
for the year ended 31 December 2006

	£	£	£
Sales			52,790
Less Returns inwards			490
			52,300
Less cost of goods sold			
Opening stock		5,690	
Add Purchases	31,000		
Carriage inwards	1,700		
	32,700		
Less Returns outwards	560		
		32,140	
		37,830	
Less Closing stock		4,230	
			33,600
Gross Profit			18,700
Less Expenses:			
Rent		1,460	
Salaries and wages		5,010	
Motor expenses		3,120	
Carriage outwards		790	
General expenses		420	
			10,800
Net profit			7,900

10.5

S Makin
Trading and Profit and Loss Account
for the year ended 30 September 2006

	£	£	£
Sales			18,600
Less Returns inwards			205
			18,395
Less Cost of sales			
Opening stock		2,368	
Add Purchases	11,874		
Add Carriage inwards	310		
	12,184		
Less Returns outwards	322		
		11,862	
		14,230	
Less Closing stock		2,946	
			11,284
Gross profit			7,111
Less Expenses:			
Salaries and wages		3,862	
Rent and rates		304	
Carriage outwards		200	
Insurance		78	
Motor expenses		664	
Office expenses		216	
Lighting and heating expenses		166	
General expenses		314	
			5,804
Net profit			1,307

S Makin
Balance Sheet as at 30 September 2006

	£	£	£
Fixed Assets			
Premises			15,000
Fixtures and fittings			350
Motor vehicles			1,800
			17,150
Current Assets			
Stock	2,946		
Debtors	3,896		
Bank	482		
		7,324	
Less Current Liabilities			
Creditors	1,731	1,731	
Net current assets			5,593
			22,743
Financed by:			
Capital			
Balance at 1.10.2005			22,636
Add Net profit			1,307
			23,943
Less Drawings			1,200
			22,743

10.8

J Smailes
Trading and Profit and Loss Account
for the year ended 31 March 2007

	£	£	£
Sales			92,340
Less Cost of sales			
Opening stock		18,160	
Add Purchases	69,185		
Add Carriage inwards	420		
	69,605		
Less Returns outwards	640		
		68,965	
		87,125	
Less Closing stock		22,390	
			64,735
Gross profit			27,605
Less Expenses			
Wages and salaries		10,240	
Carriage outwards		1,570	
Rent and rates		3,015	
Communication expenses		624	
Commissions payable		216	
Insurance		405	
Sundry expenses		318	
			16,388
Net profit			11,217

Chapter 11

11.1 (a) Materiality
(b) Business entity
(c) Prudence
(d) Historical cost
(e) Money measurement
(f) Accrual
(g) Realisation
(h) Going concern
(i) Consistency
(j) Materiality.

11.4 The *historical cost concept* is an accounting concept whereby the assets of a business are recorded in the accounts at cost price. Refer to text, Sections 11.2 and 11.4.

Advantages of using the cost method of valuation are that the assets can easily be verified since there will be an invoice available for checking the purchase price; and, also, no valuations need be carried out on assets whose value may be subjective. Refer to text, Sections 11.2 and 11.4.

J Smailes
Balance Sheet as at 31 March 2007

	£	£	£
Fixed Assets			
Buildings			20,000
Fixtures			2,850
			22,850
Current Assets			
Stock	22,390		
Debtors	14,320		
Bank	2,970		
Cash	115		
		39,795	
Less Current Liabilities			
Creditors	8,160	8,160	
Net current assets			31,635
			54,485
Less Long-term liabilities			
Loan			10,000
			44,485
Capital			
Balance at 1.4.2006			40,888
Add Net profit			11,217
			52,105
Less Drawings			7,620
			44,485

Chapter 12

12.1 (a) Sales day books/sales ledger/personal account
(b) Cash book/general ledger/nominal account
(c) Purchases day book/purchases ledger/personal account
(d) Cash book/general ledger/nominal account
(e) Sales day book/sales ledger/personal account
(f) Returns inwards day book/sales ledger/personal account
(g) Returns outwards day book/purchases ledger/personal account
(h) General journal/general ledger/real account.

12.3

Name of account	Personal	Nominal	Real
(a) Stock			✓
(b) Wages		✓	
(c) Bank		✓	
(d) Debtor	✓		
(e) Office equipment			✓
(f) Purchases		✓	
(g) Rent received		✓	

NEAB (GCSE)

Chapter 13

13.1, 13.2, 13.3 and **13.4**
The answer to each question can be found in the chapter text.

13.7 (a) Howard Photographics
(b) Central Bank
(c) Ben Brown Limited.

Chapter 14

14.1

Cash Book

	Cash	Bank		Cash	Bank
(1) Capital		4,000	(2) Fixtures		660
(4) Sales	225		(4) Rent	140	
(6) T Thomas		188	(12) Wages	275	
(8) Sales		308	(15) Cash		200
(10) J King	300		(20) Stationery	60	
(14) J Walters (Loan)		500	(22) J French		166
(15) Bank	200		(28) Drawings	100	
(30) J Scott		277	(31) Balances c/d	216	4,247
(31) Sales	66				
	791	5,273		791	5,273
(1) Balances b/d	216	4,247			

14.2

Cash Book

	Cash	Bank		Cash	Bank
2005			**2005**		
May 1 Balance b/d	14.72	820.54	May 1 Balance b/d		
3 P Wrench		432.36	2 Stationery	10.00	
3 R Whitworth		634.34	6 SW Rail		37.50
3 J Summers		341.00	9 Fabulous Fabrics Ltd		450.80
12 Sales	76.00		11 Mellors Mfg. Co		348.32
17 Trentham Traders		32.81	14 Inland Revenue		221.30
24 Sales	350.00		20 Foreign Currency		250.00
26 Cash C		300.00	20 Bank Charges		3.20
31 J Summers		1,231.00	26 Bank C	300.00	
31 Bradnop Mfg. Co		725.00	27 Salaries		5,720.00
31 Taylors		2,330.50	31 Balance c/d	130.72	
31 Balance c/d		1,824.65			
	440.72	7,851.66		440.72	7,851.66
June 1 Balance b/d	130.72		June 1 Balance b/d		1,824.65

14.4

Cash Book

	Disct	Cash	Bank		Disct	Cash	Bank
(1) Capital			6,000	(1) Fixtures			950
(3) Sales		407		(2) Purchases			1,240
(5) N Morgan	10		210	(4) Rent		200	
(9) S Cooper	20		380	(7) S Thompson & Co	4		76
(14) L Curtis			115	(12) Rates			410
(20) P Exeter	2		78	(16) M Monroe	6	114	
(31) Sales			88	(31) Balances c/d		93	4,195
	32	407	6,871		10	407	6,871

General Ledger

Discounts Allowed

(31) Cash Book	32

Discounts Received

		(31) Cash Book	10

14.5

Cash Book

	Disct	Cash	Bank		Disct	Cash	Bank
(1) Balances b/d		211	3,984	(2) T Adams	4		76
(4) C Potts	4		98	(2) C Bibby	13		247
(6) Sales			49	(2) D Clarke	22		418
(9) R Smiley	16		156	(7) Insurance		65	
(9) J Turner	13		624	(12) Motor expenses		100	
(9) R Pimlott			507	(21) Salaries			120
(18) Sales		98		(23) Rent		60	
(28) R Godfrey (Loan)			500	(31) Stationery			27
				(31) Balances c/d		84	5,030
	33	309	5,918		39	309	5,918

General Ledger

Discounts Allowed

(31) Cash Book	33

Discounts Received

		(31) Cash Book	39

Chapter 15

Note: Both in theory and in practice you can start with the cash book balance working to the bank statement balance, or you can reverse this method. Many teachers and lecturers have their preferences, but this is a personal matter only. Examiners sometimes ask for them using one way, sometimes the other. Students should therefore be able to tackle them both ways.

15.1
(a), (b) and (c)

Cash Book

Date 2006	Details	Bank £	Date 2006	Cheque number	Details	Bank £
1 Nov	Balance b/f	9,000	1 Nov	625109	R B Lawley	6,300
5 Nov	L Burger	10,000	5 Nov	625110	B&B Limited	1,100
22 Nov	D Smith	1,396	22 Nov	625111	M Parkes	300
8 Nov	B Green	3,500	22 Nov	625112	Richards Limited	9,667
			15 Nov		LBO Limited	1,300
			20 Nov		Bank charges	29
			25 Nov		HB Services	1,800
			30 Nov		Balance c/d	3,400
		23,896				23,896
1 Dec	Balance b/d	3,400				

(d)

Berry Sports
Bank Reconciliation Statement as at 30 November 2006

	£	£
Balance as per Cash Book		3,400
Add: Unpresented cheque		
M Parkes 625111	300	
Richards Ltd 625112	9,667	9,967
		13,367
Less: Bank Lodgements not yet entered on bank statement		
D Smith		1,396
		1,396
Balance at bank as per Bank Statement		11,971

15.3
(a)

Cash Book – James Baxter

2006		£	2006		£
Mar 31	Credit transfer – A May	929	Mar 31	Balance b/d	2,804
Mar 31	Balance c/d	2,003	Mar 31	Standing order – Oak plc	100
			Mar 31	Bank charges	28
		2,932			2,932

(b)

James Baxter
Bank Reconciliation Statement as at 31 March 2006

	£
Bank overdraft per cash book	2,003
Add Banking not entered on bank statement	160
	2,163
Less Unpresented cheque	490
Bank overdraft per bank statement	1,673

OR

James Baxter
Bank Reconciliation Statement as at 31 March 2006

	£
Balance per bank statement	1,673 O/D
Add Banking not entered on bank statement	160
	1,513 O/D
Less Unpresented cheque	490
Balance per cash book	2,003 O/D

15.5
(a)

Cash Book – K Talbot

	£		£
Balance b/d	4,500	RB Insurance	600
Bank interest received	720	Bank charges	90
KB Ltd	780	Dishonoured cheque: C Hill	210
Bank deposit account	4,200	Balance c/d	9,300
	10,200		10,200

(b)

K Talbot
Bank Reconciliation Statement as at 31 December 2006

	£
Balance per cash book	9,300
Add Unpresented cheques (750 + 870)	1,620
	10,920
Less Banking not recorded	2,070
Balance per bank statement	8,850

OR

K Talbot
Bank Reconciliation Statement as at 31 December 2006

	£
Balance per bank statement	8,850
Add Cash not yet credited	2,070
	10,920
Less Unpresented cheques (750 + 870)	1,620
Balance per cash book	9,300

Chapter 16

16.1 (a) Style of invoice will vary. Invoice number to be 10586

Calculations:

	£
3 sets of Boy Michael golf clubs × £240	720
150 Watson golf balls at £8 per 10 balls	120
4 Faldo golf bags at £30	120
	960
Less trade discount 33$\frac{1}{3}$%	320
	640
Add VAT 17$\frac{1}{2}$%	112
	752

(b)

D Wilson Ltd Ledger
G Christie & Sons

2005	
May 1 Sales	752

G Christie & Son Ledger
D Wilson Ltd

2005	
May 1 Purchases	752

16.2

Sales Day Book

	Total	VAT	Net
2006			
Aug 1 M Sinclair & Co	188	28	160
Aug 8 M Brown & Associates	282	42	240
Aug 19 A Axton Ltd	94	14	80
Aug 31 T Christie	47	7	40
	611	91	520

Sales Ledger
M Sinclair & Co

(1) Sales	188

M Brown & Associates

(8) Sales	282

A Axton Ltd

(19) Sales	94

T Christie

(31) Sales	47

General Ledger
Sales

(31) Credit sales for the month	520

Value Added Tax

(31) Sales book: VAT content	91

16.3

Sales Day Book – R Colman Ltd

	Total	Net	VAT
(1) B Davies & Co	188	160	28
(4) C Grant Ltd	235	200	35
(16) C Grant Ltd	141	120	21
(31) B Karloff	94	80	14
	658	560	98

Purchases Day Book – R Colman Ltd

	Total	Net	VAT
(10) G Cooper & Son	470	400	70
(10) J Wayne Ltd	282	240	42
(14) B Lugosi	47	40	7
(23) S Hayward	47	40	7
	846	720	126

Sales Ledger

B Davies & Co

(1) Sales 188

C Grant Ltd

(4) Sales 235
(16) Sales 141

B Karloff

(31) Sales 94

Purchases Ledger

G Cooper & Son

(10) Purchases 470

J Wayne Ltd

(10) Purchases 282

B Lugosi

(14) Purchases 47

S Hayward

(23) Purchases 47

General Ledger

Sales

(31) Sales day book 560

Purchases

(31) Purchases day book 720

Value Added Tax

(31) VAT content in purchase book	126	(31) VAT content in sales book	98
		(31) Balance c/d	28
	126		126

16.5 (a) Trade discount £200.
(b) Cash discount £90.
(c) VAT £299.25.

16.6 VAT payable to HM Customs & Excise:

Manufacturer	35
Wholesaler (49 – 35)	14
Retailer (56 – 49)	7
	56

16.7 (a) Debited
(b) Six years
(c) Yes
(d) Debit – Sales returns/Returns inwards 80
Debit – VAT 14
Credit – Bank/cash 94

AAT (Central Assessment)

Chapter 17

17.1

Petty Cash Book

Receipts £ p	Date	Details	Voucher Number	Total £ p	VAT £ p	Postage £ p	Cleaning £ p	Motor Expenses £ p	Stationery £ p	Sundry Expenses £ p
2007										
18.52	June 1	Balance	b/d							
131.48	June 1	Cash								
	June 1	Window cleaner	32	10.00			10.00			
	June 3	Postage stamps	33	7.60		7.60				
	June 4	Petrol	34	37.60	5.60			32.00		
	June 6	Stationery	35	9.75	1.45				8.30	
2.00	June 10	Jean Ford stamps	8							
	June 14	Office cleaner	36	20.00			20.00			
	June 16	Parcel postage	37	1.35		1.35				
	June 19	Magazine	38	3.00						3.00
	June 21	Computer disks	39	7.95	1.05				6.90	
	June 23	Petrol	40	14.10	2.10			12.00		
	June 27	Refreshments	41	4.20						4.20
	June 29	Office cleaner	42	20.00			20.00			
				135.55	10.20	8.95	50.00	44.00	15.20	7.20
152.00	June 30	Balance	c/d	16.45						
152.00				152.00						
16.45	July 1	Balance	b/d							
133.55	July 1	Cash								

Amount required to restore imprest = Float required

$$
\begin{array}{lr}
& \text{£} \\
\text{Float required} & 150.00 \\
\text{Less Cash in hand} & \underline{16.45} \\
\text{Amount required} & \underline{\underline{133.55}}
\end{array}
$$

17.4

(a)

Petty Cash Book – S Dickinson (Estate Agents)

Receipts £	Date 2009	Details	Voucher no	Total payment £	Travelling £	Postage £	Stationery £	Office expenses £	VAT £	Ledger postings £
120.00	Mar 1	Cash	CB 1							
	2	Postage Stamps	1	6.50		6.50				
	3	Rail Fare	2	23.00	23.00					
	7	Parcel	3	4.00		4.00				
	9	Window Cleaning	4	8.00				8.00		
	12	Envelopes	5	3.10			2.64		0.46	
	14	Office Tea, etc.	6	6.40				6.40		
	16	Petrol	7	10.00	8.51				1.49	
	19	Disks – Computer	8	13.00				11.06	1.94	
	20	Dusters and Polish	9	1.73				1.47	0.26	
	23	Postage Stamps	10	2.40		2.40				
	27	Ledger a/c J Cheetham	11	7.30						7.30
	31	Magazine	12	6.40				6.40		
				91.83	31.51	12.90	2.64	33.33	4.15	7.30
		Balance c/d		28.17						
120.00				120.00						
			CB 1		GL 1	GL 2	GL 3	GL 4	GL 5	C 44
28.17	Apr 1	Balance b/d								
91.83	Apr 1	Cash	CB 1							

(b)

General Ledger

Travelling Expenses Account   GL 1

2009
Mar 31 Petty Cash   PCB 1   31.51

Postage Account   GL 2

2009
Mar 31 Petty Cash   PCB 1   12.90

Stationery Account   GL 3

2009
Mar 31 Petty Cash   PCB 1   2.64

Office Expenses Account   GL 4

2009
Mar 31 Petty Cash   PCB 1   33.33

VAT Account   GL 5

2009
Mar 31 Petty Cash   PCB 1   4.15

Cash Book (Bank Column Only)   CB 1

2009
Mar 31 Petty Cash   PCB 1   91.83

Purchase Ledger   C 44
J Cheetham Account

2009				2009		
Mar 31 Petty Cash	PCB 1	7.30		Feb 1 Balance b/d		7.30

(c)

MEMORANDUM

To	Ms S Dickinson	Ref	
From	Student's Name	Date	31 March 2009
Subject	Petty Cash Imprest System		

Advantages of Imprest System:

1. *Control:* The petty cash can be checked easily at any time because cash in hand plus vouchers paid out for the period should always equal the amount of the 'float'.
2. *Responsibility:* It is an ideal opportunity to appoint junior staff and give them some responsibility and test their honesty.
3. *Efficiency:* It relieves the accountant by dealing with numerous small cash payments and reduces the posting to the general ledger.

Chapter 18

18.1   Newton Data Systems

Type of expenditure	Reason
(a) Revenue	Use up in the short term
(b) Capital	Adds to value of computer equipment
(c) Revenue	Used up in the short term
(d) Revenue	Used up in the short term
(e) Capital	Adds to the value of the computer
(f) Question is not clear	
(1) If spent on improving building Construction = Capital	Add to value of fixed assets
(2) If spent on extra wages for Security guards = Revenue	Used up in the short term

18.2   Cairns Engineering Co

	Capital	Revenue
	£	£
(a) New stationery and brochures	–	411
(b) New pickup truck	18,000	–
(c) New lathe	5,200	–
(d) Delivery costs – lathe	200	–
(e) Electricity – wiring	1,800	
– electricity costs		2,100
(f) Wages – Re: improvements	20,000	
– Other		45,000
	45,200	47,511

Brief description of capital and revenue expenditure – see text.

18.4
T Taylor
Revised Profits Year to 31 December 2008

	£
Gross profit before corrections	95,620
Add (a) Purchases overstated	311
	95,931
Less (c) Sale of building	10,000
Revised gross profit	85,931
Net profit before corrections	28,910
Less Gross profit overstated (10,000 – 311)	9,689
	19,221
Add (d) Loan interest overstated	500
Revised net profit	19,721

Error (b) does not affect gross profit or net profit calculations.

Chapter 19

19.1   Sales Day Book

(1)	J Gordon	187
(3)	G Abrahams	166
(6)	V White	12
(10)	J Gordon	55
(17)	F Williams	289
(19)	C Richards	66
(27)	V Wood	28
(31)	L Simes	78
		881

Sales Ledger
J Gordon

| (1) Sales | 187 | |
| (10) Sales | 55 | |

G Abrahams

| (3) Sales | 166 | |

V White

| (6) Sales | 12 | |

F Williams

| (17) Sales | 289 | |

C Richards

| (19) Sales | 66 | |

V Wood

| (27) Sales | 28 | |

L Simes

| (31) Sales | 78 | |

General Ledger
Sales Account

| | | (31) Sales day book | 881 |

19.3 Dabell's Stationery Supplies Ltd.

Sales Day Book

			page 26
Date	Name	Invoice No	Total £
April 1	Fisher & Co	6265	1,459
April 3	Elder (Office Supplies)	6266	73
April 5	Haigh (Mfr) Ltd	6267	56
April 11	Ardern & Co (Solicitors)	6268	1,598
April 15	I Rafiq	6269	540
April 20	Royle's Business Systems	6270	2,456
April 22	Fisher & Co	6271	23
April 22	Ardern & Co (Solicitors)	6272	345
April 25	Elder (Office Supplies)	6273	71
April 27	Haigh (Mfr) Ltd	6274	176
			6,797

Sales Ledger

Ardern & Co Account — SL 1

(1) Balance b/d	472	(30) Balance c/d	2,415
(11) Sales	1,598		
(22) Sales	345		
	2,415		2,415
(1) Balance b/d	2,415		

Elder (Office Supplies) Account — SL 2

(1) Balance b/d	75	(30) Balance c/d	219
(3) Sales	73		
(25) Sales	71		
	219		219
(1) Balance b/d	219		

Fisher & Co Account — SL 3

(1) Balance b/d	231	(30) Bank	231
(1) Sales	1,459	(30) Balance c/d	1,482
(22) Sales	23		
	1,713		1,713
(1) Balance b/d	1,482		

Haigh (Mfr) Ltd Account — SL 4

(1) Balance b/d	1,267	(30) Bank	1,000
(5) Sales	56	(30) Balance c/d	499
(27) Sales	176		
	1,499		1,499
(1) Balance b/d	499		

I Rafiq Account — SL 5

(1) Balance b/d	330	(30) Bank	330
(15) Sales	540	(30) Balance c/d	540
	870		870
(1) Balance b/d	540		

Royle's Business Systems Ltd Account — SL 6

(1) Balance b/d	750	(30) Balance c/d	3,206
(20) Sales	2,456		
	3,206		3,206
(1) Balance b/d	3,206		

List of outstanding debtors as at 30 April 2006

	Amount (£)
Ardern & Co	2,415
Elder (Office Supplies)	219
Fisher & Co	1,482
Haigh (Mfr) Ltd	499
I Rafiq	540
Royle's Business Systems	3,206
	8,361

19.5 See text, Section 19.13.

19.6 See text, Section 19.14.

Chapter 20

20.1 *Workings of purchases invoices*

(1) K King

4 radios × 30 =	120
3 music centres × 160 =	480
	600
Less trade discount 25%	150
	450

(3) A Bell

2 washing machines × 200 =	400
5 vacuum cleaners × 60 =	300
2 dish dryers × 150 =	300
	1,000
Less trade discount 20%	200
	800

(15) J Kelly

1 music centre × 300 =	300
2 washing machines × 250 =	500
	800
Less trade discount 25%	200
	600

(20) B Powell

6 radios × 70 =	420
Less trade discount 33$\frac{1}{3}$%	140
	280

(30) B Lewis

4 dish dryers × 200 =	800
Less trade discount 20%	160
	640

(a)

Purchases Day Book

		£
(1)	K King	450
(3)	A Bell	800
(15)	J Kelly	600
(20)	B Powell	280
(30)	B Lewis	640
		2,770

(b)

Purchases Ledger

K King

		£
(1)	Purchases	450

A Bell

		£
(3)	Purchases	800

J Kelly

		£
(15)	Purchases	600

B Powell

		£
(20)	Purchases	280

B Lewis

		£
(30)	Purchases	640

(c)

General Ledger

Purchases Account

		£
(31)	Purchases day book	2,770

20.3 Surprise Desserts

Purchase Day Book — *page 1*

Date 2006		Invoice No	Folio	Amount £
July 1	Barton Foods Ltd	201	PL 10	78.50
July 3	Henmore Eggs	202	PL 11	56.26
July 8	Barton Foods Ltd	203	PL 10	101.30
July 10	Fernley & Co	204	PL 12	98.00
July 12	Henmore Eggs	205	PL 11	48.20
July 14	Bridge Catering Co	206	PL 13	142.00
July 19	Ruffoni Creams	207	PL 14	132.82
July 23	Fernley & Co	208	PL 12	43.20
July 25	Ace Packaging Co	209	PL 15	217.75
July 31	Henmore Eggs	210	PL 11	62.60
			GL 28	980.63

Purchase Ledger

Barton Food's Ltd Account — PL 10

2006			£
July 1	Purchases	PB 1	78.50
July 8	Purchases	PB 1	101.30

Henmore Eggs Account — PL 11

2006			£
July 3	Purchases	PB 1	56.26
July 12	Purchases	PB 1	48.20
July 31	Purchases	PB 1	62.60

Fernley & Co Account — PL 12

2006			£
July 10	Purchases	PB 1	98.00
July 23	Purchases	PB 1	43.20

Bridge Catering Co Account — PL 13

2006			£
July 14	Purchases	PB 1	142.00

Ruffoni Creams Account — PL 14

2006			£
July 19	Purchases	PB 1	132.82

Ace Packaging Co Account — PL 15

2006			£
July 25	Purchases	PB 1	217.75

General Ledger

Purchases Account — GL 28

2006			£
July 31	Credit Purchases for the month	PB 1	980.63

Chapter 21

21.1

Purchases Day Book

(1)	H Lloyd	119
(4)	D Scott	98
(4)	A Simpson	114
(4)	A Williams	25
(4)	S Wood	56
(10)	A Simpson	59
(18)	M White	89
(18)	J Wong	67
(18)	H Miller	196
(18)	H Lewis	119
(31)	A Williams	56
(31)	C Cooper	98
		1,096

Returns Outwards Day Book

(7)	H Lloyd	16
(7)	D Scott	14
(25)	J Wong	5
(25)	A Simpson	11
		46

General Ledger
Purchases Account

(31) Purchases day book	1,096		

Returns Outwards Account

		(31) Returns outwards day book	46

Purchases Ledger
H Lloyd

(7) Returns	16	(1) Purchases	119

D Scott

(7) Returns	14	(4) Purchases	98

A Simpson

(25) Returns	11	(4) Purchases	114
		(10) Purchases	59

A Williams

		(4) Purchases	25
		(31) Purchases	56

S Wood

		(4) Purchases	56

M White

		(18) Purchases	89

J Wong

(25) Returns	5	(18) Purchases	67

H Miller

		(18) Purchases	196

H Lewis

		(18) Purchases	119

C Cooper

		(31) Purchases	98

21.3

Framework Ltd
Sales Ledger
J Forbes (Fancy Gifts) Account

(1) Balance b/d	745	(31) Bank	745
(23) Sales	1,234	(31) Balance c/d	1,234
	1,979		1,979
(1) Balance b/d	1,234		

Goodwin & Co Account

(1) Balance b/d	276	(31) Balance c/d	604
(11) Sales	328		
	604		604
(1) Balance b/d	604		

L & P Moss Account

(1) Balance b/d	390	(31) Bank	200
(27) Sales	2,500	(31) Balance c/d	2,690
	2,890		2,890
(1) Balance b/d	2,690		

Purchases Ledger

M & P Fitzsimmons Account

		£			£
(28)	Returns outwards	200	(1)	Balance b/d	800
(31)	Bank	500	(22)	Purchases	756
(31)	Balance c/d	856			
		1,556			1,556
			(1)	Balance b/d	856

L Horne Account

		£			£
(12)	Returns outwards	42	(1)	Balance b/d	450
(31)	Balance c/d	1,058	(2)	Purchases	650
		1,100			1,100
			(1)	Balance b/d	1,058

M Ward & Sons Account

		£			£
(31)	Bank	245	(1)	Balance b/d	245
(31)	Balance c/d	334	(31)	Purchases	334
		579			579
			(1)	Balance b/d	334

Chapter 22

22.1
(a)

Curtain Design Company
Sales Day Book

Date	Details	Folio	Total	VAT	Ready-made	Custom-made
2006			£	£	£	£
Nov 1	Jarvis Arms Hotel	SL 1	2,702.50	402.50		2,300.00
Nov 8	Springs Nursing Home	SL 2	1,175.00	175.00	1,000.00	
Nov 15	J P Morten	SL 3	258.50	38.50	220.00	
Nov 17	Queen's Hotel	SL 4	1,762.50	262.50		1,500.00
Nov 30	W Blackshaw	SL 5	105.75	15.75	90.00	
			6,004.25	894.25	1,310.00	3,800.00
				GL 3	GL 1	GL 2

(b)

Sales Ledger

Jarvis Arms Hotel Account — SL 1

		£			
Nov 1	Sales	2,702.50			

Spring's Nursing Home Account — SL 2

		£			
Nov 8	Sales	1,175.00			

J P Morten Account — SL 3

		£			
Nov 15	Sales	258.50			

Queen's Hotel Account — SL 4

		£			
Nov 17	Sales	1,762.50			

W Blackshaw Account — SL 5

		£			
Nov 30	Sales	105.75			

(c)

General Ledger

Sales – Ready-Made Account — GL 1

					£
			Nov 30	Day book	1,310.00

Sales – Custom-Made Account — GL 2

					£
			Nov 30	Day book	3,800.00

Value Added Tax Account — GL 3

					£
			Nov 30	VAT on sales	894.25

22.2
(a)

Hall Engineering Co
Purchases Day Book

Date	Details	Folio	Total	VAT	Engineering parts	Printing and stationery	Motor expenses
2006			£	£	£	£	£
May 1	Black's Engineering Co	PL 1	611.00	91.00	520.00		
May 3	Ace Printing Co	PL 2	170.37	25.37		145.00	
May 24	Morgan's Garage	PL 3	141.00	21.00			120.00
May 26	Martin's Foundry	PL 4	822.50	122.50	700.00		
May 28	Office Supplies	PL 5	148.05	22.05		126.00	
May 29	Black's Engineering Co	PL 1	258.50	38.50	220.00		
			2,151.42	320.42	1,440.00	271.00	120.00
				GL 4	GL 1	GL 2	GL 3

Smart Campers: Workings:

		£	£
May 2	Outdoor Centre/Moortown		
	12 Flair cool boxes at £15.90 each	190.80	
	6 Camping stoves at £29.95 each	179.70	
		370.50	
	Less Trade discount 20%	74.10	
			296.40
	Add VAT at 10%		29.64
			326.04
May 8	Premier Leisure/Horsforth		
	10 Explorer rucksacks at £34.99 each	349.90	
	Less Trade discount 20%	69.98	
		279.92	
	12 Trekker ridge tents at £59.95 each	719.40	
	Less Trade discount 15%	107.91	
			611.49
			891.41
	Add VAT at 10%		89.14
			980.55
May 16	Airedale Sport/Otley		
	8 Palma cool bags at £7.85 each	62.80	
	12 Flair cool boxes at £15.90 each	190.80	
		253.60	
	Less Trade discount 20%	50.72	
			202.88
	Add VAT at 10%		20.29
			223.17
May 28	Empire Products/Moortown		
	14 Dome tents at £47.90 each	670.60	
	8 Trekker ridge tents at £59.95 each	479.60	
		1,150.20	
	Less Trade discount 15%	172.53	
			977.67
	Add VAT at 10%		97.76
			1,075.43

(b)

Purchases Ledger
Black's Engineering — PL 1

	May 1 Purchases	611.00
	May 29 Purchases	258.50

Ace Printing Co — PL 2

	May 3 Purchases	170.37

Morgan's Garage — PL 3

	May 24 Purchases	141.00

Martin's Foundry — PL 4

	May 26 Purchases	822.50

Office Supplies — PL 5

	May 28 Purchases	148.05

(c)

General Ledger
Purchases – Engineering Parts — GL 1

May 31 Day book	1,440.00

Printing and Stationery — GL 2

May 31 Day book	271.00

Motor Expenses — GL 3

May 31 Day book	120.00

VAT — GL 4

May 31 VAT on Purchases	320.42

22.3   Sales day book – Smart Campers

Date 2006	Name of Customer	Invoice Total	Horsforth	Moortown	Otley	VAT
May 2	Outdoor Centre	326.04		296.40		29.64
May 8	Premier Leisure	980.55	891.41			89.14
May 16	Airedale Sport	223.17			202.88	20.29
May 28	Empire Products	1,075.43		977.67		97.76
		2,605.19	891.41	1,274.07	202.88	236.83

Chapter 23

23.1   Sales Ledger Control Account

(1) Balance b/d	4,560	(31) Returns inwards		460
(31) Sales day book	10,870	(31) Cheques and cash		9,615
		(31) Discounts allowed		305
		(31) Balances c/d		5,050
	15,430			15,430

23.2

Sales Ledger Control Account

	£		£
(1) Balances b/d	6,708	(31) Discounts	300
(31) Sales day book	11,500	(31) Cash and cheques	8,970
		(31) Bad debts	115
		(31) Returns inwards	210
		(31) Balances c/d	8,613
	18,208		18,208

23.6 (a)

Sales Ledger – Shery Tatupu

L Barker

2006		2006	
Mar 31 Credit sales	18,642	Jan 1 Balance b/d	62
		Mar 31 Bank	15,023
		Mar 31 Discount	142
		Mar 31 Balance c/d	3,415
	18,642		18,642

D Blackhurst

2006		2006	
Jan 1 Balance b/d	1,466	Mar 31 Sales returns	88
Mar 31 Credit sales	16,428	Mar 31 Bank	16,009
		Mar 31 Balance c/d	1,797
	17,894		17,894

H Brackenbridge

2006		2006	
Mar 31 Credit sales	19,886	Jan 1 Balance b/d	58
		Mar 31 Bank	17,332
		Mar 31 Discount	227
		Mar 31 Balance c/d	2,269
	19,886		19,886

(b)

Sales Ledger Control Account

2006		2006	
Jan 1 Balance b/d	1,346	Mar 31 Sales returns	88
Mar 31 Credit sales	54,956	Mar 31 Bank	48,364
		Mar 31 Discounts	369
		Mar 31 Balance c/d	7,481
	56,302		56,302

(c)   Sales Ledger Outstanding Balances at 31 March 2006

	£
L Barker	3,415
D Blackhurst	1,797
H Brackenbridge	2,269
	7,481
Balance per Sales Ledger Control Account	7,481

Pitman Qualifications

Chapter 24

24.1

The Journal

Date	Details	Dr	Cr
		£	£
2007			
Jan 1	Computer	4,000	
	Data Systems Ltd		4,000
Jan 5	Drawings	120	
	Purchases		120
Jan 8	Bad debts	220	
	J Oddy		220
Jan 15	Motor vehicle	15,500	
	Bank		15,500
Jan 29	Office furniture and fittings	250	
	J Street		250

24.3 (a)   The Journal as at 1 May 2008

	Dr	Cr
Bank	2,910	
Cash	160	
Equipment	5,900	
Premises	25,000	
Debtor: J Carnegie	540	
Creditors: R Smith		890
T Thomas		610
Loan: J Higgins		4,000
Capital		29,010
	34,510	34,510

Cash Book

(b)

		Cash	Bank			Cash	Bank
(1)	Balances b/d	160	2,910	(5)	R Smith		500
(31)	Sales	8,560	8,000	(12)	J Higgins		1,000
(31)	Cash C		720	(31)	Bank C	8,000	
				(31)	Loan interest		200
				(31)	Balance c/d	720	9,210
		8,720	10,910			8,720	10,910

Equipment

| (1) | Balance b/d | 5,900 | | |

Premises

| (1) | Balance b/d | 25,000 | | |

R Smith

| (5) | Bank | 500 | (1) | Balance b/d | 890 |

J Carnegie

| (1) | Balance b/d | 540 | (31) | Returns | 400 |
| (24) | Sales | 2,220 | | | |

T Thomas

| | | | (1) | Balance b/d | 610 |
| | | | (2) | Purchases | 2,100 |

J Higgins (Loan)

| (12) | Bank | 1,000 | (1) | Balance b/d | 4,000 |

Loan Interest

| (31) | Bank | 200 | | | |

Capital

| | | | (1) | Capital | 29,010 |

Returns Inwards

| (31) | J Carnegie | 400 | | | |

Sales

| | | | (24) | J Carnegie | 2,220 |
| | | | (31) | Cash | 8,560 |

Purchases

| (2) | T Thomas | 2,100 | | | |

J Green
Trial Balance as at 31 May 2008

	Dr £	Cr £
Cash	720	
Bank	9,210	
Equipment	5,900	
Premises	25,000	
R Smith		390
J Carnegie	2,360	
T Thomas		2,710
J Higgins		3,000
Loan interest	200	
Capital		29,010
Sales		10,780
Purchases	2,100	
Returns inwards	400	
	45,890	45,890

Chapter 25

K Richardson

25.1

Straight Line			Reducing Balance		
Cost		40,000	Cost		40,000
Year 1	Depreciation	7,000	Year 1	Depreciation 40% of 40,000	16,000
		33,000			24,000
Year 2	Depreciation	7,000	Year 2	Depreciation 40% of 24,000	9,600
		26,000			14,400
Year 3	Depreciation	7,000	Year 3	Depreciation 40% of 14,400	5,760
		19,000			8,640
Year 4	Depreciation	7,000	Year 4	Depreciation 40% of 8,640	3,456
		12,000			5,184
Year 5	Depreciation	7,000	Year 5	Depreciation 40% of 5,184	2,074
		5,000			3,110

$40,000 - 5,000 = 35,000 \div 5 = 7,000$

25.2

(a) Straight Line

Cost	37,500
Year 1 Depreciation	5,535
	31,965
Year 2 Depreciation	5,535
	26,430
Year 3 Depreciation	5,535
	20,895
Year 4 Depreciation	5,535
	15,360

(b) Reducing Balance

Cost	37,500
Year 1 Depreciation 20% of 37,500	7,500
	30,000
Year 2 Depreciation 20% of 30,000	6,000
	24,000
Year 3 Depreciation 20% of 24,000	4,800
	19,200
Year 4 Depreciation 20% of 19,200	3,840
	15,360

$$37{,}500 - 15{,}360 = 22{,}140 \div 4 = 5{,}535$$

25.6

(a) Reducing Balance

Dumper cost	6,000
Year 1 Depreciation 20%	1,200
	4,800
Year 2 Depreciation 20% of 4,800	960
	3,840
Year 3 Depreciation 20% of 3,840	768
	3,072

(b) Straight Line

Dumper cost	6,000
Year 1 Depreciation	976*
	5,024
Year 2 Depreciation	976
	4,048
Year 3 Depreciation	976
	3,072

*Calculation:
$$\frac{6{,}000 - 3{,}072}{3} = \frac{2{,}928}{3} = 976$$

Chapter 26

26.1 (a)

Motor Cars

2005			
Jan 1	Bank	12,500	

(b) Provision for Depreciation: Motor Cars

Date	Details	£	Date	Details	£
			2005		
			Dec 31 Profit and loss		2,500
2006			2006		
Dec 31 Balance c/d		4,500	Dec 31 Profit and loss		2,000
		4,500			4,500
2007			2007		
Dec 31 Balance c/d		6,100	Jan 1 Balance b/d		4,500
			Dec 31 Profit and loss		1,600
		6,100			6,100

(c) Profit and Loss Account (extracts) – A White

(2005)	Provision for depreciation: Motors	2,500
(2006)	Provision for depreciation	2,000
(2007)	Provision for depreciation	1,600

(d) Balance Sheets (extracts) – A White

	2005	2006	2007
Motor car at cost	12,500	12,500	12,500
Less Depreciation to date	2,500	4,500	6,100
Net book value	10,000	8,000	6,400

26.3 (a)

Computer

Date	Details	£	Date	Details	£
2005			2005		
Jan 1 Balance b/d		9,500	Jan 1 Computer disposals		9,500

(b) Provision for Depreciation: Computer

Date	Details	£	Date	Details	£
2005			2005		
Dec 31 Balance c/d		1,900	Dec 31 Profit and loss		1,900
2006			2006		
Dec 31 Balance c/d		3,800	Jan 1 Balance b/d		1,900
			Dec 31 Profit and loss		1,900
		3,800			3,800
2007			2007		
Dec 31 Balance c/d		5,700	Jan 1 Balance b/d		3,800
			Dec 31 Profit and loss		1,900
		5,700			5,700
2008			2008		
Jan 1 Computer disposals		5,700	Jan 1 Balance b/d		5,700

(c) Computer Disposals

Date	Details	£	Date	Details	£
2008			2008		
Jan 1 Computer		9,500	Jan 1 Depreciation		5,700
Dec 31 Profit and loss		450	„ 1 Bank		4,250
		9,950			9,950

Chapter 27

27.1

Data Computer Services

(a)

Bad Debts Account

2006		£	2006		£
Apr 30	H Gordon	1,110	Dec 31	Profit and loss	1,870
Aug 31	D Bellamy	640			
Oct 31	J Alderton	120			
		1,870			1,870

Provision for Doubtful Debts Account

	£	2006		£
		Dec 31	Profit and loss	2,200

(b)

Profit and Loss Account
for the year ended 31 December 2006 (extracts)

Gross profit		xxx
Less Expenses:		
Bad debts written off	1,870	
Provision for doubtful debts	2,200	
		4,070

(c)

Balance Sheet as at 31 December 2006 (extract)

Debtors		68,500
Less Provision for doubtful debts		2,200
		66,300

27.2

Date 31 Dec	Total debtors £	Profit and loss £	Dr/Cr	Final figure for balance sheet
2004	7,000	70	Dr	6,930 (net)
2005	8,000	10	Dr	7,920 (net)
2006	6,000	20	Cr	5,940 (net)
2007	7,000	10	Dr	6,930 (net)

27.4

Emford & Co

Date	Amount of provision for doubtful debts £	Amount of adjustment to existing provision £	Write either 'increase' or 'decrease' to indicate the effect on the *profit* for the year
31 December 2004	930	930	Decrease
31 December 2005	962	32	Decrease
31 December 2006	510	452	Increase

(d)

Profit and Loss Account (extracts)

(2005) Provision for depreciation	1,900	
(2006) Provision for depreciation	1,900	
(2007) Provision for depreciation	1,900	(2005) Profit on sale of computer 450

(e)

Balance Sheets (extracts)

	2005	2006	2007
Computer at cost	9,500	9,500	9,500
Less Depreciation to date	1,900	3,800	5,700
Net book value	7,600	5,700	3,800

26.4

(a)

Motor Van Disposals

Motor van	12,000	Provision for depreciation	9,700
		Bank	1,850
		Profit and loss: loss on sale	450
	12,000		12,000

(b)

Machinery Disposals

Machinery	27,900	Provision for depreciation	19,400
Profit and loss: profit on sale	2,770	Bank	11,270
	30,670		30,670

(c)

Fixtures Disposals

Fixtures	8,420	Provision for depreciation	7,135
		Bank	50
		Profit and loss: loss on sale	1,235
	8,420		8,420

(d)

Buildings Disposals

Buildings	200,000	Provision for depreciation	110,000
Profit and loss: profit on sale	59,000	Bank	149,000
	259,000		259,000

Chapter 28

28.1

C Homer

(a) Rent Account

2008			2008		
Dec 31	Bank	1,600	Dec 31	Profit and loss	2,000
Dec 31	Owing c/d	400			
		2,000			2,000
			2009		
			Jan 1	Owing b/d	400

(b) Insurance Account

2008			2008		
Dec 31	Bank	900	Dec 31	Profit and loss	635
			Dec 31	Prepaid c/d	265
		900			900
2008					
Jan 1	Prepaid b/d	265			

(c) Motor Expenses Account

2008			2008		
Dec 31	Bank	7,215	Dec 31	Profit and loss	7,381
Dec 31	Owing c/d	166			
		7,381			7,381
			2009		
			Jan 1	Owing b/d	166

(d) Rates Account

2008			2008		
Jan 1	Bank	750	Dec 31	Profit and loss	1,500
Jul 1	Bank	1,125	Dec 31	Prepaid c/d	375
		1,875			1,875
2009					
Jan 1	Prepaid b/d	375			

(e) Rents Receivable Account

2008			2008		
Dec 31	Profit and loss	2,000	Apr 15	Bank	4,800
Dec 31	In advance c/d	4,400	Dec 15	Bank	1,600
		6,400			6,400
			2009		
			Jan 1	In advance b/d	1,600

28.2

T Norton

(a) General Expenses Account

2005			2005		
Dec 31	Bank	615	Dec 31	Profit and loss	671
Dec 31	Owing c/d	56			
		671			671
			2006		
			Jan 1	Owing b/d	56

(b) Telephone Account

2005			2005		
Dec 31	Bank	980	Dec 31	Profit and loss	1,097
Dec 31	Owing c/d	117			
		1,097			1,097
			2006		
			Jan 1	Owing b/d	117

(c) Commission Received Account

2005			2005		
Dec 31	Profit and loss	3,231	Dec 31	Bank	3,056
			Dec 31	Owing c/d	175
		3,231			3,231
2006					
Jan 1	Owing b/d	175			

(d) Carriage Outwards Account

2005			2005		
Dec 31	Bank	666	Dec 31	Profit and loss	788
Dec 31	Owing c/d	122			
		788			788
			2006		
			Jan 1	Owing b/d	122

(e) Insurance Account

2005			2005		
Jan 1	Bank	1,080	Dec 31	Profit and loss	1,440
Oct 1	Bank	1,080	Dec 31	Prepaid c/d	720
		2,160			2,160
2006					
Jan 1	Prepaid b/d	720			

28.4

C Cainen
Trading and Profit and Loss Account
for the year ended 31 December 2008

Sales		18,590
Less Cost of goods sold:		
Opening stock	2,050	
Add Purchases	11,170	
	13,220	
Less Closing stock	3,910	9,310
Gross profit		9,280
Less Expenses:		
Rent (640 − 160)	480	
Wages and salaries (2,140 + 290)	2,430	
Insurance (590 − 190)	400	
Bad debts	270	
Telephone (300 + 110)	410	
General expenses	180	4,170
Net profit		5,110

28.6

J Sears
Trading and Profit and Loss Account
for the year ended 31 December 2007

Sales		80,000
Less Returns inwards		1,000
		79,000
Less Cost of goods sold:		
Opening stock	20,000	
Add Purchases	70,000	
	90,000	
Less Returns outwards	1,240	
	88,760	
Less Closing stock	24,000	64,760
Gross profit		14,240
Less Expenses:		
Wages and salaries (7,200 + 450)	7,650	
Telephone (200 − 20)	180	
Bad debts	40	
Provision for doubtful debts (1,960 × 10% − 160)	36	
Depreciation:		
Store fittings	800	
Motor van	1,200	9,906
Net profit		4,334

J Sears
Balance Sheet as at 31 December 2007

	Cost	Depreciation	Net Book Value
Fixed Assets			
Store fittings	8,000	800	7,200
Motor van	6,000	1,200	4,800
	14,000	2,000	12,000
Current Assets			
Stock		24,000	
Debtors	1,960		
Less Provision for doubtful debts	196	1,764	
Prepaid expenses		20	
Bank		600	
		26,384	
Less Current Liabilities			
Creditors	1,400		
Expenses owing	450	1,850	
Net current assets			24,534
			36,534
Financed by:			
Capital			
Balance 1.1.2007			35,800
Add Net profit			4,334
			40,134
Less Drawings			3,600
			36,534

Chapter 29

28.8

Freddy Tuilagi
Trading and Profit and Loss Account
for the year ended 30 September

Sales			30,490
Less Cost of goods sold:			
Opening stock		850	
Add Purchases (13,725 − 320)		13,405	
		14,255	
Less Closing stock		960	
			13,295
Gross profit			17,195
Add Discounts received (230 + 80)			310
			17,505
Less Expenses:			
General expenses		610	
Wages		3,880	
Advertising (420 − 46)		374	
Telephone		160	
Depreciation – Equipment		4,500	
– Motor van		1,050	
			10,574
			6,931

Freddy Tuilagi
Balance Sheet as at 30 September

	Cost £	Depreciation £	Net Book Value £
Fixed Assets			
Equipment	17,000	6,500	10,500
Motor van	7,000	1,050	5,950
	24,000	7,550	16,450
Current Assets			
Stock	960		
Prepayments	46		
Cash in hand	30		
		1,036	
Less Current Liabilities			
Bank overdraft	50		
Creditors (845 − 80)	765		
		815	
Net current assets			221
			16,671
Financed by:			
Capital			11,460
Add Net profit			6,931
			18,391
Less Drawings (1400 + 320)			1,720
			16,671

29.1

S Dickinson
Trial Balance as at 30 September 2005

	Dr £	Cr £
Capital		59,868
Motor vehicles	22,500	
Computer equipment	18,000	
Debtors	31,059	
Creditors		30,690
Purchases	245,259	
Sales		358,317
Wages and salaries	38,476	
Motor expenses	3,428	
Printing and stationery	3,600	
General expenses	8,235	
Cash at bank	5,850	
Stock 1 October 2004	23,004	
Rent and rates	31,500	
Heating and lighting	6,624	
Interest received		6,417
Insurance	10,332	
Rent received		5,175
Drawings	12,600	
	460,467	460,467

29.2

G Brammer
Trial Balance as at 31 December 2005

	Dr £	Cr £
Capital		100,000
Premises	66,250	
Motor vehicle	17,000	
Office equipment	2,438	
Wages	19,637	
Purchases	37,455	
Sales		56,170
Commission received		1,050
Electricity	925	
Telephone	1,125	
Motor expenses	1,500	
Printing, stationery and advertising	2,050	
Creditors		8,500
Debtors	12,012	
General expenses	2,371	
Bank overdraft		3,505
Drawings	6,462	
	169,225	169,225

29.4

J Steadman – Extended trial balance as at 31 January 2006

	Description	Ledger Balances Dr £	Ledger Balances Cr £	Adjustments Dr £	Adjustments Cr £	Profit and Loss Dr £	Profit and Loss Cr £	Balance Sheet Dr £	Balance Sheet Cr £
BS	Capital		58,260						58,260
BS	Equipment	11,250						11,250	
BS	Furniture and fittings	6,000						6,000	
BS	Motor vehicles	17,370						17,370	
PL	Sales		96,030				96,030		
PL	Purchases	59,220				59,220			
BS	Cash at bank	750						750	
PL	General expenses	1,800				1,800			
PL	Wages	17,820		(a) 351		18,171			
PL	Rent, rates and insurance	7,650			(b) 600	7,050			
PL	Heating and lighting	2,100				2,100			
BS	Debtors	24,000						24,000	
BS	Creditors		10,800						10,800
PL	Stock 1 February 2005	17,130				17,130			
		165,090	165,090						
BS	Accrual – Wages				(a) 351				351
BS	Prepayment – Insurance			(b) 600				600	
BS	Stock – 31 January 2006			(c) 14,730				14,730	
PL	Stock – 31 January 2006				(c) 14,730		14,730		
				15,681	15,681				
	Net profit					5,289			5,289
						110,760	110,760	74,700	74,700

29.6 (ii)

Automania – Extended trial balance as at 30 April 2005

	Description	Ledger Balances Dr £	Ledger Balances Cr £	Adjustments Dr £	Adjustments Cr £	Profit and Loss Dr £	Profit and Loss Cr £	Balance Sheet Dr £	Balance Sheet Cr £
BS	Capital		135,000						135,000
BS	Drawings	42,150		1,600				42,150	
PL	Rent	17,300				18,900			
PL	Purchases	606,600				606,600			
PL	Sales		857,300				857,300		
PL	Sales returns	2,400				2,400			
PL	Purchases returns		1,260		200		1,460		
PL	Salaries and wages	136,970				136,970			
BS	Motor vehicles (MV) at cost	60,800						60,800	
BS	Provision for depreciation (MV)		16,740		12,160				28,900
BS	Fixtures and fittings (F & F) at cost	40,380						40,380	
BS	Provision for depreciation (F & F)		21,600		1,878				23,478
BS	Bank		3,170						3,170
BS	Cash	2,100						2,100	
PL	Lighting and heating	4,700				4,700			
PL	VAT		9,200		35				9,235
PL	Stock 1 May 2004	116,100				116,100			
PL	Bad debts	1,410				1,410			
PL/BS	Provision for doubtful debts		1,050		87				1,137
BS	Debtors control account	56,850						56,850	
BS	Creditors control account		50,550	*235					50,315
PL	Sundry expenses	6,810				6,810			
PL	Insurance	1,300			100	1,200			
		1,095,870	1,095,870						
BS	Accruals				1,600				1,600
BS	Prepayments			100				100	
PL	Depreciation – Motor vehicles			12,160		12,160			
PL	Depreciation – Fixtures & fittings			1,878		1,878			
PL	Provision for doubtful debts – Adjustment			87		87			
PL	Closing stock – Profit and loss				117,700		117,700		
BS	Closing stock – Balance sheet			117,700				117,700	
				133,760	133,760				
	Net profit					67,245			67,245
						976,460	976,460	320,080	320,080

*Note: Made up of £200 purchases returns plus VAT £35 = £235

Chapter 30

30.1 (a) (i) FIFO 6 × £13 = £78 stock valuation at 31 December 2007.

(ii) LIFO

2007	Received	Issued	Stock	£	£
Jan	24 × £10		24 × £10	240	240
April	16 × £12.50		24 × £10 16 × £12.50	240 200	440
June		14 × £10 16 × £12.50	10 × £10	100	100
Oct	30 × £13		10 × £10 30 × £13	100 390	490
Nov		4 × £10 30 × £13	6 × £13	60	60

Closing stock would be valued at £60 on a LIFO basis.

(iii) AVCO

2007	Received	Issued	Average cost per unit	No. of units in stock	Total value of stock
Jan	24 × £10		£10.00	24	£240
April	16 × £12.50		£11.00	40	£440
June		30	£11.00	10	£110
Oct	30 × £13		£12.50	40	£500
Nov		34	£12.50	6	£75

Closing stock would be valued at £75 on an average cost basis.

(b) **Trading Accounts for the year ended 31 December 2007**

	FIFO		LIFO		AVCO	
Sales		1,092		1,092		1,092
Less Cost of goods sold						
Purchases	830		830		830	
Less Closing stock	78	752	60	770	75	755
Gross Profit		340		322		337

29.6 (i) Workings

(a) Rent: 1.5.2004 to 31.7.2004 = 3 months × 1,500 =   4,500
1.8.2004 to 30.8.2005 = 9 months × 1,600 = 14,400
                                             18,900
Rent paid during year 17,300
Rent owing at 30.4.2005   1,600

(b) Insurance paid in advance – 100   100

(c) Depreciation:
Motor vehicles = 20% SLM – 20% of £60,800 =   12,160
Fixtures and fittings = 10% RBM = F & F cost   40,380
Less Depreciation to date   21,600
Net book value   18,780
Therefore 10% of £18,780 =   1,878

(d) Increase in provision for bad debts to 2% of debtors
= 2% of £56,850 (new provision) =   1,137
Less Old provision =   1,050
Therefore increase =   87

(e) Stock valuation 30.4.2005   £119,360
Less Reduction in value of old stock
3,660 – 2,060 =   1,600
Less Badly damaged car door =   60   1,660
New stock valuation 30.4.2009   £117,700

(f) Debit – Creditors control   £235
Credit – Purchases returns   £200
Credit – VAT   £35

30.3

DC Ltd
Stock Valuation as at 31 December 2006

	£	£
Value at 8 January 2007		50,850
Add (*a*) Error in calculation (1,600 – 160)	1,440	
(*b*) Sales at cost (500 – 100)	400	
(*d*) Casting error (4,299 – 2,499)	1,800	3,640
		54,490
Less (*c*) Reduce to NRV (560 – 425)		135
Corrected value of stock at 31 December 2006		54,355

30.6 The Pine Warehouse

The tables and chairs sold to the customer on 30 November 2008 should not be included in the closing stock figure at the end of the financial year since they are no longer the property of The Pine Warehouse; they belong to the customer who has already paid for them and is the legal owner. Stock should be valued at the lower of 'cost' or 'net realisable value' and certainly not at selling price. In any case, the profit of £500 has already been entered in the books for the year to 30 November 2008, as it was included in cash sales.

31.3

Berry Sports
Journal

		Dr £	Cr £
Dec 1	Rates	100	
Dec 1	Rent		100
Dec 1	Creditors Control*	600	
Dec 1	Purchases Return		600
Dec 1	Bank	1,800	
Dec 1	Insurance		1,800

Note: First the error has to be cancelled:

Dr Creditors Control	300	
Cr Purchases Return		300

Then the transaction requires entering:

Dr Creditors Control	300	
Cr Purchases Return		300

Thus the amounts are double the original amount, i.e. £600

31.4

Senator Safes
Journal

	Dr £	Cr £
Rates	300	
Miscellaneous Expenses		300
Purchases Returns	99	
Creditors Control		99
(*Note:* 706 – 607 = 99)		
Bad Debts	800	
VAT	140	
Debtors Control*		940

Note: The question stated the sales ledger is a subsidiary ledger, i.e. the accounts are classed as memorandum accounts, therefore, the bad debt will need to be credited to the debtors control account.

Chapter 31

(To economise on space, all narratives for journal entries in these answers are omitted.)

31.1 (*a*) J Harkness — Dr 678 — J Harker Cr 678
(*b*) Machinery — Dr 4,390 — L Pearson Cr 4,390
(*c*) Motor van — Dr 3,800 — Motor expenses Cr 3,800
(*d*) E Fletcher — Dr 9 — Sales Cr 9
(*e*) Sales — Dr 257 — Commissions received Cr 257

Chapter 32

32.1

The Journal

	Dr £	Cr £
(a) T. Thomas	900	
Bank		900
(b) C. Charles	3	5
Discounts allowed	3	5
(c) Office equipment	6,000	
Motor vehicles		6,000
(d) J. Graham	715	
Sales		715
(e) Wages	210	
Drawings	210	
Suspense		420

32.2

Jaspa West

	Dr £	Cr £
(a) (1) Suspense	110	
Rent Received		110
Correction of error rent received £55		
debited in error to Rent Received		
(2) Bad Debts	150	
Mary Beagle		150
Debt owed by Mary Beagle written		
off as bad		
(3) Sales	350	
Suspense		350
Sales overcast by £350		
(4) Motor Vehicle	3,500	
C Williams		3,500
Purchase of motor vehicle on credit		
(5) Profit and Loss	225	
Provision for bad debts		225
Creation of provision for bad debts		

Appendices

(b) Two examples of errors which would not be revealed by the trial balance would be: Two from, errors of omission, commission, principle, original entry, compensating and complete reversal of entries.

32.4 1

The Journal

	Dr	Cr
(a) Returns inwards	100	
Suspense		100
(b) Drawings	80	
Wages		80
(c) Carriage inwards	75	
Carriage outwards		75
(d) Bank charges	270	
Suspense		270
(e) Sales ledger control (K Abbott)	385	
Sales		385
(f) Discounts allowed (2 × 218)	436	
Suspense		436
(g) Suspense	200	
Rent		200
(h) Purchases (24,897 − 24,798)	99	
Suspense		99

2

Suspense Account

	£			£
Balance b/f	705	(a)	Returns in	100
(g) Rent	200	(d)	Bank charges	270
		(f)	Discounts received	436
		(b)	Purchases	99
	905			905

3   Original incorrect gross profit   129,487

  Add (e) Sales omitted   385

                            129,872

  Less (a) Returns in omitted   100

        (c) Carriage in understated   75

        (b) Purchases understated   99   274

                            129,598

  Original net profit   77,220

  Add Increase in gross profit, i.e. it also   111

      increases net profit (129,598 − 129,487)   77,331

  Add (b) Wages overstated   80

       (c) Carriage outwards overstated   75

       (g) Rent rebate omitted   200   355

                            77,686

  Less (d) Bank charges omitted   270

       (f) Discounts allowed understated   436   706

  Corrected figure of net profit   76,980

32.5 (a)

Suspense

Balance as per T.B.	1,134	(i) Sales over-cast	350
(iv) Creditor	166	(ii) Discounts under-cast	100
		(iii) Fixtures omitted	850
	1,300		1,300

(b)

K Woodburn

Trial Balance as at 30 June 2008

	Dr	Cr
Sales (87,050 − 350)		86,700
Purchases	62,400	
Discounts allowed and received	405	410
Salaries and wages	3,168	
General expenses	595	
Fixtures (10,000 + 850)	10,850	
Stock 1 July 2007	12,490	
Debtors and creditors	8,120	4,721
Bank	6,790	
Drawings (4,520 − 490)	4,030	
Capital		17,017
	108,848	108,848

Note: Discounts allowed 305 + (ii) 100 = 405

Creditors 5,045 + (iv) 166 − (v) 490 = 4,721

32.7

The Journal

		Dr	Cr
(a)	Suspense	3,000	
	Sales		3,000
	Correction of error sales day book undercast by £3,000		
(b)	Purchases	1,147	
	Dawson & Co		1,147
	Goods purchased on credit from Dawson & Co		
(c)	Motor repairs	585	
	Motor vehicles		585
	Motor repairs posted in error to motor vehicles account		
(d)	J Greenway	675	
	J Green		675
	Goods sold on credit to J Greenway posted in error to J Green's account		
(e)	Suspense	150	
	Electricity		150
	Payment of electricity account incorrectly debited £150 too much		
(f)	Suspense	2,250	
	Teape Ltd		2,250
	Payment of £2,250 received from Teape Ltd not credited to their account		

Philip Hogan

Suspense Account

	£		£
Sales (a)	3,000	Balance b/d	5,400
Electricity (e)	150		
Teape Ltd (f)	2,250		
	5,400		5,400

Note that items (b), (c) and (d) do not pass through the suspense account, as they do not affect the balancing of the books.

Chapter 33

33.1 (a)

Total Debtors

	£		£
Balances b/d	2,760	Cash	14,610
Sales (difference)	14,940	Balances c/d	3,090
	17,700		17,700

Total Creditors

	£		£
Cash	9,390	Balances b/d	1,080
Balances c/d	1,320	Purchases (difference)	9,630
	10,710		10,710

(b) K Rogers
Trading Account for the year ended 31 October 2006

	£	£
Sales		14,940
Less Cost of Goods Sold		
Opening Stock	2,010	
Add Purchases	9,630	
	11,640	
Less Closing Stock	2,160	
		9,480
Gross Profit		5,460

33.3 (a) Capital is £6,000.

(b) D Lewinski
Balance Sheet as at 30 June 2006

	£	£
Fixed assets		
Plant		3,600
Fixtures		360
		3,960
Current assets		
Stock	1,350	
Debtors	930	
Bank	600	
Cash	135	
	3,015	
Less Current liabilities		
Creditors	720	
Net current assets		2,295
		6,255
Financed by:		£
Capital	(a) 6,000	
Cash introduced	1,855	
	7,855	
Add Net profit		
Less Drawings	1,600	
	6,255	

33.4

J Marcano
Statement of Affairs as at 31 August 2006

	£	£	£
Fixed assets			
Fixtures			3,500
Motor van			3,500
			7,000
Current assets			
Stock		16,740	
Debtors		11,890	
Bank		2,209	
Cash		115	
		30,954	
Less Current liabilities			
Creditors		9,952	
			21,002
			28,002

Statement of Affairs as at 31 August 2007

	£	£	£
Fixed assets			
Fixtures		5,500	
Less Depreciation		300	
			5,200
Motor van		3,500	
Less Depreciation		700	
			2,800
			8,000
Current assets			
Stock		24,891	
Debtors		15,821	
Prepaid expenses		72	
Cash		84	
		40,868	
Less Current liabilities			
Trade creditors	6,002		
Expenses owing	236		
Bank overdraft	165		
		6,403	
Net current assets			34,465
			42,465
Capital			
Balance as at 31.8.2006			28,002
Add Cash introduced			12,800
Add Net profit	(C)		9,223
	(B)		50,025
Less Drawings	(A)		7,560
			42,465

(A) Found as the figure to make balance sheet totals agree 42,465.
(B) Less 7,560 = (A) 42,465, therefore (B) is 50,025.
(C) Missing figure to total 50,025 = 9,223.

Chapter 34

34.1 (*a*)

Horton Hockey Club
Receipts and Payments Account
for the year ended 30 June 2006

Receipts		Payments	
Bank balance b/f	2,715	Teams' travel expenses	1,598
Subscriptions	8,570	Groundsman's wages	3,891
Donations	1,500	Postage and stationery	392
Receipts from raffles	3,816	Rent of pitches and	
		club house	4,800
		General expenses	419
		Prizes for raffles	624
		Bank balance c/f	4,877
	16,601		16,601

(*b*)

Horton Hockey Club
Income and Expenditure Account
for the year ended 30 June 2006

Income:		
Subscriptions (8,570 + 160)		8,730
Donations		1,500
Profit on raffles (3,816 – 624)		3,192
		13,422
Less Expenditure:		
Teams' travel expenses	1,598	
Groundsman's wages (3,891 + 75)	3,966	
Postage and stationery	392	
Rent of pitches and club house (4,800 + 400)	5,200	
General expenses	419	
		11,575
Surplus of income over expenditure		1,847

34.3 (*a*) Accumulated fund as at 1 June 2007:

Bar stocks		88
Equipment		340
Bank		286
		714

33.6
(*a*) *Sales*

Trade Debtors Account

2004			2005		
Apr 1	Balance b/f	23,460	Mar 31	Receipts	226,820
2005			Mar 31	Discounts	280
Mar 31	Sales (missing figure)	231,910	Mar 31	Balance c/d	28,270
		255,370			255,370
Apr 1	Balance b/d	28,270			

(*b*) *Rent*

Rent Account

2004			2004		
Mar 31	Bank: rent	12,290	Apr 1	Balance (rent owing) b/d	1,040
			2005		
			Mar 31	Profit & Loss	11,980
Mar 31	Balance (rent owing) c/d	730			
		13,020			13,020
			Apr 1	Balance (rent owing) b/d	730

(*c*) *Business Rates*

Business Rates Account

2004			2005		
Apr 1	Balance (prepaid) b/d	390	Mar 31	Profit & Loss	4,630
2005			Mar 31	Balance (prepaid) c/d	440
Mar 31	Bank: business rates	4,680			
		5,070			5,070
Apr 1	Balance (prepaid) b/d	440			

(b)   **Down Town Sports and Social Club**
Income and Expenditure Account
for the year ended 31 May 2008

	£	£	£
Income			
Subscriptions			149
Net proceeds of jumble sale			91
Net proceeds of dance			122
Contribution from Bar:			
Bar takings		463	
Less Cost of supplies:			
Opening Stock	88		
Add Purchases	397		
	485		
Less Closing stock	101		
		384	
			79
			441
Less Expenditure			
Wages	198		
Hire of rooms	64		
Loss on equipment	12		
Depreciation	30		
		304	
Surplus of income over expenditure			137

34.5

1   Bar Purchases

	£
Payments via Bank	6,400
Less Opening Creditors	1,000
	5,400
Add Closing Creditors	540
Bar Purchases	5,940

2   **Bar**
Trading and Profit and Loss Account
for the year ended 30 November 2005

Sales		8,700
Less Cost of bar sales		
Opening stock	680	
Add Bar purchases (see Task 1)	5,940	
	6,620	
Less Closing stock	890	
		5,730
Gross Profit		2,970
Less Expenses		
Wages (20% × 25,500)	5,100	
General expenses ((4,850 + 250 − 150) × 30%)	1,485	
		6,585
Net Loss		3,615

---

3   *Subscription Account*

	£		£
Balance (owing) b/d	1,000	Bank	33,000
Income and Expenditure Account (difference)	36,000	Balance (owing) c/d	4,000
	37,000		37,000

Total number of members = $\dfrac{36,000}{100}$ = 360 Members

4   **Income and Expenditure Account**
for the year ended 30 November 2005

	£
Income	
Subscriptions (See Task 3)	36,000
Expenditure	
Loss on bar (See Task 2)	3,615
Wages (80% × 25,500)	20,400
General expenses ((4,850 + 250 − 150) × 70%)	3,465
Interest on bank loan (8% × 5,400 × 11/12)	396
	27,876
Surplus of income over expenditure	8,124

5   Assets

	£
Land	12,000
Stock	890
Subscriptions owing	4,000
	16,890
Liabilities	
Bank	800
Creditors	540
Accrual (General expenses)	250
Loan	5,400
Interest	396
	7,386

6   Land is usually classified as a non-wasting fixed asset. It does not tend to go down in value and therefore is not normally depreciated.

34.6   **Amateur Dramatic Society**
Subscriptions Account

	£		£
In arrears b/d	235	In advance b/d	220
In advance c/d	140	Bank	2,600
Income and expenditure	2,630	In arrears c/d	185
	3,005		3,005
In arrears b/d	185	In advance b/d	140

Chapter 35

35.1

E Smith

**Manufacturing and Trading Account
for the year ended 31 March 2006**

	£	£
Stock of raw material 1.4.2005		2,400
Add Purchases	21,340	
Carriage inwards	321	
		24,061
Less Stock of raw materials 31.3.2006		2,620
Cost of raw materials consumed		21,441
Manufacturing wages		13,280
Prime cost		**34,721**
Add Factory overhead expenses:		
Rent and rates	2,300	
Power	6,220	
Other expenses	1,430	
		9,950
		44,671
Add Work in progress 1.4.2005		955
		45,626
Less Work in progress 31.3.2006		870
Production cost of goods completed c/d		**44,756**
Sales		69,830
Less Cost of goods sold		
Stock finished goods 1.4.2005	6,724	
Add Production cost of goods completed b/d	44,756	
	51,480	
Less Stock finished goods 31.3.2006	7,230	
		44,250
Gross profit		25,580

35.3

The Oldport Manufacturing Co

(a) Calculation of prime cost

	£
Stock raw materials 1 May 2004	31,550
Add Purchases raw materials	98,560
	130,110
Less Stock raw materials 30 April 2005	34,585
	95,525
Direct Labour – Wages manufacturing	67,525
Prime cost	163,050

(b) Variable costs are those costs that change according to the number of units produced.

Examples one from: direct material or direct labour, that may be used, for example, in the manufacture of a wheelbarrow.

35.4 (a)

CCC Ltd

Manufacturing Account for the year ended 31 December 2005

	£	£	£
Stock of raw materials 1.1.2005			4,500
Add Purchases		8,800	
Add Carriage inwards		390	
			9,190
			13,690
Less Stock of raw materials 31.12.2005 (i)			5,800
Cost of raw materials used			7,890
Stock of cases 1.1.2005		2,250	
Add Purchases		2,250	
		4,500	
Less Stock of cases 31.12.2005 (ii)		1,920	
Cost of wooden cases used			2,580
Wages (22,500 × 4/5)			18,000
Prime cost			**28,470**
Factory overhead expenses:			
Indirect wages (22,500 × 1/5) (iii)		4,500	
Manager's salary (iv)		1,650	
Power		1,820	
Rates		910	
Lighting (600 × 1/2)		300	
Depreciation		20,000	
			29,180
			57,650
Add Work-in-progress 1.1.2005			1,250
			58,900
Less Work-in-progress 31.12.2005 (v)			1,900
Production cost of goods completed c/d			57,000

(b)

CCC Ltd

**Trading and Profit and Loss Account
for the year ended 31 December 2005**

	£	£
Sales (80 × 1,000)		80,000
Less Production cost of goods sold b/d		57,000
Gross profit		23,000
Less Expenses:		
Administration expenses	2,400	
Salesmen's salaries	5,950	
Lighting (600 × 1/2)	300	
Carriage outwards	210	
		8,860
Net profit		14,140

(c) Production cost = £57,000 ÷ 1,000 = £57 per unit.

(d) Gross profit = £23,000 ÷ 1,000 = £23 per unit.

Chapter 36

36.1 (a)

Stead and Jackson
Appropriation Account
for the year ended 31 December 2005

	£
Net profit	45,000
Less Salary: Jackson	5,000
	40,000
Balance of profits shared:	
Stead ½	20,000
Jackson ½	20,000
	40,000

(b)

Capital Accounts

	Stead	Jackson			Stead	Jackson
				2005		
				Dec 31 Balance b/d	24,000	16,000

Current Accounts

	Stead	Jackson			Stead	Jackson
2005				2005		
Dec 31 Drawings	15,000	19,000		Dec 31 Balance b/d	2,300	3,500
Dec 31 Balances c/d	7,300	9,500		Dec 31 Salary		5,000
				Dec 31 Share of profits	20,000	20,000
	22,300	28,500			22,300	28,500
				2006		
				Jan 1 Balance b/d	7,300	9,500

36.4

Simpson and Young
Trading and Profit and Loss Appropriation Account
for the year ended 30 June 2005

	£	£
Sales		254,520
Less Cost of sales:		
Opening stock	18,000	
Add Purchases	184,980	
	202,980	
Less Closing stock	19,000	183,980
Gross profit		70,540
Less Expenses:		
Wages and salaries (32,700 + 500)	33,200	
Rent, rates and insurance (3,550 − 250)	3,300	
Electricity	980	
Stationery and printing	420	
Motor expenses	3,480	
General office expenses	1,700	
Depreciation: Motor van (20% of 16,000)	3,200	
Office equipment (10% of 5,600)	560	46,840
Net profit		23,700
Less Interest on capital:		
Simpson (10% of 50,000)	5,000	
Young (10% of 20,000)	2,000	7,000
		16,700
Share of profits:		
Simpson ⅗ths	10,020	
Young ⅖ths	6,680	16,700

Simpson and Young
Balance Sheet as at 30 June 2005

	Cost £	Accumulated Depreciation £		Net Book Value £
Fixed assets				
Premises	28,000	–		28,000
Office equipment	8,400	3,360	(W1)	5,040
Motor vans	16,000	8,200	(W2)	7,800
	52,400	11,560		40,840
Current assets				
Stock	19,000			
Debtors	28,000			
Prepayments	250			
Cash at bank	7,250		54,500	
Less Current liabilities				
Creditors	15,200			
Accruals	500		15,700	
Net current assets				38,800
				79,640

	Simpson	Young	Total
Financed by:			
Capital accounts			
Balance b/f	50,000	20,000	70,000
Current accounts			
Balance b/f	640	300	
Add Share of profit	10,020	6,680	
Add Interest on capital	5,000	2,000	
	15,660	8,980	
Less Drawings	10,000	5,000	
	5,660	3,980	9,640
			79,640

(W1) Provision for depreciation on office equipment:
8,400 – 5,600 + 560 = 3,360

(W2) Provision for depreciation on motor vans:
16,000 – 11,000 + 3,200 = 8,200

36.6 (a)

Bhayani and Donnell
Profit and Loss Account for the year ended 31 December

	£	£	£
Gross profit			32,000
Add Reduction in provision for bad debts			179
Add Rent received (500 – 100)			400
			32,579
Less Expenses:			
Heating and lighting (1,400 + 100)	1,500		
Wages and salaries (4,100 – 200)	3,900		
Depreciation: Vehicles (10% of 35,000)	3,500		
Fittings 15% of (12,000 – 2,000)	1,500		10,400
Net profit			22,179

(b)

Bhayani and Donnell
Appropriation Account for the year ended 31 December

	£	£
Net profit b/fwd		22,179
Add Interest charged on drawings:		
Bhayani (6% of 2,000)	120	
Donnell (6% of 600)	36	156
		22,335
Less Salary: Donnell	3,263	
Interest on capital:		
Bhayani (8% of 35,000)	2,800	
Donnell (8% of 12,000)	960	7,023
		15,312
Balance of profits shared:		
Bhayani 2/3	10,208	
Donnell 1/3	5,104	15,312

(c)

Bhayani – Current Account

		£			£
Jan 1	Balance b/d	600	Dec 31	Profit and loss appropriation account:	
Dec 31	Drawings	2,000		Interest on capital	2,800
Dec 31	Profit and loss appropriation account:			Share of profit	10,208
	Interest on drawings	120			
Dec 31	Balance c/d	10,288			13,008
		13,008			13,008
			Jan 1	Balance b/d	10,288

Donnell – Current Account

Dec 31 Drawings	600	Dec 31 Profit and loss appropriation account:		
Dec 31 Profit and loss appropriation account:		Interest on capital		960
Interest on drawings	36	Share of profit		5,104
Dec 31 Balance c/d	8,691	Salary		3,263
	9,327			9,327
		Jan 1 Balance b/d		8,691

(d)

Bhayani and Donnell
Balance Sheet as at 31 December

	Cost £	Total Depreciation £	Net Book Value £
Fixed assets			
Premises	20,000	–	20,000
Fittings	12,000	3,500	8,500
Vehicles	35,000	6,500	28,500
	67,000	10,000	57,000
Current assets			
Debtors	25,700		
Less Provision for bad debts	771	24,929	
Prepayments (wages)		200	
Cash		600	
		25,729	
Less Current liabilities			
Creditors	15,600		
Bank overdraft	950		
Accruals (heating)	100		
Rent received in advance	100	16,750	
Net current assets			8,979
			65,979

	Bhayani	Donnell
Financed by:		
Capital accounts	35,000	12,000
Balance		47,000
Current accounts		
Balance 1 January	(600)	nil
Add Interest on capital	2,800	960
Salary		3,263
Share of profits	10,208	5,104
	12,408	9,327
Less Drawings	(2,000)	(600)
Interest on drawings	(120)	(36)
	10,288	8,691
		18,979
		65,979

Chapter 37

37.1
LMT Ltd
Balance Sheet as at 31 December 2004

	Cost	Aggregate depreciation	Net book value
Fixed Assets			
Premises	45,000	18,000	27,000
Machinery	24,000	7,200	16,800
Fixtures	12,000	4,800	7,200
	81,000	30,000	51,000
Current Assets			
Stock		18,000	
Debtors		9,000	
Bank		6,000	
		33,000	
Less Current Liabilities			
Creditors	9,000		
Proposed dividend	3,000	12,000	
Net current assets			21,000
			72,000
Less Long-term Liabilities			
10% Debentures			18,000
			54,000
Financed by:			
Share Capital			
Authorised 60,000 ordinary shares at £1 each			60,000
Issued 36,000 ordinary shares at £1 each			36,000
Reserves			
General reserve		15,000	
Retained profits as per profit and loss account		(C)?	(B)?
			(A)?

(A) is the figure needed to make balance sheet total agree, i.e. 54,000.

(B) is the figure needed to add up to 54,000; therefore B = 54,000 – 36,000 = 18,000

(C) + 15,000 = B. (C) must be the missing figure of 3,000.

37.3
CA Company Ltd
Profit and Loss Appropriation Account for the year ended 31 December 2006

Net profit b/d		210,000
Add Retained profits from last year		17,000
		227,000
Less Transfer to general reserve	30,000	
Transfer to foreign exchange reserve	16,000	
Preference dividend paid (250,000 × £1 × 10%)	25,000	
Proposed ordinary dividend 10% (500,000 × £2 × 10%)	100,000	171,000
Retained profits carried forward to next year		56,000

37.4

Chang Ltd
Trading and Profit and Loss Account
for the year ended 31 December 2004

	£	£
Sales		316,810
Less Cost of goods sold:		
Opening stock	25,689	
Add Purchases	201,698	
	227,387	
Less Closing stock	29,142	198,245
Gross profit		118,565
Less Expenses:		
Wages and salaries (54,207 + 581)	54,788	
Rent (4,300 − 300)	4,000	
Lighting expenses	1,549	
Bad debts	748	
Provision for bad debts (938 − 861)	77	
General expenses	32,168	
Depreciation: Machinery (55,000 × 10%)	5,500	98,830
Net profit		19,735
Add Unappropriated profits from last year		34,280
		54,015
Less Proposed dividend		10,000
Unappropriated profits carried to next year		44,015

Chang Ltd
Balance Sheet as at 31 December 2004

	£	£	£
Fixed Assets			
Premises			65,000
Machinery		55,000	
Less Aggregate depreciation (15,800 + 5,500)		21,300	33,700
			98,700
Current Assets			
Stock		29,142	
Debtors	21,784		
Less Provision for doubtful debts	938	20,846	
Prepayments		300	
Bank		23,101	
		73,389	
Less Current Liabilities			
Proposed dividend	10,000		
Creditors	17,493		
Expenses owing	581	28,074	
Net current assets			45,315
			144,015
Financed by:			
Authorised & issued capital			100,000
Revenue reserves:			
Profit and loss account			44,015
			144,015

37.6 (a)

Jaspa West Ltd
Profit and Loss Appropriation Account
for the year ended 31 December 2006

	£	£
Net profit		80,000
Add Unappropriated profits from last year		92,000
		172,000
Less Appropriations:		
General reserve (40% × 80,000)		32,000
Proposed dividends		
Preference shares (8% × 80,000)	6,400	
Ordinary shares (4% × 150,000)	6,000	44,400
Unappropriated profits carried forward		127,600

(b)

Jaspa West Ltd
Balance Sheet as at 31 December 2006

	Cost £	Depreciation to date £	Net Book Value £
Fixed assets			
Premises	270,600	−	270,600
Machinery	72,600	18,400	54,200
	343,200	18,400	324,800
Current assets			
Stock		56,000	
Debtors (80,000 + 3,800)		83,800	139,800
Creditors: Amounts falling due within one year			
Creditors (37,000 + 4,200)		41,200	
Bank		21,400	
Dividends owing (6,400 + 6,000)		12,400	75,000
Net current assets			64,800
			389,600

	Authorised	Issued
Financed by:		
Share capital		
Preference shares	100,000	80,000
Ordinary shares	200,000	150,000
	300,000	
Reserves		
General reserve		32,000
Profit and loss		127,600
		159,600
		389,600

Chapter 38

38.1 (a) (i) Mark-up = 25%
      (ii) Margin = 20%
   (b) Margin = 25%
   (c) Mark-up = 20%

38.3 First, draw up a trading account and insert the figures given in the question. The gross profit can now be calculated. Since mark-up is 25%, therefore margin is 20%. Consequently, gross profit is 20% of £30,000 = £6,000.
Cost of Goods Sold = Sales − Gross Profit = £30,000 − £6,000 = £24,000. Purchases can now be found arithmetically.

K Young
Trading Account for the year ended 31 July 2006

	£	£
Sales		30,000
Less Cost of goods sold (a)		
Opening stock	4,936	
Add Purchases (b)	25,374	
	30,310	
Less Closing stock	6,310	24,000
Gross profit (c)		6,000

38.4 (a) Average stock value = £4,000
Therefore $\dfrac{£2,000 + (a)}{2} = £4,000$ and (a) is found to be £6,000. Mark-up is 50%,
Cost of goods sold is then calculated as £14,000. Mark-up is 50%, so sales = £14,000 + (£14,000 × 50%) = £21,000.

(b) ### T Rigby
Trading Account for the year ended 31 August 2006

		£	£
Sales			21,000
Less Cost of sales:			
Opening stock		2,000	
Add Purchases		18,000	
		20,000	
Less Closing stock	(a)	6,000	14,000
Gross profit			7,000

(c) If net profit on sales is not to be less than 10% of sales (= £2,100), this means that Rigby can afford up to £4,900 in expenses (i.e. Gross profit £7,000 − £4,900 expenses = £2,100 net profit).

38.5 (a)

	M Ltd	N Ltd

(i) *Current ratio*

M Ltd: $\dfrac{£200,000}{£50,000} = 4 : 1$

N Ltd: $\dfrac{£130,000}{£65,000} = 2 : 1$

(ii) *Acid test ratio*

M Ltd: $\dfrac{200,000 - 100,000}{£50,000} = 2 : 1$

N Ltd: $\dfrac{130,000 - 64,000}{£65,000} = 1$

(iii) *Stockturn*

M Ltd: $\dfrac{£288,000}{£120,000 + £100,000 \div 2} = 2.6$ times

N Ltd: $\dfrac{£187,500}{£60,000 + £64,000 \div 2} = 3.0$ times

(iv) *Debtors : Sales ratio*

M Ltd: $\dfrac{£60,000}{£360,000} \times 12$ months = 2 months

N Ltd: $\dfrac{£62,500}{£250,000} \times 12$ months = 3 months

(v) *Creditors : Purchases ratio*

M Ltd: $\dfrac{£50,000}{£268,000} \times 12$ months = 2.2 months

N Ltd: $\dfrac{£65,000}{£191,500} \times 12$ months = 4 months

(vi) *Gross profit %*

M Ltd: $\dfrac{£72,000}{£360,000} \times 100\% = 20\%$

N Ltd: $\dfrac{£62,500}{£250,000} \times 100\% = 25\%$

(vii) *Net profit %*

M Ltd: $\dfrac{£43,200}{£360,000} \times 100\% = 12\%$

N Ltd: $\dfrac{£35,000}{£250,000} \times 100\% = 14\%$

(viii) *Rate of return on shareholders' funds*

M Ltd: $\dfrac{£43,200}{£350,000} \times 100\% = 12.3\%$

N Ltd: $\dfrac{£35,000}{£255,000} \times 100\% = 13.7\%$

(b) Briefly N Ltd gives a better return to shareholders because of (viii) above.

Reasons include:

- M Ltd's current ratio is higher. This indicates that M Ltd is in a better liquidity position.
- N Ltd's stock turnover is higher than that of M Ltd. This shows that N Ltd manages its sales performance more effectively.
- The gross profit percentage of N Ltd is 5% higher than that of M Ltd. This is due to better purchasing and selling prices. Net profit margins differ by a smaller margin of 2%, suggesting, that M Ltd has tighter control of its overhead expenses when compared with its sales volume (8% compared with 11%).

Index